WOMEN AND MEN:
Interdisciplinary Readings on Gender

EDITED BY
GRETA HOFMANN NEMIROFF

Women and Men

Interdisciplinary Readings on Gender

Fitzhenry & Whiteside

Women and Men

Edited by

Greta Hofmann Nemiroff, New School
Dawson College, Montréal

Printed and bound in Canada
Typesetting by Jay Tee Graphics Ltd.

Canadian Cataloguing in Publication Data

Main entry under title:
Women and men: interdisciplinary readings on gender

Includes index.
ISBN 0-89902-649-1

1. Sex role — Addresses, essays, lectures. 2. Sex differences (Psychology) — Addresses, essays, lectures.
I. Nemiroff, Greta.

HQ1075.W65 1986 305.3 C86-093298-2

Contents

Biographical Notes on Contributors

Sr. Prudence Allen, R.S.M., received her Ph.D. in Philosophy from Claremont Graduate School, Claremont, California. In 1965, she immigrated to Canada; since 1967 she has been engaged in research on the concept of woman in relation to the concept of man in Philosophy. Dr. Allen has published and lectured widely in Philosophy, Theology, History and Women's Studies as Christine Allen before entering the Religious Sisters of Mercy of Alma in 1983. She is Associate Professor, Department of Philosophy, Concordia University, Montréal, and author of *The Concept of Woman: The Aristotelian Revolution (750 B.C.-1250 A.D.)* (Montréal: Eden Press, 1985).

Hugh Armstrong received his B.A. and M.A. from Carleton University and his Ph.D. from the Université de Montréal, and currently teaches Humanities and Sociology at Vanier College. Co-author with Pat Armstrong of *The Double Ghetto: Canadian Women and Their Segregated Work, A Working Majority: What Women Must Do for Pay* and several articles, he has also written articles on the state and on job creation. A manuscript editor with *Studies in Political Economy* and an elected member of the Social Policy Committee of the Canadian Sociology and Anthropology Association, he lives with his wife Pat and their two daughters in Montréal.

An activist in women's issues since the 1960s, *Pat Armstrong* co-parents two teenage daughters as well as teaches Sociology and Women's Studies at Vanier College. Her research and writing focus on broadly defined women's work. Co-author with Hugh Armstrong of *The Double Ghetto: Canadian Women and Their Segregated Work,* and *A Working Majority: What*

Women Must Do for Pay, author of *Labour Pains: Women's Work in Crisis,* Pat Armstrong's current research uses a hospital setting as a means of examining how the economic crisis influences women's jobs in and out of the labour force.

Maryann Ayim received her M.A. from the University of Toronto and her Ph.D. in Philosophy from the University of Waterloo. She is a Professor in the Faculty of Education, University of Western Ontario (London, Ontario), where she teaches Philosophy of Language Education, Women's Studies, and Philosophy of Education. She has published widely in books, journals and the proceedings of various scholarly associations in areas of pragmatism, the philosophy of education, gender in language and the philosophy of feminism. She has given talks, workshops, TV and radio interviews throughout Canada, the United States and Europe. From 1982–84, she was President of the Canadian Philosophy of Education Society and has been active in the Canadian Society for Women in Philosophy.

Elaine Batcher has her doctorate from the Ontario Institute for Studies in Education, University of Toronto, and has taught at the elementary and graduate school levels. As an independent educational theorist and mother of young children, she combines her work in research with a concern for the political process, and has recently acted as manager of the successful campaign of a local school trustee. Her project "Lunchtime at the Mall," which was funded by the Social Sciences and Humanities Research Council of Canada, continues to generate ideas, and a book detailing the findings is planned for the future.

Born in Canada in 1945 to Jewish-Polish survivors of World War II, *Judith Crawley* taught herself photography while working as a college English teacher. With the opening of Vanier College (CEGEP) in Montréal in 1970, she joined its faculty as an English and Photography teacher. She has exhibited and published her photographs in Canada and the United States. She has been a single parent of two children since 1978.

A French-Canadian born in Montréal in 1944, *Louise Dulude* obtained her B.A. from Sir George Williams University (now Concordia University) by working as a secretary and studying at night. She then earned a law degree from the Université de Montréal. She has finished a Master of Laws programme at McGill University (her thesis is on the taxation of the family in five countries), and is now working on her Doctorate in Law at the University of Ottawa. She practised law as the director of a legal aid clinic in east-end Montréal, and then worked in the field of women's rights in Ottawa, first as an officer for the Secretary of State and then as a researcher. She has written nine reports on women, including: *Women and the Personal Income Tax System, Women and Aging, Women and Poverty, The Status of Women in Federal Crown Corporations, Pension Reform with Women in Mind,* and *Love, Marriage and Money.* For the past four years she has served on the executive of the National Action Committee on the Status of Women, and became its president in 1986.

Margrit Eichler is a Professor of Sociology and Chairperson of her department at the Ontario Institute for Studies in Education. She is a co-founder of Resources for Feminist Research (previously the Canadian Newsletter of Research on Women) and a past President of the Canadian Research Institute for the Advancement of Women.

Naomi Goldenberg received her Ph.D. in Religious Studies from Yale University. She is the author of *Changing of the Gods — Feminism and the End of Traditional Religions (Beacon Press, 1979)* and *The End of God — Important Directions for a Feminist Critique of Religion in the Works of Sigmund Freud and Carl Jung* (University of Ottawa Press, 1982). She is associate professor of the psychology of religion at the University of Ottawa, where she is writing about psychoanalysis and feminism. The working title of her next book is *Returning Words to Flesh: Psychoanalysis, Feminism and the Resurrection of the Body.*

Stan Gray worked for eleven years at Westinghouse in Hamilton in a variety of jobs in the plant. Currently he is Director of a union-based Health and Safety Centre in Ontario. He has written and published other articles in Canada on workers' struggles in Ontario, particularly in the area of health and safety.

Esther Greenglass earned her B.A., M.A. and Ph.D. at the University of Toronto. She is Professor of Psychology at York University in Toronto. Dr. Greenglass has presented numerous papers and given talks throughout Canada and in other countries. She has also published widely: her main research interests include the socialization of children; abortion and its psychological effects; the social psychology of gender roles; motivation for marriage and children; and stress and Type A behaviour in women. Her latest book is *A World of Difference: Gender Roles in Perspective* (Toronto: Wiley, 1982).

M. Ann Hall is a Professor in the Department of Physical Education and Sport Studies at the University of Alberta where she teaches the Sociology of Sport. Her research interests focus on the socio-cultural aspects of gender relations in sport and leisure. Active in the women's movement, she is a past president of the Canadian Research Institute for the Advancement of Women. A recreational athlete, she enjoys jogging, squash and all manner of outdoor pursuits.

Chaviva Hošek has been active in the Canadian women's movement since 1974. She is past president of the National Action Committee on the Status of Women, Canada's largest women's lobby organization with 385 member groups. She is an Associate Professor of English at the University of Toronto, where she teaches American and Canadian literature and has been a member of the Governing Council, chair of the Academic Affairs Committee, and chair of the Women's Studies Programme Committee.

Barbara Houston, Associate Professor of Philosophy, Faculty of Education, The University of Western Ontario, has been active in the women's movement and in the development of women's studies at her university. Her current research interests are gender identity, an ethics of care, feminist ethics and a gender-sensitive approach to moral education. She has published articles on these topics in various journals and anthologies.

Hilary Lips is an Associate Professor of Psychology at the University of Winnipeg. She has specialized in the study of gender roles, and has written extensively on that topic.

Ian Lumsden teaches Social and Political Science at Atkinson College, York University, Toronto. His intellectual interests range from gay liberation to the political economy of dependent capitalist countries. Currently he is undertaking a comparative study of the social construction and regulation of homosexuality in Cuba and Central America.

Ned Lyttelton came to Canada from England in 1972. For the past few years he has been involved in various anti-sexist men's groups, including a men's child care collective. On a voluntary basis he counsels men referred to him by a local Rape Crisis Centre: male friends or relatives of women who have been raped, men who have been raped, and also rapists and wife-batterers. Recently he has been involved in gay politics. He is co-parent to two children with one more on the way, and works in a collectively managed bookstore. He says: "I owe what I have learned to the hard work of Laura Rowe and of others who cared enough to teach me about privilege and oppression and how they work in the world."

Eileen Manion was born in 1946 in New Jersey, where she lived until her father died in 1951. Afterward, she and her mother moved to Long Island, where she graduated from an all-girls Catholic high school. She earned her

B.A. at Syracuse University, her M.A. in Comparative Literature at Columbia University, and her Ph.D. in English at McGill University in 1980. Her dissertation was on Doris Lessing, about whom she has published several articles. She also has published articles on feminist theory and the women's movement, and writes book reviews for the Montreal *Gazette*. She teaches English and Humanities at Dawson College in Montréal.

Karen Messing is Professor of Genetics at the Université du Québec à Montréal, and teaches courses in genetics and on biology and women. In addition, she does research and education on workplace risks to genetics and on women's occupational health, in the context of an agreement between Québec labour unions and the university. Dr. Messing received her Ph.D. from McGill University, and is currently researching the detection of genetic damage among workers exposed to ionizing radiation.

Kathryn Pauly Morgan is Associate Professor of Philosophy and Women's Studies at the University of Toronto. She has published many articles related to gender, the philosophy of sexuality, education and other philosophical issues. Currently, she is working on two books: *Sexuality, Human Nature, and Social Structure: A Study in the Philosophy of Human Sexuality* and *The Metaphysical Politics of Gender: Collected Essays.*

Born in British Columbia in 1942, *Cerise Morris* moved to Montréal at the age of 14 when she left school to work, returning at the age of eighteen to support herself as a dancer while she acquired her B.A. and M.S.W. She has been a correctional worker, a co-ordinator of a woman's centre, a teacher, and a psychotherapist. She earned her Ph.D. in Sociology from McGill University in 1982. Her interest and commitment to feminism has permeated all of her work: her masters' thesis on the relationship between feminism and self-concept in working-class adolescent girls; her doctoral dissertation on the campaign to establish Canada's Royal Commission on the Status of Women; the work of the Commission, and its subsequent impact on federal social policy. Currently she is researching post-divorce, restructured families and shared custody experiences. Mother to two sons, Cerise Morris is married, lives in Montréal, and teaches at Dawson college.

Born in Montréal, *Greta Hofmann Nemiroff* is a writer and educator. A pioneer in Canadian Women's Studies as both a practitioner and theoretician, she has written widely on the topic. As well, she has published fiction and non-fiction in both English and French. She is Director of the New School of Dawson College in Montréal. This is an alternative programme based on Humanistic Education. She teaches English and Women's Studies there, and gives talks and workshops on feminist and educational issues throughout Canada and the United States.

Judith Nolté worked for many years counselling youth and their families in Montréal. For the past five years she has been Program Director at Planned Parenthood Federation of Canada. Judith has a Master's degree in Social Work from Carleton University, and specializes in social policy analysis and research. Published works include "Child and Family Benefits", "Social and Medical Implications of the New Reproductive Technology", "Sex Education in Canadian Schools", and "Planned Parenthood in Canada: 1977–1984".

Christine Overall earned her Ph.D. in Philosophy at the University of Toronto. She has taught Philosophy and Women's Studies courses at Marianopolis College, Montréal, and at Queen's University, Kingston. She is now a Webster Fellow in the Humanities and Assistant Professor of Philosophy at Queen's. She has published papers in philosophy of religion and in reproductive ethics, and is completing a book, *Ethics and Human Reproduction: A Feminist Analysis*, to be published by Allen & Unwin.

Susan Jean Palmer was born in southern Alberta. Two of her great-grandmothers migrated north from Salt Lake City to protect their Mormon husbands from the anti-polygamist persecution. She grew up in Europe, where her father worked for the Canadian Immigration Overseas, and returned to Canada to study literature, music and religion at McGill University. She teaches the *Women in Religion* and *Cults, New Religious Movements* courses at Dawson College, and is currently working on a thesis studying the roles of women in new spiritual groups.

Judith Posner is Chair of the Department of Sociology at Atkinson College, York University, where she also teaches a wide range of courses dealing with women's issues. She has been doing research on images of women in advertising for over a decade, speaking, publishing and broadcasting on the topic. She has also been a member of the Advertising Advisory Board sub-committee on sex-role stereotyping. Currently she is a board member of MediaWatch, a Vancouver-based feminist organisation.

Dorothy Goldin Rosenberg is a freelance film consultant and disarmament and development co-ordinator. Using film as a catalyst for action towards policy change, she has worked locally, nationally and internationally for peace and development. Associated with non-governmental organizations working on issues related to peace, disarmament, women, human rights, safe energy, and appropriate development, she is the recipient of the U.N. Environmental Program Award for Environmental Stewardship. She was principal research consultant on *Speaking Our Peace: Women, Peace and Power,* a National Film Board Studio D Film, and is currently the development and disarmament co-ordinator at the Consultative Committee on Arms Control and Disarmament, an advisory body to Mr. Douglas Roche, Canadian Ambassador for Disarmament at the United Nations.

Chuck Samuels is a photographer living in Montréal.

Born in 1944, *Alanna Janet Stalker* is the fourth child of parents who had left their farming background to work in Montréal. She lived on Jeanne Mance street until a house built by her father in St-Eustache-sur-le-Lac was ready for the family. Her father worked as a machinist at Canadair, and her mother worked at home baking bread, canning vegetables from their garden, and making the family's clothing. Alanna earned her B.F.A. from Sir George Williams University in Montréal (now Concordia University), where she is now finishing a Master's degree in Art Education. Mother of two, she teaches painting, drawing, and sculpture at Vanier College in Montréal.

Jill McCalla Vickers, Professor of Political Science and Canadian Studies, is Graduate Co-ordinator for Women's Studies at Carleton University. Co-author of *But Can You Type?: The Status of Women in Canadian Universities* and *Women in Politics in Canada: An Overview*, she recently edited *Taking Sex into Account: The Policy Consequences of Sexist Research.* President of the Canadian Research Institute for the Advancement of Women, she has been active in the Canadian Women's Movement since 1971.

Bert Young teaches Sociology at John Abbott College in Ste. Anne de Bellevue, Québec. He has for many years been a co-ordinator of Canadian / Québec Studies at John Abbott and more recently, of Peace Studies. He has been an editor of *Our Generation* for a number of years, and is currently devoting his time to a research project on participation in men's groups in Canada.

Preface

While the bulk of the work of editing this anthology was done in solitude, its creation depended on many other people in my life. *Women and Men: Interdisciplinary Readings on Gender* was undertaken as a result of my search for diverse multi-disciplinary readings for a course on Women and Men which I constructed with my students at The New School of Dawson College in the winter term of 1984. Without their critical reading and discussion on a variety of works, as well as their expression of a need for Canadian material with which they could identify, I might not have thought of editing this book. I would, then, like to thank them for their inspiration, and I hope that their good teaching was reciprocated ... and all debts discharged by this book.

To defray some of the expenses in assembling this book, I was helped by a grant from the office of Julia Newell, Academic Dean of Dawson College. The process would have been much slower without the uncomplaining help of Deborah Blacklock, Moira Egan, Deborah Gaudet and Carol Gordon.

Murray Lamb, the book's editor at Fitzhenry and Whiteside, has been a wonderful partner in considering with me the merit of almost all the submissions received.

Debra Martens provided astute and speedy work in indexing this book; without Francine Geraci's gimlet editorial eye, this would have been a lesser volume.

Stanley Nemiroff has contributed the benefit of his mercilessly logical and critical eye, often interrupting his own work to do so. Carla, Daniel and Rebecca Nemiroff have tolerated interruptions and upheavals in their own lives with considerable grace and patience ... most of the time. Without the work and organization of our household by Rina Marchei, there would be little energy left for research, editing and writing. I thank her for twenty-three years.

Introduction

The original concept of this book was that it should be multi-disciplinary in nature, should refer wherever possible to the Canadian context, and should be symmetrically arranged so that there would be an equal number of articles by women on women, by men on men, and by women or men on women and men. In order to achieve this goal, I designed a sequence of subject matter not unlike the present sequence of the book, solicited articles wherever possible, and also conducted a library search for articles. I was fortunate in that some of the people I contacted provided me with leads to others, whether or not they themselves were ready to contribute. I also had to complete this project in less than a year.

While I was able to locate many articles by women on women, and by women on women and men, and even an article by a woman on the male image in advertising (Posner), I was not equally able to find articles by men on men or on women and men. Three of the ten articles submitted by men related to violence in male culture. While I received several articles on mothering, I received nothing on fathering. I regret not having received any submissions on the socialization of pre-schoolers. While several submissions covered the politics of the family and of sexuality, I was not able to find work that focussed intensively on the experiential aspects of family life or sexuality. I thought that the latter would be of great interest to young people in colleges and universities.

As mentioned above, the articles by men that included male-female relations did so in the context of violence. While these articles are not included, primarily owing to their length, it might have been interesting to see attention paid to such other aspects of the male-female relationship as romantic love or marriage. Perhaps, though, violence is an eliptical way of treating the way that many men in our society ultimately respond both to romantic love and marriage.

There were many submissions I would have liked to include and could not because of length or general suitability to the total work. Editing a book requires a constant shift of emphasis in its process; each work can change the tone and focus of the whole. A primary consideration was that this book will be used in colleges and universities; for this reason, I placed great importance on clarity of language and the diversity of topics raised in consideration of gender. I was anxious to encourage the development of visual literacy by the inclusion of articles requiring visual analysis. I was also interested in breaking down some of the traditional disciplinary boundaries. The moment we consider subjects from the standpoint of gender, the usual categories can become skewed and new ones must be constructed. Hence, Naomi Goldenberg's chapter, "Resurrecting the Body," appears in the section *The Body / Sexuality* rather than under religion or theology. When power is addressed, it appears that men's true liberation might stem from redefining power, or at least giving up some of their privilege, according to Ned Lyttelton's article on men's liberation.

In structuring this book, it seemed to me that it was essential to begin by addressing epistemology: what do we think about, and how do we think about it, when we think about gender? Many of the issues related to gender have to do with the pre-conditions of people's lives, with life's stages and with the choices — or non-choices — that women and men make separately and together. Language and communication are two of the ways in which all humans attempt to bridge the gap of our existential isolation as well as the isolation imposed by social conventions and restrictions. And finally, all humans experience in varying degrees both powerlessness (especially as children) and power (wherever we best find it). While there are, without doubt, many ways of schematizing a treatment of the subject of gender, the above structure suited both the intentions and submissions of this book in the most adequate way.

I would have liked to include, and did try to solicit, an article by a military man on the military. It seemed to me that when we talk about power in this world, ultimately we are forced to acknowledge that it is not conceived entirely in the eyes of the beholder. Right this moment, as you are reading this Introduction, missiles are aimed close enough to where you sit to destroy everything understood as essential to your life. I was, however, unable to find anyone willing to show *explicitly*, from a male point of view, in what respects the very structure of thought underlying warfare can be characterized as fundamentally male, owing to its historical development within a purely patriarchal context. While there are references to the military in articles written by women in this anthology, we still must wait to hear how the men involved in the practice of warfare describe their culture in terms of gender. This subject is especially timely in Canada, where there is current debate regarding the issues of women's participation in active warfare and homosexuals' participation in the armed forces. An analysis of warfare as a male construction of reality is long overdue in Canada, where naive biographies of military men abound.

There is an under-representation of male writers in this book: only six out of thirty-one, slightly less than 20%. This simply reflects the state of the art. Male scholars still seem most likely to strive for the patriarchal ideal of "universality" by treating concepts related to "human nature", which often means men's experience mildly tempered, if at all, by token references to the sub-stratum of women. I hope that more men will write about men *qua* men and retrieve from the body of men's studies those elements specific to men, examine them, and structure an epistemology that takes gender into account. Perhaps a close perusal of Margrit Eichler's chapter will clarify some of the issues and problems for them. It is difficult for a power group, which has had the privilege of defining reality, to undertake such a re-examination. On the other hand, it is an exciting project, one that should stimulate and challenge both male and female scholars ... but especially men who, after all, can then gauge the universality of their claims against their own unmediated experience without even token considerations of the supposed "anima" hidden within the concept of "Mankind".

After studying, soliciting articles, editing, and reflecting on this anthology on gender, I have concluded that this fascinating subject begs for more extensive research. Most questions raised by a serious consideration of gender seem ultimately to boil down to "nature versus nurture"; reflecting on the innate versus the acquired, of course, can make us swerve from hard-core determinism to hard-core free will and back. This exercise in the examination of assumptions, values, and facts is worth undertaking with the most fastidious scholarship because its conclusions can be crucial. Our conclusions will influence us in deciding how free and powerful we may actually be to effect change in our own lives, in the lives of those we love, and in the world that we inhabit.

My hope, then, is that this anthology will stimulate its readers into further questions and scholarship on the subjects explored within its covers; that it will encourage its readers to investigate subject matter not addressed here (like androgyny, the family, or women's self-defined sexuality for instance, and so much more); and that all these efforts will result in more writing, talks, works of art and theory, which will open our minds and hearts to a greater understanding of ourselves and others through consideration of gender and human identity.

Greta Hofmann Nemiroff
Montréal, October, 1986

I. THE EPISTEMOLOGY OF GENDER

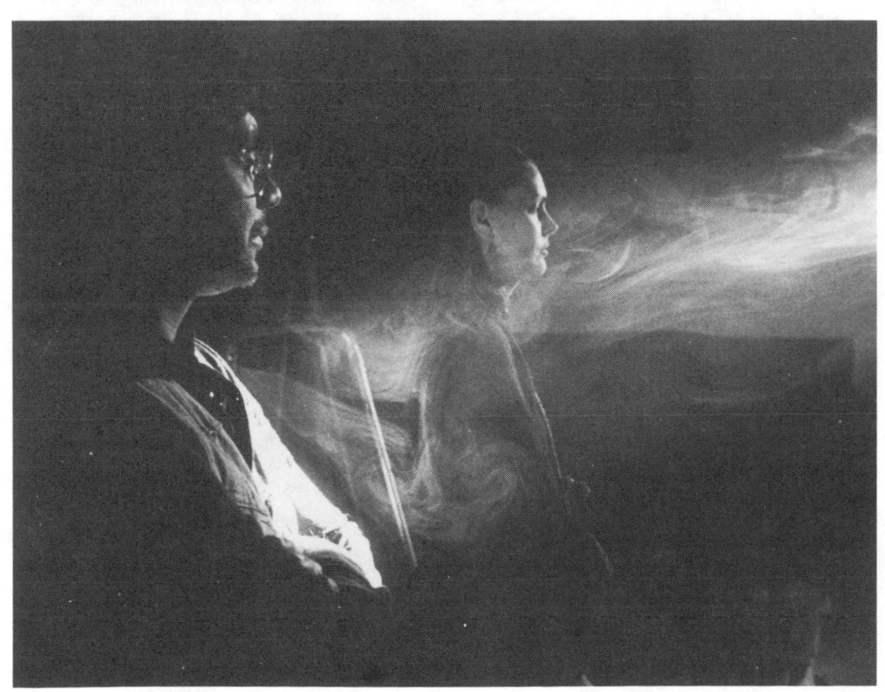

INTRODUCTION

How can we arrive at the truth about gender? What do we know? How do we know it? How can we be certain that the ways in which we approach this contentious and affect-laden subject are objective? Given that to date scholarship has, for the most part, been developed and perpetuated by men, can the methodology developed in a male-dominated academy apply to the subject of gender?

This first section of the book addresses some of these questions. Sister Prudence Allen, in "Sex Unity, Polarity, or Complementarity," examines some of the historical roots to philosophical positions or concepts of gender. Margrit Eichler discusses various paradigms of scholarship, distinguishing among them in the hope that eventually the Social Sciences will develop non-sexist criteria and methodology. Armstrong and Armstrong examine another aspect of Social Science research: its dependence on quantitative data and some of the biasses underlying those questions which produce quantitative data that can, in turn, lead to erroneous conclusions. Karen Messing shows how all stages of scientific research can be "contaminated" by various evasions and sexist assumptions. Ann Hall's chapter demonstrates how the social analysis of gender and sport raises various epistemological and methodological questions and how some of these issues may be resolved.

The epistemology of gender is a huge subject and a fascinating one. It is most encouraging to see that it interests scholars in many disciplines. The chapters here raise all the important questions of objectivity, bias and methodology. There is still much to be done in this area. Perhaps a good place to begin is by applying some of the concepts gleaned from these articles to areas of study of specific interest to each reader.

SR. PRUDENCE ALLEN, R.S.M.

Sex Unity, Polarity, or Complementarity?

INTRODUCTION

The current debate about women and men is in desperate need of a new model of sex identity, for it is frequently trapped between two models of sex identity, which I call *sex polarity* and *sex unity*. If the concepts of "equality" and "differentiation" are taken as central to theories of sex identity, then the difference between sex polarity and sex unity can be described as follows:

Sex polarity claims that the sexes are significantly different but not equal. In its traditional form, as defended by Aristotle, man is thought to be superior; in its reverse form, as defended by radical feminists, woman is thought to be superior.

Sex unity claims that the sexes are equal and not significantly different. Plato first articulated this theory, but it is commonly found in the unisex philosophies present in much contemporary feminist thought. A derivative form of sex unity, which I call *sex neutrality*, merely *assumes* that the sexes are not significantly different. Sex unity, on the other hand, attempts to *prove* this philosophical assumption.

The failure of philosophy to develop and defend a third alternative to sex unity and sex polarity has had serious repercussions for Western culture and civilization. This third alternative would have as its basic concepts the equality as well as the significant differentiation of women and men. Although this particular theory was first tentatively expressed by Hildegard of Bingen, a twelfth century philosopher, for a number of important historical reasons it was soon overpowered by versions of sex polarity and sex neutrality.[1]

Originally published under the authorship of Christine Allen in the *International Journal of Women's Studies,* Volume 6, No. 4, September / October 1983, pp. 311 - 325.

There is some difficulty in settling on an effective name for this third theory of sex identity, which defends both the equality and the differentiation of the sexes. After considering several alternatives, *sex complementarity* appears to be the most suitable name, even though in the past it has been abused by sex polarity theorists. Their abuse consisted in the claim that complementarity implied the equality of the sexes while, in fact, it really involved the superiority of man over woman. In other words, their complementarity collapsed into a hidden form of sex polarity. Even with this history of abuse, however, it would seem that sex complementarity, at the deepest level of understanding, demands a true equality of woman and man.[2] Authentic sex complementarity, should, therefore, be able to resist a fall into either sex polarity or sex unity.

If the above theories of sex identity are summarized, then their key concepts would fall into a pattern suggested by the following chart:

	Equality	Differentiation
Sex Unity	X	
sex neutrality	X	
Sex Polarity		X
reverse sex polarity		X
Sex Complementarity	X	X

It would take a great deal of serious study and evaluation to consider the detailed way in which various theories of sex identity fall into the above categories. They must be taken as guidelines rather than as rigid classifications. At the same time, there is a certain truth to the suggestion that the concepts of equality and differentiation offer a key to the orientation of various theories of sex identity. Therefore, it is useful to pursue the classification further in this introductory essay.

In this chapter I would like to consider the theory of sex complementarity from two different, but interrelated, perspectives. First, I will examine some of the practical consequences of the theory; and second, I will suggest a possible way to establish a theoretical foundation for its philosophical defence.

PRACTICAL APPLICATIONS OF SEX COMPLEMENTARITY

While a theory of sex identity is bound to affect nearly every aspect of personal existence, I will try to sketch some very specific consequences of sex complementarity in four specific areas: law, education, research, and personal lives.

Sex Identity and the Law

The law, for centuries dominated by a sex polarity model of sex identity, has shifted radically in our century towards a model of sex neutrality. This shift has caused such contortions as considering whether to classify pregnancy under the category of a disease, in order to avoid a special differentiation for women. Pregnancy is clearly not a disease, and it should not be legally recognized in the same category as testicular cancer, for example. A sex complementarity model would allow for the true differentiation between the sexes under the law, without endangering the legal equality of woman and man.

Another example of the artificial "either / or" between sex polarity and sex unity was seen in recent debate about the Equal Rights Amendment in the United States and the Charter of Rights in Canada. A problem arose because equality before the law appeared to imply non-differentiation of men and women. This led to the following emotionally charged claims, which were reported in U.S. and Canadian media during the years 1980 and 1982: that the passage of ERA, or the adoption of the Charter of Rights, would mean the end of separate public restrooms for women and men; the drafting of women to fight in wars; the end of preferential automobile rates for women drivers; the end of sexually segregated rooming houses; and the end of the right of a woman to be supported by her husband.

In all of the above examples, a hidden premise implied that equality before the law would necessitate the non-differentiation of women and men in all situations. It must be admitted that the rationale for this implication flows from the rather frequent practice of members of the judicial system of making the mistaken judgement that equality means non-differentiation. With this accumulation of erroneous practice, it is all the more crucial for philosophers to point out that equality and differentiation are not incompatible.[3]

Affirmative action and preferential hiring would also be aided by the introduction of a theory of sex complementarity. Many contemporary sex unity and sex neutrality theorists are extremely perplexed by the problems of justice posed in these two practices.[4] If a man and a woman are equal, they ask, how can preferential treatment of women be justified? Sex complementarity could provide a rationale for considering collective as well as individual justice because differentiation between the sexes could involve an historical as well as a biological component.[5]

Sex Identity and Education

The application of a theory of sex complementarity to educational issues can be seen in a consideration of various views about the proper place and longevity of women's studies. After the exclusion of women from higher education, beginning with the University of Paris in the thirteenth century, most universities embodied a sex polarity structure. The teaching of philosophy within this structure, on the other hand, embodied a sex neutrality perspective that was, in part, derived from an emphasis on logic and mathematics as the proper methodology for the discipline.

Today, we are offered various options for women's studies that seek to overcome this tradition of the sex polarity structure of universities, combined with the sex neutrality curriculum of courses. Radical feminists who hold a model of reverse sex polarity, that is, of belief in the superiority of woman over man, assert that women's studies must take place outside the university.[6] Traditional sex polarity theorists, on the other hand, argue that women's studies is faddish and non-academic. Sex unity theorists claim that within the university, women's studies might be needed as a temporary measure until all information about the sexes is integrated into regular curriculum. They long for the day when women's studies will cease to exist.

When the underlying premises of these views are examined, it becomes apparent that reverse sex polarity theorists devalue the contribution of men to scholarship and learning and that, conversely, traditional sex polarity theorists devalue the contribution of women to knowledge as well as the historical contributions of women to society. For both of these theories, the differentiation of the sexes leads to their inequality. On the other hand, the sex unity theorists appear to believe that there are ultimately no significant differences between women and men, and that there will not be any perpetual value in studying one sex in distinction to the other. For sex unity theorists, then, equality leads to non-differentiation.

The value of sex complementarity for this debate about the nature and future of women's studies is that it promotes a flexible attitude towards both the structure and curriculum of universities. To understand the sexes as being both significantly different and equal would allow the possibility of a variety of structural opinions, such as men's colleges, women's colleges, and co-educational colleges.[7] To differentiate a college by sex usually would involve reference to the administrative orientation and tradition of the college, rather than to the sex of all students. In this way, a women's college could be open to male students and vice versa.

A model of sex complementarity could also provide a flexible approach to curriculum. Most courses in a university will eventually include reference to sexually integrated data. However, there will always be room for a few courses that would focus on women's history and situation in distinction from other more inclusive assessments; in a similar way, it would be of value to have courses that differentiate men's history and situation. Once again, attendance at such courses should be open to members of both sexes. I might even be so bold as to suggest that, ideally, all women and men should be required to take a course in women's studies and a course in men's studies before graduating from university. In any event, the sex complementarity model appears to be the most useful in countering the pressures of sex polarity and sex unity in contemporary education.

Sex Identity and Research

Research is an area related to, but not identical with, education. A model of sex complementarity could be useful for research by opening up a new avenue for funding mechanisms, and for the publication of results of studies about sex identity. It has become apparent that journals have a tendency to publish articles that support their hidden assumptions. For example, a journal that carries an editorial board with a sex unity model of sex identity would not be interested in publishing a study that claimed that boys were different from girls in some aspect of the reasoning process. Or, conversely, a journal with an editorial preference of the sex polarity model might dismiss a study that indicated no significant differences between boys and girls in some area of scholastic achievement.[8] The dominance in our culture of the theories of sex unity and sex polarity means that a study that would tend to support the thesis of sex complementarity, that is, of significant differentiation and equality of men and women, might have difficulty being published. Barring the conversion of sex polarity and sex unity editors, it might be useful to establish some journals with an editorial openness to a sex complementarity model of sex identity.

For an individual researcher as well, sex complementarity offers a possibility that is not available to the other two options. To enter into research with an open mind about differences between the sexes, but with a belief in the inherent equality of women and men, would allow the researcher to explore the actual ways in which the sexes relate to the world. The question is not whether we are different by virtue of our sex, but how are we different.[9]

A cursory study of some of the historical examples of research within the sex unity or sex polarity models leads me to make the following observations. When a theory of sex unity is deeply probed, it almost invariably reveals a devaluation of the materiality of human existence. This devaluation might be of the body, of one's historical situation, or of what is sometimes called the "facticity" of human existance. Plato, the Cartesian feminists or, more recently, Shulamith Firestone, serve as examples of this tendency.[10]

On the other hand, sex polarity theorists tend to isolate and inflate one specific material aspect of woman or man. Aristotle chose the capacity to concoct seed, Freud chose the male sexual anatomy, Sartre chose the activity of the male sexual organ, and Stephen Goldberg chose the hormone "testosterone" for the philosophical basis of male superiority.[11] Conversely, Henrich Cornelius Agrippa chose the material of a woman's body, Ashley Montagu and Valerie Solanis chose the female chromosomal structure, and Jill Johnson chose woman's capacity to give birth as a philosophical basis for the superiority of woman.[12]

Faced with this tendency to devalue the materiality of the human condition by the sex unity theorists, or to overvalue one aspect of the materiality of the human condition by the sex polarity theorists, it would seem that sex complementarity theorists have an important challenge to keep human materiality in balance with such other aspects of the human situation as rationality, individuality, spirituality, and so on.[13] Indeed, I would like to suggest, although this cannot be proved here, that sex complementarity may very well be the only theory that could provide a balanced view of the identity and proper relation of the sexes.

Sex Identity and Personal Lives

The last area I would like to mention as involving a practical application of the philosophical theory of sex complementarity is what I have called simply "personal lives". In the last two years, it has been my privilege to speak with two women who are on the frontier of women's accomplishments. Anne LaBastille is a well-known conservationist, who frequently travels by herself for long periods of time into wilderness areas.[14] Arlene Blum is the leader of the successful women's climb of Annapurna.[15] Both of these women have found that their success in traditionally male kinds of activities has led many within the sex polarity tradition to consider that they "want to be men", instead of understanding their motivation as a love of wilderness, conservation, mountain climbing, camping, and trekking. Indeed, they both eschew the claim that they are examples of a new "female machisma", or women who love competing with, and beating, men.[16]

At the same time, it is important to both Anne LaBastille and Arlene Blum that they are *women* who have achieved their respective extraordinary goals. The sex unity theorists would argue that their sex should not matter, that they are merely individuals who have accomplished something. A theory of sex complementarity would enable them to claim their success as women, without forcing them into competition with men. Perhaps it is worth concluding this example by simply stating that they have both expressed to me that a philosophical defence of the theory of sex complementarity would be of great help to them in their lives and work. If this can be achieved, then philosophy could have a concrete effect on people outside the academic milieu.

Sr. Prudence Allen

A Theoretical Foundation for Sex Complementarity

What can philosophers do to develop a theory of sex complementarity? Perhaps one of the first things would be to analyse arguments presented about sex identity throughout the history of philosophy. Beginning with the pre-Socratics, philosophers have approached the question of the respective identities of woman and man through asking one or more of the following four questions:

1. What do woman and man contribute to generation?
2. Are women and men wise in the same way?
3. Are women and men virtuous in the same way?
4. How are women and men opposite?[17]

The answers that traditional philosophers gave these questions were influenced by the scientific data available to them, by their own intellectual schema, and by the social conditions of their times. The questions they asked, however, seem to transcend a particular time and place. They point to fundamental categories of human existence. Therefore, even though we might want to reject many of the answers that various philosophers gave to these questions, the questions themselves can be useful to any search for the truth about sex identity.

To be more precise, the above four questions reflect our material, thinking, and acting nature as woman or man. In addition, they bring into focus our relation to one another as well as to the world. It would seem, then, that one method for developing a theoretical base for sex complementarity could be to reflect again on these fundamental questions in order to determine whether our own contemporary scientific data, intellectual schema, and social conditions can offer a solid foundation from which to defend the equality and differentiation of women and men.

WHAT DO WOMEN AND MEN CONTRIBUTE TO GENERATION?

For nearly two thousand years the Aristotelian theory of generation suggested that woman was inferior to man because she was incapable of providing seed in generation.[18] The invention of the microscope has allowed us to discover that women do contribute seed to this activity. This material given of our situation has thus repudiated one of the fundamental defences of traditional sex polarity.

Many philosophers did accept the claim that woman provided seed to generation. However, most of them believed that female seed was infertile;

some believed that the seed was merely a glandular secretion.[19] The discovery that both the mother and the father provide 23 chromosomes to the embryo repudiates the sex polarity claim that woman is a passive contributor to generation because her seed is impotent. Indeed, the discovery that both mother and father provide the same structural contribution, and that both are equally active in the ensuing structure of the foetus, suggests evidence for a theory of equality of the sexes.

At the same time it is important to note that even though each sex provides half of the necessary structure of the new life, it is not possible for two contributions from the same sex to have the same result; i.e., two female seeds or two male seeds will not be able to generate a child. The female seed must approach by way of the egg; the male seed must approach by way of the sperm. Another way of saying this is that the two contributions must have a differentiated route of access, a different pathway, one provided by male biology and the other by female biology.

If we were to diagram this relationship of the sexes in generation, it might look as follows:

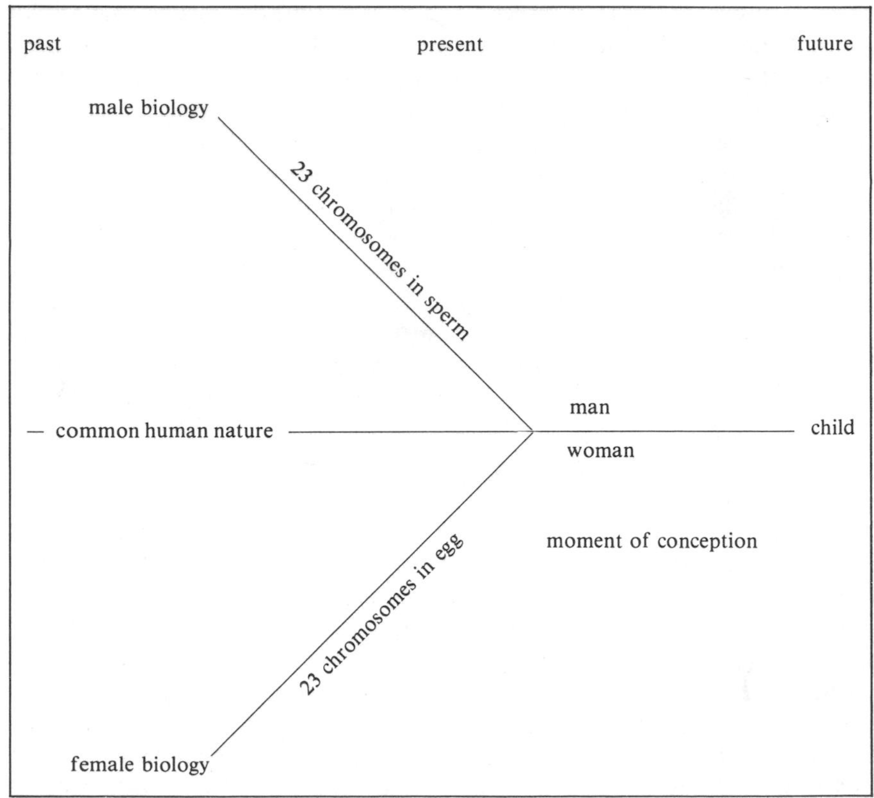

FIGURE 1.1

It can be seen then, that just by considering the barest facts about generation, we have found an initial support for the two basic concepts of sex complementarity; namely that the two sexes are equal and significantly different. Their equality is derived from the chromosomal structure of the seed, and their differentiation is derived from the respective pathways that the seed follows.

ARE WOMEN AND MEN WISE IN THE SAME WAY?

It is not possible here to enter into a consideration of the full nature of wisdom. However, we can say that it involves, at least, the capacity to think or reason well. When we reflect on what we know about the thinking capacities of women and men today, once again we find an interesting shift in scientific knowledge from what had been believed in the past. It has often been argued, although never proven, that women and men have different reasoning capacities.[20] Philosophers in the sex polarity tradition have claimed that men were superior because of their capacity for discursive reasoning, and now theorists from the reverse sex polarity tradition argue that women are superior because of their capacity for intuitive thinking.[21] There has been no scientific evidence that shows that one sex or the other, by virtue of sex, is limited either to discursive or to intuitive reasoning. In fact, it has become clearer that women and men have potentially the same capacity for discursive and intuitive thinking. It would seem to follow from this, then, that women and men are equal with respect to their reasoning capacities.

Sex unity theorists often imply that wisdom demands a complete lack of differentiation between men and women as reflected in language and in thought. They seek to remove all words with sex differentiation from language, to change institutional structures so that no differentiation between the sexes will be possible, and to change the physical appearance so that no differentiation between the sexes will be visible.[22] The sex unity theorists conclude, from the equality of the capacity for reasoning in women and in men, that the thought content of the two sexes is, or should be, sexually non-differentiated. This argument, however, neglects one important fact. Although the reasoning capacity is the same for women and men, the content of consciousness may be different in a number of significant respects.

The difference between the content of thought for woman and man is drawn from their relation to a specific kind of body, to a specific recent past (since their birth), a specific inherited past (within their culture), a present context, and future options. This means that when a person thinks about his or her own identity, the data that are available to his / her mind are different. We could say that the pathway of information differs according to sex. The lived experience of the body is different for a man than it is for a woman; being brought up in the Western world as female or male brings to consciousness an entirely different range of data; being born into a world of stereotypes, archetypes, and historical facts provides a different range of information for a man's reason to appropriate as a specific history than for a woman. Therefore, we can say that reflection on the different data available to the reason of woman and man points to a significant differentiation between the sexes.

This difference in data of consciousness for woman and man does not deny that there may be a large range of common data for individual women and men. There are a great many other factors, such as race, religion, class, domicile, etc., to consider. Therefore, while there is a common bond of data for women and men with similar historical situations, each person has a small band of data for consciousness which is specifically related to sex differentiation. A visual summary of this explanation is found in the following diagram.

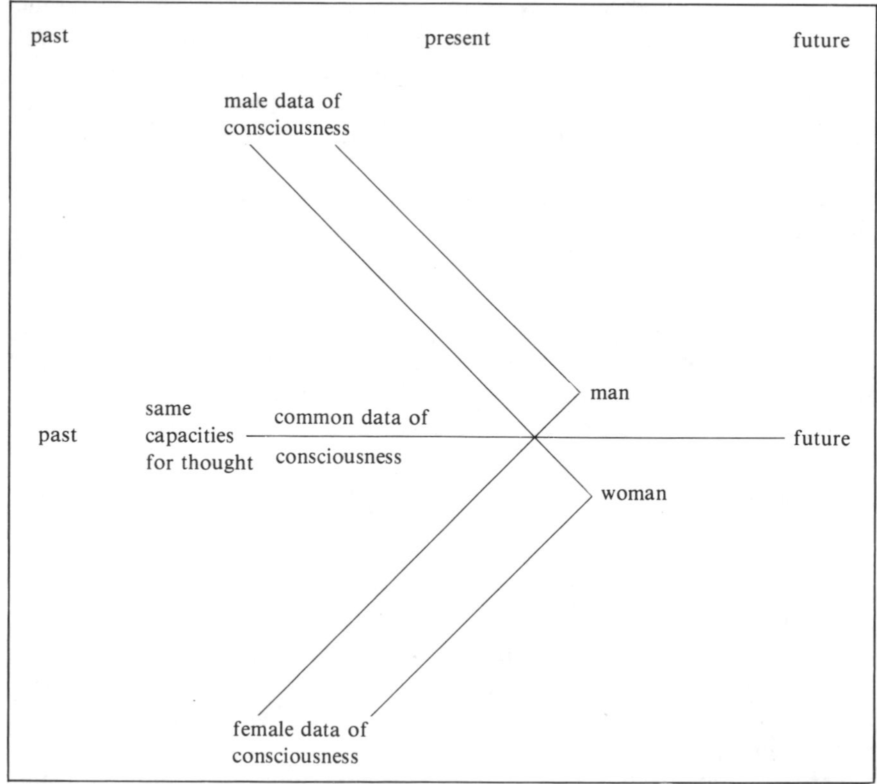

FIGURE 1.2

The question originally posed in this essay concerned whether or not women and men are wise in the same way. Since wisdom invokes using the reason well, it would seem to follow that in terms of having the same capacities for reasoning, women and men are wise in the same way, but that in terms of the particular kind of data they reason about, women and men are wise in different ways. Therefore, this initial consideration of the way in which a person aims towards wisdom also supports the two basic claims of sex complementarity, that women and men are equal, but significantly different.

ARE WOMEN AND MEN VIRTUOUS IN THE SAME WAY?

Once again, without giving a philosophical explanation for the origin and nature of virtue, it can at least be said that virtue involves an ability to act well. Reflection on virtue, then, raises the question: do women and men have the same or different capacities for action?

In order to answer this question it is useful to describe action as involving three phases: assessment, decision making, and forward movement. It has been argued by theorists in the sex polarity tradition that women have a different capacity for assessing situations than men. For example, it has been suggested that women merely have opinions while men have knowledge, or that women jump to conclusions while men consider things more carefully.[23] In a similar way, it has also been argued that women are not capable of making decisions, because their emotions overpower their reason. Certainly, contemporary experience has shown that women as well as men have the same potential for assessing what needs to be done in the world, for deciding what they ought to do, and for carrying this decision forward in action. In short, it is becoming increasingly clear that women and men have a similar capacity for action.

However, does this similarity of capacity imply that women and men ought to do the same things? Sex unity theorists would conclude that it does. They argue that the similarity of acting capacity, or ability to shape the world, demands a rigorous effort to get rid of anything that hinders a person because of his or her sex. In the extreme, it is suggested that all differences in biological contexts for action should be eliminated through the introduction of the test tube baby.[24] The sex unity theorists, in this way, view male or female identity as something to be gotten rid of.

It seems, however, that while it may be correct to argue for the equality of the acting capacity of women and men, that there is also an important difference in context for action given to woman and man. Therefore, just as the fact that the two sexes have the same reasoning capacity is compatible with the conclusion that they have a different context of consciousness, so the fact that the two sexes have the same acting capacity is compatible with the conclusion that woman and man may have a significantly different context for action in many situations. Therefore, women and men under certain conditions ought to act differently.

If we take two traditional virtues associated with the two sexes, a different historical context will emerge. Two of the inheritances of Western patriarchal society are the following moral claims:

> Men ought to rule and women to obey.
>
> Man's actions ought to be directed towards the public sphere and woman's actions ought to be directed towards the private sphere.[24]

One of the basic assumptions of sex complementarity is an aim to develop shared authority of woman and man in both public and private spheres of activity. Sex complementarity claims that women and men bear equal responsibility for the quality of life at home and in society in general. However, the way in which they approach the goal may differ in some respects because of their different natural, historical, and contemporary contexts. That is, women and men have a different pathway of access to the same goal. Figure 1.3 visualizes this difference.

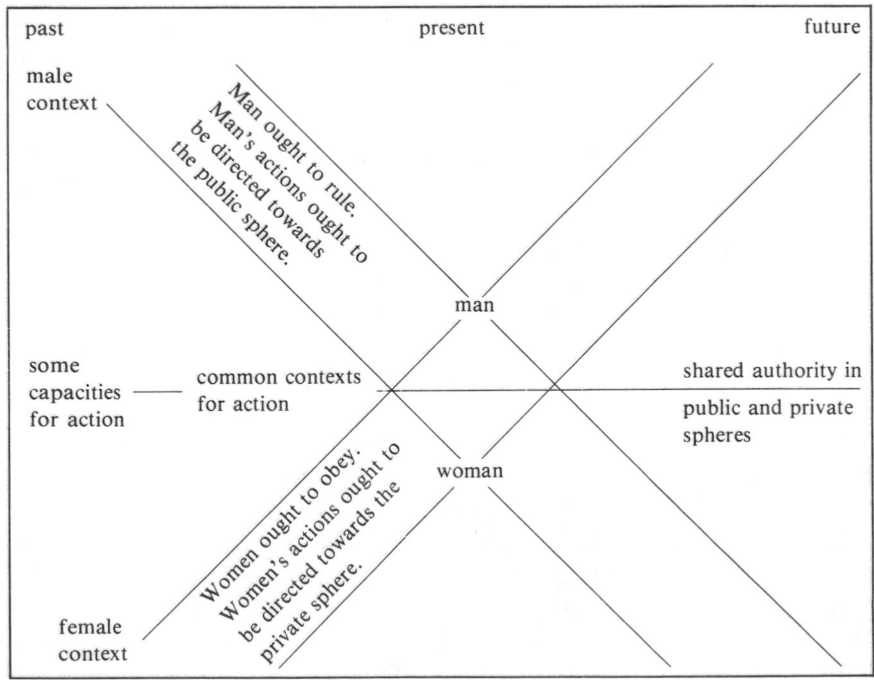

FIGURE 1.3

Women and men inherit different contexts for action because patriarchal society in the Western world embodies the basic views expressed through the sex polarity theory. A woman with an inheritance of patriarchy has a different context for action from a man with an inheritance of patriarchy. It can be seen that women inherit a context for action in which it is considered virtuous for her to obey man, while man's virtue is associated with ruling. This means that if there is a common goal of society to move towards shared authority, it might be more virtuous for a woman to practise the skills of ruling in assuming authority in a particular context, and more vurtuous for a man to practise the skills of obeying in sharing authority, than the other way around. Therefore, an assumption of leadership could be understood as a virtuous act for a woman, and the abdication of leadership for a man in the same situation. A man would be virtuous precisely by not ruling, but by electing to follow, while the woman would be virtuous in the same situation by attempting to rule and giving up the position of follower. Therefore, the different pathways of access to the same situation lead to the choice of different virtuous actions for the woman than for the man.

Another example of the same phenomenon can be seen in an analysis of the second context mentioned above. Patriarchy has often left the legacy that a woman ought to practise her virtues primarily in the home, while a man ought to practise his virtues primarily in society at large. Sex complementarity, as I have defined it, seeks to make women and men aware of their responsibility in both the public and private spheres of activity. It could follow from this that a woman or a man might be virtuous by performing the opposite act in the same situation.

It must be mentioned in passing that this suggestion is not meant to apply to all women and men without exception. Obviously, individuals have a variety of other factors that influence their contexts of actions. There are, for instance, women who have all their lives been able to take leadership positions in public life without any difficulty, and there are men who have equally shared in responsibility in the private sphere. These persons, however, are the exceptions in our society. A philosophy of sex complementarity ought to be established upon the common context of women and men. Therefore, the exceptions ought to be properly understood within the broader framework of the general pattern of activity common to both sexes.

It must also be emphasized that the above examples are not meant to imply that in all situations women ought to lead and men to follow, or that in all respects women ought to move into the public sphere of activity and men into the private sphere of activity. On the contrary, the goal is to have a society in which authority is shared by women and men in all areas of life. The sex unity theory would agree with the goal of shared authority, but would claim that it makes no difference whether the people involved in the authority are male or female. The sex polarity theory, on the other hand, would argue that men ought to have the primary authority. The reverse sex polarity argues sometimes that women ought to have the primary authority, and other times that there ought not to be any authority in society. Sex complementarity insists that the equality of women and men demands a society with shared authority, but that the sharing of authority by significantly different kinds of persons will be reflected in a creative dynamism which this difference unleashes. Only in specific situations will a woman and a man be able to make these dynamics more precise. However, we can tentatively suggest that women approach authority from a different pathway from men in both the private and public spheres of activity.

In this brief consideration, the two examples mentioned merely indicate an application of the basic theory of sex complementarity to the context of virtuous activity. We have seen in this brief study of virtue that there appears to be equality in capacity for action along with a differentiation in contexts for action that are present to women and men. Therefore, once again the two basic concepts of sex complementarity, equality, and differentiation have been supported.

HOW ARE WOMEN AND MEN OPPOSITE?

Although historically, the question of the kind of opposition of the sexes was posed in terms of the opposition of male and female or of the masculine and feminine, today I am posing the question in terms of the opposition of woman and man. The reason for this particular formulation is due to a central emphasis upon the concept of person. The opposition of male and female included the sexual differentiation of a wide variety of animals, while the opposition of masculine and feminine concentrated instead upon qualities of character. Only the sexual opposition between women and men concentrates on their identities as persons.

The first claim of sex complementarity, that women and men are equal, arises in and through their identity as persons. This inherent quality of dignity and worth is the natural birthright of each boy or girl, present even if everyone who receives a child into the world devalues it in relation to the opposite sex. It is also present even if experiences in the world twist and destroy any visible trace of this fact in a particular way in which the individual person's character develops.

The second claim of sex complementarity, that women and men are significantly different, arises through their inheritance as different kinds of persons. Rational consciousness, the particular gift of human life, reveals this difference. Women and men are significantly different in their most important human activities. This difference has been characterized as a difference in pathways to the world. In generation, this occurred through the different ways in which female seed and male seed travel to meet one another for conception. In wisdom, this occurred through the specific delineation of sex-related data of consciousness. Finally, in virtue, this occurred in the different contexts of action for woman and man.

It is possible, now, to summarise the ways in which this consideration of generation, wisdom, and virtue had produced evidence for the philosophy of sex complementarity.

	Equality	**Differentiation**
Generation	The seed of woman and man have the same basic structure.	The seed of woman and man approach one another from a different pathway.
Wisdom	Women and men have the same capacities for thought.	Women and men have different pathways of data for thought.
Virtue	Women and men can have the same capacities for action.	Women and men have different pathways or contexts for action.

If the generation, thinking, and acting capacities of woman and man are integrated, then a kind of picture of their complementarity begins to emerge. Once again a diagram (Figure 1.4) might help to unify the explanation.

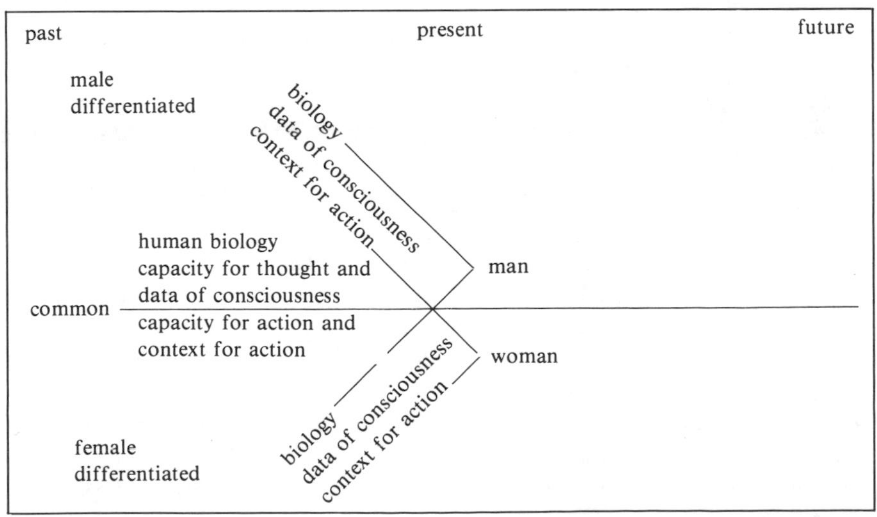

FIGURE 1.4

As human beings we move forward into the future out of a specific past. Just as our generative capacities mature over time, so our thinking and acting capacities develop from a concrete past into a dynamic present. Similarly, just as a future child calls forth the equal and differentiated contribution of a mother and father, so also the future of the world calls forth the interaction of equal and differentiated thinking and acting women and men.

In conclusion, it appears that the limited goals of this chapter have been met. Some practical areas of application, as well as a theoretical foundation for a theory of sex complementarity, have been indicated. In an historical and contemporary context of many sophisticated arguments in support of sex polarity, reverse sex polarity, and sex unity, I am aware of the controversial aspect of some of my claims. I hope, therefore, that they will be received with the recognition that it is simply a beginning of a work that will need to unfold further through the co-operative efforts of women and men far into the future.

REFERENCES

Acknowledgement — This article has been presented as papers at the following conferences: The Canadian Philosophical Association, Learned Society Meeting, Ottawa, June 1982 and The World Congress of Philosophy, Montréal, August 1983.

1 Hildegard of Bingen, *Heilkunde* (Salzberg: Otto Muller Verlag, 1957). Sex polarity, as a theory, gained dominance in Europe through the influx of Aristotelian theory at the University of Paris in 1255. Sex unity was later developed through Cartesianism in the 17th and 18th centuries.

2 It is interesting to note that the concept of "complementarity" is surfacing again in many high-quality feminist works. See Carol Gilligan, *In A Different Voice* (Cambridge: Harvard Univ. Press, 1982); "Development for both sexes would therefore seem to entail an integration of rights and responsibilities through the discovery of the complementarity of these disparate views" (p. 100).

3 It is interesting to note the difference between the United States and Canada here. The ERA was rejected while the Charter of Rights was finally adopted. Could it be that Canada is more comfortable with the concept of "different but equal" through its preservation of distinct cultural and linguistic groups?

4 See, for example, Lisa Newton, "Reverse Discrimination as Unjustified" in *Sex Equality,* ed. Jane English (Englewood Cliffs, N.J.: Prentice-Hall, 1977).

5 The best discussion of this issue is found in Janet Radcliffe Richards, *The Sceptical Feminist: A Philosophical Enquiry* (London: Routledge and Kegan Paul, 1980).

6 See Mary Daly, *Gyn / Ecology: The Metaethics of Radical Feminism* (Boston: Beacon Press, 1978).

7 See the following sources for further discussion of this issue: Jane Gould, "The Case for Barnard College: A Feminist Statement", unpublished article, 1976; "History of Smith College", an excerpt from *Smith College Calendar*, 1977 / 78, Series 71, Sept. 1977; and Elizabeth Tidball and Vera Kistiakowsky, "Baccaulaureate Origin of American Scientists and Scholars", *Science*, 193(1976), 646 - 52.

8 See Olga Eizner Favreau, "Sex Bias in Psychological Research", *Canadian Psychological Review*, 18, 1(1977), 56 - 65.

9 See Gilligan, op. cit.

10 Plato, *Republic, Laws;* Poulain de la Barre, "De l'égalité des deux sexes", 1673; Ann (Finch) Conway, *The Principles of the Most Ancient and Modern Philosophy,* 1690; Margaret Cavendish, Duchess of Newcastle, *Observations Upon Experimental Philosophy,* 1666, *Grounds of Natural Philosophy*, 1688, *Descriptions of a New World, Called the Blazing World*, 1688, and "Female Orations" in *Orations of Diverse Sorts*, 1668; and Shulamith Firestone, *The Dialectic of Sex* (New York: Bantam, 1971).

11 Aristotle, *The Generation of Animals;* Sigmund Freud, "Femininity" in *New Introductory Lectures* XXXIII; Jean Paul Sartre, *Being and Nothingness* (New York: Philosophical Library, 1956); Stephen Goldberg, *The New Inevitability of Patriarchy* (New York: William Morrow, 1973).

12 Heinrich Cornelius Agrippa von Mettlesheim, *On the Superiority of Woman Over Man,* 1529; Ashley Montagu, *The Natural Superiority of Women* (New York: Macmillan, 1953); Valerie Solanis, "The SCUM Manifesto" in *Sisterhood is Powerful*, ed. Robin Morgan (New York: Random House, 1970), pp. 514 - 19; and Jill Johnson, "Woman Prime" in *Lesbian Nation* (New York: Simon and Schuster, 1973).

13 For a consideration of the importance of rationality see Jean Bethke Elshtain, *Public Man, Private Woman, Women in Social and Political Thought* (Princeton: Princeton Univ. Press, 1981); of individuality, see Simone de Beauvoir, *The Second Sex* (New York: Random House, 1974); and of spirituality, see Rosemary Ruether, *New Woman, New Earth: Sexist Ideologies and Human Liberation* (New York: Seabury Press, 1975).

14 Ann LaBastille, *Woodswoman* (New York: E.P. Dutton, 1976); *Women and Wilderness* (San Francisco: Sierra Club Books, 1980); and *Assignment: Wildlife* (New York: E.P. Dutton, 1980).

15 Arlene Blum, *Annapurna: A Woman's Place* (London: Granada Publishing Limited, 1980). I would also like to mention that I met Arlene through Luree Miller, author of *On Top of the World: Five Women Explorers in Tibet* (London: Paddington Press, 1967). It was Luree's recognition of the practical application of the theory of sex complementarity that led me to write this paper.

16 See Grace Lichtenstein, *Machisma: Women and Daring* (Garden City, N.Y.: Doubleday, 1981).

17 I have traced the historical roots of these questions in ancient and mediaeval philosophy in a text entitled *The Concept of Woman: The Aristotelian Revolution* (750 B.C. - 1250 A.D.) (Montréal and London: Eden Press, 1985).

18 Aristotle, *Generation of Animals, 728a - 775a.* See also "De formationis corporis" in *Giles of Rome and the Medieval Theory of Conception,* ed. M. Anthony Hewson (London: The Athena Press, 1975).

19 See *The Concept of Woman,* op. cit., for a detailed explanation of these theories.

20 See Aristotle, *Politics,* 1260a, 1 - 15.

21 See Daly, op. cit.

22 See Firestone, op. cit.

23 See Arthur Schopenhauer, "On Women" in *Studies in Pessimism* (Michigan: Seabury Press, 1970).

24 Firestone, op. cit.

FURTHER READING

Allen, Sr. Prudence, R.S.M., *The Concept of Woman: The Aristotelian Revolution, 750 B.C. - 1250 A.D.* (Montréal and London: Eden Press, 1985).

Anderson, Margaret, *Mother Was Not a Person* (Montréal: Black Rose Publishing Ltd., 1972).

Clark, Lorenne and Lange, Lynda, *The Sexism of Social and Political Theory* (Toronto: University of Toronto Press, 1979).

English, Jane, *Sex Equality* (Englewood Cliffs, New Jersey: Prentice-Hall, Inc., 1977).

Mahowald, Mary Briody, *Philosophy of Woman: Classical to Current Concepts* (Indianapolis: Hackett Publishing Company, 1978).

Warren, Mary Anne, *The Nature of Woman: An Encyclopedia and Guide to the Literature* (Inverness, California: Edgepress, 1980).

MARGRIT EICHLER

The Relationship between Sexist, Non-sexist, Woman-centred and Feminist Research in the Social Sciences

INTRODUCTION

Over the past fifteen years, much effort has been expended on demonstrating that, by-and-large, research in the social sciences is sexist.[1] For the time being, I will define social science as sexist if it is informed and shaped by a male viewpoint, resulting in a distorted picture of social reality. A more detailed definition of sexism in the social sciences will be offered below.

For the purposes of this chapter, I will take as a starting point the conviction that indeed the social sciences are, by-and-large, sexist. The major aim here will therefore not be to demonstrate once more that a sexist bias exists in some particular aspect of scholarship (although the continued exploration of this bias continues to be an extremely important task, by no means completed), but rather to pose the question: where do we go from here? Once we have accepted the verdict that at present most social science is, in fact, sexist, how do we go beyond this bias?

This is a point on which feminist scholars differ. There are some who would propose particular methods as particularly appropriate for overcoming sexism and incorporating women into our knowledge-generating processes. Bernard (1973), for instance, has argued for a communal rather than an agentic approach. McCormack (1981), by contrast, suggests simulations as a particularly useful tool for going beyond the restrictions of current sexist society. Oakley (1981:41) identifies the use of prescribed interviewing practice as ''morally indefensible'', and argues for a relationship between interviewer and interviewee that is non-hierarchical and in which

Originally published, in slightly modified form, in Thelma McCormack (ed.), *Studies in Communication III*, JAI Press, 1986.

the interviewer is prepared to invest his or her own personal identity in the relationship. Thus, there is "no intimacy without reciprocity" (Oakley, 1981:49). Smith (1979) argues to take the everyday world, in which we are located physically and socially, as our problem and to look from the women's standpoint at the location of organizing processes in externally structured and differentiated relations. O'Brien (1983) argues for an historical dialectical method that takes the reproductive process into account. Some Marxist feminists argue for a Marxist approach that, at the same time, recognizes patriarchy as an independent force in history (e.g., Hartmann, 1976). In my opinion, all of the above suggestions for proceeding (as well as others not mentioned here) have merit. This suggests that the answer to the puzzle posed by the existence of sexism in the social sciences does not lie at the level of any one particular method employed, but at a meta-level.

The question then is: what is our ultimate vision of the direction that knowledge should take? Should it be non-sexist? If so, what would this mean, and is this thinkable in a profoundly sexist society? Or should our ultimate aim be the creation of a new form of scholarship, whether it be called women's studies, feminology, feminist studies or anything else that runs parallel to what Kuhn (1970) has called "normal science" and what I will refer to as "normal social science" in this paper?

Here again, feminist scholars will disagree, but much less clearly, since much of this argument has not been put forward explicitly. Instead, the argument has been largely implicit. My primary goal here is to make the point that we must explicitly identify the goal of feminist scholarship beyond the level of criticizing sexist social science. In order to do so, I will distinguish between two modes of conducting feminist studies, namely woman-centred research and non-sexist research. The distinction will be drawn rather sharply in the beginning, but will become more blurred as we examine the interaction between these two modes of engaging in feminist research. Both modes are in opposition to sexist social science, thus necessitating a reflection on the nature of sexism in the social sciences. In order to locate the discussion within a historical context, I will draw on Kuhn's (1970) essay, *The Structure of Scientific Revolutions*, in order to identify the stage of the current discussion and to propose what I see as the desirable ultimate goal for feminist research.

THE PROCESS OF PARADIGM SHIFTS

Kuhn describes the process of major theoretical reorientations within science — events that he calls scientific revolutions — as a process that starts with the existence within a particular science of a crisis which may be externally or internally generated. Prior to the crisis there exists a paradigm that guides research. At its most general level, this paradigm can be identified as "normal science". For a paradigm of this sort to exist it is not necessary for practitioners to be aware of a set of rules and assumptions that underlie their work for as long as there is agreement on this unstated body of rules and assumptions.

> Scientists work from models acquired through education and through subsequent exposure to the literature often without quite knowing or needing to know what characteristics have given these models the status of community paradigms. And because they do so, they need no full set of rules. The coherence displayed by the research tradition in which they participate may not even imply the existence of an underlying body of rules and assumptions that additional historical or philosophical investigation might uncover. (Kuhn, 1970:46)

The existence of such a paradigm (which, as stated, may be unconsciously followed) determines the choice of problems to be studied within its framework:

> ... one of the things a scientific community acquires with a paradigm is a criterion for choosing problems that, while the paradigm is taken for granted, can be assumed to have solutions. To a great extent these are the only problems that the community will admit as scientific or encourage its members to undertake. Other problems, including many that had previously been standard, are rejected as metaphysical, as the concern of another discipline, or sometimes as just too problematic to be worth the time. (Kuhn, 1970:37)

The transition from one paradigm to another commences with a feeling of crisis. This crisis is evoked by an anomaly that is so weighty that it calls the entire paradigm into question if the latter is unable to provide a solution for it. "When ... an anomaly comes to seem more than just another puzzle of normal science, the transition to crisis and to extraordinary science has begun." (Kuhn, 1970:82) People begin to search for alternative solutions. This is a lengthy process, one that is impossible to time exactly or to attribute with precision to one individual only, since we are discussing a collective process rather than an individual shift in thinking.

Once a new paradigm has been formulated, it will in time come to replace the previous paradigm, but only against concerted resistance (Kuhn, 1970:64 - 65), and no existing paradigm will be rejected simply because flaws within it have been uncovered: rejection of an existing paradigm *at the collective level* always implies acceptance of an alternative paradigm. In other words, "a scientific theory is declared invalid only if an alternate candidate is available to take its place." (Kuhn, 1970:77).

If we accept the above description as an accurate description of shifts in scientific world views, where do woman-centred and non-sexist scholarship fit into this picture?

SEXIST SOCIAL SCIENCE AS "NORMAL SCIENCE"

In the last decade and a half, there has been a concerted effort by feminist scholars to demonstrate that normal social science is, indeed, sexist. By now, there is an impressive array of literature that makes this point in detail and with great care.[2]

There seems to be some dawning awareness on the part of, I would suspect, the majority of social scientists that women have so far been unjustifiably excluded from consideration, and that there is some need to integrate women's concerns into social science. In Canada, this is manifested in many conferences geared towards women; a strategic grant area on the topic of "Women and the Work World" at the Social Science and Humanities Research Council of Canada; some modest tendency in various new textbooks to include at least one chapter or section on women, and / or to discuss some aspect of sex roles, or the position of women with respect to the subject area under discussion, etc. In addition, there has been some concern about sexist language, and several publishers and scholarly journals have accepted policies on publishing only materials written in non-sexist language. Universities and colleges have courses on women, or on sex roles, and occasionally even on feminist theory. The federal government has created five endowed Chairs of Women's Studies, one for each region of the country.[3] There are a host of special publication outlets for specifically feminist outputs.[4]

In other words, there is some tangible evidence that women now constitute a legitimate area of interest, counter to earlier times, in which many of the same criticisms and the same suggestions as are being made today were made then but did not penetrate institutional structures sufficiently to appear on official agendas.[5] Nevertheless, the estimation of the importance of the issues raised will vary tremendously among different social scientists. For some feminist scholars, including myself, the problem of sexism in the social sciences is seen as of such pre-eminent importance that it needs to be solved before we can proceed with business as usual. For other social scientists, concern about feminist issues and sexism in social science may at best constitute a bit of unrest that is taking place at the distant margins of their respective fields, just barely at the periphery of their field of vision, and therefore only most dimly perceived.

As far as mainstream social science — normal social science — is concerned, there is at best the dawning awareness that there may be a problem, but then, research is beset with problems of all kinds. In spite of the impressive amount of work done by feminist scholars in a very short time,[6] the impact of feminist scholarship on normal social science has, in my opinion, so far been quite negligible.

If we recall Kuhn's observation that one paradigm will not be abandoned before there is another to take its place, it follows that the struggle to eliminate sexism from the social sciences will *not* be won by further demonstrating that social science is, indeed, sexist. The most likely response from the majority of normal social scientists will probably simply be to say, "Okay, so it is sexist, but what would you have us do instead?" We therefore need to develop a response to the question of how to go beyond sexism once its existence has been demonstrated, and this is a point on which feminist scholars do not at present agree.

POSSIBLE RESPONSES TO THE PROBLEM OF SEXISM IN THE SOCIAL SCIENCES

There are at least four possible responses to the realization that there is, indeed, sexism in social science scholarship. The first response is to consider this an issue of marginal importance and effectively to ignore it by going on with business as usual. At present, I would suggest that this is the response of normal social science and therefore of the vast majority of social scientists involved in the collective process of knowledge generation.

The second response acknowledges that sexism is an important issue and tries to deal with it by attempting to incorporate women, wherever possible, and however much something needs to be stretched, into one's existing framework. This results in studies that show that one's own theoretical framework — Marxism, phenomenology, ethnomethodolgy, demography, symbolic interactionism, role theory, etc. — are in fact admirably fitted to incorporate women. It results in publications that have, typically, one chapter or one section on women, often connected by an "and", namely whatever the topic is "and women". This could be identified as a liberal response.

The third response to the dilemma posed by sexism in the social sciences starts from the premise that women have been excluded from consideration and that this cannot be remedied by simply adding them to otherwise unchanged ways of proceeding. New questions, this response would argue, need new answers, and we will be able to generate both the questions and the answers only by concentrating wholly on women. The starting point is, therefore, the position of women, and the goal is to reach a better understanding of the particularities of the female condition. This response, which can be identified as a woman-centred approach, may or may not be combined with a concomitant commitment to a particular way of proceeding. In cases of conflict between a particular method or theoretical framework and the central concern of understanding women, the commitment to the latter is stronger than the commitment to the former. This is a position that would seem to describe the work of a number of feminist scholars in at least some portion of their writings.[7]

The fourth response shares the premise of the third, that sexism in the social sciences cannot be solved by simply incorporating women into existing theories, but draws a quite different conclusion as to what should be done: while the third response logically would ultimately result in a new field of study, whether it be called women's studies, feminist studies, feminology, or anything else, the fourth response to the dilemma of sexism in the social sciences asks for a transformation of all social science itself such that it becomes non-sexist, not only by the creation of a new paradigm centred around women, but the integration of the concern for women into social science in such a manner that transforms both the current male-centred (sexist) approach and the incipient female-centred approach into a non-sexist approach.

When choosing between the four possible responses as outlined above (in reality, the distinctions are not quite as sharp as is suggested here), it becomes very obvious that the choice of what is considered the most appropriate response hinges on one's definition of the nature and the gravity of the problem, whether it is seen as a marginal or as a core issue for the social sciences.

If the answer is that the problem is marginal, responses one or two (business as usual or the liberal response) would seem appropriate; but if the issue is seen as one of fundamental importance, one might still legitimately choose either response three (the woman-centred approach) or response four (the non-sexist approach). This being the case, I will next consider the nature of sexism in the social sciences, arguing that it is indeed a fundamental rather than a marginal problem, and thus ruling out responses one and two as appropriate responses. I shall then demarcate, in a somewhat exaggerated manner, the differences between the woman-centred approach and the non-sexist approach and look at the consequences of choosing the one over the other as an ultimate goal for feminist scholarship. Both the woman-centred and the non-sexist approach shall be seen as two alternative modes of conducting feminist research. Subsequently, the relationship between woman-centred and non-sexist research will be explored in both an ahistorical temporal sense as well as in an historical logical sense.

THE NATURE OF SEXISM IN THE SOCIAL SCIENCES

Trying to identify and isolate the various elements that make a particular piece of research sexist is a bit like trying to determine, in a general sense, the various conditions that may render a person incapable of walking on his or her own two feet. In any case, the condition always results from a complex net of interrelated factors, and in different cases different factors will be present. Some that are crucial in some cases will be absent altogether in others (e.g., some persons simply may no longer have one or two feet), and any attempt to disentangle the various combinations of factors that lead to comparable outcomes (not being able to walk on one's two feet) will by necessity make some artificial distinctions.

One way to isolate sexist elements in research would be to follow the sequence of doing research. This is an approach taken by Kelly (1978), who divides the research process into three crude stages:

1. Choosing the research topic and formulating hypotheses
2. Carrying out the research and obtaining results
3. Interpreting results (Kelly, 1978:227)

She argues that feminism can and must enter the first and third stages, but not the second one. If, however, one is convinced that data collection (or, in general, "carrying out the research and obtaining results") can also be done in a sexist or in a non-sexist manner, this sequencing is of no great help, since it does not break down the syndrome of sexism into manageable bits.

Instead of following some sequence of the research process, I will therefore identify elements of sexism that may appear in any, all, or some stage of the research process, and generate them by drawing on such feminist analyses of sexism as are helpful in this context. I will therefore discuss sexism in social science research in seven major forms: in language, concepts, questions posed, methods used, interpretations made, and (where applicable) policy recommendations made, as well as in overall perspective.

As is obvious from this simple listing, the various elements are not independent. Concepts are inseparable from an overall perspective; questions posed interact with methods used; the medium of language affects (with the exception of some highly mathematical studies) all other elements, etc. Nevertheless, isolating these elements may serve as a useful heuristic tool as long as we keep in mind that the distinctions thus created are, in reality, artificial. Overall perspective is the most important and the least specific element: it is, in a sense, a residual category, and in our attempts to identify sexism it will be desirable to specify the overall perspective through detailed analyses of other elements as much as possible. It will thus be considered last, as a catch-all category.

1. LANGUAGE

It is by now fairly well recognized that the use of male terms for generic purposes constitutes a sexist practice that has two major flaws: for one, the male terms are not experienced as truly generic. Silveira (1980), in reviewing fourteen empirical studies that examined this issue found that:

In all 14 studies the GM [generic male] terms caused more male-biassed responses than did the more neutral wording. Thus, pictures illustrating generic *man* contained more males than pictures illustrating people. Characters referred to as generic *-man, he* or *his* were given a male identity more often than characters referred to as *-person, their, they, he or she* or *his or her.* (Silveira, 1980:170).

For the other, one of the most important aspects of scientific discourse is clarity, accuracy, and non-ambiguity. Therefore, to use terms that have two quite different meanings is highly confused and confusing. If we take a non-sexual analogy this becomes quite clear. Let us assume we lived in a society in which right-handed people were dominant, considered this a very important characteristic, and discriminated against left-handed people as well as anything that is "left." Let us further assume that this was reflected in the language such that "right" was seen as both a specific directional term as well as a generic directional term, incorporating both left and right. Let us now assume that we wanted to find Main Street and got as a response to our question that it was quite close — "all you have to do is turn right at the first corner, right at the second corner after that and right again." Given the ambiguity in the meaning of "right", we would not know whether to turn right, right and right, or right, left and right, or left, left and right, etc. The unsatisfactory lack of precision becomes immediately clear. The situation really is not much different with respect to the use of male terms for generic purposes, which has been examined quite carefully and from a variety of perspectives and is now widely seen as unsatisfactory.[8] However, there is another aspect to the issue of sexism in language that has not drawn as much attention but is equally important: namely the use of generic terms for sex-specific situations, for instance by calling boys "children", mothers "parents", wife abuse "spouse battering", delinquent boys "delinquent adolescents," etc. This practice as effectively confuses issues as the use of male terms for generic purposes, and for parallel reasons. This practice may be engaged in, however, in an attempt to use non-sexist language! Using non-sexist language, therefore, must definitely not be confused with removing sex from language, but instead to use it in its proper form and place. To put this into abstract terms, language is non-sexist if it uses sex-specific terms to describe sex-specific situations; by the same token it never uses sex-specific terms to describe generic situations. Instead, it uses generic terms to describe generic situations. Sexist language commits either one or both of the above identified errors: it may use sex-specific terms to describe generic situations and / or may use generic terms to describe sex-specific situations. Either usage must be seen as unacceptable for scientific discourse, because it obscures and confuses descriptions of social phenomena rather than elucidate and accurately describe them.

2. CONCEPTS

Recognizing concepts as sexist is much more difficult than recognizing language in general as sexist, and touches more upon their meaning than their wording. In other words, concepts may be sexist because of the context in which they are located, the meaning that is attributed to them, and the manner in which they are used. In general, concepts are sexist if they are based on some form of double standard, although the ways in which such double standard may manifest itself may vary greatly. Let us consider some examples.

When suburbs were characterised as "bedroom communities", we must ask ourselves: "For whom?" Obviously, the answer is — only for employed people who work elsewhere, and twenty years ago that meant primarily men. Housewives, children, the unemployed, those on social assistance, the handicapped, and the retired (all together constituting the majority of people), as well as those people working in the suburbs — store clerks, bank tellers, waitresses, etc. (many of them women) would spend their daytime in the suburbs. By characterising an entire community, which consists of members of both sexes, from primarily the perspective of one sex only (and not even all members of that sex, either) the experience of a select group of men has been allowed to describe a collectivity that far surpasses those men. The concept is sexist, then, because it takes the experience of a portion of one sex and elevates it to the level of a *general* statement that is false for most of the other sex and portions of the same sex.

If, by contrast, the concept had specified that "suburbs are bedroom communities for employed men and women", and then focussed attention on the community structures of those who stayed, there would have been absolutely nothing wrong with that. Instead, we might have had a series of studies that explored the rich texture of community relations from a female perspective. That did not happen, as Lofland (1975) has so eloquently demonstrated.

To take another example, consider the concept of "maternal deprivation", applied (as used to be the case) to designate the experience of children with "working mothers" (meaning mothers who had to leave their children in the care of somebody else during specified portions of the day because they worked for pay). This concept is sexist because it is asymmetrical in the way in which it considers male and female parenting. Children have fathers and mothers, yet fathers who were working for pay were not therefore considered to deprive children of their presence and therefore to produce "paternal deprivation". If we wish to equate regular absences from home with deprivation for the children at all (and this view seems finally to be waning), then a non-sexist expression of this thought would be "parental deprivation" of which there would be two sub-forms: "maternal deprivation" and "paternal deprivation", and each would need to be considered in its own right as well as how it interacts with the other.

Another form of sexism involves a differential valuation of female and male traits as expressed in value-laden terms. Spender (1980:164 - 65) has noted that the habit of calling the male capacity to recognize embedded figures in surrounded fields as "field independence" and the female capacity to perceive the overall pattern rather than special segments of it "field dependence" carries rather clear evaluative overtones. They would be reversed if we were to label the respective capacities as "context awareness" (instead of field dependence) and "context blindness" (instead of field independence). Other instances in which male attributes are very clearly seen as desirable in a general sense include such words as "of seminal importance" (some feminist writers will use instead "of ovular importance".

Yet another form of sexism in concepts involves the implication of a hierarchically structured sexual relationship where such does not adequately reflect social reality. The concept of "head of household" provides one such example. Although the use of this concept seems to be somewhat on the wane in sociological analyses, it seems still to be seen as appropriate in economic analyses.

In Canada, since the revisions of the various provincial family laws, starting with the Ontario Family Law Reform Act of 1978, husbands and wives have, by-and-large, equal responsibilities towards each other, their children, and themselves. By now, the majority of Canadian wives are in the labour force and therefore earn an independent income. In such situations, the use of the concept of head of household, which implies an authoritarian position of one adult over others — this adult always being a male, providing there is one in a household — is therefore inappropriate. By contrast, the use of the concept is appropriate where it designates an authoritarian relationship that in fact exists.

Finally, concepts that are based on some notion of sex appropriateness when in fact we are dealing with human qualities (which may or may not be differentially distributed among the sexes) must be seen as sexist. For instance, such psychological traits as dependency, leadership capacity, talkativeness, etc. are often identified as masculine or feminine traits, meaning that they are represented as being seen as more *appropriate* for one sex than for the other, not that they appear only in one sex. Such labelling distorts actual differences and similarities between the sexes because it grossly exaggerates what may be a *statistical* difference (meaning an unequal distribution) into an *ontological* difference (meaning a difference of being). This is even more obvious with such concepts as the "male" and "female" hormones, which also appear in both sexes, albeit in different proportions.

To summarise, then, concepts are sexist if they (a) construct ego as of one sex only but apply the concept generally, (b) are asymmetrical, in the sense that identical behaviours of females and males are evaluated differentially, (c) involve a differential evaluation of male-identified and female-identified traits, (d) are premised on a hierarchical sexual ordering that does not, in fact, obtain in social reality, and lastly (e) are premised on notions of sex appropriateness when in fact we are dealing with a human attribute.

3. QUESTIONS POSED

One of the most important and least obvious ways in which sexism creeps into scholarship is through the questions that are posed to and about the sexes. Questions can be posed in two ways: either directly to a person or indirectly about a person. We are here concerned only with the second type of question, since the first type will be considered later under the methodology section.

"Question" in this sense, then, means overall research question, irrespective of what methods are being used to pursue an answer. For example, if we ask only women about the conflict they experience between their home life and their paid work, we will be able to document that yes, indeed, there is such a conflict. However, if we neglect to ask men this same question, we cannot draw any inferences about conflict between "the female sex role" and paid labour since we do not know whether the conflict is due to any particular feminine experience or whether it is symptomatic of a general tension that exists between paid labour and home life — and which may also be experienced in some form (although possibly a different form) by men.

Or, if we fail to ask what women (or people not in formal positions of power in general) have contributed to history, we will indeed get the impression that history has been shaped by some men only. Or, if we fail to ask about the men who impregnate women where such conceptions result either in abortions or in births to unmarried women, we will get the impression that both these phenomena are female problems — rather than products of a male-female interaction. It is, for instance, possible that a rather small number of men are responsible for the creation of a rather large proportion of one-parent households. If so, we would have discovered a peculiar *male* behaviour that would require documentation and explanation rather than a peculiar female behaviour, as it is currently perceived.

All of these examples involve one-sided questions that are one-sided by virtue of the fact that they are being asked of one sex only although relevant to both. However, they are *assumed* (not shown) to be irrelevant for the other sex, and thereby any conclusions drawn on such one-sided information must by necessity be suspect if they are elevated to the level of *general* conclusions.

There is another way in which questions posed may be sexist although asked of both sexes, namely by ignoring sex as a variable. This is a practice that seems to be particularly widespread in economics, in which, for instance, workers may be split into full-time and part-time workers and compared on a number of variables, but researchers will not ask of the data whether they show differential patterns by sex. Male-female differences thus may average out and result in an inaccurate picture for both males and females, given that there are gross differences between the sexes with respect to such economic variables as pay, type of occupation, propensity to engage in full-time vs. part-time work, and access to promotions, etc.

Questions posed, then, may introduce a sexist bias into research in either of two ways: either by asking differential questions of the sexes, which necessarily result in different answers, thus reinforcing the stereotype that the sexes are very different; or by collecting data about both sexes but failing to analyse them by sex, thus potentially distorting conclusions drawn about both sexes.

4. METHODS USED

There is probably no other area in which feminist scholars will disagree more strongly with respect to sexism in scholarship than with respect to the issue of sexism in methodology. Some feminists will argue that methods are essentially neutral and that a discussion of sexism in methods is therefore misplaced. Others will argue that particular methods are particularly appropriate for feminist research, and some will argue that particular methods are particularly inappropriate (this argument is sometimes put forward with respect to quantitative methods in general, and in defence of qualitative methods — or one particular qualitative method, such as ethno-methodology).

In my view, such arguments suffer from two misconceptions: first, and more importantly, they confuse methods with their applications, and secondly (when arguing for qualitative over quantitative methods) they confuse a particular state of knowledge (or lack of knowledge) with a question of principle.

With respect to the first of these misconceptions, any method, without exception, can be used in a sexist manner. I am not so certain about the reverse, but until convinced by some cogent argument, I would proceed on the assumption that any method can also be used in a non-sexist manner.

With respect to the second misconception, the argument for qualitative methods usually centres around our collective lack of knowledge about women, and the inherent flaw in using instruments developed for male subjects on female subjects. Women, it is argued, should be able to tell their own story. That is undoubtedly true, and indeed very desirable, but does not really address the issue of appropriateness of certain methods in principle. With respect to certain issues (for instance the birthing experience of women) qualitative methods are highly appropriate, not because they are particularly appropriate for the study of women, but because they are particularly appropriate for exploring subjective experiences about which little is known at the collective level, and about which therefore no reasonable decisions can be made as to what would be the most important variables on which to collect information on a broad basis. Nor can reasonable hypotheses be formulated that might be subjected to large-scale testing in the absence of basic knowledge about the phenomenon under study.

Returning to the issue of sexist use of methods, any discussion of this topic must by necessity be quite sketchy in a chapter of the length of this one. What would ideally be required would be a systematic listing of various methods currently in use in the social sciences, and a thorough examination of representative recent applications with respect to any sexist elements present. Instead, we will here consider only some *examples* of how some methods are often put to use in a sexist manner.

One of the simplest and most obvious ways in which sexism can enter the use of methods can be found in survey research. It can enter through selection of *whom* is being asked *what* as well as through the formulation of questions. For instance, in family sociology it used to be established practice to ask only wives about family issues but to treat their responses as if they reflected reality as experienced by wives as well as husbands. This practice has been severely criticised by Safilios-Rothschild (1969), and since that time there have been a few studies that have asked both husbands and wives about their feelings and afterwards correlated the answers. When this is done, typically large discrepancies in responses can be found.[9] Asking members of one sex about the life circumstances of the other and treating the responses as if they represented reality rather than simply the perception of such reality on the part of the respondents is one form in which sexism can enter into survey research.

Another manner in which sexism enters concerns the formulation of questions asked of respondents. One issue already discussed in the preceding section involves asking questions of one sex but not the other and then drawing general conclusions about the issue *per se*. (For an example, see Eichler, 1983:65 - 104.) Another form of sexism involves questions that allow only a limited spectrum of responses for one of the sexes, for instance, such questions as: "Do you think that women drivers are as good as men drivers?" (or women as bosses, lawyers, or surgeons). This type of question allows responses only up to the level of stating that women drivers (bosses, etc.) are as good as men, but it does not allow the statement that the respondent may think that they are *better*. Correspondingly, men drivers cannot be characterised as worse than women drivers. A non-sexist example of how this question might read follows: "I would like to know what you think about male and female drivers: do you think that, in general, women and men are equally good drivers, that women are better drivers than men, that men are better drivers than women?"

The use of male terms in survey questions for generic purposes generates the same problems. Responses to such statements as "Man is responsible for shaping his own destiny" must always be ambiguous in their meaning, since it remains unclear whether the responses would have been the same if the question had read "Woman is responsible for shaping her own destiny". In such cases, the question must either be rephrased in general terms (e.g., "Humans are responsible for shaping their own destiny") or be asked specifically with respect to both sexes.

In general, and cutting across a large range of methods, the sex of all participants in the research process as well as in all materials used (whether written, visual or otherwise) must be taken into account. This includes the sex of the experimenter, interviewer, coder, subject, interviewee, informer, recorder, experimenter's accessory, etc. In such research instruments as statements to which subjects are asked to respond, cue cards, interpretation of other visual materials, etc., sex of any persons (and possibly animals or such things as dolls) must be noted and be taken into account when interpretations of responses are made. Failing to do so is one common way of using methods in a sexist manner. Finally, the sex of the originators of sources (diaries, pictures, artifacts, etc.) should be taken into account whenever this information is available. Neither sex can speak *for* the other, but only *about* the other. If, for instance, it is impossible either to establish the sex of an originator, or if access to members of both sexes is impossible, at a minimum such gaps should be noted and their significance considered.

A quite different way in which a very serious sexist error is committed occurs if any instruments used have been validated on one sex only but are subsequently used to measure and compare both sexes. This practice has, for instance, been criticised with respect to Kohlberg's model of stages of moral development (Gilligan, 1979). It applies, as a general rule, to all research instruments that are meant to be used by both sexes. *If* they are meant to apply to both sexes, they must be validated on both sexes, or else any findings of discrepancy will not be very meaningful.

Finally, as a matter of course, whenever data are collected on both sexes, they should be manipulated in such a manner that sex can be analysed as a variable.

Although this discussion of sexism in the use of methods has not been an exhaustive one, several general statements can be made: Methods are used in a sexist manner if (a) questions are asked of one sex about the other and the responses are subsequently used as if they represented the reality for the other sex; (b) questions are asked that do not reflect the theoretically possible spectrum of female-male behaviours, attitudes, capacities, traits, characteristics, etc.; (c) the sex of the participants in the research process is not properly taken into account; (d) any sexually identified objects or persons (whether through verbal, visual, or any other means are not properly controlled for); (e) research instruments are validated on one sex only but used on both; and (f) data collected on both sexes are manipulated in such a manner that they cannot be analysed (or the researcher(s) fail(s) to analyse them although it is possible to do so) by sex.

5. INTERPRETATIONS MADE

To discuss sexism in interpretations is a rather dangerous issue, since supposedly we are always guided by our data in our interpretations. It turns out, however, that one can be guided in quite different directions by the same data.

One of the major ways in which sexism enters into interpretation of data is through overgeneralisations, which often take the form of using data collected on males only but treating them as if this represented the issue under discussion in its entirety. Social stratification studies are among the worst offenders on this score. To take just one example, a recent book on *The Fragmentary Class Structure* (Roberts, Cook, Clark, and Semeonoff, 1977) is based on a sample of male workers only, but neither the title nor the subsequent discussion limits itself to, e.g., the "fragmentary male class structure". The authors note the exclusion of women as follows:

> The sample was restricted to the economically active because our interest lay in stratification amongst the working population, and, confined to males because the division of labour between the sexes was not an issue with which we were concerned and, by excluding women, we were able to hold the gender variable constant in the research design. The changing position of women in the class structure is a subject worthy of study in its own right. Little is yet known about women's images of class. As in some other spheres of life, the knowledge codified in "the literature" relates almost wholly to the male half of the population. The female's role has traditionally centred around home and family and her status in the wider society, apart from simply being a woman, has been regarded as dependent upon her husband's. This may be changing and the topic deserves investigation but it was not one of the problems which our enquiry addressed. (Roberts, Cook, Clark and Semeonoff, 1977:12 - 13)

Nevertheless, the authors continue happily to discuss stratification, class formation, systems of inequality, etc., as if they were, in fact, discussing them for all of society, and not excluding the majority of people (i.e., all women, all children and men not in the labour force) from any relevant discussion.

One avoids overgeneralisations by generalising one-sex studies to one sex only. Such restriction must also be obvious in the central concepts used which should reflect their partial applicability by a sexual specification where such is the basis on which they have been created.

Another way in which sexism creeps into interpretations consists of ignoring findings of no sex differences, as Maccoby and Jacklin (1874:4) have noted. This leads, in a cumulative manner, to an exaggeration of sex differences rather than sex similarities, by distorting the balance. Findings of no sex difference should be as big news as findings of sex differences, and should be routinely noted. Too often, however, significant information is equated with the finding of a statistically significant difference between groups.

There are at least two other major ways in which sexism can enter the interpretation of data. Whenever a double standard is used to explain any findings — e.g., when sexual activity of adolescent girls and boys is evaluated differentially, or seen as of differential importance, or when some behaviour (trait, attitude, etc.) is seen as appropriate for one sex but as inappropriate for the other, we are dealing with a sexist interpetation.

Finally, although sex must be considered as an extremely important variable for *descriptive* purposes, in *social science research* it is not a useful explanatory variable: when a social sex difference has been identified, it is insufficient to "explain" it by the biological variable "sex". (Eichler, 1980)

Sexism enters into the interpretation of data, then, through overgeneralising findings made on one sex to all of humanity (or at least by presenting it in such a manner that such is the impression that is created), by ignoring findings of "no sex difference" in favour of findings of "sex differences", by using a double standard in the interpretation of findings, and by using the biological variable of sex as an explanatory variable for *social* behaviours.

6. POLICY RECOMMENDATIONS

Policy recommendations stand in a different relationship to the research process as a whole than do all the other elements. First, many studies do not make policy recommendations. Second, there seems to be no logical connection between findings obtained and policy recommendations made. When looking over theories concerning the origin of sex inequality over the ages, for instance, I was struck by the fact that theorists who subscribe to more or less the same explanation (e.g., social differentiation as a consequence of some crucial biological sex difference, whether this be brain size, overall body type, or whatever) may nevertheless end up with opposite policy recommendations (see Eichler, 1979).

To give just one example: if it is found that boys are physically stronger than girls, one may therefore argue that some type of physical education is particularly relevant for boys, since they are better fitted to engage in it; or, one may argue that it is therefore more important to train the girls in this particular type of physical activity so that they catch up with the boys. In the first case more expenditures might be recommended for boys' sports; in the second for girls'. The difference between the two recommendations — based on the same finding of a sex difference in physical make-up — is due to a different value: in the first case to train the "best" athletes best, in the second to raise the level of physical fitness of all members of a particular group.

Essentially, then, policy recommendations must be evaluated in terms of the goal(s) with respect to which they have been formulated, and it is the goal that is either sexist (by trying to create or maintain a socially generated sex difference) or non-sexist (by trying to maintain or create social equality between the sexes). This implies that in cases in which the conditions of the sexes are comparable, recommendations should be comparable for the two sexes, and where the conditions are different, recommendations should be geared towards minimising social differences.

Many policy-oriented studies, however (e.g., many economic studies) simply will not consider the issue of sex explicitly. It is then a much harder process to identify potential differential effects of proposed policies on the sexes, and may, indeed, be impossible if the preceding analysis did not break down the relevant information by sex. In such cases, a sexist research design will make the generation of non-sexist policy proposals impossible, although a non-sexist research design does not, unfortunately, guarantee that any recommendations made will also be non-sexist.

7. OVERALL PERSPECTIVE

The overall perspective that characterises any piece of research is the most pervasive and most important way in which sexism can and does enter the research process. Those issues that have been considered so far are in a sense nothing but specifications of an overall perspective, which may or may not be sexist. In general, a piece of research must be considered sexist if it adopts the viewpoint of one sex only, but presents this as if it encompassed all of social reality. Since the social positions of the sexes are systematically different, by necessity the perceptions of one sex will be limited as to their applicability to the other. It is for this reason that feminist writers have gradually evolved different descriptions of social institutions, such as "his" and "her" marriage (Bernard, 1972) or "his" and "her" polity (McCormack, 1975), or "his" and "her" work (Oakley, 1974), without necessarily using just these terms.

Another way in which the perspective that characterises research may be sexist consists in seeing one sex (usually women) only as they are relevant to the other sex (usually men), rather than as persons in their own right.

Yet another way in which sexism enters is through conceptualising women (or females in general) as passive, acted upon, and men (or males in general) as active, initiators of actions, rather than starting from the assumption that both males and females have the capacity to act and be acted upon, and that one must search for both aspects in both sexes.

Finally, if one sex is seen as more important than the other, in whatever form, or if a double standard is applied in the evaluation of any behaviours, traits, or attributes of the sexes, we are dealing with sexism in its quintessential form.

Having briefly discussed the specifics of the nature of sexism in the social sciences, we may now give a definition of the problem, using the same words, without being totally tautological, since the operationalisations can be found above. Research, then, is sexist if it displays any sexist elements in any or all of the following: in language, concepts, questions posed, methods used, interpretations or policy recommendations made, as well as in overall perspective. Having finally arrived at a definition of the problem, we can now consider its gravity.

THE PROBLEM OF SEXISM IN THE SOCIAL SCIENCES

Overall, it is no exaggeration to state that, by-and-large, the social sciences are sexist; specifically, that the overall perspective that informs them is androcentric.

So far, we have treated sexism theoretically, as it may take either a male or a female direction, but in fact, of course, at the present time the problem is a male bias, and not a female bias. Beyond such a sweeping statement, our knowledge about the problem of sexism in the social sciences is very limited. For instance, we do not know at the present time what elements of sexism most frequently go together, and why. Likewise, we have not researched the question of whether there is some social science research that is *not* sexist, even though it was developed in an overall sexist intellectual environment. If we could find such unbiassed work, it would be important to understand why and how it managed to escape the sexism that characterises most social science work. At this point, we can address the issue of the gravity of the problem of sexism in the social sciences only in an exemplary manner.

Let us, then, consider one of the central cases in which sexism displays itself within sociology and for which we clearly lack a remedy at the present time. Most sociologists would probably agree that social stratification is one of the most important issues for sociology. The fact that stratification theory in its various versions is sexist has, by now, been noted repeatedly (for example, see the work of Acker, 1973; Eichler, 1973, 1980; Delphy, 1981; Hartmann, 1976 and many others). The issue is not simply one of integrating women into existing frameworks[10] (although such attempts are interesting as far as they go), but of being able to deal with the issue of sex stratification itself *within* (not beside) an overall framework of stratification. Sex stratification manifests itself at the work level, not only in terms of sexual segregation of occupations, or sexual harassment which may take place at all occupational levels (see Backhouse and Cohen, 1981), or in the systematic exclusion of women from positions of power in public institutions, but also at the familial level in the form of wife battering and marital rape (irrespective of the husband's socio-economic status), and in the danger of being assaulted when walking on public streets. In other words, if we truly want a theory of stratification that deals with systematic social inequalities of major kinds, those forms and consequences of inequality that particularly affect women must be integrated not as marginal but as equally important aspects with other forms of social inequality into any theory that claims to be a comprehensive, non-sexist theory of stratification.

In such cases, questions that have previously been considered irrelevant — or at best pertinent in the most ephemeral manner — take on central importance. As Kuhn suggests, a new paradigm leads to new questions. *If* we take women's experience of inequality as having the same importance as men's experience of inequality, then it becomes impossible to argue that women's experiences just do not fit the model and therefore obviously are not so important. This, then, is where the watershed occurs: women's experiences of social inequality are demonstrably *not* represented in current theories of stratification, and a choice must be made either to consider the experiences as of minor importance in order to save the model (of course with some revisions) or else to consider the experience as primary and therefore be prepared to let go of the model, even in the absence of an alternative model.

We have previously identified four possible responses to the problem of sexism in the social sciences: the "business as usual" response; the liberal response; the woman-centred approach; and the non-sexist approach.

Once it has been demonstrated that significant aspects of women's experience are not reflected in any given model, the scholar will have to make a choice as to his or her primary commitment, whether it is to a given model or to an adequate representation of social reality. If the choice is the former, then either the "business as usual" or liberal response will be chosen. (I am inclined not to argue strongly against the liberal response, because it is one step ahead of the "business as usual" one and will, if well done, perform a valuable service: either women turn out to be integratable, in which case this is a sufficient response; or their experience turns out not to be integratable, in which case such efforts at least pave the way for the woman-centred or non-sexist approaches.) However, if the liberal response turns out to be unsatisfactory, the question still repeats itself, and the scholar will have to decide whether her or his deepest commitment is to an already existing model or to the task of capturing the lived experience of women.

If one's commitment is to finding an adequate expression of experience over a commitment to a model *per se*, there are still two alternative responses possible: one may argue that a separate paradigm must be developed for women (the woman-centred approach), or that a model must be developed that is equally applicable to both males and females, and which will therefore not only improve our understanding of the situation of women, but also of the situation of men. Ignoring sex as a variable not only leads us to ignore women, but also blinds us to seeing men as men, since they are treated as if they represented all of humanity (Morgan, 1981).

It is at this point, then, that we find a branching off among feminist scholars. While the "business as usual" response is typical of a scholar untouched by (or perhaps hostile to) the feminist debate, the "liberal" response derives from an awareness that there is a problem, but a lack of understanding of its true dimensions. Adherents of the woman-centred or non-sexist approaches, by contrast, share the view that the scope and gravity of the problem make a continued use of sexist models impossible, but differ on the solutions they consider appropriate, at least at a given point in time.

We shall now examine in more detail the nature and logic of the woman-centred and non-sexist approaches.

THE WOMAN-CENTRED VS. THE NON-SEXIST APPROACHES AS SOLUTIONS TO THE PROBLEM OF SEXISM

Above, we identifed seven ways in which sexism may enter research. We also noted that sexism in the overall perspective is the most pervasive and encompassing aspect of all, and that at the present time the form that this sexism takes is an androcentric (rather than a gynocentric) perspective. Since the overall perspective incorporates the other elements that have been identified as sub-aspects within itself, it can be used as a shorthand expression for discussing the problem of sexism. Concentrating, then, only on the single criterion of overall perspective, we can graphically represent sexist scholarship as a circle in which men (and sometimes women) circle around a social universe that is constructed around males (Figure 2.1):

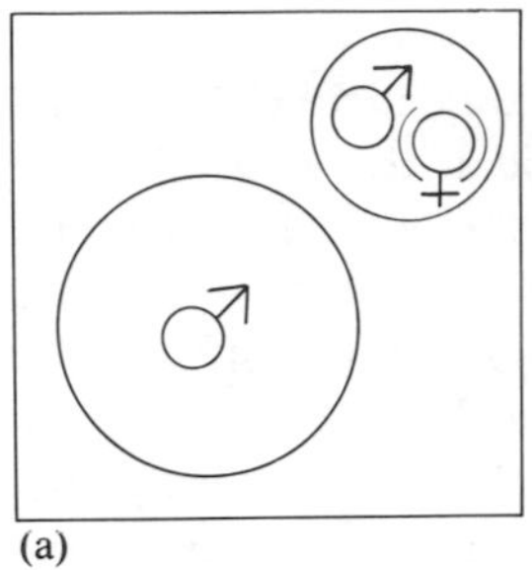
(a)

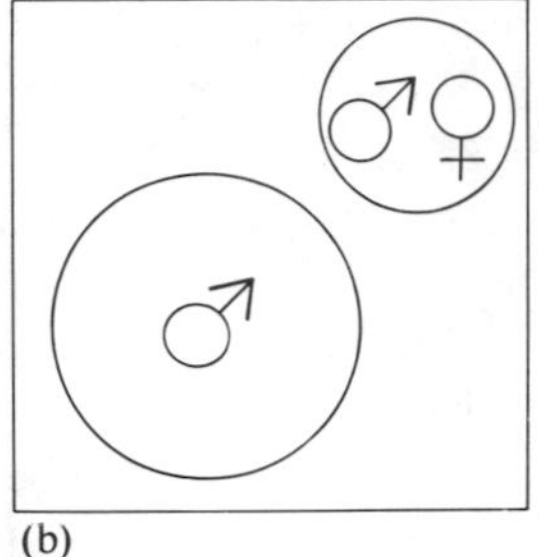
(b)

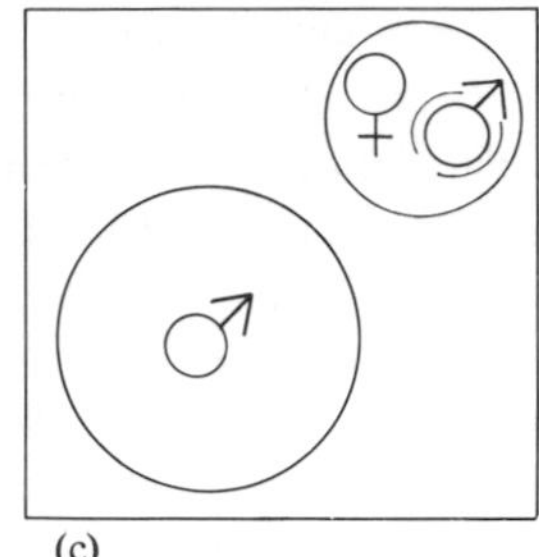
(c)

FIGURE 2.1

This depiction displays that research can be sexist irrespective of its subject matter. A study may focus totally on women, but if these women are seen only in relation to a social universe constructed around males, it remains as sexist as if the work were focussed totally on males. Figure 2.1(a) represents a large bulk of social science, in which both the focus of investigation is on men and the operative model is built on a male perspective, e.g., social mobility studies that measure social mobility between fathers and sons. In model 2.1(a) women are present only as incidental and marginal, shadowy figures. Figure 2.1(b) has as subject matter both women and men, but they are both likewise seen in the context of a male perspective model, e.g., social mobility studies that measure the mobility between sons, daughters and fathers or between sons and fathers and son-in-laws and fathers. Figure 2.1(c), finally, has as subject matter women, but places them firmly into the context of a male-oriented model of social reality. At the non-scholarly level, the "total woman" literature is a prime example of this type of approach. At the scholarly level, Freudian psychology would provide an example of this type of thinking.

A fair amount of feminist research places a gynocentric model in opposition to this androcentric model of the world. As Mary O'Brien (1983:12) says: "Feminist theory has to be biassed because it is anti-bias." Some feminist research, then, constructs a model of social reality that centres around women (Figure 2.2):

(a)

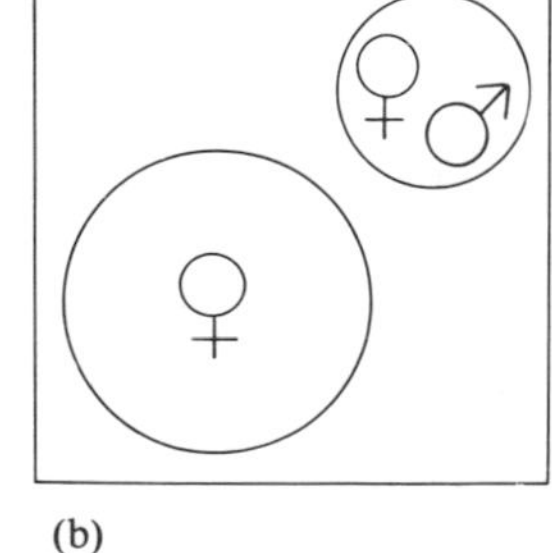
(b)

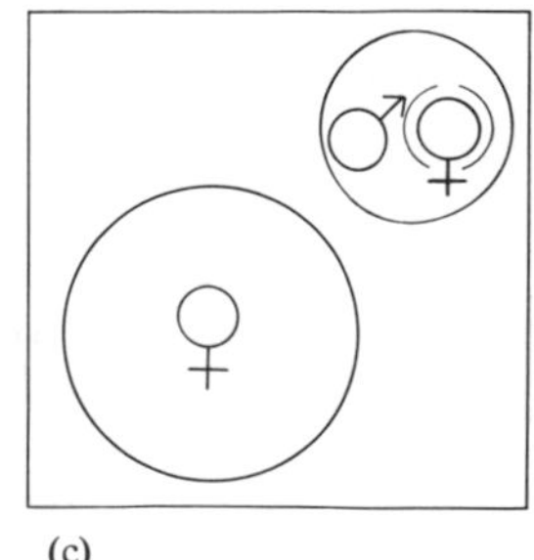
(c)

FIGURE 2.2

Most woman-centred feminist research seems to take the form of model 2.2(a), rather than (b) or (c). When either women and men (b) or men only (c) are placed into the context of a gynocentric model, this is often done tongue-in-cheek, to expose the androcentric bias in models 2.1(a), (b) and (c). Since sexist social science of the type of model 2.1 is, unfortunately, normal social science, users of model 2.1 sometimes seem to confuse their model of reality with reality itself. When there are at least two competing paradigms, or when one uses a model that has been constructed in opposition to a prevailing model, this error would be much harder to commit. It is probably partially for this reason that feminist scholars are less likely to mistake their model of reality for reality itself, and that models 2.2 (b) and (c) are often used as heuristic devices rather than as permanent replacements for models 2.1(b) and 2.1(c) (see, for example, Marsden, 1981).

The third model, the non-sexist model, conceptualises the social universe as constructed around both women and men. Since, however, the position of women and men is not, at present, comparable, we can no longer conceptualise the social universe as a circle that has a focal point, but must instead imagine two equally important focal points. This takes us out of the metaphor of the circle and into the metaphor of an ellipse:

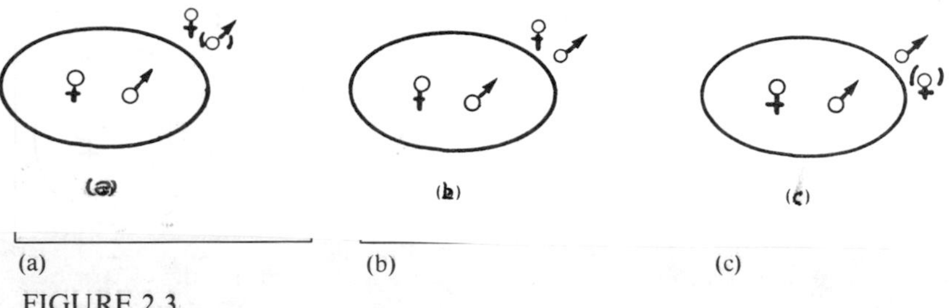

(a) (b) (c)

FIGURE 2.3

This shift of metaphor illustrates the need to re-examine *all* social aspects once we conceptualise the social universe as circling around women *and* men, including male-female relationships. Neither the relationships constructed in model 2.1 nor in model 2.2 can be transferred in unaltered form, irrespective of whether the subject matter is women, men, or women and men both.

Whether one wishes to give primacy to model 2.2 or model 2.3 depends partially on one's view of timing. It can be legitimately argued that it is premature to try to develop a non-sexist model of society before the sexism in prevailing normal social science has been more fully explored and before we have more fully explored the possibilities contained in model 2.2. We need therefore to distinguish between ultimate goals and proximate goals for feminist research.

As an *ultimate goal* I consider woman-centred research undesirable, since it is much too limited; but as a *proximate goal* it constitutes a necessary stage through which we must pass in order to be able even to think about a non-sexist approach.

Identifying the development of a non-sexist approach to scholarship as the *ultimate goal* of feminist scholarship does not imply a devaluing of woman-centred studies, although it does imply a relativising of them. Woman-centred studies are antithetically tied to male-centred studies, and while they provide us with the means of recognising androcentric scholarship as such, they do not give us the means to replace it. If we recall Kuhn's dictum that an old paradigm will only gradually be abandoned by its adherents when there is a new one to take its place, we must ask ourselves what might take the place of the currently existing sexist paradigm.

It cannot be woman-centred studies, because they will exhibit the same limitations as male-centred studies, only in the reverse direction. In addition, they do describe a subject matter: namely the world as it is experienced by women. While this is admittedly a pretty large subject, it is not all-inclusive. In addition, researchers will continue to be largely male for quite a while to come, and even if the sex ratio were 50 / 50, one would not expect all female researchers to adopt a woman-centred approach, especially if their primary interest were quite divorced from issues that are presently seen as relevant to women. Understanding the process of paradigm shift as not only a scholarly but also as a political process, feminist researchers need to be able to suggest a paradigm that could be used by all researchers, whether male or female, and whether interested in feminism or not. Failing such a possible substitution, problems with existing models may be recognised but the models will continue to be used, possibly with some attached disclaimers, such as stating that the choice to continue to use an adequate model is entirely a pragmatic one.

By contrast, if we manage to develop viable non-sexist models, one may hope eventually to replace current sexist models, and can argue that, given the choice, continuing to use old sexist models can no longer be seen as acceptable scholarly behaviour.

THE RELATIONSHIP BETWEEN WOMAN-CENTRED AND NON-SEXIST RESEARCH

I have been suggesting that the development of a non-sexist approach to scholarship must be the ultimate goal of feminist research. However, this is easier said than done. I do not think that it is possible to go directly from sexist research to non-sexist research. At a minimum, there must be two intervening steps: one, the realisation that the old approach is, indeed, sexist, and second, an exploration of what the issue under consideration would look like if it were examined from a female perspective in order to know what questions should be asked with respect to it. At least at a preliminary level, we must regard an issue from a female perspective in order to be able even to think about it in a non-sexist manner.

The identification of sexism in prevailing models, concepts, and research in general is itself one extremely important aspect of feminist research, towards which a major part of the collective effort has so far been, and continues to need to be, directed. It is neither simple nor easy to recognise a theory, a piece of work, or a concept as sexist, and even harder to communicate the methods by which such recognitions can be achieved. Once a piece of work, or an aspect of a work, has been recognised as sexist, it is still an equally, if not more, difficult step to try to identify how the issue might be approached in a non-sexist manner.

Let me come back to the example of social stratification cited before. Since I teach at a graduate school, I am involved in directing a fair number of master's and doctoral theses. Although I am keenly aware of the inadequacies of current ways of measuring stratification, I am nevertheless incapable at the moment of telling my students how to measure stratification in a non-sexist manner. I therefore advise them to use some traditional approach (some type of class analysis, or some form of measuring socioeconomic status), and to use these traditional approaches in more than one way (e.g., by determining the social class of a husband and a wife separately and to record the discrepancy, if any). Clearly, this is a highly unsatisfactory response to the problem. On the other hand, since these theses have to be passed by committees, not dealing with the issue of stratification might be mistaken as incompetence on the part of the student rather than as dissatisfaction with existing measures. I therefore request students to display their competence in using measures that I firmly believe are highly inadequate, and to point out in addition some of the flaws within these measures. This gets the theses passed, but does not solve the problem of inventing a method of dealing with social stratification that is, indeed, non-sexist. In other words, having identified a particular method (theory, model, concept) as sexist does not necessarily enable one to create a non-sexist alternative.

Returning, then, to the issue of the relationship between female-centred and non-sexist research, I believe that in most cases we will have to pass through a stage of female-centred thinking before we will be able to work towards a non-sexist approach. This relationship needs, furthermore, to be put into a time perspective. We are not describing a process in which there is a clear progression from sexist to woman-centred to non-sexist research; we are describing a muddy, unclear, complex process that winds its way back and forth, and it will often be unclear what the ultimate goal is or should be.

Recognising something as sexist is neither simple nor easily achieved. Sometimes we will be able to recognise something as sexist because some other element has previously been so recognised, and an effort has been made to substitute a non-sexist version, only to realise eventually that there are other sexist elements in the supposedly non-sexist model.

One final personal example may suffice to illustrate this process. Sexist language was one of the earliest targets of feminist critiques and the one in which, I believe, we have progressed furthest in creating non-sexist alternatives. Like most other feminist scholars, I have been at some pains, once having become aware of the issue, to acquire the habit of speaking and writing in a non-sexist manner — which at the time I interpreted to mean to avoid the use of male terms for generic purposes. In my efforts to express myself accordingly, I therefore often used generic expressions for all purposes. Recently, while teaching a graduate seminar on family policy, one of my students (Maureen Killoran) pointed out in a carefully written critique that my use of generic terms in situations in which the referent was in fact sex-specific was itself a sexist practice. So, for instance, I had been talking about spouse abuse. Pointing out that spouse abuse, in about 95 per cent of the cases, takes the form of wife battering, she suggested that it was sexist to hide the fact that we are dealing with a sex-specific phenomenon by using a truly generic term. Of course it is! Once it had been pointed out, and my initial shock at being caught red-handed at something I had identified as unacceptable behaviour wore off, it was immediately obvious that the use of generic terms for sex-specific situations is simply the obverse form of sexism that uses sex-specific terms for generic situations. The proper way of communicating in a non-sexist (and therefore adequate) manner consisted in using sex-specific terms for sex-specific situations and generic terms for generic situations.

Using the insight, once it had been formulated, was simple and straightforward, but having the insight and communicating it in an effective manner involved a creative leap that cannot be derived in a linear manner.

Our definition of what constitutes sexism in the social sciences will continue to evolve as our knowledge about previously hidden aspects of sexism in scholarship will continue to grow. This implies that the relationship between sexist, woman-centred and non-sexist research is a dynamic one in which different parts will continue to evolve in interaction with each other. Perhaps it can be represented as a spiral that moves towards (but does not reach) a non-sexist point, and where at any one level woman-centred research makes it possible to recognise some non-sexist version which, placed in a different context, is still seen to contain a sexist element, which, when examined from a female perspective, will allow substitution by a non-sexist element, and so on (Figure 2.4) . . .

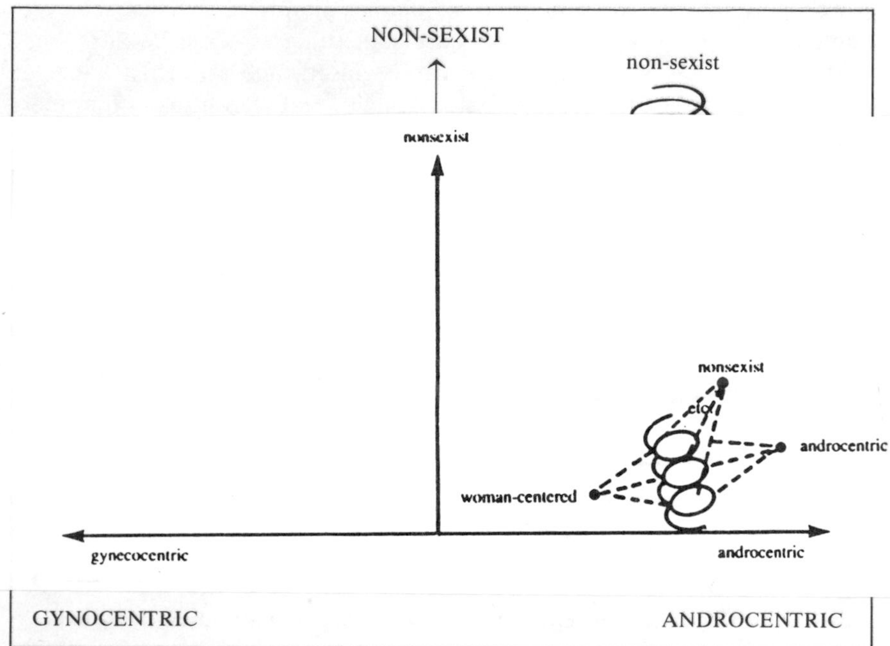

FIGURE 2.4

It should be noted that in this chapter, feminist studies have been treated as a collective endeavour. There is no reason to suppose that any one researcher would follow this pattern of evolution in thought as has just been suggested for the collectivity of feminist researchers. Some researchers may, indeed, switch from concentration on a woman-centred perspective to a critique of sexism to an attempt to develop a non-sexist alternative. Some may switch from one mode of analysis to the other even within one paper or book. Others may devote their energies only to one aspect — for instance, to explore one topic from a female perspective — and indeed that may be more than enough for a lifetime. The distinction that has been drawn between the different modes of analysis exists therefore only in an abstract sense, not necessarily in a concrete sense within any one researcher or group of researchers. Nevertheless, it is an important distinction, because it allows us to examine the relationship that various modes of feminist research have with each other, and to value each in its own right.

WOMAN-CENTRED AND NON-SEXIST RESEARCH AS FEMINIST RESEARCH

So far I have given no definition of feminist research, although it has been implied that both woman-centred and non-sexist research constitute alternative modes of feminist research. If we define feminism, with Richards (1980:4), as "a movement for the elimination of sex-based injustice", feminist research can be defined as research that is informed by a commitment to social justice for women and / or research that exposes prevailing sexist biasses and / or creates unbiassed alternatives and / or constructs reality from a female perspective. Although this is an extremely broad definition, it nevertheless does make a statement about the content of feminist research: although feminist research may deal with any subject matter — relocation of the aged, uranium mining, solar energy, urban planning, leisure activities, the micro-chip, etc. — unless we can establish some connection between the topic and the achievement of social justice for women, either in concrete terms, or in abstract terms through the manner in which the knowledge is generated, it does not qualify as feminist research. This implies an asymmetry with respect to sexist and non-sexist research: although all social science research can be conducted in a sexist manner, once it has been put into a non-sexist mode, much of it will cease to be feminist research and will become simply good social science.

Identifying the creation of a non-sexist mode of knowledge generation and transmission as the goal of feminist *research* (not of the feminist movement, whose goal is the establishment of social justice for women) implies that the ultimate goal of feminist research must be to make itself superfluous. Reaching the goal of non-sexist scholarship is, then, at one and the same time, an ultimate goal for feminist scholarship as well as beyond it. Therefore, establishing the *rules* of how to conduct non-sexist research is a central aspect of feminist scholarship; but using the rules once they have been identified becomes a matter for all scholars irrespective of their concern (or lack of it) for social justice for women.

In other words, the most urgent task of feminist research is to make itself unnecessary by replacing the overall sexist paradigm with a non-sexist one. That, I am afraid, will not happen quickly. So far, the impact of feminist scholarship on normal social science has been quite negligible, in spite of a most impressive array of publications, conferences, and a clearly demonstrated interest on the part of large segments of the scholarly community, as witnessed by the number of courses and programmes oriented towards women's studies or feminist studies. As Kuhn suggests, in the final analysis an old paradigm is abandoned because its adherents eventually die off, or, perhaps more kindly said, retire. Since at present the labour market is such that newcomers find it difficult to enter universities (where most of the paradigm building seems to be taking place), this is not going to speed up the process of replacing the prevailing sexist paradigm with a non-sexist one. However, equally or perhaps more importantly, until we have developed a non-sexist paradigm that can be used by all social scientists irrespective of their interest in and commitment to the notion of social justice for women, the current sexist paradigm will not be abandoned. Scholars will give up one paradigm only if there is another ready to take its place, and *not* simply because flaws in the old paradigm have been convincingly demonstrated. This suggests a natural limitation to the effectiveness of critiques of sexism in the social sciences: although they are an integral aspect of feminist scholarship, and indispensable to the development of a non-sexist paradigm (just as woman-centred research is indispensable for it), their effectiveness and importance consists only in being a transitionary step towards the elaboration of a non-sexist model of social reality. In and of itself, critique will not lead to the abandonment of what has been criticised, even if the criticism is acknowledged as justified.

A SMALL PARADOXICAL POSTSCRIPT

Having started out this chapter with the premise that social science at the present time is largely sexist, I find myself in a somewhat paradoxical situation: having re-read Kuhn's book for the purposes of this chapter, I was amazed to find how well it lends itself to analysing the current situation of feminist research. Yet there is no doubt that this book was written in an overall sexist intellectual environment, and that it in no way distances itself from this intellectual tradition. Women do not even seem to exist for Kuhn, and all scientists are obviously men for him. How then is it that his framework is so admirably useful in understanding the process of transition from a sexist to a non-sexist paradigm that we are currently experiencing?

This is a question to which I have at the present no answer, and I simply present it as a puzzle that may be worth some exploration: under what circumstances, and why, do certain explanations, although developed within an overall sexist framework, lend themselves with only minimal changes to pursuing non-sexist scholarship? It may be that this is the flip side of the coin, which we have so far ignored in our attempts to expose sexist elements in social science: the seeking out of elements of current normal social science that continue to be useful even after a critique of sexism has been undertaken. Perhaps answering this question might aid us in the formulation of a non-sexist paradigm. This chapter thus ends with a question, rather than with an answer, as is quite proper given that we are in the middle of a paradigm shift, rather than at the end of one.

REFERENCES

1 See, for example, Bernard, 1972; Boulding, 1976; Eichler, 1980; Eichler and Lapointe, 1985; Glazer and Waehrer, 1977; Miles and Finn, 1982; Millman and Kanter, 1975; Roberts, H., 1981; Roberts, J., 1976; Sherman and Beck, 1979.

2 For example, Bernard, 1972, 1973, 1981; Boulding, 1976; Eichler, 1973, 1977, 1980, 1983:65 - 104; Hubbard et al., 1979; Huber, 1973; *Journal of Marriage and the Family*, 1971; Maccoby and Jacklin, 1974; McCormack, 1975, 1981; Miles and Finn, 1982; Millman and Kanter, 1975; O'Brien, 1983; Pierson and Prentice, 1982; Roberts, H., 1981; Roberts, J., 1976; Sherman and Beck, 1970; Spender, 1980; Smith, 1974, 1975; Vickers, 1982. For a selected annotated bibliography of critiques of sexism in research see Eichler, with the assistance of Lenton, Brodribb, Haddad and Ross, 1985.

3 The chairs have been awarded to Mount St. Vincent University, Simon Fraser University, Ottawa University and Carleton University (a joint chair), the Universities of Manitoba and Winnipeg (a joint chair), and Laval University.

4 See, for example, *Signs, Women's Studies International Forum, Atlantis, Feminist Review, Hecate, Women and Politics*, and many more. For an international guide to women's periodicals and resources up to 1982, see Zavitz and Kleipool, 1982. See also *Women's Studies Abstracts, Resources for Feminist Research*, and the CRIAW *KWIC Index* for abstracting services.

5 For some of the historical writings, see the collections edited by Rossi, 1974; Scheir, 1972; Spender, 1983; and the quite funny book by Hershberger, 1970, which raised many of the issues of a sexist bias in scholarship in 1948.

6 For an overview of the work done in Canadian anglophone sociology alone, see Eichler, 1985.

7 See, for instance, Bernard, 1981; Boulding, 1976; O'Brien, 1983; Daly, 1978; Smith, 1977.

8 For some literature on this issue, see Blaubergs, 1980; Moulton, 1981; Miller and Swift, 1980; Yaguello, 1970; Spender, 1980; Katz, 1981; Vetterling-Braggin, 1981.

9 For one example, see Lupri and Frideres, 1981.

10 This is sometimes done by computing, for instance, the socio-economic status of a family by taking the occupation, education and income of both wife and husband into account, or by stipulating that patriarchy and capitalism are two forces that run parallel to each other through history (Hartman, 1976).

Acker, Joan, "Women and Social Stratification: A Case of Intellectual Sexism", in *American Journal of Sociology*, 1973, Vol. 78, No. 4, pp. 174 - 83.

Backhouse, Constance and Leah Cohen, *Sexual Harassment on the Job: How to Avoid the Working Woman's Nightmare*. Englewood Cliffs, N.J.: Prentice Hall (A Spectrum Book), 1981.

Bernard, Jessie, *The Future of Marriage*. New York: Bantam Books, 1972.

Bernard, Jessie, "My Four Revolutions: An Autobiographical History of the ASA" in *American Journal of Sociology*, 1973, Vol. 78, No. 4, pp. 11–29.

Bernard, Jessie, *The Female World*. New York: The Free Press, 1981.

Blaubergs, Maija E., "An Analysis of Classic Arguments against Changing Sexist Language", in *Women's Studies International Quarterly*, 1980, Vol. 3, No. 2 / 3, pp. 135 - 48.

Boulding, Elise, *The Underside of History. A View of Women through Time.* Boulder, Colo.: Westview Press, 1976.

Daly, Mary, *Gyn / Ecology: The Metaethics of Radical Feminism.* Boston: Beacon Press, 1978.

Delphy, Christine, "Women in Stratification Studies", in Helen Roberts (ed.), *Doing Feminist Research.* London: Routledge and Kegan Paul, 1981, pp. 114 - 28.

Eichler, Margrit, "Women as Personal Dependents: A Critique of Theories of the Stratification of the Sexes and an Alternative Approach", in Marylee Stephenson (ed.), *Women in Canada.* Toronto: New Press, 1973, pp. 38 - 55.

Eichler, Margrit and C.A. Nelson, "History and Historiography: The Treatment of Significant Events Concerning the Status of Women in American Histories", *The Historian*, 1977, Vol. 40, No. 1, pp. 1–15.

Eichler, Margrit, "The Origins of Sex Inequality: A Comparison and Critique of Different Theories and Their Implications for Social Policy", in *Women's Studies International Quarterly*, 1979, Vol. 2, No. 3, pp. 329–46.

Eichler, Margrit, *The Double Standard: A Feminist Critique of Feminist Social Science.* London: Croom and Helm, 1980.

Eichler, Margrit, *Families in Canada Today: Recent Changes and the Policy Consequences.* Toronto: Gage, 1983.

Eichler, Margrit and Jeanne Lapointe, *On the Treatment of the Sexes in Research.* Ottawa: Social Sciences and Humanities Research Council of Canada, 1985.

Eichler, Margrit with the assistance of Rhonda Lenton, Somer Brodribb, Jane Haddad and Becki Ross, *A Selected Annotated Bibliography on Sexism in Research.* Ottawa: Social Sciences and Humanities Research Council of Canada, 1985.

Eichler, Margrit, "And the Work Never Ends: Feminist Contributions to Canadian Anglophone Sociology", *Canadian Review of Sociology and Anthropology*, December 1985.

Gilligan, Carol, "Women's Place in Men's Life Cycle", *Harvard Educational Review*, 1979, Vol. 49, No. 4, pp. 431 - 46.

Glazer, Nona and Helen Youngelson Waehrer (eds.), *Woman in a Man-Made World: Socioeconomic Handbook*, 2nd ed. Chicago: Rand McNally, 1977.

Hartmann, Heidi, "Capitalism, Patriarchy, and Job Segregation by Sex", *Signs,* 1976, Vol. 1, No. 3, Pt. 2, pp. 137 - 70.

Herschberger, Ruth, *Adam's Rib*. New York: Harper and Row, 1970.

Hubbard, Ruth; Mary Sue Henifin and Barbara Fried (eds.), *Women Look at Biology Looking at Women.* Cambridge, Mass.: Schenk Publications, 1979.

Huber, Joan (ed.), *Changing Women in a Changing Society*. Chicago: The University of Chicago Press, 1973.

Journal of Marriage and the Family, Special Issue: *Sexism in Family Studies,* 1971, Vol. 33, No. 3, and Vol. 33, No. 4, pp. 734 - 99.

Katz, Wendy R., *Her and His: Language of Equal Value.* (A Report of the Status of Women Committee of the Nova Scotia Confederation of University

Faculty Associations on Sexist Language and the University, with Guidelines.) Halifax, N.S.: The Nova Scotia Confederation of University Faculty Associations, 1981.

Kelly, Alison, "Feminism and Research", in *Women's Studies International Quarterly*, 1978, Vol. 1, No. 3, pp. 225 - 32.

Kuhn, Thomas S., *The Structure of Scientific Revolutions,* 2nd enl. ed. Chicago: University of Chicago Press, 1970.

Lofland, Lyn H., "The 'Thereness' of Women: A Selective Review of Urban Sociology", in Marcia Millman and Rosabeth Moss Kanter (eds.), *Another Voice: Feminist Perspectives on Social Life and Social Science.* Garden City, N.Y.: Anchor Books, 1975, pp. 144 - 70.

Lupri, Eugen and James Frideres, "The Quality of Marriage and the Passage of Time: Marital Satisfaction over the Family Life Cycle", *Canadian Journal of Sociology*, 1981, Vol. 6, No. 3, pp. 283–305.

Maccoby, Eleanor Emmons and Carol Nagy Jacklin, *The Psychology of Sex Differences.* Stanford, Cal.: Stanford University Press, 1974.

Marsden, Lorna R., " 'The Labour Force' is an Ideological Structure: A Guiding Note to the Labour Economists", *Atlantis*, 1981, Vol. 7, No. 2, pp. 57 - 64.

McCormack, Thelma, "Towards a Non-sexist Perspective on Social and Political Change", in Marcia Millman and Rosabeth Moss Kanter (eds.), *Another Voice.* New York: Anchor Books, 1975, pp. 1 - 33.

McCormack, Thelma, "Good Theory or Just Theory? Toward a Feminist Philosophy of Social Science", *Women's Studies International Quaterly*, 1981, Vol. 4, No. 1, pp. 1 - 12.

Miles, Angela R. and Geraldine Finn (eds.), *Feminism in Canada: From Pressure to Politics.* Montreal: Black Rose Books, 1982.

Miller, Casey and Kate Swift, *The Handbook of Non-sexist Writing.* New York: Lippincott and Crowell, 1980.

Millman, Marcia and Rosabeth Moss Kanter (eds.), *Another Voice: Feminist Perspectives on Social Life and Social Science.* Garden City, N.Y.: Anchor Books, 1975.

Morgan, David, "Men, Masculinity and the Process of Sociology Enquiry", in Helen Roberts (ed.), *Doing Feminist Research.* London: Routledge and Kegan Paul, 1981, pp. 83 - 113.

Moulton, Janice, "The Myth of the Neutral 'Man' ", in Mary Vetterling-Braggin (ed.), *Sexist Language.* Totowa, N.J.: Littlefield, Adams, and Co., 1981, pp. 100 - 15.

Oakley, Ann, *The Sociology of Housework.* New York: Pantheon Books, 1974.

Oakley, Ann, "Interviewing Women: A Contradiction in Terms", in Helen Roberts (ed.), *Doing Feminist Research.* London: Routledge and Kegan Paul, 1981, pp. 30 - 61.

O'Brien, Mary, *The Politics of Reproduction.* Boston: Routledge and Kegan Paul, 1983.

Pierson, Ruth and Alison Prentice, "Feminism and the Writing and Teaching of

History'', in *Atlantis*, 1982, Vol. 7, No. 2, pp. 37 - 46.

Richards, Janet Radcliffe, *The Sceptical Feminist. A Philosophical Enquiry.* London: Routledge and Kegan Paul, 1980.

Roberts, Helen (ed.), *Doing Feminist Research.* London: Routledge and Kegan Paul, 1981.

Roberts, Joan I. (ed.), *Beyond Intellectual Sexism. A New Woman, A New Reality.* New York: David McKay Co., 1976.

Roberts, K., F.G. Cook, S.C. Clark, and Elizabeth Semeonoff, *The Fragmentary Class Structure.* London: Heinemann, 1977.

Rossi, Alice S. (ed.), *The Feminist Papers. From Adams to de Beauvoir.* New York: Bantam Books, 1973.

Safilios-Rothschild, Constantina, ''Family Sociology or Wives' Family Sociology? A Cross-Cultural Examination of Decision Making'', in *Journal of Marriage and the Family*, 1969, pp. 290 - 301.

Schneir, Miriam (ed.), *Feminism: The Essential Historical Writings.* New York: Vintage Books, 1972.

Sherman, Julia A. and Evelyn Torton Beck (eds.), *The Prism of Sex: Essays in the Sociology of Knowledge.* Madison, Wisc.: University of Wisconsin Press, 1979.

Silveira, Jeanette, ''Generic Masculine Words and Thinking'', in *Women's Studies International Quarterly*, 1980, Vol. 3, No. 2 / 3, pp. 165 - 78.

Spender, Dale, *Man Made Language.* London: Routledge and Kegan Paul, 1980.

Spender, Dale (ed.), *Feminist Theories: Three Centuries of Women's Intellectual Traditions.* London: The Women's Press, 1983.

Smith, Dorothy E., ''Women's Perspective as a Radical Critique of Sociology'', in *Sociological Inquiry*, 1974, Vol. 4, pp. 7 - 13.

Smith, Dorothy E., ''An Analysis of Ideological Structures and How Women are Excluded'', *Canadian Review of Sociology and Anthropology*, 1975, Vol. 12, No. 4, Part I, pp. 353 - 69.

Smith, Dorothy E., ''Some Implications of a Sociology for Women'', in Nona Glazer and Helen Youngelson Quehrer (eds.), *Woman in a Man-Made World*, 2nd ed. Chicago: Rand McNally, 1977, pp. 15 - 29.

Smith, Dorothy E., ''A Sociology for Women'', in Julia A. Sherman and Evelyn Torton Beck (eds.), *The Prism of Sex.* Madison, Wisc.: University of Wisconsin Press, 1970, pp. 135 - 87.

Vetterling-Braggin, Mary (ed.), *Sexist Language: A Modern Philosophical Analysis.* Totowa, N.J.: Littlefield, Adams and Co., 1981.

Vickers, Jill McCalla, ''Memoirs of an Ontological Exile: The Methodoligical Rebellions of Feminist Research'', in Angela R. Miles and Geraldine Finn (eds.), *Feminism in Canada: From Pressure to Politics.* Montreal: Black Rose Books, 1982, pp. 27 - 46.

Vickers, Jill McCalla (ed.), *Taking Sex into Account.* Ottawa: Carleton University Press, 1984.

Yaguello, Marina, *Les mots et les femmes: Essai d'approche socio-linguistique de la condition feminine*. Paris: Payot, 1979.

Zavitz, Carol and Hans Kleipool, "International Guide to Women's Periodicals and Resources, 1981 / 2", *Resources for Feminist Research*, Vol. 10, No. 4, Dec. 1981 / Jan. 1982, pp. 33 - 95.

FURTHER READING

Bowles, Gloria and Renate Duelli Klein (eds.), *Theories of Women's Studies*. London: Routledge and Kegan Paul, 1983.

Eichler, Margrit, *The Double Standard*. London: Croom and Helm, 1980.

Eichler, Margrit and Jeanne Lapointe, *On the Treatment of the Sexes in Research*. Ottawa: Social Sciences and Humanities Research Council of Canada, 1985.

Roberts, Helen (ed.), *Doing Feminist Research*. London: Routledge and Kegan Paul, 1981.

Vickers, Jill McCalla (ed.), *Taking Sex into Account*. Ottawa: Carleton University Press, 1984.

PAT ARMSTRONG
HUGH ARMSTRONG

Beyond Numbers: Problems with Quantitative Data

As C. Wright Mills put it so clearly many years ago, "Social research of any kind is advanced by ideas; it is only disciplined by fact" (1959:71). Ideas, particularly the systematic organisation of ideas into theory, are however all too often forgotten in social research. Facts are frequently identified with numbers, and numbers with neutrality or even truth. This is especially the case when the numbers are collected by a state agency like Statistics Canada.

In this paper we argue that numbers, and the methodology used to gather them, cannot and should not be separated either from their social context or from the ideas that direct their selection. Moreover, numbers cannot be viewed as the sole, or even necessarily the most accurate and relevant kind of fact.

The inadequacy of numbers as an aid to gaining a full understanding of the position of women is camouflaged by researchers' references to "scientific" methodology, by the adoption of non-sexist language, by the use of similar questions for both sexes, and by the tabulation, according to sex, of most data. But for the most part, women and men do different work, in different places, for different pay. Given this segregation, and given the different reproductive capacities of the sexes, many questions are women's questions, many answers are women's answers, many categories are women's categories, many omissions primarily affect women.

From this perspective, we begin with a critical examination of Statistics Canada, our chief source of the numbers so often accepted as factual. Explicit, and more often implicit, assumptions are built into the collection and

Revised and abridged from a paper that appeared in *Alternate Routes* 6 (1983), pp. 1 - 40.

tabulation of these data, assumptions that may serve to conceal or distort important aspects of women's work. Moreover, some information that is crucial for understanding the nature and conditions of women's work is inaccessible to or lost from quantitative measures, however carefully structured their questions and explicit their ideas. Building on this critique of Statistics Canada in particular and quantitative approaches in general, we go on to suggest how qualitative techniques can expand and correct our view of women's work, complementing and checking the information gathered through quantitative measures.

In what follows, examples from Statistics Canada data collection are introduced only to illustrate the argument. We should make it clear that we do not hold the view that some sort of arbitrariness and / or conspiracy is reflected in the methodological choices made by Statistics Canada. Rather, in a context of competing pressures and perspectives, and thus of compromises, these choices reflect more the relative absence to date of feminist pressures and perspectives.

ASSUMPTIONS AND CONCEPTS

According to Mills (1959:67), all empirical research involves "a choice as to what is most real." But the basis of these choices, the theoretical assumptions inherent in the collection and tabulation of data, are often obscure, sometimes to the statisticians themselves. As John Irvine, Ian Miles and Jeff Evans (1979:5) explain in their introduction to *Demystifying Social Statistics,*

> it is not enough, however, merely to make the case that statistical data cannot be interpreted without reference to their underlying theoretical assumptions. All data, whether produced in the course of academic research or by state bureaucracies, are structured by the conceptual framework that is applied as well as by the technical instruments used in their production. It is the precise nature of these practical and theoretical commitments that needs investigating for each set of data.

While the technical instruments are usually clearly described in Statistics Canada material, the theoretical commitments are seldom discussed. Few publications explore the assumptions behind the research or the specific selection of questions, responses and techniques of analysis.[1] This alone suggests a perspective that considers their theoretical approaches unimportant (or absent), their methods scientific, their numbers objective reflections of reality. As a result, it is not always a simple task to determine what is being measured and why, let alone what is being ignored and for what reasons.

Explicit statements outlining theoretical approaches are rare, but an examination of concepts and how they are operationalised does reveal some of the assumptions behind the data. For women, probably the most obvious example is the definition of work.

> It includes working for wages, salary, tips or commission, working in their own business, farm or professional practice, or working without pay in a family business or farm owned or operated by a relative in the same household. "Work" excludes housework or other work around the house, and volunteer work. (Statistics Canada, 1982a:17)

What Statistics Canada is interested in counting is not all the ways people spend their days or their energy, not how they survive on a daily basis, not how food gets to their tables, nor even how they improve their standard of living. On the other hand, interest is not limited to paid employment, to work that brings individuals cash income. Rather, the focus of concern is work that results directly in profit and exchange. As the *Guide to Labour Force Survey Data* explains,

> the concepts of employment and unemployment are derived from the concept of the supply of labour as a factor of production measured over a short interval of time. The production referred to is in turn defined as those goods and services included in the National Accounts. (Statistics Canada, 1979:15)

The interests served are not those of women, since the work most women do at home for their families, as well as the important volunteer work they do in hospitals, schools, playgrounds, and a wide variety of other institutions, disappears.

This is not to suggest that counting housework or volunteer work would change the nature of that work. That they are not considered reflects the perspective of Statistics Canada. The omission indicates that there are assumptions behind the data, assumptions that produce a picture that excludes much of the work most women do.

Less obvious than the assumptions about the work that counts are the assumptions related to the structure of families. When collecting data on households, Statistics Canada seems to assume that each household has one person primarily responsible for financial support, that this person is normally male if there is a man in the house, and that women, by themselves, have the babies. Here too the concern seems to be with the connection of the household to the economy outside the home rather than with what happens within this domain.

Largely in response to feminist protests, Statistics Canada has dropped the term "head of the household" and replaced it with "Person 1." For the 1981 Census, respondents were instructed to:

Choose one of the following as Person 1:
- either the husband or the wife in any married couple living here
- either partner in a common-law relationship
- the parent, where one parent only lives with his or her never-married son(s) or daughter(s) of any age.

If none of the above applies, choose any adult member of this household.

But in spite of the introduction of non-sexist terminology, little change in the data was anticipated. Indeed, alterations in other sections of the Census helped ensure that this would be the case. According to the *1981 Census Dictionary,*

> in 1981, the criterion for determining family type was changed. A new question was added to the census questionnaire to determine a person responsible for paying the rent, or mortgage, or taxes, or electricity, and is used to identify primary and secondary families.
>
> In previous censuses, the primary family was defined as the family of the head of the household. While we anticipate that in the majority of cases the person responsible for household payments will also be considered as the household reference person (Person 1), this will not always be the case. (Statistics Canada, 1982a:63)

Research in the United States (Vickery, 1979) and in Canada (Armstrong and Armstrong, 1983) suggests that the income of employed women who live with men pays for food, clothing and services rather than shelter and energy. Thus the criteria selected to determine the family maintainer favour men, even though the actual amount allocated for mortgages, taxes and electricity may be lower than that spent on food (Canada Department of Finance, 1981:13). The primary family, then, becomes another way of reinstating men as the head of the household.

Men's headship is further reinforced by the decision to record only one family maintainer. If respondents write in that these expenses are jointly paid, one will be selected by the statistician. Maintenance, the Census assumes, cannot be shared. Once again, it is women's contribution that is the more likely to disappear.

One aspect of the household, however, does seem to be recorded for women alone. Census question number 37 states:

> For WOMEN [emphasis in the original] who are married or have ever been married: How many children were EVER born to you?

Furthermore, according to the *1981 Census Dictionary*, "childless families refers to those families where the wife has reported that no children were ever born to her'' (Statistics Canada, 1982a:62). Biological reproduction does require male participation. Marriage is not required for conception. Yet the Census records the fertility of ever-married women only. While women always know how many babies they produce and while some men may be in doubt, the lack of male precision hardly seems large enough to warrant their exclusion from these parenting records. In the absence of a clear justification for this approach, it is tempting to assume that *women's* child-bearing responsibilities — the social extension of biological reality — are the focus of concern. However, given that some men retain alone the responsibility for their children, and given that some never-married women also keep their children, the data obscure actual child-care arrangements.

The same is true of the practice of counting only never-married children living at home.[2] Divorced and separated offspring may be returning to their parents' homes, seeking financial and emotional support as well as baby-sitting and other family care services. Failing to record these dependencies, like the omission of data on the financial and work contributions of each member, hides the actual economic relationship within the family. It also conceals the additional work that such dependencies may mean for women. Moreover, given the growing unemployment and inflated housing costs facing young people, it seems plausible that more and more young marrieds will be looking to their parents for financial support and accommodation. Statistics Canada seems ready to provide little assistance in monitoring these growing dependencies.

The conceptualisation and operationalisation of work, maintainer and fertility illustrate the importance of assumptions to findings, of choices to the selection of facts. The development of the problem, of the hypothesis, takes place at least as much *before* the information is collected, as *after* Statistics Canada publishes its numbers. However, in the absence of explicit theoretical justification for these choices, it is possible only to speculate about the theoretical framework guiding the data collection. Consequently, debate has focussed on the techniques, which are explicit, rather than on the hypotheses, which are obscure. In Canada, theoretical work has been divorced from, and has taken second place to, empirical research. Both suffer in isolation. The theoretical assumptions behind the data should be brought to light for examination, and the development of theory should be strongly supported as legitimate social science work.

COLLECTION OF DATA

The methods used to gather data both reflect the assumptions behind the research and affect the information collected. Techniques cannot be fully evaluated or understood outside the social and economic structure of their particular historical period. Who is interviewed, how they are interviewed, the information sought, the alternative responses offered and the consequences of the answers are all significant factors in the production of statistics. Here too choices are necessary, and the choices have important consequences for our view of women's work. The point, of course, is not to argue that everything is relative; it is not to deny the existence of the 'real' world in some phenomenological sense. Rather, it is to advocate theoretically informed and skeptical caution in the use of data as we, quite reasonably, seek more reliable knowledge about the world.

Deskilling

Harry Braverman (1974), in his perceptive analysis of work in the twentieth century, describes how the pursuit of profit has encouraged the separation of manual and mental labour as well as the progressive deskilling of both white-collar and blue-collar jobs. In these times of government restraint, a similar process seems to be taking place in the collection of statistics. Many of the tasks are simplified to allow their completion by untrained persons. While the Labour Force Survey continues to employ trained enumerators, the Census now depends heavily on self-enumeration. However, as Statistics Canada (1980a:14) points out in the *Social Concepts Directory,* "The questions are usually phrased to be suitable for self-enumeration for a reasonably well-educated respondent." The assumption of "reasonably well-educated" respondents can be made neither about the population covered by the Census nor about those included in the more comprehensive questions of the 1 / 5 sample. Thus, not only does this procedure encourage the simplification and perhaps even the omission of important questions, it also makes errors in the interpretation and responses to questions much more likely. Those many women who have not had the opportunity to learn to read and write one of our major languages cannot be sure they are included.

Restraining Legislation

Even if the respondents clearly comprehend the questions, they may be unwilling to expose their position to government scrutiny, in spite of assurances about confidentiality. According to the women we interviewed, a range of government programmes and regulations discourage them from reporting their employment and earnings (Armstrong and Armstrong, 1983). For example, veterans' allowances, disability pensions and welfare payments set a low maximum on family income. Reporting employment and pay thus often means a reduction in much-needed benefits. Low maximum earnings set for day-care subsidies have a similar effect. For those relatively low-income families, the effective tax rate on paid employment may well be 100 per cent or even more. And the income tax regulation that sets a low maximum on the amount a spouse may earn and still be claimed as a deduction itself also frightens some away from declaring their employment to any government representative conducting a survey. Employers may discourage their employees from reporting income, wishing to evade regulations and contributions to government programmes. Rules related to contributory plans like unemployment insurance and Canada/Québec Pension also encourage women to hide their employment, sacrificing their future and current protection in order to take home a little more money at the end of the week. Many of these people are unwilling to take the chance on promises of secrecy. That such factors can have a significant effect on data collection has not been entirely ignored by Statistics Canada. The *1981 Census Dictionary* (Statistics Canada, 1982a:13) notes that tax changes allowing for the deduction of spouse's wages as expenses "may have changed the status of some self-employed persons from 'without paid help' to 'with paid help' if they decided to pay wages to their spouses." Few of those disappearing from, and appearing in, the unpaid spouse category are male.

That this hidden economy, this invisible work force, is composed primarily of women is of course difficult to prove. However, our research suggests that many of them are women who do hairdressing or typing at home, look after children in their own or other people's houses, scrub floors and do errands for pay, sew baby clothes and stick labels on bottles, or sell their sexual services on the street. It seems likely then that labour force data fail to capture many of the women who work for pay, especially those who are employed in the lowest paid and least protected work.

Employers as well as individuals may be influenced in their responses by government regulations. For example, the Statistics Canada monthly publication *Employment, Earnings and Hours*, which provides the current information in this area, is based on employers' answers to survey questions. But laws related to minimum wages and equal pay, to hours and overtime, to piece rates and benefits may discourage some employers from accurately filling in the blanks. It should also be noted that the survey includes only those establishments with 20 or more employees. Since many women are employed in smaller workplaces, this information may not only count some women inaccurately but also excludes entirely many of those in the lowest-paid jobs.

Sampling

Financial and respondent burden considerations frequently make sampling techniques necessary. However, important data can be lost through the choice of sample over comprehensive methods, or through the choice of a small sample size. When many people are in a category, they are easily picked up by sampling techniques, but the method is much less precise when few people fit into the group. With women highly concentrated in some occupations and industries and virtually absent from others, the use of samples in collecting labour force data in both the monthly surveys and the 1981 Census means that some women will not show up in non-traditional occupations and industries, because the estimates are unreliable. The female electricians in PEI, for example, are extremely unlikely to become visible, although the female professors in Ontario have a better chance.

Machine Processing

When large numbers of responses must be processed quickly, the tendency is to rely on those questions and responses that can be read by a machine and easily categorised into neat tables. It is difficult, of course, to tell what is left out as a result of being difficult to measure numerically, or to determine the extent to which questions are structured by methodological as against theoretical considerations. But the two kinds of consideration are clearly linked, and the consequence is that we miss out on some important issues. For example, the absence of questions on the labour process is perhaps a result of both theoretical and technical considerations. The absence of statistics on the nature and conditions of work influences our understanding of women's employment situation, since it is on the shop floor, and in the bank, the restaurant, the hospital and the grocery store that sex segregation and inequality become reality.

The Wording of Questions

Statistics Canada argues in its *Social Concepts Directory* that "the key consideration to be borne foremost in mind, when constructing questions, is the viewpoint of the respondent with the needs of the survey sponsor in the background" (1980a:15). While the viewpoint of the respondent is certainly important, sponsor needs are seldom explicitly revealed to those using the data. Moreover, it is not simply the viewpoint of the respondent that should be thought about but also the structural constraints influencing the answers. Thus, in developing the wording of questions, more than their clarity, brevity and simplicity should be considered; sex segregation of work should also be taken into account.

The Census asked, for example, "Last week, how many hours did you work (not including housework or other work around the house)?" Our research suggests that such questions are answered in a variety of ways, depending on the nature and conditions of the work. Women who work part-time frequently have short daily hours of steady work, with few, if any, paid breaks. The hours they report working are fully spent at the desk, behind the counter or on the line. With few, if any, paid holidays, the days per week they report may also not be comparable to those with full-time jobs. Moreover, those who work in non-unionised establishments often work without breaks, have short lunch periods and stay late to finish up. Yet they calculate their hours from when they are required to be at work until the formal quitting time. Not only are they not paid overtime, but they do not view these extra minutes as time on the job. Finally, those who work in homes as domestics, babysitters, cleaners and piece workers normally have very long, but inaccurately recorded, hours.

The point, of course, is that these part-time, non-unionised and/or home workers are disproportionately women. The recorded sex differences in hours worked are only in part the result of actual differences. They are also in part the result of how the question is asked and answered. To ignore the sex segregation of the labour force is to produce faulty data on such issues as hours worked.

Excluded Questions

Not only the questions that are asked, but the ones that are not asked, should be considered in light of women's structural segregation in and out of the market. For instance, the monthly survey of *Employment, Earnings and Hours* requests information on the total number of female employees as well as the proportion that are wage and salary earners. However, employers are not questioned on how much they pay these female wage and salary workers. Nor are they asked about turnover rates, about which people leave which jobs after what period of time for what reasons. Once again, it is women who are most concerned about revealing wage differentials, and who are accused (in the absence of evidence) of having high turnover rates resulting from their low level of commitment to their paid jobs.

While people are asked about their formal education, they are not asked about their skills. In assuming competence can be measured by formal certification, Statistics Canada fails to measure the actual skills people employ in their jobs. Women's skills in particular disappear because, as one woman explained to us about the requirements of her job, "It's what every woman knows how to do." Furthermore, the absence of such a question means that there is no real assessment of the resources available for coping with the new micro-electronic technology. Because these skills are new and constantly changing, many are learned on the job and therefore cannot be measured by questions on formal education. And many more women are learning how to use this equipment on the job than are acquiring these skills in credit courses.

Although fringe benefits are an increasingly important part of workers' incomes, the sex differences in this field are virtually ignored by Statistics Canada. Various factors — like the ineligibility of some part-time, salaried and young workers, not to mention the wage and salary basis of most benefits — may mean that female employees receive fewer rewards in this area as well. Yet the monthly survey reported in *Employment, Earnings and Hours* does not cover fringe benefits. And between 1967 and 1975 several surveys of labour costs in various industries were conducted and then jointly published by Statistics Canada and the Department of Labour, but with no data on the benefits by sex. Finally, only in Saskatchewan are workers' compensation records published by sex of claimants, and these figures indicate significantly lower claims for women (Statistics Canada, 1980b:27). In part because Statistics Canada produces so little information on occupational health and safety, it is difficult to learn just why this is the case.

The failure to ask a question about relatives requiring special care has a similar effect. Information is collected on the number and ages of children but not on aging grandparents or disabled younger people who make up part of the "personal or family responsibilities" fulfilled by women as part of the invisible work that reduces their labour force participation. In general, by not asking these questions, and by not collecting information by sex, significant aspects of women's, and men's, work are hidden from view.

Selecting Alternative Responses

The data are not only conditioned by the questions asked, or not asked, but also by the choices of responses that are offered. In the Census question on major source of income, for instance, one choice was "working for wages, salaries, tips or commissions". That Statistics Canada asks employers answering their monthly survey to distinguish between wage and salary earners clearly indicates that these differences are seen to be significant, yet they disappear in the Census, in what is supposed to be the more complete source of information. Workers may well be concentrated by sex into each of these categories, but it is impossible to tell, given the choices offered.

Perhaps the problem is more obvious in another possible response to this question. The "retirement pensions, superannuation and annuities, and other money income" choice includes "alimony, child support, periodic support from persons not in the household, net income from roomers and boarders, non-investment income such as retirement income from abroad, scholarships, etc." (Statistics Canada, 1982a:24). By lumping together these diverse sources, Statistics Canada does not facilitate the analysis of income sources by sex.

In not offering technological change as a reason for leaving last job, the

Labour Force Survey is missing the opportunity to monitor the effect of micro-electronic technology on employment. Since the research to date (e.g. Menzies, 1981) suggests that women will be hit first and hardest, omitting this alternative conceals important factors influencing female labour force work.

Denying History

If the purpose is to understand what is happening to women today and what will happen to them in the future, it is necessary to examine the changes that have been taking place, to take an historical perspective that exposes the factors influencing these changes. But Statistics Canada makes such analysis difficult by failing to ask historical questions and by changing questions or categories.

Few historical questions can be found in the Census. In the questionnaire distributed to the 1/5 sample, those designated "Person 1" are asked how long they have lived in their current dwelling. Everyone is asked where they lived five years ago. Ever-married women are asked how many children were ever born to them. Labour force information is collected only for the last year, or at most for the last year and a half, and job search for the last four weeks. For personal history, then, the only information available from the Census is ever-married women's life-long fertility, most people's residence change from five years ago, and some people's recent labour force experience.

Nor does the monthly Labour Force Survey collect much historical data, although some occasional publications do look at labour force activity over time. For example, in 1976 Statistics Canada published *Earnings and Work Histories of the 1972 Canadian Labour Force*. Based on the 1973 Survey of Consumer Finances, the study reported data on male and female earnings differentials and work history between 1967 and 1972. Respondents to the sample were asked what was their *main* activity while not working for periods of one year or more, with "kept house, raised children" as one possible answer. They were not asked why they left their last job. The analysis of the data suggests that the higher turnover and lower wages reported for women were related to their decision to stay home with the house and children, to their choice of dropping out of the labour force to do their unpaid women's work. Yet, since most women continue to do the house work and child care whether or not they have paid employment, it seems unlikely that many women without a paid job would not be mainly keeping house and raising children. With the rare historical investigations based on such questions and alternative responses, it is difficult to find out what is happening to women over time and what factors influence these patterns.

Little, if any, information is available on the historical impact of new technologies, particularly of the micro-electronic technology now so important to women's work. Nor is it possible, from Statistics Canada data, to examine the effect over time of different kinds of work on the health of men and women. It is also extremely difficult to relate alterations in the resources and structure of families to labour force changes. If the data followed some families, recording the hours, duration, type and wages of work for both spouses and for children, as well as their health situation, their skills and their reasons for entering or leaving specific jobs, it might be possible to understand the factors structuring people of different ages and sexes into and out of labour force jobs. Without such information, any explanation is necessarily partial and superficial, focussed on individuals outside their historical, familial and even much of their economic context.

Changes in the collection and categorisation of data also make historical investigation difficult. Of course, the alterations may primarily reflect changes that are taking place in the labour force. This was the case, for example, in the separation of file clerks and receptionists from the secretarial category and in the new definition of part-time work (a reduction in weekly hours from less than 35 to less than 30). In other cases, the changes may result in part from new government policies and programmes. For farm workers,

> the data between 1971 and 1981 may not be strictly comparable because of small changes in definitions. Females who were unpaid family workers, worked as farm labourers and did less than 20 hours of unpaid work a week, were excluded from the labour force according to the 1971 definitions. These persons are now included in the employed labour force. Due to changes in the tax laws and Census procedures, some persons formerly identified as unpaid family workers may now be classified as paid workers. The tax changes permitted for the first time, in the 1980 tax year, the deduction of a spouse's wages as expenses. This may have resulted in some changes in the status from unpaid family workers to paid workers. As well, Census editing of this category was more stringent in 1981. (Statistics Canada, 1982a:12)

Some alterations, like the switch from "head of household" to "Person 1", may be related to pressure from feminist groups. But some changes seem unrelated to any of these concerns. For example, the *Census Dictionary* reports that:

> In all the 1981 tables on "Occupation Based on the 1980 Classification," the 1971 "Not stated" category will no longer appear. This category has been redistributed by imputation into new "imputed groups" within each minor group. (Statistics Canada, 1982a:37)

Since clerical employees, part-time workers, unpaid employed spouses, workers with unstated occupations and people not heading households are usually women, these new definitions and categories primarily affect the analysis of women's work. Whatever the reasons for the changes, the need for historically comparable data should be a central concern. In explaining the objectives of the Labour Force Survey Revision Project, Statistics Canada (1977:19) indicated an awareness of the problem, noting a

> demand for new information on the dynamic aspects of the labour force to supplement the monthly "snapshots" the new survey provides, much more information is required on the gross movements between various labour force categories each month, along with somewhat longer-term longitudinal data covering the six month period over which the respondents are surveyed.

The problem is, however, far from solved.

Comparing Data Sources

The problem of comparable data is not confined to history. Many government agencies and departments collect statistics, but the definitions, categories, responses, techniques, time periods and tabulations are often different, making comparisons difficult. Even within Statistics Canada, these differences sometimes exist. While Statistics Canada is working to eliminate these discrepancies, some do remain, obscuring the actual situation of women at work. For example,

> for the Unemployed and the Not in the labour force groups, data from the Labour Force Survey refer to the last job held by persons who have worked in the last five years. Since no question is asked on the most important activities or duties in the job held, as in the Census, the Labour Force Survey may classify more persons to the "Managerial" group on the basis of job titles than would be the case with the Census. (Statistics Canada, 1982a:37)

While the numbers are probably not large, the discrepancy still makes comparisons difficult. And once again, it is most likely women who are the extra persons classified by the Labour Force Survey into the managerial group, since they are the ones most likely to have jobs that are labelled managerial but whose actual tasks would place them lower on the hierarchy of Census occupational categories.

TABULATION OF DATA

Not only the collection but also the tabulation of data can influence the view of women at work. As Statistics Canada (1979:13) points out in its *Guide to Labour Force Survey Data*, "virtually any combination of questionnaire values can be cross-tabulated on request, subject to a 'reliability' criterion which is related strictly to the sampling variability and size of the estimate." However, such extra tabulations often cost money, limiting their access to those with research funds. And of course, the information available for tabulation is restricted by the problems with data collection cited above. Furthermore, the tabulations that are published, since they are the most accessible, are the most widely used, especially by the media. Thus, although most information is now collected by sex and could be tabulated for men and women, the published compilations form the basis for most of the public commentary on women as well as much of the research. These tabulations therefore deserve particular attention for the view of women they present.

Tabulations may both reflect and confirm assumptions about women. The proposed tables on census families to be drawn from the 1981 Census offer a case in point. According to Statistics Canada's (1982b:32–36) *Products and Services of the 1981 Census of Canada*, tables will be published on husband-wife families in private households by the wife's age and highest level of schooling. These are the only listed tables on husband-wife families in private households that use the wife's characteristics as the basis for compilation. Data will be tabulated for these households by both the husband's and wife's highest level of schooling, labour force activity, and age. The rest of the tables for these households will be compiled primarily on the basis of the husband/parent's characteristics. This is particularly the case for the income data that will be tabulated by husband/parent's age, highest level of schooling, work activity and period of immigration. That income tables are not based on the wife's characteristics indicates a particular view of women's place as well as reinforcing the perspective that sees wives' economic contribution as secondary. Perhaps their child-bearing and child-rearing responsibilities account for the concern about their age and schooling.

The categories used in tables also influence the perception of women's work. The Labour Force Survey's "managerial, professional, etc." category, for example, lumps together laboratory technicians and neurosurgeons, library technicians and full professors, managers of small shops and senior executives from General Motors.[3] The wide differences in power and pay, as well as the sex segregation, disappear. Indeed, the growth in the proportion of women in this category has helped to create the false impression that there has been a significant improvement in women's position.

In publishing tables by occupation and industry separately, the Labour Force Survey data also create the impression that women have been moving into prestigious management jobs and into traditional male fields like construction work. However, cross-tabulations of industry and occupation data indicate that, in 1980, three-quarters (74.8%) of female managers worked in the service industries while less than half (42.8%) of the male managers were employed there. In the construction industry, less than 10 per cent (9.3%) of the women actually did construction work; over 70 per cent of the women employed in that industry held clerical jobs (Armstrong and Armstrong, 1983; Tables 3 and 10). When such cross-tabulations are unpublished, segregation is camouflaged. Furthermore, change may be suggested where little has in fact taken place.

THEORY AND METHODOLOGY IN QUANTITATIVE RESEARCH

Counting women in means much more than including a question on sex and tabulating the results separately for women and men. It requires a recognition that the experiences of women and men are segregated in many ways, that policies, programmes, concepts and questions have a differential impact on women and men, that some questions are women's questions while others ignore or denigrate their contribution. The intention here is not to attack Statistics Canada. Indeed, it should be noted that Statistics Canada has been willing to alter some concepts, to bring them more in line with the actual contributions of women and men. Note, for example, its abandonment of the Census policy permitting respondents' paternal ancestry only to be recorded. Nor is the intention to draw up a shopping list of changes required in established techniques. The examples provided here are designed merely to illustrate problems with its methodology and thus to indicate that official data collection and the funding of research need to be re-examined if women's work is to be counted in.

But to begin such a re-examination, it is necessary to start with theory, with the systematic organisation of ideas, both because theory is the major way of advancing our understanding, and because methodology is inseparable from the perspective that guides the choice of what is real. The assumptions behind the data should be drawn out for critical appraisal. However concretely the questions surrounding the collection and tabulation of statistical information are posed, the methodological answers must be theoretically informed if they are to be useful. Thus, in order for statistical information to be improved, theoretical work as well as theoretically informed methodological work must be undertaken. In particular, problems of deskilling, restraining legislation, sampling, machine readability, the wording and avoidance of specific questions, the selection of possible response choices, the denial of history, the comparability of data sources, and the choices about what to tabulate and what tabulations to publish need to be examined from a theoretical perspective that takes the sexual division of labour into account. And that theoretical perspective itself needs to be refined.

However, no matter how finely tuned and sex-conscious the theory and techniques, some information will continue to evade quantitative approaches, whether based on sample or universal surveys. Some of the information collected through such methods, no matter how carefully the questionnaires are structured and the data collected and tabulated, may create an inaccurate view of women's work. At best, such techniques can produce only a partial picture of Canadian women's daily working lives. Quantitative data miss, and may misrepresent, many aspects of women's experiences in and out of the labour force. The final section of this paper draws on material and lessons learned from lengthy interviews conducted with women in working-class jobs to argue that qualitative data are at least as important as quantitative data in developing an accurate view of women's work.

QUALITATIVE RESEARCH

From Horace Miner's 1939 study of a French Canadian parish to Meg Luxton's 1980 examination of women's work in the home, qualitative research has provided valuable insights into women's daily experiences. However, such studies are rare, in part because they are expensive and time-consuming, but mainly because they are considered somehow less legitimate than statistical analysis. As a recent letter to the public from the 1981 Census Manager makes clear, Statistics Canada views itself as producing "facts", profiles that are "useful, convenient, complete". And many social scientists would agree that these facts, these numbers, are more reliable and accurate than data collected from lengthy hours spent in conversations with women in Flin Flon. But the bias in favour of "hard" data is seldom based on a rigorous comparison of the findings of quantitative methods with those of qualitative research, or of their value in explaining or predicting women's actions. Nor is the bias often based on respondents' assessment of the facts' accuracy, on the ability of these facts, in Lillian Rubin's (1976:13) phrase, "to generate an 'aha' experience". Nor is the bias sex-neutral, as Pauline Bart has so eloquently pointed out:

> We speak of hard data as being better than soft data, hard science better than soft science, hard money better than soft money. In the fifties, one was criticized for being "soft on communism." This is of course a male sexual metaphor, so since discovering this, I have substituted a metaphor based on female sexual experience and refer to wet and dry data. (quoted in Roberts, 1981:22)

The bias is not, however, simply a matter of metaphor. It reflects the priority given to the collection of some kinds of data, those that are easily counted, frequently repeated, and amenable to statistical analysis. But, as feminists have long made clear, the personal is political. Daily work and family relationships have a profound impact on work activity; physical and social conditions influence ideas and actions. To leave them out — and many are difficult or impossible to include in sample survey and statistical analysis — is to create not only huge gaps in the data but often inaccurate information as well. Our experience in interviewing women about the nature and conditions of their work suggests that qualitative research provides a necessary complement to quantitative analysis because it can test the reliability of quantitative data, can collect information not accessible to survey techniques, and can indicate areas that should be included in quantitative analysis.[4]

Checking the Facts

Keeping questions clear, simple and direct does not necessarily guarantee the accuracy of responses. Because the approaches used in gathering qualitative information take many aspects of the individual's life and relationships into account, and because the less rigid and more informal style of data collection often encourages a more open exchange, these qualitative "facts" can frequently be used to test the results of quantitative research. Interview procedures that are flexible, unstructured or partially structured, and wide-ranging, permitting people to offer their own responses and views, frequently draw out quite different information than that collected through highly structured, official-sounding questionnaires that allow only machine-readable choices.

In our experience, direct questions may elicit responses that are often contradicted by information gathered through more probing and indirect techniques. For example, when we asked women if they knew of any health dangers in their jobs, some simply said no. Yet, when describing in detail an average day on the job, various work-related problems emerged. A clerical worker who uses visual display terminals (VDTs) in a trust company responded negatively to the health question but earlier had told us that during the day, "Sometimes I'll go down to the lounge and fall asleep, my eyes are so sore." A factory worker who offered a similar response also told us that, with her right foot operating the sewing machine, her right hand adding cloth, and her left hand guiding the material as quickly as possible all day to ensure a survival wage from her piece work job, her arms, feet and legs hurt. "Sometimes when I come home, I can't make more job in my house." Various explanations were offered for this discrepancy. They expect work to hurt, so sore arms, legs, heads and hands may not be defined as health hazards but simply as part of the job. Many of the dangers women face are invisible, and have a slow, cumulative affect. Thus, they are less likely to be associated with the job than are the broken toes or burned hands that men more often suffer. And a few do not want to think about the dangers, because they have to go back there to work tomorrow. Whatever the reasons for these seemingly contradictory responses, they indicate that simple, direct questions will not always reveal the simple truth.

Like the questions on health and safety, those on sexual harassment also suggest that direct questions provide only limited, or inaccurate, pictures of the situation. When we asked women if they had ever been sexually harassed, some had difficulty answering the question — even when examples were given — often because they had come to accept this behaviour as part of the job. One woman offered a very definite no to the question. However, when reminded that she had said, in describing her work history, "That was something else, if you could keep out of the boss's hands," she explained that she had made it clear to "knock it off." Therefore, she felt "you don't have to write a book about it." Some said it was unlikely, given they worked with women only or had a lone male boss.

What this evidence suggests is that, if a question on sexual harassment were asked of all employed women, there would probably be an overwhelmingly negative response because of the way women perceive and respond to advances, and because many women are segregated into jobs where there are few men to do the harassing. Moreover, if the only answers recorded are those given for this question — as is the case with most machine-readable questionnaires — then much of the counter-evidence would disappear.

There are also often quite valid reasons for women to hide information from official government statisticians or from written questionnaires they fill out for the government. When we asked one woman for her age, she requested that the tape recorder be turned off so she could tell us her real age. Her boss, she explained, thought her below retirement age. She could not live without her employment income and thus she could not risk exposure. This woman not only had our assurances that we would not link her age to her name, job or employer, she also lived in a large metropolitan area where any identification was extremely unlikely (as was the possibility that her employer would read a book on work by a couple of sociologists writing for the Canadian Advisory Council on the Status of Women). However, she was not alone. Barely making ends meet, one woman collects a small unemployment insurance cheque, takes in foster children, babysits on weekends and does odd clerical jobs while the children are in school. Although willing to exchange this information over coffee in the kitchen, she made it very clear that, since her survival was at stake, there was no way she would write that information down on a questionnaire. Thus, even on such seemingly straightforward questions as age and employment, the facts may not be accurate. The qualitative data can help us become more accurate and more skeptical about the supposedly hard data.

In other cases, the answers given may be literally correct but hide a significantly different reality. One waitress, for instance, is paid the required minimum wage, but her employer then forces her to sign the cheque back to him. The taxes are paid, law is obeyed to the letter. However, her real income is low and irregular.

These examples are designed to illustrate how qualitative data can be used to check quantitative data. But this methodology can do more than suggest where the figures do not measure what they are supposed to measure. It can also indicate where there are holes in the data, where information could be, but is not, collected in quantitative research.

Exposing the Holes

Whole areas of women's lives remain virtually untouched by government and other quantitative research, and it would be impossible to do an inventory here. However, in the course of our interviews, many conditions were exposed that could be measured by existing quantitative techniques, and thus serve to illustrate the oft-complementary nature of these approaches. For example, some women indicated that they could not join the company pension plan until they had been with the organisation for a specified period of time or until they had reached a certain age. General questions on persons covered by pensions overlook policies like these, which have the effect (and perhaps the purpose) of preventing women from adequately protecting themselves in their old age.

The women we interviewed also drew attention to sick-pay policies. Simple to measure but seldom enquired about, sick leave is not covered by most labour codes. For many women, "if you sick, you sick." No work means no pay. Given their meagre earnings, most simply cannot miss work if they are ill. "Clerks cough in your face because they can't afford to be sick. I know I do." The significance of workers' health to the transmission of disease was recognised many years ago when special labels were attached to homework goods to warn potential customers that they might spread contagious diseases from workers' homes (Johnson and Johnson, 1982:47). But today, women who are not well may process food, sew clothes, care for other people's children, and serve meals in restaurants because they cannot miss a day's wages. Once again, the interview response indicated an important issue easily measured by quantitative methods but all too often ignored.

Another example of the contribution that qualitative research can make to the collection of quantitative data comes from the investigation of procedures for promotion. Many of the women we interviewed told us, "I don't think there's such a thing there as promotion," suggesting that enquiries into women's upward mobility should begin by examining whether or not such movement is possible. Although many people have pointed out that women are often locked into dead-end jobs, few have exposed another difficulty mentioned by these women. Some refused promotions because a move to a higher position meant little if any increase in power or pay and because it would eliminate the only satisfying aspect of their work — companionship with other women. One woman turned down a promotion because it meant working at night, with more responsibility and virtually no increase in pay. Here too, questions on what rewards are offered by promotion, if promotion is possible, are not difficult to get at through survey techniques, but the researcher must first be aware of such possibilities.

In quantitative research, the problems revealed are likely to be technical. In qualitative research, the difficulties exposed are more frequently substantive, suggesting new areas for investigation, ones that are often amenable to quantitative techniques. The examples of pensions, sick pay and promotions serve to indicate some ways in which qualitative data can improve the collection of facts in quantitative research, and can aid in the selection of what is real.

Collecting Data Inaccessible to Quantitative Techniques

Qualitative research can do more than indicate ways to improve quantitative techniques. It can provide complementary (or contradictory) information that brings life to the statistics, fills in the numbers, and explores relationships. Moreover, such methods can look at the meanings of experiences in a way that cannot be measured by multiple-choice questionnaires that generate machine-readable answers. They can permit the investigation process to be an exchange that allows those being studied to participate actively in the description and definition of their lives.

How could a survey take into account the pride of a home worker who is paid by the number of skirts she sews?

> My sister-in-law says, "I don't know how you work so fast," but I have to do fast. Everything I have to do fast. On Thursday I have 74 skirts. My husband said, "You don't finish this week." I said, "Sure." ... and I finish on Friday night."

Or the reality of working on a line?

> Basically, I stand there all day and slash the necks of chickens. You make one slash up on the skin of the neck and then you cut around the base of the neck so the next person beside you can crop it ... The chickens go in front of you on the

line and you do every other chicken or whatever. And you stand there for eight hours on one spot and do it. On a regular day [five people] can do maybe about 30,000 fryers.

Or the dangers that many women face?

One day the propane dryer caught on fire. They never evacuated the plant. They just tried to put the fire out. I think when a propane dryer that size catches on fire, it's a big fire. The plant should have been evacuated. That's my opinion now. And there are people working right by that dryer. If you die, you die. If you don't, you get the work done.

Such things cannot be easily measured, tabulated and fed into a computer for the analysis of statistical relationships.

Not only descriptions emerge from qualitative analysis. Often some of the most important processes at work, some of the most potent forces, are missed in quantitative data collection. For example, the implied threat of firing and the awareness of a huge reserve of women desperately searching for work have a powerful influence on women's performance on the job. According to one clerk,

to get fired from office staff, all you gotta do is look sideways. It's got to the point where everybody knows that you've got to do your work to keep your job. There's always another person ready to take your job.

Such research can also show how women are not merely passive. They actively participate in shaping their working conditions. From the women who adjust the thermostat when the boss is not looking, to the women who develop elaborate strategies to vary their tasks and eliminate boredom, there are many examples of women individually resisting the structure of their work. But women also get together to slow down the line when it is going too fast, or to force changes in their work environment, as was the case in one plant.

When I'm working, it is hot ... We don't have ventilation enough. Where I'm working, there are three big fryers and the fat is hot and when that fish strikes the fat, it gives smoke. And there's times when you go in there, you can just about see through the place. Now, we're inhaling this all day.... They have fans and half the time they are not working for the simple reason that it's the fat that clogs them. We have walked out already and I was the head one on our line too. I told my supervisor, "There's no way I can stand it in there. I'm choking and I cannot stand it. I'm going out 'till it's cleared up. And the girls followed us.... They got it fixed the next day.

Although justified by the conditions, this woman was frightened. "My heart pounded like you'd never believe. I hate doing anything like that 'cause I'm scared of getting fired." It was not her sex but her lack of job security that had discouraged this kind of resistance in the past.

Qualitative research can also capture, in a way that is impossible in quantitative investigations, what it is like to be an employed woman. For example, the women we interviewed reported that they were frequently asked to do extra tasks that were unrelated to their job description but fell into that all-too-broad category "women's work". As a woman hired to fill mail orders explained, "I hate dusting and cleaning. I don't go to work to do these things. I can do them at home.... Yeah, I do it." Most women go home to yet more of these same kinds of tasks. Our research was unable to explore the relationship between home and work in any detail, but the recent case study of an east-coast fishing village (Connelly and MacDonald, 1983) clearly illustrates the importance of relating domestic and wage labour to each other and to the wider economic structure. Such relationships and such an integrated approach are missing from quantitative data, which usually measure individual activity, for short periods of time, in a restricted context.

And quantitative research misses what technological change means to the workers. "Before, everyone was a typesetter. Now everyone works on a typesetting machine." "I went through tests two years ago and they found out that my hearing is poorer in one ear than the other. When I started there they told me that my hearing was very good." Perhaps even more elusive are the silent, psychological firings that never appear in the statistics. One long-time secretary described how she was refused training on the new electronic equipment, how her job slowly disappeared, how she spent hours at her desk with nothing to do, how she had to stay at her desk in order to get paid and how staying there meant it was difficult to look for alternative work. Finally she quit and was therefore not defined as a victim of the new technology.

Qualitative data are often dismissed as anecdotal, as unscientific, as unrepresentative because they do not include a statistically selected sample of the target population. Researchers often respond to this criticism by resorting to statistical analysis alone or by transforming their information into numbers. Komarovsky (1962:204), for instance, takes the group of 58 marriages and tells us that "among the older couples," "only 3 per cent of the less-educated husbands" complained that "we have nothing interesting to talk about." Yet the way our examples resonate in the lives of women suggests that they tap many shared experiences. They may not only provide a fuller, more humane picture of women's daily lives, but a more accurate one as well.

CONCLUSION

Theory, statistics and qualitative data are all necessary for rigorous research. Theory guides the selection of the real, the techniques employed to expose it, and the explanations used to understand it. Statistics can help to establish the broad outline of the picture, a picture that can only be fully developed with the aid of qualitative data.

We have argued that, like all methodologies, those of Statistics Canada reflect a perspective, one that, whatever the intent, has the effect of serving more the interests of men and the economy than those of women and the home. Available data do not permit a thorough examination of the sex-segregated labour force; they offer little assistance in examining the labour process, health and safety, hiring, promotion, wages and benefits, job security — to mention only a few issues — as they affect women. The priorities of the agency thus allow only a partial, and sometimes distorted, view of women's work.

We have also argued that statistics are not all they have been cracked up to be. The way data are collected and tabulated, the way questions are asked and not asked, the way government programmes and policies are structured, the way history is considered, all influence the data and in the process often leave out and sometimes misrepresent the position of women. Qualitative data, while not free of faults, can provide an effective complement to quantitative techniques, checking the results, suggesting alternative areas and methods for research, and filling in the numbers with the actual experiences of women.

REFERENCES

Acknowledgements — This paper was originally presented to the Conference on "Data Requirements to Support Research into Women and the Canadian Economy", organised by the Institute for Social and Economic Research, University of Manitoba, for the Social Sciences and Humanities Research Council of Canada. The Conference was held in Winnipeg in December 1982. Our thanks to Patricia Grainger, Edward T. Pryor, Bob Stirling and Maryanne Webber for comments, some of which we heeded, on the original version.

1 Statistics Canada does explain its methodology, but the justification for particular kinds of techniques rests on the assumption that these are primarily scientific and practical rather than theoretical issues. The tools are not related consistently to the theoretical framework. For example, Statistics Canada's *Methodology of the Canadian Labour Force Survey* (1977:23) offers the following justification for the use of a stratified sample:

Though the main advantage of stratified sampling is the possible increase in efficiency per unit cost in estimating the population characteristics, stratification also introduces considerable flexibility in the sense that, depending upon the information available, sampling and estimation procedures may differ from stratum to stratum. Further, in a continuous survey like the LFS, stratification provides an added flexibility of updating or redesigning the sample of a specified stratum or groups of strata, without affecting the design in the remaining strata.

See also the tool-kit orientation of Statistics Canada's (1980a) *Social Concepts Dictionary*. For a contrary example, however, see Kim Farrall's (1975) article on the impact of Keynesian and post-Keynesian developments in economic theory on labour force survey measures.

2 The Census does publish data on additional persons in the household (see, for example, Statistics Canada, 1982c: Table 6), but the nature of this relationship, and particularly the consequences for the household economy and domestic labour, are difficult to determine from such figures. The assumption seems to be that only never-married children are dependent.

3 Some LFS occupational data are now available at the minor group (three-digit) level of detail, at which the broad "managerial, professional, etc." category is broken down into 26 distinct occupations. Shortcomings remain, however. This information can be obtained in unpublished form only, and, because of the reliability criterion, as part of only a few general cross-tabulations.

4 The 65 interviews included in our study (Armstrong and Armstrong, 1983) were conducted by seven researchers selected for their expertise in interviewing techniques, knowledge of feminist issues, and familiarity with a particular area of Canada. The interview schedule was designed as an outline of areas to be covered rather than as specific questions to be asked. Interviewers were instructed to gather as much information as possible in each area, to record conversations on tape and to view the work site. We wish to acknowledge the assistance of Sonja Greckol, Sharon Kirsh, Judy Mosoff, Shirley Pettifer and Martha Tracey in the interview stage of the project.

Armstrong, Pat and Hugh Armstrong, *A Working Majority*. Ottawa: Supply and Services Canada, 1983.

Canada Department of Finance, *Economic Review*. Ottawa: Supply and Services Canada, 1981.

Connelly, M. Patricia and Martha MacDonald, "Women's Work: Domestic and Wage Labour in a Nova Scotia Community." *Studies in Political Economy* 10 (winter), 1983.

Farrall, Kim, "Theories, Concepts and the Art of Measurement: Economic Theories' Relationship to the Labour Force Survey Concepts." *Notes on Labour Statistics 1973* (Statistics Canada Cat. no. 72-207), 20–28. Ottawa: Information Canada, 1975.

Irvine, John, Ian Miles and Jeff Evans (eds.), *Demystifying Social Statistics*. London: Pluto Press, 1979.

Johnson, Laura C. and Robert E. Johnson, *The Seam Allowance: Industrial Home Sewing in Canada*. Toronto: The Women's Press, 1982.

Komarovsky, Mirra, *Blue-Collar Marriage*. New York: Random House, 1962.

Luxton, Meg, *More Than a Labour of Love: Three Generations of Women's Work in the Home*. Toronto: The Women's Press, 1980.

Menzies, Heather, *Women and the Chip: Case Studies of the Effects of Informatics on Employment in Canada*. Montreal: The Institute for Research on Public Policy, 1981.

Mills, C. Wright, *The Sociological Imagination*. New York: Grove, 1959.

Miner, Horace, *St. Denis: A French-Canadian Parish*. Chicago: University of Chicago Press, 1939.

Roberts, Helen (ed.), *Doing Feminist Research*. London: Routledge and Kegan Paul, 1981.

Rubin, Lillian Breslau, *Worlds of Pain*. New York: Basic Books, 1976.

Statistics Canada, *Employment, Earnings and Hours* (Cat. no. 72-002). Ottawa: Supply and Services Canada, monthly.

Statistics Canada, *The Labour Force* (Cat. no. 71-001). Ottawa: Supply and Services Canada, monthly.

Statistics Canada, *Earnings and Work Histories of the 1972 Canadian Labour Force* (Cat. no. 13-557). Ottawa: Industry, Trade and Commerce, 1976.

Statistics Canada, *Methodology of the Canadian Labour Force Survey 1976* (Cat. no. 71-526). Ottawa: Industry, Trade and Commerce, 1977.

Statistics Canada, *Guide to Labour Force Survey Data* (Cat. no. 71-528). Ottawa: Supply and Services Canada, 1979.

Statistics Canada, *Social Concepts Directory* (Cat. no. 12-560). Ottawa: Supply and Services Canada, 1980a.

Statistics Canada, *Workmen's/Workers' Compensation: Social Security, Provincial Programs* (Cat. no. 86-501). Ottawa: Supply and Services Canada, 1980b.

Statistics Canada, *1981 Census Dictionary* (Cat. no. 99-901). Ottawa: Supply and Services Canada, 1982a.

Statistics Canada, *Products and Services of the 1981 Census of Canada*. Ottawa: Supply and Services Canada, 1982b.

Statistics Canada, *1981 Census, Volume 1. Census Families in Private Households*. (Cat. no. 92-935). Ottawa: Supply and Services Canada, 1982c.

Vickery, Clair, "Women's Economic Contribution to the Family," in Ralph E. Smith (ed.), *The Subtle Revolution: Women at Work*. Washington: The Urban Institute, 1979, pp. 159–200.

FURTHER READING

Canadian Research Institute for the Advancement of Women, *Knowledge Reconsidered: A Feminist Overview*. Ottawa: CRIAW/ICRAF, 1984.

Eichler, Margrit and Jeanne Lapointe, *On the Treatment of the Sexes in*

Research. Ottawa: Supply and Services Canada for Social Sciences and Humanities Research Council of Canada, 1985.

Kinnear, Mary and Greg Mason (eds.), *Women and Work*. Proceedings of a Conference on Data Requirements to Support Research into Women and the Canadian Economy, December 9–10, 1982. Winnipeg: Institute for Social and Economic Research, 1983. (Available from Social Sciences and Humanities Research Council of Canada.)

Roberts, Helen (ed.), *Doing Feminist Research*. London: Routledge and Kegan Paul, 1981.

Vickers, Jill McCalla (ed.), *Taking Sex into Account*. Ottawa: Carleton University Press, 1984.

M. ANN HALL

Knowledge and Gender: Epistemological Questions in the Social Analysis of Sport

In this chapter I want to focus on how taking account of gender influences our knowledge structures and the ways in which knowledge is produced. I will be operating from the assumption that although we have constructed a world of two genders, we must uncover how gender differences have become the basis of social, economic, and political inequality. In my view, there is an ideology of gender that not only influences our understanding of the social world but also the ways or methodologies we use to comprehend the world — in short, our conduct of inquiry. The questions I want to ask here are rooted in that rather formidable branch of modern philosophy known as epistemology: the study of the origin, nature, methods and limits of knowledge.[1] Over the last decade we have witnessed an explosion in research and theory about women's experience in the world.

We have learned much, but by necessity our intellectual journeys have become more profoundly radical simply because "we cannot understand women and their lives by adding facts about them to bodies of knowledge which take men, their lives, and their beliefs as the human norm" (Harding and Hintikka, 1983:ix). The question then becomes whether there can be a distinctive feminist epistemology, and if there is, what would it look like.[2] To put this another way, we must ask what counts as knowledge. Our experiences as women in an androcentric world must differ from those of men who clearly do not live in a gynocentric cosmos. What has counted as knowledge, until recently, has been based not on *human* experience but essentially on male experience seen through male eyes. Our knowledge of the social world and social life, and possibly even the natural world, is distorted so that often this "knowledge" does not make sense to women.

Originally published in *Sociology of Sport Journal* 2(1), 1985:25–42, by Human Kinetics Publishers.

In asking whether there is a unique feminist epistemology, we are challenging the origin, nature, methods, and limits of knowledge that have shaped our understanding of social life. In the end I want to explain why it is so important to comprehend this challenge and what implication it has for the social analysis of sport.

FROM SEX DIFFERENCES TO GENDER RELATIONS

The terms "sex" and "gender" have become particularly problematic in the feminist literature. In our earlier thinking it seemed entirely possible to distinguish between sex and gender in a fairly straightforward manner. After all, sex, when used in a nonsexual context, referred to dichotomous distinctions between male and female based on physiological characteristics that are genetically determined. Gender, so we argued, defined the psychological, cultural, and social dimensions of maleness and femaleness. The distinction was between what was biological and what was cultural, and it seemed to work. However, we now know that the meaning of a biological sex difference varies according to the culture through which it is mediated (Eichler, 1980). We know also that sex and gender make distinct contributions to a very complex sex / gender system. There is also considerable confusion over the meaning of "sex roles" and "gender roles," but there is agreement that gender roles, being an intricate blend of social and psychological behaviors, represent a more complex concept than sex roles (Lipman-Blumen, 1984).

It is not very useful to think in terms of a dichotomous category, male versus female, for either sex or gender. As social beings we have constructed a world in which there are two, and only two, sexes. In fact, it is extremely difficult to imagine any other kind of world.[3] We often forget that sexual dualism is socially constructed in such a way that it *appears* to be an immutable fact. For instance, Kessler and McKenna (1978) argue that often we construct sexual dimorphism when there is continuity. Biological, psychological, and social differences do not lead to our seeing two genders, they suggest; rather, our seeing two genders leads to the "discovery" of these sex differences. The implication of their argument is a paradigm shift away from the results of seeing someone as female or male (specifically sex-difference research) to seeing gender attribution, or the process by which we classify someone as female or male, as primary and gender itself as the practical accomplishment.

They argue against the very "facticity" of two biological sexes as a view of objective reality when what they want us to understand is how the gender attribution process creates and sustains androcentric reality. In the context of sport, they point to the "sex test" for female athletes in international competition as an example of science providing evidence of a biological continuum, whereas we insist on discrete categories because of the way reality is constructed. What is more, we legislate against this continuum and in this case we actually decree a person's sex.

We may or may not wish to accept Kessler and McKenna's insistence upon the primacy of gender attribution for our understanding of social reality. It is important that we abandon the notion that gender is a dichotomous social category determined for all time by biology. It makes more sense to think of sex / gender as a *system of social relations between females and males.* I prefer to call these *gender relations,* and I mean by this a system of relations structured by gender. The term is being used here in the same way marxists[4] describe "class relations" — not as abstract categories based on income, occupation, or ownership, but as real-life groupings that involve relationships among people and their relationships to aspects of social structure (schools, business, churches, sport, etc.). Gender relations, like class relations, are in essence power relations whereby men, as a social group, have more power over women than women have over men. These relations are characterised by male dominance and female subordination in both a sexual and economic sense. But since they are *socially constructed,* not biologically given, they are not fixed; rather, they are subject to historical change and can be transformed.

Thus far I have been arguing that in order to answer our sociological questions about gender inequality in sport, we must abandon our insistence that gender is a dichotomous category. To see gender in this way, rather than as a system of relations, means that our questions remain distributive rather than relational. For instance, we continue to ask what factors, what barriers, prevent women from achieving full equality in sport rather than to examine the nature of the social relations, both past and present, that determine gender inequality. It is important to ask how sport came to embody and recreate male power and domination. What are the connections between women's sporting practice and the broader ensemble of patriarchal relations? Can women's experience in sport challenge and eventually transform gendered social arrangements as they exist today (Theberge, 1983)? However, before pursuing such questions, I want to describe some of the theoretical approaches to the sex / gender system and gender relations in particular that have evolved over the past decade or so.

THEORETICAL PERSPECTIVES ON GENDER RELATIONS

A work has been published recently that brilliantly provides a comprehensive synthesis of feminist writing, theory, and politics. Alison Jaggar, in *Feminist Politics and Human Nature*, has, as one reviewer suggested, "shown us the rich diversity in activity, attitude and analysis of the contemporary women's movement, and has taken it all very seriously as philosophy and politics" (Young, 1984:12). I do not wish to recount much of Jaggar's work here except to outline briefly the four strands of feminist theory and politics she finds most basic, because for our purposes it is necessary to understand the breadth and depth of feminist theory. What I will do in more detail is to examine, using Jaggar's work as a guide, the epistemological and methodological assumptions that stem from these theoretical variants. As I have repeatedly suggested, "feminism" and "feminist" are not monolithic concepts; there is no *one* feminism.

Jaggar divides feminist theory and politics into four fundamental categories she finds most useful: liberal, traditional marxism, radical, and socialist. She examines the theory of human nature inherent in each as well as the potential of each framework for understanding and eliminating women's oppression.

Very briefly, and perhaps too simplistically, *liberal feminism* has been inspired by the traditional liberal ideals of human dignity, autonomy, equality, and individual self-fulfillment. Liberal feminists argue that women in contemporary society suffer unjust discrimination on the basis of their sex alone, thereby depriving them, as a group, of equal opportunities for pursuing their own self-interest and self-fulfillment as they define it. Therefore, the abolition of sex discrimination is not only required by justice but will also maximise each individual's contribution to society as a whole. To bring about the abolishment of sex discrimination, liberal feminists make extensive use of the state (for example, limited legal reform and affirmative action programmes) but at the same time believe that in certain areas state intervention is unjustified (for example, in our sexual lives). In the context of sport, liberal feminists have sought fairness, equity, and equality of opportunity for all females through such mechanisms as Title IX in the United States and human rights legislation in Canada.[5] For liberal feminism, therefore, the just society is a fair meritocracy, and the strategy for achieving that society is to use rational argument coupled with legal reform to secure equality of opportunity.

Traditional *marxist feminism,* on the other hand, maintains that the liberal feminist goal of equal opportunity can never be achieved under capitalism. Women are oppressed in their exclusion from public production, but the marxist feminist would argue that class relations primarily determine all forms of oppression. The problem, of course, is that traditional marxism does not and cannot account for women's specific oppression. In direct contrast, *radical feminism* (which for Jaggar includes lesbian and anarchist feminism) argues that it is in fact the oppression of women that is at the root of all other systems of oppression. The sex / gender system from this viewpoint is an elaborate system of male domination that structures virtually every aspect of our lives and is so pervasive that it often goes unrecognized. According to Jaggar, radical feminism is inadequate in its failure to provide theoretical explanations for the social relations between women and men that it so richly describes. Their explanations have, unfortunately, become biologically deterministic rather than historical.

It is so-called *socialist feminism* in which Jaggar finds the most coherent liberatory body of theory because it seeks to historicise the insights of radical feminism. Drawing on the marxist method of historical materialism, it "redefines the material base as that set of social relations which structures the production and reproduction of the necessities of daily life, the production of people, including the production of sexuality, as well as the production of goods and services" (Young, 1984:11). Socialist feminism attempts therefore to transcend the "gender-blindness" of the traditional marxist categories by focussing on the *sexual* division of labour.

With the exception of radical feminism, which at present has no coherent paradigm of human nature, it is possible to distinguish the essentially incompatible views of human nature present in liberal feminism versus marxist and socialist feminism. The liberal tradition posits that humans are essentially separate rational agents with no connection with each other or even the non-human world. Traditional marxism has always challenged this liberal notion of human nature, claiming instead that individuals exist necessarily in a dialectical interrelation with each other and the physical environment. Socialist feminism is committed to this basic marxist concept of human nature but insists on a more adequate theoretical understanding of the sex / gender system through the sexual division of labour. Now, whether or not we are willing to accept Jaggar's categories of feminism, or any categorisation for that matter, and indeed where we ourselves "fit" theoretically and politically as feminists, is quite irrelevant to the discussion here. The point is that there are distinct and sometimes incompatible epistemological assumptions stemming from our differing views as feminists on human nature and how our society is or should be organised.

What Jaggar argues, having elaborated the theory and politics of these feminist frameworks, is that "every conception of human nature involves a characteristic conception of human knowledge — its sources, its extent and the proper criteria for distinguishing truth from falsity" (p. 355). She states, in other words, that "commitment to a theory of human nature carries with it commitment to a certain epistemology."[6] The epistemological tradition associated with liberalism is positivism, or at least some version of positivism. Inherent in positivism is the notion of objectivity or lack of bias insofar as the same scientific conclusion will follow from all research that adheres to strict methodological rules of valid inference. Also part of objectivity is the requirement of value neutrality in that researchers should scrupulously control their own values, interests, and emotions. "Liberal feminism," says Jaggar (1983:357), "makes a sharp distinction between what it takes to be the normative and the empirical aspects of the theory... [It] relies on values that are claimed to be universal values and which in consequence...cannot reflect only the special interests of a particular group." Finally, because liberalism views humans as essentially separate rational agents, the attainment of knowledge then becomes an individual project.

Traditional marxism, on the other hand, sees knowledge not only as a social activity but also as growing out of human productive activity (work or praxis). Therefore this view of knowledge challenges the liberal concept that knowledge is the achievement of isolated individuals; rather, it is socially constructed. It also challenges the liberal notion of value-neutrality since all forms of knowledge are historically determined by the prevailing mode of production (in our society, capitalism). Moreover, according to Marx and Engels, the generally accepted system of knowledge within a society reflects the interest of the dominant or ruling class. Therefore, within traditional marxism, all existing claims to knowledge are "ideological" insofar as they are distorted representations of reality because the dominant class must justify the reality of domination. In general, inherent in marxism is the belief that all systems of thought are constructed from some standpoint within the social world. In traditional marxism, the standpoint of the proletariat (working class) is the most unbiassed and objective representation of social reality. Unfortunately, this does not allow for the fact that women might have their own epistemological standpoint.

Such a view is fundamental to the epistemology of radical feminism, which seeks to construct a new picture of the world as seen through the eyes of women. Similar to traditional marxism, it criticises the liberal / positivist paradigm of knowledge and it assumes that the dominant group (men not the ruling class) will inspire its own distorted and mystifying version of reality. However, there are differences, and they seem to lie in the lack of radical feminist interest in political theory, which leads Jaggar to conclude that their epistemology provides a description of reality rather than an explanation of it. The final epistemological position is that which stems from socialist feminism. It is this perspective that brings us to consider the notion of representing the world from the standpoint of women.

TAKING THE STANDPOINT OF WOMEN

Central to any feminist epistemology or theory of knowledge is the notion of taking the standpoint of women.[7] But what does this mean? Let us examine the notion of a "standpoint" first. Put simply, and using a marxist interpretation, the premise of a standpoint is that "those suffering oppression have no interest in appearances passing for reality and so can really show how things work'' (Haraway, 1981:481). Therefore, those on the bottom of the social heap, so to speak, be they members of the working class, women, racial minorities, the mentally and physically challenged, and so forth, see the world from a different perspective, a more ''correct'' one, than those on top. In more theoretical terms, Hartsock (1983b:285) has described the notion of a standpoint as follows:

> A standpoint is not simply an interested position (interpreted as bias) but is interested in the sense of being engaged. It is true that a desire to conceal real social relations can contribute to an obscurantist account, and it is also true that the ruling gender and class have material interests in deception. A standpoint, however, carries with it the contention that there are some perspectives on society from which, however well-intentioned one may be, the real relations of humans with each other and with the natural world are not visible.

Given the idea of a standpoint *per se*, what then are the implications and meaning of the ''standpoint of women''? The first point is that women's lives differ systematically and structurally from those of men such that women's lives ''make available a particular and privileged vantage point on male supremacy'' (Hartsock, 1983a:231). The way in which men's and women's lives are structurally different is usually described as the sexual division of labour. For women, their experience within the institutionalised sexual division of labour is both one of production (of goods) and reproduction (of human beings) which profoundly influences how they view themselves and the world, in other words, an epistemology. More specifically, the differences in the sexual division of labour in child rearing and housework purportedly give women a deeper and more thoroughgoing vision of reality than that available to men.

Let's illustrate what this means. As every woman who is a full-time housewife and / or mother can tell us, there is little distinction between being at work and not being at work in the home. Once it is recognised that housework and child care are work, and that being responsible for the lives of other human beings means that one is always at work in some sense, then distinctions between work and non-work are simply not appropriate. Yet we have innumerable accounts that make use of a work-leisure dichotomy, and sociologists do research on the ''leisure'' of housewives and mothers. ''If we had started with housework as the basis,'' says Smith (1979:154), ''the categories of 'work' and 'leisure' would never emerge.'' In fact, she points out that if we were to use housework as our basic framework, it would be difficult to imagine how to make work and leisure observable.

The second implication that comes from positing a standpoint of women is that there must be an equivalent masculinist world view. How should it be characterised?[8] Words such as manliness, virility, power, and domination come to mind, but what Hartsock (1983a) argues is that the vision of each will represent the inversion of the other. More importantly, since the sex / gender system is characterised by male dominance, the vision available to the rulers will be both partial and perverse. It is partial because "interests in ruling require repression, blindness to what social relations look like from the perspective of the ruled, and to the real relations of everyday life which make possible a life of privilege for some and of subjugation for others" (Harding, 1984b:19). It is perverse because "men persistently have insisted that only their death-risking and death-dealing activities mark truly human life activity, and that women's life-creating and life-preserving activities are sub-human, no different in kind from the life of brute necessity claimed to be characteristic of other species" (Harding, 1983b:20).

The fact of men's insistence on the primacy of "death-risking and death-dealing activities" has, I think, rather remarkable implications for the social and philosophical analysis of sport, many forms of which exist *because* of the exhileration gained from cheating death (e.g., skydiving, car racing, and even American football — which is purportedly a very dangerous sport if measured by the number of deaths). On the other hand, women's "life-creating and life-preserving activities," or reproductive capacities, have been used repeatedly against us in our attempts to participate fully in the sports world.

The third point is that the ruling group can make their false vision of the world become apparently true. Let me clarify this with a brief example: A friend, who for several years now has been attempting to sort through the implications of a long marriage and the rearing of several children, relates bitterly the ways in which her world was severely restricted by this very vision of the ruling group (men). She tells of countless summer days when the men in her family would be off playing tennis, which they took very seriously. But as each day ended and the women's housework and child care eased, they were "permitted" to play tennis with the men — but here the game was treated as an obligation by the men and never taken seriously. It was, by everyone's account, the natural order of things. More generally, "women's biology appears to be their destiny, when in fact it is the structuring of women's lives to match men's belief in women's biological destiny that creates the appearance" (Harding, 1984b:20).

Fourth, political struggle has revealed to women the entirely *social* nature of their oppression. Coupled with political activity is the process of revaluing women's experience so that the liberatory possibilities present in that experience can be identified and developed (Hartsock, 1983a:246). The standpoint of women, therefore, can form the basis for moving beyond gender relations characterised as inhumane and oppressive (specifically in this case for women) to relations that are humane and liberatory.

Finally, it is recognised, of course, that not *all* women share a common viewpoint. For some women, class and race will be much more significant. However, what is implied by "the standpoint of women" is that we do have something in common. "What we have in common," suggests Dorothy Smith (1979:163), "is that organisation of social relations which has accomplished our exclusion."

FEMINIST EPISTEMOLOGY AND METHODOLOGY

Is there a distinctly feminist epistemology? The answer to this question depends very much on whether one considers the rapidly accelerating feminist challenge to Cartesian epistemology, on which is grounded not only modern science but also liberal philosophy, as evidence of something unique. Certainly marxists have mounted the attack long before this, but the feminist critique itself does constitute at least the beginnings of an alternative epistemology. It is as yet in a vague and ambivalent form, but there nonetheless. Imagining the alternatives, as Elizabeth Fee (1981:389) has pointed out, is "rather like asking a mediaeval peasant to imagine the theory of genetics or the production of a space capsule; one's images are, at best, likely to be sketchy and insubstantial."

In this section I will develop the major assumptions or principles that I believe identify a distinctly feminist epistemology. These principles are based on my reading of the literature, and they may differ in content from those of others who have investigated the same literature.[9] Moreover, since all of the material is so recent and certainly not extensive, there are few fully articulated feminist theories of knowledge; so the principles as I state them here are far from definitive and are at best tentative. In addition, these principles are at present more in the form of "rebellions" rather than philosophically refined statements about what constitutes a feminist epistemology. They may be perceived as reactive and oppositional. But it is important to realise, as one rebellious feminist has put it, "that most of our thought is still conditional, constrained and limited by the fact that we first learned to think using the tools and categories devised by men to understand their reality, not ours" (Vickers, 1982:44).

In the same way that we have asked whether there is a distinct feminist epistemology, we must also ask if there is a unique feminist methodology. By "methodology" I mean here the science or study of methods and not the specific research techniques or processes themselves. I also assume that we could argue for a distinctly feminist methodology if we were able to show that its underlying epistemological assumptions were those that are distinctly feminist. These are not abstract principles that have no relevance to feminist methodological practices. In fact, they help define them, and for there to be any claim to a feminist methodology they, or some other agreed-upon set, should be followed.[10] There can be no gap between how these epistemological assumptions are discussed in the abstract and how they are incorporated into feminist research. But like a feminist theory of knowledge, a feminist methodology is still "in the process of *becoming* and is not yet a fully articulated stance" (Cook & Fonow, 1983:2).

My third task in this section is to spell out the implications of both a feminist epistemology and its methodology for the social analysis of sport, in particular our understanding of gender relations. I want to deal with the questions asked earlier, and to suggest how an analysis of sport along these lines could contribute to feminist debates more broadly defined.

The Necessity of a Standpoint and of the Standpoint of Women in Particular

In the same way marxists have maintained that the standpoint of a politically self-conscious proletariat is conceptually and empirically preferable to the bourgeois perspective on reality, I have argued (following others) that an epistemological standpoint of women has even further advantages; indeed, it can be a superior grounding for knowledge claims relative to men's. It is superior in perhaps two ways. One is because of the sexual division of labour whereby men's and women's experience differ in ways that tend to limit men's understanding of social relations and social life more than women's. Second, although differing men's and women's experience within the sexual division of labour seem to have their root in biologically different bodies, these differences are socially constructed. This gives women further epistemological advantage because of the possibilities this holds for demystifying social reality. Sandra Harding (1984a:27 - 28) is worth quoting on this point:

> The feminist epistemological standpoint argues that the existence of inverted visions of material life within the sexual order gives women an epistemological advantage. If those inverted visions did not exist, it would be because we did not have humans constructed as women and men; there could be no women's experience and thus no feminist epistemological standpoint. Thus it is differences in social experience, not 'bare biology,' which is claimed to create epistemological advantage for women's experience.

What all this means is that the standpoint of women provides for a more accurate and comprehensive representation of reality than the standpoint of men.

Here I wish to make three major points about sport (as well as play and games) that are consistent with the notion of a standpoint, and the standpoint of women in particular. The first concerns how sport is conceptualised and theorised. Play, games, and sport are real *social* practices; they are neither idealist abstractions, as liberals / positivists would have us believe, nor are they simple products of material conditions, as some neo-marxists insist. They are, as Gruneau (1983:50) puts it: "constitutive social practices whose meanings, metaphoric qualities, and regulatory structures are indissolubly connected to the making and remaking of ourselves as agents (individual and collective) in society." Play, games and sports, then, are forms of cultural production and as such they are creations of human agency. They too can be transformed.

The second point is that as cultural forms they are tied to modes of domination such as those between social classes and between the sexes. This does not mean that play, games, and sports have been created in some determinate way by those who have more resources due either to their "superior" class position or sex. What must be specified is exactly *how* these cultural representations come to embody capitalist class relations and patriarchal gender relations in the first place.

The third point follows from the second: even though sport depends upon and reflects the material conditions in the society in which it exists, it also opposes those conditions. In other words, in a cultural sense it is viewed as largely inconsequential, disconnected, and somewhat autonomous from the dominant economic and political structures that govern social necessity. Therein lies the fascinating paradox of sport.

Given this very brief explanation as to the social nature of play, games, and sport, where does it lead us regarding the standpoint of women? Alison Jaggar (1983:384) makes the point that those who construct the standpoint of women *must begin from women's experience as women describe it.* Moreover, she suggests, we must go beyond that experience theoretically, and it is only through a protracted political and scientific struggle that the intricate, systematic reality of male dominance becomes clear. Therefore, I am calling for an emphasis on research that not only addresses the actual concrete conditions of women's experience in sport both past and present, but also recognises that knowledge, to be useful, must contribute to the practical reconstruction of the sports world in which women's interests are no longer subordinated to those of men. We must study not only how women are constructed as subordinate but also how male sport structures operate to keep them that way (Imray and Middleton, 1983). "Left to our own devices," as someone has asked, "would women invent a model of sport that includes physical aggression, exclusive rewards, scholarships, sophisticated recruitment systems, free cars and carpeted offices for coaches, and powerful economic cartels?" (Birrell, 1984:132).

From a methodological point of view, the notion of an epistemological standpoint of women means that the vertical relationship between researcher and "researched" must be abolished. In other words, the view from above must be replaced by the view from below (Mies, 1983). This is the process of "conscientisation" whereby the study of an oppressive reality is not carried out by experts but by the objects of the oppression. As women studying sport, we ourselves have experienced discrimination in some form; therefore we must learn to take this experience as a starting point and integrate it into the research process.[11] There are very few examples of this approach, but three come to mind: Fritschner (1978), who studied the karate dojo, discovering how the "weakest" (women, children, and unathletic males) survive in an exaggerated physical environment; Prendergast's (1978) fascinating examination of female solidarity in an English village maintained through the game of stoolball; and Imray and Middleton's (1983) tantalisingly brief look at how cricket in a Yorkshire village marks the boundaries between the public and private spheres which dictate the reality of women's lives.

Research that takes women's experience as its starting point and is committed to an eventual reconceptualisation of social reality will also be characterised by meaningful "consciousness raising" during the research process itself. Women simultaneously oppose and conform to the conditions that deny their freedom, but when social knowledge and self-knowledge become mutually informing, there is at least the possibility of imagining one's freedom (Westkott, 1983). Meaningful change for women in sport will come only through a collective feminist consciousness that comprehends the dialectical relationship between knowledge and action.

The Challenge to Objectivism and the Rejection of Positivism

It has been said that feminist epistemology rejects *objectivism* but advances *objectivity* (Harding, 1984b). There is an important point here. As I have already noted, traditional marxist feminism and socialist feminism are at odds with the norm of objectivity because it also implies value neutrality. The latter is inherent in liberalism and its epistemological cousin, positivism. Feminist epistemology, like that of marxism, challenges the claim that what we know, or what best "corresponds" to our reality, is value free. It is in this sense that it rejects objectivism. Our knowledge claims depend upon who we are as social persons, and as I have argued previously in discussing the notion of a standpoint, those committed to emancipatory political struggles are "less likely to have reasons to obscure or mystify to themselves or others the regularities of nature and social life and their underlying causal tendencies" (Harding, 1984b:41). From a feminist standpoint it can be argued that a theory of knowledge and the "science" to be guided by it *follow logically from feminist moral and political truths, not the reverse.* The moral and political "truths" held by feminists state simply that it is unfair and unjust to exclude women from any area of social life. As Harding (1984a:3) argues,

> what the feminist epistemology requires is a disorienting, estranging, uncomfortable intellectual, moral and emotional break with the Enlightenment assumption that *all* claims to moral and political truths are on shakier justificatory grounds than are *any* widely confirmed factual truths.

Therefore, what is being challenged here is the notion of an objective reality which is "out there" and can be studied, grasped, researched by anyone using universally applicable rules of inquiry. It is this sort of objectivism and norm of objectivity that a feminist epistemology challenges. What it reaffirms, on the other hand, is that knowledge claims of women, at least those engaged in liberatory struggles, are indeed more objective because they place far more importance on moral and political truths than they do on scientific rationality. In this sense it can be said that a feminist epistemology rejects objectivism and positivism but reaffirms a new concept of objectivity.

Methodologically this means that feminist researchers are likely to challenge the rigid separation between researcher and researched, and we will be wary of any methodology that results in dichotomy, duality, linearity, and fixity (Du Bois, 1983). We will also want to avoid decontextualisation or "context-stripping," which means allowing women's experiences to disappear or become invisible. Instead, we will employ methods that restore human agency rather than take it away by substituting sterile "forces, factors, roles, structures, stereotypes, constraints, attitudes" for the real-life experiences of women (Vickers, 1982). As one commentator succinctly puts it: "Our scientific methods, as women, as feminists, require seeing things *as they are*: whole, entire, complex" (Du Bois, 1983:111).

Just what this particular rebellion means in a practical sense is the subject of continuing debate among feminist researchers. Sociological research strategies range all the way from using several techniques simultaneously to creative ways of gathering data in a non-reactive manner.[12] The general trend is for feminists to place more faith in methodologies that reinforce the epistemological assumption that the only way of knowing a socially constructed world is to know it from within. This entails more of an emphasis on reflexive sociologies, such as symbolic interactionism, phenomenology, ethnomethodology, and perhaps Marx's dialectical materialism, all of which proceed by locating social phenomena in actual practical activities (cf. Smith, 1981; Stanley and Wise, 1983). As Dorothy Smith (1981:17) argues, "it is not individual social behaviour which is our interest, but the social determinations of our everyday experience."

Within the context of our research on gender and sport, I would suggest that there is virtually no recognition, even understanding, of what I have just described. Others have shown that where gender has been taken into account in any meaningful way (infrequently), it usually means either "controlling for gender," describing the differential effects of gender on sport involvement, or a documentation of male dominance in sport (Birrell, 1984). In one specific area of gender research, namely, sex role and sex identity studies, I have pointed to the unavoidable and futile reification in this research that hinders political attempts to criticise the cultural ideologies that maintain the stereotypes in the first place, and to find at least a starting point for social change (Hall, 1981).

It would be much better if we redirected our research energies to a totally different set of questions. As a starting point, we need to devote a great deal of attention to exactly how sport, both women's and men's (because they usually are separate), helps encourage and maintain patriarchy. We must gain a much better historical understanding of women's sporting experience than we have at present — *all* women — not just those who were most visible. For example, we know virtually nothing about working-class women and how they have participated. From here we need to examine the extent to which sport, for women, has the potential to take on a set of oppositional meanings within a patriarchal ideology.

Paul Willis (1982), for instance, brilliantly discusses the role of sport in the reinforcement of common-sense ideologies that assert the superiority of men and how women actually collude in these ideological definitions. Admittedly his is an "essay in ideas," as he puts it, but it is a superb example of the sort of analysis that will help us see that which is so difficult to see. I would want to extend his work further to examine how sport has and could represent sites of resistance to a specifically patriarchal social order. I am convinced that an examination of the relationship between female sexuality and physicality will provide us with useful insights about the potential for resistance because of the very longstanding hegemonic control men have had over women's bodies (cf. Lenskyj, 1984; Bray, 1984). I raise these questions to stimulate discussion about what sort of research we should do in this area, given the feminist challenge to empiricism and positivism.

The Rejection of a Hierarchy of Dualisms

Inherent in liberal political philosophy is a series of rigid conceptual dualisms — culture / nature, mind / body, rationality / emotionality, public / private, objective / subjective. What is interesting about these dichotomies is how the "culture, mind, rationality, public, objective" side is associated with males and the "nature, emotionality, private, subjective" side with females. Liberals claim, however, that these dualisms are sex-blind and not intended to promote sexual hierarchy. Yet the liberal notion of rationality is itself based on the primacy of culture over nature, mind over body, private over public, objective over subjective, and so forth. As we saw earlier, this view has been challenged most clearly by radical feminists and certainly by traditional marxist and socialist feminists.

Scientific rationality seems also to be based on this rigid set of sex-linked dualisms. Fee (1981:381) has identified this as the "ideology of gender" which pervades scientific thought:

> We find that the attributes of science are the attributes of males; the objectivity said to be characteristic of the production of scientific knowledge is specifically identified as the male way of relating to the world. Science is cold, hard, impersonal, "objective"; women, by contrast, are warm, soft, emotional, "subjective". Even the hierarchy of the sciences is a hierarchy of masculinity: as the language suggests: the "hard" sciences on the top of the hierarchy are seen as more male than the "soft" sciences at the bottom.

A feminist epistemology evaluates and rejects this (sexual) hierarchy of dualisms because it sees them as central to maintaining the androcentric nature of science. Their existence also denies, in a very real way, the validity of women's specific claims to knowledge. Our knowledge is based on experience, and although it is often far more within the nature / body / private side of the dichotomy, as women we do participate in the culture / mind / public arena. Our experience, quite literally, has been denied its own rationality because it does not fit scientific rationality. Even marxism insists upon a rigid dichotomy between production and reproduction. Although marxists claim that these categories are sex-blind, they are not. How else to explain the undue importance placed on production while reproduction is virtually ignored?[13]

Sport poses an interesting problem here because the *body as subject* underlies all human physical activity including, of course, sport. In fact, it has been observed that the identity of body and active subjectivity reaches its paradigm in sport (Young, 1979). Unlike other physical activities with more utilitarian purposes, sport "calls upon the body's capacities and skills merely for the sake of determining what they can achieve" (Young, 1979:46). Therefore, sport exhibits the essential body-subject. Patriarchal culture has defined woman, on the other hand, as the essential body-object. Limited space precludes developing this assertion here, but so much of modern feminist literature and theory beginning probably with de Beauvoir's *Second Sex* has focussed on this problem. What follows for women and sport, however, is that a culture that defines sport as body-subject and women as body-object forces an incompatibility between women and sport. In the end it means that women have either been excluded from the symbols, practices, and institutions of sport or, when they do participate, what they do is not considered true sport, nor in some cases are they viewed as real women.

This is certainly not a new idea, and many others have already made the same points. Moreover, as greater numbers of women enter masculinist sport (swifter, higher, stronger) or attempt to change the essential masculine meaning of sport (e.g., the introduction of rhythmic gymnastics and synchronized swimming in the 1984 Olympics), the patriarchal nature of sport will change. It can also work in reverse. As more and more women have entered the "fitness industry", they have become increasingly defined, at least through media images, as body-objects, not unlike the way women are objectified and commodified in pornography.

Therefore, the problem posed by sport is a reversal of the culture / mind / objective versus the nature / body / subjective dualism. Sport is clearly identified with the latter and so are women, yet women are excluded in many ways from sport. I do not think we fully understand how and under what historical conditions this has been allowed to happen. Nor, as I pointed out earlier, have we focussed sufficient attention on how female sexuality and physicality have come to be defined in patriarchal culture so as to necessitate women's exclusion from an activity which, symbolically at least, should include us. I strongly suspect that often our methods in the sociology of sport have prevented us from seeing its importance.

By and large, the concepts and methods of sociology as a discourse constitute women as object rather than subject. Dorothy Smith (1979:159) argues, "By insisting that women be entered into sociology as its subjects, we find we cannot escape how its practices transform us into objects." The main point is that the theory and practice of women's experience cannot be split; what is required is conscious subjectivity, whereby the subjective experience of women is validated and acknowledged (Klein, 1983). The specific methodological implications include, for example, interactive interviewing, collaborative and participatory techniques where there is a dialectic between researcher and researched, finding ways not to manipulate and objectify *everyone* (including support staff) in the research process, and avoiding quantitative objectification because it has its own inherent biasses and distortions.

The Recognition of a Transformative Potential in a Feminist Theory of Knowledge

Feminism, say some (cf. Rose, 1983), has been quick to point out its methodology but much slower when it comes to an epistemology. The essential debates have only begun to emerge within feminist scholarship, primarily in the social sciences, and very little has been said about their relevance to the natural sciences. However, there is a growing recognition among some that perhaps Virginia Woolf (*Three Guineas*) was right: "Science it would seem is not sexless; she is a man, a father and infected too." Calls for an epistemology for the natural sciences, indeed an alternative feminist science, are slowly developing beyond mere critique to the laborious work required in creating them.[14]

The point I wish to make here is that the epistemological challenge to both the social and natural sciences, by feminists, is a radical one and has transformative potential. The question has become, "if and how we can use for human ends forms of inquiry apparently inextricably enmeshed with distinctively masculine identity projects" (Harding, 1984a:1). For some, this has become the science question in feminism. The emerging debates at present point to an answer in the negative. The epistemologies of liberalism's empiricism, positivism, and objectivism, as well as marxism's dialectical materialism, are the main targets and cannot be simply reformed. Needed is something radically new and different, certainly feminist: a revolutionary theory of knowledge.

What implications does this have for the sociology of sport and in particular the consideration of gender? In recent years there has been an increasing awareness that taking serious account of gender means far more than describing sex differences or documenting male dominance. In other words, there is a growing recognition that taking account of gender means at the very least an incorporation of feminist theory and critique into the analysis. What is so interesting in the sociology of sport is that this is more likely to be carried out by our male colleagues and especially those writing from a neo-marxist or materialist perspective. For instance, Garry Whannel (1983) in *Blowing the Whistle*, a useful little book about the place of sport in socialism, makes some very meaningful observations concerning the role of feminism in sport. He notes also that there is surprisingly little discussion of sport in feminism, and he is right. I'll return to this point in a moment.

In a recent article, David Whitson (1985) carefully examines some of the issues and debates emanating from the domination / subordination and reproduction / transformation literature in the sociology of sport and finds them wanting in their consideration of gender. His argument is that it has been disabling to conceive of domination in traditional class terms alone, and he suggests that the sex / gender system as it is reproduced in sport is one site where patriarchal cultural hegemony is being challenged. We must address its theoretical significance. My colleague Bruce Kidd has consistently recognised the importance of gender and feminism in his work and writing. There are probably others, but this is just to mention some of the material with which I am familiar.

Despite these welcome additions to the analysis of gender relations in sport, I am concerned that it will be deemed enough. Certainly there is much more work to be done in extending the analyses and incorporating issues of gender into the central debates. However, I am afraid that we will again engage in a fruitless exercise to modify that which cannot be reformed because whatever "it" is has an inherent logic that simply cannot accommdate the epistemological standpoint of women. Does this mean that we should begin all over again? No, I believe that the starting point is always feminist theory and, for myself, that is some combination of radical and socialist feminism which has not only the greatest potential for transforming how women come to know their social reality, but also that reality itself.

CONCLUSION

It is tempting to suggest that the reason feminist theory has virtually ignored sport is that it simply is not considered a very significant issue. Some say it cannot be compared with the more important gender issues that stem from the economy (e.g., labour force participation, equal pay legislation, affirmative action), our political and legal institutions (electing female politicians, fighting for the ERA), our sexuality (sexual harassment and sexual assault), and those that threaten our very existence (domestic violence). It is also tempting to suggest that most feminist theorists have little conception of sport as an ideological institution with enormous symbolic significance that contributes to and perpetuates cultural hegemony. Whenever feminists have taken sport seriously, it has either been in practical terms of attempting to incorporate feminist values into women's sporting experience or found in the writings of some radical feminists who see sport as yet another example of sexual violence. Robin Morgan (1984:119), for example, writes:

> If sports are, as the saying goes, America's "national pastime", and pornography is one of America's fastest-growing industries, what does this tell us about the way we regard human flesh, the way we play, express sexuality, and transmute excitement — into violence?

The point is that nowhere is there a recognition among feminist theorists / scholars as to the fact that sport plays a considerable role in the reproduction of a specifically patriarchal social order and could, therefore, be significant in the transformation of that order. At the very least, it can provide a site of resistance. Let us get on with the analysis and historical work necessary. By doing so, we will be making an important contribution to some essential rethinking within the sociology of sport — as well as to feminist theory.

REFERENCES

Acknowledgements — This is a much-revised version of a paper presented at the AAHPERD National Convention, Anaheim, CA, March 29 - April 2, 1984. I want to thank Margrit Eichler, Richard Gruneau, and Robert Sparks for their very helpful suggestions.

1 I am using here a straightforward dictionary (*Webster's New World*) definition of epistemology rather than a more formal philosophical one. O'Connor and Carr (1982), for example, suggest that epistemology is concerned with knowledge in four ways: (a) it seeks to give an account of the nature of *knowing* in general; (b) it is concerned with the *sources* of knowledge, with the investigation of the nature and variety of *modes of acquiring* knowledge; (c) it is concerned with the *scope* of knowledge, and (d) it is concerned with defending our criteria for knowledge against the attack of *skepticism*.

2 In the end, the question is whether there is a distinctive feminist perspective on the philosophy of science that includes not only epistemology but also metaphysics and methodology. For a discussion in this broader context, see Harding and Hintikka (1983).

3 For a fascinating "thought experiment" concerning the possibility of human society without gender, see Cucchiari (1981) who postulates the existence of an ungendered stage in human cultural evolution in order to explain gender hierarchy or universal male dominance. See also Ursula LeGuin's marvelous science fiction novel, *The Left Hand of Darkness*, which depicts a world in which both sexes are embodied in each person.

4 I have purposely not capitalised "marxist" and "marxism" throughout this chapter because even though it is customary to capitalise terms that are derived from a proper name, to do so juxtaposes marxism and feminism unequally. To capitalise "feminism" makes no sense because it cannot be named after a single individual.

5 For an excellent philosophical discussion of these issues in the context of women's sport, see Postow (1983).

6 I would also argue the reverse in that commitment to a certain epistemology also carries with it commitment to a theory of human nature. As I will try to show later in the section on feminist methodology, I do not think that many feminist researchers deem this important.

7 I have been aided greatly in this discussion by Nancy Hartsock's work, but also by Sandra Harding, who recently gave a talk about a book she is writing (Harding, 1984a, 1984b). The terms "feminist standpoint" or "standpoint of women" or "women's standpoint" are sometimes used interchangeably in the literature, but their usage by Nancy Hartsock (1983b) and Dorothy Smith (1979) appears to be different. Hartsock prefers the term "feminist standpoint" because of its achieved character and liberatory potential. When

Smith uses the term "standpoint of women", I believe she means that "we have not known how to begin from our experience, how to make ourselves as women the subjects of the sociological act of knowing" (p. 154). But I prefer to use the term "standpoint of women" because there are many variants of feminism, and taking a feminist standpoint does not mean the same thing to those who adhere to one variant over another.

8 Hartsock (1983a) elaborates this characterisation in great detail and places enormous stress on the nature and character of both sexuality and eros because she believes they are fundamental to an understanding of the structuring of human community. Unfortunately, I have had to oversimplify her arguments here, but I hope the essence of her ideas remains intact.

9 For instance, see Cook and Fonow (1983) and Eichler (1983), whose assessments of some of the same literature differ from my own. However, I am indebted to them for pointing out that it is now possible to articulate a set of principles or assumptions in the first place.

10 I am aware of the problems in this statement. These epistemological principles are very slippery indeed. If they are defined differently, then the implications for a methodology change considerably. For instance, Cook and Fonow (1983) argue for epistemological principles based on an analysis of feminist methodology in the field of sociology, whereas I argue from a reading of feminist *epistemology*, which I think is a more valid process.

11 This raises the question of whether this double vision of reality, which better equips feminist researchers to comprehend and interpret women's experience, also equips them to comprehend men's experience. Conversely, can male researchers (some of them convincingly feminist) comprehend and interpret women's experience? I think the answer in both cases is a qualified yes. It is possible to "take the role of the other" through one of the reflexive / interpretive sociologies. If this is denied then there can be no comparative social science, and what remains are worlds of mutual incomprehension. (I am indebted to Rick Gruneau for this valuable point.)

12 For a description of some of these strategies, see Cook and Fonow (1983).

13 A great deal of socialist feminist theoretical work is focussed on rectifying the imbalance in marxism between production and reproduction. An excellent example of this sort of important work is Mary O'Brien's *The Politics of Reproduction.*

14 For the emerging debates within the development of a feminist epistemology for the natural sciences, see Harding (1983, 1984a, 1984b), Rose (1983), Keller (1978, 1982), Haraway (1978, 1981), Hubbard et al., (1982), Fee (1981), and Stehelin (1976).

Birrell, S., "Studying Gender in Sport: A Feminist Perspective," in N. Theberge and P. Donnelly (eds.), *Sport and the Sociological Imagination.* Fort Worth: Texas Christian University Press, 1984, pp. 125 - 35.

Bray, C., "Gender and the Political Economy of Canadian Sport," in N. Theberge and P. Donnelly (eds.), *Sport and the Sociological Imagination.* Fort Worth: Texas Christian University Press, 1984, pp. 104 - 24.

Cook, J.A. and M.M. Fonow, "Knowledge and Women's Interests: Feminist Methodology in the Field of Sociology." Paper presented at the American Sociological Association, Detroit, August, 1983.

Cucchiari, S., "The Gender Revolution and the Transition from Bisexual Horde to Patrilocal Band: The Origins of Gender Hierarchy," in S.B. Ortner and H. Whitehead (eds.), *Sexual Meanings: The Cultural Construction of Gender and Sexuality.* Cambridge: Cambridge University Press, 1981, pp. 31 - 79.

Du Bois, B., "Passionate Scholarship: Notes on Values, Knowing and Method in Feminist Social Science," in G. Bowles and R.D. Klein (eds.), *Theories of Women's Studies.* London: Routledge & Kegan Paul, 1983, pp. 105 - 16.

Eichler, M., *The Double Standard: A Feminist Critique of Feminist Social Science.* London: Croom Helm, 1980.

Eichler, M., "The Relationship between Sexist, Non-sexist, Woman-centred and Feminist Research." Paper presented at the American Sociological Association, Detroit, August, 1983.

Fee, E., "Is Feminism a Threat to Scientific Objectivity?" *International Journal of Women's Studies* 4 (1981): 378 - 92.

Fritschner, L.M., "Karate: The Making and the Maintenance of an Underdog Class." *Journal of Sport Behavior* 1 (1978): 3 - 13.

Gruneau, R., *Class, Sports, and Social Development.* Amherst: The University of Massachusetts Press, 1983.

Hall, M.A., *Sport, Sex Roles and Sex Identity. The CRIAW Papers / Les Documents de l'ICRAF*, Number 1. Ottawa: The Canadian Research Institute for the Advancement of Women, 1981.

Haraway, D., "Animal Sociology and a Natural Economy of the Body Politic." *Signs: Journal of Women in Culture and Society* 4 (1978): 21 - 60.

Haraway, D., "In the Beginning Was the Word: The Genesis of Biological Theory." *Signs: Journal of Women in Culture and Society* 6 (1981): 469 - 81.

Harding, S., "Why Has the Sex / Gender System Become Visible Only Now?", in S. Harding and M.B. Hintikka (eds.), *Discovering Reality.* Dordrecht, Holland: D. Reidel, 1983.

Harding, S., "The Science Question in Feminism." Unpublished paper, 1984a.

Harding, S., "Towards a Feminist Epistemology." Lecture given at the Ontario Institute for Studies in Education, Toronto, February, 1984b.

Harding, S. and M.B. Hintikka, *Discovering Reality: Feminist Perspectives on Epistemology, Metaphysics, Methodology, and Philosophy of Science.* Dordrecht, Holland: D. Reidel, 1983.

Hartsock, N.C.M., *Money, Sex and Power: Towards a Feminist Historical Materialism.* New York: Longman, 1983a.

Hartsock, N.C.M., "The Feminist Standpoint: Developing the Ground for a

Specifically Feminist Historial Materialism,'' in S. Harding and M.B. Hintikka (eds.), *Discovering Reality*. Dordrecht, Holland: D. Reidel, 1983b.

Hubbard, R., M.S. Henifin and B. Fried, *Biological Woman — The Convenient Myth*. Cambridge, MA: Schenkman, 1982.

Imray, L. and A. Middleton, ''Public and Private: Marking the Boundaries,'' in E. Gamarnikow et al. (eds.), *The Public and the Private*. London: Heinemann, 1983, pp. 12 - 23.

Jaggar, A., *Feminist Politics and Human Nature*. Totowa, NJ: Rowman & Allanheld, 1983.

Keller, E.F., ''Gender and Science.'' *Psychoanalysis and Contemporary Thought* 1 (1978): 409 - 33.

Keller, E.F., ''Feminism and Science.'' *Signs: Journal of Women in Culture and Society* 7 (1982): 589 - 602.

Kessler, S.J. and W. McKenna, *Gender: An Ethnomethodological Approach*. New York: John Wiley & Sons, 1978.

Klein, R.D., ''How to Do What We Want to Do: Thoughts about Feminist Methodology,'' in G. Bowles and R.D. Klein (eds.), *Theories of Women's Studies*. London: Routledge & Kegan Paul, 1983, pp. 88 - 104.

Lenskyj, H., ''Sport, Femininity and Sexuality.'' *Resources for Feminist Research/ Documentation sur la recherche feministe* 13 (1984): 66 - 8.

Lipman-Blumen, J., *Gender Roles and Power*. Englewood Cliffs, NJ: Prentice-Hall, 1984.

Meis, M., Towards a Methodology for Feminist Research,'' in G. Bowles and R.D. Klein (eds.), *Theories of Women's Studies*. London: Routledge & Kegan Paul, 1983, pp. 117 - 39.

Morgan, R., *The Anatomy of Freedom*. Garden City, NY: Doubleday (Anchor Books), 1984.

O'Brien, M., *The Politics of Reproduction*. London: Routledge & Kegan Paul, 1981.

O'Connor, D.J. and B. Carr, *Introduction to the Theory of Knowledge*. Brighton: The Harvester Press, 1982.

Postow, B.C. (ed.), *Women, Philosophy, and Sport: A Collection of New Essays*, Metuchen, NJ, and London: The Scarecrow Press, 1983.

Prendergast, S., ''Stoolball — The Pursuit of Vertigo?'' *Women's Studies International Quarterly* 1 (1978): 15 - 26.

Rose, H., ''Hand, Brain, and Heart: A Feminist Epistemology for the Natural Sciences.'' *Signs: Journal of Women in Culture and Society* 9 (1983): 73-90.

Smith, D.E., ''A Sociology for Women,'' in J.A. Sherman and E.T. Beck (eds.), *The Prism of Sex*. Madison: The University of Wisconsin Press, 1979, pp. 135 - 87.

Smith, D.F., ''The Experienced World as Problematic: A Feminist Method.'' University of Saskatchewan Sorokin Lectures, Number 12, 1981.

Stanley, L. and S. Wise, *Breaking Out: Feminist Consciousness and Feminist Research*. London: Routledge & Kegan Paul, 1983.

Stehelin, L., "Science, Women and Ideology," in H. Rose and S. Rose (eds.), *The Radicalisation of Science,* London: Macmillan, 1976, pp. 76 - 89.

Theberge, N., "Towards a Feminist Alternative to Sport as a Male Preserve." Paper presented at the NASSS, St. Louis, October, 1983.

Vickers, J.M., "Memoirs of an Ontological Exile: The Methodological Rebellions of Feminist Researchers," in A. Miles and G. Finn (eds.), *Feminism in Canada: From Pressure to Politics*. Montréal: Black Rose Books, 1982, pp. 27 - 46.

Westkott, M., "Women's Studies as a Strategy for Change: Between Criticism and Vision," in G. Bowles and R.D. Klein, *Theories of Women's Studies*. London: Routledge & Kegan Paul, 1983, pp. 210 - 18.

Whannel, G., *Blowing the Whistle*. London: Pluto Press, 1983.

Whitson, D., "Structure, Agency and the Sociology of Sport Debates." *Theory, Culture and Society* 3(1), 1985.

Willis, P., "Women in Sport and Ideology," in J. Hargreaves (ed.), *Sport, Culture and Ideology*. London: Routledge & Kegan Paul, 1982, pp. 117 - 35.

Young, I., "The Exclusion of Women from Sport: Conceptual and Existential Dimensions." *Philosophy in Context* 9 (1979): 44 - 53.

Young, I. "From Fireworks to Frameworks." *The Women's Review of Books* 1 (1984): 11 - 12.

FURTHER READING

Harding, S., and M.B. Hintikka (eds.), *Discovering Reality: Feminist Perspectives on Epistemology, Metaphysics, Methodology and Philosophy of Science*. Dordrecht, Holland: D. Reidel, 1983.

Hartsock, N.C.M., *Money, Sex and Power: Towards a Feminist Historical Materialism*. New York: Longman, 1983.

Keller, E.F., *Reflections on Gender and Science*. New Haven: Yale University Press, 1985.

Jaggar, A., *Feminist Politics and Human Nature*. Totowa, NJ: Rowman & Allanheld, 1983.

Stanley, L., and S. Wise, *Breaking Out: Feminist Consciousness and Feminist Research*. London: Routledge & Kegan Paul, 1983.

KAREN MESSING

The Scientific Mystique: Can a White Lab Coat Guarantee Purity in the Search for Knowledge about the Nature of Women?

In the 1950s and 1960s, Yale professor Stanley Milgram reported results from a series of experiments that shocked many academics.[1] In these experiments he asked his subjects to press a button which they believed delivered painful electric shocks to people, in an ostensible attempt to find out how much electricity the human body could stand. The "victims" were confederates of the experimenter and simulated increasing pain and anguish as the subjects thought they were intensifying the shocks. To Milgram's surprise, 20 per cent of the subjects could be induced to administer "shocks" that they believed were lethal, when told by the experimenter that the study required it. And if the investigator wore a lab coat, the percentage of "killer" subjects who would do this increased to 65 per cent. These experiments were commonly interpreted as showing that people are very obedient to authority. It is clear that they also demonstrate the tremendous respect lay people have for the authority of scientists and for scientific experiments.

Part of this scientific mystique comes from the image of science as the search for objective truth, a pursuit of knowledge carried out in neutral surroundings by disinterested observers. This view is based on a romanticism that most scientists do not actively discourage, but which has, as all of us engaged in science know, very little to do with reality.

In the present chapter I will show that the scientific community is in fact molded by the society of which it is a part. Scientists, and the data we produce, are not and cannot be free from the prejudices, ideologies, or interests of the larger society. This lack of objectivity is manifested in the ways scientists are selected and in the scientific results themselves. The examples I use

Originally published in Marian Lowe and Ruth Hubbard (eds.), *Woman's Nature: Rationalizations of Inequality*. Toronto: Pergamon Press, 1983.

will relate primarily to the treatment of women[2] by the scientific community, but similar mechanisms affect working-class people, blacks, or any other group that is under-represented in the scientific establishment.

It will be useful to look at several components of the scientific process; they can be divided roughly into those relating to the scientists themselves and those pertaining to the process.

The scientist

1. The selection of scientists
2. Their access to facilities for scientific work.

I will show that research scientists are a highly selected group whose interests are not typical of a cross section of society. This situation has a strong influence on the scientific process.

The process

3. The choice of research topic
4. The wording of the hypothesis
5. The choice of experimental subjects
6. The choice of appropriate controls
7. The method of observation
8. Data analysis
9. The interpretation of data
10. The publication of results
11. The popularisation of results

For each of these components, I will give examples of how the ideology and background of the researcher can influence the results, and how these results then become accepted scientific truth.

THE SELECTION OF THE SCIENTIST

Many articles have been written lately on the difficulties facing women who want to be scientists. These barriers have been of various kinds: exploitation of women scientists,[3] undervaluing of their contributions,[4] and exclusion of them from "old-boy" communication networks.[5]

In addition, many women are cut off at the start by the forced choice between child bearing and graduate studies.[6] It usually takes eight to nine years of post-secondary education to get a Ph.D. in the sciences. For a person to get through this, he or she must have a great deal of persistence and confidence and either a good supply of money or the time to earn it. Financial needs go up and available time, of course, goes down when child care is involved. The demands of research can produce major conflicts for those of us with children. Chemical reactions, physical phenomena, and cell behaviour do not fit neatly into an eight-hour day. Therefore, the laboratory scientist must be available at all hours and often on weekends.

The same is true of field work in ecology or geology, for example.

For this reason, conciliation of research schedules with child bearing and child raising is nearly impossible to do well. At 5 P.M., just as one has finally got conditions for an experiment right, it is time to pick up the children. One has the unacceptable choices of rushing off to the day-care centre, thereby wasting the day's work, or making the phone calls to the day-care centre, arranging a sitter, changing the arrangements for supper, and staying to do the experiment, afterward facing one's own guilt and the eventual revenge of children and mate. The total exhaustion associated with this period is not conducive to creative work of any kind.[7] One of my graduate students supports her two children, aged 1 and 2, by taking part-time jobs. By the time she gets to the lab in the morning, she feels she has already put in a full work day.

The scientific community does not tolerate the temporary lowering of productivity associated with child raising, although the years of graduate studies are also those in which most people have children. The Canadian NSERC fellowships for gifted students have an absolute limit of two years in which to obtain the Master of Sciences degree. While maternity leave (unpaid) is granted, no provision is made for a slower rhythm of work once the mother returns to the laboratory or field. If she takes longer than two years for the M.Sc., she can get no Ph.D. support.

These conditions make it equally difficult for anyone to hold a part-time job, so that the student who must earn money in order to stay in school faces the same problem as someone with family responsibilities.

ACCESS TO FACILITIES FOR SCIENTIFIC WORK

Doing science requires space, equipment, and infrastructure. While some world-shaking results have been obtained using minimal facilities, most modern biological endeavours, for example, are facilitated by the latest models of spectrophotometers, computer-assisted chromatography, scintillation counters, ultracentrifuges, and so on. Plenty of these machines are found in the top-rated universities, where up-and-coming scientists are hired to tenure track positions if they have been superstars in graduate school. Less successful scientists are found in underequipped universities and in less secure jobs, where even access to a laboratory may be a problem.

In the United States, female Ph.D.s are more than four times as likely as males to be unemployed and constitute only 6.6% of tenured Ph.D. faculty in the sciences. Most of the scientific community is now white and male.[8] This is not to say that blacks or females necessarily would do neutral, nonsexist research, but that science is done primarily by only certain people, who seek recognition from peers who are similar to them.

THE CHOICE OF RESEARCH TOPIC

The choice of topic is influenced by several factors: the interest of the scientist, that of his or her present and future employers, and the ability to get funding for the work. Because of their sex and class, the large majority of scientists are less likely than the general population to be interested in such topics as the occupational exposures that present a risk to the nursing mother, alternate (non-hormonal) treatments for the discomforts of menopause, how a woman can give herself a safe (and, where necessary, secret) abortion, what work postures increase the likelihood of menstrual cramps, and how a low-income family can provide itself with nutritious meals. On the other hand, there is plenty of research, supported by drug companies, on drug therapy for menopausal women,[9] by government on what racial and income groups have the most abortions,[10] by employers on the relationship between women's physiological cycles and productivity,[11] and by private charity on how to prevent a rich, fat-laden diet from causing heart disease.[12]

THE WORDING OF THE RESEARCH HYPOTHESIS

Articulating the hypothesis is crucial to the scientific method. Research is done in order to find an answer to a specific question, and the way the question is posed often determines the way the research will be carried out and how the eventual data will be interpreted. John Money and Anke Ehrhardt, for example, have done a good deal of research on whether prenatal hormone exposures explain sex-specific behaviours. In one study[13] they looked at children who have only one sex chromosome, an X, rather than the usual two (XX for girls, XY for boys), a condition that is called Turner's syndrome and is symbolized XO. Money and Ehrhardt hypothesised that since XO children, like normal girls, are less exposed than males to prenatal androgens (so-called male hormones) they should be "feminine," just as normal XX girls are. They defined "femininity" as not being a tomboy, preferring "girls' toys", wearing dresses rather than pants, being marriage-oriented rather than career-oriented in early adolescence, and so forth. By these criteria, their XO subjects were indeed found to be even more feminine than normal XX girls. It is unlikely that an investigator who was less accepting of present-day sex role stereotypes would have shaped the hypothesis this way, since she or he would consider "femininity" an inappropriate variable on which to study individuals with Turner's syndrome, who, though they have a vulva and not a penis, in fact lack most primary and all secondary female sexual characteristics. They are further distinguished by being unusually short, and many have a webbed neck and are mentally retarded. Hence, they probably have quite different social and biological experiences than most ordinary girls. A more critical investigator might also question the criteria of "femininity" chosen by these authors.

The controversy surrounding XYY males a few years ago is a similar example of a hypothesis that was based on a socially-defined point of view, this time involving prejudice about males. Early investigators, finding a large number of men with an extra male (Y) chromosome in prisons, formulated the hypothesis that people who have an extra Y chromosome (XYY) must be "supermales", which they took to mean that these people would be especially prone to violence. They failed to consider the fact that XYY males are unusually large, slow, and somewhat retarded. Thus, it was only after much money and time had been wasted that another hypothesis, that XYY males had the same chance as other retarded males of being in prison, was tested and confirmed.[14]

THE CHOICE OF EXPERIMENTAL SUBJECTS

The clearest example of bias in the choice of a study population is the simple and extremely common exclusion of *women* from studies in which one wishes to obtain information about *people*. In a study of occupational cancers in the lead industry, all 950 women (but not blacks or short people) were excluded in order to keep the sample uniform.[15] In another study, as reported by Jeanne Stellman, 370,599 males were studied by the National Institutes of Health, in order to identify risk factors for heart disease.[16] Heart disease is also the leading cause of death in women, but women's risk factors were not studied. In reporting the results of such studies, authors rarely state clearly that they apply only to men.

Another way that a poor image of women (especially poor Third World women) conditions research strategies is by a callous disregard for the welfare of female subjects. For example, the birth control pill, though developed in Massachusetts, was first tested in Puerto Rico. And in 1971, long after its efficacy had been established, Dr. Joseph Goldzieher decided to test the Pill once more at his clinic. *Without their knowledge*, eighty of his 398 patients were given placebos (pills that looked and tasted like the Pill but were ineffective) instead of the Pill. All of the women chosen for this study had proven themselves fertile by having at least three previous children. Within a few months, ten of the women who were receiving the fake pills had become pregnant with unwanted foetuses.[17] Legal abortion was not available for these women.

THE CHOICE OF APPROPRIATE CONTROLS

The choice of controls is probably the factor that has the most influence on research results. Our research group was recently confronted with this issue when trying to determine whether rates of congenital malformations were higher than usual among the offspring of men occupationally exposed to a radioactive dust. These men lived near the factory, which discharged its untreated effluent into the air. If we used neighbours as controls, we would underestimate the effects of *factory*-caused exposures, since both groups would have some exposure to the dust. If we used as controls people who lived elsewhere, the measured effect might be greater, but we would be unable to identify the proportion due to specifically occupational exposures. Yet the usefulness of the results in bargaining with employers might be enhanced, because of the greater difference between the workers and the unexposed control population.

A glaring example of a poor choice of control group comes from a study of the effects of occupational exposure to radium.[18] Sharpe examined the incidence of stillbirths and miscarriages among female workers exposed to radium and compared them to pregnancy outcomes of the wives of their male co-workers, calling this "a not unreasonable control group". Not unreasonable, that is, if one forgets that males can also suffer genetic damage from radium exposure and pass it on to their children. The common idea that child bearing is an exclusively female province may account for Sharpe's forgetfulness.

Another example of the selection of a control group by sex-biassed assumptions occurred at a seminar given in 1977 at the Université du Québec by an ethologist from the Université de Rennes in France. The speaker described a study of the mating behaviour of large mammals, in which three female goats, sheep, or cows were tethered in separate stalls and offered serially to 100 males. The subsequent pawing, sniffing, and copulatory behaviour of the males was recorded. When asked why 100 males were necessary, the speaker replied that it was necessary to observe the full range of behaviour. When asked why, in that case, there were only three females, he answered, "To keep the conditions standard." In studying the most bilateral of behaviours, sexual intercourse, a feminist would find it less reasonable to select females to represent "standard conditions" and males to study the "range of behaviour". She would assume that results would be as skewed by the choice of a limited number of individuals of one sex as of the other.

THE METHOD OF OBSERVATION

The data an investigator collects are affected by the choice of tools (questionnaires, interview schedules, observations, biochemical tests) and the data that are considered valid and relevant. Ideology can affect all of these.

For example, in their study of the prevalence of warts among poultry slaughter-house workers, Mergler, Vezina and Beauvais[19] recorded the incidence by asking workers on a questionnaire how many warts they had. The study showed that workers who reported that they worked with saws, that their workplace was humid, and / or that their protective gloves did not fit correctly, had a significantly higher incidence of warts. During a presentation of these results at a scientific meeting, the study was criticised on the basis that the workers were incompetent to count their warts and that counting should be done by a qualified medical practitioner. This criticism ignored the fact that doctors are in general less familiar with these warts than are the affected workers, some of whom had upwards of a hundred warts on their hands.

Crucial data can also be ignored because of ideological bias. In a 1963 study of the effect of work on pregnancy outcome by the U.S. Public Health Service, the worker's *husband's* occupation was recorded, but that of the pregnant worker herself was not.[20] This expensive study was thus useless for identifying working conditions that pose a risk to pregnant women and their foetuses, and the absence of such data has rendered protection very difficult.[21] Nevertheless, a recent (1980) study of the causes of premature delivery did not even include in its parameters the question of *whether* the mother was employed, let alone her particular occupation.[22] The bias that blinds investigators to the fact that many married women work outside the home prevents research results from helping employed women.

A methodological weakness found in many studies of sex-specific behaviour is the reliance on a single observer who is aware of the hypothesis being tested, and who may therefore be biassed. The Money and Ehrhardt studies,[23] for example, compared girls of various hormonal statuses with respect to "femininity" on the basis of an interview with a single counsellor who knew the girl's history. Another example of a single-observer study comes from sociobiology. David Barash formulated the hypothesis that male ducks rape females because the males need to ensure a maximal number of descendants to maximise their own "reproductive success". Based on this, he predicted that a female who had been raped by a strange male would be re-raped as soon as possible by her usual consort (ducks live in couples). To test this complex hypothesis, Barash (alone) observed mallards for 558 hours, decided (alone) which male ducks were "husbands" and which were "strangers", and also which copulations were rape and which were mutually desired. He found, unsurprisingly, that his observations squared with his hypothesis.[24]

Even when experiments are performed under controlled laboratory conditions, observers may be biassed by their political or social interests. A technical study of the chromosomes (hereditary material) of people exposed to industrial pollutants ran into this problem. For many years, the Hooker Chemical company discharged waste products into Love Canal, New York. Residents noticed a high rate of congenital malformations and illness among their children and pets and asked the Environmental Protection Agency to do a study. Eleven of 37 residents were found to have abnormal-looking chromosomes. When the residents demanded to be evaluated, a review panel was set up to look at the chromosomes. The panel did not see the same abnormalities as the EPA.[25] Thus started a long exchange in the pages of scientific journals. Each side has its scientists, but the scientists on the two sides did not perceive the chromosomes on the microscope slides in the same way.

DATA ANALYSIS

There is a large literature on "demand characteristics" of experimental situations; that is, the tendency of experimenters, their subjects, and their research assistants to produce by unconscious manipulations the data desired by the investigator.[26] Steven Gould has illustrated this point in his re-analysis of data on cranial capacity of different races, showing how a distinguished nineteenth century investigator manipulated his data to prove (incorrectly) that blacks had smaller brains than whites.[27] Another study of experimenter bias showed that research assistants made three times as many errors in arithmetic that favoured the chief's hypothesis as errors that went against it.[28]

Few non-scientists are aware of how many simple errors can be found in the scientific literature and in well-known, respected journals. For instance, the previously cited Money and Ehrhardt article used a statistical (chi-square) test under conditions where the use of this test is forbidden by elementary statistics texts (too many expected values were less than five). The Barash study contained an arithmetic error that rendered results statistically significant, in that the probability of the situation occurring by chance is given as less than .001, when the data in fact yield a probability of its occurring through chance alone as greater than .05.

There are also instances of intentional mis-analyses of data. A case that has recently come to light is that of Sir Cyril Burt, a prominent British psychologist and educational planner, who is now known to have manipulated data supposedly collected from twins reared apart so as to demonstrate a strong genetic component in I.Q.[29] The fact that it took nearly 50 years for Burt's deceptions to be revealed is perhaps evidence that his conclusions, used for many years to argue for racial and class differences in intelligence, agreed so closely with widely held prejudices that a critical eye was never cast on the data.

THE INTERPRETATION OF DATA

One of the major questions in the occupational health and safety field, as well as in the anti-nuclear movement, is the degree of genetic damage induced by low levels of ionising radiation. In Québec, a case is under arbitration in which a radiodiagnostic technician applied for leave with pay during her pregnancy in accordance with a contract clause that provides for such leave if working conditions endanger a foetus. The employer argued that radiation below a certain threshold level poses no problem for the foetus; the union argued that there is no threshold, and that any exposure is associated with some probability of damage.[30] Scientists were found to testify on both sides, since the argument turns on the extrapolation of a particular dose-responsive curve, for which it is prohibitively time-consuming and expensive to obtain complete data to the lowest possible doses.[31,32] Scientists testifying on behalf of the union or the employer interpreted the same data in opposite ways; each found that the data supported the contention of her or his side.

There are many such cases where interpretation of data depends on one's point of view; the controversies about race and I.Q.,[33] about male "genes" for mathematical ability,[34] and about the effectiveness of chemical spraying in insect control[35] are examples of areas where an intensive research effort has not succeeded in settling a scientific question, owing to the involvement of opposing groups with a vested economic or social interest in opposite conclusions.

THE PUBLICATION OF RESULTS

After writing up the research results, the scientist submits a paper to a journal, which sends it to a few people working in the same field for review. This process is meant to guarantee that no slipshod work is published, that errors will be corrected, and that worthy articles find an audience. In practice the system is far from ideal. Once a scientist has made a name, he or she (though, of course, usually he) can often get an article published quickly after only perfunctory review. Less well-known scientists can have considerably more difficulty, especially if their results depart from accepted dogma.

Results that reinforce prevalent biasses are often accepted without question. For example, recently, the anthropologist C.O. Lovejoy published an article in *Science* with the ambitious title, "The Origin of Man"[36]. Some weeks later, he informed journalists that he had played a little joke. He had stated in his discussion that "the human female is continually sexually receptive." As authority for this statement he cited not research results, but "D.C. Johannsen, personal communication." This is the learned equivalent of saying, "My buddy told me in the locker room." Presumably because the original statement did not seem unreasonable to the reviewers, none of them picked up the faulty citation. A feminist reviewer might have, of course.

THE POPULARISATION OF RESULTS

Many research papers have been published on the cause of superior male performance on mathematics tests in high school.[37] Some papers support the hypothesis that males have superior genes, others that they have an environmentally conferred advantage. Therefore, it is hard to find a scientific basis for the fuss and furour that followed the publication of a recent study by Benbow and Stanley showing that one proposed environmental determinant — number of mathematics courses taken — could be eliminated from consideration.[38] There was no attempt by the authors to eliminate all environmental influences, and no evidence for genetic determination was offered. Yet the paper elicited editorial comment in the issue of *Science* magazine in which it appeared, and within a few weeks of publication *Time, Newsweek*, and local newspapers were publishing articles with titles like "Sex differences in achievement in and attitudes toward mathematics result from superior mathematical ability."[39] No similar publicity had accompanied Elizabeth Fennema's article of a few years earlier,[40] in which, based on the same data, she had argued for an environmental determination. The ideology of the media greatly influences which scientific results enter into the popular culture.

Some results lend themselves to use in political and social battles. Money and Ehrhardt's research on hormonal determination of sex-typical behaviour has slipped into the givens of popular science. They are quoted extensively in the sexology courses at the Université du Québec and in popular magazine articles.[41]

And David Barash, after studying rape in birds, wrote a widely read *Psychology Today* article in which he suggested that the double standard of sexual behaviour among humans follows the bird pattern, owing to men's biologically-based need to inject their sperm into as many women as possible.[42] This view was also quickly picked up and published by *Playboy*, under the title, "Do Men Need to Cheat on Their Women? A New Science Says Yes."[43]

On the other hand, ideology and special interests may prevent some research results from becoming publicised. In 1979, Dr. David Horrobin was fired from the Clinical Research Institute of Montreal for having "prematurely" publicised research results suggesting that the tranquiliser Valium may promote cancer of the breast in women. These results, subsequently confirmed by other investigators, were certainly of immediate practical value for women, since one woman in eleven gets breast cancer and Valium is the most commonly used prescription drug on the market.[44] No such censorship has been practised on Benbow's and Stanley's results or interpretations, which are prejudicial to women's education, on those of Barash, which justify rape, or on those of Burt, which support racism, although Horrobin's studies were based on much more data than any of these.

In fact, as we have seen in the preceding examples, scientists, protected by their image as zealous seekers after truth, have been allowed to say the most outrageous things about women with impunity. Such statements have been used to limit women's access to educational and occupational opportunities and have damaged our health. And, of course, scientists have also done damage to minority and working-class men. The problem of scientific objectivity is therefore not simply an academic one.

It is about time that scientists be regarded with the same skepticism as other members of the establishment. If and when we achieve an egalitarian society, we may hope for a science more in touch with people's needs. Industrial hygienists will listen to workers when they look for risks associated with working conditions. Biologists will consult with, rather than experiment on, women who want contraceptive devices, and psychologists will search for the basis of co-operative rather than aggressive behaviour. Until that time, since we still have a long struggle ahead of us, we would be wise to examine closely, even belligerently, what scientists have to say about the nature of women.

REFERENCES

Acknowledgements — I would like to thank Lesley Lee for bringing the methodological issues in the mathematics and sex research to my attention, and Jean-Pierre Reveret and Luc Desnovers for reading the manuscript.

1 Stanley Milgram, *Obedience to Authority* (New York: Harper & Row, 1973).

2 The treatment of women is more specifically covered in Ruth Hubbard, Mary Sue Henifin and Barbara Fried, eds., *Biological Woman — The Convenient Myth* (Cambridge, MA: Schenkman Publishing Co., 1982). This book contains an extensive bibliography.

3 Naomi Weisstein, "Adventures of a Woman in Science", *Fed. Proc.* 35 (1976): 2226 - 2231.

4 Anne Sayre, *Rosalind Franklin and DNA: A Vivid View of What It Is Like to be a Gifted Woman in an Especially Male Profession* (New York: W.W. Norton and Co., 1975).

5 Nancy Hopkins, "The High Price of Success in Science", *Radcliffe Quarterly* 62 (June 1976): 16 - 18.

6 Liliane Stehelin, "Science, Women and Ideology", in *Ideology of / in the Natural Sciences*, H. Rose and S. Rose, eds. (Cambridge, MA: Schenkman Publishing Co., 1979).

7 I speak from my own experience and that of my graduate students.

8 Betty Vetter, "Degree Completion by Women and Minorities in Science Increases", *Science* 214 (1982): 1313 - 1321; Betty M. Vetter and Elinor L. Babco, "New Data Show Slow Changes in Science Labour Force", *Science* 216 (1982): 1094 - 1095.

9 M. Whitehead et al., "Synthetic Absorption from Premarin Vaginal Cream", in I.D. Cooke, ed., *The Role of Estrogen / Progesterone in the Management of the Menopause* (Baltimore, MD: University Park Press, 1978).

10 Centre for Disease Control, *Abortion Surveillance*, 1978. (Issued November 1980. U.S. Department of Health and Human Services.)

11 F.S. Preston et al., "Effects of Flying and of Time Changes on Menstrual Cycle Length and on Performance in Airline Stewardesses", *Aerospace Medicine* 44 (1973): 438 - 443.

12 A. Kurkis et al., "Effect of Saturated and Unsaturated Fat Diets on Lipid Profiles of Plasma Lipoproteins", *Atherosclerosis* 41 (1982): 221 - 241.

13 Anke Ehrhardt, Nancy Greenberg, and John Money, "Female Gender Identity and Absence of Fetal Gonadal Hormones: Turner's Syndrome", *Johns Hopkins Medical Journal* 126 (1970): 237 - 248.

14 Herman A. Witkin et al., "Criminality in XYY and XXY Men", *Science* 193 (1976): 547-555.

15 W. Clarke Cooper, "Cancer Mortality Patterns in the Lead Industry", *Annals N.Y. Acad. Sci.* 271 (1976): 2250 - 259.

16 Jeanne M. Stellman, *Women's Work, Women's Health: Myths and Realities* (New York: Pantheon Books, 1977), pp. 32 - 33.

17 Gena Corea, *The Hidden Malpractice* (New York: HBJ Books, 1977), p. 16.

18 William D. Sharpe, "Chronic Radium Intoxication: Clinical and Autopsy Findings in Long-term New Jersey Survivors", *Environmental Research* 8 (1974): 243 - 383, 310.

19 Donna Mergler, Nicole Vezina, and Annette Beauvais, "Warts amongst Workers in Poultry Slaughter-houses", *Scand. J. of Work, Envi. and Health* 8, suppl. 1 (1982): 180 - 184.

20 U.S. Department of Health, Education and Welfare, *Employment During Pregnancy: Legitimate Live Births 1963* (Washington, D.C.: U.S. Government Printing Office, 1963).

21 Karen Messing, "Est-ce que la travailleuse enceinte est protegée au Québec?" *Union Médicale* (February, 1982).
22 Gertrud S. Berkowitz, "An Epidemiologic Study of Preterm Delivery", *Am. J. Epidemiol.* 113 (1981): 81 - 92.
23 Anke A. Ehrhardt, Ralph Epstein, and John Money, "Fetal Androgens and Female Gender Identity in the Early-treated Androgenital Syndrome", *Johns Hopkins Med. Journal* 122 (1968): 160 - 168; see also study in note 13.
24 David Barash, "Sociobiology of Rape in Mallards (Anas platyrynchos): Responses of the Mated Male", *Science* 197 (1977): 788 - 789.
25 Gina B. Kolata, "Love Canal: False Alarm Caused by Botched Study", *Science* 208 (1980): 1239 - 1240.
26 Robert Rosenthal, *Experimenter Effects in Behavioural Research* (New York: Appleton-Century-Crofts, 1966).
27 Steven J. Gould, "Morton's Ranking of Races by Cranial Capacity", *Science* 200 (1978): 503 - 509.
28 J.L. Kennedy and H.P. Uhoff, "Experiments on the Nature of Extransensory Perception, III. Recording Error Criticizer of Extra-chance Scores", *J. Parapsychol.* 3 (1939): 226 - 245.
29 D.D. Dorfman, "The Cyril Burt Question: New Findings", *Science* 201 (1978): 1177 - 1180.
30 Arbitration hearing on the case of Mme. Adrienne Robichaud, before Judge Jean-Jacques Turcotte, Québec, 1980 - 82.
31 Charles E. Land, "Estimating Cancer Risks from Low Doses of Ionizing Radiation", *Science* 209 (1980): 1197 - 1203.
32 John W. Gofman, *Radiation and Human Health* (San Francisco: Sierra Club Books, 1981).
33 Joanna J. Ryan, "I.Q. — The Illusion of Objectivity", in Ken Richardson and David Spears, eds., *Race and Intelligence* (Baltimore, MD: Penguin Books, 1972): 36 - 55.
34 Jon Beckwith and John Durkin, "Girls, Boys and Math", *Science for the People* 13, No. 5 (Sept. / Oct. 1981): 6 - 9; 32 - 35.
35 Robert Van den Bosch, *The Pesticide Conspiracy* (New York: Doubleday, 1978).
36 C. Owen Lovejoy, "The Origin of Man", *Science* 211 (1981): 341 - 350.
37 Lynn H. Fox et al., eds., *Women and the Mathematical Mystique* (Baltimore, MD: Johns Hopkins University Press, 1980).
38 Camilla P. Benbow and Julian C. Stanley, "Sex Differences in Math Ability: Fact or Artifact", *Science* 210 (1980): 1262 - 1264.
39 D.A. Williams and P. King, "Sex Differences in Achievement in and Attitudes toward Mathematics Result from Superior Mathematical Ability", *Newsweek* (December 15, 1980): 73.
40 Elizabeth Fennema, "Sex-Related Differences in Mathematical Achievement:

Where and Why?'' in L.H. Fox et al., eds., *Women and the Mathematical Mystique* (Baltimore, MD: John Hopkins University Press, 1980).

41 For example, Pierre Sormany, ''Le Cerveau a-t-il un sexe?'' *L'Actualité* (November 1980): 35 ff.

42 David Barash, ''Sexual Selection in Birdland'', *Psychology Today* (March 1978):81 - 86.

43 Scot Morris, ''Do Men *Need* to Cheat on Their Women? A New Science Says YES: Darwin and the Double Standard'', *Playboy* (May 1978): 109 ff.

44 Francie F. Pelletier, ''La belle au bois dormant se meurt: le valium et le cancer du sein'', *La Vie en Rose* (Juin, Juillet, Août 1981): 33 - 37.

FURTHER READING

Bleier, R., *Science and Gender.* Toronto: Pergamon Press, 1984.

Gould, S.J., *The Mismeasure of Man.* New York: W.W. Norton, 1981.

Lewontin, R., Rose, S. and Kamin, L., *Not in Our Genes.* New York: Pantheon Books, 1984.

Keller, E.F., *Reflections on Gender and Science.* New Haven, CT: Yale University Press, 1985.

Hubbard, R., Henifin, M.S. and Fried, B., *Biological Woman: The Convenient Myth.* Cambridge, MA: Schenkman Publishing Co., 1982.

II. LIFE'S CONDITIONS, STAGES, AND CHOICES

INTRODUCTION

Most discussions concerning gender-linked human characteristics distill themselves into the issue of "nature versus nurture". While it is fairly simple to demonstrate, for example, that parturition is linked to the female gender, it is becoming increasingly evident that many of the tasks and actions previously understood as "mothering" are not necessarily linked either to biological mothers or to women. For this reason, when we speak about gender, we are trying to understand what conditions seem to be biologically determined, what conditions may be socially determined, and what conditions may be determined by free choice. It is also clear that the way in which various stages of life are experienced are linked to gender in many ways.

Philosophical biasses and fashions change from period to period in our history and from culture to culture. Thus the prevailing articulation of the human freedom to act wavers over time and space from determinism to free will. For feminist theoreticians, both positions have an attraction. Determinism is helpful in explaining why self-consciousness has not always been enough to empower women. It is clear that over the centuries, women often realised and articulated their oppression. However, conditions such as their own biology and social and economic positions made it virtually impossible for them to break out of oppressive social constraints. On the other hand, underlying much feminist theory and research is the notion that knowledge can liberate women ... that free will can be exercised not only to change one's place within the social structure, but to change the social order itself.

Beginning with Cerise Morris' provocative essay, "Against Determinism: the Case for Women's Liberation," preoccupation with the issues of free will and determinism is a sub-text to this section of the book. It touches subjects like the early socialisation of girls and boys through schools and their own informal social structures. This preoccupation is essential in determining the extent to which we internalise current social attitudes to the very bodies we inhabit and to our own sexuality. We will see that the new fertility technologies and changing sexual mores have thrown many social and ethical questions up for our reconsideration. As respect for the power of societal control on individual lives changes, so do many of our expectations regarding relationships, such as friendship, romantic love, marriage, and even the possible benefits of solitude. We might, on the other hand, find it difficult to believe that we have sufficient free will in determining our destinies when we read Louise Dulude's analysis of aging, "Getting Old: Men in Couples and Women Alone".

One condition over which most humans have little choice is that eventually we must all work to sustain ourselves ... whether or not that work is rewarded by wages. We are living in times of vast technological change as well as increasing unemployment, which is often due to the very changes that should make people's lives less arduous. These changes have an enormous impact on both women and men, on the division of labour in our society, and on their possibile sharing of power in the public domain. Some people will argue that men and women cannot, on the whole, do the same jobs; others argue that they can and should. Most of the contributors to the section on work in this book would argue that the energy devoted to work-related conflict between women and men should really be turned to changing the oppressive relationship between management and labour, that is, that the primary conflict is not based on gender, but on class. However, they would also agree that women are discriminated against in the work force. Hilary Lips, a psychologist, and Stan Gray, an advocate for workers' rights, both address the issue of women and power in the workplace from very different, but not necessarily opposing, perspectives.

There are many areas of the human experience begging for a gender-related analysis that are not covered in this section. I think here especially of in-depth discussion regarding the family in its many manifestations in our society. There is much more to be said on education, sports, sexuality, inter-gender relationships, homosexuality and lesbianism. I would have welcomed an article on what "fathering" means to men. However, these are the articles among those examined that are most complementary to one another and best suited to this section of the book. I hope you will find them as informative and provocative as I do.

A. INTRODUCTORY ESSAY

CERISE MORRIS, MSW, Ph.D.

Against Determinism: The Case for Women's Liberation

Sometimes the most obvious things are those which do not get said, and so we carry on as if they *cannot* be said. Once the utterance is made we then have to ask ourselves: why was the silence exacted from us? It is in this spirit that I wish to confront the unspoken problem of determinism in feminist theory.

Determinism assumes that people's thoughts, feelings, attitudes and behaviour are caused by specific conditions or structures "out there". People are not understood to be actively creating, choosing or negotiating their situations — predictable things happen *to* them. And feminist theory, so radical and path-breaking in its challenge to our male-centred social structure, has been decidedly traditional in adopting the deterministic assumptions and methodology of conventional social science. "Normal" social science has, of course, been heavily criticised by feminist writers for its inherent androcentric biasses which, prior to feminist scrutiny, were passed off as nothing less than "objective reality". Yet the feminist critique has stopped short of questioning the positivistic assumptions on which social science rests.

Positivism assumes that there is a knowable social reality "out there" beyond the subjective experience and interpretation of individuals, and that the researcher, armed with the right scientific instruments, can uncover the "real truth" about social phenomena. But what may be useful for knowing physical reality is quite unsuitable, I believe, for thinking about social reality. "Grand theories" purporting to explain human social behaviour (e.g., Marxism, structural-functionalism) postulate the existence of fixed (deterministic) laws that explain social phenomena; yet these models are all abstracted from the lived experience of individuals whose behaviour *determines and constructs* a social reality.

By their very nature, grand theories rest on abstracted generalisations, and they cannot do more than approximate reality as we live and experience it. Nowhere are those tendencies more evident than in Marxist-feminist theory, as Liz Stanley and Sue Wise have argued so cogently in their paradigm-challenging work, *Breaking Out* (1983). Marxism can be seen as a "grand theory" rooted in patriarchy and primarily concerned with abstract debates disconnected from everyday experience. Marxist-feminism tries to "fit women in" to a male-centred world view in which the personal gets lost in a realm of "ideas" and "structures". Other dominant theoretical models do the same, albeit in somewhat different terms.

But why do I wish to argue that the determinism of social science theories constitutes a particular problem for feminist thinking? I contend that positivistic and deterministic accounts of our situation as women deny the primacy of our personal experience, ignore our active participation in shaping our reality and question our capacity to make meaningful individual choices about our lives.

I have felt discomfited by — and increasingly distanced from — the kinds of feminist ideas that tell me "how it is" and that I've "got it wrong" if I articulate a lack of fit between my own life experience and the given categories of "female socialisation" and "woman-as-victim". Though dissimilar on the surface, the different ideologies in feminist theory (e.g., socialist-feminism, Marxist-feminism, even so-called liberal feminism) share common and quite conventional deterministic assumptions about our social and psychological reality. What Stanley and Wise (1983) call "feminist orthodoxy" refers to the body of feminist thinking that uses deterministic explanations to show how women are oppressed by social structures and social systems (whether conceptualised on a grand scale, like "patriarchy", "capitalism", or some amalgam of the two; or on a smaller scale, like "the family", "the educational system", "the media", etc.)

I find it both significant and disturbing that these troublesome contradictions have been virtually ignored by feminists. On the one hand, we firmly rejected deterministic theories that use biological, psychological or social arguments to explain the "natural" dominance of the male in the social order. On the other hand, it seems that we readily accept the notion of "feminist determinism", a notion that portrays women as (more or less) passive victims of social conditioning and family-based oppression, designed to serve the requirements of the capitalistic and / or patriarchial system.

I see two central problems arising from our belief in "feminist determinism" — and they combine to produce an effect that is, ironically, anti-feminist. The first problem lies in the assertion that our personal experiences are invalid whenever these do not fit the deterministic framework. I am thinking, for instance, of having been told that make-up and conventional feminine attire is the badge of my submission to male expectations and the result of being brainwashed to believe that we have to decorate, disguise and otherwise alter our appearance in order to be considered acceptable. Now, I believe that "appearance" is an important and interesting topic for feminists. I also believe that *sometimes* the theme of "oppression-through-image" needs to be named for what it is. But I nonetheless do not experience my act of, say, using make-up as a direct expression of my oppression. To the contrary, I am conscious that I have choices about how I present myself. Naturally, each choice carries its consequence, and if I am unwilling to accept a given consequence then I avoid the choice that carries it. To be sure, I might want the range of my available choices to be narrower, less demanding. I might wish, for instance, that make-up cease to exist altogether in order to free me from having to make choices about its use. But the existence of make-up in no way alters my option to use it (or not use it) with respect to my own sense of comfort. (I am also aware that the meaning I give to using make-up may be quite different from that given by another woman. For that matter, the meaning I give it now as a mature woman is quite different from the meaning I gave it at age fifteen, as an insecure and unformed girl.)

I think also of having been told that I was socialised to place other people's needs (especially those of men and children) above my own. This theme certainly has some resonance in relation to established patterns of interaction among men, women and children in our society. However, it fails to explain the "deviations" from this supposedly embedded pattern and, as I shall show, it does not adequately explain *why* some women persist systematically in behaviour that seems self-denying and servile.

To address this question we must move to a consideration of the socialisation model that has been at the centre of feminist theorising about women's oppression. In its crudest, simplest formulation, the socialisation account of "how we got this way" begins with the observation that "girl babies are wrapped in pink blankets, boy babies in blue", and goes on to show how we internalise our gender role through imitation, identification, exhortation, positive and negative reinforcements and so on, until we are made into finished feminine products. The feminine personality thus produced is assumed to be in some sense "unreal" — we are not what we would or should have been in the absence of sexual stereotyping.

More sophisticated feminist formulations of the socialisation paradigm (see, for example, Barrett, 1980) rightly avoid the excesses of this reductionist, mono-causal approach. These formulations generally recognise the complex network of social variables in the real world and they consider the *personal* realm in which people negotiate meaning in their transactions with the environment. However, they are still unable to escape the flaws that derive from a fundamental acceptance of deterministic assumptions about "society" and "the family".

When I taught undergraduate sociology I became increasingly uncomfortable with the deterministic ideas I presented to students in my own lectures and in assigned feminist textbooks. The first time round, it all made near-perfect sense to talk about "the self-fulfilling prophesy of sex-role socialisation" (see Chafetz, 1974), but less so with each repetition. I recall marking an essay by one of the better students, in which everything deemed wrong or problematic about the position of women in society was attributed to "what society has done to us". I was led to comment in the margins, "*Who* and *what* is society, finally?" I wrote this in recognition of the problem, not because I felt I knew the answer.

Similarly, we can ask, who and what is "the family"? Stanley and Wise (1983:90) describe the model used by many feminists to explain the process of socialisation:

> ... the processes of socialization are seen as those by which "social structures" are internalized by children. Parents are seen as a kind of funnel through which stereotyped behaviours of all kinds are presented to children who then obligingly internalize them.

And here I was, teaching a model that bore only a tenuous relationship to how I made sense of things in my personal life. I believe that people — including myself — express aspects of "gender socialisation" in complex, variable, and unpredictable ways. People's behaviour does not fit neatly into predictable patterns that have been programmed since infancy. I used to be mistaken when I considered the behaviour of those around me as a "predictable product" of a patriarchal socialisation process.

For instance, a long-time woman friend always seemed to distance herself from the feminist ideology, often affirming her dislike of "strident feminists" and her enjoyment of many gender-based social conventions. I used to consider her "unenlightened", less interesting and less substantial than women with feminist identification. Yet one day I became aware that this woman had acted to challenge established policy and practices in her place of work in order to move from a clerical to an administrative rung on the ladder. The fact that she was a woman was central to her analysis of the resistance she was fighting. Did she have a "feminist conversion"? No; and the very question is patronising in its assumptions. The feminist / non-feminist dichotomy might be useful if feminism were a political party with members and non-members; but it has little to teach us about how women experience their lives.

My mother — burdened as she was by traditional notions about "the weaker sex" and the immutability of the differences between the sexes — is also the person who introduced me to Simone de Beauvoir's book *The Second Sex*. Although she conveyed to me her own sense of powerlessness, she also conveyed a great lack of interest in serving men, a certain rebelliousness against convention, and she certainly never inculcated in me the slightest inclination toward housework as a calling. I could go on. The point to be made is that people are not living sex-role stereotypes, and parents do not give one-dimensional messages about being male or female. Moreover, people continually evaluate and negotiate their reality, which means that interpretations change, and new decisions are not bound to reflect old ones.

The subjective processes by which people construct their realities are far too complex and dynamic to be captured even in the most sophisticated version of the current socialisation model. I join Stanley and Wise (1980) in criticising the assumptions of this model as at once "overly socialised" (since it depicts the female child as passive, malleable, and living at the mercy of social conditioning) and "psychologistic" (because it suggests that there exists within the child certain innate traits). The model also tends to reify abstract concepts such as "the family" and "the social system". Finally, Stanley and Wise identify a problem that had puzzled me for a long time: the socialisation model fails to explain the very activities of feminists themselves! somehow, in a way never explained by feminist writings, feminists would have to be "special" or "outside the determined order of things" in order to have escaped the fate held to be unavoidable for women in general.

I have frequently observed the questionable tendency — in myself as well as other feminists — to characterise women as victims of their conditioning or their "false consciousness", while exempting oneself without a word of explanation. Or, even while speaking about herself as constrained by sexist conditioning, the feminist would not address the contradiction inherent in recognising her condition yet not acting to change it.

If certain women can refuse to live and behave in ways deemed inimical to personal dignity and autonomy, then why can't others? It is not of much use to rush in here with more deterministic notions about the influence of such other variables as class, culture and the like — they merely restate, but do not answer, the question. I maintain that we do not know why particular people make particular choices, though we can often make fairly reliable predictions on the basis of sociological variables like race, class and sex. But even here, to state descriptively that people belonging to a given social category are statistically more likely than others to be located in a certain situation is not to explain *why* and *how* that is so. The assumption of social-structural determinism is only an assumption, and an example of *a posteriori* reasoning — "if something is so then it had to be so, and was caused to be so".

Determinism would have us believe that people's "station in life", or their situation at a given moment, is as complex as the cumulative effect of all the stimuli (of which we are for the most part unaware) that have ever influenced the individual from within and without. But at the centre of all these stimuli there is an individual who mediates and orchestrates her own reality. People have far-reaching capacities to determine their own lives, even though given circumstances may be working against them. (If this were not true, I could not have written this article, for gender and class barriers would have presumably prevented me from ever conceiving it.) If we selectively deny aspects of our own experience so that we can fit neatly into a theoretical paradigm, then we do ourselves damage of the sort that male-based values have done to us. Further, if we refuse to question our basic assumptions, we will remain wedded to them forever. This, I believe, would be a tragic mistake. Stanley and Wise (1983) for example, believe that feminism does *not* really understand *how* and *why* women are oppressed; and until we possess this knowledge we cannot claim that we know how to liberate ourselves.

The other major problem with "feminist determinism" concerns the attribution of responsibility. When we use the model of social determinism we are inevitably led to attribute responsibility for our personal situations to external sources, be they "my husband", "my mother", "men", "patriarchy" or "the capitalist system". As Stanley and Wise assert:

> ... structural explanations ... enable people to hide in collectivisms, in the sense that they can avoid taking responsibility for their own lives and actions. (1983:107)

I have been working as a psychotherapist for nearly a decade, and I've also been a psychotherapy client myself for several years. This continued experience has taught me that the hardest thing for most people to do is precisely this — to take responsibility for their everyday choices and for the course of their lives. Yet it is this very willingness — and capacity — that defines autonomous adulthood. The individual who operates at a childlike level will excuse herself from unfamiliar and frightening responsibility. And I do assume that women, like men, have the freedom to make choices that will shape their lives. Obviously, if we are the owners of this freedom, we also bear responsibility for having made our choices and having constructed the realities of our daily lives.

Let me be clear: I am not "blaming the victim" here. I do believe that women have been oppressed — this fact remains incontrovertible. But I do *not* believe that we live in a continuous state of victimisation. What is the distinction? Victims — at least to the extent that they *are* victims — are helpless; we are not. Like Stanley and Wise (1983:82), I view oppression as something people do to other people in myriad different ways: "Institutions, structures do not oppress. *People* oppress people — they make decisions to do so, and the oppressed sometimes comply in acts of oppression." As women we actively define, interpret and participate in this process. Sexism, then, is not a disembodied system "out there" beyond our reach; rather, at its root it is "a set of practices, contextually located and daily enacted, which fix us within them" (Stanley and Wise, 1983:183).

What about these practices? In the past few years some feminist writers have begun to discuss what they call women's "collusion with patriarchy" (e.g., Barrett, 1980; Hamilton, 1980; Mitchell, 1974). This "collusion" is theoretically linked to women's psychic formation under patriarchy, and may be viewed as stemming from "unconscious" forces (another form of determinism!). Again, the concept of collusion is negative, and certainly implies that women who collude do so because they have unconscious needs, or in the language of feminism, because they are victims of "false consciousness". Here too I'd prefer to talk about women's *intentional participation* in all those practices that feminists define as "sexist."

Let's take housework as an example. A vast body of literature — most recently the Marxist-feminist treatises on domestic labour — portrays women in Western industrial societies as "trapped housewives" or as workers forced to work a "double day" (see, for example, Luxton, 1980; Meissner, 1975). There must be some truth to these portrayals; women evidently do perform the great majority of domestic labour from which they, but also men and children, benefit directly. Everyone (including men) agrees that, in general, men do much less than what could be called their "fair share". The external and statistical portrait thus obtained seems to support the deterministic view. But what are the internal processes by which this "reality" gets created in each household? If we were to question those women who perform more than their share of domestic labour we would probably hear many different answers. For example: their mothers did it that way (and they don't believe they should do it differently); their husbands expect it (and they don't believe that they can legitimately challenge these expectations); their husbands demand it (and they don't elect to view such a demand as unreasonable and unacceptable); they believe that it is appropriate for them to be doing it this way (and they don't choose to examine that belief critically); they actively enjoy doing it this way (and may or may not acknowledge the sense of power and importance that comes with having control of this work). These kinds of responses show how a woman might perceive or justify her work in the home. Whether it is in any individual woman's best interest to assume more than her share of domestic labour is a different question. But what seems evident to me is that as long as women are willing — *for whatever reason* — to do the work, the pattern of male uninvolvement can be expected to continue.

Of course the standard deterministic rebuttal to this is that the domestic role of women is a structural problem, so individual women cannot change it. A recent personal experience is instructive. At a feminist workshop, a presenter was arguing that only a "structural revolution" could bring to an end the injustice of working women's "double day". From the floor, I offered the view that individual women could act to change their double day by refusing to put up with it — I, for one, had never accepted to live with a man who would not do his share of domestic work. The presenter then suggested that perhaps for a few "professional women" like myself there might be a personal solution, but for "working women in general" personal solutions were not possible — only global, structural ones. In this response I saw an attempt to dismiss the significance of my personal choice (which includes my freedom to reject a man's behaviour if I find it objectionable).

This person, like so many others, *assumes* that working women generally experience their domestic labour as "oppressive". My contention is that only when individual women really do come to see their situation as oppressive, and are prepared to act on it, will a particular "sexist" practice be altered. But, some will ask, what about the real fact of "male power" — women can't be expected just to change the terms of their established relationships without reprisals. Again, "male power" is a disembodied abstraction: each one of us lives with a particular man whom we know in his complexity, weaknesses and strengths. He does not hold the power of life and death over us, even though we might have a great stake in maintaining the relationship with him. But not at all costs, surely. When the cost is estimated to be disproportionate to the benefits, the reasonable response is to reshape the relationship or terminate it. To say that I do not wish to confront my partner about housework because I risk termination of my relationship with him is thereby to say that the issues of "fairness" in doing domestic chores takes second place to my desire to maintain my relationship. This choice might be based either on one's expressed values or on personal insecurity, but *it would be the woman's choice nonetheless*, for it is not predetermined that women perform domestic services for men.

Why is it so difficult for us to confront and change everyday situations that compel us to behave in false or demeaning ways? I have already pointed to the broad, existential avoidance of personal responsibility, which is a human tendency. Many people make the interpretation that it is "safer" to take direction from external authorities and to blame the environment when things go wrong — this approach is certainly familiar and deeply instilled from the experience of childhood. And the residue of unresolved childhood fear in our individual personalities leads us to shun conflict or confrontation (or sometimes actually to seek these out inappropriately, and thereby arrange our own failure).

Women in particular have learned to behave deferentially toward men in many situations, and to act as if we were putting the other person's wishes ahead of our own. I remember (with some regret) many situations and times in my own life when I tolerated and participated in "sexist" practices that made me quite uncomfortable: smiling at remarks that I actually found embarrassing or offensive; allowing a male companion to direct our conversation, even encouraging him to do so while suppressing my own inclinations; dealing with unwanted sexual aggression by using feminine "strategies" like coyness and politeness. (There are many more examples.) Sometimes my only clear motive in such situations was to avoid conflict or prevent someone else's anticipated displeasure (my own somehow not being of any importance). At other times my intent was to maintain or achieve some benefit, practical or symbolic, that I believed I was deriving from the situation.

As I subsequently worked toward becoming a person who would not choose or accept to participate in demeaning practices, the incidence of such situations in my daily life declined. It is not "male power" that has changed — it is my own sense of personal comfort and integrity that has changed. I used to blame men constantly for the discomfort I suffered when interacting with them, and for this reason I often felt hostility and rage toward them. I now can react calmly (even tolerantly) to many "sexist" practices, and reserve my anger for truly stupid and/or menacing behaviour.

One last example of supposed female victimisation concerns the work women do in what has been called the "sexual industry": soft- and hard-core pornography, striptease dancing, and prostitution. Recently, much feminist energy has been directed toward undermining this industry in both ideological and practical terms, because of its embodiment of sexist, male-supremacist values. I am basically in agreement with this position to the extent that the sex industry portrays women — and actually treats them — in degrading ways. However, I strongly disagree with the assumption that all women who work in these fields do so unwillingly or as virtual "sexual slaves". It is common on the one hand to hear the most extensive vituperation heaped upon the men who consume, enjoy or otherwise profit from the sexual industry, and on the other hand to hear either elaborate excuse-making or total silence about the women without whom "the show could not go on". In my experience, these women frequently do profit from their work, and are likely to make the calculation that, all said and done, such work is "easier", "more lucrative", "more interesting", or at least "less boring" than other conventional options open to them.

Without a doubt, it is deplorable that the most conventional and accessible job options open to women tend to be low-paid and menial, and that the sex trade is likely to be the most lucrative field for women who do not have specialised skills or training. Nonetheless, a *choice* is still there to be made. (Obviously I exclude very young or vulnerable females who do not have the personal resources to resist coercion.) Also, the circumstances of these jobs can vary enormously from utterly disagreeable to quite appealing conditions that a woman might choose for a time, in the absence of a better perceived option.

Nor is the sexual pleasing of men *inherently* degrading to women, or inimical to our own pleasure. Some of us do enjoy the sense of power that derives from possessing attributes or abilities that are in great demand. Along the "sexual continuum", we need not assume that actresses or models renowned for their beauty are motivated in a very different way from the model in a *Playboy* centrefold, the stripper, or even the call girl. As Janet Radcliffe Richards observes in *The Skeptical Feminist* (1980:243):

> Women do enter beauty competitions which are supposed to be run because men enjoy seeing the parade of women. They do earn livings by pleasing men as strippers or prostitutes. If, therefore, there is something bad about the men who want these things and the women who go along with them, why is there not something equally bad about people who are interested in musicians only for their musical ability, and musicians who are happy to go along with that interest, and earn their livings by means of it?

Richards argues that the sexual services offered by these women are not *inherently* degrading. Rather, the women are degraded by their exploitative working environment and by the hypocrisy of "public morality". Feminist energy then can rightly be directed toward the issue of work choices for women: acknowledging the validity of the ones that women do presently make and fighting to expand the array of choices available to women. Again, we should not deny that women make deliberate choices about their lives — though we might disagree with the nature of these choices.

I now turn to a brief discussion of men's behaviour toward women. Here I wish to make two central points. Firstly, if we are to reject the deterministic view of women's behaviour then we must do the same for men. We cannot speak of a "male nature" or "male role", whether in biological or social terms. Men collectively enjoy the prerogatives of their dominant social status, to be sure, but each man operates in concrete everyday situations: with his mother, wife, daughter, lover, secretary and others. And within its own framework each situation is open to reinterpretation and change. In this regard, Stanley and Wise (1983) write,

> it would be sensible to...conclude that the "masculine role" (like the "feminine role") exists as a *stereotype* to which the self may feel lesser or greater similarity and adherence, depending upon a multitude of circumstances. (1983:103)

This conclusion accords with my own experience. When I was younger and more fearful, I made many assumptions about the motives and behaviour patterns of the men who related to me. Not surprisingly, my perception of men would usually fit the standard gender stereotypes: sexual aggressiveness, lack of respect for women, obsessive motivation toward sexual gratification, lack of emotional and interpersonal sensitivity, and the like. (Of course, I frequently had real evidence for these perceptions.) But I gradually came to realise that men, like women, make *individual* choices which may or may not conform to traditional sexual stereotypes. The point to be made is that when you examine men as individual human beings you find complex people rather than walking "masculine roles". Furthermore, behaviour that appears as distinctly sexist can in fact be motivated by something quite different. Women frequently experience and label "sexist" what is actually motivated by something other than "the need to affirm male power over women". Just as behaviours can share a common motive, so can the same behaviour have various meanings. For example, men often volunteer to perform large or small physical tasks for women — simply because they wish to be helpful.

(An important note: we have every right to avoid or reject objectionable behaviour regardless of the perpetrator's motives. As in every other area of my life, I make personal choices that allow me to feel comfortable in my environment. So whatever the personal motives of my husband might be, I would object if he brought a magazine like *Playboy* into the home — simply because I personally find these magazines disagreeable.)

This brings me to my second point: if a man's behaviour is objectionable, he can often be persuaded to change it. And the most effective way to convey a request for change is to be direct and specific — just what many women find hardest to do in situations that are emotionally charged. But in order to convey our request we must begin by telling men what we expect, or by changing our own behaviour toward them. Consider, for example, our interaction with men in the sexual realm. A woman may complain that the man in her life is insensitive to her sexual needs, overly controlling, or by his own inhibitions doesn't let her feel free in their love making. What should she do to change things? For one thing she can simply tell him, directly, explicitly, and at the time, what she would like from him. Or, she can exercise her privilege to go ahead and do whatever she would like to do with him, without waiting for his permission. Either way, she is provoking desired change in her relationship. It is not that we are or should be responsible for promoting behavioural change in men. Rather, we should take responsibility for arranging to get what we want and eliminating what we don't want, as much as possible. (It is to be expected, though, that some change would gradually take place in an individual's personality as he begins to assimilate new realities in his relationships.)

When I think of men as individual people rather than as agents of "the patriarchy'' or embodiments of ''male power'' I am able to bring them down to proper size, making it easier for me to deal with them and work toward the kind of changes that I really want in my life. ''Change'' does not exist in the abstract, nor is it co-terminous with innovative laws and policies enacted by the state. The kind of revolution we require is not a major event ''out there'', but rather many little revolutions in our daily lives. Change stops, or fails to expand, exactly at the point where people are unwilling or unable to examine their everyday patterns and break with the old way of doing things.

I have observed acquaintances of mine — feminists, to be sure — who get uneasy and defensive when their sex-typed child-rearing practices are questioned. One woman, a devoted campaigner for women's rights, insists on dressing her young daughter in pink and frills, indulging all the girl's ''feminine whims'' in appearance and activities. Granted, the child wants to do these things, but her mother appears unwilling to challenge, question or set limits to her child's enthusiastic mimicry of the feminine stereotype. Another self-proclaimed feminist will not insist that her twelve-year-old son contribute to the housework, even though she grumbles about being expected to be a ''household drudge''. Such blind spots set the limits to growth and change at any given time. Yet these limits are not determined — the ''drudge'' may one day decide to be a drudge no longer! And only then, when individuals start to behave differently, will social structures start to crumble or fade away.

What about the women who do not make the type of choices we think they should, *even when it is perfectly obvious that they can do so if they wish*? We can choose to blame ''men'', ''conditioning'', ''the family'', or even the women's ''false consciousness''. But we do so at our own peril, for we would be perpetrating the same wrongs as those who have oppressed us: to deny the validity of other people's perceptions and to impose on them our own standards of conformity. And no matter how defensible our intentions are in themselves, our demand for conformity would necessarily act as a brake on women's freedom of choice.

In calling for a more interpretive, non-dogmatic expression of feminism, I am affirming that each woman must define her own reality and accept responsibility for her own choices. For me, the *raison d'être* of feminism is just this: to validate women's own experiences of reality, and to open up the maximum possible choices for us. It is because ''orthodox feminism'' could subvert this goal that I speak out against determinism. It is my rallying call for other feminists to debate and challenge our own limiting assumptions, which act to impede women's liberation.

REFERENCES

Acknowledgements — I would like to acknowledge the considerable influence that two recent books have had upon the ideas presented in this article: *Breaking Out: Feminist Consciousness and Feminist Research*, by Liz Stanley and Sue Wise; and *The Skeptical Feminist*, by Janet Radcliffe Richards. This chapter, in fact, grew out of a review, which appeared in *Atlantis* (Fall, 1985), of Stanley and Wise's book.

I wish also to thank my husband, Uri Ravel, for his critical comments and editing assistance which have resulted in a much-improved presentation of my ideas.

Barrett, Michèle, *Women's Oppression Today*. London: Verso Editions, 1980.

Chafetz, Janet Saltzman, *Masculine/Feminine or Human?* Itisca, IL: F.E. Peacock Publishers, Inc., 1974.

Hamilton, Roberta, "The Collusion with Patriarchy: A Psychoanalytic Ac count." Montréal: Unpublished paper, 1980.

Luxton, Meg. *More Than a Labour of Love*. Toronto: The Women's Press, 1980.

Meissner, Martin et al., "No Exit for Wives: Sexual Division of Labour and the Cumulation of Household Demands." *Canadian Review of Sociology and Anthropology* 12: no. 4, part I, 1975, pp. 429–439.

Richards, Janet Radcliffe, *The Skeptical Feminist*. Middlesex, England: Penguin Books, 1980.

Stanley, Liz and Sue Wise, *Breaking Out: Feminist Theory and Feminist Research*. London: Routledge & Kegan Paul, 1983.

FURTHER READING

Barrett, Michèlle, *Women's Oppression Today*. London: Verso Editions, 1980.

Berger, Peter L., and Luckman, Thomas, *The Social Construction of Reality*. Garden City, NY: Anchor Books, 1967.

Richards, Janet Radcliffe, *The Skeptical Feminist*. London: Penguin Books, 1980.

Stanley, Liz and Sue Wise, *Breaking Out: Feminist Consciousness and Feminist Research*. London: Routledge & Kegan Paul, 1983.

Vetterling-Braggin, Mary, Elliston, Frederick and English, Jane, eds., *Feminism and Philosophy*. Totowa, NJ: Littlefield, Adams, 1977.

B. THE EARLY YEARS

BARBARA HOUSTON

Should Public Education Be Gender-free?

INTRODUCTION

Discussion of the question, "should public education be gender-free?" should begin with a sorting out of the different possible meanings of the term "gender-free".[1] In the context of this discussion I assume the following three distinct meanings. In the first sense, the strong sense, a "gender-free" education would be one that makes active attempts to disregard gender by obliterating gender differentiations arising within the educational sphere. Ruling out items on I.Q. tests that give sex-differentiated results in scores is an example of a gender-free educational practice in this strong sense. Such efforts are sometimes described as attempts to de-institutionalise sex differences to create a form of gender blindness.[2] Another example of this approach is that of abolishing such activities as wrestling, in which there are thought to be significant gender differences in achievements due to natural and ineradicable biological differences between the sexes.[3]

In the second case, the weak sense, "gender-free" means that gender is ignored, not attended to. In this meaning a gender-free education is one that refuses to take notice of gender. No longer using gender as an admissions criterion to educational institutions or to specific educational programmes is an example of this weak sense of "gender-free".

In the third sense, I take "gender-free" to mean freedom from gender bias. On this understanding, a gender-free education would be one that eliminates gender bias.

In this last, weakest sense we could all be said to favour gender-free

Originally published in *Educational Theory,* Vol. 35, No. 4, Fall 1985.

education. Even the traditionalist who holds to false accounts of sex differences and inadequate justification for gender roles within education might well argue that gender differentiations within education are not meant to constitute a gender *bias*. So, the interesting interpretation of the question, "should public education be gender-free?" is not "should public education be free of gender bias?" This question is not the issue, since all positions, at least in their rhetoric, already agree that public education should be free of gender bias. The question is rather what is the best way to achieve this freedom from gender bias. Should we undertake to ignore gender, or obliterate gender differentations, or should we in some way pay deliberate attention to gender?

I assume in this chapter the viewpoint of an educator who is already committed to sex equality and to equal educational opportunity but who recognises that a number of practical questions and policy matters are still undetermined with respect to the question of whether we should or should not institute a kind of gender blindness. I shall argue that, in the present cirucmstances, the adoption of either version of the strategy is likely to cause us to miss, or even to reinforce, the more subtle forms of gender bias. Through an examination of three prevalent forms of gender bias and actual examples of the gender-free strategy, I shall show that general recommendation of this strategy would likely ensure that females continue to have unequal educational opportunity. The strategy is problematic in a second way because both versions of it presuppose an ideal of sex equality that prematurely forecloses on important questions central to the issue. In conclusion I shall defend a more promising strategy for achieving freedom from gender bias, a strategy first suggested in the work of Jane Roland Martin and labelled by her "gender-sensitive".[4]

GENDER BIAS

Unequal Access, Unequal Opportunity for Participation and Genderised Valuation

That girls and women have had unequal access to educational institutions is news to no one. Undoubtedly significant progress toward sex equality was made when it was decided that we should ignore gender, that is no longer pay attention to it in deciding who should get an education, who should be admitted to schools, allowed to study certain subjects, and to have no access to particular educational activities. Having come to the realisation that much sex-segregated education has been both different and unequal, ignoring gender has enabled us to move to co-education in a stricter sense. For example, no longer do we have home economics and typing for girls only or physical sciences and industrial arts for boys only.

Physical education is an especially interesting case in point. Sex-segregated classes have fostered different and unequal education for boys and girls in this domain.[5] One reasonable attempt to eliminate the gender bias that has developed in physical education has been to adopt both the weak and strong versions of what I have called the gender-free strategy. This approach has urged that we ignore the gender of those in the physical education class and ignore the gender of those on the teams, allowing all to have equal access to the educational resources. Under such a policy, one would expect girls' and women's opportunities to increase. But often quite the opposite is true. Solomon's observations of game interactions in a fifth grade co-ed class showed that:

> Girls tended to be left out of game interactions by the boys. This was true even when the girls had a higher skill level than boys did. Additionally, both girls and boys regarded boys as better players even when the girls were more highly skilled. Boys preferred to pass the ball to an unskilled boy rather than to a skilled girl. Girls tended to give away scoring opportunities to boys. Unskilled girls were almost completely left out of game action. However, both skilled and unskilled girls received fewer passes than boys did.[6]

Of course it is a good thing to remove access barriers to education, and in this case, ignoring gender has allowed us to do that. However, equal participation in the educational process is also a crucial dimension of equal educational opportunity. In this case, the strategy that removes access barriers has also had the effect of bringing about a *greater loss* of educational opportunities for girls.[7]

Research findings suggest that this basketball game, where males keep passing the ball to each other, is a metaphor for all types of mixed-sex classrooms and activities. From the research we have on student-teacher interactions and on student-student interactions, essentially the same picture emerges, though there are some differences dependent upon the race and class of the students.

Studies on teacher-student interactions indicate that within co-educational classrooms, teachers, regardless of sex, interact more with boys and give boys more attention (both positive and negative), and that this pattern intensifies at the secondary and college levels. Girls get less teacher attention and wait longer for it. When they do get attention, it is more likely that the teacher will respond to them neutrally or negatively (though this depends somewhat on the girls' race and class). The reinforcement girls do get is likely to be for passivity and neatness, not for getting the right answer.[8]

Equally distressing is the indication we have from research findings that student interactions with one another also appear to dampen female participation in mixed-sex classes. At the post-secondary level often the brightest women in the class remain silent, women students are in general likely to be less verbally assertive, they are likely to be called on less often than men students, and those who do participate may find that their comments are disproportionately interrupted by teachers and male classmates and that teachers are less likely to develop their points than those made by men students.[9]

Part of the explanation for these classroom inequities may be that the everyday linguistic patterns of how women and men talk together in mixed-sex groupings is carried over into the classroom. In mixed-sex groupings men talk more than women; men talk for longer periods of time and take more turns at speaking; men exert more control over the conversation; men interrupt women more than women interrupt men; and men's interruptions of women more often introduce trivial or inappropriately personal comments that bring women's discussion to an end or change its focus. It is also indicated that what men say carries more weight. A suggestion made by a man is more likely to be listened to, credited to him, developed in further discussion and adopted by the group than a suggestion made by a woman.[10]

There are also linguistic styles of speech that can affect women's participation opportunities in the classroom. For example, there are certain features that occur more in women's speech than in men's such as hesitations, false starts, a questioning intonation when making a statement, an extensive use of qualifiers which serve to weaken what is said, an extensive use of modals and forms of speech that are excessively polite and deferential. In addition, in mixed-sex interactive patterns the speech of women is more supportive than that of men, inasmuch as it exhibits an effort to elicit and encourage the contributions of the other speakers to the conversation. Male patterns, on the other hand, include highly assertive speech, an impersonal and abstract style and "devil's advocate" exchanges.[11]

The problem, as one researcher suggests, is that in the school setting these "male" ways of talking are often "equated with intelligence and authority".[12] If someone speaks hesitantly or with numerous qualifiers, she is perceived by her teachers and classmates as unfocussed and unsure of what she wants to say. It is also clear than an overly polite style more easily allows interruptions or inattention from both teachers and students.[13] The same points made in a "masculine", assertive way are taken more seriously. But more significant perhaps is the fact that while it is thought to be perfectly proper for boys to "conduct argument, air their views and query information", it is not thought proper for girls to do the same thing.[14] This genderised valuation of classroom talk poses special problems for girls who seek to take on those ways of talking associated with "intelligence and authority".

What are the consequences for girls if the classrooms are male-dominant in this way? Clearly, we think it important that learners be able to talk about their own experiences as a starting point for learning; we regard the classroom as an opportunity for discovering new insights and understandings which need not depend upon received knowledge. Here, we say, "students can find out things for themselves, they can ask questions, make new connections, describe and explain the world in different ways".[15] Indeed, we even claim they can criticise the received texts. But what if one-half of the students are not free to make such explorations, to take up the topics of their choosing, to articulate and validate their own experience? What if this opportunity is blocked for them?

Teacher behaviour can directly or inadvertently reinforce those patterns that make it difficult for half the class population to talk, particularly to the teacher, but also to have their own experience be perceived as interesting and appropriate to discuss. If teachers fail to notice the gender of who is talking, who is interrupting whom, whose points are acknowledged and taken up, who is determining the topic of discussion, then she or he will by default perpetuate patterns that discourage women's participation in the educational process.

The *teacher* may well try to ignore gender, but the point is that the *students* are not ignoring it in their sense of how the interactions should go and who is entitled to speak in the educational arena. Gender may be excluded as an *official* criterion, but it continues to function as an *unofficial* factor.

In a recent study designed to measure the effects of efforts to correct sexism in education a tenth-grade girl said, "If I were a boy I would be more outspoken and confident, but I really don't know why." It has been suggested that "the why is that boys usually know that they are valued whereas girls are not always sure".[17] Although they may not articulate it, students of both sexes have a clear perception of the devaluation of girls in the culture.[18] Obviously, in these circumstances if we simply ignore gender differentiations in the mode in which students can participate in the educational process, we will reinforce the message that girls don't count, at least they don't count as much.

This suggestion of some of the influences of gender in educational interactions has been necessarily brief. The picture is nowhere as simple as time forces us to sketch. Nevertheless, although gender bias will vary in texture and complexity depending upon many other factors, notably race and class, our picture points to the fundamental issue with which we should be concerned, namely, the manner in which the school can confirm girls in subordinate positions. This, I would stress, should be a matter of concern regardless of girls' school achievements.

EVALUATION OF THE GENDER-FREE APPROACH

When gender differentiations exist in the opportunity to participate in the educational process, what are we to do to eliminate bias? Within the gender-free strategy there are two approaches, one more radical than the other. We have seen that the first approach, that of deciding to ignore gender by no longer letting it count where it had before, is certainly effective in removing gender as an access barrier. However, we cannot count on this passive ignoring of gender as an effective means to the elimination of other types of gender bias. In fact, it appears that it may simply have the effect of masking other types of bias, for example in opportunities for participation.

There are two general difficulties with the approach suggested by the weak sense of "gender-free". First, it is doubtful that teachers *can* ignore gender in this sense because they often do not recognize when gender is exerting an influence. It is startling just how unaware teachers are of the phenomenon we have described. Their perceptions of how they interact with students are often grossly inaccurate. Saying that they treat girls and boys equally in the classroom, they are shocked to discover through objective observation measures that they spend over two-thirds of their time with boys who constitute less than half the class; or that they reward boys for getting the right answers and girls for neatness; or that they criticise boys for poor work and criticise girls for being assertive; or that they explain a boy's achievements in terms of his abilities and a girl's in terms of the degree of difficulty of the text or in terms of luck.[19] Students, however, are often clear in their perceptions of the gender differences in student-teacher interactions.[20]

But the second and equally important difficulty is that even if the teacher were successful in ignoring gender, it is obvious that students do take cognizance of it. The gender-connected conventions and expectations that students themselves bring to their classroom interactions will continue unaltered, if not actually strengthened, if teachers do not intervene to change the patterns.

Perhaps mindful of these difficulties, the other version of the gender-free strategy would have us press for interventions to eliminate any gender differences in achievements in the hopes of creating in us a kind of gender blindness. As with the first approach, this more active pursuit of gender blindness can be useful. But it is also problematic. There is the very real danger that in restructuring activities we are likely to be unduly influenced by a male valuation scheme. For example, it would have us intervene to eliminate or restructure sports at which either of the sexes had a natural advantage because of physical differences, such as football in which males are favoured, or certain forms of gymnastics work, such as the balance beam, in which girls are favoured. The idea behind restructuring sports activities has been to allow girls and boys equal rates of success. However, there are a number of dubious assumptions at work here, for instance, the assumption that girls' performance levels are accurately perceived and that these levels do determine their opportunities.

But the case is not that simple. The problem is not how well girls do in relation to boys; the problem is that *even when girls do as well or better than boys at the same activity*, their performance is undervalued by themselves and by others and their opportunities remain relatively limited.[21] A more radical critique would note that, even if we could straighten out the misperceptions about performance and opportunities, we should still question the further value assumption that only winning matters, rather than the enjoyment of playing or the development of a sporting attitude.[22]

In the case of gender-differentiated speech patterns, a male valuation scheme might well recommend a single classroom speech pattern, an assertive one, and offer girls and women special training in this form of "educated speech". But giving girls lessons in how to be assertive in the classroom can be problematic when it merely puts girls in a double bind in which they must adopt what are perceived as "masculine" speech patterns if they are to succeed. As we have noted earlier, the patterns of speech in boys and men that are regarded as forceful are often regarded as negative and hostile when used by girls and women.[23] More to the point, women's conventional patterns of speech have been demonstrated to be helpful in so far as they foster participation by others and encourage a co-operative development of ideas rather than adversarial relations.[24] If we attempt to eliminate gender differentiations, we will have to bear in mind that often our evaluation of the differences has itself been gender-biassed.

There are two other significant problems that need to be addressed in the discussion of the interventionists' gender-free approach. How accurate are teachers' perceptions of fairness? And more significantly, what influence can we expect students' efforts to have on teachers' efforts to bring about change?

Even those teachers who undertake to correct genderised patterns of participation have been, in the words of one of them, "spectacularly unsuccessful". Dale Spender notes with dismay how she and others seriously underestimated the amount of attention they gave to boys rather than to girls *even when they were trying to be fair about it*. When teachers feel they are being fair, or even showing favouritism to girls, the empirical evidence shows otherwise. For example, giving 35 per cent of one's attention to girls can feel as though one is being unfair to boys. Giving just over one-third of one's attention to girls can feel as though one is making a significant effort, even compensating girls.[25]

It is important to notice that students share this perception. For example, when a teacher tries to eliminate gender bias in participation by giving 34 per cent of her attention to girls who constitute one-half the class, the boys protested: "She always asks girls all the questions"; "she doesn't like boys and just listens to girls all the time."[26] In a sexist society boys perceive that two-thirds of the teacher's time is a fair allotment for them, and if it is altered so that they receive less, they feel they are discriminated against. And of course they resist, and they protest, and teachers often give in in order to foster the co-operation that gives the appearance that they are in control of the classroom. Anyone who has tried to correct the bias will recognise the phenomenon.

In other words, even a strong interventionist strategy may at best achieve a gender-free inequality that gives two-thirds time for attending to males. As Spender notes, even when teachers do want to treat the sexes equally, the difficulty is that "our society and education is so structured that 'equality' and 'fairness' means that males get more attention".[27] Our own existing perceptual frameworks are themselves too gender-biassed to provide reliable guides as to whether or not our approaches are actually gender-free. Of course these difficulties will plague all methods we use to get rid of gender discrimination. However, their presence represents a powerful argument against the suggestion that the best route to sex equality in education is simply to ignore gender and, as I shall argue, careful attention to these difficulties can point to a better approach to the problem of the elimination of gender bias.

Thus, as with the weaker version of the gender-free strategy, I find two major difficulties with the stronger version: (1) it fails to aid us in the identification and elimination of genderised valuations; and (2) because of this, in employing the strategy we run a serious risk of encouraging an assimilation of women's identity, interests and values to men's.

It should be clear that I do not object to all suggestions coming from the gender-free approach. As I have indicated, I think it is useful, indeed imperative, at times to ignore gender in the weak sense, and at other times I think it is useful to try to obliterate gender differentiations to ensure the absence of improper gender influence. However, it is also clear that both recommendations may, on occasion, fail to eliminate bias. More importantly, on some occasions we may need to use gender as a criterion in designing a practice useful to eliminating gender bias.

For example, we might restructure the basketball game so as to introduce new rules requiring alternative passes to females and males. In other sports such as volleyball one might introduce a temporary rule change: boys must set up spikes for girls. We may even want to introduce single-sex schooling.

Some studies indicate that in certain contexts it may be necessary to have single-sex classrooms for particular subjects such as math or science for a period of time to ensure that in co-educational classrooms girls will have an equal opportunity to participate and attain equal educational results.[28] The point is that these equalising practices require those involved to be sensitive to gender in a way that appears to be ruled out by the gender-free strategy.

My most general objection then to the gender-free strategy, both the strong and the weak versions, is two-fold: (1) it is likely to create a context that continues to favour the dominant group; and (2) it undermines certain efforts that may be needed to realise an equalisation of educational opportunities.

The central problem with the gender-free mandate is that it misleadingly suggests that in order to free ourselves of gender bias, we have to stop paying attention to gender. It is singularly odd to call this approach "gender-free" or "gender-blind" if it involves paying attention to gender. If we look closely, we find that any significant success of the gender-free strategy would require that one continue to pay scrupulous attention to gender to make sure that the strategy is effective in eliminating bias. Either the strategy recommends this attention to gender or it does not. If it does, its rhetoric is misleading; if it does not, its method is mistaken.

In response to my evaluation of the gender-free strategy, it may be said that I have created a straw strategy. In particular, a gender-free enthusiast might claim that the strategy can be more effectively used than is suggested by my choice of examples. This response to my criticism has some merit. It is not ever wholly convincing to argue that a strategy or method is a poor one because its use is liable to error. In the wrong hands, or in difficult circumstances, any method for eliminating gender bias will suffer an increased likelihood of failure.

A critic might also contend that any persuasive force my remarks or examples may have is due to my equivocation upon the notion of ignoring gender. Proponents of the gender-free approach would undoubtedly claim that the gender-free strategy, in recommending that we ignore gender, is not recommending that we stop attending to it. But no, my criticism cuts deeper than this. My point is that the gender-free strategy presupposes that we have *a priori* decided that gender should have no educational relevance attached to it. This, I contend, could never be decided once and for all *a priori*. The greatest danger of the gender-free approach is that it prematurely forecloses on two important questions: (1) Are there gender-related differences? and (2) How are we to evaluate them?

With the growth of women's studies in the past decade we are only now beginning to catch a glimmer of the powerful and subtle ways in which gender has been and continues to be a basic social organising principle in all known societies. In taking gender itself as a matter of study, women's studies has produced a revolutionary means of viewing the form and subject matter of a variety of disciplines. It is too early to pronounce that we know all the forms of gender bias and that we know that they are best eliminated by invoking a gender-free ideal and a gender-free strategy. We need to pay yet *more* attention to gender, not ignore it. We need to inquire further into gender differences, not try to get rid of them.

For the first time in history, we are now actually in a position in which women are beginning to create a study of themselves by themselves. There is now the opportunity for us systematically to articulate, theorise about, and evaluate our own experience. We need this opportunity especially to investigate what is or might be uniquely female experience, the better to understand the human condition. We will not achieve the understanding we seek if we ignore or try to obliterate gender differences, or attend only to those experiences that the genders share in common, without first being sure that we have accurate information about differences and a proper evaluation of them.

ASSUMPTIONS ABOUT GENDER

Thus far I have attempted to show that the gender-free strategy is suspect because both versions of it, the strong and the weak, fail us in the identification and elimination of the type of gender bias I have called gender valuation. I wish now to explain why the strategy has this effect in some cases. Thc explanation lies in an examination of the assumptions about gender that underlie the strategy and the ideal of sex equality at which it aims.

The ideal of sex equality urged by those who advocate the gender-free strategy is one that gives gender the status that eye colour now has in our society. In short, gender is taken to be totally irrelevent to social organisation. I have no special quarrel with the claim that this is precisely how a good, a just society ought to treat gender. My worry is that this ideal is not especially helpful in the detection and elimination of present gender bias.

This difficulty arises, I suspect, because there is a tendency to see gender as a trait of individuals. If gender were simply a characteristic of individuals that was linked to sex, could be easily marked, correlated with achievements and used as a criterion for qualification or exclusion, then it would make good sense to talk about ignoring gender or treating it as an irrelevant characteristic. However, although we do speak of individuals as gendered, if we see gender solely or primarily as a trait of individuals, we shall be seriously misled.

Gender is also a structure of power; it is a structuring *process*. As one group of researchers puts it, we are better to "...treat gender not just as a matter of existence of two categories of people, male and female, but primarily as a pattern of *relations* among people".[29] They note further:

Relationships between the sexes are not just a matter of distinctions leading to inequalities. They are also relations of power. When we talk about gender we are talking about ways in which social relations get organized in the interests of some groups, overriding the interests of others.[30]

It is equally important to notice that these social relations are systematic, not random, and historical, not static. They change constantly and they are influenced by such other social structuring processes as race and class. But matters are extremely complex because the influence of race and class are not in any way straightforward.

Class and gender do not occur jointly in a situation. They abrade, inflame, amplify, twist, negate, dampen and complicate each other. In short, they interact vigorously, often through the schools and often with significant consequences for schooling.[31]

If we want to make any significant difference to the educational opportunities of girls, we shall have to take cognizance of the precise nature of the femininity that the school is helping to construct, how it is aided or subverted by race and class influences, and we shall have to map the consequences of alternative interventionist policies. This will not be an easy task. The structuring processes of race, class, and gender have different dynamics and attempts to remedy equal educational opportunities from the point of view of one of these interests can have different and even contrary effects for the others. We have learned, for example, that in some cases policies undertaken with class interests in mind have had differential effects for girls and boys.[32] In other instances we have learned that the educational sex segregation of girls which once served to marginalise them and socialise them to a subordinate role now works, in some class contexts, to erode their subordination.[33]

Because gender is a set of relations that are constantly changing and are constantly affected by other structuring processes in social relations, the gender-free strategy has to appear somewhat simplistic. It is misleading to think of gender as something that can be ignored or treated as irrelevant. Gender relations can be ignored, but only at the risk of entrenchment, and while they are changeable, it misses the mark to think of them as eliminable. Eliminating gender bias may often be a matter of seeing gender differently rather than becoming blind to it. It is not always a question of making some characteristic of individuals irrelevant, it is often a matter of recognising that some activities, characteristics or interests of individuals are more valuable than we thought. We need to learn to assess them independently of their location in gender relations.

A GENDER-SENSITIVE PERSPECTIVE

But there is another, a better approach to the elimination of gender bias, one is that is conceptually distinct from the gender-free one, although it does not necessarily foreclose on any particular suggestions recommended by that strategy. Jane Martin has suggested that we employ a gender-sensitive perspective which recommends that we pay attention to gender when it can prevent sex bias or can further sex equality.[34] It is a perspective that requires careful monitoring of our gender interactions and urges direct intervention when necessary to equalise opportunities. In considering alternative strategies for eliminating bias, I think Martin's is the most defensible.

What differentiates a gender-*sensitive* strategy from a gender-*free* one is that a gender-sensitive strategy allows one to recognize that at different times and in different circumstances one might be required to adopt opposing policies in order to eliminate gender bias.[35] A gender-sensitive perspective is not a blueprint for education that will answer all our questions about particular practices. It is, rather, a perspective that constantly reminds us to question the ways in which students and teachers make sense of and respond to a sexist culture. It is a situational strategy, one that lets the patterns of discrimination themselves determine which particular action to take to eliminate bias. This is an important feature to bear in mind. It is the chief virtue of this perspective, for new unsuspected types of gender bias will continue to emerge.

We have already seen how a significant school policy on gender relations, *viz.* co-education, designed to remove access barriers has revealed that women do not have equal participation in the educational process. Once equal participation is achieved, it will become more evident that women do not have an equal say about what knowledge is to be distributed, or about what the styles of pedagogy should be, or about what the goals and ideals of education should be.[36]

A gender-sensitive perspective is a higher-order perspective than that involved in the gender-free strategy. It encourages one to ask constantly: is gender operative here? How is gender operative? What other effects do our strategies for eliminating gender bias have?

A gender-sensitive perspective can also be differentiated from a gender-free strategy by the kinds of questions it leaves open — questions which a gender-free strategy threatens to close, for example, questions about possible differences in learning that might be correlated with gender relations. It is not that a gender-sensitive perspective claims there *are* significant differences, only that there *could be*, given the way in which gender has functioned as a creator of species within our culture.

The superiority of the gender-sensitive perspective is secured by the fact that it can yield a methodology that is self-correcting. For it is a vew that can acknowledge that gender is a set of relations between the sexes, a process that is constantly organising and reorganising our social life. It can recognise the dynamic nature of the gender system, one that exerts pressures, procedures reactions and generates changes.[37] Thus it is a perspective, the only perspective of the three considered, that maintains a constant vigilance and reckoning on the significance that gender acquires in particular contexts. Only if we adopt a perspective of this sort will we be able to catch our own errors, alter policies and practices that no longer work, and introduce new policies for new circumstances. It is in this sense that a gender-sensitive perspective can be a self-correcting methodology for realising the elusive ideal of sex equality.

CONCLUSION

In this chapter I have tried to address the transitional problem of moving from a gender-biassed education in a sexist culture to an unbiassed education that will continue for some time to be influenced by the wider culture. I have argued that the most effective way to deal with gender bias is by adopting a gender-sensitive perspective. It is fundamentally a perspective that encourages a critical and constant review of the meaning and evaluation attached to gender. In this it offers greater hope for the elimination of all types of gender bias than does a gender-free strategy.

REFERENCES

Acknowledgements — This paper has benefitted from my discussions with Susan Franzosa, Jennifer Radden, Janet Farrell Smith and especially Jane Martin and Ann Diller.

1 One of the common distinctions employed in the literature on sex roles and sex equality is that drawn between sex and gender. When the distinction is drawn, "sex" refers to the biological differences between females and males, and "gender" refers to the social differences between the sexes. However, the matter is far from simple; usage of the terms is often inconsistent, and some have argued that the distinction itself is unsuccessful because of the complex linkage between the biological and social aspects of sex (see M. Eichler, *The Double Standard: A Feminist Critique of Feminist Social Science*, London: Croom Helm Ltd., 1980). I grant the difficulties and nevertheless employ the distinction in this chapter. I use the term "gender-free" precisely because I believe that not only biological differences between the sexes are relevant to the discussion of sex equality in education. I do not wish to beg any questions about the nature or causal explanation of gender differences but I am in-

terested in the implications we think gender relations should have for educational theory and practice. Hence I invoke the notion of gender but I use it solely as a descriptive term. For an elaborate clarification of the notions of gender, gender identity and gender role that attends to educational implications, see M. Ayim and B. Houston, "The Epistemology of Gender Identity: Implications for Social Policy", *Social Theory and Practice*, 2, No. 1 (Spring 1985).

2 So far as I know, the term "gender blindness" was first introduced by Richard Wasserstrom in his paper entitled, "Racism and Sexism" in *Philosophy and Women*, ed. S. Bishop and M. Weinzweig (Belmont, CA: Wadsworth Publishing Co., Inc., 1979).

3 For a discussion of the merits and difficulties with this attempt to pursue gender blindness, see R. Wasserstrom, "Racism and Sexism", and Benard Boxill, "Sexual Blindness and Sexual Equality", *Social Theory and Practice*, 6 (Fall 1980): 281 - 299.

4 Jane Roland Martin, "The Ideal of the Educated Person", *Educational Theory*, 31, No. 2 (1981:97 - 109. For further discussions of Martin's critique of philosophy of education and her views about the best ways to include women in educational theory and practice, see her papers "Sophie and Emile: A Case Study of Sex Bias in the History of Educational Thought", *Harvard Educational Review*, 51, No. 3 (1981):357 - 72; "Excluding Women from the Educational Realm", *Harvard Educational Review*, 52, No. 2 (1982):133 - 48; "Sex Equality and Education", in *"Feminity", "Masculinity", and "Androgyny"*, ed. Mary Vetterling-Braggin (Totowa, NJ: Littlefield, Adams, 1982); and "Bringing Women into Educational Thought", *Educational Theory*, 34, No. 4 (1984):341 - 355.

5 This point has been argued in many places. Noteworthy discussions occur in A. Fischel and S.J. Pottker, eds., *Sex Bias in the Schools* (New Brunswick, NJ: Rutgers University Press, 1977); T. Saario, C. Jacklin, and J.C. Tittle, "Sex-Role Stereotyping in the Public Schools", *Harvard Educational Review*, 43, No. 3 (1973):386 - 416; and S.D. Eitzen, *Sport in Contemporary Society: An Anthology* (New York: St. Martin's Press, 1979).

6 Quoted in P. Griffin, "Developing a Systematic Observation Instrument to Identify Sex Role Dependent and Sex Role Independent Behaviour among Physical Education Teachers". Doctoral Dissertation, University of Massachusetts (*University Microfilms International*, No. 8101326, 1980), p. 10.

7 A. Diller and B. Houston, "Women's Physical Education: A Gender-Sensitive Perspective", in *Women, Philosophy, and Sport*, ed. B. Postow (Metuchen, NJ: The Scarecrow Press, 1983), p. 251.

8 These studies and their findings are reported in P. Mahoney, "How Alice's Chin Really Came to be Pressed against Her Foot: Sexist Processes of Interaction in Mixed-Sex Classrooms", *Women's Studies International Forum*, 6, No. 1 (1983):107 - 115; D. Spender, *Invisible Women: The Schooling Scandal* (London: Writers and Readers Publishing Cooperative Society Ltd., 1982); D.

Spender and E. Sarah, ed., *Learning to Lose: Sexism in Education* (London: The Women's Press, 1980); M. Stanworth, *Gender and Schooling: A Study of Sexual Divisions in the Classroom* (London: Hutchinson & Co. Ltd., 1983); N. Frazier and M. Sadker, *Sexism in School and Society* (New York: Harper and Row, 1973); J. Stacey, S. Bercaud, and J. Daniels, ed., *And Jill Came Tumbling After: Sexism in American Education* (New York: Dell, 1974).

9 For a summary and discussion of these findings see the report issued by the Project on the Status and Education of Women of the Association of American Colleges entitled, *The Classroom Climate: A Chilly One for Women* (1982).

10 These findings are reported in D.H. Zimmerman and C. West, "Sex Roles, Interruptions and Silences in Conversations", in *Language and Sex: Difference and Dominance*, ed. B. Thorne and N. Henley (Rowley, MA: Newbury House Publishers, Inc., 1975); Dale Spender, *Man Made Language* (London: Routledge and Kegan Paul, 1980); Dale Spender, "Talking in Class", in *Learning to Lose*, ed. D. Spender and E. Sarah (London: Women's Press, 1980), pp. 148 - 154.

11 For an account of these findings see M.R. Key, *Male/Female Language: With a Comprehensive Bibliography* (Metuchen, NJ: The Scarecrow Press, 1975); B. Thorne and N. Henley, ed., *Language and Sex: Difference and Dominance*; and M. Ayim, "Wet Sponges and Bandaids: A Gender Analysis of Speech Patterns", *Semiotics 1982*, Proceedings of the Seventh Annual Meeting of the Semiotics Society of America.

12 Association of American Colleges, *The Classroom Climate, op. cit.*

13 Spender, "Talking in Class", *op. cit.*, p. 150.

14 *Ibid.*

15 Spender, *Invisible Women, op. cit.*, p. 61.

16 C. Tavris, "How Would Your Life be Different If You'd Been Born a Boy?" ed. A. Baumgartner, *Redbook*, 160 (February 1983), 94.

17 *Ibid.*, 94.

18 *Ibid.*

19 Spender, *Invisible Women, op. cit.*, p. 82.

20 E. Sarah, "Teachers and Students in the Classroom: An Examination of Classroom Interaction", in *Learning to Lose: Sexism and Education*, ed. D. Spender and E. Sarah (London: The Women's Press, 1980). See also M. Stanworth, *Gender and Schooling.*

21 Stanworth, *Gender and Schooling: A Study of Sexual Divisions in the Classroom*. See also P. Griffin, *op. cit.*

22 Diller and Houston, *op. cit.*, p. 252.

23 Spender, *Invisible Women, op. cit.*, pp. 60, 63. For a more general discussion of the genderised valuation of educational traits, see J. Martin, "The Ideal of the Educated Person", *op. cit.*

24 P. Fishman, "Interactional Shitwork", *Heresies, A Feminist Publication on Art and Politics*, 2:99 - 101.

25 Spender, *Invisible Women, op. cit.*, p. 55.
26 *Ibid.*, p. 57.
27 *Ibid.*, p. 55.
28 J. Finn, J. Reis, and L. Dulberg, "Sex Differences in Educational Attainment: The Process", *Comparative Educational Review*, 24, No. 2:333 - 352; J. Laviqueur, "Co-education and the Tradition of Separate Needs", in *Learning to Lose: Sexism and Education*, ed. D. Spender and E. Sarah (London: The Women's Press, 1980), pp. 180 - 190.
29 R.W. Connell, R.W. Ashenden, D.J. Kessler, and G.W. Dowsett, *Making the Difference* (Boston: George Allen and Unwin, 1982), pp. 34 - 35.
30 *Ibid.*, p. 173.
31 *Ibid.*, p. 182.
32 *Ibid.*, p. 181.
33 *Ibid.*, p. 182.
34 Martin, "The Ideal of the Educated Person", *op. cit.*
35 If the complexities of gender relations were acknowledged and taken seriously in education, one should expect those interested in sex equality to recognise that different social contexts can make the same educational policy at one time effective in realising equality and at another ineffectual. A differential evaluation of the effectiveness of a particular educational policy such as a common curriculum need not make us think the ideal of sex equality has altered, nor should it lead us to doubt either the sincerity or intelligence of feminist reformers who offer differential evaluations of it at different times. For an example of just this sort of serious misunderstanding of feminist proposals for reform that is based on an ignorance of the complexities of gender, see G. Partington, "Radical Feminism and the Curriculum", *The Salisbury Review* (July 1984): 4 - 9.
36 Martin, "Excluding Women from the Educational Realm", *op. cit.*
37 Connel *et al., op. cit.*, p. 180.

FURTHER READING

Connel, R.W., R.W. Ashenden, D.J. Kessler, and G.W. Dowsett. *Making the Difference*. Boston: George Allen and Unwin, 1982.

Kessler, Suzanne, and Wendy McKenna. *Gender: An Ethnomethodological Approach*. New York: John Wiley & Sons, 1978.

Martin, Jane, *Reclaiming a Conversation: The Ideal of the Educated Woman*. New Haven: Yale University Press, 1985.

Rich, Sharon Lee, and Ariel Phillips (eds.). *Women's Experience and Education*. Harvard Educational Review Reprint Series No. 17. *Harvard Educational Review*, Longfellow Hall, 13 Appian Way, Cambridge, MA 02138

Spender, Dale, *Invisible Women: The Schooling Scandal*. London: Writers and Readers Publishing Cooperative Society Ltd., 1982.

ELAINE BATCHER

Building the Barriers: Adolescent Girls Delimit the Future

INTRODUCTION[1]

Within the past decade, the sprinkling of information that permeates and typifies North American life has given us the truth that teenage girls, living in a post-feminist era,[2] have the world of possibilities before them and are no longer limited by the restrictions placed on previous generations. "Girls today can do anything," is the way it is often put by people all along the age range, and they point invariably to the large presence of females in institutions of higher learning, the professions and in the general work force, and to the number of choices available to girls, greater now than in any earlier time.

Nowhere does assurance of this fact receive greater credence than among adolescent girls, old enough to have caught many times over the messages on all sides, and too young to have translated them into personal realities. Those who have been raised on the myths of social progress and advertising see women as having come a long way,[3] in a move toward equality that will be achieved when this generation of modern mothers raises the current crop of children. Adolescent girls see equality as an accomplished fact, and not as something that they personally need to win. They are post-feminist in the sense that feminism does not speak to them.

But if there is anything we have learned from our past, it is surely that we cannot become complaisant about social progress for women. As Antonia Fraser admirably documents, women in England gained and then lost, both socially and politically during the 1600s, so that they occupied about the same societal position at the end of the century that they had at the start.[4] The historical, political and social forces against the achievement of equality have been foci of extensive research from various quarters over the past two decades and will not be reiterated here. Instead, I wish to examine some of the processes at work in individual adolescent girls that contribute toward the setting of psychological as well as practical limitations on what they may expect to achieve.

At the risk of sounding like the Victorian feminists, who found the source of female inequality in the sexual subjugation of women in marriage,[5] I wish to put forth the observation, based on recent research, that adolescent girls learn the nature and extent of traditional societal expectations for the female sex in the social group or groups to which they attach themselves. Further, the girls themselves, with varying degrees of self-knowledge, and like all their foremothers, seek these attachments actively and feel themselves deficient if they cannot attain them. The social construction of attachments and their significance forms a persistent pattern over time, in the face of rapid change and growth in many other areas of current life. It is this web, partly of the girls' own construction, wherein lie the barriers to a future of equality.

We tend to see young women as very free, but observations of individuals and groups have shown that sex, drugs and rock music, specifics of the teen culture, are not advancements in young women's freedom, but further pathways of their control by the social group, within which girls play very conventional roles. A girl may be planning a future of accomplishment, but in giving up individuality in favour of acceptance she is throwing her destiny into the hands of others. The message is an old one, but the details are ever fresh.

THE STUDY

The data emerge from a larger study of adolescents and their attitudes to school, family and life, undertaken over a period of six months, which began with the observation two years earlier that a particular mall, in a middle-class suburban setting in Metropolitan Toronto, acted as a focus for a sizable group of teenagers from the local high schools. At the mall, they escaped the requirements of adult culture while establishing their own. This mall culture was surprisingly stable over a period of two years, even though the individual members appeared to change. The group, I was told, were not just friends — they were like family.

The method of participant observation for the gathering and analysis of data began with this group, a process that involved gaining access to the setting, with full disclosure as to intent, and then seeing the culture from inside.[6] The group numbered anywhere from thirty to sixty by various estimates, and there were usually a few members present throughout the twelve hours that the mall was open weekdays. The largest numbers appeared at lunch and after school and commandeered many tables, but those who held part-time jobs in the mall took their breaks here; many cut classes to be here; others who were neither working nor attending school gathered here; and if they were planning any excursion, here is where they collected their forces. I had observed and then met some of the members in previous months while preparing for the study, and in January 1984 I began systematic observation.

Description and analysis were qualitative, like those of Glaser and Strauss for the discovery of grounded theory.[7] This methodology relies on the human instrument to make sense of and convey to the reader the meaning of another culture. Initially, I sat in with members of the group, later in the day recording events in observational, methodological and theoretical notes. Events, the episodes of human activity that were the units of observation, emerged through my personal experience with the individuals in the setting and through tape-recorded interviews done with volunteers.

Because the quantity of information was potentially limitless, one of the guiding principles was to gather only enough to generate theory — which for this study was seen as the depiction of adolescent life, with the principles of organization of this picture made evident. Guides for adequate subjectivity and objectivity were incorporated into the observation process, and multiple perspectives of events were encouraged, each being considered valid from within the context of its emergence, each being seen as a slice of data.

Analysis began after a few weeks of observation and consisted of the placement of events in categories of understanding. By the constant comparison of events as they were placed within a category, the properties of the categories emerged, and memos were written to elaborate these. Sense-making comparisons were at first internal to the group, but soon more information had to be sought outside, and now, in order to make theoretical sense of events, the selection of external comparison groups became important.

Using the help of my student research assistant,[8] I observed in a number of public gathering places, such as malls, restaurants and video-game parlours, and spent time with adolescents from ages thirteen to over twenty. I interviewed specific willing individuals.[9]

Observation and coding for analysis continued in all original and comparison groups, and as general ideas emerged they were written as memos. By the end of the observation period, there was a set of inter-related memos from which theory could be written.

FORWARD TO THE FINDINGS

For purposes of the research, a social group is seen as a group of people, however large or small, cohesive or disjointed, composed of adolescents of both sexes. It can be an actual group, like the group at the mall, or a potential group, like the preps — people with similar styles and interests who might be friends if they met. Any social group implies selection and exclusion.[10] Girlfriend and boyfriend, who pair under the observation of others, never in isolation, constitute a social group, but not single-sex groupings of any size.

The examination of the lives of adolescents revealed four major concerns, which I have set out as four questions central to daily existence: Who am I? Who are my friends? What are my skills and talents? and What can I accomplish? It will be shown how answers to these questions are sought and found within the social group, how each feeds on the others, and how all are meshed in individual experience. What follows is an outline of my findings in these areas.

What Are My Skills, Talents and Interests? The Problem of Knowledge

For an adolescent, there are several kinds of special knowledge. The first comprises those skills, talents and interests unique to the individual, and is variably accepted within the adult and school worlds, depending on the nature of the talent (for example, the ability to speak French or develop photographs). The second comprises group knowledge or talent in a skill that the group values, and which puts the individual in the know (for example, knowing how to party or breakdance). The third is knowledge about how the social group works, its rules of conduct, inclusion and exclusion of people (for example, knowing when and how to freeze out an intruder).

It is the search of adolescence to find some talent or talents that bring satisfaction — a finding of the research aptly affirmed by one boy's exclamation, "Wow! I've finally found something that I can do that I like!" The rewards for skills in the different realms, however, are very different, and there are varying penalties also.

Individual achievement, the sort of knowledge that adults and schools prize, is often a lonely business. Not everyone has the drive, patience and individual strength to work alone for long periods of time, for a future that is not only in doubt but of questionable value.

> I hate being by myself. I'd rather be out with people, so I go out all the time. I should stay home and do my homework but I don't.

This is the explanation of Karen, who was so far advanced in Grade 2 that she twice skipped a grade (was double-promoted). She knows she is capable of 90s but just gets through, preferring to meet her friends at the mall rather than to prepare for class and study for tests.

Girls are not necessarily rewarded within the group for what would be considered knowledge in the adult world. One girl reported being told by some boys that they didn't understand her — the words she was using were too big. Another spoke of her ten-year background in piano and her love of Beethoven and Mozart, which was not understood even by her closest friend. A strong talent or knowledge of the first sort may isolate an adolescent from others. She or he is then in the postion of having to translate that talent or knowledge in order to be understood and appreciated by social peers. The girl who studied piano found herself buying popular sheet music so she could play for her friends. The girl with the decent vocabulary reported her dilemma to her parents; what was she to do? If she wanted to communicate with these boys, she would have to use smaller words, diminishing herself. If she were rightly to see this as an attempt to control her or put her in her place, her choices were the same — translate or remain out. And she wanted in.

Within the group, boys' knowledge is seen as real knowledge, boys' talents as real talents. It is not that girls are not seen as having the potential for talent, in some cases the very same talents as boys, but that there is much more public support for boys than girls. Whether it is an individual skill, like breakdancing, or a group talent in football or basketball, boys are more likely to be found doing things, and girls found cheering them on. Boys who win a championship are school heroes and receive acknowledgement within the group; girls who come tops in their league win the championship game in an empty gym, to the amused tolerance of others in the group.

An additional problem for girls in today's social group is that the activities that were once part of the group agenda, and for the performance of which girls could once achieve recognition, such as dancing, bowling, skating, amateur theatrics, have largely been replaced as sources of group amusement by doing drugs, drinking alcohol and getting into sex. Girls' acquiescence in these activities works to boys' advantage, not just because of the relative inequity of the possible outcomes for either side, but for what these activities prevent girls from doing.

Drug use, whose process embodies watching and surrogate feeling, works against the development of individual action and achievement. The power of the group to chastise sexual activity spreads out to inhibit carefree exploration in a general sense. Although in some cases the boundaries have been loosened somewhat to allow "softer" drugs for girls, and sex for girls with boyfriends, the old double standards still apply, so that girls who are "good" at these are seen as bad girls.

Social knowledge develops early, and the rewards for it are considerable. One boy, who had come from the "wrong" elementary school, spent all of Grade 7 and part of Grade 8 looking on and worshipping the preps at his junior high. When he had the information he needed, he cut his hair, changed his style of dress, and went after one of the prep girls — and he was in.

Both sexes display knowledge of all three sorts, but they do so in different ways. Whereas the above boy was amused at himself for learning about and going along with the crowd, happy to have achieved his goal but able to assess his own role in the process, girls tend to learn the rules too well and then see them as having a life of their own, apart from the individuals who made them up. One of my initial informants told me,

> all the popular kids sit at the tables. But if a guy asks you, you can sit there. Like, if you're going around with a guy, you'll sit at the tables.

This was a public mall, and the local high school kids, however popular, certainly had no monopoly on tables anywhere but in her mind.

Regarding knowledge, then, girls with a skill in the first area, which is individual, specific and accepted within the adult world, must often choose between being lonely in the development of that skill or debasing or translating it for the benefit of others in the social group. The second, group-oriented kind of skill, is dominated by the boys, acceptable within limits in girls, and the old double standards still apply. Lastly and most importantly, girls are simply too good at knowledge of the third sort, and too accepting of it. They do not see "the rules" as structures within which to work, but as solid artifacts of life, even if they personally disagree with them.

Who Are My Friends? The Problem of Popularity

Adolescents accept groups — their existence, their importance in people's lives, and their function as centres of activity and acceptance. Criticism of another group, of which there is plenty ("Those preps are rich and spoiled and addicted to Daddy's money"), is usually an affirmation of the group's own values ("Punks buy our clothes cheap!"). That adolescents need friends can hardly be disputed, but in accepting membership in a group, girls accept a lot of unexamined baggage. This may be loosely summarised as follows.

Groups are centred around boys who like power and girls who like boys. Girls no doubt enjoy being part of a powerful "family" and having access to power through their boyfriends, but they do not seek it for themselves. They accord the group the status of fact and the boys the leadership, asking mostly to belong to the family and often unaware of their role in maintaining the boys in power. Girls accept in the group attitudes and values that they reject at home. They have different definitions about what is happening in the group than do boys, and are both attracted and repelled by the idea that precocious behaviour and experimentation creates leaders out of boys and groupies of girls.

One girl, for example, who was strongly supportive of group members, displayed this sort of confusion in her attitudes to alcohol. She felt herself mature and socially acceptable, on a par with others, since she had been drinking for four years, while her sister, two years younger and now fifteen, had not yet begun to drink and was regrettably growing up slowly. Boys' drinking habits governed the spending of time and money on weekends, so that they might get roaring drunk and be the life of the party, or they might pass out. Girls, however, were cheapening themselves when they drank to excess and came on to men, and she herself rarely took more than a glass or two of wine or beer.

Every step toward popularity is a step against singularity, against self. The question of how many people any one individual is willing to share her/himself with is an important one. Popularity may be seen as a power, the power to impose one's will on many others, and indeed the cultural image of a popular girl is that creature on a pedestal ordering her suitors about. But better understanding would be achieved by examining the number of people allowed access to her talents, and the types of behaviour necessary to being of the group (dressing correctly, for example), at the front of the group (trying new things, like alcohol, first) and yet not so far out in front that she loses the others (not becoming an alcoholic). Common sense, if nothing else, would indicate that an adolescent with a few same-sex friends is more likely to have time to devote to individual achievement than one who is involved with a large group. She may consider this as lonely time, however.

Girls are said to belong to groups in two ways: as girlfriends to the guys who belong, and on their own. The following two vignettes, related by Paul, a boy identified by everyone as central to his group, illustrate exactly how an insider sees everyone else.

A lot of people...see a relationship between myself, Gary and Clark, and they get jealous or they get upset because we're so close, and we'll stick together through thick and thin all the time. Where some people....try and try to get into our little group, which is not a little group to us, it's a family to us, and people don't seem to understand that, they think we're just friends. And we don't mind people hanging around with us. It's just when they start saying, "us four," "us four," "us four," and "we're going to do this and this," where *we* like to do what we want to do, and if *he* happens to be there when we do it, he also can. But, see, we always considered ourselves The Three Musketeers...because us three are really the closest.

Clark had a girlfriend and she was upset because me and Clark hung around so

much and she came on to me one night at a party, and tried to make me come on to her, which I didn't want to [do] because she was my best friend's girlfriend, and Clark saw it and she went up to him and said, "Yeah, Paul was trying to pick me up"...and Clark turned around...and he said, "Listen...get the hell out of my house. I know Paul would never do that."
...And he just forgot that girl that night and it was over. It's because she tried to break up our friendship that way.

Outsiders give public recognition to this group. It is well-known who belongs, what they wear, how they do their hair and make-up, what music they like, what they drive and how they party. And at the centre of this group, estimated in size by various members at as few as eight, as many as fifty or sixty, are three boys with some rules of exclusion that seem iron-clad: when the three feel like it, certain boys are in; girls are in only on good behaviour.

Within the group, acceptable girls assume a range of roles that is recognisable. They are pals who can chum along and be the occasional butt of boys' humour, act as go-fers and remain good sports. They are the trial material on which boys can practise their social-sexual skills and may serve, in turn, as romantic interest ("When the guys in that group break up with one girl, they immediately start going out with another girl in the group"). Girls act as family members, mothers to the patriarchy, with supportive roles ("The girls are just there"). And there are the housekeeping functions of tidying the tables ("There's always such a mess when everybody leaves"), buying or paying for food ("While you're there get me a burger!"), and keeping track of commitments and class schedules ("When did he say that assignment was due?"). In short, while a friendly guy uses his contacts to build a power base, a friendly girl becomes part of someone else's power base. While a friendly guy becomes a wheel, a friendly girl becomes a go-fer.

The model of a successful group girl, in fact, conflicts with the model of a successful adult. Talking and thinking about eating less, buying and wearing clothes and doing hair and make-up to be noticed, and getting a protector (boyfriend) may all be considered as clinging to immaturity, not developing to maturity, a state where the body is fully fed, fully grown and the emphasis is on independent action and accomplishment rather than on being seen.

One girl, described by one of the group members, Ian, as a "muffin", meaning sweet, kind and caring, considered herself a marshmallow, a weak person who let others walk on her and "It's O.K." Ian said of her and her friend of similar personality that they were very strong individuals and that it was impossible to think that they would ever take second place to anybody. Ian was very committed to the group — in fact, had transferred from a school he described as top-notch to one he thought merely mediocre, in order to be with "these guys". The glow of people's acceptance, as well as his male perspective, masked knowledge that the girls had — that taking second place was exactly what they were training themselves to do.

What Can I Accomplish? The Problems of Power and Strength

As men have done for centuries, boys secure for themselves anything they consider good and keep it away from girls. A breakdance enthusiast gave the following reasons why girls do not breakdance.

They're not interested.
It doesn't look right.
It's more for guys.
Girls like slow dancing.
Not too many girls do it.
They can do it but it looks different.
Everybody is shocked when they see a girl who does.
Girls haven't found the interest.
I don't know how people would accept it.
They would think this girl's a tom-boy.
She'd get the reputation of being a tom-boy who's into boys' stuff and sports.
It would be like seeing a girl play hockey.

If everything else were equal, which of course it is not, this capacity to grab and keep resources would alone ensure the supremacy of boys over girls at every level of the Byzantine hierarchy of social groups in a high school.

Given the rhetoric on equality current in society, it is unexpected to find either sex being open about claims of superiority or inferiority. Given the assertiveness of adolescents, these claims nevertheless emerge in conversation. Bob, for example, labelled a classmate "Queen of Africa" for daring to announce herself tops both on the courts and in the classroom. He claimed male superiority — for it is men who have testosterone, men who get the big muscles — although he did allow women their intellectual merit, admittedly because intellectual ability was not the source of his pride. Girls who would never assent to their own inferiority would nevertheless agree that boys occupy superiority of position. "Yeah, but it's changing," is the way it is often put, affirming both the truth of it and their hopes for the future.

It is a simple fact of life today that men hold power. If it is understood that both sexes use the social group partly to explore their future as adults, it is easy to see how boys, who will be men, can gain strength individually and as a boy-class by borrowing on the future. Glimpses of such a future often act as wonderful incentives to boys to grow themselves quickly.

Girls, on the other hand, grow up to be women, and although this is slowly changing in our lifetime, women at the moment do not hold as much power as men. Girls do not borrow on their future as women. First, they may correctly see adult women as less powerful than men and hardly worthy of adolescent emulation. Second, they are ambivalent about their futures, not always identifying with other females, thinking they will never be like their mothers, rejecting friends as potential rivals, and therefore unable or unwilling to group cohesively together in their own interests.

The fact that boys are a cohesive group gives them a distinct advantage, which girls see but do not emulate. When girls attempt to bind, it is with their boyfriends, who are themselves bound first with other boys, second with their girlfriends. The girls' attachment, then, is to the whole male-dominated group, where girls are separated from each other like spokes on a wheel. At the hub is the tight little family arrangement whose core is the boys' trio described earlier, and from which a spoke can easily be replaced. A wheel thus constituted would fall apart without its spokes, and without girls' participation, the group would simply not exist.[11] There is among females a very deep belief in this very point, but little in the way of linkage among spokes that would create force from understanding — little in the way of insistence that this viewpoint prevail.

Indeed, girls generously allow boys to structure everyone's view of events. A trip to Buffalo by the boys in a group was explained to me by one of the girls (as it was explained to her) as a quest for American beer and cigarettes. The girls never went to Buffalo and didn't want to go, I was told, for the boys all piled in two or three cars to save on gas, and stayed in truck stops. While the girls got together in twos and threes, they did not report adventures comparable to the boys'. They did, however, drink at parties. Another girl, describing her first experience of sex, recalled how "aggressive" her partner had been, so that she was bruised for several days following, and also how he had talked about his girlfriend after the act. She said of the experience, "I was so infatuated by him, it was fine." The editor of the yearbook installed her boyfriend as co-editor, and then stepped back to allow him to assume command. His dictatorial attitude was resented by others on the yearbook staff, but she supported his actions. Girls are seen to make allowances for boys, and reciprocity does not exist.

If power is seen as a group function, strength as a function of the individual, then Hannah Arendt's statement, "It is in the nature of a group and its power to turn against independence, the property of individual strength,"[12] may be seen as an apt assessment of what happens in adolescent social groups. Eccentricity even of the faintest sort is discouraged, as would testify the young teen who really preferred Heavy Metal music but who wore Duran Duran buttons favoured by the "in" crowd at school, for the sake of his image.

Boys, however, get and keep power in groups, while girls in conformity lose strength. For boys, going with group power reaffirms male values. If a girl abrogates strength for power, it is male power, once again, that is reaffirmed, because there is no female equivalent of group power — no female power. There are strong individuals, and girls' groups seen as powerful from the outside, as prep girls may be seen, but the precocity and exploration on which this "power" is built occur in the male-directed areas of sex and drugs, and work, ultimately, against them. Girls would have more strength *out* than power *in*, but it is hard to persuade them of this.

Girls seem to go along willingly with the pull of the group. A strong girl will give up the possibility of her own leadership to support the candidacy of a boy in the group, much in the way that a candidate for political leadership who is trailing may pull her or his support behind another candidate, trading uncertain victory now for influence at a later time. If the girl and boy are attracted to each other, then a very traditional solution, sexual pairing with its usual inequities, may "solve" the problem for the group. Girls are pulled into the group by the lure of popularity, the promise of fun.

Not all are pulled in, of course. Not all are muffled by the group. There are many who would try new paths — girls who thirst for experience, yearn for satisfaction of a strength, or just want to be themselves. It is against these individuals that group tools, applied by both females and males, are most effective. Labels are powerful means of bringing free-thinkers into line. "Tom-boy" calls up an entire history of past associations the girl cannot begin to combat. "The clamp" is one girl who has sex because she likes it, not because she is doing it for her boyfriend. And what defence is possible against terms like "dirty rocker hosebag", "sleaze bucket", and the all-purpose "slut"?

There is also gossip. Gossip was the main event at the tables at the mall. Everyone of the extended group had access to the most intimate details of the lives of every one of them, including those who became pregnant, those who married for the sake of the child, the one who refused to acknowledge a child that was his, although the mother was a member of the group and everyone knew he was the father, and those who had recently yielded to their boyfriends' urging. One interviewee described the group as "just a big soap opera".

There are warnings also to those who escape implicit messages. There was one girl who not only *could* breakdance but who *did*. One of her classmates followed her after the dance and beat her up for her presumption. The police were called and the boy was charged, and everyone spoke of how "crazy" he had been and how wrong. But the warning was not lost on the girl, nor on the other girls, and there were no girls currently breakdancing when I heard about it a few months later.

Finally, people who play to win change the rules to suit themselves. People who follow along are forced to keep up a path not of their own pace or direction. Teenage fads, like multiple ear-piercing, shaved heads, ripped clothing are brief and work against those who are their slaves. There will always be another fad to follow, another group to get in with, another male-oriented set of directives to learn. Some girls set a track record in moving through groups in just this way, as do some boys. People who are slaves to fads are pulled away from their own individual strengths. Change of speed and speed of change keep boys in charge, and girls who follow contribute to their own limitation.

Who Am I? The Problem of Identity

Who are girls and who should they be today? That adolescents actively seek ways of being emerges through every interview. Quite rightly, they see these years as the decisive ones.

> [Teenagers] have a lot of things to face...they have to decide what they want to do for the rest of their lives and it's a hard thing to do...you have to make sure that you make the right decision and you can't be rushed into that.

It is possible for a teen to seek refuge from a demanding world within the social group, accepting there an identity she dismisses at home. One girl who escaped her parents every evening and weekend was actively planning to repeat her mother's life — training for a job that she knew paid little so that self-support would be difficult, hoping for an early marriage and children immediately.

Within the group, the search for something to do well, to avoid the ignominy of being "nothing special", can be achieved in very traditional ways — by being "pretty", or "good; you know what I mean?" or a "muffin". There was more than one girl interviewed who indicated a mind to the future by reference to the wealth of her boyfriend's family, which was seen as accessible. A young couple in the group had recently married to legitimate an unplanned pregnancy, and were being supported by their families in secure middle-class life style while he completed school and she looked after the infant.

When one can receive love, approval, acceptance and fun any time one chooses to show up at the mall, it is tempting to be there often and to go along with events until circumstances decide the future. As long as one's education is proceeding and one's high school credits are accumulating, all things are possible. But "circumstances" are not always pleasant. The unplanned marriage had halted the young mother's education, although she was still coming out to parties and parking the infant in the bedroom. The boy who refused to accept responsibility for a pregnancy was still welcomed in the group, while the girl, who "had so much going for her" was waiting it out alone. Where was the group for her now?

The search for oneself is not one that can properly be conducted within the group, where certain lines may be blurred, for example those of race, religion or class, but where others remain firm, and where the emphasis is not on individuation. Friendship and loyalty are paramount in this age group, but in remaining involved with a group, a girl must be able to separate how she sees an issue from how the group sees it, how she sees herself from how others see her.

When you are seventeen, you know a lot more about what you don't want than what you do want. One boy said of the boss where he worked that if he knew he was going to be like him when he was an adult, he'd party his brains out and never grow up. But one of the tragedies of life is that we often do end up with what we didn't want, because it was what we knew, and the other was so uncertain.

Individual talent and achievement thrive on this uncertainty. They cannot be made comfortable because they are singular and not always appreciated by others. Girls who understand this need not worry about the lack of confirmation they find in their surroundings, and lack of confirmation may be all they find. Even the fantasy books, now popular because of their escapist quality, portray women in the conventional ways.[13]

Of all the people interviewed, the ones who seemed to have the brightest future, boys as well as girls, were those who had stepped outside, if only for a time, to find the individual within. It did not mean abandoning friendships. The one girl who was so insistent on lighting her own cigarette, humorously blowing out several times the lighter held for her by a young gallant, until he finally conceded the point to her, was still a member of the group about which one of the boys had said, "The girls are just there." Her minor rebellion was not taken seriously, but she took *herself* seriously.

SUMMARY: HOW THE BARRIERS ARE BUILT

The social world, in which we all live, is essentially the creation of its participants. It is built through belief, shared experience and inter-subjectively shared meanings over time. It has no "real" existence in the way that a table has real existence, yet it is more real to us than any furniture.

It is the task of youth, in a positive way, to set the delimitations to action — to define what one will and will not do, what one hopes to do and never wants to do. Think of this as a model. Within these boundaries individual action can take place. Within these boundaries also, youth must find something the doing of which brings satisfaction and wins admiration. The boundaries are not firm walls — they are constantly being measured, moved and re-established as part of the process we call growth.

Each person's self-definition takes place in the midst of people who are also finding themselves and stretching the boundaries. The process of self-definition is reflexive in the sense that each individual creates and is created by the group, within which one lives, grows and measures oneself. Model-making is also reflexive, both creation and creator of future action.

If every adolescent is seen as her own theorist, actively applying sense-making methods to a wealth of data, actively evaluating action in the light of what she wants to be, it is obvious how any limitations of the model can create barriers to achievement, barriers to the future. It might appear that the application of sense-making methods will bring her to an understanding of the inferiority of a limited model, and this sometimes does occur. It is the "click" perception popularised by *Ms Magazine*, the phenomenological "shock" experience of passing from one reality to another[14] — the sudden realisation that one's past ideas must immediately be overturned. Why this does not happen more frequently, in the face of the overwhelming evidence that women's experience provides daily, has of course been the subject of much of feminist inquiry, including this study.

It has been my contention in this paper that the model is initially limited by its conventionality, its control within the social group, its male-centred direction. Girls must reclaim it, for every girl who allows others control over her reality is blocking her own path to success. Girls must build and believe, believe and build better models of their own existence and thus overcome the barriers of their own making.

REFERENCES

1 This paper was originally presented in abbreviated form at the Canadian Research Institute for the Advancement of Women Conference in Montréal, November, 1984, and subsequently published in the conference proceedings. The author wishes to thank the Social Science and Humanities Research Council of Canada for financial support of the research on which this paper is based.

2 I first read the term in Gloria Steinem, "The Good News Is: These Are Not the Best Years of Your Life", *Ms.*, September 1979.

3 "You've come a long way, Baby." Virginia Slims cigarette advertisements inform that where once we were not allowed to smoke, now we have our own cigarette, shaped like ourselves.

4 Antonia Fraser, *The Weaker Vessel: Women's Lot in Seventeenth Century England*. London: Weidenfeld & Nicolson, 1984.

5 The lives of Harriet Taylor and John Stuart Mill, as discussed in Phyllis Rose, *Parallel Lives* (New York: Vintage, 1984) are illustrative of this.

6 See Elaine Batcher, *Emotion in the Classroom: A Study of Children's Experience*, New York: Praeger, 1981, for a complete discussion of field methodology.

7 Barney G. Glaser and Anselm L. Strauss, *The Discovery of Grounded Theory.* Chicago: Aldine, 1967.

8 Research for this study was aided immeasurably by Stephen Chadderton.

9 Parental permission was obtained for all those under the age of nineteen. Those nineteen and over signed the consent form themselves.

10 The disuse of the words "peer group" is deliberate, the term having taken on a meaning among teenagers for which it was never intended — as that group of people older and more experienced than oneself, by whom one desires to be accepted, and whom one therefore emulates. Interestingly, this gives real understanding of how peer pressure actually operates.

11 I am indebted to Russell Batcher for the extention of the wheel analogy to its present form.

12 Hannah Arendt, *On Violence.* New York: Harcourt Brace Jovanovich, 1969, p. 44.

13 I investigated fantasy fiction because so many adolescents spoke of it as very different from life as we know it. I found it not to be so. See Anne McCaffrey's Dragon series (*Dragonsong, Dragonsinger, Dragondrums*), for example.

14 See, for example, "Transcendences and Multiple Realities", in Helmut R. Wagner (ed.), *Alfred Schutz on Phenomenological and Sociological Relations.* Chicago: University of Chicago Press, 1970, pp. 245-262.

FURTHER READING

Batcher, Elaine, *Emotion in the Classroom: A Study of Children's Experience.* New York: Praeger, 1981.

Baker, Maureen, *"What Will Tomorrow Bring?..."* Ottawa: Canadian Advisory Council on the Status of Women, 1985.

Elkind, David, *The Hurried Child: Growing Up Too Fast Too Soon.* Reading, MA: Addison-Wesley, 1981.

Mead, Margaret, *Coming of Age in Samoa: A Psychological Study of Primitive Youth for Western Civilization.* New York: Morrow, 1928.

Munro, Alice, *Lives of Girls and Women.* New York: McGraw-Hill, 1971.

Waller, Willard, "The Rating and Dating Complex", in Harry Silverstein, *The Sociology of Youth — Evolution and Revolution.* New York: Macmillan, 1973, pp. 284 - 92. Orig. pub. *American Sociologist Review* (ASA, Vol. 2, No. 5, October 1937).

C. THE BODY/SEXUALITY

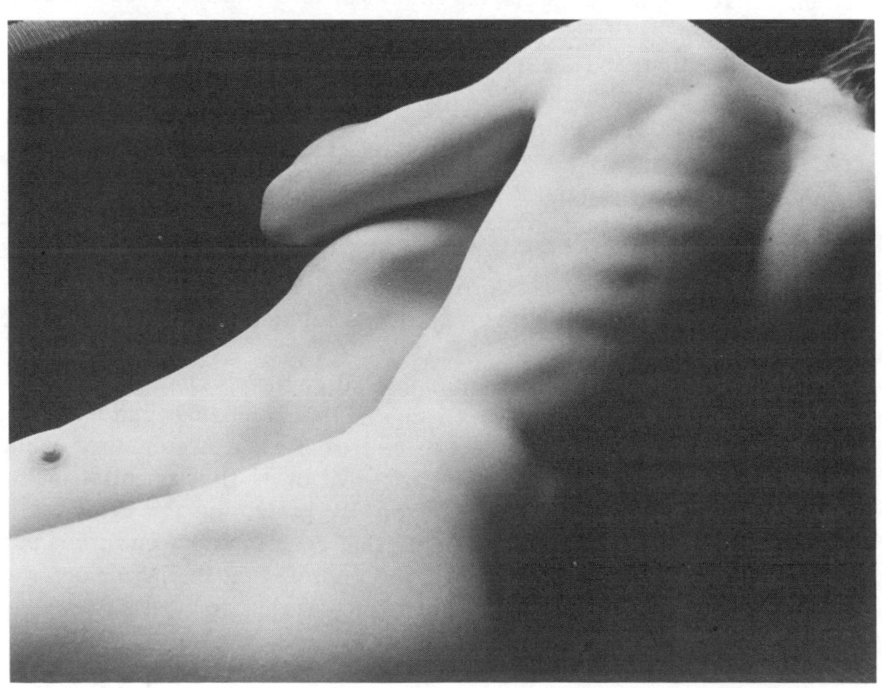

NAOMI GOLDENBERG

Resurrecting the Body: An Agenda for Feminist Theory

A brochure for a recent conference on feminism and spirituality announced that "patriarchy has reached a deadly, dead end."[1] This is an accurate statement even though the words "deadly, dead end" are tautological. Stylistically, it might have been better to use only one dead word — such as "patriarchy is deadly" or "patriarchy has reached a dead end." But correct style isn't everything. To me, saying that "patriarchy has reached a deadly, dead end" suggests that we live with two different, but related feelings of deadness. The first, and the more obvious to us all, is that nuclear bombs can literally bring an end to all of human culture. However, the threat of sudden and fiery death, although certainly very real and frightening, may in some way mask concern about a more typical and mundane deadness that pervades our culture. To put it another way, the fear of death from nuclear weapons is the most common expression of the daily sense of deadness that is so much a part of modern life. Our absolutely realistic fear of a final and spectacular end to the planet is probably the clearest image we have of the death that patriarchal culture conveys to us subliminally and subtly every day.

Now, when I say that modern patriarchal culture is characterised by a feeling of deadness, I do not mean to suggest that any human culture or any human being can realistically expect to be free of some awareness of death. I think that sensitivity to anger and the threat of death is essential for the health of both individuals and cultures. By presenting the deadness of modernity as a problem, I am asserting that contemporary culture is particularly and excessively *deadening*. I am arguing that the pernicious sapping of vitality that is now typical of our culture is altogether different from the consciousness of limitation and mortality which we all need to live wisely.

An important task of feminist theory, whether we conceive of that theory as spiritual or routine, religious or secular, is to address the deadness within modern culture. We must figure it out. We must arrive at a better understanding of the death within our lives in order to respond with life — in order to conceive of enterprises and institutions that can better sustain and nourish life.

I want to begin discussing the feeling of deadness in patriarchal culture by talking about machines. What does it mean to be in a culture so thoroughly pervaded by man-made machinery?

Besides the deadening effects of our collective preoccupation with war machines in particular, there is a sense in which all machines loosen our connection to life. An increased reliance on machines means a decreased reliance on other people, because machines tend to make human beings less necessary for each other. Consider these examples:

1. In warfare, troops are less necessary for generals now that so much killing can be done automatically.
2. In sex, real women and men are less necessary for arousal now that technology makes pornography so widely available.
3. In play, television, stereo and video games make other humans inessential for entertainment.
4. In reproduction, women and men become less important to one another as reproductive technology becomes more sophisticated.
5. In education, professors are becoming less necessary for students as pre-packaged video classes become more popular.
6. In medicine, many things that doctors used to do are now done by machines that diagnose and treat diseases. The cold physician is being replaced by even colder steel.
7. In the work place, colleagues and co-workers could become less a part of working life as more people work at home on computer terminals.

These examples illustrate my contention that machines, or more specifically, our uses of machines, are making our communal ties to one another less obvious and less physical. I think McLuhan was right about technology's ability to turn the world into a global village. However, he failed to take sufficient notice of the discarnate quality of the majority of the village's citizens. As we become increasingly more aware of the presence and activities of people all over the globe, we become increasingly less acquainted with the felt physical presence of people in our immediate environment. It becomes increasingly easy for us to avoid each other. I suggest that the disappearance of people from the world contributes to a sense of deadness and loneliness in modern culture.

In addition to blurring our sense of the body politic, machines alter our relationship to our own bodies. We use machines for the purpose of extending all our senses and capacities. With machines we live more — see more, hear more, taste more, play more, work more, travel more and heal more. Machines are likenesses of body parts. They are mechanised bodily functions that have been severed from their total human context in order to expand sensual range and possibility. Machines are supposed to heighten sensibilities and extend life and, in many ways, they do. But, unfortunately, that is not all they do.

Machines and the culture they foster and permit do expand and improve life but also damp it down. Modern mechanised culture is tranquillised and deadened. Paradoxically, the machines that enable us to live more also allow us to feel less. This deadness, I suggest, comes from the progressive dissolution of the physical context for human emotions — from the dissolution of the human body.

I started thinking about the importance of what I call the context of body when I read Susan Sontag's book, *On Photography*. Sontag explored how the camera has altered our sense of self and world. She wrote that there are many ways in which the photographic image has become more real than what we actually see. The camera, she argued, has altered our sense of sight and perhaps has even begun to define reality for us. We often try to see things as cameras do, and thus distance ourselves from being involved in what we see. Real seeing becomes dispassionate, "objective", mechanised seeing.[2]

Sontag's work led me to understand how the technology of photography enables us to take the world out of context. Photography enables us to break things up into abstracted images which then seem more real than the things themselves. In fact, reality is often felt to be inferior to the photographic images of it with which we are continually bombarded. Women in particular, I think, have suffered from photographic objectification. We have been pictured and posed in order to be formed by the artificial images of ourselves posing. As French feminist Hélène Cixous has suggested, male culture behaves toward women as does a photographer-director who says "Hold still, let me take your picture so you can begin looking like it right away".

But this is only an example. The point I want to make is more general than the objectification of women by photographic technology. I think women and men are pushed by technology to objectify all of life — that is, we are pushed to abstract life like a photographic image and experience it in dissociated parts. The prevalence of photography in the modern world probably reflects how many of us feel a good deal of the time. Machine-age mobility cuts us off from relationships and communities. Our jobs and career-paths lead us away from each other — from our pasts, from our friends, from our families. We live out our lives in a series of places — in a series of relationships. The segregation of age groups contributes to the sense of discontinuity. As our individual lives are discontinuous, so too are our collectivities. Babies stay in their places. Yuppies in theirs. Old people in theirs. Isolation. The lack of sustained human contact. Transience. The lack of a sense of inheritance. These are some of the very disquieting characteristics of modern culture. We are all somewhat displaced. We are all very much in mourning.

I have just painted a bleak picture. Let me take a step back by saying that I realise that not all of us feel the weight of this deadness with the same severity. There are people whose satisfying childhoods and close families enable them to feel more connected to life than others do. There is a great deal of variation possible. I am arguing that our culture does not push us into life — that it does not encourage close ties. The dominant direction of culture is to dissociate, to disembody, to cut off, to abstract, and to dehumanise. Although our individual histories make us more or less prone to feel this, we all are affected by it in some degree. Thus the daily deadness of patriarchy is a general problem even though some people manage to live "counter-cultural" existences and even though we all manage to improve our own circumstances to some degree.

But what should we do in a larger sense — in a collective sense? I don't propose to banish machines from the world. What I suggest is that we all become much more sophisticated about how the typically male fantasies of distance and dissociation[3] are expressing themselves in technology and pressuring us all to feel and act more and more like machines. Instead of a return to nature, I propose a return to human nature — in our institutions, in our communities, in our theories.

The deceptively simple answer I suggest to the problem of deadness in culture is a return to the body. *Body* is the name of the ground on which I want to see our theories built. Body is the word I am using to refer to all that is human about us, to all that distinguishes us from machines, to all that we need to feel alive.

The course that can return culture to the body is very complicated, but probably not infinitely so. Our feminist movement has done a lot of the initial thinking already. We simply need to keep going. That is our work.

A basic insight of feminism is that no one thinks very effectively about revitalising culture without thinking a lot about women. It is interesting to see how the work of male theorists like Norman O. Brown and Herbert Marcuse, who both advocated "the body" and "eros" as solutions to modern deadness, never really went beyond a visionary stage of invoking physicality and sensuality as cultural forces. Brown and Marcuse could not provide more direction because they failed to think sufficiently about women. (Attention to their maestro Freud did not help them with this, since Freud himself had failed to think very extensively or very well about women.) Listen to one of Brown's concluding statements in *Life Against Death*:

The resurrection of the body is a social project facing mankind as a whole, and it will become a practical political problem when the statesmen of the world are called upon to deliver happiness instead of power,...[4]

Feminists know that "statesmen" are unlikely to do anything significant to change "power" into happiness. As long as societies are run by men who behave according to traditionally male codes, nothing can change and there can be no resurrection of the body.

There are many feminist thinkers who have pointed out how hatred of the body and hatred of women are linked. [I have reviewed some of this work in an article in the first issue of the *Journal of Feminist Studies in Religion*.[5]] Such feminist theory builds on the truths that we all live daily. Women are in charge of the body; that's what women's work is all about. We feed bodies, clean bodies, and comfort bodies. We come to represent sensuality itself with our clothing and decoration. Our culture tends to prescribe uniforms for men — suits and clothes that standardise their bodies and make them monochromatic. Women, in contrast, are encouraged to use a range of fabrics, colours, styles and adornments. We present ourselves as the varied ones — as the textured, embodied members of the species.

We women are human beings who have never been allowed to entertain the illusion that our minds are separate from our bodies, or that we have a public life that is discontinuous with our private selves. Karen Brown once said that no matter what job a woman has, it is she who will always have to know how much milk is in the refrigerator. On the same theme, French feminist Christiane Rochefort has written, "We have a body: university degrees don't obliterate the fact. When Kristeva got a prize not long ago, a critic wrote in a so-called liberal newspaper: 'She has beautiful legs.' We have a physiology: after de Beauvoir's novel *La femme rompue* the critic of *Le monde* said, 'She's an old woman.' He himself was about to die, but he was a man and consequently had no age."[6]

We women act as everyone's body. And we are naturals for the role. We are body because we are mothers. Everyone first comes to know her body or his body next to a female body. Or, to put it another way, everyone begins her life or his life in the context of a female body.

It is this deep connection of women with body that enables women to resurrect the body in civilisation now. This mission is highly problematic. For at the very time that we must stand up for the body, we must also refuse to stand for it exclusively. We must continually insist that men have bodies too. We must continually challenge the illusion that women are the more physical sex. We cannot allow men to continue to imagine themselves as either gods or machines. They too must be bodies. Our survival as a species could very well depend on correcting the male imagination — on rendering obsolete the notion that people are ever anything else than human beings enmeshed in human subjectivities, enmeshed in human bodies.

I think that Dorothy Dinnerstein is probably correct in insisting that we must involve men in early child care if we are to have any profound effect on future conceptions of the male or female gender.[7] But changes in child care practices will not occur without changes in the gender politics of contemporary life. Thus, even though psychoanalytic theory can help us see how the association of women with body begins in the mother-child relationship, it is political change now that will enable us to write new scripts both for ourselves and for future generations.

The agenda of feminist theory must be to articulate the body. This is the only sane direction, the only direction of life. I think body is a good word to describe this vital orientation. But there are certainly others. Other modes of discourse can illuminate the same ground.[8]

The goal I have named for myself in my own work is that of grasping the body in theory, with theory. For a number of years I have meditated on this goal by calling to mind some statues that Michelangelo sculpted toward the end of his life. They are human figures that are still embedded in the rough stone. They are co-extensive with their backgrounds, with the material in which they are created. Each formed figure thus illuminates the substance that formed it. I think theory should be like that: that theory should illuminate more and more of the body, more and more of the context in which we theorise. To be specific:

First, by body I do not mean the body as exaggeratedly praised by many back-to-nature movements. I distrust natural food, fibre, and medicine zealots almost as much as I do born-again Christians. The smile of both sorts of devotees hides anger, I think. I suspect that many back-to-nature movements have scapegoated technology by making it represent all the impurities of self and world that they find so confusing. The answers of the back-to-nature movements disguise too many problems. We need to learn to see more complexity in our environment, and not to reject energetically large portions of our world. I would like to define body as something that includes nature as a part of itself. I do not want to think of "body" as an isolated "pure nature" that is separated from a total environmental context.

Second, what I am calling "body" stands in contrast to the notion of transcendence in traditional theology. Transcendence is a wish for something beyond body, beyond time and beyond specific relationships to life. Such a male notion of perfect safety involves a negation of this world and is probably motivated by a characteristically (but not exclusively) male fear of being merged with life.[9] The male imagination has envisaged salvation as up, out and beyond. Men have called this hoped-for state of dissociation the ultimate reality. In fact, it is no reality at all but rather a death-wish which Christianity has aptly symbolised by a male dying on a cross. In the course of Christian history, men have much preferred to promote this image of suffering and agony instead of any image of comfort and love such as that of Mary with her baby. The crucifixion is therefore now the central image of modern Christianity. And the medium is the message.

The particularly male obsession with a dying man dominates and limits the work of most male theologians. For example, deathly transcendence is a key theme in the work of Hans Küng, a theologian who is trying to improve traditional theology. Küng writes: "Why should I not be allowed to wish that the sweat, blood and tears, all the sufferings of millenia may not have been in vain, that definitive happiness may finally be possible for all human beings...? Why should I not...feel an aversion to being required to be satisfied with rare moments of happiness and — for the rest — to come to terms with 'normal unhappiness'?... May I not feel an aversion...in regard to the idea that the life of the individual and mankind is governed only by the pitiless laws of nature, by the play of chance and by the survival of the fittest, and that all dying is a dying into nothingness."[10] When Küng looks at this world, he finds it insufficient and disappointing. Because daily life seems so unsatisfying, another world becomes necessary — a world of God, which in Küng's work is described as being "Unconditioned".[11] For Küng this "unconditioned" reality that he says is "independent of our thinking, willing and feeling, of psyche and society"[12] is where truly good things can be found.

Like many male theologians, Hans Küng has written a fair bit about life after death. Note how such issues have never fascinated feminist theologians, who are concerned with hopes for life before death. Life after death is a question that is symptomatic of structures of thought that spring from deadened feelings.

It might be possible to have a concept of transcendence which is not death-like. A transcendence with body, a transcendence that is life-oriented would involve feelings of connection instead of separation. It might be possible for transcendence to refer to a state of knowing oneself to be part of other human lives — to knowing that one's life is linked to other lives. Feeling part of an enormous effort at social reform such as the woman's movement has been an avenue of such an experience of transcendence for many of us. The feeling of participation in the body politic not only provides a tie to a present collective community, but also links our lives to those who lived before us and those who will live after us. Such "transcendence" is a quality of now — a feeling that is part of the present moment and that gives contemporary lives a significant tie to human history and society. This "transcendence" is a sense of involvement in one's own and other human lives. It fosters feelings of being alive. It is far removed from the death-like hope for a static "unconditioned" detachment which patriarchal theology has presented as paradise. One of the tasks of feminist theology is to name the out-of-body fantasies of male theology as the death-wishes they are.

Our visions of happiness, of peace, of contentment must be as embodied as life itself. To extol salvation as something other than a human condition is to envy the dead, unfeeling presence of machines. The only transcendence worth working for is one based on an awareness of our own contingency.

A second point I want to emphasise about "body" is that it is much more than dumb flesh. Bodily experience has a complexity that is often denied. Human bodies experience everything, even the most specific sensation, in a complex context of memory and wish. If our theories and social practices are to foster an awareness of body, they must show reverence for those parts of physicality which we usually call "emotions". Much of modern body culture treats our emotions as if they were separable from our physical selves. Hospitals, for example, are notorious for treating bodies like machines with defects to be fixed like broken parts on an assembly line.

The same is true of many modern sports in which athletes train to turn their bodies into mechanisms to perform tasks with absolute perfection. Medicine and sports are examples of practices that often disembody the body and turn it into a thing or an instrument. The awareness of body that I want to see would entail sensitivity to feelings, to histories and to the physical presence of friends and families. Our bodies would be understood as the sum of all our particular situations as created by a complex web of physical, social, emotional and historical contingencies.

Third, I want a feminist notion of body to expand the sense of the body politic. We must learn to feel the presence of more and more people on the planet. Survival probably depends on fostering sympathy among races and cultures. Feminism has a part to play here by exposing the objectification of all groups that are treated as "others". Our sense of self must permit an increasing identification with more and more of the human community.

In order to tolerate a more realistic relationship with more and more people, we must learn to stop both idealising and vilifying each other. We have to become much more sophisticated in our understanding of the human dynamics of envy and hatred.

This brings me to the last factor I want to see included in theories based in the body. I want to see "body" include what psychoanalysts have called the unconscious. Theories with body should be theories that take account of rage and desire; they should be theories that put our conscious awareness in the context of our unconscious wishes and fears. They should be theories that take cognizance of the "baser" drives of all human beings.

Now, religion has not been very good at taking account of what psychoanalysis has termed "instinct". Bodily loves and hates have been largely repressed in the name of goodness, godliness and spirituality. The result is that religion has functioned to cut us off from essential parts of ourselves.

The very words that we use to describe religious feelings depict those feelings as disembodied.

For example, a typical definition of "spiritual", taken from *Webster's New World Dictionary*, goes as follows:

> 1. of the spirit or the soul, often in a religious or moral aspect, as distinguished from the body.
> 2. of, from, or concerned with the intellect, or what is often thought of as the better or higher part of the mind.
> 3. of, or consisting of spirit; not corporeal.
> 4. characterized by the ascendancy of the spirit; showing much refinement of thought and feeling.[13]

In accordance with these definitions "spirituality" is identified as "spiritual character, quality, or nature: opposed to sensuality, worldliness" and "the fact or state of being incorporeal".[14]

Is "spirituality" a good word for what feminists are up to in Religious Studies? Or is it a limiting word — a word which implies that some parts of life are elevated and some are not? Doesn't "spirituality" say that some things are "sacred" and some are not? Doesn't "spirituality" give us an elitist, hierarchial notion of what experience is worth having?

Much feminist thought about religion is better than the word "spirituality". For example, in her work on women and religion,[15] Carol Christ analyses literature by women to arrive at an understanding of what she terms women's "spirituality". However, Christ does not idealise incorporeality nor does she praise states of being that are greatly set apart from the typical experiences of a life. Instead, she is interested in the expansion of sensibility and awareness within the stuff of women's lives. Christ's work, I would say, is thus better characterised as being about body than being about spirit. Perhaps our words have not yet caught up with us. Perhaps "spirituality" is a word that limits us in our conceptions of what we are doing by mystifying the direction of our best theories.

One domain of experience which the usual notions of "religion", "wholeness" and "spirituality" do not adequately address is that of human aggression. Anger is probably the aspect of body that is most poorly contained by our religious systems. An adequate understanding of rage could explain why we are motivated to split up our world in the first place. Therefore, I want to conclude on an angry note — by discussing aggression and how it is distorted by religiosity.

The theories of Melanie Klein, the late British psychoanalyst, say a great deal about the ways in which aggression underlies both our sense of vitality and our concern for others. Let me outline her theory.

Klein posited two psychological stages that culminate in the perception of oneself and other people as complex beings with good and bad aspects. The first stage of psychological life predominates in the first three or four months of infancy. It is characterised by the feeling that each event or experience is a separate concrete thing. The thing, or "object" in Klein's terms, corresponds to the infant's feelings at the moment. For example, the breast or bottle that feeds her is good; while the breast or bottle that frustrates her by its absence is bad. Klein thought that immature visual perception causes a baby to see the world in fragments. Her own body and that of her mother seem to be just so many disconnected good and bad parts that correspond to her experiences of satisfaction and frustration.

But in addition to visual immaturity, there is another reason for seeing the world in parts. Klein thought that babies and young children are afraid that the good, satisfying things in their world may be destroyed by the bad, frustrating things. The baby's sense of well-being, she believed, initially depends on the ability to keep the good and bad objects widely separated. Keeping absolutely good things far away from absolutely bad things is the baby's only defence against the fear that the two objects will meet and that the good things will be destroyed. The fear of the annihilation of good things, she wrote, amounts to the fear of death. Thus, maintaining experience in good and bad fragments is the earliest method each of us has for coping with this basic terror.

To keep good things far away from things that threaten them, Klein believed that young children split both themselves and other people into good and bad aspects. For example, negative feelings about parents are sometimes projected onto strangers who then seem terrifying. The strangers represent the fear and anger the child feels toward her own parents. The split object of parents/strangers is paralleled, Klein thought, by a split of love/hate in the child's ego. The frightening parts of both self and world are thus isolated and controlled.

Another way of making sure that aggressive feelings in the first stage of psychological development are kept at bay is for the child to exaggerate the goodness of pleasant things and people in her experience. Klein thought that children tend to idealise parents in order to control their fear of them and anger toward them. Although she thought that the ability to idealise parents provided important reassurances in childhood, she thought that it was essentially motivated by a fear of persecution. In order for the world to be seen more realistically, this fear must abate.

In Kleinian theory, what enables the world to come together for the child is confidence in the continuing presence of good objects inside her body. Klein believed that if the child could take in enough love and comfort, she would know that goodness existed inside her and that destruction was not imminent. The growing conviction that goodness resides within allows the child to permit aggression to be felt toward good objects. At this point, the second stage of psychological development begins.

In the second stage, psychic reality becomes "increasingly poignant"[16] as the child faces her own destructive feelings. In Klein's terminology, "persecutory anxiety" now changes to "depressive anxiety". Fear for oneself becomes fear for others. Klein suggested that the various inhibitions that small children develop might be techniques to keep depressive anxiety at bay. The refusal to eat, for example, might be an attempt to restrain the wish to bite — an action which, in the child's fantasy, might signify a desire to harm people she loves.

When self and world are more unified, compassion for people becomes possible. Klein wrote that "when...destructive impulses and phantasies are felt to be directed against the complete person of a loved object, guilt arises in full strength and, together with it, the over-riding urge to repair, preserve or revive the loved injured object."[17] Klein labelled the tendency to cherish and maintain good internal feelings as the desire to do "reparation". She saw all constructive activities in life, all creative work, all caring behaviour as expressions of this urge to aid, nourish and sustain what she terms "the good object".

I want to stress that for Klein the key motive behind the need to care both for people and for work was guilt. Because the person can feel the capacity to destroy life, she or he is continually moved to protect and nourish life. If aggression is not experienced, it will be split off; and thus the motive for concern about the world will be absent. Then the person will experience his or her own aggression solely in paranoid form as an alien force threatening the self. This persecutory anxiety will dominate; and the intellect and personality will be restricted along with the capacity to care about other people. Klein believed that it is in the second state that the so-called depressive type of anxiety spurs the child "to project, deflect and distribute desire and emotion...on to new objects and interests."[18] In Klein's thought, it is the guilt and concern that we feel over our desires to destroy our first loved objects which urges us both to explore the world and to cherish it.

Klein told us that aggression is essential to life. She saw it as an instinct and thus as a source of vitality. If we can not digest aggression, her theory says, we lose interest in the world and we feel frightened. We are then moved to split the world and ourselves into idealised all-good parts and despised all-bad parts. It is then that aggression becomes very dangerous.

Now, if Klein is right, religion has encouraged us to become perilously out of touch with our aggression. Let me illustrate this with two arguments.

First, I suggest that the idea that we have "bodies" and "souls" functions as a way of splitting off anger. The body is where religious thought has dumped aggression. While the soul has been seen as pure, valuable, loving and eternally alive, the body has been viewed as tainted, expendable and the vehicle of death.

This image of the physical, human world as the place of death and fault is preserved in such modern dualistic psychologies as Jungian psychology or archetypal psychology. Although these systems of thought try to place value on the physical world, they fail because the concepts of the deathless "archetypes", of a cherished trans-human "psyche", or of a grandiose "self" or "spirit" become the idealised, split-off portions of people and their world.

I suggest that these religions and religious philosophies that separate the body from the soul are really separating anger and love. And, if Klein is right, it is the splitting off of human anger from human love that truly promotes a deadened world and causes hate to search out a scapegoat.

A second idea that puts us dangerously out of touch with aggression is our idealisation of God. The Old and New Testaments are rife with examples of parent-child hostility. In the Old Testament we have God's frequent punishment of Israel; and in the New, we have God's complicity in the murder of his son. ("My God, my God why hast thou forsaken me?") God's portrait as an angry, jealous and sadistic parent depicts an awareness of the aggression we feel within ourselves and our parents. Christian theologians thoughout the ages have largely turned away from the negative aspects of the divine parent-child relationship. Their refusal to recognise hostility within the paternal image of God has encouraged some devotees of the Christian God literally to blame Christ's murder on a group of outsiders, the Jews. By identifying themselves with an idealised concept of God, Christians have, perhaps, at certain periods in history, escaped adequate recognition of their own malice.

Let me quickly add that I have the same concern about the idealisation of God in Judaism. Although the God of Judaism is often wrathful, his anger is continually justified as being caused by the transgressions of His children. All of God's deeds, no matter how disproportionate in their cruelty, are generally explained away. Fairness and humane treatment of others is thought to be a given in the Jewish way of life, partly because the God whom the rules honour is Himself just. Jews, I think, tend to idealise themselves as followers of such a God and perhaps have become too complacent about the danger of their own aggression. Part of the Jewish unwillingness to criticise the state of Israel about its violations of human rights might stem partly from a long-standing idealisation of the Jewish sense of justice.

We ought not to allow our religious systems to ignore the wrath of God or Goddess. It is the idealisation of a deity that encourages us to ignore important portions of ourselves. In 1933 Melanie Klein wrote that "the repeated attempts that have been made to improve humanity — in particular to make it more peaceable — have failed, because nobody has understood the full depth and vigour of the instincts of aggression innate in each individual. Such efforts do not seek to do more than encourage the positive, well-wishing impulses of the person while denying or suppressing the aggressive ones. And so they have been doomed to failure from the beginning."[19]

In contrast to many "repeated attempts to improve humanity", I think feminist theory has a better chance. Feminism may well give birth to ways of thinking that successfully promote compassion and vitality. The deadness of modern patriarchy arises from the fragmentation of human experience and human communities. Women are countering this deadness by bringing to light what has been split off. In our thinking we oppose fragmentation and stand up for liveliness and peace when we concentrate on what I have called body — when we concentrate on bringing more and more of human experience into the purview of theory.

REFERENCES

1 The conference on "Feminism, Spirituality and Wholeness" was held at the Institute for Religion and Wholeness, at the Claremont School of Theology, Claremont, California in April of 1985.

2 Susan Sontag, *On Photography* (New York: Farrar, Straus and Giroux), 1973.

3 For the classic argument about why men tend to distance themselves from intimate experience see Nancy Chodorow, *The Reproduction of Mothering* (Berkeley: University of California Press), 1978.

4 Norman O. Brown, *Life Against Death* (New York: Random House), 1959, p. 317.

5 Naomi Goldenberg, "Archetypal Theory and the Separation of Mind and Body". *Journal of Feminist Studies in Religion*, Vol. I, No. 1, 1984, pp. 55 - 72.

6 Elaine Marks and Isabelle de Courtivron, eds., *New French Feminism: An Anthology* (New York: Schocken Books), 1981, p. 183.

7 Dorothy Dinnerstein, *The Mermaid and the Minotaur: Sexual Arrangements and Human Malaise* (New York: Harper & Row), 1976.

8 See, for example, the discussion of politics, science and philosophy in the essays included in *Discovering Reality*, Sandra Harding and Merrill B. Hintikka, eds. (Boston, MA: D. Reidel Publishing Co.), 1983. "Gender and Science", pp. 187 - 206, by Evelyn Fox Keller is particularly interesting.

9 Nancy Chodorow, *The Reproduction of Mothering, op. cit.*

10 Hans Küng, *Does God Exist?*, trans. Edward Quinn (Garden City, New York: Doubleday & Co., 1980), p. 301.

11 *Ibid.*, p. 333.

12 *Ibid.*, p. 329.

13 *Webster's New World Dictionary, College Edition* (Cleveland and New York: The World Publishing Co.), 1955, p. 1406.

14 *Ibid.*, p. 2.

15 Carol Christ, *Diving Deep and Surfacing: Women Writers on Spiritual Quest* (Boston: Beacon Press), 1980.

16 Melanie Klein, "The Emotional Life of the Infant", in *Envy and Gratitude and Other Works 1946 - 1963* (Delacorte Press, Seymour Lawrence), 1975, p. 73.

17 *Ibid.*, p. 74.

18 *Ibid.*, p. 83.

19 Melanie Klein, "The Early Development of Conscience in the Child," in *Love, Guilt and Reparation and Other Works 1921 — 1945* (Delacorte Press, Seymour Lawrence), 1975, p. 257.

FURTHER READING

Chodorow, Nancy, *The Reproduction of Mothering* (Berkeley: University of California Press), 1978.

Christ, Carol, *Diving Deep and Surfacing: Women Writers on Spiritual Quest* (Boston: Beacon Press), 1980.

Dinnerstein, Dorothy, *The Mermaid and the Minotaur: Sexual Arrangements and Human Malaise* (New York: Harper & Row), 1976.

Harding, Sandra, and Merrill B. Hintikka, eds., *Discovering Reality* (Boston, MA: D. Reidel Publishing Co.), 1983.

Spretnak, Charlene, ed., *The Politics of Women's Spirituality — Essays on the Rise of Spiritual Power within the Feminist Movement* (New York: Doubleday/Anchor Books), 1982.

JUDITH POSNER

The Objectified Male: The New Male Image in Advertising

The burgeoning literature on pornography, and the escalating debate on censorship have developed in large part out of the contemporary feminist movement. This association implies that the commodification or commercialisation of sex is strictly a woman's issue.[1] Although it is evident that to date North American and even Western society as a whole has exploited female sexuality in particular, the changing imagery of thc male is also of interest. If one result of the contemporary women's movement has been the general liberation from traditional sex stereotyped behaviours, then an important aspect of male liberation is the gradual softening and objectification of masculine demeanour. Even an analysis of something as trivial as the male purse or pouch directs our attention to the relationship between changing fashion and demeanour and sex-role ideology; for example, the male purse is associated with tighter-fitting pants that make billfolds and other pocketed paraphernalia obsolete. The proliferation of beefcake and male stripping are other examples of this trend. In short, the analysis of changing images of men in fashion, the media, and advertising in particular, reveals that sexual exploitation is not just a feminist issue. In this chapter I will delineate some of the visual configurations that constitute a changing male image, and discuss its socio-political implications. Specifically, I wish to address the question of whether the softening of the male media depiction reflects equalitarian ideology or part of the burgeoning elaboration of the commodification of sexuality.

In the tradition of Erving Goffman[2] who applies a dramaturgical or theatrical perspective to the analysis of print ads, it is possible to identify

Originally published in the *Atkinson Review* (Toronto: York University), Vol. 1, No. 2 (Spring 1984), pp. 17-22.

PLATE 10.1

PLATE 10.2

PLATE 10.3

PLATE 10.4

body language, facial expression and proxemic patterns that are associated with dominance and submission. While Goffman focusses specifically on the female, as does most research on sex-role stereotyping, it is also possible to apply reciprocal concepts to the male. If women are associated with head cocks, pelvic tilts, knee bends and smiling expressions (see Plate 10.1), then men are by definition full frontal, straight and stern (see Plate 10.2). Such a dichotomy accounts rather neatly for traditional images of men and women in advertising. In looking at Plate 10.2, the traditional macho male, our attention is drawn especially to the dominant jutting jaw and accompanying stiff upper lip; "real" men don't smile.

Objectification refers to the object-like character of the visual image. Such an image connotes passivity, vulnerability and property. In its most extreme form it alludes to victimisation. This can be contrasted with the traditional masculine image which is subject-like: powerful, active, and doing. Furthermore, a major feature of women's objectification is her trivialisation or infantilisation. The notion that children are objects or non-persons in our society is certainly not a new one. What is interesting here, however, is the extent to which the female presentation of self — that is, body language, facial expression, and so on — is based on a child's interaction style. It is cute, silly and trivialised (see Plate 10.3). It is also relevant to point out that there is a very obvious association here between infantilised posturing and "cheesecake", i.e., the traditional erotic posing.[3] This relationship merely reflects the fact that women are erotic by virtue of their innocence and naïveté. This theme is particularly applicable in contemporary pornography with its emphasis on prepubertal-looking models.

This discrepancy in erotic gender presentation is also reflected in the double standard of nudity revealed in both popular and high culture. Because nudity connotes vulnerability we are more accustomed to seeing the

PLATE 10.5

PLATE 10.6

male form clothed even in classical painting; for example, Manet's *Le dejeuner sur l'herbe*, which depicts fully clothed males and fully disrobed females enjoying an eroticised picnic. Contemporary imagery still reflects this double standard. (See Plates 10.12 and 10.13 to follow.)

The relationship of objectification, infantilisation, and eroticisation to gender is also inadvertently suggested by Linda Nochlin in her analysis of a classic nineteenth century French magazine image titled *Achetez des pommes*. It depicts a half-nude female, complete with pelvic tilt, head cock, and breasts hanging over a tray of apples. In order to understand how the fruit metaphor works Nochlin asked a male to strike a reciprocal pose *vis-a-vis* bananas. A picture speaks a thousand words! The male parallel is nothing short of ludicrous and reveals to us our deeply ingrained notions of male-female eroticisation. In fact, although Nochlin does not discuss these concepts explicitly, her work reveals the association of infantilisation and trivialisation with female eroticisation. Because male eroticisation has been more intimately connected to dominance, power and aggression, mass media portrayal of male sexuality has tended to take the form of the Marlboro Man, fully dressed and stooped over an open fire. Similarly, *Playgirl* magazine, at least in its earlier issues, seemed to have difficulty coming up with successful erotic male depiction, therefore resorting to awkward looking nude males, attired only in sneakers, leaning casually against a Camaro.

Before turning to some recent imagery in men's fashion magazines, a few comments are in order about the source of these materials and their regional specificity. Many of these images are taken from *Gentleman's Quarterly*, the top men's fashion magazine in North America, analogues to *Vogue* for women. While such magazines are not statistically representative of popular fashion, they certainly reflect the tip of the iceberg and the shape of things to come. In other words the underlying aesthetics of more avant garde publications eventually filter down to the general public, albeit in diluted form.

In regard to the Canadian question, it is quite impossible to separate American and Canadian fashion trends and advertising imagery. Since top American fashion magazines dominate the Canadian market, there is no basis for positing a distinct aesthetic. More importantly, while the Canadian advertising industry is somewhat more conservative and more regulated than its American counterpart, we receive much of the imagery in its original American-produced form.[5]

If Plate 10.2 represents the traditional '60s male, then Plate 10.4 represents the contemporary male image. Although the actual body position is still full frontal, the men exude a more relaxed casual air, with hands in pockets. More importantly, even their body type reflects the new male image in that they are significantly more slight than their predecessors. It is

PLATE 10.7

PLATE 10.8

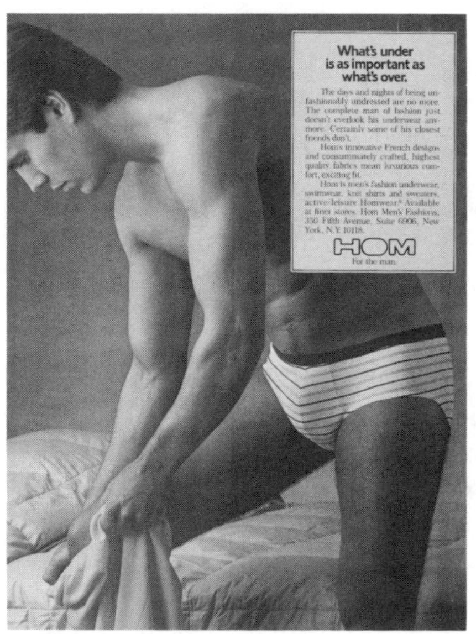

PLATE 10.9

PLATE 10.10

also noted that their more vulnerable physique is accompanied by less pronounced jaw structures and concomitantly smiling facial expressions. Plate 10.5 is interesting because of the crossed-leg posture, once considered effeminate for North American men. In Plate 10.6 the model exhibits a casual hand-in-pocket stance combined with a modest head pose. While it may be hard to prove that any one set of pictures or particular magazine fully reflects the ideal male at any particular point in time, it is certainly true that Plates 10.5 and 10.6, although undramatic examples of contemporary male depiction, would never have appeared ten or fifteen years ago in a major men's magazine or advertising brochure. Now such images are relatively commonplace.

A more unusual example of changing body language and facial expression for men, however, is Plate 10.7, which illustrates a full-fledged head cock that is striking in its infantilisation. Additionally, Plate 10.8 is an excellent example of role reversal *vis-à-vis* the concept of gaze.[6] The female presents a cool, disinterested demeanour complete with sunglasses, while the male sex object, complete with pelvic tilt, maternal hand-to-hip pose, connects quite directly with the viewer's gaze. Note, too, the new addition of male genital bulge. Until recently, male erotic parts were air-brushed out while female ones were frequently air-brushed in. And Plate 10.9 is a classic example of a toilette depiction in the tradition of classical painting, such as Degas or Lautrec. The self-touching, narcissistic quality to the depiction is surely something Goffman never envisioned when he wrote *Gender Advertisements*!

> Self touching can also be involved, readable as conveying a sense of one's body being a delicate and precious thing.[7]

Plate 10.10 is a classic example of disrobement. The depiction of the process of undressing can be more erotic than the naked form itself, because the process of disrobement engages the viewer voyeuristically. Finally, Plate 10.11 is such an extraordinary example of popular male depiction that it is almost too much to bear. Yet we are practically immune to seeing women in similar portrayals. First of all, the image emphasises the buttocks both by posture and photographic angle, thus reflecting research that indicates that, contrary to what most men think, the rear, not the phallus, is the focus of visual arousal for women. Secondly, the presentation of the male to the viewer is a vulnerable one, reminiscent of cheesecake poses in which the model looks back over the buttocks at the viewer. But thirdly, and more importantly, is the use of the wet bathing suit, which emphasises the body's contours. In fact, the perfect parallel to this particular male pose is a classic poster from the '70s which depicted Raquel Welch in a wet T-shirt. Yet, even though these examples do depict the male as more vulnerable, he is still

PLATE 10.11

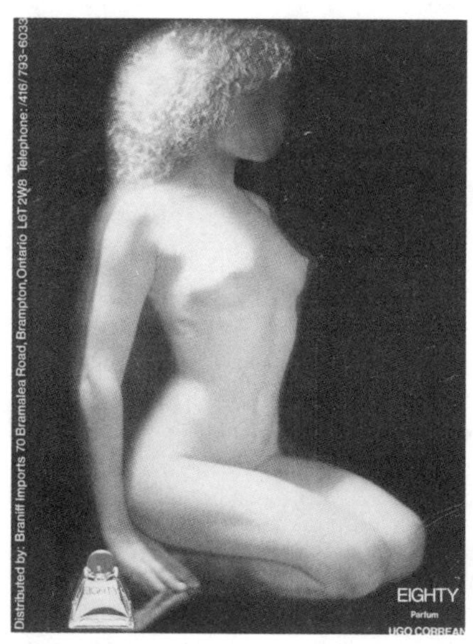

PLATE 10.12

PLATE 10.13

not as passive as his female counterpart. In this regard it is interesting to note that one of several slide shows in the States dealing with images of men in advertising is called *Stale Roles, Tight Bums*, a title that reverberates rather nicely the nature of male depiction. In short, no matter how elaborate the eroticisation, the male body still tends to be muscularly taut as epitomised by Plate 10.11, thus contradicting the otherwise voyeuristic, objectified component.

It should come as no surprise to anyone, then, when it is suggested that there is a peculiar similarity between a gay aesthetic, even gay pornography, and the middle-class androgynous ideal, reflected in contemporary fashion magazines, store windows and a variety of other forms of popular culture. In fact, when presenting slide materials on this subject it is not uncommon for the audience to react with disbelief at some of the *Gentleman's Quarterly* ads. And inevitably, there are remarks concerning the sexual preference of its readership. Since a major men's fashion magazine could not possibly afford to direct its efforts to an exclusively homosexual audience, we cannot understand the appeal of its imagery by dismissing it in this way. Rather, the popularity of such magazines as *G.Q.* must be saying something quite general about a changing masculine aesthetic, and one that is strangely compatible with gay ideology.[8]

What is surprising, however, is the peculiar paradox that underlies the changing demeanour and visual depiction of the North American male. We live in a culture that is obsessed with gender and sex-role segregation, and concomitantly one which is decidedly homophobic. Yet we are witnessing a change in masculine demeanour which seems to contradict traditional macho ideology.[9] While, for women, the increasing eroticisation and sexual exploitation has been viewed as another example of sexist patriarchal ideology, there is something peculiarly paradoxical about the concomitant increasing eroticisation of men. On the one hand, it tends to equalise the power dimension inherent in such an issue; in fact, it suggests a sort of androgynous ideology that might be compatible with feminist ideology. On the other hand, the eroticisation of males may have very little to do with any ideological issues whatsoever. Rather, it may merely reflect the increasing commercial exploitation of sexuality, a trend that was once "for women only", and has recently been extended to include men, children, the aged and even cats and dogs. (We know that the commercialisation of sex has reached a new high when even cat food is presented in an eroticised format — as epitomised by the long-running TV commercial "Miss Mew, Miss Mew, how are you?" which features a buxom feline complete with false eyelashes and sultry voice being lusted after by a variety of toms.) Just as women's liberation rhetoric has been co-opted by the advertising industry (for instance, sanitary napkins called *New Freedom*), so has a feminine/gay aesthetic.

Lastly, it is appropriate to end with current examples of contemporary advertising from a recent issue of a Toronto magazine that illustrate this point succinctly. Plates 10.12 and 10.13 are two side-by-side, full-page ads that promote corporate cousins, female and male perfumes respectively. Both ads are erotic. Both depict nude models. Both use light and shadows to produce a dramatic, sensual tone. The female is reminiscent of something from *Playboy*, and the male counterpart is reminiscent of images in gay magazines. But what is most striking about this unusual instance of gender parallel advertising is the degree to which the female image is objectified *vis-à-vis* the male. This is epitomised by her anonymity: she lacks a face. Similarly, only the female's entire nude body is depicted. Although the male image is also highly eroticised and objectified (he poses like a pin-up; he is involved in no other activity beyond his presentation of self; in short, he is narcissist) the gender gap is still apparent. This example reveals quite clearly that the new style of male eroticisation has little to do with sex-role liberation, and much to do with the increasing commercialisation of sexuality. In short, if men are being more eroticised and objectified, then women are as well. In the final analysis, when it comes to the commodification of sexuality, the gender gap is not really changing. Rather, it would appear, we have merely upped the ante.

REFERENCES

1 Contemporary feminist literature on pornography that reflects this bias includes Andrea Dworkin, *Pornography: Men Possessing Women*, New York, 1979; Susan Griffen, *Pornography and Silence*, New York: Harper & Row, 1981; and Laura Lederer, ed., *Take Back the Night*, New York: Bantam, 1980. In Canada, Susan Cole, an editor of *Broadside*, and well-known public commentator on the subject, reflects a similar view.

2 *Gender Advertisements*, New York: Harper & Row, 1976.

3 Although Mark Gabor does not actually discuss the issue, a quick scanning of his book on the history, *The Pin-up*, New York: Universe Books, 1972, illustrates this point rather nicely.

4 Linda Nochlin, *Woman as Sex Object*, New York: Newsweek Inc., 1972.

5 An unusual but interesting case in point is a recent Calvin Klein ad for men's-style women's underwear. It depicted an erotically reclined female in underwear and matching undershirt pushed up over her breasts. While the Canadian company has recently adapted this image for Canadian billboards so that almost all the breast is covered, we still receive the original depiction in *Vogue* magazine and a variety of other imported publications.

6 John Berger's excellent series, *Ways of Seeing*, Part II, is relevant here. In it he focusses on the female nude in nineteenth century European painting, and elaborates on the gaze of the objectified female *vis-à-vis* the male spectator.

7 *Gender Advertisements*, p. 31.
8 For example, Michael Jackson, recent recipient of a variety of pop music awards, epitomises the androgynous demeanour of the contemporary male.
9 In a similar light, it is quite instructive to analyse male stripping from this perspective. The costumes worn, the body movements and facial expressions all suggest a similar style of changing eroticisation, and it is interesting to note that it is certainly not unusual to find male strippers who are gay. Given that in our culture straight males are traditionally not socialised into presenting themselves as sexual objects, this is not really very surprising.

FURTHER READING

Berger, John, *Ways of Seeing*. London: Penguin Books, 1972.
Courtney, Alice, and Tomas Whipple, *Sex Stereotyping in Advertising*. Lexington, MA: D.C. Heath & Co., 1983.
Gabor, Mark, *The Pin-up*. New York: Universe Books, 1972.
Goffman, Erving, *Gender Advertisements*. New York: Harper & Row, 1976.
Root, Jane, *Pictures of Women*. London: Routledge & Kegan Paul, Pandora Press, 1984.

IAN LUMSDEN

Sexuality and the State: The Politics of "Normal" Sexuality

The good Lord created woman for man. God created man and woman; that is normal, natural and proper.

Real Caouette, M.P.[1]

We live in a society in which sexuality has become pre-eminent. We are saturated by its images on outdoor billboards and on indoor television screens. It permeates our private fantasies and our pursuit of happiness. Our politicians and public figures are judged by their sex appeal; and they, in turn, increasingly manipulate our sexual preoccupations.

In Ontario, and perhaps even more so in the rest of Canada, sexuality has not yet acquired the polarising force it has attained in the United States — home of the Moral Majority and the New Right. But recent public struggles over pornography, abortion, gay rights, and sex education in schools, to name but a few issues, increasingly compel people to respond to the new sexual politics.

This has taken many Canadians by surprise, for sex is experienced by most people as something intensely personal and private. As Robert Kaplan, former Solicitor-General once noted, "There are few Canadians who would believe that laws exist governing voluntary private sexual conduct between a husband and wife or between unmarried couples of the opposite sex."[2] Sexual acts, at least insofar as they involve heterosexual couples, are perceived as being "natural". It follows that they should not, and even could not, be subject to public regulation. Hence the long-standing reluctance to acknowledge — let alone eradicate — the violent sex-

Originally published in the *Atkinson Review* (Toronto: York University), Vol. 1, No. 2 (Spring 1984), pp. 3-9.

ual abuse of women and children that takes place within the privacy of many homes.

The largely uncontested power of husbands and fathers offers a clue to the character of "normal" sexuality. It is heterosexual and patriarchal.[3] It is legitimised by the fact that it takes place between males and females, preferably within the privacy of family homes. If these conditions are met, anything goes. As John Turner, then Minister of Justice, admitted in 1969 during a parliamentary debate over homosexuality, "homosexual" [sic] and "indecent" acts, otherwise illegal if committed by two people under twenty-one years of age, are not an offence if they are committed in private by a husband and wife under that age.[4] The absurd contradiction of "homosexual" acts being committed by heterosexual couples is also an illustration of the fact that the contemporary state is more concerned with the regulation of sexual *identities* than sexual *acts.*[5]

Parents, according to the dominant ideology, have primary responsibility for upholding respectable sexual standards amongst their offspring. Only when parents are unable to do so should society intervene. Once the borderline has been crossed separating "abnormal" from "natural" behaviour, a variety of public institutions should be resorted to — the church, welfare agencies, psychiatric medicine, police, reform schools and even prisons — so as to uphold "normal" sexual practices, and to contain deviancy. This is as true today as it was in 1969, when Stanley Knowles, M.P., noted approvingly that society and state were "doing [their] best to prevent the spread of sexual irregularities."[6]

Related to the belief in the essentially private nature of sexuality is the notion that, in spite of the widespread representation of sexuality in the mass media and popular culture, information about actual sexual practice should be restricted. It is not to be depicted in all its variety on the screens; furthermore, it is not to be taught in schools; nor is it to be discussed between parents and children within the home other than in terms of the most narrow heterosexual norms. Consequently, most of us are deprived of any opportunity to learn about the diversity of sexual fantasy, desire and practice that is probably far more extensive than we imagine (or are allowed to imagine). Women, in particular, have suffered most in this respect.

The prevalent assumption, then, is that something that is as "natural" as sexuality should be allowed to develop freely within the individual, in the belief that it will naturally accord with the behaviour that is believed to be appropriate to one's biological sex. From one point of view these sexual arrangements work very well insofar as the vast majority of people, at least until very recently, are perceived as subscribing to the values that revolve around assumptions about "natural" sexuality. At no time has this been more clearly illustrated than in the lengthy parliamentary debate over the revision of the Criminal Code's treatment of homosexuality and abortion in

1969. Every single speaker, of whatever political persuasion, agreed upon the "normal" and "natural" character of (hetero)sexuality, even as they disagreed as to whether "abnormal", "unnatural" (homo)sexuality was a voluntary deviation, a sickness, an illness, a perversion, a sin or a crime.

Nevertheless, in large part as a result of the feminist and gay movements, questions about the "naturalness" of sexual desire have been increasingly raised in public. There is increasing agreement, too, amongst academic scholars, that sexuality is "normal" only in the sense that in every society there seem to be dominant norms regarding sexuality and gender that are socially and politically enforced.[7] It is equally apparent, however, that beliefs and practices related to sexuality have varied historically and continue to do so across contemporary cultures. As Jeffrey Weeks, the British sexual historian, explains:

> The sexual potentialities of the body have been integrated into a vast range of different social contexts; from pedagogic relations and puberty rites, to fertility cults and religious ceremonial. Some cultures have seen no connection between sexual intercourse and conception; others have seen the only justification for sex is reproduction. Some cultures have made little distinction between heterosexual and homosexual forms, concentrating on the age or class of the partner; our culture has made the distinction of prime social significance. In some societies, sex is a simple source of pleasure, a key to the glorification of the erotic arts; in others it is a source of danger and taboo, of mortification of the flesh.[8]

Thomas Szasz, the radical psychiatrist and social critic, offers a graphic illustration. "In the nineteenth century, masturbating was an illness and not masturbating was a treatment; today, not masturbating is a disease and masturbating is a treatment."[9] In this light, it is obvious that there is nothing natural or normal about sexual practice.

Biological factors cannot be discounted as having some impact in determining sexual behaviour — for example, with respect to the relationship of conception and reproduction to the physiology and sexual responses of women. But the wide variation in the manifestation of sexual practice coupled with the hegemonic enforcement of specific norms within given societies, leads to the conclusion that sexuality, particularly the content of sexual desire, is primarily a social construct. Thus, the need for sex is not determined by its relationship to human procreation; rather, this need is determined by the way in which social relations, particularly family and kinship ones, are affected by the organisation of work, consumption and knowledge, and by the intervention of a variety of religious, medical and state agencies. These in turn are mediated for individuals, at unconscious as well as conscious levels, by their experience of growing up with specific class-bound families. "Sex will always be permeated with meanings that attach to individual and social parameters.''[10] It follows, then, that sexual desire, for the most part, originates in our heads rather than in our groins or hearts.

Insofar as there is no inborn sexual desire, it is misleading to talk about the repression of natural sexuality with respect to individuals or to whole societies. It is equally misleading to posit the existence of unencumbered sexual practice in either romanticised Polynesian islands or in idealised future sexual nirvanas freed from all social constraints. Future states may well vary in the degree to which individual sexual expression is regulated, but it is unlikely that sexual desire can ever be unaffected by the social environment.

Nevertheless, it is true that many people experience their sexuality as being repressive; that is, they feel that their desires and needs cannot be expressed or satisfied, either because of external compulsion or because of internalised restrictive social mores. The frustration and anger of women and of homosexuals at having been denied the right to express and gratify their sexual needs as freely as heterosexual men is by now commonplace knowledge. Their growing resistance to this situation is a reminder of something that has always been the case — the social construction and regulation of sexuality is not totally imposed upon us from above.

The major institutions that affect collective sexual behaviour in our society are subordinate to the interests of the dominant economic class, which in turn is largely composed of men imbued with heterosexual and patriarchal values. The institutions that I have in mind include the large corporations, which control not only the content of advertising and hence of consumption, as well as the mass media, which depend upon advertising revenue, and the entertainment industry. Schools, universities, and most non-profit foundations also fit into this category. These institutions promote and disseminate economic and political beliefs consistent with the interests of the dominant economic class. Moreover, they also further the heterosexist values, which legitimise the prerogatives of heterosexual males, encourage the sexual and emotional dependence of women upon men, and invalidate homosexuality. For neither radical feminists nor openly gay men are to be found at the pinnacle of power in our society. In addition to these institutions, which support the hegemony of heterosexual patriarchal values, there are state agencies that are specifically empowered to intervene in and regulate our sexual lives, such as law courts, the police force, censor boards and welfare agencies.

Public institutions that affect the social construction and regulation of sexuality are dominated by the male corporate rich in a capitalist society, but do not and cannot have total control, particularly in a society such as Canada's that is imbued with liberal market values. The remainder of the population are not mere spectators, incapable of affecting society's culture and public policy. At the very least, there are always minorities that resist and defend their positions, and fight for political change.

Struggles over sexual rights and freedoms have recently become more evident, be it in the streets, the law courts or the legislative buildings. Though the women's and gay liberation movements took the initiative in bringing the sexual dimension into the political arena, they have increasingly been surpassed by the forces of what have become known as the Moral Majority and the New Right. The latter's ability to mobilise anxious and alienated elements within the middle and skilled working classes, who see the chances of being able to enjoy the American way of life threatened at every turn, should not be underestimated, as evidenced by the defeat of the Equal Rights Amendment, and the growing support for the proposed constitutional amendment that would outlaw any form of abortion.

In Ontario the repressive underbelly of Progressive Conservatism has begun to show itself, seeking to reverse many of the gains made by women and gays in the previous decade. The police and former Attorney General Roy McMurtry have paved the way onto which the extreme Right, epitomised by former *Toronto Sun* editor, Peter Worthington, will try to steer the new conservatism of Brian Mulroney. In Canada, as in the United States, the New Right offers no effective solution to the deepening social crisis, but it can reassure the middle class by counter-attacking those who have dared to question its values. The interminable vendetta against the *Body Politic*, prosecuted for publishing allegedly obscene material despite its double acquittal in the lower courts, the violent bathhouse raids, reminiscent of Grade B movies, by hundreds of police, and similar dramatic raids upon the Morgentaler Abortion Clinic have led the way.

The Ontario Board of Censorship plays a particularly important role in demonstrating more subtle ways to control women. In the name of decent community standards, it censors feminist films, like *Not a Love Story*; and its chairperson, Mary Brown, has harangued the film industry for producing anti-war films, like *Coming Home*, which allegedly undermine family values.[11] The family role model which she, like the Ontario Government, advocates, is no less than the Trapp family in *The Sound of Music*![12] Though the new anti-pornography crusaders claim to be concerned with the rights of women, their policies have little to do with the basic concerns of the feminists who raised the issue of pornography in the first place — namely, the real economic and sexual oppression of women, which underlies their devaluation in pornography and which is part and parcel of any patriarchal capitalist society. In fact, the movements that now purport to protect women from sexual exploitation are increasingly being dominated by forces that would curtail their freedoms with respect to reproductive rights, sexual orientation and sexual fulfilment *per se*, as well as the right to equal pay, and day care.

Heterosexist agitation is clearly an integral component of the Right's response to the deepening social and economic crisis of the United States and Canada. It need hardly be added that the volume of its denunciations is, in part, a reflection of the irreconcilable contradictions that are increasingly undermining the traditional family, that bastion of male domination and women's oppression. True, far more women than men are materially deprived by divorces, which verge on terminating one out of every other marriage, but it is unreconstructed men rather than women who have proved incapable of responding positively (in sexual and non-sexual terms) to these new trends. Heterosexual males and the dominant economic class may control the representation of sexuality in our society, but they no longer have overwhelming control over the practice of sexuality.

Women are frequently and typically poorer if they decide to terminate a dependent monogamous relationship with their husband: inevitably so, so long as they receive 60 per cent of men's incomes, and fathers renege on support payments for their children. Despite this, women are discovering in ever-increasing numbers that there is life beyond marriage. Women have rediscovered women, whether their relationships are sexual, despite all efforts to make such an option invisible, or are composed of platonic bonding and support networks. Homosexual men, too, have created an ever-expanding gay community to develop a wide variety of social ties with other men. The overwhelming majority of heterosexual married men, on the other hand, have remained "straight", not merely in the popular usage of the word, but in their failure to develop alternative or additional means of satisfying needs for companionship, intimacy and sexuality. Their lives are still dominated by their work and careers. They may bond with other men in public rituals, but no intimacy is developed; they may have sex with new female conquests, but never friendship. Unlike their wives, there is no life beyond marriage for them, a fact that is compounded by the increasingly oppressive and alienated character of their work and leisure. Only women can give meaning to the personal life of heterosexual men. Isn't this the explanation behind the urgency with which separated men seek replacement substitutes for their former wives? For masculinity has been constructed in such a way, particularly at the psychic level, that men "have come to suppress relational capacities and repress relational needs."[13] The material domination of women by heterosexual men in the public and private spheres masks men's utter dependence upon them for emotional and personal sustenance.

Heterosexual males are dominant in the main regulatory institutions of the state — a logical consequence of its patriarchal character. But it is also significant that they predominate in the political and intellectual institutions from which a critical response to the New Right's sexual politics might be expected to emerge. Most heterosexual males, while not necessarily homophobic and anti-feminist, do not recognise the centrality of sexual politics to other people's lives largely because their own sexual and gender needs are relatively accommodated and reinforced by the system. While we must be cautious about making facile parallels between the oppression of women and gays, and so obscuring real differences — particularly economic ones — in the process, most feminists and gay men have no difficulty in agreeing upon one fact: the virtual impossibility of communicating to "straight" men of all classes that cultural and sexual oppression is every bit as real and concrete for its victims as is economic exploitation.

We should not be surprised to find that the NDP, for example (barring isolated and honourable exceptions such as Svend Robinson, M.P.) is at best a co-opter of issues raised by feminists and gays at the grass roots outside the party. While an NDP government in Manitoba prosecutes abortion clinics, and NDP opposition leaders like Michael Cassidy in Ontario reassure voters prior to elections that "gay rights are not a priority for the party,"[14] the NDP will continue to vacate the field of sexual politics to the Right. It also becomes marginalised from the vast majority of activists within the women's and gay movements. In as much as feminists, gays and lesbians remain within the NDP, it is clearly *faute de mieux*, and explicable only in terms of the belief that, for the moment, it is the sole significant party that can pretend to have links with the working class whose potential strength is an indispensable element for any effective challenge to the patriarchal capitalist state.

The response of male academics is very similar to that of their counterparts in the NDP. If it is true that a significant number of radical scholars have emerged in Canadian universities over the last two decades, it is no less true that their analysis of Canadian politics and society has primarily been concerned with questions of political economy. If academics in Canadian universities — typically heterosexual males — have any concern about the relationship of heterosexism to the social relations of the contemporary capitalist state, or about the legitimacy of the resistance of dominated groups, be they feminist women, lesbians or gays, with respect to sexual oppression, they have muted it. Even when the centrality of sex is recognised, it is desexualised insofar as the focus of analysis is restricted to questions of biological reproduction and gender roles.[15] The oppression of women, for example, tends to be intepreted in terms of raising children, domestic labour, and unequal wages. These are important issues, to be sure, but the impact upon women of sexuality, of its social construction and regulation in a heterosexist society, is simply ignored. To overlook the fact that our roles and identities stem from other aspects of sexuality than gender and biological sex is to make a profound mistake that is not only complicit in the silencing of lesbians but has implications for all women. Tiresome as it may seem to repeat the obvious, women become pregnant and raise children, but they also have sex to meet a variety of non-procreative needs 99 per cent of the time. In our culture, sexuality is not only motivated by the pursuit of pleasure but also by the need to express a range of other feelings related to intimacy, dependency and even hostility.[16]

In actual practice, the regulation of the reproductive role of women is connected to limiting their autonomy and non-procreative sex. The "pro-life" forces are as concerned with punishing women who dare to assert their sexual independence as they are with protecting the future of the foetus. If the latter were their real concern, they would not give their allegiance to governments such as those of Ronald Reagan, and William Bennett in British Columbia, whose savage cutbacks in social security benefits and employment opportunities for women have done more to destroy the possibility of a mother being able to care for her future child than anything else.

Furthermore, since patriarchal society is based upon the hegemony of heterosexual masculine men, it must also perforce respond to those whose presence puts it in question. Thus lesbians threaten heterosexist men as role models for women with respect to their economic as well as sexual independence. For these reasons it is as important to render them invisible as it is to attack them directly. The absence of all but a fleeting reference to lesbians in the lengthy debate over homosexuality when it was partially decriminalised in 1969 illustrates the point. Gay men, on the other hand, are constantly denounced since the advent of the contemporary gay liberation movement, not merely on account of their sexual acts, but also because their social behaviour offers the most visible challenge to the equation of manhood with participation in the patriarchal structures of the nuclear family.

The New Right is seeking to deprive people, young people in particular, of access to sexual role models, sexual freedom and sexual information, even as the state that it supports is inextricably bound up with the corporations that have saturated the environment with (hetero)sexual stimuli.

Though there has been too much public exploitation of sexuality in commerce and entertainment, we cannot go back to privatising sexuality. In a society that remains patriarchal, addressing itself to the desires of heterosexual patriarchal males, this would be a disaster for women in particular, but also for other sexual minorities. Heterosexual women, lesbians and gays have all in diverse ways suffered in the past by being denied access to information and to the means of communication that could overcome our isolation, and which are so crucial to the maintenance of patriarchal, heterosexist hegemony. In any event, the notion of returning to the past (usually a mythologised past) for solutions to contemporary problems invariably leads to repressive as well as regressive policies. Privatising sexuality in a reconstructed conventional heterosexual family would entail forcing women back into male-dominated homes, and gays into closets. Even if this could be done it would not affect the declining real incomes of working-class husbands, less and less capable of supporting a full-time wife, or the fragmenting impact of monopoly capitalism upon the family as it commercialises more and more needs whose satisfaction previously structured family life — for example, eating and leisure activities.

What is needed is a recognition and validation of the idea that greater autonomy and choice in meeting sexual and emotional needs in economically wealthy, and therefore potentially diverse and pluralistic, societies is indeed as desirable for individuals and society as a whole as is the enlargement of choice in any other sphere of life, be it in work, consumption or leisure. In fact, what is needed is an extension to the rest of society, particularly to the working classes, of the conditions that permit the sort of freedom that upper-class men already largely enjoy.

Those of us who question the family are often portrayed as fleeing from commitment and intimacy. There is a germ of truth to this in that our beliefs are no doubt influenced by the way in which these values have been *enforced* in our own families, particularly with regard to children. However, we are also reacting to the sacrosanct elevation of the nuclear family in society as a whole insofar as it presupposes certain specific structured relations between men, women and children. The personal experience of many is that the family is based upon oppression and dependence as much as on love; nevertheless, it is still considered sacrilegious to say so in public.

What is oppressive is not necessarily the family *per se*, but the imposition of the nuclear family role model, which underlies the familial ideology, upon the rest of us, not merely in terms of structuring individual sexual relationships, but also in the way in which society is organised to meet the needs of a specific type of family. No one is suggesting, as Michele Barrett emphasises, that we don't need intimacy and love in our lives, or that the need for "intimacy, sexual relations, emotional fulfilment, parenthood and so on are in themselves oppressive. What is oppressive is the assumption that the present form of such needs is the only possible form, and that the manner in which they should be met is through the family as it is today."[17]

A society that permits, indeed encourages, sexual autonomy and choice will be possible only when heterosexual males have been stripped of their privileges, and when the sexual division of labour within the home and within society as a whole has been transformed. The latter is crucial, for it is the public sphere of paid work that elevates the twin values of domination and competition that reinforce men's age-old tendency to control women's sexuality. And it is men's absence from the personal sphere within the home, particularly with respect to nurturing and parenting the next generation of men, that hinders the development of the relational capacities that are now exclusively associated with femininity.

The struggle to dispossess heterosexual males of their power while reconstructing the meaning of masculinity will be a lengthy task. In the meanwhile the remainder of us must continue to struggle on two fronts. First, we must create and defend institutions and practices that satisfy some of our needs; and second, we must resist the hegemonic role of the familial ideology that mystifies the role of the conventional family, and invalidates the experience and needs of a growing proportion of the population who live outside it.

REFERENCES

1 *Hansard*, April 21, 1969.

2 *Ibid.*, February 11, 1969.

3 I am using the term patriarchal in the contemporary feminist sense to refer to the dominating power of males imbued with masculine values over the rest of society. See Zillah R. Eisenstein, ed., *Capitalist Patriarchy and the Case for Socialist Feminism*, New York: Monthly Review Press, 1979. See also Varda Burstyn, "Masculine Dominance and the State", in Ralph Miliband and John Saville, eds., *The Socialist Register 1983*, London: Merlin Press, 1983.

4 House of commons, Standing Committee on Justice and Legal Affairs, March 4, 1969.

5 The reverse was true in the seventeenth century. See Introduction to Part I, Jonathan Ned Katz, *Gay/Lesbian Almanac*, New York: Harper and Row, 1983.

6 *Hansard*, April 17, 1969.

7 See Ann Oakley, *Sex, Gender and Society*, New York: Harper & Row, 1972. See also Jeffrey Weeks, *Sex, Politics and Society*, New York: Longman, 1981.

8 Weeks, *op. cit.*, p. 11

9 Quoted by Sheila Kitzinger, *Woman's Experience of Sex*, New York: G.P. Putnam's Sons, 1983, p. 24.

10 Ethel Spector Person, "Sexuality as the Mainstay of Identity: Psychoanalytic Perspectives" in Catherine R. Stimpson and Ethel Spector Person, eds., *Women, Sex and Sexuality*, Chicago: University of Chicago Press, 1980, p. 58.

11 See *Globe and Mail*, February 7, 1983.

12 *Ibid.* and "Rediscover Each Other", the Community Booklet published by the Ontario Secretariat for Social Development with respect to the proclamation of May as the Family Unity Month, Toronto, 1984, p. 5.

13 Nancy Chodorow, *The Reproduction of Mothering: Psychoanalysis and the Sociology of Gender*, Berkeley: University of California Press, 1978, p. 207.

14 See *Body Politic*, No. 70, February, 1981, pp. 10 - 11.

15 See, for example, Pat Armstrong and Hugh Armstrong, "Beyond Sexless Class and Classless Sex: Towards Feminist Marxism", *Studies in Political Economy*, No. 10, Winter, 1983.

16 See Person, *op. cit.*, p. 47.

17 Michele Barrett, *Women's Oppression Today*, London, Verso Editions, 1980, p. 251.

FURTHER READING

Burstyn, Varda, and Dorothy Smith, *Women, Class, Family and the State*, Toronto, 1985.

Burstyn, Varda, ed., *Women Against Censorship*, Toronto, 1985.

Kinsman, Gary, "Heterosexual Hegemony and Homosexual Resistance", OISE MA thesis, University of Toronto, 1983.

Lumsden, Ian, ed., Atkinson Review ("Sexuality and the State"), Vol. 1, No. (2), 1985.

Feminist, gay and counter-culture magazines such as *Broadside, Body Politic, Rites*, and *Fuse* provide the best source of information with respect to current struggles over the state's regulation of sexuality.

D. FERTILITY

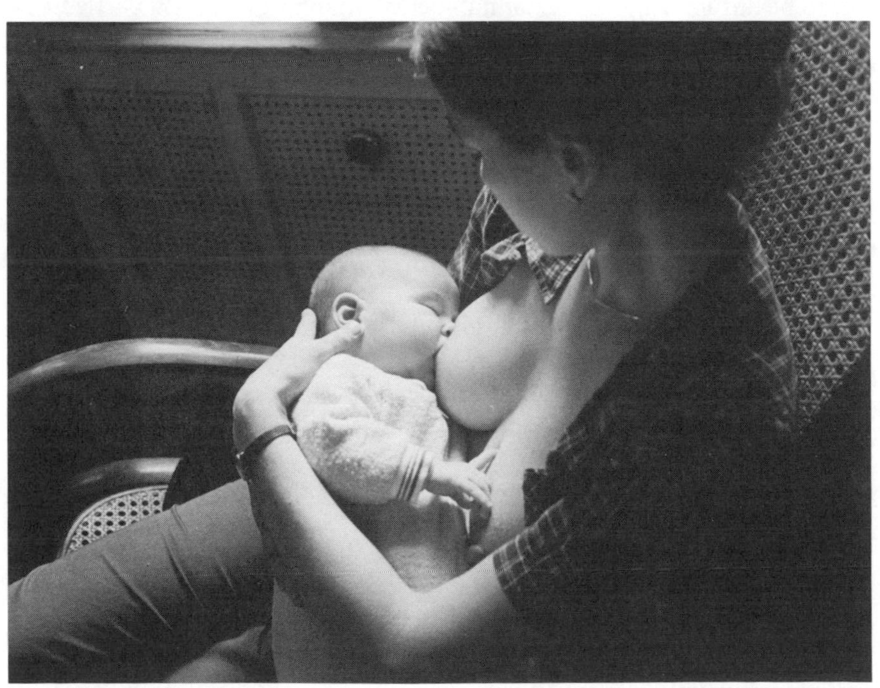

JUDITH NOLTÉ

Sexuality, Fertility and Choice: On Becoming a Woman in the Eighties

The way in which a young woman deals with her sexuality has always had a greater effect on her life than the manner in which a young man "disposes" of his. For women's sexuality is inextricably linked with her fertility. This connection impresses itself indelibly on any woman at the time of her first encounter with a possible pregnancy. While for many women this fear turns out to be unfounded, for a great number of young women, and particularly teenagers today, the fear turns into a well-founded reality.

Each year over 40,000 Canadian teenage women become pregnant. The extent of these pregnancies has become a serious social issue in Canadian society. The phenomenon seems surprising since there is a general agreement, both popularly and among social scientists, that the '60s and early '70s were distinguished by a growing liberalisation of our attitudes towards sex, sexuality, and birth control. This should have resulted in a more responsible and successful use of contraception, while not only aiding, but actually furthering the advancement of the status of women in Canadian society. Yet, for a number of reasons these advances are being threatened by growing contradictions between liberal tradition and a sweeping tide of conservatism which is becoming increasingly evident in Canada. This polarised debate is played out in the scientific arena, with each side manipulating data to its own end.

INTRODUCTION

Traditionally, a woman's sexuality and especially her fertility were her most marketable commodities. Today, this trend continues in a modified form. Central to her identity as a developing and maturing individual are a woman's biological forces, which bring her into contact with and are influenced by a variety of inter-related social, philosophical, technological, medical, and economic realities of our post-industrial consumer culture. Among the forces having a direct bearing on a young woman's sexuality and fertility are the acceptance of sexuality as a crucial force in our individual and social existence; the greater availability, variety and effectiveness of contraception; the women's movement; the increasing distortion and acceptance of sex in public discourse (advertising, pornography and violence) particularly in the mass media of music, print, pictures, video, movies and television; the steady decline of traditional religions and the lapse of structures that limit premature, unrestricted sexuality; the resultant vacuum which offers no well-established modes for sexual behaviour; the lack of role models within a rapidly shifting demography of climbing divorce rates and single-parent families; the collapse of the prosperity of the early '70s, with its concomitant rise in expectations contrasting unfavourably with today's unemployment, inflation and the reality of a society with receding options; and the lack of meaningful employment, as well as increased leisure time, which is more often than not filled by passive watching of television, movies and videos that promote the shallow values of money and sex as the commodities most important to a successful, happy life.

While there is some awareness among young people that "TV is TV", or "it's only a movie", the general level of visual literacy in this society is very low. Most people, lacking real-life experiences, are not equipped to assess and criticise what is presented to them. As an ever-present and persuasive force, the media seldom portray sexuality in a responsible manner. Rarely do we see evidence of sex within a caring relationship. Emphasis is on pre-or extra-marital sexual encounters. References to birth control are non-existent, so the viewer receives no tips on how to combine contraception with the romantic flow of rising sexual excitement in real life.

The romantic myth surrounding sexuality is also being perpetuated through films and television. A variance on the long-established tradition of women having to choose between being a "madonna" (pure, chaste and virginal) or a "whore" (tainted, promiscuous and wanton) continues. It is further compounded by the confusion between reality and fiction when many well-known actresses and models become single parents under circumstances paralleling their fictitious roles in movies and television dramas. This "love baby" trend is glamourised through a whole species of glossy magazines specialising in biographical gossip, e.g., *People, U.S.*, as well as "people sections" in *Vogue* and general interest weekly news magazines. Is it any wonder that adolescents are seduced by this romantic portrayal of women as sex objects? Even educated people, aware of the influence of the media, are seduced by images depicting the ideal partner.

Although it is easy and fashionable to blame the media, a realistic assessment has to recognise their offerings as a reflection of society's lowest common moral and intellectual denominator. As such, the media provide symptoms of what we are about, rather than a cause. There are many other factors and forces that contribute to teenagers' unresolved dealings with their sexuality and fertility as they come of age in our age.

Despite the supposed sexual liberalisation, adults responsible for running society are still the products of their past repressions. This becomes evident in the increasing polarisation of progressive liberal values versus the growing traditional reactionary causes (Moral Majority, Right to Life, etc.). Little in our society encourages an open, rational discussion of sexuality to help young people come to grips with that part of their nature. Schools, families and the medical system mirror the factional indecision described above. Many parents find it difficult to talk to their children about sexuality.

The level of discomfort often increases as their children reach adolescence, when parents assume "no news is good news". School programmes reflect the ambivalence of society in dealing with this matter. Sex education programmes, where they exist, often do not discuss contraception until the later grades of high school — when many of the students are already sexually active. Few medical services are geared to teens, so many young people are reluctant to seek help from what they perceive as a disapproving medical system. The failure of parents, schools and medical practitioners to discuss sex openly means teens have little information upon which to base decisions about their sexual activities. This void perpetuates the aura of mystery that surrounds sexuality, confusing teens and mitigating against the possibility that they will carefully plan their reproductive lives.

The complex problem of growing up in the eighties seems to produce two almost simultaneous reactions in young women. One is denial, while the other is a fatalistic attitude that they have no control over their lives. A recently released study by Canadian Advisory Council on the Status of Women[1] demonstrated that girls, with little or no exception, expect a future with exciting jobs, adequate income, loving mates, trouble-free children, and international travel. Conspicuously absent from this image are diapers, divorce and poverty — the bitter reality for an increasing number of women. On the other hand, the girls surveyed hope that when the third world war comes they will be vapourised as quickly as possible. With girls envisioning either scenario, there is an alarming absence of any effort to control some of the events that are shaping their lives. Teenagers are not participating in droves in the anti-nuclear protest movement, nor are they planning for their futures in any concrete way — they're just hoping things will work out.

This ambivalence is also reflected in the way in which teens handle their sexuality. There is rarely a conscious decision to become sexually active. Rather, many girls put themselves in situations where they are out of control (either through passion, drugs or drinking) before they engage in sex for the first time.

To be prepared is to seem promiscuous, and to become a target for the label of an "easy lay". But it is acceptable to engage in sexual activity if you "did not plan on it". As a result, even in 1985, women are becoming pregnant through lack of foresight.

These behaviours and attitudes are extreme and perhaps are part of growing up. Yet in all areas of development except the sexual one, teenagers are given guidance or training before they can indulge in so-called adult activities. To drive a car or graduate from school a certificate must be obtained. To vote or drink in public a certain age must be attained. But to be sexually active requires no such certification — anyone can do it. Little is being done to help young people make informed, rational decisions about when and why they should become sexually active. Yet the decision to become sexually active has important consequences not only for the individual involved but for society as a whole — particularly if a pregnancy occurs.

This chapter will examine some of the contradictions existing in our society today. The very existence of these contradictions prevents a reliable resolution in the immediate future. However, it is hoped that the following discussion of this particular reality might help establish a base for future policy making and action.

ATTITUDES AND BEHAVIOUR

I think sex before marriage is O.K. — especially if you are in love. All my friends feel that way too.

I love my boyfriend and we enjoy having sex. But I want to finish school and start a career before I get married.

I have a good relationship with my parents but I know how upset they would be if they knew I was having sex.

The results of Gallup Polls show there has been a growing acceptance of sexual relations before marriage. In 1970, Canadians were equally divided on the issue, but by 1979, 78 per cent of Canadians felt that sex before marriage was acceptable (although many felt it was more acceptable for men than for women, evidence that the double standard lives on).

While no national survey has been conducted to ascertain the attitudes of young women and men, a number of small studies of high school and university students have been conducted.[2] The results show that the attitudes of teenagers closely mirror those of Canadians in general. "Love for your partner" seems to have replaced the more traditional vows of marriage as a prerequisite to sexual activity.

One study found that almost 80 per cent of teenagers said that, if they were in a committed relationship, sex before marriage was acceptable. Students who were religious and attended services at least once a week were less accepting of premarital sex. Only half of this group accepted "sex with affection".

Over 60 per cent of Canadians are sexually active by the time they reach age 18. This figure has remained fairly constant since the Badgley Commission conducted its 1976 survey. The major change is found in the rates of sexual activity among younger women. In 1976, eight per cent of girls under age 15 were sexually active. A decade later the figure has risen to 26 per cent.[3]

The rate of decline in teenage pregnancy for the under-15 group has not kept pace with that of older women. While the overall decline is due to increasing use and effectiveness of contraception, there is concern about the ability of young women to use contraception because they have not accepted their sexuality.

Most teens are engaging in sex and most of those interviewed believed their friends were also sexually active. Many felt their parents would be upset if they knew they were having sex (86 per cent of females and 68 per cent of males).[4] While this perceived disapproval causes guilt and confusion, many teens see the beginning of sexual activity as their rite of passage into adulthood. By not confronting their parents, they can enjoy the privileges of "adulthood" without relinquishing the comforts that dependence on families often provides.

While the perception of parental disapproval may not stop teens from engaging in sex, it is an important predictor of how they will handle their fertility. The attitudes that parents pass on to their children, either implicity or explicitly, greatly influence children's feelings about their sexuality and, consequently, their fertility.

In families where parents accept their own sexuality and show affection for each other in front of the children, children grow up with a more positive feeling about sexuality. Taught about their genitals in the same way as other body parts, they are more likely to accept sexuality as a "normal" part of themselves, and less likely to have negative experiences and guilt feelings.

In contrast, in families where little affection is shown, where genitals are referred to as "down there", children perceive sex as "dirty". Punished for masturbating, the children are confused when the "badness" of sexual acts conflicts with pleasure that they feel. This guilt can remain with the child throughout life.

Unfortunately, many parents do not recognise the importance of integrating their child's sexual development with other learning processes.

Without proper names for sexual parts, open and rational discussion about sexuality is difficult. It is more difficult to introduce sex education as the child grows older and begins dealing with his or her sexuality in a more overt way.

If children believe that sex is "bad" or "dirty", they are also unlikely to use contraception successfully. In one survey, respondents were ranked on a scale from erotophilic (very comfortable with their sexuality) to erotophobic (very uncomfortable with their sexuality).[5] Those closer to the erotophilic side of the scale have a greater knowledge about their sexuality and birth control methods, are more sexually active and are likely to use contraception consistently.

A number of other studies[6] showed that high guilt levels about sexuality interfered with learning about sex and birth control. Erotophobics scored significantly lower on birth control knowledge after a lecture on sexuality and contraception than did those closer to the erotophilic side of the scale. Without such knowledge, it is less likely that contraception will be used on a regular basis.

The development of a positive attitude toward sexuality and birth control is a long and complex process. Acceptance of one's sexuality is first influenced by the manner in which the subject of sex is handled in the early developmental years of childhood. Healthy sexual self-awareness is promoted only when sexuality is treated as an integral part of a child's emotional, physical and intellectual development. In this context, attitudes that parents impart to their children become the major influence on a life-long ability or inability to deal with fertility.

SEX EDUCATION

My mother talked to me a bit. My phys-ed teacher said there were three methods of birth control — the pill, safes, and vasectomy.

My parents never talked to me about it. By the time they told us about birth control in school, it was too late.

I got my sex education from my friends, reading magazines sort of piecing it together for myself.

The comments above illustrate how inadequate sex education is in Canada. Yet, the debate continues — a debate that reflects the attitudes towards sexuality held in our culture. The confusion about whether sex education should be taught in the home or the school, and about what should be taught, mirrors the ambivalence toward sexuality in general.

Proponents believe information is a necessary component of decision making — that children need information about their sexuality to decide when and why to become sexually active. Opponents believe information about sex will encourage experimentation and lead to promiscuity. Those that oppose sex education in schools tend to believe it is the parents' responsibility to talk to their children about sex.

Yet a comparative American/Swedish study[7] that graded knowledge about childbirth (how the baby got in and out) showed that American parents are not giving their young children correct information about birth. When asked to describe how the baby got in there, many American eight-year-olds did not know or said that their mother had to eat a certain type of food. They believed the doctor would have to punch holes in the mother's stomach or cut it open to get the baby out and that it would hurt a lot. The Swedish group scored significantly higher on the test by citing both male and female involvement in reproduction, referring to sexual intercourse and having more accurate knowledge of prenatal development and birth through the vaginal canal. The results of this study would suggest that American parents are not doing a great job in educating their children about the facts of life.

Still, according to a recent Gallup Poll,[8] 94 per cent of Canadians believe parents should talk to their children about sexuality. While many adolescents cite their parents as the preferred source of information about sexuality, 70 per cent of the adolescent respondents in one study[9] could not talk comfortably to their parents about sex, pointing out the difference between the ideal and the reality.

Students say they get their sex education from the media and their peers in over 60 per cent of cases.[10] This ad hoc method of education results in incomplete information or misinformation. The Canada Health Survey published in 1984 by Health and Welfare Canada showed that over half of 12- to 15-year-olds thought it was impossible to become pregnant before the age of 16. The implications are especially serious when one considers that it is among this younger age group that sexual activity and pregnancy are increasing.

The level of knowledge does not increase dramatically with age. Only 41 per cent of university students in one survey could identify the fertile time of the woman's menstrual cycle (despite the fact that many were using the rhythm method as birth control).[11] According to the Gallup Poll only 50 per cent of Canadians surveyed knew (or guessed) that more than five methods of birth control were available to Canadians. Of this group, 64 per cent would have liked more information on sexuality and birth control when they were growing up.

Despite the fact that a great number of Canadians would like more information about their sexuality, their parents are not providing it; and while groups like the Canadian Medical Association have been advocating the fourth "R" (reproduction) as a required subject at school for over twenty years, sex education is not available to all Canadian children.

A national survey of schools conducted in the spring of 1984 by Planned Parenthood Federation of Canada[12] showed that only half of Canadian schools offer sex education or family life education (as it is euphemistically called). Half of these schools bury content in such courses as physical education, home economics or health. Only 25 per cent offer it as a separate course.

Family life education courses were developed to teach students about interpersonal relationships, communication skills, family life, responsible decision making, and coping in this rapidly changing world.

When instruction about sex is given, it is likely to be too little, too late. Contraception and venereal disease are only taught in grades 9 and 10, when students are 15 and 16 years old (26 per cent of this age group is already sexually active). Teachers themselves say that students react quite favourably to the classes but often want more information.

Most of the teachers surveyed by Planned Parenthood were enthusiastic about such courses, and said they were comfortable teaching the subject. Most felt the majority of parents either supported the courses or were ambivalent about them. They believed only 3 per cent of parents were actually opposed to the courses. This estimate, a far cry from the impression created by reports of parent opposition in the press, is supported by two other surveys. The 1984 Gallup Poll found that 83 per cent of Canadians believed sex education should be taught in school. A 1985 survey, designed to obtain parents' attitudes about sex education of their children, found that 82 per cent of parents believed that the school had a role in this area.[13]

Parents seem to support sex education at school because many of them are not comfortable talking with their children about sex. They recognise the need for information but they are more comfortable if someone else provides it. Others are concerned that their children, not always comfortable talking to them, may prefer the relative anonymity of the classroom.

A disturbing finding of the Parent's Survey was that 50 per cent of the respondents did not know what their children were being taught in family life education (i.e., facts or values) or did not respond to the question. So while parents seem to support sex education in general, they are not, for the most part, informed about what is being taught to their own children.

Proper sex education in school can replace the silence about sex in some homes and work to reinforce what parents who do talk to their children say about sexuality. It would seem from the survey of schools that teachers are not interested in taking over the parental role. They are, however, genuinely concerned about the children's sense of self, want them to be well adjusted and to understand their bodies. Most "sex education" programmes are founded on basic values that include caring about self and others, avoiding pregnancy until the people involved are willing and able to raise a family, and having sexual contact only after understanding the responsibilities and possible consequences. Such values should not conflict with home or religious-based values.

Conflict does arise around the issue of how much information students need. It appears students are still woefully ignorant, yet there are those who believe knowledge will promote promiscuity. There are others who take a more rational approach which acknowledges that lack of information does not inhibit sexual activity, but lack of knowledge will inhibit contraceptive use.

Sex education is only a minor part of a much larger sexual environment and it cannot be expected to remedy all the problems associated with sexuality. Although education has been a method of alleviating ignorance and social ills in our society, competing ideologies are now denying adolescents information on sexuality, sexual activity and contraceptive use. These issues need to be discussed openly and thoroughly in both our public and private institutions.

CONTRACEPTIVE USE AND NON-USE

I was too shy, I guess; mostly, I was too shy to see the doctor. I didn't want him to know that I was having sexual relations. I thought he might tell my parents.

I couldn't take the pill home. My mother is against girls going on it. She says that if you go on the pill you're tempted to have sex with anyone. She'd be really mad if I went on it.

It's too dangerous to use the pill. I mean you hear about women dying from it. I don't know much about the other things — they don't work anyway.

Many young women are not sure how to deal with their need for birth control. Yet, the prevention of pregnancy through contraceptive use is an active rather than a passive process. This often conflicts with the common view of "femininity" or a female sex role that expects the men to do all the desiring, initiating and directing of sexual activity. For women to take a rational approach to sex and to plan to have contraception available is a major departure from this traditionally nurtured, romantic notion of sex.

Many women face the reality of sex only after the fact — i.e., if they have a pregnancy scare. However, even after such a scare, many women still do not always take precautions to prevent unprotected intercourse from recurring. In an effort to understand why contraception is not consistently used, the effect of personality factors, societal attitudes and the availability of services must be considered.

A number of researchers have worked to develop a model of contraceptive use that incorporates these factors. Bogue, Byrne, Fisher and Herold posit that there are five steps that must be taken before contraception will be used effectively:[14] learning about birth control, anticipating intercourse, acquiring contraception, discussing contraception with the partner, and using contraception consistently.

While these steps seem straightforward, considering them in conjunction with personality and social factors gives some insight into how a process that seems simple can become a complex matter for so many sexually active couples.

The findings of the Sexual Opinion Survey[15] show that the level of comfort with sexuality affects learning about sex and birth control. Studies have shown that those who are close to the erotophobic end of the scale (uncomfortable with their sexuality) tend to absorb less information than those who are more comfortable with their sexuality. Erotophobics also tend to remember the more negative aspects of contraceptive methods more frequently than their erotophilic counterparts, and are less likely to ask questions about sexuality or to put themselves in situations where discussions about sex or birth control occur.

A low level of information about contraceptive methods has a negative impact on contraceptive use. For example, many women who equate birth control with the pill just stop using it if they suffer side effects. They do not start using another method because they do not understand other options or believe in their effectiveness.

As no one contraceptive will be suitable throughout a lifetime, women need to adopt a "cafeteria approach" to birth control — changing methods when side effects occur or needs change. Erotophobic women are not likely to have either the knowledge or the flexibility to consider options.

In the second step of the model, successful contraceptors must be able to anticipate when they will be having sex. The ability to predict sexual activity helps ensure that contraception will be available for use. A prerequisite for predicting intercourse is the acceptance of sexual activity. Erotophilics are more likely to accept their sexuality, enjoy sex, and look forward to the next occasion. Erotophobics often do not enjoy sex, feel guilty about having it and often put themselves in situations where they are not "in control". Using passion, alcohol, or drugs as an excuse, they rarely make a decision to have sex; it is something that happens to them. Reaction the next day is often denial — although they did it this once, they will never do it again. This denial is often the reason many teenagers postpone seeking contraception for up to a year after they have become sexually active. But while their level of guilt is high enough to prevent them from enjoying sex, or anticipating it, it is not sufficient to prevent them from having sex again.

Another problem young people face in trying to anticipate sex is caused by the lack of acceptance of teenage sexuality in our society. Young people rarely have predictable sexual patterns as they often do not have a place for sex. Consequently, even if they have contraceptives, the "equipment" is often not in the right place at the right time.

The stability of a relationship is another major influence in anticipating intercourse. If a couple has been going out for some time and has established a routine, they can predict that they will have sex on a certain night, allowing for preparation. However, because most young people are not involved in a stable relationship, they are afraid that if they have contraceptives they will look promiscuous.

The third step in the model, acquiring contraception, involves public declaration of one's sexual activity. Many young people are very sensitive to reactions about their sexuality. A nurse asking the reason for a visit in a crowded waiting room can create a very embarrassing situation. Disapproval from a doctor or a judgemental comment from a pharmacist serve to discourage rather than reward young people who behave responsibly.

While some judgemental behaviour inevitably occurs, erotophobics are more likely to perceive a situation as negative than are those people more comfortable with their sexuality. A study conducted by Fisher, Fisher and Byrne[16] showed that men who scored closer to the erotophobic end of the scale rated the experience of purchasing condoms less positively than did other men. They thought the pharmacist was judgemental and reacted to them negatively. This perception carried over to their ratings of the effectiveness and convenience of condoms.

Discussing contraception with a partner, the fourth step in the process, plays a central role in the successful use of contraception. If both partners have been part of the discussion and decision making regarding the method of choice and both believe in its effectiveness, they are more likely to use it consistently.

Unfortunately, contraception is still considered a female domain by many people and although they may be comfortable enough "doing it", they have difficulty talking about contraception. Just as young women have trouble asking, "Do you have a condom?", young men find it difficult to ask, "Are you using something?"

The consistent use of birth control, the fifth step in the model, is more likely to occur if both partners understand contraception, can plan for intercourse, have discussed sex, and have acquired contraception. This is more likely to take place in a stable relationship, where both partners are comfortable with their sexuality.

A number of other factors also influence whether young women will manage their fertility responsibly. Successful contraceptors tend to be independent and self-reliant and hold less traditional views about the roles of women. Sex is often part of a mature, loving relationship. They tend to place a high value on the opinions of their parents, their family life and their achievements at home and school, and envisage a positive future for themselves. In other words, they have good reasons to avoid unplanned pregnancy.

On the other hand, unsuccessful contraceptors hold more traditional views of male/female roles, tend to indulge in sexual activity because it is expected of them, and follow the adage that "biology is destiny", valuing peer opinions over those of their parents. Although they desire independence, they do not accept the value of either academic or work experience to help them achieve this goal.[17]

A longitudinal study found that adolescents who became sexually active at an early age were often rebellious, confrontational and highly inclined to engage in such other problematic behaviour as drinking, smoking and drug use. These adolescents were also less likely to be concerned with the consequences of unprotected sex, and apt to subscribe to the belief that "to be protected was to be promisicuous", but to "be swept off your feet was O.K."

In describing adolescents who became sexually active at a later age, Jessor[18] pointed out the importance of family and personal relationships. These support systems encourage a delay in sexual activity, which allowed teenagers to pass through a phase in which they could accept their own sexuality and integrate knowledge about sex and birth control with their own behaviour. Not only did this delay protect teens from pregnancy, but it also allowed them time to develop both socially and psychologically. Thus they were prepared to manage their fertility more responsibly.

To be truly effective, use of contraception should begin at first intercourse and be used during every sexual contact. Yet, only one-third of young people use contraception at first intercourse,[19] and only 20 per cent use it every time.[20]

Subjective experience also affects the decision to use birth control. If a woman or one of her friends has had a pregnancy scare, she is more likely to use birth control and to use an effective method. On the other hand, if she has been having sex for a long time and did not get pregnant, she may become convinced it will not happen to her. In the words of one young woman, "It took so long to get pregnant, I just didn't think it would happen. I just thought I would be lucky and not get pregnant."

The fear of parental disapproval plays a major role in determining whether young women will use birth control. If young women believe their parents support birth control use, they are more likely to use contraception. One study describing the differences between young women who obtain the pill before intercourse and those who delay obtaining contraception concluded that those girls who had talked to their mothers about contraception were more likely to avoid risk-taking behaviour.[21]

As mentioned previously, to be motivated to obtain birth control, young women have first to perceive themselves as needing it. Yet, a recent study conducted in Ottawa[22] showed that teenagers were generally more concerned with appearance-related disorders (acne and obesity) than with their sexual health. While many of those interviewed were sexually active, only 35 per cent sought advice on birth control during a visit to the doctor.

The general discomfort that young people experience in seeking medical advice has often surfaced as a reason for unintended pregnancy. In the words of some teens, "I was too embarrassed to go up and ask the doctor for the pill", "I felt guilty having premarital relations", "I guess mostly, I was too shy to see the doctor, I didn't want him to know that I was having sexual relations, and I thought he might tell my parents."

Yet another Ontario study showed that in cities where sex education was given in schools and youth-oriented clinics were responsive to the needs of young people (i.e., convenient hours, no need for appointments) the rate of teen pregnancy was significantly lower than in those areas where no special efforts were made to serve the younger population.[23]

The province of Québec provides another example of how service delivery can effectively reduce unintended pregnancies. Since the establishment of family planning clinics in local community service centres across the province and the introduction of sex education programmes in schools, the incidence of teenage pregnancies has declined to one of the lowest in the country. The young of Québec also benefit from a more liberal attitude toward sexuality in general, a result of the province's emergence from the dominance of the Roman Catholic church in the last decade, thus forcing a re-examination of issues surrounding sexuality. The open attitude that resulted seems to have helped reduce the confusion surrounding sexuality in more repressive societies and to encourage a more responsible management of fertility.

TEENAGE PREGNANCY

I would have preferred not to be pregnant. But I hated school anyway. This way I get to move in with my boyfriend. My parents were always bugging me.

I didn't think I was doing it often enough to get pregnant. We'd been doing it for a year, it hadn't happened yet, so I thought I was just lucky — it wasn't going to happen to me.

My mother drilled into me that I had to finish school. She taught me that I had to have a career and be in control of my own life. I knew I couldn't do it with a child, so I had an abortion. I didn't tell her....

The comments above show that women's feelings about pregnancy are often influenced by the attitudes of those around them. The belief that women make decisions about reproduction on an individual basis is naîve, as we are clearly influenced in this area, as well as in others, by societal attitudes.

Essentially, ours is a pro-natalist society, which sees birth as a positive event. Women have often had to choose between their career and their reproductive capacities, influenced by the traditional belief that child bearing demonstrates a women's femininity and gives true meaning to her life. This notion has been reinforced by recent developments in reproductive technologies that attach additional importance to motherhood. Artificial insemination allows single women to have children on their own, and infertile women may be encouraged to have children through in vitro fertilisation, embryo transplant, etc.[24]

However, this idealisation of the maternal role is deceptive. The anti-natal attitudes of society become evident after the reproductive miracle has occurred. The lack of post-natal counselling (to help parents deal with the reality of their new role), adequate maternity benefits, and accessible, quality day care clearly demonstrate the value that society places on children.[25] The first message — the pro-natalist — contributes to the soaring number of teenage pregnancies.

In 1983, there were 40,384 pregnancies to teenagers in Canada.[26] While one-third of the pregnancies end in abortion, young women are shifting away from the traditional responses to pregnancy — marriage or adoption. About one-third are choosing to keep their baby, creating a phenomenon popularly called "children raising children". Of these women, 20 per cent will give their children up for adoption, either voluntarily or through court order, by the time the child is two.

While the numbers themselves show little reason to believe in the "epidemic of teenage pregnancies" that we hear about in the media, the individual situations of the young women who keep their babies each year must be considered in order to realise the severity of the problem.

Early child bearing is strongly associated with limited education. It is rare that young mothers are able to catch up with their former classmates who have postponed child bearing. This gap in educational and work experience results in a situation where 90 per cent of the young mother's life script is written for her, a script that likely includes unemployment, poverty, and marital problems.

Births by very young adolescents have a greater incidence of health risks to mother and child. Marriages following teenage childbirth have a much higher risk of dissolving than do marriages of those who postponed child bearing until after the age of 20. And finally, teenage mothers have a suicide rate ten times higher than that of the general population.[27]

Research to determine the differences between women who terminated an unwanted pregnancy and those who kept their children showed that women who had abortions typically did so because they did not want the pregnancy to interfere with their educational and career aspirations. Those who kept the baby had lower educational goals, did not foresee much of a future for themselves in the labour market, and believed that having a child would not interfere with an uncertain future.

A bleak picture is emerging of "teenage moms" who are poor, unskilled, and discouraged. In one Ontario study[28] 85 per cent of the teenage single mothers were on social assistance throughout the first 18 months following the birth of the baby (with an average monthly income under $400). Those working were living well under the poverty line. Three-fifths of the group had completed grade 10 or less. Only a minority were trying to complete high school. The majority of mothers spent most of their time with their infant, but many lacked parenting skills as they were only 14 to 16 when the baby was born.

Many of the mothers became more discouraged as the baby got older, ceasing to look for help to find suitable housing, schooling or employment. A substantial number reported greatly lowered expectations about what they hoped to achieve within five years.

The lives of these women contrast sharply with those who delay child bearing. Older women are more likely to be established in their careers, to be able to take maternity leave, and to re-enter the work force with satisfactory child-care arrangements, suffering fewer consequences of child bearing.

A study that assessed the long-term economic consequences of child bearing on both mother and child reinforces the conclusion that the consequences of teenage marriage and child bearing are negative.[29] Among women who married at 19 or younger, 50 per cent had not received a high school diploma and only 6 per cent had been to university. In the group of mothers who had a child while an adolescent, 64 per cent had less than a high school education and only 4 per cent had enrolled in university. In considering the occupational structure of Canada in 1981, it appears that lower proportions of women in the professional occupations are associated with early child bearing and marriage.

Unequivocally, the data show that adolescent marriage and fertility have a negative impact on the economic prospects of women. It is probable that these effects are cumulative across generations. The consequences are almost as severe for women who began child bearing before the age of 25. It would appear that women at age 30 are in the best economic circumstances to have children. These findings have serious implicatons for women deciding to have children, particularly in light of the increasing number of women raising their children alone.

It is obvious that ways must be found to allow women to participate fully in the economic life of society while still having the number of children they desire. But the present lack of such support structures as day care means this is not possible. Therefore, it is crucial that young people know the facts and probabilities associated with teenage marriage and child bearing. They must be afforded the ability to implement their choices based on those facts and a clear understanding of the consequences.

CONCLUSION

While there are mixed reactions to adolescent sexual activity, most Canadians are concerned about the consequences of early parenthood, its effect on social security systems, and its implications for the future. Yet, government, while willing to document the extent of the problem, does little more. Private industry continues to reap profits by marketing sexually desirable scenarios. It has little reason to promote a more realistic image of human relations in the field of sexuality. After all, "sex sells"; in fact, potentially and precisely through pregnancies, it increases the number of future consumers.

One of the major reasons that solutions to the problem of teenage pregnancy are not being developed is that so much of the discussion surrounding the subject focusses on whether or not teenagers should be sexually active. Canadian approaches do not accept the sexual activity of teenagers and address the prevention of pregnancy *per se*. The rationale for this approach is supported by research such as an international study on adolescent pregnancy[30] that looked at seven countries and concluded that the rate of teenage pregnancy is lower in those countries where sexual activity of teenagers is accepted.

The researchers looked at attitudes, social services, sex education and medical services in the United States, Canada, Sweden, France, Holland and England to determine factors that work to reduce teenage pregnancy. The results showed that the lowest rates of teenage pregancy occurred in countries that had liberal attitudes toward sex, had easily accessible contraceptive services for young people (with contraceptives being offered free or at low cost and without parental notification), and had comprehensive sex education programmes in schools.

The findings show that teenage pregnancy cannot be ascribed to teenage unemployment, since unemployment for youth was fairly consistent in all countries and the pregnancy rates differed greatly. The study also dispelled a number of myths about the determinants of teenage pregnancy: i.e., young teenagers are not too immature to use contraceptives effectively; the availability of welfare benefits and services does *not* act as an inducement to teenagers to have babies; low teenage birth rates are *not* achieved by greater recourse to abortion; teenage pregnancy rates are *lower* in countries with *greater* availability of birth control and sex education.

In the countries that have lower pregnancy rates, government actions have demonstrated a determination to minimise the incidence of teenage pregnancy, abortion and child bearing. In no country has the government attempted to reduce or eliminate teenage sexual activity or placed any restrictions on confidential access to birth control. In all countries, the pill is widely prescribed and accepted as the most appropriate method for teenagers.

Yet each has developed its own unique approach to the problem. In the Netherlands, the country with the lowest pregnancy rate, sex education in the schools is perfunctory, but all the media contain an abundance of clear information about contraception. Mobile sex education teams operate under the auspices of a government-subsidised family planning association. In Sweden, which liberalised its abortion laws in 1975, a concerted effort was made to ensure teenage abortion rates did not rise as a result. The primary vehicle was a link between schools and contraceptive clinic services for adolescents. As a result, the teenage abortion rate *declined* dramatically after 1975.

There is no reason to believe that a comprehensive approach to solving the problem of teenage pregnancy would not work in Canada. If the government took a pro-active role in trying to prevent teenage pregnancy, rather than withdrawing from the area (as it has with the recent closure of the family planning division of Health and Welfare), they could conduct a public awareness campaign aimed at enhancing the information Canadians receive about sexuality.

Public awareness campaigns should be on the level of "Participaction" or the anti-smoking campaign developed by the federal government. To be most effective, a multi-faceted educational campaign aimed at parents of young children, young women and young men should be launched.

The message designed for parents of young children would alert them to the importance of their role as the primary sex educators of their children. A soft-sell approach would encourage them to discuss sexuality openly. Supplementary information packets would give parents the background material they need to be effective in this role. The results of this campaign would be long-term. Children who grow up with this information would be more able to accept their sexuality and deal with their fertility responsibly.

A public awareness campaign designed to achieve more immediate results would be aimed at young women. These messages would give girls guidelines on how to respond to the exploitative lines that boys use to influence them to have sexual relations. They would also work to give girls a sense of opportunity, and encourage them to invest in their futures through educational and career experiences before undertaking parenting.

The third approach would be designed to encourage male involvement in the contraceptive process. Using role models, young men would see the desirability of talking about sex and contraception. Using a harder line, young men should be aware of the cost of unintended pregnancies and be forced to pay child support. If the father is a minor, then his parents would be held accountable. With this negative incentive, parents would become aware of the importance of educating both male and female children.

The government should reduce the restrictions on the advertising of contraceptives. If restrictions were lifted, it seems likely that aggressive manufacturers would develop effective campaigns to increase their share of the market. Introducing these products in the media in a positive light (we hear of them now only when another negative side effect is suspected) would increase the knowledge about the number of methods available and would help young women and men see the desirability of contraceptive use.

While the government cannot legislate sex education, asserting the value of such programmes would help legitimise their inclusion in curricula. It would also be feasible for the government to sponsor demonstration projects that would integrate sex education and clinic services in schools or community settings (two factors that, in combination, have been shown to reduce adolescent pregnancies).

Unfortunately, there are many forces working against government involvement in this area. While many Canadians believe information is readily available, studies show that sex education is not universally available in Canada. Vocal minorities, fueled with money from the United States, are seeking to limit further the right to information. These fundamentalist groups promote chastity as the cure to the problem of teenage pregnancies. While abstinence will undoubtedly prevent pregnancies, the denial of adolescent sexuality will only confuse the issue further and discourage teens from using birth control. The promotion of chastity will be successful only if there are major changes in society and in its messages about sex and sexuality.

The universality of access to family planning services is also being eroded. In small communities and rural areas, young women are often subjected to the judgemental behaviour of doctors who do not approve of pre-marital sex. Ironically, these small communities often have the highest rates of teenage pregnancy. It is also unfortunate that because access to information on birth control is denied, the need for abortion increases. Yet, abortion services are not now universally available, and opposition groups are seeking to limit access even further.

This fight for the foetus is clouding the issue that most of the anti-abortion movement is also anti-contraception. Most members of this male-dominated movement believe the role of women is in the home raising children — a return to tradition which they believe would also help cure the problem of unemployment.

Finally, special services for adolescents need to be developed. In areas where these exist, the results have been encouraging. In Ottawa, for example, a converted school bus travels the city in the summer, offering medical advice on fitness, drugs, alcohol, acne and smoking. The bus shows videos on a wide range of issues, including birth control. This casual approach has had great success in serving the hardest-to-reach adolescents — young males. In other communities, public health units offer special clinics for young people.

While the problem of teenage pregnancy is a serious one, it is not insurmountable. Programme initiatives designed for youth have been successful in reducing teenage pregnancy. Canadians must direct their attention to designing effective programmes to give young people the information and services they need to prevent unintended pregnancy.

By remaining unresponsive, the government has made a decision — one in favour of non-action. If initiatives are not forthcoming, young people will continue to receive mixed messages about their sexuality. They will remain caught between the glitter and glamour promised by the media and the stark reality of life as a young woman in the '80s.

REFERENCES

1 Baker, Maureen. "*What Will Tommorrow Bring?...A Study of the Aspirations of Adolescent Women*. (Ottawa: Canadian Advisory Council on the Status of Women, 1985.)

2 Herold, E.S., and Thomas, R.E., "Sexual and Contraceptive Attitudes and Behaviour of High School and College Females". *Canadian Journal of Public Health*, 1969, 311 - 314; Meikle, S., Pearce, K.I., Peitchinis, J., and Pysh, F., "An Investigation into the Sexual Knowledge, Attitudes and Behaviour of Teenage School Students". Unpublished manuscript, Department of Psychology, University of Calgary, Alberta, 1981.

3 While no one study has been done, this figure was arrived at by considering the results of studies conducted from 1974 - 81 by Badley, Herold, Stennett, Handleby, Gemme, Planned Parenthood Ontario, Meikle, Weston and Frappier.

Males	1976 Badgley national	1974 Herold	1974 Stennett	1975 Handleby	1975 Gemme	1979 Frappier	1980 Meikle	1980 Weston	1981 PPOnt.
15	30%			22%			24% (both)		N/A
16 - 17	42%			33%				35% (both)	
18 - 23	73%	57%	53%		60%	55%	66%	61% (both)	
Females									
15	8%			15%			24% (both)		26%
16 - 17	19%			25%				35% (both)	44%
18 - 23	60%	33%	39%		45%	53%	66%	61%	

4 Herold, E. *Sexual Behavior of Canadian Young People* (Toronto: Fitzhenry and Whiteside Ltd., 1984), p. 12.

5 Fisher, W., Byrne, D., and White, L.A., "Emotional Barriers to Contraception", in Donn Byrne and William Fisher, eds., *Adolescents, Sex and Contraception*. (New Jersey: Lawrence Erlbaum Associates, 1983), p. 215 - 216.

6 Schwartz, S., "Effects of Sex Guilt and Sexual Arousal on the Retention of Birth Control Information", *Journal of Consulting and Clinical Psychology,* 1973, 61–64.
Mosher, D.L., "Sex Guilt and Sex Myths in College Men and Women", *Journal of Sex Research,* 1979, 224–234.
Mendelsohn, M.J. and Mosher, D.L., "Effects of Sex Guilt and Premarital Sexual Permissiveness on Role-played Sex Education and Moral Attitudes", *Journal of Sex Research,* 1979, 174–183.

7 Koch, P.B, "A Comparison of the Sex Education of Primary-aged Children as Expressed in Art in Sweden and the United States", in *Adolescents, Sex and Contraception, op. cit.* p. 153.

8 "Canadians Demand an End of Sexual Ignorance", *Tellus,* Journal of Planned Parenthood Federation of Canada, Volume 5, Number 3 (1984), p.2.

9 Sorenson, Robert. *Adolescent Sexuality in America* (New York: World Publishing, 1973), p. 77. Also see "Gallop Poll Reveals Canadian Attitudes", *Tellus,* Volume 6, Number 2, 1985.

10 Allgeier, A.R., "Information Barriers to Contraception", *Adolescents, Sex and Contraception, op. cit.*, p. 149.

11 Zelnik, M., and Kanter, J.F., "Sexual and Contraceptive Experience of Young Unmarried Women in the United States, 1976 and 1971", *Family Planning Perspectives,* 1977, pp. 55-71.

12 Nolté, J. "Sex Education in Canadian Classrooms", *Tellus*, Volume 5, Number 3, 1984.

13 Nolté, J. "Parents' Opinions on the Sex Education of Their Children", unpublished manuscript, Planned Parenthood Federation of Canada, 1985.

14 Bogue, in Schlesinger, Ben, ed., *Family Planning in Canada* (Toronto: University of Toronto Press, 1974); Bryne and Fisher, *Adolescents, Sex, and Contraception, op. cit;* Herold, *Sexual Behavior of Young People, op. cit.*

15 Fisher, W., Bryne, D., "Emotional Barriers to Contraception", in *Adolescents, Sex and Contraception, ibid.,* p. 212–222.

16 Fisher, W.A., Fisher, J.D., and Byrne, D., "Consumer Reactions to Contraceptive Purchasing", *Personality and Social Psychology Bulletin*, 1977, p. 3.

17 Devlin, M.C. and Hornick, J.P., "A Study of Psychological Determinants of Reproductive Behaviour". Unpublished manuscript; study funded by The Family Planning Division, Health and Welfare Canada, December 1982.

18 Jessor, Richard, et al., "The Time of First Intercourse: A Prospective Study", *Journal of Personality and Social Psychology* (publication pending).

19 Herold, E.S., *Sexual Behaviour of Canadian Young People, op. cit.*, p. 89.

20 Gvetkovich, G., and Grote, B., "Adolescent Development and Teenage Fertility", *Adolescents, Sex and Contraception*, Byrne and Fisher, eds., *op. cit.*, p. 113.

21 Herold, E.S., and Samson, L. "Differences between Women Who Begin Pill Use Before and After First Intercourse", *Family Planning Perspectives*, 1980, Number 12.

22 Feldman, W., et al., "Adolescent Health Needs — Health Concerns and Health Related Behaviour", unpublished manuscript, Children's Hospital of Eastern Ontario, Ottawa, 1984.

23 Orton, M. and Rosenblatt, E., "Adolescent Birth Planning Needs," Planned Parenthood Ontario, 1981.

24 The advances of technologies in this area beg the question of whether these processes give women more control over their bodies or make them passive recipients of medical treatment. The new reproductive technologies have far-reaching implications in a reassessment of the abortion issue. If this "clump of tissue" has such high value in the petri dish, how can it have so little value in a woman's womb? Kathleen McDonnell discusses these issues in *Not an Easy Choice — A Feminist Re-examines Abortion* (Toronto: The Women's Press, 1984).

25 For a more thorough (albeit biassed) discussion of this see Germaine Greer, *Sex and Destiny* (London: Picadour, 1985).

26 Statistics Canada, Number 91-210, June 1, 1983, p. 48, Table 3.

27 Allgeier, A.R., "Informational Barriers to Contraception", *Adolescents, Sex and Contraception, op. cit.*, p. 155.

28 McKay, H., and Austin, C., *Single Adolescent Mothers in Ontario* (Ottawa: Canadian Council on Social Development, 1983).

29 Grindstaff, C., "Longterm Economic Consequences of Adolescent Marriage and Fertility", *Tellus*, Volume 5, Number 2, 1984.

30 The Allan Guttmacher Institute, "An International Study on Adolescent Pregnancy", 1985 (publication pending).

FURTHER READING

Boston Women's Health Collective, *The New Our Bodies Ourselves*. New York: Simon & Schuster Inc., 1985.

Byrne, D., and Fisher, W., eds., *Adolescents, Sex and Contraception*. New Jersey: Lawrence Eilbaum Associates Publishers, 1983.

Carrera, Michael, *Sex: The Facts, The Acts and Your Feelings*. London: Mitchell, Beazley Publishers, 1981.

Hatcher, Robert et al., *It's Your Choice — A Consumer's Guide to Birth Control*. New Jersey: Irvington Publishers, 1981.

MacDonnell, Susan, *Vulnerable Mothers, Vulnerable Children: A follow-up study of unmarried mothers who kept their children*. Nova Scotia Department of Social Services., P.O. Box 696, Halifax, B3J 2T7, 1981.

SUSAN J. PALMER

The Cult of Birth: Natural Childbirth and Feminine Charisma

It was during my own pregnancy that I began to observe the cult of natural childbirth. Birth has become a verb. Women these days "birth" their own babies — with a hard "th". There is now an aesthetic of birth, as elaborate and precise as the art of bullfighting. Friends began to treat me to blow-by-blow descriptions of "birthings" with all the gusto and discernment of true *afficionados*. A proud father whom I encountered on the bus produced a photo-essay of his wife in labour. I felt a queer thrill of terror and tenderness as I stared at his fat lady, whose face was a study in ecstasy and pain as a foetus-baby squirmed out of her private parts. As my own term approached and the baby refused to turn around, I was plied with raspberry leaf tea, illegal midwives (who, my friends claimed, could massage the baby into place), upside-down postures, and conflicting advice. Deciding between a natural and caesarian birth was more than a medical issue — it was a feminist and religious one. One friend insisted that pushing through the birth canal was an important spiritual process for the baby and, of course, submitting to the doctor's scalpel was letting a man poach on woman's preserves. Out of my own confusion and indecision two things emerged: a healthy son and the conviction that the natural childbirth movement has become a cult.

The natural childbirth movement can be traced back to Ivan Pavlov's experiments in 1912. The Lamaze method, introduced in the 1958 classic, *Painless Childbirth*, has spread so widely that today a pregnant woman can choose from a variety of pre-natal classes offered by local community centres and hospitals. There have been many developments of Lamaze's analgesic methods and many approaches to the subject of natural childbirth — medical, political, and philosophical. This chapter, however, will explore the spiritual aspects of the movement and focus on the highly elaborate cult of birth as it is practised in two utopian communities, The Farm in Tennessee, and the Institute for the Development of the Harmonious Human Being in California. The significance of these rituals within the context of these communities and their relevance to the larger society will be discussed and compared to parallel trends among "ordinary couples". Finally, the evolution of a feminine idea of the sacred through the iconography and symbols of birth within the feminist movement will be examined.

NATURAL CHILDBIRTH AS A CULT

The natural childbirth movement can be termed a cult in that it has its own set of myths and rituals. Pre-natal literature has created the myth of the perfect birth. Couples who have produced perfectly healthy babies expressed in interviews their disappointment at the doctors' intervention — that it didn't "go right", that "the experience wasn't what we hoped for."[1] Women who prepared for natural births and ended up having caesarean surgery expressed a sense of failure; of not being "real women". Even couples with children will enroll in pre-natal classes, reinforcing the myth that there is a correct way to give birth. These classes tend to present birth as an Olympic event in which the wife/athlete tests her mettle as the husband/coach cheers her on. Perhaps because of the techniques of breathing, relaxation, and concentration which form part of the Lamaze method, there is great attention paid to the inner state of the participants. Birth is seen as an "experience" that has intrinsic value rather than a biological process with instrumental value. It becomes a stylised activity with ritualised breathing postures. It contains the tradition of generations of women, as authoritatively designed by Lamaze and the classes, and stereotyped by the myth of the perfect birth. Thus it has all the ingredients of a ritual, according to Fred Bird's definition in "The Pursuit of Innocence": "Ritual is a stereotyped, stylised, repeated, authoritatively designated, objectively posited, intrinsically valued activity."[2]

If birth has become a ritual, this raises the question of what kind of ritual it is. With the new emphasis on the labouring woman's state of consciousness, one could argue that birth is a meditation ritual. Its sacred function in utopian communities will be discussed below. For the "ordinary" couples interviewed, the events of birth appeared to have a time-out-of-time significance that boded well or ill for their new career as parents. Thus one can argue that birth is an initiation ritual, which, if performed correctly, successfully prepares the couple for their new role. Many couples, in describing their birth experience, gave an occult or magical interpretation of obstetrical events. For feminists who feared they might revert to the old style of motherhood, which they perceived as a life of drudgery and enslavement, a brilliant performance of a natural birth was hoped for. Control over the birth process symbolised control over their new lives in which they would be expected to juggle the demands of child, husband, and work. A correct performance of birth represented an initiation into the new style of motherhood which means sharing domestic tasks and child care with the father, and maintaining a career.

The spiritual trends in this movement appear to come from three sources: first, the birth process by its very nature tends to evoke a sense of awe; it is a mystery, a transition between life and pre-life, and Tillich claims that awe is the essence of religious emotion. Secondly, the human potential movement has influenced pre-natal classes and literature since the late 1960s, particularly in California. The human potential movement represents a merging of the scientific and religious world view. The concept of mind was expanded to include the soul, and the group-oriented therapies of encounter were fused with oriental meditation techniques. The aim was to tap a sacred source of power and use it for therapeutic and secular ends. This magical approach to healing has greatly influenced natural childbirth. Thirdly, the hippie psychedelic movement of the '60s has influenced the way women view their own "birthings". Ex-hippies describe it as "the ultimate trip", or "being stoned out of my head". The quest for mystical states of consciousness led former hippies to replace the artificial, uncontrolled highs of drugs with the organic, self-induced highs found in meditation rituals. As a result, attention is focussed on the labouring woman's state of consciousness, and ritual breathing or touching is a preferred analgesic to the use of drugs.

The two alternative spiritual communities whose rituals are described below manifest the influence of these movements. The Farm in Tennessee originated from the hippie psychedelic movement of the '60s, and the Institute for the Development of the Harmonious Human Being in California has all the characteristics of a cult originating from the human potential movement.

The Cult of Birth at the Farm

The Farm is situated on 1,000 acres of farmland near Summerton, Tennessee. It was founded by Stephen Gaskin, a former graduate student in semantics from San Francisco, whose charisma is based on his spiritual awakening through the use of psychedelic drugs. He expounded his philosophy in the famous Monday Night Meetings in the late 1960s. In 1971 he led a caravan of 300 long-haired vegetarians in remodelled busses and vans across the country on a national lecture tour, and they eventually settled down on 1,000 acres of wild land in Tennessee which they cultivated. Today the community numbers over 1,200 people and is called The Farm.

The Farm is, in Stephen's words "a telepathic society". One of the revelations he had on LSD was that an unseen field of communication does exist, and therefore thought has an impact on other people's well-being. As a result, it is essential to feel love and compassion for others. "What is the etiquette of a telepathic society?" he asked in 1967. One of the utopian aims of The Farm is to create such an etiquette.

Ina May, Stephen's wife, writes of The Farm:

> We are not just a community. We are a church. We hold our land in common and share fortunes as in The Book of Acts 2:44 - 45.[3]

Besides sharing their property, members exchange no money for goods or services, and everyone works hard in the fields. They live simply and close to nature in early American frontier style. They believe in God and read the Bible, but their Christianity is heavily influenced by the psychedelic world view, by nature worship, and by a sort of popular oriental mysticism. The body is sacred, the mind suspect. Touch and sexual contact are "telepathic", and astral travel and psychic experiences are not unusual and prove the "Unity of All Life".

Ina May and her team of midwives have delivered over 780 babies at The Farm. She developed her midwifery skills through her own five birthings, her mother's advice and a free seminar conducted by a kindly obstetrician who was worried about all the births occurring on the caravan. Now The Farm has its own clinic with a staff of 15 midwives, a doctor, nurses, paramedics, and technicians. They own two ambulances, and each midwife has access to a jeep with a band radio.

Spiritual Midwifery by Ina May Gaskin, published in 1978,[4] is an account of the highly elaborate ritual of birth at The Farm. It resembles a sacred text in its content, layout and graphics. Part One consists of "Amazing Birthing Tales" which are personal accounts of birthings by the mother, father or midwife. They have a strong mystical flavour and read like popular Sufi stories or Zen koan. The graphics emphasise their sacred character. Each story begins with an illuminated capital letter and is illustrated by a photograph of the family in a natural setting or a madonna-like pose of mother and infant.

These stories constitute half of the book; the second half is more conservative and scientific, offering information on pre- and post-natal care, stages of labour, and possible complications. However, quotations from Zen and Sufi masters, Chassidic rabbis and Stephen Gaskin serve to leaven the scientific tone and remind us of the sacred nature of birth.

The centrefold painting separates the two parts of the book and is a sort of mystical feminist variation of the Nativity. A beautiful naked mother lies on a bed giving birth. Her husband supports her back and three midwives crouch at the foot of the bed receiving the child. Everyone has a halo, or "aura" in Farm terminology, and the style is self-consciously primitive.

The birthing stories are testimonials of the participants' direct experience of Stephen Gaskin's mystical world view. Life is perceived as a flow of energy or a scale of vibrations. The "rushes" felt during labour are simply a speeding up of this flow.

The testimonials share a similar structure. They begin with a description of the onset of contractions, called "rushes". Ina May explains, "I like to use the term 'rush'...because I think it describes better how to flow with the birthing energy."[5] Then help is sought and given in the person of the husband and midwife. The midwife prepares the space and the participants for the ritual. Then ensues a description of the mother's state of consciousness and performance. The language breaks down at this point and becomes abstract and poetic. Dangers threaten which are overcome by the skill and wisdom of the midwife or through the husband's healing power of touch. The epiphany of the ritual is when the baby's head pops out or alternatively, after a suspenseful, timeless moment, he takes his first breath. The story concludes with a general affirmation of love for everyone involved, especially the baby, and an expression of gratitude to God, or a mystic revelation ("All is One", "I realize the Unity of all Beingness"). Many accounts contain incidents of telepathy, precognition, astral travel or levitation.

From these testimonials it is clear that birth at The Farm is a ritual central to the life of the community, a ritual organised and directed by the midwife, whose role as a healer is closer to that of shaman than to that of doctor. Like the shaman, the midwife must understand and work with forces of nature. Ina May says,

> birthing mothers are elemental forces, in the same sense that gravity, thunderstorms, earthquakes and hurricanes are elemental forces. In order to understand their energy flow you must love and respect them for their true magnificance...[6]

She emphasises the sacred character of her work ("Every birth is Holy") and interprets birth in a Christian context: "Every birth is the birth of the Christ child." She describes the way of the midwife as a spiritual path:

> The Vow of the Midwife has to be that she will put out one hundred percent of her energy to the mother and child that she is delivering until she is certain that they have safely made the passage. This means she must put the welfare of the mother and child first before that of herself and her own family if she has to make a choice of that kind.[7]

The midwife's sacred power lies in her touch:

Great changes can be brought about by the midwife's touching the woman or the baby....For this touch to carry the power it must, the midwife must be in a state of grace. She has to take a spiritual vow...if she is to have a touch with any potency.[8]

The midwife's role is also to be a spiritual guide or yoga instructor to the birthing mother:

One of the midwife's most valuable tools is the same intimate knowledge of the subtle physiology of the human body that is the province of yoga. The spiritual midwife brings about states of consciousness in ladies that allow physical energy transformations of great power, great beauty, and great utility.[9]

The births possess the sacred character of ritual. No profane spectators are allowed; Ina May claims they "slow down or halt the energy".[10] The mother is clothed in the sacred "costume" of nudity and the husband is naked above the waist. The rationale behind this seems to be that the body as nature is sacred, therefore the mother becomes more animal and filled with sacred power. Also, she and the husband are more accessible to the magical, healing "telepathic" power of touch. Touching and postures are stylised and stereotyped. The home becomes the sacred space and the bed the altar. Participants speak of an altered perception of their ordinary environment: "everything looked golden", "the walls looked misty and glowing". One husband said, "suddenly the bed started to shake and roll like the surf".[11] Similarly, perceptions of time are altered or distorted. In many of the testimonials the epiphany of the ritual is written in italics: "*It all felt timeless*" or "*It felt like one of those timeless life and death moments when everything is supsended.*"

The ritual actors are all necessary to direct the energy, and each has a different role.

The father sits behind his wife, supporting her back; his job is to touch her, massaging her back, breasts and legs, to "smooch with her" and tell her she looks beautiful. Cara, who seems to be the second most charismatic midwife, says:

Those loving sexy vibes which got the baby in there in the first place are what will help get him out.[12]

Stephen advises the fathers to "Be Tantric with your lady." "Tantric" on The Farm means "telepathic in the language of touch". This term underlines the belief at The Farm that touch is sacred and has a magical power. Therefore, the husband is encouraged by the midwife to make love to his labouring wife, to arouse her sexually, behaviour that would be considered entirely inappropriate anywhere else. However, on The Farm it is part of a sacred ritual and represents the telepathic communication between husband and wife, channeling of "The Energy" which will help facilitate the birth. Some husbands claim feeling sympathetic "rushes", and many mothers declare their husband's touch helped them handle the "energy". Some couples report a "falling in love all over again" or feeling like newlyweds after this experience.

The role of the mother has different aspects. She is a channel of the life force and is identified with nature. Beneath a photograph of waves crashing against rocks, Ina May writes "labouring birthing mothers are elemental forces...tornados, volcanoes, hurricanes...you can't predict what they will do."[13] Admiring husbands compare their wives to animals: "she looked exactly like a bullfrog with its eyes bulging out,"[14] and Stephen affectionately addresses a labouring mother as "monkey lady".

The pregnant woman is considered to be in a wise or sacred state. A photograph in the preface shows a pregnant lady in Buddha-pose, cradling her belly and contemplating her navel. On the other hand, the birthing mother is undergoing an ordeal in which her courage is being tested along with her ability to flow with the life force. Stephen says, "It does a man good to see his lady being brave about having his child." Finally, the birth is her chance to achieve a high spiritual state, and even a mystical experience. Ina May advises her "get your head in a place where you can get as high as possible."[15] Some husbands describe their wives as performing yoginis with amazing breath and physiological control. Midwife Cara presents a mother as a goddess-creator though the magic power of speech (like *mantra* and *logos*) in the text accompanying the centrefold nativity scene:

> Nancy taught me what heavy magic speech is, when she'd say, "I just want to open wide" and her cervix would dilate another two centimeters. Then she'd say, "I want to let go and let the baby out," and she started to push the baby out..."I want the very best for this baby," and he came out into vibes full of crystal clear life force.[16]

There are many accounts of magical flight in the mother's stories:

> I was somewhere on the astral plane, feeling all the forces of the Universe... pounding my body. I felt like my brain and upper body were separate from the rest and looking down on the action.[17]

The idea that a pregnant or birthing woman is every woman and one with all creation is expressed.

> I flashed on all the mothers around the world who must be having babies at the

same time, and felt telepathic with them. Then I felt it all go back in time to include *all* mothers. It just felt like giving birth is such a pure eternal thing, always happening somewhere, always Holy.[18]

The baby, however, is the ritual actor who is the most sacred. Babies are compared to angels and also to eastern gurus. Stephen says, "Your child is your spiritual guide and teacher."

The people on The Farm are Christians and the "sacrament of birth" is a communication with God. The following passage conveys a clear idea of Stephen Gaskin's unique intepretation of Christianity. Adoration is "telepathic virbrations", the Holy Spirit its manifested through "sexual love vibrations", and halos are "auras".

A nursing mother is really a Holy and sacred thing. If she'll really give her kid some and really let it go, she can become a tremendous generator of psychic energy. That energy is for the baby. They say, "Man does not live by bread alone." A kid that's been breast-fed for the first few months of his life is not making it on just the milk, he's making it on pure energy, which is being given to him in the form of — call it sexual if you like — vibrations. Those sexual love vibrations are a manifestation of Holy Spirit. When a child is nursing and soaks it up, it's good for the child and it makes him prosper and it makes him fatter, just as if it had put something material on him. You can come up to any lady who has a new baby and who's in love with that baby, and you can tune into it and it's just like the Christ child. The Catholic Church shows those pictures called "Adoration of the Infant". To adore is to put your attention on somebody and become receptive to them, feel their vibrations in a telepathic and loving place, and it's the way you approach babies and Holy men and people like that. In religious art there are pictures of a bunch of people sitting around a baby and the baby has all these power lines coming out of his head and glows and has auras. You can see that on all new babies if you pay good enough attention and be pure in heart.[19]

This passage is interesting in that it presents a feminine idea of the sacred. Nursing is a ritual, an acting out of the Madonna's Adoration for the Christ Child. The milk is identified with the Holy Spirit. A nursing mother is "a Holy and sacred thing", identified with the Virgin and also with the nurturing forces of nature. Nursing and birthing are two rituals that can be performed only by women and are evidently rituals with a high spiritual status on The Farm. The mother is the star of the birthing ritual until the baby appears and upstages her. She is compared to a Goddess Creator in the text accompanying the centre fold-out, her "heavy magic speech" creating life. This is a self-conscious imitation of the Creation in the Bible. Thus the meaning of the birthing ritual at The Farm is a recreation of the universe with the mother as goddess.

The social function of the birth is in binding the nuclear family closer to the community. The birth is an initiation ritual, a direct experience of The Farm's philosophy, and a powerful psychological transformation in which Gaskin's world view is impressed on the minds of the participating couple. A "beautiful" birth is evidence of the telepathic power of the community to create its own reality. Stephen says, "A community of beautiful vibrations can bring about refined, pure creation".[20] This is why the mothers don't need hospitals; if enough people are present at the birth and believe it will be perfect, then it will be. It also explains why birth is a public and relatively crowded event. A group of people form a sort of telepathic field and each healthy baby is seen as physical proof of the power of The Farm's "telepathic society".

The Cult of Birth at The Institute for the Development of the Harmonious Human Being

Cybele Gold's book, *Joyous Childbirth* describes the beliefs and rituals surrounding childbirth in the IDHHB, a spiritual community in Grass Valley, California. In 1964 Cybele became a disciple of E.J. Gold, later married him, and took over the administration of the Institute. In 1974 she gave birth to their first child.

It is difficult to describe the IDHHB. To call it eclectic, protean and theatrical is an understatement. E.J. Gold, the founder-leader, has a background in science fiction (his father was editor of *Galaxy Magazine*), Scientology (Hubbard was a friend of his father's) and Gestalt Theraphy. The ideas of Gurdjiev, the Russian mystic, are perhaps the most pervasive in his system. He is a mime artist and comedian who disorients his students by administering shocks or jolts. His professed aim is "The education of the universe, one idiot at a time". He creates a new cult with a new name every year. One season the theme will be Tibetan, the next it will be Sufi. Gold rechristens himself accordingly and will become Mr. G. with a fake moustache and a fez for the Gurdjiev-style "Work Groups", and then sport blackface for "The Wudshalo Handbook" which claims to present a hitherto-undiscovered martial art from Ethiopia.

The underlying philosophy is consistent throughout the changes, and is best described as neo-gnostic. Gold believes in reincarnation. The soul is immortal, but utterly alien and machine-like in the sense that it will repeat the same life over and over again with the same boring obsessions unless it is de-automatised by conscious "Work". The first step in this process is to free the soul or "Being" from identification with the body, the personality and the social role so that one can achieve the "waking state", a Zen-like awareness in the present that will enable the "Being" to stay conscious between lives. The powers resulting from this not only include dying fearlessly and choosing one's next body, but mobility and efficiency within the roles one plays in this lifetime. E.J. Gold's techniques emphasise role playing, and the ritual death-rebirth of his cult or "outer school" can be interpreted as practice in staying awake between roles or lives. Since Gold describes life as a process of constant dying and being reborn it would seem his techniques aim at cultivating a shamanic ability to travel through "between" states that can apply to social roles and life crises as well as physical death.

Cybele, by creating a cult of birth in which she, not her husband, was clearly the expert, became a spiritual leader in her own right. Following in Gold's entrepreneurial footsteps she chose a spiritual name, Cybele, indicating her identification with the ancient fertility goddess from Asia Minor, and set up a course in Conscious Birth. From all accounts, most of the women who attended were not pregnant and the emphasis was on learning how to give birth to your own soul. The course in 1974 culminated in a simulated birth experience which resembled a shamanic ordeal of initiation. Participants reported reliving their former births and deaths and travelling on weird astral planes.

Joyous Childbirth, A Manual for Conscious Childbirth appears to be handbook on natural childbook, until one reads the preface in which Cybele states her aim:

> This book, unlike any other, focuses on the specific problems and solutions of spiritual birth — that is, the birth of a being in a created atmosphere which makes it possible for the being to come through childbirth completely intact, with its eternal memory and meditation unbroken and uninterrupted. Most methods of childbirth do at least one thing which prevents the being from maintaining its meditation through the process of rebirth. This system, if followed exactly, is capable of assisting the being in maintaining its full spiritual identity throughout the birth process.[21]

The Leboyer system is the basis of her method, but adapted to Gold's ideas. The birth environment is controlled — no noises, bright lights, or drugs, and mother and child maintain close contact immediately after birth. For Leboyer the purpose is to promote the psychological welfare of mother and child and to facilitate bonding. For Cybele, the purpose is to avoid shocks to the "Being" which would cause it to forget its divine nature and identify with its human form. It also allows the mother to concentrate on maintaining psychic contact with the baby. Thus she shifts the emphasis from psychological to spiritual trauma, from emotional bonding to psychic contact.

The preparation of the expectant mother is rather like the shaman's apprenticeship. The first exercise is *Centering Meditation*[22]: the mother says "I AM" 100 times daily and imagines a corresponding vibration in her solar plexus. This meditation is to be practised during the first stages of labour.

The aim is to develop the will or "Attention" which, Castaneda-style, is located in the solar plexus. Once this is mastered, the next exercise is *Getting in Touch with Baby*. This is a focussing of the will on the I AM of the baby in order to make psychic contact. The mother is in a sort of mediumistic trance during birth, acting as the baby's spirit guide. This not only facilitates the delivery, but helps the "Being" maintain its spiritual identity so that it will not suffer a "massive memory blackout" and forget its previous existence.

The remaining three exercises featured in *Joyous Childbirth* symbolise an inner detachment from the outer mask of the body and social personality. *The Draining Exercise*[23], as the name suggests, is a purification ritual in which, through focussing on the moment between the "out" breath and the "in" breath, thoughts and emotions are allowed to fall away. It is an interesting combination of Lamaze and yoga breathing techniques. The next exercise, *The Mask* (this involves relaxing the face and wiping it free of expression) is reminiscent of African masks which identify the wearer with his or her mythic ancestor. In the IDHHB, the "Mythic ancestor" is the "Being" ancient, immortal and formless, and therefore free from the pain of birth. *The Confront*, in which the mother and father sit two feet apart and maintain eye contact without physical or emotional reactions, is strikingly similar to the Confrontation exercise in the Scientology Communications Course. When two Scientologists gaze into each other's eyes they are Thetans (immortal, omniscient omnipotent spirit beings) floating in space, zapping each other like sci-fi heroes with a psychic exchange of energy. The ritual holds a similar significance for IDHHB members. One is reminded of the shaman's magical power of seeing.

The physical exercises outlined in *Joyous Childbirth* are the usual strengthening and flexibility exercises featured in pre-natal courses. Cybele, however, has chosen names for them which imbue them with a mystical significance. For example, perineum clenching is called *Tantric Exercise*. She describes a meditation called *Solarisation* which is interesting as an attempt to create a feminine idea of the sacred. The uterus becomes the source of all life and the mother becomes the Goddess-Creator:

> *Solarisation* — Imagine your uterus to be the central point of all beginning life....As you exhale imagine the life force radiating outward, filling the universe with life and love.[24]

These pre-natal exercises are part of a spiritual discipline that prepares the mother for a possible mystical experience, during the final stage of expulsion. This experience is Tunnel Vision, often described in pre-natal courses as a moment of distortion in sensory perception, but Cybele presents it as an out-of-body experience. Her description reminds me of the shaman's magical power of flight:

A Note About Tunnel Vision: Your vision changes radically when you are pushing to deliver the baby during expulsion. So does your state of being relative to your body and the environment. You may notice a gradual change, or you may become aware of it suddenly at the most extreme point. Everything around you goes into the background and your attention refocuses within yourself in the deepest area of being. Sometimes sound perceptions will take on a distant quality. Your eyes may change color. Mine are normally brown, but during pushing they change to bright green. The energy sensation is a burst of waves similar to heat, but in the electromagnetic band. You may be able to combine all perceptions into one, in which you see/hear/smell/feel/know/remember, etc., everything happening for miles around all at once. If you were under medication, you would lose this experience.[25]

The style of birth in the IDHHB is described by members in Chapter I of *Joyous Childbirth*, "Conscious Birth Experiences". In each case birth is a public and communal event involving the nuclear and sometimes extended family, friends, and E.J. Gold. The event is videotaped or filmed. Everyone maintains a strict silence so as to avoid shocks to the baby's Being. The husband's role is to be a coach and to assist his wife in her spiritual work by "Holding the Confront" with her. As soon as the baby is born the husband solemnly reads out *The Address to Being*.

This is the planet Earth in the solar system Ors of the galaxy Milky Way. You have just been reborn into a human body. The time and day are _______, _______, in the month of _______, of the year _______. The location of this room is in _______ (city, town, or country) in the state of _______, in the country of _______. My human name is _______, and I will act as your planetary father. This (indicating the mother) is your planetary mother. Her human name is _______. We will be taking responsibility for the development of your psyche and body until the maturation of that body.[26]

No one is allowed to refer to the sex of the newborn child lest the Being forget its spiritual nature and identify with its new body. E.J. Gold's ritual function appears to be that of welcoming the child into his community. In one account he kneels beside a freshly born infant, gazes into its eyes and says, "Welcome back, old friend. Ready to get to work?"

This is a joke, of course, but it is reminiscent of the way Cybele met her guru-husband. She wandered into his perfume stall and he looked up and asked, "Well, are you ready to get to work this time around?"[27] There are references in IDHHB literature to ancient "schools" of which Gold's group is a reincarnated congregation. For example, in 1974 they called The Second Council of Nicea to discuss the coming "Dark Ages" and announced solemnly, "The Same Souls Are Present."[28] Thus it is clear that the birth is a ritual of initiation in which the baby is formally admitted into Gold's "School".

Several points emerge from these accounts of ritualised birth:

1. The theological significance of birth in the IDHHB is that it is a ritual enactment of their belief in reincarnation. The central mystery is not birth but rebirth. The purpose of the controlled environment and the rituals is to reinforce the spiritual identity of all the participants. The baby is welcomed to the planet with the same cautious respect one might extend to a visiting Martian.

2. For the mother the occasion is not unlike the initiatory ordeal of the shaman's apprentice. She displays her mettle as a "Being" through her magical control over the birth process. Her relationship with her baby resembles that of the shaman with the helping spirit, and she communicates through the "spirit language" of the I AM exercise. She undergoes a sort of ritual dismemberment through the disassociation exercises, and her courage is tested; she is not only impervious to pain, but unmoved while confronting her own death, for birth in Gold's system, like the shaman's initiation, is a symbolic death. Consequently, the woman approaches giving birth as if it were a dress rehearsal for her own death.

3. Cybele's analgesic method is very different from Ina May's. The Farm lady is encouraged to identify with her body which, as a part of nature, is sacred, and to abandon herself to the contractions or "rushes", which are perceived to be higher universal forces. Her closeness to her own body, and to other people, is ensured through touch. Cybele's system depends on breathing and eye contact and emphasises control over physical sensations by disassociating the real inner self from the body. Gold's neo-gnostic view envisages the human as a solitary alien Being, essentially sexless, inhabiting a machine-like body. It is interesting to compare photographs from the two books. After the sensual, long-haired "ladies" of The Farm, writhing in their husband's arms, their sweaty faces expressing the full range of human emotion, one turns to a picture of Cybele and E.J. demonstrating the *Confront*. E.J. is bald, and they both have shaven eyebrows which lend an eerie mask-like quality to their fleshy faces, as they stare, like rival sorcerors, into each other's eyes.

In both communities the birth experience is an initiation ritual that not only marks the woman's progress up the spiritual ladder but also serves to bind the family unit closer to the community. One could argue that these rituals are control mechanisms that discourage dyadic withdrawal from the group and regulate the exclusive couple relationship. Rosabeth Moss Kanter in her study, *Community and Commitment*,[29] found that successful communes weakened family bonds by practising celibacy, for example. It is interesting to examine the birth rituals from this perspective.

Bryan Pfaffenberger's study is useful, providing the social background to The Farm ("A World of Husbands and Mothers: Sex Roles and Their Ideological Context in the Formation of The Farm").[30] Challenging Kanter's theory, he finds evidence that the couple is very strong. Gaskin frowns on extramarital sex; in their Sunday morning Church meetings, couples are invited to air their problems, and Stephen encourages them to be loving and devoted to each other. Ina May plays the role of marriage counsellor as well as midwife during birth. However, the couples' marriages are very much regulated by the group. Two sets of couples live together in "complex households" so that they can intervene in instances of macho domination, or intimidation. Stephen believes that if couples are left alone inevitably the male will intimidate the female and destroy her "beautiful female energy".[31] In the early days of The Farm they practised "Four Marriage" in which two couples would marry each other and swear eternal fidelity. This was abandoned when Stephen's own four marriage, which had been contracted during a telepathic LSD trip, broke down. This background explains the public nature of the births. Stephen describes his society as a "mental nudist camp",[32] and even toilets are doorless. Therefore group regulation serves to strengthen the marriage and produce faithful, loving couples, particularly when one considers that these people came from the permissive society of the hippie era.

In the IDHHB the couple is not as important, if the life of the leader is any indication of the status of marriage in the group. Cybele and E.J. have been divorced since the book was published, and he now lives with 5 of his female students who are all giving birth regularly. Although there are a few long-term couples in the group, my impression as a participant in a weekend workshop in New York City, July 1984, was that there was a high proportion of divorced people among his students. The group is run by women, and in Grass Valley they have communal day care so that the mothers are free to do "The Work".

Rosabeth Kanter also claimed that in successful communes there was equality between the sexes. Although The Farm is the most successful contemporary commune in North America in terms of size and longevity, the equality of the sexes is arguable. There is a strong differention in sex roles. Men work in the shops and fields and dominate the governing board. Women are relegated to the domestic sphere as homemakers. However, a Farm insider would consider women to be equal to men (certainly they are in Stephen's ideology), and holier than men in their power to give birth. The more babies a Farm "lady" has, the holier she is. Pfaffenberger mentions that the normal dress for women is a maternity smock. One lady who wanted to drive a tractor was discouraged by the group because women's reproductive power is very holy and they must not endanger it by emulating men's roles. Thus, although woman might be seen as degraded in her social role by outsiders, within the ideology of The Farm she is seen as equal and even superior. Certainly the ladies themselves, judging from Pfaffenberger's study and from Ina May's book, seem to consider themselves as happier and more fulfilled than outsiders.

In Gold's ideology women are equal to men, but there are two ways of viewing his polygamous situation. When I first heard of Cybele's demise and his five wives who create and destroy his series of cults for him, I interpreted the situation as a triumph of male power in the group. However, after meeting the "wives" in the New York workshop, my impression was not of an oppressed harem. They were strong, outspoken women who appeared to be enjoying life and were very affectionate with each other. I began to see the group as a matriarchy behind which Gold was the brain. It was the ex-husbands of these women who seemed to be the oppressed ones.

The historian Frank Manuel once observed that "the utopia may well be a sensitive indicator of where the sharpest anguish of an age lies". Reading through these alternative pre-natal books I was struck by the authors' sensitivity to the pain of our fragmented and transitional age. Ina May's book ends with the following invitation,

> Don't have an abortion. You can come to The Farm and we'll deliver your baby and take care of him, and if you ever decide you want him back, you can have him.[33]

In the section on abnormal births she tells the story of Ira, a baby who was born with no skull over his brain. He was given to the hospital where, expecting him to die within a few hours, the nurses did not feed him. When after five days his mother heard he was still alive she was shocked that he had not been fed, and brought him home. The midwife writes,

> he and the parents stayed at our house, and we fed him with an eye dropper because he was too weak to nurse....His mother made him little hats and they sunned him on the porch. He never cried but now and then he called us....He was no longer a baby; he was like a wise old teacher. We felt very privileged to have a Holy thing like that in our house...He lived for 5 more days....When Dr. Williams used the medical term, "anencephalic monster", we'd say, "no, a baby, not a monster, a baby."[34]

These passages are a defiant assertion of the sacredness of human life in the face of a technological society which often treats birth and pregnancy as a purely medical phenomenon. A new father I interviewed recently expressed his uneasiness at viewing a TV report on the birth of septuplets. "I couldn't understand the father's attitude. One of his babies had just *died* and he was telling jokes to the media, 'Well, we always wanted a baseball team', and the media crew was right in there in the intensive care unit, filming the poor little creatures — it was tasteless, to say the least.''[35] Similarly, a few women I talked to who were unanimously pro-abortion, nevertheless revealed feelings of grief and guilt concerning their own past abortions. One woman even invented a ritual to allay her guilt: ''I made a little stick man out of twigs and buried him in the woods. Every once in awhile I return to the spot and ask the spirit's forgiveness.''[36]

The depiction of labouring women as sacred, beautiful, and powerful forces of nature is not only a reaction to the traditional Christian view of childbirth as suffering and punishment for The Fall, but also a conscious departure from the callous and irreverent treatment women sometimes receive in hospitals, as the following story from *Spiritual Midwifery* illustrates:

> One of the most insensitive things I ever saw a doctor do was during a caesarean section....The doctor put his hands on either side of the incision and moving the wound as if it were a puppet mouth, said ''Hi, Steve'' to the young intern across the operating table...The remark was intended to be funny, but wasn't because the doctor was ignoring so totally the human dignity, not even to mention the bravery of the lady whose life was in his hands.[37]

Every woman I interviewed had heard similar stories. The ritualisation of birth in the IDHHB reveals a different concern: an anxiety concerning the fragmentation and impermanence of today's urban life. The determination not to identify with what is going on in birth might well be due to a fear of being stuck in the limiting, demanding role of mother. In order to survive in an insecure, changing world, the ability to shift roles and maintain an inner identity separate from these roles is vital. Thus the birth ritual in the IDHHB can be seen as an expression of the anguish of the contemporary woman who fears the loss of mobility, social flexibility, and control over her life that motherhood entails. When the woman ''holds the confront'' with her husband and ''drops the mask'' she is telling him, the world and herself, ''I am not really a woman; motherhood is one of my many masks. My real self is utterly alien and free, a Being with infinite powers.''

Another concern reflected in these ritualised births is an anxiety concerning the strength and durability of family life. At The Farm couples have returned to the earlier values of frontier life. Their births are a public display of their devotion in which they seek to conform to Gaskin's model of the ideal male-female relationship. In the IDHHB the opposite strategy is employed. The pain of separation is handled by avoiding attachments, perceived as false because they belong to the fake self of the body and social role. The baby is treated as a free soul, not to be owned or talked down to. The husband and wife encounter each other as free, alien, sexless beings. The impermanence of life and relationships is stressed in Gold's system, and his techniques emphasise mastery over "between" states so that his students are equipped to handle separation, solitude, divorce, and eventually, death. "Ordinary couples" I interviewed expressed the same concerns and believed that the husband's participation in the birth would strengthen their relationship and facilitate bonding between father and baby.

"ORDINARY" BIRTHS

In focussing upon the pre-natal preparation and birth experiences of "ordinary" couples I found in the course of the interviews many instances of ritualistic approaches to and magical interpretations of birth. From these accounts and from an interview with Joanne, the midwife's assistant and administrative head of the Centre de Naissance Alternative, several main themes emerged:

1. The idea that birth was a primal event. Pre-natal books and courses stress bonding between parents and child, claiming that the minutes following birth are crucial in this process. Conrad Lorenz's study of imprinting in geese is often cited. As a result, parents often feel their future family relationships will be conditioned irrevocably by their performance of the birth ritual. For example, women feel that the father's participation in the birth will mark his initiation into the new-style fatherhood, which involves an equal sharing of the "nurturing" tasks.

2. Parents often create their own rituals in response to an inner psychological pressure. Some of these rituals are recreations of primitive fertility rites or taboos of the type described in Fraser's *Golden Bough*. For example, Joanne described burying her afterbirth in the garden of her farmhouse and planting a tamarack tree over it. "The placenta was so beautiful, all red and blue, smooth on one side and so complicated on the other. It was like a miniature planet, a whole system of life support. I felt it was part of me and part of my daughter, so I felt like doing something special with it."[38] Two midwives reported having sampled Placenta Stew, served up to them after the birth by the participating husbands.

3. The hypno-suggestibility of the woman in labour. Midwives rely upon the power of suggestion. Joanne said they emphasised a positive attitude to the approaching birth and avoided discussing abnormalities or possible complications. "If they believe it will go well, it will go well." Her accounts of the sumbliminal techniques and psychological intervention of the midwife are remniscent of the pre-Pavlovian hypnosis, with the hocus pocus put back in.

When Isabel (the Midwife) is talking she uses her voice to emphasise certain words. She *sings* them so they go straight into the woman's mind. All the good midwives can do that. For example once we had a woman who was very independent, very strong and she got pregnant through a casual encounter and decided to have the baby on her own. The labour went very well, but when it came time to push, she was using her muscles to hold the baby in. Isabel interpreted this as an unwillingness to let the baby take over — she was still trying to control it. Some of her friends were there so Isabel told her to relax into the hands of her friends, who lifted her up — to let other people help her. She sort of sang it and the woman relaxed, we lifted her up and the baby soon came out. But I was worried that she might relax too much and start to haemorrhage after, so I took Isabel aside. Then she sang to the woman to tighten up as soon as the baby was born — she would feel her uterus clamping down — and she did — she was all right. You see, when you are in labour your whole mind opens up to a new dimension. You are very susceptible during this time.

4. Magical applications and interpretations of obstetrical events. One woman used her pre-natal exercise in a magical way. "Whenever I felt frightened about the birth, I would clench my perineum and chant, "It's going to be all right." Many parents have occult interpretations of the events of birth, and turn it into a ritual of divination or see portents in events preceding the birth: "Driving to the hospital my contractions were getting closer together. It was 6:00 A.M. and the streets were deserted but suddenly we saw a little boy sitting on the front steps of a house. At that moment I knew it would be a boy."[39]

5. The idea that natural childbirth was both a spiritual and a political event. For many women, choosing natural and home births was a political choice and a feminist issue. Hospitals were seen as male-dominated, patriarchal institutions where the woman was reduced to the passive role of patient. Home births were seen as spiritual, hospital births as secular. Some women even went so far as to describe the doctor's intervention as a "desecration". Some women felt men had taken over a field which by rights should belong to women, and that all obstetricians and gynaecologists should be women. The main issue was the woman's rights to power and control over her own body. These ideas are reinforced by and perhaps originate in pre-natal books coming out of the feminist movement. Every woman I interviewed had heard stories illustrating the callous and irreverent treatment of women and babies in hospitals.

THE CULT OF BIRTH IN THE FEMINIST MOVEMENT

An investigation of the books in the feminist section of a library or bookshop will reveal that the only books that are religious in tone are the pre-natal books. The few exceptions are studies of ancient fertility goddesses and of witchcraft, and the works of Reuther and Daly, although these are religious in content rather than in tone. Most feminist writers tend to view the Catholic Church as an oppressive patriarchal institution. This view is expressed in Mary Daly's *The Church and the Second Sex*. With the rejection of traditional "phallic" symbols of the sacred, a search has begun for new, female symbols that reflect women's psyche and culture.

The work of artist Judy Chicago is a good example of this. Her current show, *The Birth Project*, has been described by a critic as "creating an iconography of birth, a way of depicting the female genitalia, at once tasteful and explicit." Chicago says, "Nowhere in western art are there images of the birth process itself, unless you believe God touching man on the finger."[40]

There is a certain narcissism in the cult of birth, in the close-up explicit photographs which many pre-natal books contain of babies and female genitalia in the moment of expulsion. There is a vogue among parents to photograph the birth and show it to their friends in an album, or to tape, film, and videotape the event. One might ask why there is this sudden need for exposure of what was traditionally a private event. It could be dismissed as just another aspect of the new narcissism, satirised by Tom Wolfe in *The Me Decade*, or explained as an attack on the establishment, a defiant demonstration on the part of women that the female body is beautiful and powerful, or alternatively as an offshoot of the sexual revolution. However, these images could also be seen as playing a part in the forging of a new iconography of the sacred. They have a heavy emotional impact as a depiction of pain, ecstasy, defecation and creation. Teenage students I interviewed who had just seen a film on birth in their sex education class found it either utterly revolting and terrifying or else inspiring and deeply moving. By its very nature, the birth process is a strong symbol of the triumph of life over death — of immortality.

The significance of the cult of birth within the feminist movement seems to be a turning to the self as a source of sacred power. The cult of birth has a certain grass-roots quality. One woman interviewed said that when she got pregnant she felt like she'd suddenly joined an underground movement. Strangers would warn her against the medical establishment, friends gave her clothes and baby furniture. "It was like I was part of a secret society." The feminist movement is concerned with the issue of woman's power, and until recently, procreation was seen as a weakening of her power in the sense of interfering in her career. Ten years ago birth control was a bigger issue than styles of birth. But perhaps because the "baby boomers" who have established themselves in their careers are beginning to procreate in their middle-to-late 30s, birth and fertility are "hot" issues now. Even Germaine

Greer's latest book is a *volte face* on her former arguments. Birth is self-expression, "the one experience I haven't tried yet". The need to ritualise the experience appears to lie in the individual's feelings of powerlessness in the face of society's institutions — and women who regard themselves as part of an oppressed minority within a patriarchal culture would be particularly prone to these feelings. Through ritual these individuals are seeking a source of hidden power which is believed to be located within the self. One woman who had recently attended a workshop conducted by the witch, Starhawk, claimed, "The word *empowerment* was used about a thousand times".[41] Thus women who control their birth through ritual feel they are tapping a hidden source of power within themselves, a power that can be used to make them more effective in their new life as a parent.

REFERENCES

1 Interview with Trevor, 1982.
2 Frederick Bird, "The Pursuit of Innocence", sociological analysis, 1979.
3 Ina May Gaskin, *Spiritual Midwifery*. Tennessee: The Book Publishing Co., 1978.
4 *Ibid.*, p. 14.
5 *Ibid.*, p. 239.
6 *Ibid.*, p. 354.
7 *Ibid.*, p. 283.
8 *Ibid.*, p. 283.
9 *Ibid.*, p. 284.
10 *Ibid.*, p. 238.
11 *Ibid.*, p. 238.
12 *Ibid.*, p. 327.
13 *Ibid.*, p. 354.
14 *Ibid.*
15 *Ibid.*, p. 355.
16 *Ibid.*, centrefold.
17 *Ibid.*, p. 350.
18 *Ibid.*, p. 352.
19 *Ibid.*, p. 102.
20 Brian Pfaffenberger, "A World of Husbands and Mothers: Sex Roles and Their Ideological Context in the Formation of The Farm" in Jon Wagner, *Sex Roles in Contemporary Communes*. Bloomington, IN: Indiana University Press, 1982.
21 Cybele and E.J. Gold, *Joyous Childbirth*. California: And/Or Press, 1977.
22 *Ibid.*, p. 67.
23 *Ibid.*, p. 68.
24 *Ibid.*, p. 252.

25 *Ibid.*, p. 123.
26 *Ibid.*, p. 143.
27 Cybele Gold, "My Life with Mr. Gold", Part One. IDHHB pamphlet, n.d.
28 Susan Palmer, *Shakti, The Spiritual Science of DNA*. M.A. Thesis, Department of Religion, Concordia University, 1976.
29 Rosabeth Moss Kanter, *Community and Commitment: Communes in a Sociological Perspective*. Cambridge, MA: Harvard University Press, 1972.
30 Pfaffenberger, *op. cit.*
31 *Ibid.*, p. 202.
32 *Ibid.*, p. 197.
33 Gaskin, *Spiritual Midwifery, op. cit.*, p. 448.
34 *Ibid.*, p. 456.
35 Interview with J.K.
36 Interview with S.P.
37 Gaskin, *Spiritual Midwifery, op. cit.*, p. 455.
38 Interview with Joanne.
39 Interview with Karla.
40 *Globe and Mail*, Nov. 1984.
41 Interview with Anne.

FURTHER READING

Arms, Suzanne, *Immaculate Deception*. San Francisco: Houghton Mifflin, 1975.
Leboyer, Frederick, *Birth without Violence*. New York: Knopf, 1975.
Milinaire, Catherine, *Birth*. New York: Harmony, 1974.
Nilsson, Ingelman-Sundberg, *A Child Is Born*. New York: Dell, 1982.

CHRISTINE OVERALL

Reproductive Technology and the Future of the Family

INTRODUCTION

This chapter examines some of the ways in which recent developments in the technology of reproduction may affect the kinds of relationships that now exist primarily within the so-called nuclear family. I am concerned with how these new relationships between men and women and between parents and children may change what we are able to be and do and become, as children, as parents, and as spouses.

Reproductive technology is burgeoning, and so is discussion about it by sociologists, legal experts, feminists, and philosophers. Many — but especially doctors, lawyers, and scientists — are willing to sing the praises of reproductive technology, yet they seldom stop to consider its implications for our future. The general rule appears to be: what can be done should be done; if it is possible to manipulate human reproduction, then human reproduction should be manipulated. In contrast to this approach, I argue that we must consider carefully what may be the potential effects of reproductive technology on human relationships.

Some forms of reproductive technology are already very familiar. Today contraception, abortion, and often birth involve the use of some form of reproductive technology. But in this article I shall discuss several procedures and devices that are much more recent: foetal sex pre-selection, pre-natal diagnosis and surgery, in vitro fertilisation and embryo transfer, and surrogate motherhood. I shall briefly describe each of them, and suggest what implications each has for the future of the family.

There are two general themes that unify this discussion. The first concerns reproductive freedom and choice. I argue that new reproductive technology has a paradoxical effect on reproductive freedom, particularly the reproductive freedom of women: on the one hand, it appears to enhance our capacity to make choices, but on the other hand, a closer examination suggests that there are many ways in which reproductive technology may serve to reduce the reproductive choices we can make.

The second theme concerns the tendency towards the commodification[1] of human beings and the introduction of certain sorts of economic considerations into social relationships. Children, in particular, are commodified by reproductive technology, for it permits them to be treated in some respects as consumer goods that can be made to order and purchased on the open market. A child becomes a product with an exchange value, a luxury item that one might or might not want or need. At the same time, reproductive technology permits men to become primarily the consumers of reproductive services and reproductive products. Finally, reproductive technology also transforms women into reproductive consumers, but, more directly and more significantly, it makes women the suppliers of reproductive services and products. Thus, the economic relationships of buying, selling, and leasing are transforming traditional family alliances.

FOETAL-SEX PRE-SELECTION

The term "foetal sex pre-selection" refers to various means that have been proposed for the purpose of determining, at the time of conception, the sex of the foetus.[2] A variety of techniques for sex pre-selection have been experimentally tested.[3] Most promising among them are methods that involve separating X-bearing and Y-bearing sperm by means of filtering or centrifugation. The woman is then artificially inseminated with a sperm sample containing a significant concentration of the type of sperm that will produce a child of the desired sex. Thus, the woman's chances of conceiving a child of the "right" sex are increased, although success is by no means guaranteed.

At least two important questions about the use of foetal sex pre-selection could be raised: first, is it ever the case that individuals are justified in making use of pre-selection techniques to determine the sex of their children? If so, when and why are they so justified, and if not, why are they not justified?[4] Second, what sort of social policy about research into, and development and availability of, sex pre-selection should we have?[5] I shall concentrate mainly on the second of these.

In order to reflect on the issue, it is necessary to consider, first, the possible effects of the use of foetal sex pre-selection. At the moment, these effects are chiefly a matter of speculation. But we do know that there is a world-wide preference for male offspring over female offspring. Study after study has shown that this preference is held by men even more strongly than by women; that if a couple is to have only one child, they prefer a boy; that people want their first-born to be a boy; and that if they want an odd number of children (three, five, etc.) then they want more boys than girls.[6] In light of this well-documented preference for male offspring, it seems likely that widespread use of sex pre-selection techniques would result in a change in the sex ratio: that is, far more males than females would be born. Would this mean that, because of our fewer numbers, women would be more cherished and valued?[7] Or would it mean even greater restrictions on and control over women, in order to "safeguard" our scarce sexual and reproductive services?[8] Would the use of foetal sex pre-selection produce a decrease in population, since people would get exactly the kinds of children they want?[9] Or would it mean an increase in crime, violence and war (since men are primarily responsible for these)?[10] Would human freedom expand or diminish?

At least superficially, it looks as if the use of foetal sex pre-selection would increase our reproductive choices and control. But we must consider who makes the choices and who is in control. Fetal sex pre-selection enables people to act upon their biasses against females. Who would make that choice? Would it be women, who often express no preference of their own for the sex of their offspring,[11] but may tend to want a male child for the sake of their husbands? Would it be men, who may make the choice for male offspring, perhaps with the goal of obtaining a son to carry on their name?

Or, in impoverished countries, and in those subject to stringent state control, would the choice of foetal sex be imposed by governments anxious to set limits on the numbers and kinds of children produced by their citizens? Several social scientists who support the widespread use of foetal sex pre-selection advocate it because they believe it will reduce the population explosion. This would occur, it is claimed, because parents would no longer need to have "just one more child" in order to obtain a child of the desired sex. More radically, it has also been proposed that the use of sex pre-selection techniques, inevitably resulting in the birth of far more boys than girls, would reduce the population because there would be so many fewer women to bear children.[12] In this scenario, the price of foetal sex pre-selection is state control of reproduction, and, perhaps, considerable sacrifice of individual autonomy.

We must also consider the possible effects of this technique on the children themselves. On the one hand, it has been argued that the use of foetal sex pre-selection would produce happier families:[13] the parents get the kind of children they want; the children, whether boys or girls, are wanted as boys or girls. On the other hand, it has also been suggested that the use of foetal sex pre-selection would exaggerate existing gender roles: parents who want a son so much that they use sex pre-selection methods to obtain one would expect that son to act like a "real boy", and pre-selected daughters might be expected to be "little ladies".[14]

These stereotypes could be further exacerbated by the fact that sex preference is related to desired birth order: particularly in North America, people usually prefer a son first, then a daughter.[15] But studies have consistently found certain important differences between first- and second-born children, regardless of their sex. In terms of ability and academic and professional success, first-borns are over-represented.[16] Second-born children, however, are likely to be socially adept and popular.[17] Thus the use of sex pre-selection techniques could confirm existing stereotypes about the sexes and relegate women to "second class" status, because they would be denied the advantages of being the first-born.[18] On this view, gender stereotyping of children would be increased, to the detriment of their freedom to develop.

The use of foetal sex pre-selection also exemplifies the tendency toward the commodification of children. While apparently being valued for their own sake, through foetal sex pre-selection children are treated as a type of consumer good. The parents — perhaps most often the father — pay their money and take their choice: instead of being stuck with whatever nature brings, they purchase the type of child they want. But unfortunately, unlike some other forms of technology, the use of foetal sex pre-selection does not permit unsatisfied parents to return a defective product. Assuming, as I think we must, that the technology would not be fail-safe, we might wonder about the fate of those children — primarily females — who would be the "wrong" sex.[19] The use of foetal sex pre-selection appears to imply that children are wanted, not for their own sake, for their own individual characters and abilities, but rather for the sake of the gender they represent.

PRE-NATAL DIAGNOSIS AND FOETAL SURGERY

This tendency toward the commodification of children is even more evident in the use of pre-natal diagnosis and foetal surgery.

Pre-natal diagnosis involves the use of such procedures as ultrasound tests, chorionic villi sampling, and amniocentesis. These techniques permit the acquisition of a great deal of information about possible structural and chromosomal defects in the foetus, as well as its sex. In an ultrasound test, high-frequency sound waves are projected into the woman's uterus, and the waves reflected back are resolved visually to allow the foetus to be "seen" on a display screen.[20] In chorionic villi sampling, a tube is inserted through the vagina and cervix to the placenta, from which a small amount of tissue is removed. The tissue can be examined for evidence of foetal defects. This test can be performed as early as eight or nine weeks into the pregnancy, but it is not yet widely available in Canada.[21] On the other hand, amniocentesis is easily available. It involves the insertion of a needle through the woman's abdomen and into the amniotic fluid which surrounds the developing foetus. Fluid containing cells from the foetus is removed and can then be examined in the laboratory. However, amniocentesis cannot be performed before about sixteen weeks into the pregnancy, and, unlike chorionic villi sampling, a further two or three weeks are necessary to wait for the results of the analysis of the fluid.[22]

In the context of pre-natal diagnosis, the assumption is that a foetus found to be defective will be aborted. For example, the use of chorionic villi sampling permits an early abortion, in the first trimester of pregnancy, but a verdict of foetal defects detected through amniocentesis results in a very late abortion, at about five or six months' gestation.

In addition to diagnostic tests of the foetus, foetal surgery is also being developed.[23] This involves cutting open the woman's uterus during the pregnancy, temporarily removing the foetus, correcting a defect (such as a block in the urinary system), and then replacing the foetus in the uterus to enable the pregnancy to continue to term.

In general, once again, these technologies appear to enable us to obtain the kind of child we want, by repairing correctable defects and eliminating foetuses with non-correctable handicaps. Yet this very factor may contribute to the growing tendency to treat the child as a material commodity, a consumer good to be purchased by means of money and medical technology. Pre-natal diagnosis and foetal surgery permit us to make more and more detailed specifications of the type of child we want. The techniques encourage us to raise our standards for what are considered to be acceptable offspring. The development of these tests means that men and women become the consumers of special reproductive services designed to enhance the quality of the child-product. Although there can be no doubt that they permit the birth of more and more healthy babies, some ethicists and some handicapped persons themselves[24] fear that the widespread use of pre-natal diagnosis and foetal surgery will mean that in the future any children born with handicaps will tend to be regarded as unfortunate mistakes who should have been eliminated prior to birth.

These technologies also appear to increase our information and choice about reproduction. However, some recent writers have also challenged this assumption. Some forms of pre-natal testing are not always easily available. For example in Canada, chorionic villi sampling is so far available only to women who are enrolled in a scientific trial of the technique.[25] On the other hand, other diagnostic procedures, such as ultrasound, are now so routine that women do not have the opportunity and the right to refuse them — in spite of the fact that the long-term effects of ultrasound are not yet known.[26] It is taken for granted that the pregnant woman will submit to an ultrasound test twice in her pregnancy and that, if she is thirty-five or over, she will undergo amniocentesis. And then, if the foetus is found to be defective (to have, for example, Down's Syndrome) can she freely choose to continue the pregnancy if she so desires, or is pressure exerted on her to have an abortion?[27] In this context the autonomy of the woman is not augmented but decreased.

Another problem attendent upon pre-natal testing and surgery is that these processes draw more and more attention to the status and well-being of the foetus, and tend to treat the woman as no more than a sort of carrier or environment for it.[28] This sets the stage for what some legal experts see as a potential conflict between the alleged rights of the foetus and the rights of the pregnant woman.[29]

This conflict has already manifested itself in at least two areas. In the United States there have been landmark cases in which a caesarean section has been ordered to be performed on an unwilling woman for the sake of the supposed well-being of her foetus, as determined by still-fallible pre-natal tests. In those cases, the courts found that the safety of the foetus took priority over the autonomy and reproductive control of the mother.[30] In Canada certain cases have found that a child was the victim of pre-natal abuse as a result of the mother's use of alcohol or drugs.[31] These findings, while they seem to give a greater and greater protection to the foetus (and I do regard that as a desirable goal) may also provide a sturdy background for the erosion of maternal freedoms.

Some writers have wondered, then, whether the growing concern for the welfare of the foetus can be considered to be consistent with our current regulation of abortion. On the one hand, the abortion law, both here and in the United States, permits the killing of the foetus under specified conditions. On the other hand, more and more steps are being taken in other circumstances to safeguard the health of the foetus. Are these tendencies compatible with each other? Is it consistent to attempt to protect the health of the foetus at various stages of its existence, and yet also to sustain the mother's right to terminate its existence?[32]

These questions suggest that in evaluating the implications of pre-natal diagnosis and foetal surgery we should be assessing the relative claims of foetal rights and women's autonomy. Reproductive technology encourages physicians and scientists to see the pregnant woman as an adversary of the foetus.[33] The possibility exists that proposals to require certain restrictions on the mother's behaviour, in the interests of allegedly protecting foetal life and well-being, could be the result of the growing technological focus on the state of the foetus.[34] In the future we should therefore consider whether or not these technologies actually increase our reproductive control and choice, or whether in fact they subtly detract from the freedom of pregnant women.[35]

Christine Overall

IN VITRO FERTILISATION

The technology of in vitro fertilisation (IVF) must be evaluated in conjunction with embryo transfer and the storage of frozen embryos. In IVF a woman is treated with hormones which stimulate her to produce several ova (eggs) simultaneously. Under general anaesthesia, these ova are removed from her body. A sperm sample is obtained from her partner and is added to the ova in a petri dish. It is hoped that at least one and possibly more than one fertilised egg will be produced. The fertilised eggs are permitted to develop to the eight- or sixteen-cell stage; they are then transferred to the woman's uterus. Sometimes not all of the fertilised eggs are implanted; they can be frozen for possible use at a later date.[36]

The main rationale for the use of IVF and embryo transfer is the treatment of infertility — ordinarily, the treatment of infertility in the woman. In the typical case, the woman produces ova, but they are unable to reach the uterus because her fallopian tubes are blocked. When surgery to open the tubes is unsuccessful her only hope for a pregnancy lies in the IVF technique. Less frequently, the procedure can also be used for one type of male infertility. In this case, the man produces sperm, but in insufficient quantities and concentrations to permit fertilisation of the ovum in vivo, that is, within the woman's body. It is thought that in this instance the artificial environment of IVF permits fertilisation to take place more easily than it would within the environment of the woman's body.[37]

Like the other technologies discussed so far, IVF and embryo transfer appear to expand human control over reproduction, by enabling childless individuals to reproduce. And there can be no doubt about the very real grief experienced by many infertile couples.[38] Once again, however, it is necessary to look a little more closely at what the technology really accomplishes, and at who is in control of it.

This technology is not, first of all, available on demand. Specific criteria are used by the medical profession to determine who will have access to it. In most writings on infertility, the impression given is that infertility is only significant and worth treating in persons who are heterosexual and married, and have a so-called "stable" relationship with their partners.[39] Thus, women who are single and/or lesbian, for example, and in some cases those who are judged by the physician not to have the appropriate potential for parenting, often do not have access to these forms of reproductive technology.[40] It seems that the way in which IVF and embryo transfer are made available serves to reinforce the traditional connection between motherhood and marriage, and the dependence of women upon men.

Furthermore, for couples who are judged to be eligible for the procedure it is not an unmixed blessing. The process of extracting ova involves rather painful surgery. If it is not successful, the woman may have to undergo the surgery more than once. Moreover, at most Canadian clinics, the woman has no choice as to whether or not all of the fertilised eggs will be implanted in her. Thus, despite the increased probability of multiple birth, if the clinic's policy is to transfer them all, then regardless of what the woman thinks of the prospect of giving birth to twins or triplets or quadruplets, they are all transferred.[41]

It should be noted that in such countries as Britain, the United States, and Australia, the fate of so-called "spare embryos" — those which are produced by means of IVF and not subsequently transferred to the mother's uterus — is a hotly debated moral issue. Should spare embryos be discarded, or frozen for possible future use?[42] The attitude toward this appears to depend mainly on one's beliefs about the personhood, or lack of it, of the embryo.[43] But there may be other reasons for being concerned about issues pertaining to the so-called spare embryo. The fact that embryos can be frozen for future use emphasises the fact that the procedure of IVF permits women to become suppliers of reproductive products.[44]

There is already a century-long social history of men supplying sperm, for a price, for the purpose of artificial insemination. Now technology permits women to be vendors in a comparable fashion. Women can donate or sell their ova to women who do not ovulate, or whose ova cannot be extracted from their bodies. Moreover, women can also donate or sell embryos, by means of a new process known as uterine lavage. In this procedure, the donor woman is artificially inseminated. If conception takes place, the fertilised egg travels from the fallopian tube to the uterus. Before the embryo implants in the uterine wall, it can be washed out of the uterus and recovered; it can then be transferred to the uterus of another woman who is unable to ovulate.[45] Thus women become, through reproductive technology, the suppliers of reproductive products — ova and embryos — which can be purchased by infertile individuals. The commodification of reproduction now extends to both sexes.

The embryo transfer stage, whether it follows IVF or uterine lavage, is a perilous one. Very often, a number of attempts will have to be made at transferring embryos; most failures in IVF occur at this stage.[46] And in fact, the procedure has a rather low success rate. One Canadian clinic claims a success rate of 20 per cent,[47] but that estimate seems rather optimistic; a 12 per cent success rate is more usual.[48] The procedure is also quite expensive: in this context, the acquisition of a child-commodity requires an investment of several thousand dollars. The total amount depends on how many attempts must be made until either a pregnancy is achieved or the couple gives up.[49]

Finally, the idea of "giving up" is itself significant. Some writers on infertility and artificial reproduction have suggested that the development of reproductive technology has drastically changed the significance of and attitude toward infertility. While IVF appears to expand our options, it may in other ways reduce them. The use of IVF and embryo transfer may help to sustain traditional ideas about the importance to women of child bearing. For it exacerbates what has been called "the moral pressure to have children".[50] The infertile couple can no longer merely accept their infertility as a sort of mysterious incapacity inflicted by fate; instead they must resort to lengthy, expensive, painful, exhausting diagnostic and surgical procedures. If they fail to make full use of all that medicine offers them, then they seem to have willfully chosen their infertility.[51]

I believe, therefore, that while the development of procedures such as IVF can help a very few fortunate individuals with specific sorts of infertility, it also encourages us to think of infertility as a disease, a treatable disease. It encourages us to see the infertile as persons who are handicapped and in dire need of help. Instead of possibly assisting them to adjust to and accept the fact that they do not have a child who is genetically related to them, or, better still, instead of encouraging all of us to feel concern and responsibility for all children, it drives home the idea that a family without children is not a "real" family. It implies that an individual is not complete, not a real woman or a real man, without her or his "own", genetically related child, and that childless persons should explore all possible means of obtaining one.[52]

SURROGATE MOTHERHOOD

Like IVF, surrogate motherhood is resorted to as a corrective for infertility. When a woman, for a variety of reasons, is unable to sustain a pregnancy, her husband can hire a woman to bear "his" child. There are two possible procedures here. First, if the wife produces ova, one or more of these can be extracted from her and fertilised with her partner's sperm. This would make use of the IVF technique. The embryo or embryos which are thereby produced could then be transferred to the surrogate who would gestate them and surrender the baby or babies to the couple at the end of the pregnancy.

The more usual case of surrogate motherhood as it presently is practised involves not IVF but the much older process of artificial insemination of the surrogate with the sperm of the man who hires her. Conception then takes place within the surrogate's body, the pregancy proceeds, and the woman surrenders the baby to the couple after its birth.[53]

Thus, in the first case, the surrogate provides only her reproductive services: the use of her uterus and all of its capacities for nurturing a foetus. In the second, actual, case, the surrogate not only provides reproductive services but also supplies, in her ovum, a reproductive product: that is, one-half of the baby's genetic inheritance. So, one question that arises immediately is whether there are any important moral, psychological, or social policy differences between the two forms of surrogate motherhood. However, I think that most of the important questions about surrogate motherhood, in either form, arise in connection with its potential effect on the children that are thereby produced, and also in regard to what the practice suggests about the social position of women and about women's relationships to men.

It seems clear, first of all, that there is some potential for problems arising from surrogacy, problems which, first and foremost, can affect the well-being of the child that is produced. Because the practice of hired surrogacy is so new, no one yet knows what all of the possible effects on a child might be, when that child has been ordered and purchased by its parents. For example, we already know that adopted children in later life very often feel a longing to search for their genetic parents; it seems possible that a child born to a surrogate might later want to seek her out.

However, other problems pertaining to surrogate motherhood are not merely hypothetical, but have actually occurred in surrogacy arrangements in the United States. It is particularly clear in these contracts that once again the child is being treated as a commodity. Perhaps we should wonder generally about our social attitudes toward children if buying babies becomes a widespread and acceptable practice.

The baby produced by a surrogate is an expensive commodity: the going rate for hiring a surrogate is now twenty to twenty-five thousand dollars.[54] Presumably the hiring couple wants a top-quality product. As a result, some surrogacy contracts even specify both that the surrogate explicitly forgo her right to choose an abortion, and also that she agree to undergo an abortion if foetal testing indicates the presence of a handicapped child.[55] But what happens if the baby is born with a defect anyway, or is not of the sex for which the couple was hoping? Does the commissioning couple have to accept damaged goods? What is the fate of a child for whom no one wants to take responsibility?[56] Or perhaps the mother produces not one baby but two. In a way, the commissioning couple seems to get double their money's worth. Are they entitled to both children? What if they only want one? A more serious possibility is that the baby is born dead. Has the mother then fulfilled her responsibility; is she entitled to payment?

One of the most serious complications which has so far arisen with some frequency in surrogacy arrangements is that some mothers are no longer willing to surrender the child after it is born.[57] The other side of the coin is that some couples have been known to change their minds about taking the baby they have ordered, if their circumstances change drastically: if, for example, one of them dies, or the marriage breaks down.[58] If the surrogate also does not want the baby, it again becomes an unwanted child.

More subtle, perhaps, but just as important, are the questions that the practice of surrogate motherhood raises about the position of women in society and about women's relationships to men and to their offspring.

First, the existence of surrogacy emphasises the fact that we can now clearly distinguish between different forms of motherhood and fatherhood.[59] Thanks to reproductive technology, a baby could, potentially, have five different parents: its genetic mother and genetic father, who supply the ovum and the sperm; its carrying mother, who gestates the embryo produced by the union of ovum and sperm; and finally its social mother and father, the individuals who rear the child produced by the carrying mother.

The possibility of making these distinctions also permits the development of a distinctly commercialised form of reproductive labour. Medical and legal writers, as well as the surrogates themselves, tend to see surrogacy as a type of job.[60] But if it is a job, it is a most peculiar one. The incumbent is required to be on duty twenty-four hours a day. The pay is very low, far below the present minimum wage: even though the hiring couple may pay twenty thousand dollars, the surrogate receives only about ten thousand of that; the rest goes for lawyers' fees, medical expenses, psychological and physical tests, and travel expenses.[61] It is also a job that can drastically reduce the surrogate's personal autonomy. Often, surrogacy contracts will include provisions that severely limit what the woman eats and drinks, the timing of her sexual activities, her leisure pursuits and physical activities, and her use of medical services, including her right to an abortion.[62]

I think it is important to ask whether in fact this is the sort of "job" we would value and would want to encourage for women. Would you want your daughter or sister to take up a "career" as a surrogate mother? Should surrogacy be presented by vocational counsellors as a new job option? Is this the sort of thing you would want to put on your curriculum vitae or résumé?[63] Surely the answer to each of these questions is no. From the point of view of the women involved (whatever its benefits for those who are infertile), surrogacy does not seem to be the sort of practice we would want to encourage, at least in its commercialised form.

Surrogate motherhood represents the final step in the commodification of reproductive relationships. Some feminist writers, in fact, have compared it to prostitution. A prostitute sells her sexual services; a surrogate mother sells her reproductive services.[64] In this latter context, the consumer of the services is, usually, a man, not a woman: the surrogacy contract is ordinarily an agreement between the surrogate and the man who hires her; the infertile wife is a legal non-entity for purposes of the arrangement.[65] And the lawyer who recruits surrogates and negotiates the contract with the hiring couple is very like a pimp, for he derives great economic benefit from handling the sale of reproductive services.

I want to emphasise here that in comparing surrogate mothers to prostitutes, I am not condemning the women themselves who make money in these ways. Instead, I am concerned about the sort of social system in which women see their future only in terms of selling their reproductive capacities. The women who now seek work as surrogate mothers are often poor and uneducated.[66] For them surrogacy may appear to be a sort of last resort, when more lucrative and prestigious forms of employment are unobtainable. In becoming surrogates, they take on work that denies their individuality, that places value upon them only to the extent that they are successful and healthy reproductive machines. In that respect, surrogate mothers are interchangeable and anonymous.[67] Although the hiring father has the freedom to choose which woman he wants to have bear his child,[68] the surrogate herself has little choice in the matter, especially if she is recruited through one of the surrogacy agencies such as operate in the United States.

Thus, once again, although the practice of surrogate motherhood appears to increase our reproductive freedom by allowing some infertile women and the men to whom they are married (at least those who are wealthy) to acquire a baby, in fact in other respects, in its highly commercialised form, it diminishes at least some women's reproductive freedom and control. For, as the popular press has so aptly suggested, surrogacy amounts to no more than a depersonalised rent-a-womb arrangement.

CONCLUSION

There is much more that could be said about the impact of reproductive technology on the future of the family. But even a brief examination suggests that this technology raises serious questions in regard to the commodification of reproduction and reproductive relationships within the family, and the scope and meaning of reproductive freedom and choice, particularly for women.

New reproductive technology generates many conflicts and contradictions. It has the potential to be both an asset and a liability for the future of human relationships. Perhaps the main source of this ambiguity is the question of power that it raises. If women and men, both as individuals and as members of groups, share control over reproductive technology, it may be put to uses that benefit us all. But if, as now seems to be the case, most people are able to exert very little control over research into and the development and applications of reproductive technology,[69] then it may be a real threat to our hopes for a humane future.

REFERENCES

1 I use the term in the Marxist sense. See, for example, Frederick Engels, "The Origin of the Family, Private Property and the State", in *Karl Marx and Frederick Engels: Selected Works* (Moscow: Progress Publishers, 1970), p. 580.

2 I shall exclude from consideration the topic of post-conception foetal sex selection, which involves the discovery of the sex of the foetus through the process of amniocentesis or chorionic biopsy, and subsequent abortion if the foetus should turn out to be of the "wrong" sex. See Viola Roggencamp, "Abortion of a Special Kind: Male Sex Selection in India", in *Test-Tube Women: What Future for Motherhood?*, ed. Rita Arditti, Renate Duelli Klein, and Shelley Minden (London: Pandora Press, 1984), pp. 266 - 277 for discussion of a specific case.

3 Jalna Hanmer, "Sex Predetermination, Artificial Insemination and the Maintenance of Male-Dominated Culture", in *Women, Health and Reproduction*, ed. Helen Roberts (London: Routledge & Kegan Paul, 1981), p. 175; M. Ruth Nentwig, "Technical Aspects of Sex Preselection", in *The Custom-Made Child? Women-Centred Perspectives*, ed. Helen B. Holmes, Betty B. Hoskins, and Michael Gross (Clifton, NJ: The Humana Press Inc., 1981), pp. 181 - 186; Betty B. Hoskins and Helen Bequaert Holmes, "Technology and Prenatal Femicide", in Arditti et al., eds., *Test-Tube Women, op. cit.*, pp. 238 - 241; Gale Largey, "Reproductive Technologies: Sex Selection", in *Encyclopedia of Bioethics*, ed. Warren T. Reich (New York: The Free Press, 1978), 4: 1439 - 1441; Robert H. Glass and Ronald J. Ericsson, *Getting Pregnant in the 1980s: New Advances in Infertility Treatment and Sex Preselection* (Berkeley, California: University of California Press, 1982), pp. 113 - 129.

4 Tabitha M. Powledge, "Unnatural Selection: On Choosing Children's Sex", in *The Custom-Made Child?*, pp. 193 - 199; Michael D. Bayles, *Reproductive Ethics* (Englewood Cliffs, New Jersey: Prentice-Hall, 1984), pp. 33 - 36.

5 Amitai Etzioni, "Sex Control, Science, and Society", *Science*, Vol. 161, No. 3846 (September, 1968): 1107 - 1112; Marc Lappé and Peter Steinfels, "Choosing the Sex of Our Children", *The Hastings Center Report* 4 (February, 1974): 1 - 4; John Postgate, "Bat's Chance in Hell", *New Scientist*, Vol. 58, No. 540 (April 5, 1973): 12 - 16; Charles F. Westoff and Ronald R. Rindfuss, "Sex Preselection in the United States: Some Implications", *Science* Vol. 184 (May 10, 1974): 633 - 636.

6 See Nancy E. Williamson, *Sons or Daughters: A Cross-Cultural Survey of Parental Preferences* (Beverly Hills, CA: Sage Publications, 1976); Nancy E. Williamson, "Sex Preferences, Sex Control, and the Status of Women", *Signs: Journal of Women in Culture and Society* 1 (1976): 847 - 862; Anne R. Pebly and Charles F. Westoff, "Women's Sex Preferences in the United

States: 1970 to 1975'', *Demography* 19 (May 1982): 177 - 189.
7 Nathan Keyfitz, ''Foreword'', in *Sex Selection of Children*, ed. Neil G. Bennett (New York: Academic Press, Inc., 1983), p. xii; cf. Nancy E. Williamson, ''Parental Sex Preferences and Sex Selection'', in *Sex Selection of Children*, p. 142.
8 Postgate, *op. cit.*, p. 16.
9 Richard L. Meier, ''Sex Determination and Other Innovations'', in *Population in Perspective*, ed. Louise B. Young (New York: Oxford University Press, 1968), p. 410; Postgate, *op. cit.*, p. 14.
10 Etzioni, *op. cit.*, p. 1109; Robyn Rowland, ''Reproductive Technologies: The Final Solution to the Woman Question?'', in Arditti et al., eds., *Test-Tube Women, op. cit.*, p. 362.
11 In the United States, women are likely to say that they want a balance in the sex of their offspring. See Pebley and Westoff, *op. cit.*, p. 178.
12 Postgate, *op. cit.*, p. 14.
13 Tabitha M. Powledge, ''Toward a Moral Policy for Sex Choice'', in Bennett, ed., *Sex Selection of Children, op. cit.*, p. 202.
14 Lappé and Steinfels, *op. cit.*, p. 2.
15 Westoff and Rindfuss, *op. cit.*, p. 635.
15 Williamson, ''Sex Preferences, Sex Control, and the Status of Women'', *op. cit.*, p. 859.
17 Lucille Forer with Henry Still, *The Birth Order Factor* (New York: Pocket Books, 1977), passim.
18 Williamson, ''Sex Preferences, Sex Control, and the Status of Women'', *op. cit.*, p. 860; Rowland, *op. cit.*, pp. 361 - 362.
19 Hoskins and Holmes, *op. cit.*, p. 248.
20 Abby Lippman, ''Access to Pre-natal Screening Services and Trials: Who Decides?'', paper delivered at the Policy Workshop on Medical Control: Pregnancy Issues, Sixth National Biennial Conference of the National Association of Women and the Law, Ottawa, Ontario, February 22, 1985, p. 3.
21 *Ibid.*, pp. 3 - 4, 14.
22 *Ibid.*, pp. 1 - 2.
23 William Ruddick and William Wilcox, ''Operating on the Fetus'', *The Hastings Center Report*, Vol. 12, No. 5 (October 5, 1982): 10; Ruth Hubbard, ''The Fetus As Patient'', *Ms.* (October, 1982): 32.
24 Marsha Saxton, ''Born and Unborn: The Implications of Reproductive Technologies For People With Disabilities'', in *Test-Tube Women, op. cit.*, pp. 298 - 312.
25 Lippman, *op. cit.*, p. 14.
26 *Ibid.*, 12 - 14.
27 Barbara Katz Rothman, ''The Meanings of Choice in Reproductive Technology'', in *Test-Tube Women, op. cit.*, pp. 29 - 30.
28 Ruddick and Wilcox, *op. cit.*, p. 12; Hubbard, *op. cit.*, p. 32.

29 Janet Gallagher, "The Fetus and the Law: Whose Life Is It Anyway?", *Ms.* (September, 1984): 65, 66, 134, 135; Ruddick and Wilcox, *op. cit.*, p. 11; Hubbard, *op. cit.*, p. 32; John A. Robertson, "Procreative Liberty and the Control of Conception, Pregnancy, and Childbirth", *Virginia Law Review* 69 (3) (April, 1983): 437 - 450; Sandra Rodgers-Magnet, "Foetal Rights and Maternal Rights: Is There a Conflict?", paper delivered at the Policy Workshop on Medical Control: Pregnancy Issues, Sixth National Biennial Conference of the National Association of Women and the Law, Ottawa, Ontario, February 22, 1985.

30 Gallagher, *op. cit.*, p. 66; George J. Annas, "Forced Cesareans: The Most Unkindest Cut of All", *The Hastings Center Report* 12 (3) (June, 1982): 16, 17, 45.

31 Madam Justice Proudfoot, "Judgement Respecting Female Infant 'D.J.' ", in Wesley Cragg, ed., *Contemporary Moral Issues* (Toronto: McGraw-Hill Ryerson Ltd., 1983), pp. 16 - 18; Ian Gentles, "The Unborn Child in Civil and Criminal Law", in Cragg, ed., *ibid.*, pp. 24 - 25.

32 Gentles, in Cragg, ed., pp. 19 - 29; E.W. Keyserlingk, "Balancing Prenatal Care and Abortion", in Cragg, ed., *ibid.*, pp. 29 - 37.

33 Gallagher, p. 134; Gentles, p. 23; Robertson, p. 463.

34 Annas, p. 45; Robertson, pp. 443-444; Edward W. Keyserlingk, "The Unborn Child's Right to Prenatal Care" (Part 1), *Health Law in Canada* 3 #1 (1982): 10 - 12; Margery W. Shaw, "Conditional Prospective Rights of the Fetus", *The Journal of Legal Medicine*, Vol. 5, No. 1 (1984): 83 - 89.

35 John F. Leeton, Alan O. Trouson, and Carl Wood, "IVF and ET: What It Is and How It Works", in *Test-Tube Babies: A Guide to Moral Questions, Present Techniques and Future Possibilities* (Melbourne: Oxford University Press, 1982), pp. 2 - 10.

37 R.G. Edwards, "The Current Clinical and Ethical Situation of Human Conception In Vitro", in *Developments in Human Reproduction and Their Eugenic, Ethical Implications*, ed. C.O. Carter (New York: Academic Press, 1983), p. 95.

38 See Barbara Eck Menning, "The Psychology of Infertility", in *Infertility: Diagnosis and Management*, ed. James Aiman (New York: Springer-Verlag Inc., 1984), pp. 17 - 29; Carolyn Coman, "Trying (and Trying and Trying) to Get Pregnant", *Ms.* (May, 1983): 21 - 24; Germaine Greer, *Sex and Destiny: The Politics of Human Fertility* (London: Secker and Warburg, 1984), pp. 46 - 47; Melvin L. Taymor, *Infertility* (New York: Grune & Stratton, 1978), pp. 94 - 96; Robert Edwards and Patrick Steptoe, *A Matter of Life: The Story of A Medical Breakthrough* (London: Hutchinson, 1980), p. 121; Isabel Bainbridge, "With Child in Mind: The Experience of a Potential IVF Mother", in *Test-Tube Babies, op. cit.*, pp. 119 - 127.

39 See, for example, Leon R. Kass, "Babies by Means of In Vitro Fertilization: Unethical Experiments on the Unborn?", *The New England Journal of*

Medicine 285 (November 18, 1971): 1176 - 1177; Leon R. Kass, "Making Babies — The New Biology and the 'Old' Morality", *The Public Interest* 26 (Winter, 1972): 20; Anibal A. Acosta and Jairo E. Garcia, "Extracorporeal Fertilization and Embryo Transfer", in *Infertility: Diagnosis and Management*, p. 217.

40 Rita Arditti, Renate Duelli Klein, and Shelley Minden, "Introduction", in *Test-Tube Women*, p. 5; Barbara Katz Rothman, "How Science is Redefining Parenthood", *Ms.* (July/August, 1982): 156; Somer Brodribb, "Reproductive Technologies, Masculine Dominance and the Canadian State", *Occasional Papers in Social Policy Analysis #5* (Toronto: Ontario Institute For Studies In Education, 1984), pp. 15 - 16.

41 Brodribb, *op. cit.*, p. 16.

42 George J. Annas, "Redefining Parenthood and Protecting Embryos: Why We Need New Laws", *The Hastings Center Report*, Vol. 14, No. 5 (October, 1984): 50 - 52; Clifford Grobstein, "The Moral Uses of 'Spare' Embryos", *The Hastings Center Report*, Vol. 12, No.3 (June, 1982): 5 - 6; Great Britain, Department of Health & Social Security, "Report of the Committee of Inquiry Into Human Fertilisation and Embryology", Command Paper 9314 (July, 1984), pp. 55 - 69.

43 There is an enormous amount of philosophical discussion of this issue, usually in connection with the abortion debate. For a discussion of the issue in the context of IVF, see Brian Johnstone, and Helga Kuhse and Peter Singer, "The Moral Status of the Embryo: Two Viewpoints", in *Test-Tube Babies, op. cit.*, pp. 49 - 63.

44 Annas, "Redefining Parenthood and Protecting Embryos", pp. 51 - 52.

45 Council for Science and Society, *Human Procreation: Ethical Aspects of the New Techniques* (Oxford: Oxford University Press, 1984), p. 91.

46 "Report of the Committee of Inquiry into Human Fertilisation and Embryology", *op. cit.*, p. 30.

47 Dr. Murray Kroach, LIFE Program, Toronto East General Hospital, Toronto, Ontario, personal communication, March 22, 1985.

48 Leeton, Trounson, and Wood, *op. cit.*, pp. 7 - 8.

49 For example, the LIFE Program at the Toronto East General Hospital charges $1,500 per attempt at embryo transfer. However, that amount is described as a "bargain" compared to the costs at some clinics in the United States, which charge $5,500 on average per cycle. (Dr. Murray Kroach, personal communication, March 22, 1985.)

50 Jeremy Laurance, "The Moral Pressure to Have Children", *New Society* 5 (August, 1982): 216 - 218.

51 Rothman, "The Meanings of Choice in Reproductive Technology", pp. 31 - 32.

52 These ideas are given dramatic expression throughout Edwards' and Steptoe's

A Matter of Life, which narrates the full history of the production of the first "test-tube baby", Louise Joy Brown.

53 See Alan A. Rassaby, "Surrogate Motherhood: The Position and Problems of Substitutes", in *Test-Tube Babies, op. cit.*, pp. 97 - 98; Peter Singer and Deane Wells, *The Reproduction Revolution: New Ways of Making Babies* (Oxford: Oxford University Press, 1984), pp. 107 - 114; Bayles, pp. 22 - 23; John A. Robertson, "Surrogate Mothers: Not So Novel After All", *The Hastings Center Report*, Vol. 13, No. 5 (October, 1983): 28 - 34.

54 Robertson, *ibid.*, p. 29.

55 Linda Silver Dranoff, "Ask a Lawyer", *Chatelaine* (January, 1984): 26; Sarah Helm, Rowena Webster, Robert Wilsher, and Mark Hosenball, "Nothing Left to Chance in 'Rent-A-Womb' Agreements", *Toronto Star* (January 13, 1985).

56 The result of the surrogacy arrangement in 1981 between Judy Stiver and Alexander Malahoff was a baby with microcephaly, who was wanted by neither of the two parties to the contract. See Singer and Wells, pp. 118 - 119.

57 Rassaby, *op. cit.*, pp. 101 - 102; Singer and Wells, *op. cit.*, pp. 120 - 121.

58 For example, in the Stiver/Malahoff case, Malahoff's marriage to his infertile wife ended before Stiver's baby was born.

59 Barbara Katz Rothman, "How Science is Redefining Parenthood", *Ms.* (July/August, 1982): 154, 156, 158.

60 Margaret Munro, " 'Rent-a-Womb' " Trade Thriving Across Canada - U.S. Border", *The Montreal Gazette* (January 21, 1985): D-11.

61 Munro, p. D-11.

62 Dranoff, *op. cit.*, p. 26; Theresa M. Mady, "Surrogate Mothers: The Legal Issues", *American Journal of Law & Medicine*, Vol. 7, No. 3 (Fall, 1981): 332 - 338.

63 I owe this suggestion to Lorraine Code.

64 Andrea Dworkin, *Right-Wing Women* (New York: Perigee Books, 1983), pp. 174 - 188.

65 Susan Ince, "Inside the Surrogate Industry", in *Test-Tube Women, op. cit.*, pp. 101 - 102.

66 See Philip J. Parker, "Motivation of Surrogate Mothers: Initial Findings", *American Journal of Psychiatry* 140:1 (January 1983): 117 - 118.

67 Dworkin, *op. cit.*, p. 182.

68 Munro, *op. cit.*, p. D-11.

69 This is a major theme of Brodribb's paper.

FURTHER READING

Arditti, Rita, Renate Duelli Klein, and Shelley Minden, eds. *Test-Tube Women: What Future for Motherhood?* London: Pandora Press, 1984.

Bayles, Michael D. *Reproductive Ethics.* Englewood Cliffs, NJ: Prentice-Hall, 1984.

Brodribb, Somer. "Reproductive Technologies, Masculine Dominance and the Canadian State". *Occasional Papers in Social Policy Analysis.* Toronto, Ontario: Ontario Institute for Studies In Education, 1984.

Singer, Peter, and Deane Wells. *The Reproduction Revolution: New Ways of Making Babies.* Oxford: Oxford University Press, 1984.

Walters, William, and Peter Singer, eds. *Test-Tube Babies: A Guide to Moral Questions, Present Techniques and Future Possibilities.* Melbourne: Oxford University Press, 1982.

E. RELATIONSHIPS

KATHRYN PAULY MORGAN

Romantic Love, Altruism, and Self-respect

In this chapter, I focus on Simone de Beauvoir's analysis of romantic love as it is presented in Chapter 23, "The Woman In Love", in *The Second Sex*.[1] There, de Beauvoir cites three men who claim that there are gender differences in the nature and significance of human love. Balzac says,

> Among the first-rate, man's life is fame, woman's life is love. Woman is man's equal only when she makes her life a perpetual offering, as that of man is perpetual action. (SS,742)

Similarly, Byron claims,

> Man's love is of man's life a thing apart;
> 'Tis woman's whole existence. (SS,712)

Third, de Beauvoir quotes these remarks from Nietzsche's *The Gay Science*:

> The single word love in fact signifies two different things for man and woman. What woman understands by love is clear enough: it is not only devotion, it is a total gift of body and soul, without reservation, without regard for anything whatever. This unconditional nature of her love is what makes it a *faith*, the only one she has. As for man, if he loves a woman, what he *wants* is that love from her; he is in consequence far from postulating the same sentiment for himself as

---

This article is reprinted from *Hypatia: A Journal of Feminist Philosophy,* Vol., No. 1 (Spring 1986), by permission of the publisher, Hypatia, Inc., c/o Department of Philosophical Studies, Southern Illinois University of Edwardsville, Edwardsville, Illinois 62026-1437.

for woman; if there should be men who also felt that desire for complete abandonment, upon my word, they would not be men.

De Beauvoir's own view is that the *vocation* of loving involves massive self-deception, inevitably leading to personal annihilation for the woman concerned.

In the first part of this chapter I highlight central philosphical and empirical assumptions which constitute the framework for de Beauvoir's discussion. In the second part, I examine her account of the process of loving, underscoring four devastating paradoxes faced by the woman in love, and endorse her conclusion that this kind of "vocation" leads ultimately to maximum servility in the woman who loves. In the third part of my discussion, I ask whether, outside the framework of existentialist ethics, it is morally wrong for a woman to aspire to and choose this form of servitude. In my response, I distinguish two categories of moral considerations: (1) those having to do with the intrinsic moral nature of the decision and the type of life to which one is thereby committed, and (2) considerations based on the notion of harm: harm to the woman who loves; harm to the loved Other (whether man or woman); harm to the quality of the relationship undertaken; and, finally, harmful social consequences.

PHILOSOPHICAL AND EMPIRICAL ASSUMPTIONS

Central to belief in this gender theory of love are three claims which de Beauvoir explores in the chapter on "The Woman in Love":

1. The claim that loving is woman's central *vocation*, i.e. that it is the most important form of life a woman, *qua* woman, can engage in, that it is her fundamental purpose in life.[2]

2. The claim that loving is what confirms a woman in her *womanliness* (as contrasted with her biological femaleness which is confirmed through maternity and lactation). Without the experience of full commitment to a Great Love to a superior being[3] a woman is likely to feel unfulfilled as a woman, according to this theory.

3. The claim that the moral principle proper to this ideology of love is that of person-specific *altruism* as a life-governing principle (as contrasted with simply a flurry of altruistic acts). According to this principle a life of self-sacrifice to her lover is not only a woman's duty but her highest glory as a woman. Thus is forged the crucial link between altruism, self-respect, and womanliness. The woman in love gains self-respect *as a woman* through the self-abnegation which is central to her commitment to her lover. As a consequence, self-regarding dispositions and actions come to be labelled "selfish" and are regarded as moral flaws.

Dualism 1: Life vs. Spirit

In *The Second Sex*, de Beauvoir works with three important dualisms in addition to the central dualism of Self and Other. The first of these is a distinction between a life oriented towards Life as its primary focus and a life of the Spirit.[4] For an individual committed to life and life processes, life giving and life sustaining are the dominant values. Such activities as giving birth, nursing a child, and preparing food are paradigmatic life-oriented activities according to de Beauvoir. Central to the focus on life is a commitment to the domain of the temporal and the ephemeral. The processes of organic life — the ripening of fruit, the rising of dough, the moment of birth; growth, aging, decaying, going mouldy — are processes largely out of one's control, requiring waiting and passivity. In general, a life oriented toward Life is essentially a life lived in common with other animals, because its ultimate goal is simply the *replication* of life. Thus, to the extent that the lives of women are defined in terms of biological and social reproduction of Life, theirs are not truly human lives.[5]

By contrast, the life of Spirit rises above the biological level. De Beauvoir uses fishing to illustrate her distinction. Someone who regards fishing as a life-sustaining activity to be undertaken in harmony with nature would simply go fishing, sit on the bank, catch the fish, clean them, cook them and eat them. This ritual could conceivably be repeated day after day with no thought of change in the life-oriented catcher of fish. Contrast this individual with a person who thinks of the water as a domain to be mastered, and of fish as alien species to be conquered. Such an individual might invent canoes or boats and fashion various fishing implements, subtle detecting devices and forms of bait and lures.[6] This individual would be interested in creative adventure, in experimentation, perhaps even to the point of risking life. We can identify a life committed to Spirit, de Beauvoir suggests, by noting the primacy placed on inventions, technology, symbols and idealised values, i.e. entities whose permanance often outlasts the perishable domain of biological life, whether it be that of the individual or the species.[7] This commitment is manifest in situations in which an individual is willing to risk life for a higher value such as the Nation or Peace or the Public Good or Justice, the implication of this risk being that there are values more important to human life than biological life. Since de Beauvoir regards the life of the Spirit as the only genuinely human life, one of her primary projects is the fight for women to have access to this life. As she says,

> ...it is regardless of sex that the existent seeks self-justification through transcendence — the very submission of women is proof of that statement. What they demand today is to be recognized as existents by the same right as men and not to subordinate existence to life, the human being to its animality. (SS,73)[8]

Dualism 2: Immanence vs. Transcendence

De Beauvoir's second dualism is the distinction between immanence and transcendence. The sphere of immanence involves lived repetition.[9] According to de Beauvoir, the physically confined and repetitious life of many women is simply the material replica of their psychological confinement. Psychologically, the life of immanence is a life in which one thinks within pre-determined limits, within already established conditions and conventions, submitting to identity-determining roles that are perceived as necessary and given. It is a life without adventure, without risk. Its chief attraction is security through predictability. Metaphysically speaking, it means living a life immersed and trapped within the domain of the *given*, the present and the immediate, which are then equated with all that is real. Optimally, it is a life undisturbed by thoughts or situations that would introduce genuinely new possibilities. Carried to its ultimate limit, it approximates the predictable life of the non-human object. For de Beauvoir it is a life of human stagnation. But it is also a life which at a deep level many of us find tempting.

A life directed towards transcendence, by contrast, is a life open to the future, a life self-originated rather than based on a pre-existing identity. Transcendent subjects invent, act, make choices. They view the future as something indeterminate to shape and bring into existence rather than as a fate to which one can only submit. Individuals oriented toward transcendence test their own limits, experiment, take risks in order to define themselves in terms of future projects, not of past accomplishments. They think of themselves as self-determining, as having the power to create. Metaphysically speaking, the transcendent subject is oriented towards the domain of the possible. Concomitant with this experience of the self, however, is a pervasive feeling of dread at the resulting responsibility for one's life and identity.

Again it is clear that de Beauvoir regards only the life of transcendence as worthy of human respect.[10] But she also notes that one or another form of a life of immanence is built into virtually all the acceptable roles open to women.

Dualism 3: Life Situations of Women and Men

As de Beauvoir studies the life-determining situations and roles of adolescent girls, married women, mothers, and aging widows, she argues that since women's consciousness is constantly directed to concerns that are concrete, immediate, and particular, concerns that seldom transcend the limits of the given, women are committed to lives of immanence.[11]

Further, she claims that the situation of women defines the heterosexually desirable feminine women in terms of dependency, vulnerability, and submissiveness, along with a commitment to self-sacrifice. For the feminine woman to lead a life of autonomy or self-determination would be a living contradiction.

On the contrary, the social situations of men characteristically require a "masculine" boy or man to strive to be independent, achievement-oriented, courageous, assertive, and decisive; to have a sense of adventure and risk-taking; and to be rational: all these qualities can and must be integrated into growing virility.

> The advantage man enjoys, which makes itself felt from his childhood, is that his vocation as a human being in no way runs counter to his destiny as a male. Through the identification of phallus and transcendence, it turns out that his social and spiritual successes endow him with a virile prestige. He is not divided. Whereas it is required of woman that in order to realize her femininity she must make herself object and prey, which is to say that she must renounce her claims as sovereign subject. It is this conflict that especially marks the situation of the emancipated woman. She refuses to confine herself to her role as female, because she will not accept mutilation; but it would also be a mutilation to repudiate her sex. (SS,758).

Intellectually, de Beauvoir sees the consciousness of men as permeated with abstractions, theories, and universal principles. Men live and think in a world that is essentially constructed by transcending the particular and the personal in order to generate the universals required by science and other forms of theorising necessary for a life of transcendence. In general, then, de Beauvoir claims that as the world has been and is presently structured, it is only the situation of men's lives that begins to allow for the possibility of fully human, revolutionary life.[12]

De Beauvoir's treatment of these three dualisms reveals her profound commitment to what might be called a Platonic preference for the permanent, the transpersonal, and the self-transcending. She associates these characteristics with a life of existential transcendence, the human life of the Spirit whose highest manifestations are found in lasting human inventions of technology, theory and aesthetic symbols. She sees the world so structured as to encourage this life in men and deplore it in women. Insofar as the worlds of women are variant worlds of immanence; insofar as women's lives are committed to personal altruistic support through temporal, perishable life processes, de Beauvoir devalues and mourns for the lives of women.

Within this general dualistic framework, de Beauvoir argues that three factors contribute to generate in women the desire for romantic love: (1) the general human desire to avoid a life of responsible self-determination (the phenomenon of bad faith or *mauvaise foi*); (2) the specific social and economic circumstances of many women, and (3) a romantic ideology which is carefully inculcated in girls and women from an early age. I shall examine each of these in turn before describing the phenomenology of the inter-subjective dynamic of romantic love and its multiple double binds.

(1) BAD FAITH

The first factor contributing to women desiring romantic love is what de Beauvoir and other existentialist thinkers see as a primary, defining form of motivation in human subjects, *viz.* the desire for inauthenticity, objectification or bad faith (*mauvaise foi*). Basically, this notion refers to the desire of any conscious subject to flee from a life of self-determination in which we strive to surpass our given self. Glimpsing the uncertainty and concomitant dread that characterise this work of self-determination, we sink softly and securely into some self-deceptive form of objecthood. We relax into a state of crippling contentment based on an illusion of necessity.

Although the desire for inauthenticity is seen as a universal human desire, it can assume any of a myriad of possible forms. There are at least four ways in which a woman can be tempted into bad faith. Unfortunately these ways are not mutually exclusive.[13]

First, a woman might regard the values that permeate and regulate her life as absolute and necessary. For example, a woman might think, "As a woman, I must be nurturant, compassionate, self-sacrificing. I have no choice." De Beauvoir argues that this is a self-deceptive frame of mind because all human values are of human origin and consequently open in principle to revision and change. Pretending that these values are necessary and absolutely binding is simply one way of abdicating responsibility for having chosen them.

A second form of bad faith consists in completely identifying with a role or set of roles and, again, pretending that that role is *normatively* binding. For example, the woman who says that "As a good Christian mother, I must do X, feel Y..." or that "As the wife of Professor X, I must always say..." or thinks "As a feminist, I must feel..." would be practising self-deception. In general, for many women, the roles of "good wife" and "good mother" appear to have this kind of self-deceptive binding power.

A third form of bad faith involves subordinating oneself to the status of instrument or object. The "doormat" view of motherhood or the singular perception of women in the Napoleonic Code as sub-human breeders would be instances of this. A woman who experiences pleasure when hearing her husband say, expansively, "These are my fields, my livestock, my wife..." may be experiencing herself as a treasured possession, an object which confers status on the possessor but denies the subjectivity of the possessed.

The fourth form of bad faith which tempts women is that of becoming an identity parasite. Women are tempted to deny their uniqueness, their separateness, and are urged to identify themselves with and commit their lives to the support of a superior male and his offspring. This fourth form, de Beauvoir argues, must be invoked in order to explain the desire that women have for a great romantic love either with a human being, or through mysticism, with a divine being. It is this fourth form that de Beauvior is particularly interested in in her discussion of the woman in love.[14]

(2) GENERAL SOCIAL AND ECONOMIC CIRCUMSTANCES OF WOMEN

In explaining the appeal of romantic love to women, it is important to note general features of many women's lives which in many cultures lead women to see romantic love as a form of salvation. At least three such circumstances need to be mentioned here. First, women are relegated to the essentially repetitive tasks of domestic labour because of biological maternity and the requirments of nursing. Secondly, women are devalued because of their role in the family, according to an ideology that views the family as natural, pre-cultural and private. Those whose labour involves young children are assumed to be emotional and irrational. Thirdly, the young girl is taught that her life as a woman is, properly, a life destined to be lived for others. Her social position, her economic security are essentially bound up with the social and economic position of her father, husband, or other significant male kinship figure. Her own situation, as a woman, is one of minimal power. In this context, falling in love and being loved by a superior being come to be seen as a desirable way of acquiring identity and access to power. Thus romantic love within an oppressive set of social and economic circumstances comes to be seen as a way of escaping this oppression.

(3) BELIEFS THAT ARE CENTRAL TO A ROMANTIC IDEOLOGY

> ...It is agonizing for a woman to assume responsibility for her life. It is man's good fortune to be obliged to take the most arduous roads, but the surest; it is woman's misfortune to be surrounded by almost irresistible temptations; everything incites her to follow the easy slopes; instead of being invited to fight her own way up, she is told that she has only to let herself slide and she will attain paradises of enchantment. (SS,715)

According to de Beauvoir, girls and women, particularly in Western cultures, are bombarded with a complex belief set which one can refer to as the Romantic ideology. Throughout *The Second Sex*, de Beauvoir attempts to expose the central precepts of this ideology which seizes hold of the young girl and pervades the consciousness of women of all ages. It is transmitted to young girls not only by the "great" male writers and poets but by their own mothers.

Central to this ideology are the following beliefs. First, it is crucial to convince the young girl that as a female she will throughout her life be seen as less important and less valuable than a male, and that this situation is normal. As a consequence, the young girl learns to prize the wishes and companionship of men over those of women. This is the crucial premise of male supremacy. The second crucial premise is the belief in the essential incompleteness of the young girl and single woman. Prior to or lacking affiliation with a male, a girl or woman passes her life in a state of suspension, because the locus of her identity has not yet appeared. Encouraged by the popular and religious mythologies of the culture, she dreams of being found by the appropriate Prince Charming who will confer a sense of identity upon her along with, in many cases, social and economic status.[15] The third, crucial belief in the Romantic Ideology is the belief that it is possible for each woman to have a Great Love in her life and until that Love happens to her, she will not be truly fulfilled as a woman.

Once these three beliefs are internalised, de Beauvoir argues, it is easy to understand what motivates a woman to want to love. First, women have been taught that until they fall in love with a superior being who has already formed an identity of his own, they do not have an identity. *A woman wants to fall in love to find out who she is.* De Beauvoir asks us to witness Catherine in *Wuthering Heights*, who says "I am Heathcliff": "...her own world collapses in contingence, for she really lives in his." (SS,725). For de Beauvoir, this is the fatal mirage of the ideal of romantic love: transcendence by way of immersion in the transcendence of the Other, the superior male who is perceived as free.

Her second important motive is that in the process of loving and acquiring her identity, a woman's past and present become *meaningful* in relation to the loved one.

> Love is the developer that brings out in clear, positive detail the dim negative, otherwise as useless as a blank exposure. Through love, woman's face, the curves of her body, her childhood memories, her former tears, her gowns, her accustomed ways, her universe, everything she is, all that belongs to her, escape contingency and become essential. (SS, 718).

What had been indeterminate now has significance. Think, for example, of the positive value assigned to Lady Diana Spenser's virginity prior to her marriage to Prince Charles. As a biological state of the organism, one might regard virginity as a value-neutral property. In the eye of the royal loved one, it obviously was of prime importance. By being loved, the woman in love is no longer in a state of suspension of significance — if he prizes her giggle, her blush, then these are part of her desirability; if he deplores her tomboy youth, her history is written in that light.

The third important motive is to acquire a *locus of values*. Ideally, the woman in love looks to her lover to be *her* world. The extent to which this can take place is limitless.

> The measure of values, the truth of the world, are in his consciousness; hence it is not enough to serve him. The woman in love tries to see with his eyes; she reads the books he reads, prefers the pictures and the music he prefers; she is interested only in the landscapes she sees with him, in the ideas that come from him; she adopts his friendships, his enmities, his opinions; when she questions herself, it is his reply she tries to hear; she wants to have in her lungs the air he has already breathed; the fruits and flowers that do not come from his hands have no taste and no fragrance. Her idea of location in space, even, is upset: the centre of the world is no longer the place where she is, but that occupied by her lover; all roads lead to his home and from it. (SS,724).

In sum, for the woman in love, her lover becomes the source of meaning and significance in her world, the limits of her world, thc infallible judge of her life, and the locus of her own freedom.[16]

Throughout this process, an element of prudential judgement enters it. In order for the woman in love to acquire maximum value it is crucial that she seek out a superior man, one who will represent the essence of transcendent manhood. As a consequence, the woman in love holds back her commitment until she has evidence that the man in question is genuinely worthy of her love and her devotion. Virility, physical strength, distinction of manner, wealth, cultivation, intelligence, a sense of authority, social status and the courage suggested by military uniforms — these are taken as signs of superiority by women (SS,714). Moreover, the woman in love demands some sort of proof that she is valued or treasured before abandoning herself to love — given the totality of the commitment involved, it is foolhardy not to demand some assurance.

A fourth motive for the woman to love is that it provides for the possibility of legitimising and integrating her sexuality with her sense of her own identity. De Beauvoir points out that in a situation devoid of affection and commitment, many women who are taught to regard their own erotic responses as forms of animal-like debasement feel used by men as sexual instruments. Sexual fervour in the context of love legitimises a woman's erotic passion; sexual pleasure is experienced in a genuinely human way.

What is particularly treacherous about this whole situation, for de

Beauvoir, is that inauthenticity and self-deception are being camouflaged in the powerful guise of "freedom". Loving is perceived as a move towards her *own* self-realisation, as one of the few avenues open to her to escape the stultifying worlds of feminine immanence. The woman in love desires and seeks love as a form of liberation, as one of the few genuinely creative acts open to her. Loving is the closest, gender-appropriate way of approximating the Life of the Spirit to which she, as a naturally inferior human subject, can aspire. Rather than being identified as a form of temptation, the ideal of the woman in love is advanced not only as a normal ideal worthy of any woman, but as the highest form of existential aspiration open to her. This is why de Beauvoir's critique is so ruthless. She is committed to exposing romantic love as an existential fraud. Where the woman in love sees in her love a form of transcendence, a form of genuine liberation, de Beauvoir sees it as an inevitable downward spiral into abject servility imcompatible with any notion of self-respect.

Having sketched out the background assumptions of de Beauvoir's analysis, I now turn to her examination of the process of loving.

THE PHENOMENOLOGY OF ROMANTIC LOVE: PROBLEMS AND PARADOXES

Phase One: Identification

In describing the phenomenology of the romantic love dynamic, I distinguish four separate phases or moments each of which leads to a devastating paradox. In the first part of this chapter, I noted that the deepest, most important motives that lead a woman to seek out a great love are the acquiring of identity, value, meaning, and integration. In her love for a superior being who instantiates all that is desired by way of freedom, the woman in love sees herself as creative, as transcending her initial situation of feminie powerlessness. Moreover, in glorying in her love and serving this superior person, she glories in her essential womanliness. This is the initial experienced state of loving. Confident that she is treasured by the superior person she loves, the woman in love abandons herself to her vocation of loving.

But this leads to the first paradox: the woman in love abandons herself, in a blaze of altruistic splendour, in order to save herself from a lifetime of contingency and irrelevance. Such salvation is achieved only through loving immersion in and identification with the loved one, so that her transcendence is achieved through participation in his. So that this metamorphosis of identity can take place, submissiveness and passivity are required on her part. But through this process the woman in love succeeds only in becoming a metaphysical dependent: for genuine transcendence requires *action*, a sense of authority, and independence. As the woman in love identifies more and more with her lover — which is how she defines "falling in love" — she loses and destroys the very possibility of her ever having her own identity. The more deeply she loves, the more the necessary conditions for genuine transcendence are eliminated by that very process. Believing that just the opposite is taking place, the woman in love has moved into an enveloping state of self-deception which will be celebrated and approved of by any culture that celebrates romantic love. This is, then, the first paradox: that in seeking transcendence, the woman in love chooses precisely those means which annihilate the possibility of her transcendence. (SS,722)

The course of love is not, however, a static one. Often an initial euphoric romantic beginning shades into some darker phases of the relationship. The most important phase to succeed the first one is, in crucial ways, an inversion of it.

Phase Two: Inversion

As mentioned earlier, de Beauvoir believes that every human subject desires to experience self-determination. Although the woman in love initially celebrates her vulnerability and dependency as proof of the intensity of her love, she gradually comes to perceive her need for some power and control in the relationship. This desire becomes more urgent as the woman in love comes to see the fragility of her situation. Having given all, she is in a position to lose all should her lover abandon her. In response to a resurgence of her desire for genuine transcendence, the woman in love strives to invert the power situation through her sacrifice.[17] She conveys to her lover the magnificence of the gift of her love, the totality of the gift of herself and the absoluteness of her devotion. Even more sensitively, more completely, the woman in love expresses her devotion. The clever woman in love strives to become indispensable to her lover even to the point of cultivating wants in him that only she can satisfy.[18] Should the lover feel uneasy about this situation, he has little recourse. It is virtually impossible for him to resist without appearing brutishly ungrateful. Nevertheless, a mortal struggle is taking place here: "...the woman requires him to accept gratefully the burdens with which she crushes him." (SS, 729)

But the woman in love cannot logically win this struggle. This is the second paradox: If she succeeds in gaining control at this stage of the relationship, if she takes camouflaged possession of her lover, then he ceases to be a worthy object of her love. She has destroyed that transcendence which attracted her to him in the first place. Having guaranteed the continued presence and interest of her lover through her masquerade of devotion and self-sacrifice, she finds herself without a worthy lover. She is lost. She is degraded and unhappy. She knows that a truly transcendent free subject could not be so controlled. Consequently, if she succeeds, she demonstrates her own ridiculousness in her choice of a lover, the relationship is shattered, and her sacrifice is exposed as worthless.

If, on the other hand, the woman in love fails, if her lover remains free of her tyranny of devotion, the woman in love sees her own powerlessness, her failure as a free subject. Thus, she is unhappy with this second alternative as well. Once she knows that she will never be able to possess him, her fear and existential anxiety intensify. She knows that she is in greater jeopardy than before her attempt at inversion. In short, either way she loses.

At this stage, the woman in love is subject to two powerful temptations.

TEMPTATION 1: LYING

Acknowledging her own vulnerability, the woman in love tells herself that their love is a genuinely reciprocated relationship of mutuality, that her lover is just as dependent on her as she is on him. But the relief and satisfaction provided by this state of deception is short-lived. It cannot be sustained without generating a third paradox similar to the second. It is this: what attracted the woman in love to her lover initially was his sense of separate and complete identity, his sense of superiority and independence which had been achieved quite apart from her. Postulating a relation of mutual *interdependence* destroys precisely those features of the lover that have made him worthy of her love. Asymmetry of both power and significance was required at the outset. The longer her relationship of dependency and identification continues, the more crucial it is that the transcendent power of the lover continue to be demonstrated to sustain the totality of her commitment. Demonstrated reciprocity would destroy the very grounds of her commitment. Her inessentiality to her lover is necessary for him to be, genuinely, a free subject. If the woman in love catches herself out in this lie, she returns to her original state of fearful servility.

Suppose, on the other hand, that what she is telling herself is the truth, namely, that her lover *is* dependent upon her, that her existence and identity are just as central to his sense of himself as his are to hers. In an existential context of interpretation, what this means is that the lover really has lost the strength, the sense of independence, of the transcendent subject. He is no longer free. He too has been destroyed by this relationship. But then, from the point of view of romantic ideology, he is a fallen idol, not worth her love. If her love is to continue at all, the lie must be exposed as a lie. In short, if the lie is recognised as a lie, it signals a return to a state of fear and dread. If the lie is *not* a lie, or is not recognized as a lie, then the conditions for romantic love are no longer satisfied and the love shatters.

TEMPTATION 2: JEALOUS MANIPULATION

De Beauvoir argues that the experience and significance of jealousy are metaphysically different for the woman in love than for her lover.[19] The lover's identity and sense of self-worth is presumed to be formed prior to entering into this relationship. Thus, the loss of his loved woman, at best, might be akin to the loss of a treasure, or a servant, or a mirror, or all three. The definition of the nature of romantic love prevents his loss from being of any greater significance for him. (Again, should the loss prove more profound, this would testify to his lack of transcendent completeness and would be evidence of his existential inferiority. Such a lover would not be worth feeling jealous over.)

The woman in love, on the other hand,

> ...loving her man in his alterity and in his transcendence, feels in danger at every moment. There is no great distance between the treason of absence and infidelity....Her entire destiny is involved in each glance her lover casts at another woman, since she has identified her whole being with him....She has received all from love, she can lose all in losing it. (SS,736)

The slightest indication of interest in another woman can trigger feelings of jealous terror in the woman in love. Because she has, literally, come into existence through this relationship, if she loses it, she loses all that she is: her sense of identity, her sense of herself as a person of value, her social world and, almost invariably, her sense of economic security.

Because of her experience of jealousy and her fear of its consequences, the woman in love sees the world as a competitive place in which it is crucial for her to perceive and assess all other women as potential rivals. If such feelings are sparked by the perception of waning interest on the part of the lover, the woman in love is tempted to engage in one of two manipulative tactics. She might try returning to the manipulations involved in the inversion stage of the relationship, this time in more hyperbolic form using more gentleness, more devotion, more smiles, more mystery.

> Even a proud woman is forced to make herself gentle and passive; maneuvering, discretion, trickery, smiles, charm, docility, are her best weapons...Her hair was carefully done, her lips and cheeks had unaccustomed coloring, she was dressed up in a lace blouse of sparkling white. Party clothes, weapons of war! (SS, 738)

This tactic is likely to fail. This time, her very servility will undermine her efforts. For, as de Beauvoir notes, "giving herself blindly, the woman has lost that dimension of freedom which at first made her fascinating. The lover seeks his reflection in her; but if he begins to find it altogether too faithful, he gets bored.'' (SS, 738)

A slightly more subtle tactic is to feign a lack of interest in the lover in order to conjure up a tantalising dimension of freedom. Often she will engage in flirtation and seduction with others in hopes of rekindling his interest. But this situation leads to the fourth paradox: if either of these manipulative strategies succeeds and the lover fails to see through them, she cannot help but see how gullible and imperceptive he is. So although she is a success as a manipulator, she leaves the lover exposed as a gullible, imperceptive fraud. Thus she ultimately sees herself and her commitment as a failure.

If, on the other hand, her manoeuvres fail and the perceptiveness of the lover is thereby revealed, so, too are her manipulations seen for what they are, games played by an abject and fearful dependent. Consequently, her identity and existence continue to be imperilled and she is left without recourse.

In short, though praised and celebrated for her love, the woman in love becomes in reality silly, insecure, dependent, and powerless. Her own life now is one of servility, devoid of the conditions or the possibility of self-respect. Romantic love is a dehumanising relation also for her lover, but she is the only one whom it can completely destroy:

> It is, again, one of the loving woman's misfortunes to find that her very love disfigures her, destroys her; she is nothing more than this slave, this servant, this too ready mirror, this too faithful echo...Her salvation depends on this despotic free being that has made her and can instantly destroy her....love is a supreme effort to survive by accepting the dependence to which she is condemned; but even with consent a life of dependency can be lived only in fear and servility. (SS, 738, 742).

Thus far I have worked within the framework of existential ethics. Within this perspective, the moral assessment of romantic love is clear. As noted above, de Beauvoir believes that if a woman genuinely chooses romantic love, then she chooses a clear moral evil. If it is not a choice but is experienced as a ''necessity'' in the context of oppressive social and economic circumstances through internalisation of the mythology of romantic love, it is a destructive form of self-delusion. In either case, it is morally wrong.

The question then arises: Is it only the value system of existentialist ethics that leads to a negative moral assessment of romantic love? If we leave aside the lofty language of transcendence and the model of human nature that depends upon a theory of objectifying self-deception as a universal human desire, what moral assessment should we make of romantic love? This question occupies my attention for the remainder of this chapter.

AN ASSESSMENT BY A MORAL ECLECTIC

Although one might acknowledge the psychological demands and the likely emotional complications of romantic love, the fundamental moral question remains: is it morally wrong to aspire to and to choose a life commitment of romantic love?

At the first stage of the assessment it is important to determine whether or not the choice is really a choice. That is, we need to know whether the necessary pre-conditions of genuine choice have been satisfied. As a minimum, genuine choice requires knowledge, freedom from coercion, and access to other real alternatives. Therefore, we need to ask whether the choice of romantic love satisfies these conditions.

Turning first to the question of coercion, one can distinguish at least two types. One is the obvious knife-at-your-throat, gun-at-your-back variety of overt physical coercion. Usually, though not always (remember the Stockholm syndrome), this form of coercion is not at work in romantic love. Two other forms need to be considered: covert deliberate coercion, and unintentional institutional coercion.[20] Both can take subtle and insidious forms. Human beings grow up and are socialised in a culture that indoctrinates them into a complex set of beliefs about what their essential nature is, what their corresponding permitted and proper roles will be, and how access to economic and social privileges can be gained. Described in a formal way, this process appears (relatively) morally neutral. Consider, however, someone being socialised in a culture in which an assumption of white supremacy is generally accepted as an "empirical truth". When faced with a significant choice, a person of colour who believes in white supremacy may believe that it is "fitting and right" to choose an inferior position on the grounds that this is what is commensurate with one's abilities. To do otherwise would be a display of deplorable and punishable social and moral arrogance. Deference and institutionalised inferiority are seen as the appropriate postures to assume.[21]

In this situation, the individual's self-image has been shaped in powerful ways.[22] Even if we omit the negative social consequences of choosing otherwise, I think it is fair to say that although a particular choice is alleged to be "open", the person of colour would experience strong internal pressure in the direction of an inferior alternative.

Not all female babies are given complete sets of Harlequin Romances at birth. Nevertheless, women in many cultures are socialised, completely and profoundly, into heterosexist ideologies of male supremacy. In some cultures and in some historical periods, this ideology is supported by more specific ideology of romantic love. Again, central to romantic ideology is the axiom of male supremacy and essential female inferiority.[23] Raised in a male supremacist society, a woman comes to have an image of herself as inferior. This gets lived out in the selection of inferior roles and alternatives.[24] Such "choices" then reinforce the perception of women as inferior and provide material support to existing male supremacist practices. Thus, I would argue, a woman's "choice" of romantic love, defined as including affiliation with a superior male, is not a genuinely free choice.

Similarly, I think a strong case could be made that in many cultures women do not have genuinely human alternatives to choose from. Any culture that *defines* women totally in terms of reproductive and domestic roles cannot be said to offer women a full range of alternatives. If romantic love is believed to be the necessary catalyst in leading a woman into her life as a domestic reproducer and that is the only legitimate life held open to her, then the choice of romantic love is, again, not a genuine choice.

Finally, it is clear that where knowledge of the consequences is lacking, a person cannot be said to have made an informed free choice. In many cultures, the praises of romantic love are sung and celebrated. The consequences often remain camouflaged.[25] A woman who has accepted the illusory message of romantic love as literal truth cannot be said to be informed about the situation. Again, her choice is not a free one.

Suppose, however, that we consider the morally difficult case. Let us assume that we are looking at a woman whose choice has not been coerced, either overtly or covertly, who has other significant alternatives in her life, and who has knowledge of the consequences of her choice. She has read and understood *The Second Sex*, she has even read this chapter. She has seen numerous friends disappear into the quagmires of romantic servility, and she does not regard herself as, in some way, idiosyncratically exempt from the servile consequence. Is it immoral for her to choose a life of romantic love if *HE* comes along?

I believe it is immoral for two very different sorts of reasons. First, because the choice of romantic love, as defined here, is the choice of an intrinsic evil; and, second, because the life of romantic love leads to significant harm. In the remainder of this chapter, I argue for these two claims.

Claim 1: Romantic Love Is Intrinsically Evil

This type of objection can be found in the writings of a variety of moral theorists. For example, in *On Liberty* John Stuart Mill argues that one cannot, with moral approbation, knowingly enter into a relationship or situation that will terminate the very possibility of moral choice.[25] That is, voluntary servitude is always immoral. This moral evaluation is based on a view of human nature (not completely unlike that of de Beauvoir) on which the making of moral choices is central to any life properly regarded as a human life. The voluntaristic stress in both classical Kantian moral theory and in Mill's formulation of liberalism prohibits choosing a life of committed inevitable servility whether it is in the form of romantic self-abasing attachment or in some other form of servitude such as economic slavery *when one has other real options that might preserve and even enhance one's capacity and range of choice.*[26] If one accepts the stress on the importance of human choice, it follows that it is immoral for any human being to use their human capacity for choice in such a way as to annihilate that capacity for choice. Any choice which by virtue of the completeness of the servility required is humanity-destroying must be regarded as immoral if there are humanity-preserving alternatives available. From this perspective, then, the choice of romantic love as a life-determining form of voluntary servitude must be regarded as an intrinsically immoral choice if it satisfies the conditions for genuine choice.

In addition to this line of argument, one might argue that the choice of romantic love is bad because of the consequences of the choice which are lived out by lovers in situations of romantic love. This line of argument leads to the second type of moral assessment which is a consequentialist analysis.

Claim 2: Romantic Love Is Harmful; Therefore It Is Bad

As mentioned at the beginning of this chapter, we can distinguish at least four possible categories of harm:

(1) harm to the woman who loves
(2) harm to the lover
(3) harm to the quality of the relationship
(4) harm to the social community ("the greatest number")

Although several significant types of harm can be argued for in each of these categories, space does not permit a detailed articulation of all these in the present context. Consequently, I sketch out one characteristic type of harm in each category.

ROMANTIC LOVE HARMS THE WOMAN WHO LOVES

As noted earlier, when the woman in love begins to fear the loss of her lover, she uses the only form of power available to her: manipulative power. This can be roughly characterised as power the successful exercise of which depends essentially on its remaining unperceived. The effect of the exercise of covert power on the manipulator is a complicated issue;[27] but in this context the following point is the crucial one. Anyone who uses manipulative power in a situation in which no other forms are available to them (because they are not of the "right" gender or the "right" race) will be crippled and mutilated through the very use of that power.

The manipulating woman must simulate a posture of weakness and vulnerability. This has the harmful consequence that even though the particular manipulative tactic may work, the woman herself can only continue to be falsely perceived as weak and powerless and, hence, open to exploitation. Often the woman internalises this perception of herself (this may be precisely why she turns to manipulation in the first place) and comes to see herself as genuinely weak. Moreover, because she will be seen as a *typically* "weak woman", the property of being naturally weak is ascribed to other women as well.

Secondly, the use of manipulative power is seldom cumulative. Because the manipulative woman is not perceived as powerful by those whom she manipulates, she is not accorded the minimal amount of respect that is directed toward individuals who use power in publicly acknowledged ways. This lack of power is underscored in the situation of romantic love which, at its core, emphasises a woman's vulnerability, her childlike weakness and awesome dependency on the lover. Reinforcing these real weaknesses in the name of "loving attraction" is obviously harmful to the woman concerned. To the extent that she has recourse to manipulative tactics in order to preserve and intensify her relationship of dependency, she is harming herself even further. Needless to say, the person manipulated, in this case the lover, is also harmed by this use of power, since by being deceived his own capacity for self-determination is being undermined.

ROMANTIC LOVE IS HARMFUL TO THE MALE LOVER[28]

As seen earlier, the ideology of romantic love calls for the lover to be an incarnation of an ideal transcendent hero. Romantic love requires that the appropriate loved person be a *world-constituting*, meaning-conferring subject. This cannot help but be a deeply falsifying picture of the lover. Even when the social acceptability of the demands of masculinity support the development of such males, it is difficult to imagine any human being able to satisfy, unwaveringly, the demands made of them by a woman in love. In short, no one can *be* the transcendent existentialist hero that the woman in love requires to justify her passion and her commitment. This is the first sort of harm that is done to the lover: impossible and falsifying demands are placed upon him.

Moreover, the lover is invited to participate in a situation of double metaphysical duplicity. He is encouraged, often both by the culture and by the woman who loves him, to believe that he really *is* the "Hero", this superior being. Forbidden any weakness, he himself may well forget that he too, like any other subject, is vulnerable, fragile, and subject to anguish. Thus not only is he being forced into a mould by his lover (and his culture) as a foil for her weakness; he is praised for accepting this falsifying perception of himself. Although some beneficial consequences might result from this false picture (for example, he might be likely to act more courageously or more steadfastly than if he did not have this view of himself), this situation is harmful because it makes genuine self-knowledge impossible.

In addition, it is a perception that encourages and legitimises exploitative arrogance in the name of normal love. As noted above, the woman who is socialised to desire romantic love has often been socialised into feeling that she should tolerate and accept servility because she has internalised a view of herself as essentially inferior. In complementary fashion, the romantic ideology instructs a male, as the potential legitimate recipient of this life, to regard his arrogance as the normal behaviour of a superior individual. In a situation like this, the avoidance of arrogant exploitation is almost impossible.[29]

Thus, romantic love requires a falsification of the lover which is harmful because it prevents genuine self-knowledge and leads to the further harm of camouflaging the vice of arrogance as an indelible mark of superior virtue. That arrogance can be as morally corrupting a moral disposition as servility is clear.

ROMANTIC LOVE HARMS AND CAN DESTROY ANY RELATIONSHIP OF LOVE

I have already argued that the relationship of romantic love is based on multiple deeply destructive illusions that harm each of the participants. I would now argue that the relationship of love itself suffers accordingly with yet more resultant harm to the participants. A specific example of harm to the quality of the relationship can be seen in situations of romantic love where the woman in love tries to carry out her inversion of the original power relationship by preserving or even cultivating emotional primitiveness in her lover. This is designed to establish the woman's indispensability as a kind of expert in the life of the emotions, an expertise often conveniently already assigned to her in many western capitalist societies.[30] Using a feminine stereotype entrenched in a social context that routinely assigns emotional maintenance work to women, the woman in love can encourage a perception of herself as an indispensable empathic companion. Blum *et al.* discuss the harmful effects this process can have for wife and husband. This dynamic can occur in the relationship of romantic love as well.[31] Although the woman in love may be successful in cultivating such emotional dependency, in so doing, she harms the quality of the relationship (as well as herself in the process). Such an asymmetrical relationship is bound to remain emotionally primitive while all potential for emotional growth in intimacy is stunted and thwarted by both participants. I see this as a clear case of harm.[32]

More generally the relationship of romantic love is claimed not only to *be* a love relationship but, for a woman, her most significant and fulfilling adult relationship.[33] I would hold that, at the minimum, any genuine love relationship should provide support and caring in an atmosphere of mutual trust and communication. Each of the parties should strive to be present to the other in a forthright way so that the relationship can be based on shared and mutual knowledge — albeit partial and open to change.

When under the influence of romantic love, however, lovers are incapable of satisfying these minimum conditions for genuine love. So the relationship of love suffers. Instead of knowledge, we find double illusions necessary to sustain the dynamic of romantic love. Instead of trust, we find, at best, an intermingling of dependency, fear, and manipulation on the part of the woman in love, and a prohibition of genuine intimacy and sharing by the lover. Instead of mutual support, we find a situation of double-victimisation involving the woman whose total dependency is encouraged and in the lover whose solitary self-sufficiency is required as the *raison d'être* of the relationship. If we regard the love relationship as I have just sketched it to contain morally good and beneficial characteristics in itself, then the effect of romantic love can only be seen as noxious. Romantic love is a clear case of harm both to the potentiality and to the actual existence of genuine love.

ROMANTIC LOVE PRODUCES SOCIAL HARM

In this section I am assuming that interpersonal alientation is bad. And I am assuming that any process that produces alienation on a large scale by creating an atmosphere of fear and hostility should be avoided if possible. More specifically, where participation in a particular dynamic diminishes the potential for caring and trust among human beings and intensifies loneliness and dependency, I would argue that this dynamic is harmful.

I would, like de Beauvoir, argue that the situation of romantic love provides an illustration of such a dynamic. As mentioned above, in the discussion of jealousy, the woman in love is likely to fear abandonment. Her situation is, psychologically, a life-and-death situation for her. Thus, at the very least, prudence would seem to require that she monitor her environment for potential threats. Given identity and a feeling of worth through her love, the woman in love exists in a state of metaphysical dependency upon her lover. Should he leave her for another, in an important sense she perishes, *qua* individually defined consciousness. For the most part, women form the threatening social group.

In this context, it is important that the woman in love be able to assess other women in male-identified terms, using those categories which she knows attract her lover (which might be quite distinct from those categories she herself employs when she finds another woman attractive and valuable).[34] In this evaluation process, it is crucial that the woman in love be able to see other women *through* her lover's eyes. Two categories of women emerge: women who are assessed as (potential, illusory, or real) threats and those women who appear to be "safe". The woman in love knows that this latter judgement is never infallible. There is always the lurking suspicion that even "safe" women are capable of being metamorphosed by the "right" lover into potential threats. Thus, in principle, no woman is completely safe for the woman in love.

This leads to at least two harmful consequences. First, as mentioned above, the woman in love employs — and must employ — standards of assessment derived from male criteria of attractiveness and desirability (and is herself continually being evaluated by these criteria by *other* women in love). In the best of all possible worlds, male-derived criteria of assessment can lead only to a partial perception of any individual woman. What is more likely is that these male criteria of evaluation are seen, both by the woman in love and the culture at large, as the *only* standards of evaluation worth employing. Thus the use of these standards not only distorts but simultaneously devalues women on a large scale, thereby reinforcing male supremacist attitudes and practices.

Secondly, since the woman in love carries out this process of monitoring in the name of assessing threats, any positive assessment of another woman by her is bound to generate feelings of suspicion, fear, and hostility — feelings that make it impossible to form relationships of support and affection with any of these women. Any positive significant relationship with another woman is thereby closed off. Since in our culture and in many others romantic love is encouraged on a large scale (remember the universalistic language of Byron, Nietzsche, and Balzac), the resulting social alienation and hostility between women is potentially massive. As I suggested above, if we know that a particular process is likely to generate this much social harm and we can avoid participation in that process, we are morally bound to do so. Thus, I conclude that romantic love should be avoided because of its profoundly harmful effects to the social community at large.[35]

In sum, I have argued in this section that the choice of romantic love can be seen as morally bad. If other alternatives are open to women (and men), romantic love should be avoided because of its harmful effects to the woman in love, her lover, the quality of the relationship itself, and the social community at large.

CONCLUDING POSTSCRIPT

Is There Life After Romantic Love?

Unlikely...at least for a while. But there certainly is life before romantic love, a life that contains the possibility for genuine love. And de Beauvoir thinks so too. She's even willing to spell out the conditions for authentic love. But that's the subject of another paper.

REFERENCES

1 All references in this paper are to the following edition: *The Second Sex*, trans., edit. H.M. Parshley. New York: Random House, 1952. Such references will be abbreviated as *SS*.

2 De Beauvoir distinguishes this from nurturance which is simply one form that this loving might take. This claim interestingly parallels Carol Gilligan's research findings concerning the question of whether the parameters of women's moral judgements are the same as those of men. Gilligan argues that a concern for interpersonal relations and affiliations dominates women's moral judgements, as contrasted with the more individualistic, potentially adversarial rights-oriented models of moral thinking which appear to be dominant in men. For the most recent statement of Gilligan's theory see Carol Gilligan, *In a Different Voice: Psychological Theory and Women's Development*. Cambridge, MA: Harvard U. Press (1982).

3 For the remainder of this chapter I will be using the term 'man' in place of 'superior being' because de Beauvoir assumes (uncritically) a heterosexist model throughout. Insofar as the socialisation of males is directed towards producing a sense of superiority and male supremacy as an ideal end state, an "appropriately" socialised male will be more likely to be perceived as the "proper" recipient of love. However, I do not believe that de Beauvoir's analysis applies solely to heterosexual situations. What is necessary to generate the dynamic under discussion is the presence of someone (most likely a woman) who has internalised these three central tenets. That this same dynamic can be generated between two women is clear from Kate Millett's account in *Sita* (New York: Ferrar, Straus and Giroux, 1977). Whether it is likely to be generated between two men neither of whom has been indoctrinated into this set of beliefs is an open question at this point.

4 See the chapter "The Nomads", *SS*, pp. 69 - 73, for a fuller discussion of this distinction.

5 Cf. Sherry Ortner, "Is Woman to Man as Nature is to Culture?" in *Women, Culture, and Society*, ed. Michelle Zimbalist, Louise Lamphere (Stanford, CA: Stanford University Press, 1974), pp. 265 - 80. Ortner develops the theme of the partial identification of women with Nature, accepting de Beauvoir's

devaluation of the natural domain. It should be noted that there are at least two critical ways of dealing with the claim that women are closer to Nature and therefore inferior. One way is to argue against the primary association of women and Nature; the second is to challenge the consequent assessment of inferiority alleged to follow from this association. In *Women and Nature* Susan Griffen adopts this second tactic. See Susan Griffen, *Woman and Nature, The Roaring Inside Her* (New York: Harper and Row, 1978).

6 De Beauvoir offers a parallel example with respect to agriculture, *SS*, p. 85.

7 In the Chapter on "Situation and Character", De Beauvoir expands this distinction into a full theory of human consciousness in which characteristic feminine and masculine sensibilities are sharply differential along cognitive, emotional, physical, moral, political, and metaphysical lines.

8 To many contemporary feminist thinkers, much of de Beauvoir's discussion of this dualism with its Platonic commitment to the non-corporeal appears to be not only somatophobic but misogynistic. See for example Mary Lowenthal Felstiner, "Seeing *The Second Sex* through the Second Wave", *Feminist Studies*, Vol. 6, No. 2 (Summer 1980), pp. 247 - 276. I concur with this assessment.

9 An example that de Beauvoir examines at length is the situation of a housewife in industrialised societies whose labour is entirely of a domestic sort. She is involved in non-cumulative cyclical processes of cleaning and cooking, cleaning and cooking with no obvious product of any sort to show for this labour.

10 "Every subject plays his part as such specifically through exploits of projects that serve as a mode of transcendence; he achieves liberty only through a continual reaching out toward other liberties. There is no justification for present existence other than its expansion into an indefinitely open future. Every time transcendence falls back into immanence, stagnation, there is a degradation of existence into the "*en soi*" — the brutish life of subjection to given conditions — and of liberty into constraint and contingence. This downfall represents a moral fault if the subject consents to it; if it is inflicted upon him, it spells frustration and oppression. In both cases, it is an absolute evil." (*SS*, xxxiii).

11 Note that one can accept de Beauvoir's descriptive analysis of women's situations and roles without accepting her value judgement. Such an approach has been attempted recently, with admirable success, by Sara Ruddick in "Maternal Thinking", *Feminist Studies*, Vol. 6, No. 2 (Summer, 1980), pp. 342 - 367.

12 This is not to say that the actual lives of all men are those of authentic human subjects — de Beauvoir herself cites the example of the *petit bourgeois* white-collar male worker as exemplifying some of the worst aspects of a life of immanence. Rather, it is a claim that it is only within the *kind* of situations which, until now, have been available only to (white) men, that any form of a life of transcendence is possible. Whether this *caveat* ultimately saves de Beauvoir from this charge of male identification is unclear.

13 This notion of bad faith has recently been lifted out of its existentialist theoretical framework and is being marketed in a current best seller by Colette Dowling called *The Cinderella Complex, Women's Hidden Fear of Independence* (New York: Simon and Schuster, 1981).

14 In general, I believe it is fair to say that the second half of *The Second Sex* consists of an extended analysis of the ways in which the various roles ascribed to women, as lived by "normal women", generate situations of bad faith, lives that are less than fully human. De Beauvoir is convinced that the "normal", "good" woman, as defined in patriarchal cultures, must live in bad faith and cannot be fully human. Her analysis of the woman in love is simply one form of a much larger sustained feminist project.

15 Eli Zaretsky, *Capitalism, the Family, and Personal Life* (New York: Harper and Row, 1976).

16 Although de Beauvoir's descriptions here might seem to be hyperbolic, something like her theory is needed to account not only for women like Nancy Reagan, but also for the accounts of the profound loss of identity experienced by women who are suddenly abandoned or widowed, a loss that does not always diminish with time. Translated into a social practice, the suttee as it is practised and understood in India illustrates the total identification expected of a wife with her husband.

17 In this and other sections of *SS*, de Beauvoir's debt to Hegel's analysis of the master-slave dialect in the *Phenomenology of Spirit* is clear.

18 The devastating moral consequences of this process have been explored in a perceptive article by Larry Blum, Marcia Homiak, Judy Houseman, and Naomi Scheman, "Altruism and Women's Oppression" in *Women and Philosophy*, ed. Gould and Wartofsky (New York: G.P. Putnam's Sons, 1976), pp. 222 - 247.

19 For an interesting alternative account of jealousy see J. Neu, "Jealous Thoughts", in A.O. Rorty, ed., *Explaining Emotions*, Berkeley: University of California Press, 1980.

20 See Richard Wasserstrom's analysis of this corruption in his essay, "Racism, Sexism, and Preferential Treatment: An Approach to the Topics", *U.C.L.A. Law Review* (Feb., 1977) pp. 581 - 615.

21 I am grateful to Thomas E. Hill for suggesting an analogous example. See Hill's exceedingly ovarian article, "Servility and Self-Respect", *The Monist*, Vol. 57, No. 1 (January, 1973), pp. 87 - 104.

22 Bem and Bem make this point in their discussion of the socialisation of American women. They say, in their discussion of the claim that American women are perfectly free to choose amongst a variety of roles, that "this argument conveniently overlooks the fact that the society which has spent twenty years carefully marking the woman's ballot for her has nothing to lose in that twenty-first year by pretending to let her cast it for the alternative of her choice. Society has controlled not her alternatives, but her motivation to

choose any but one of those alternatives. The so-called freedom to choose is illusory...". *Roles Women Play*, ed. Michele Garskof, pp. 84 - 96, p. 88 - 89. See also Sandra Bartky, "On Psychological Oppression", in *Philosophy and Women*, ed. Sharon Bishop and Marjorie Weinzweig. (Belmont, CA: Wadsworth Publishing Co., 1979), pp. 33 - 41.

23 This consideration leads me to distinguish morally and politically between heterosexual love and lesbian romantic love. Although lesbian romantic love may involve some of the same emotional and moral pitfalls from the point of view of de Beavoir's analysis, the situation of a woman committed profoundly and completely to another woman challenges at its very core the premise of male supremacy.

24 Think of the documented tendency of women, in sexist capitalist societies, to name lower starting salaries for themselves than their male counterparts as a result of an internal devaluation of themselves as workers.

25 See Chapter V of *On Liberty* for Mill's discussion of this issue. John Stuart Mill, *On Liberty*, ed. Elizabeth Rapaport. Indianapolis: Hackett Publishing Company, 1978, pp. 99 - 101. It is interesting to note that Mill objects less to actual suicide than to lives of voluntary servitude.

26 This is a crucial assumption. The actual life situation of any particular woman must be carefully looked at to determine whether real alternatives exist before one passes moral judgement. For many women, this condition may not be met although, to be sure, girls and women in many cultures enter into — or are entered into — marriages devoid of romantic love and completely circumscribed by domestic toil. Whether this latter situation is a more or less desirable form of servitude than advanced romantic love is an open qestion. My present feeling is that in relationships devoid of romantic love at least a woman stands a chance of having her identity left more intact. The extent to which her situation is one of social and economic oppression coupled with domestic violence will be determining factors here.

27 See my "The Morality of Manipulative Power" (in progress).

28 I am speaking here specifically of a male lover because it is not entirely clear to me that the same harm is done to a lover who is a woman.

29 An analogous argument is made by R.M. Hare regarding the moral well-being of slave owners. See R.M. Hare, "What is Wrong with Slavery", *Philosophy and Public Affairs*. Vol. 8, No. 2., pp. 103 - 117.

30 See Eli Zaretsky, *Capitalism, the Family, and Personal Life* (London: Pluto Press, 1976) for a good general discussion of the rise of this perception of women as emotional experts.

31 See Blum, Homiak, Housman, Scheman, "Altruism and Women's Oppression", *art. cit.*

32 Similarly, if the woman in love is led to overlook real difficulties in the relationship or to excuse them because sustaining that relationship is the most important part of her life, then she is undercutting the potential for change and growth in the relationship. A similar point is made by Blum *et al., ibid.*

33 This is to be distinguished from a possible relationship she might have with a child which many (of the same) theorists argue is — or ought to be — a woman's most fulfilling relationship *per se*.

34 Here again important gender differences might be drawn between heterosexual and lesbian romantic relationships. In a lesbian relationship, although the potential for abandonment may be present, the woman in love does not need to use male-generated criteria of assessment in calculating her risks. This removes at least one layer of alienation from the situation. In a male supremacist society, the woman in love in a heterosexual relationship must adopt the criteria of assessment of the dominent group. This entails a devaluation and rejection of values that women may hold important.

35 Now it may be that the prevention of significant forms of bonding among women is precisely one of the main consequences desired in a patriarchal situation. It is important to test the hypothesis that a stress on the importance of heterosexual romantic love is inversely correlated with high social expectations and approval of friendships between women. Some work has already been done in this area. See, for example, Lillian Faderman, *Surpassing the Love of Men: Romantic Friendship and Love Between Women from the Renaissance to the Present*. New York: William Morrow and Company, Inc., 1981; Adrienne Rich, "Compulsory Heterosexuality and Lesbian Existence", *Signs: Journal of Women in Culture and Society*. Vol. 5, No. 4, pp. 631 - 660; and Carroll Smith-Rosenberg, "The Female World of Love and Ritual: Relations between Women in Nineteenth-Century America." *Signs: Journal of Women in Culture and Society*, Vol. 1, No. 3.

FURTHER READING

Bishop, Sharon, "Love and Dependence", in *Philosophy and Women*, ed. Bishop, Weinzweig (Belmont, CA: Wadsworth, 1979).

Eshleman, J. Ross and J. Clarke, eds., *Intimacy, Commitment, and Marriage: The Development of Relationships* (Boston: Allyn and Bacon, 1978).

Greer, Germaine, *The Female Eunuch* (New York: Paladin, 1971), especially the section on "Love".

Rapaport, Elizabeth, "On the Future of Love: Rousseau and the Radical Feminists", in *Women and Philosophy*, ed. Gould, Wartofsky (New York: G.P. Putnam, 1976).

Safilios-Rothschild, D., *Love, Sex, and Sex Roles* (Englewood Cliffs, NJ: Prentice-Hall, 1977).

ESTHER R. GREENGLASS

A Social-Psychological View of Marriage for Women

Traditionally, the family has been a blessing for men at the expense of women. In the traditional family the man is the sole breadwinner, and the woman takes primary if not sole responsibility for child care and housekeeping and is the emotional mainstay of the family. Although the traditional family has been assumed to be natural and normal, research findings have revealed that psychologically it is devastating for women. Jessie Bernard (1971) cites studies suggesting that in the traditional marriage, wives lose ground in personal development and self-esteem during the early and middle years of adulthood, whereas husbands gain ground in these respects during the same years. Moreover, the housewife role has been identified as the role accompanied by the greatest amount of psychological disturbance. Housewives have been shown to be at the highest risk for psychological disorders: they have the highest rate of entry into psychiatric treatment of any occupational group, and they request and obtain the greatest quantity of prescribed mood-modifying drugs (New York Narcotic Addiction Control Commission, 1971). Physical and social isolation, along with economic dependency which affords little opportunity for autonomy or alternatives to marriage, are just some of the factors associated with the housewife role that may lead to psychopathology. Psychiatric symptoms may also appear in women as a result of their having to give up power to their husbands in traditional marriages. In this regard, loss of power has been shown to lead to psychopathology (Marecek, 1976).

Further research has shown that considerable stress may be associated with motherhood when sole responsibility for child care is placed on the

Originally published in *International Journal of Women's Studies* 8 (1) (1985): 24 - 31.

woman, who is expected to give 24-hour loving care. A poem by J. Echegaray (quoted in Bernard, 1974) captures the essence of the normative prescriptions associated with the traditional role of the mother:

There was a young man loved a maid
Who taunted him, "Are you afraid,"
She asked, "to bring me today
Your mother's head upon a tray?"

He went and slew his mother dead:
Tore from her breast her heart so red
Then towards his lady love he raced
But tripped and fell in all his haste.

As the heart rolled on the ground
It give forth a plaintive sound.
And it spoke in accents mild:
"Did you hurt yourself, my child?"

With the rise in feminist consciousness and the growing awareness of the psychological costs of the traditional marital role for women, increasingly they have been redefining their role in ways that would allow greater opportunity for their individual growth. Moreover, according to the media, a decade of feminism has brought about social changes that have made marriage equally beneficial to women and men. But is it true that women have achieved equality with men in marriage? What is the woman's experience in marriage today? Are the problems that women experienced in the past really gone? And, what are women's expectations of marriage today?

There is evidence that women are now expecting and demanding greater equality in marriage than they did in the past. According to some marriage counsellors (Prochaska and Prochaska, 1978), the most common reason for couples coming into marital therapy is that the marriage is being shaken by the wife's struggle for equality. For many people, the companionship marriage is being held up as the ideal. Moreover, a trend that seems to have intensified in the 1980s is that marriage has become saddled with unprecedented ideological burdens. It has become the framework for *couple* relationships supposedly based on perfect mutuality, intimacy, sexual ecstacy and mutual growth. The companionship marriage, with its emphasis on egalitarianism and democracy, is characterised by the development of an interpersonal relationship based on mutual respect and affection, understanding and friendship. Where the traditional marriage has been highly institutionalised and held together by external forces, the companionship marriage is regarded as held together by the couple's interpersonal relationship. Moreover, everyone is encouraged to strive for the companionship marriage. What is more, people generally expect that companionship will be an important basis of their marriage.

WHAT DO UNMARRIED PEOPLE EXPECT OF MARRIAGE?

In a pilot study, Marsha Eisner and I have recently found that companionship, sharing, and love were among the answers most frequently given by unmarried people (both women and men) who were asked what benefits were associated with marriage (Greenglass and Eisner, 1981). The respondents in this pilot study were a random sample of 25 never-married women and 25 never-married men between the ages of 20 and 30 who were living in Metropolitan Toronto (including the City of Toronto, North York, and four boroughs). Respondents for the study were recruited over the telephone, using a sample of telephone numbers generated by computer with the Random Digit Dialing Technique. The average number of benefits given by men and women did not differ; it was a little more than two for both groups. Although the numbers in the various cells are small, certain trends relating to gender differences nevertheless emerged. Although love was cited as a benefit almost equally often by women and men, companionship, mutual help and sharing tended to be regarded more often by men as benefits of marriage. Women, on the other hand, tended more to cite benefits relating to security, including emotional security and the legal security that stems from a marriage certificate. Additional benefits cited by both women and men included sex, children, and those of a financial nature. In summary, then, whereas men may want marriage more for interpersonal support, women seem to be opting more for security. The security that the women regarded as emanating from a legal marriage supports the traditional idea that the status of being married is more important to women than to men. On the other hand, women are less likely to rely on their marital partner for interpersonal support, no doubt partly because they are less likely to get such support from men who were not socialised to be nuturant or emotionally supportive to any great extent. Women may also be less likely to rely on their male partner for emotional support because they, more than their male counterparts, have established a close interpersonal relationship with others, particularly their female friends.

In the same study, respondents were asked what drawbacks they thought were associated with marriage. Both women and men named an average of two drawbacks. Men, more than women, perceived "loss of freedom" as a drawback; 72% of the men cited "loss of freedom" as a drawback, compared to 8% of the women. It is interesting to note that although men are looking to marriage for intimacy and interpersonal support, they seem also to be wary of the loss of freedom that may result from such a commitment. Emotional dependency on a woman, or even the thought of it, may arouse anxiety in a man because it seems to condradict our society's norms for the masculine role, which include independence and emotional invulnerability. In effect, the man himself probably believes he should be in control at most times. Therefore, marriage, or even the thought of it, may be considered by a man with some ambivalence. On the one hand, his needs for intimacy and interdependence may motivate him toward marriage, and in this regard, marriage is defined as the socially appropriate or "safe" area for men to allow themselves intimacy. However, on the other hand, the man may be motivated to avoid marriage because he fears that loss of control that may result from his dependence on a woman. Although both women and men cited interpersonal difficulties and financial expense as drawbacks, these tended to be mentioned more by men. Women were more likely to consider marriage a risky venture. An interesting paradox in the case of the female sample is that, although they tended to regard the legal security of marriage as a benefit, they — more than the men — also regarded the legal commitment associated with marriage as a drawback.

MARRIED WOMEN AND EMPLOYMENT

The belief that women have achieved equality with men in marriage is largely based on the fact that a significant proportion of married women today, compared to the past, are holding outside employment. Whereas in 1941, only 4.5% of married women in the Canadian population were employed, this figure rose to 47.4% in 1979 (see Table 16.1). In 1979, married women represented 60% of the female labour force (Canada, Labour Canada, 1980). Similar trends have been observed in the United States. Some of the reasons for their increasing employment are inflation, rising expectations in a society that places heavy emphasis on materialism and acquisition of goods, and the growing perception of the need to provide environments for children that are considered educational and stimulating (e.g., lessons of various kinds, sports, records, tapes, etc.). But according to Sylva Gelber (1972), past director of Canada's Women's Bureau, "the vast majority of women, particularly married women with young children, who double their own burden by going out to work, are employed because of economic need" (p. 7).

Employment does benefit married women psychologically — employed wives have been found generally to enjoy better physical and psychological health than housewives. Bringing home a paycheque may be regarded as a tangible symbol of competence, and employed wives have been found to have higher self-esteem, more self-confidence, and a greater sense of personal competence and autonomy (Birnbaum, 1971; Feldman and Feldman, 1973; Ohlbaum, 1971). In society's view, holding outside employment is generally regarded as more valuable than occupying an unpaid position (housewife) which supposedly requires little skill (at least according to the popular view). To some extent, women themselves probably internalise this view; this may explain why employed mothers have been found to have a more positive image of themselves than housewives (Feld, 1963).

Although employment may benefit the married woman in some ways, in others, it is clearly a liability. For example, research evidence reveals that even when women hold outside employment, they continue to take the main responsibility for housework and child care, and employment considerably increases the total number of hours women work (Walker, 1973). These women are sacrificing time from other activities, such as eating, sleeping, television viewing, gardening, and visiting (Meissner, Humphreys, Meis and Scheu, 1975). In their study, Williams, Zabrack and Harrison (1980) report that married female members of the Canadian Psychological Association (CPA) in their sample had an *increased* workload of about two working days per week. Conversely, as a result of services contributed by their spouses, male CPA members had a *reduced* workload of about three days per week. Couples may profess a commitment to equality that they find difficult to implement. Hall and Hall (1979), in their study of two-career couples, report that the most serious fights among such couples occur *not* in the bedroom but in the kitchen.

Despite research that shows that employed wives are healthier than their unemployed female counterparts, sizeable numbers of women suffer from role strain when they simultaneously occupy the roles of mother and employee. When women (as opposed to men) take on paid employment, they are regarded as taking on the additional role of employee while maintaining their traditional primary responsibility for children and the home. So, whatever else a woman does, her roles of wife and mother are expected to take precedence. As a result of carrying a double load, employed wives are reported to be suffering from "weekend stress syndrome", which is characterised by tension, irritability, and occasionally physical malaise (Szinovacz, 1978). It is most easily recognised by its periodicity — symptoms peak every Monday, Friday and Saturday, diminish on Sunday, and are hardly noticeable from Tuesday through Thursday. The syndrome presumably stems from the woman's knowledge that she actually holds not one but two jobs — breadwinner and housekeeper. "Blue Monday" comes about because of the anxious feelings most people, regardless of sex, experience when anticipating another hard week at the office. However, whereas men cheer up as the weekend approaches, employed women become tense because they feel they have to catch up on all the child care and housework they put off during the week. Even if the husband takes on some of these tasks, it does not help much because the wife still considers herself fully responsible for both child care and housework.

TABLE 16.1

Married Women's Labour Force Participation Rate in Canada[1]

Year	*Participation Rate* %
1941	*4.5*
1951	*11.2*
1961	*20.8*
1971	*33.0*
1977	*44.1*
1979	*47.4*

[1]*For 1941 and 1951 only, separated women are included with married women.*

Sources: For 1941 and 1951, Canada, Ministère du Travail, Division de la main-d'ocuvre féminine, *La femme canadienne au travail* (Publication No. 1), Ottawa: Imprimeur de la Reine, 1957, pp. 10 & 13.

For 1961 and 1971, Canada, Labour Canada, Women's Bureau, *Women in the labour force 1971: Facts and figures*, Table 9, 1972.

For 1977, Canada, Labour Canada, Women's Bureau, *Women in the labour force 1977: Facts and Figures,* Table 14b, 1978.

For 1979, Canada, Labour Canada, Women's Bureau, 1978-79 *Women in the labour force*, Table 24b, 1980.

The problem of role strain worsens in the relatively small contingent of families in which the woman is raising a family and simultaneously occupying a career role which demands a high level of commitment. Although she is more likely than her less affluent counterpart to be able to afford outside help with housework, nevertheless, she and her husband will probably have high achievement aspirations for both their marriage and their children's psychological development. Such aspirations require considerable time for planned activities, within both the family and the community. Since normative expectations disproportionately place the responsibilities for children's psychological development on the mother, the extent of these burdens will likely be felt more by the woman involved in a demanding career than the man (Johnson and Johnson, 1976). Thus, women "know" that if anything goes wrong with the children, i.e., if they seem disturbed, deprived or even upset, it is *they*, not the men, who will be held responsible. One of the ways that women can alleviate their role strain is by lowering their commitment level in their careers and settling for lower rewards. Unlike men who are highly motivated in their careers, women usually cannot place familial demands below that of career because of societal expectations and resulting powerful, deep-seated feelings regarding these familial obligations. Whereas a man may find that his family accommodates his career demands, it is doubtful whether the same thing would occur in the case of a woman with similar career ambitions.

The psychological cost of role proliferation for women is illustrated very well in a study by Ruth Moulton (1977), who compared a sample of 50 female patients, 25 of whom were in psychotherapy between 1953 and 1956, and the other 25 between 1973 and 1976. Women in the first group tended to seek treatment for problems that centred around sex (including frigidity), marriage, and child rearing. The most prominent symptom in ten of these patients related to desperation about finding a husband. In contrast to the women seeking help in the 1950s, women patients in the 1970s often regarded marriage as a trap. For female patients in the 1970s, anxieties emerged that were a direct result of greater role proliferation. For example, one quite prominent syndrome was anxiety resulting from conflict between the woman's sense of personal identity — to which marriage was supposed to contribute positively, and her autonomous professional identity — to which marriage was often regarded as a threat. Other syndromes included re-entry anxiety, when a long-homebound woman resumed her employment, and performance anxiety, such as a woman's difficulty asserting herself. So, although new paths are opening up for women, new anxieties have also emerged when women have combined home and employment roles.

Work overload — when simultaneously occupying the roles of mother and employee — will no doubt contribute to feelings of frustration and dissatisfaction in the woman. At the same time, when a woman holds employment, she has less time for child care and housework. If, however, family members continue to hold expectations of the woman along traditional gender-role lines, then their satisfaction also will likely decrease when the woman is employed. Although the relationship between women's employment and divorce is not clear-cut, it is possible that the feelings of dissatisfaction described above could contribute to marital instability. On the positive side, since the family enjoys a higher total income when both spouses are employed, the marriage may be improved by their higher standard of living.

IS THERE EQUALITY IN MARRIAGE?

Some have predicted that the situation for women will improve when men gradually decrease their commitment to their employment and increase their participation in the home; that this will result in a "symmetrical" family (Young and Willmott, 1973) in which both husband and wife are employed outside the home, and in which they share responsibility for work within the home equally. However, it is not likely that this will occur soon. For one thing, middle-class men who regard their jobs as careers are likely to feel that any greater commitment to work in the home may jeopardise their career advancement. What is more, they are likely to consider part of their wife's job, whether she holds outside employment or not, as helping them in their advancement on the job. Additionally, for a great many men, not only are household chores thought to be demasculinising, but work on a "woman's turf" is even considered degrading (Bernard, 1981). So, even if men had jobs that would allow them to take greater responsibility in the home, it is unlikely that they would do so spontaneously because of the norms for male dominance.

Symmetry, however, is not identical to equality. Even if household tasks and child care were shared equally along with the breadwinner role, equality would still not be achieved for the spouses. Another important deterrent to equality, even when both spouses hold outside employment, concerns the type of employment in which women and men are likely to find themselves: the wife is more likely to occupy low-paying, low-prestige service or office jobs, and the husband, higher-paid, more prestigious jobs. Data for 1979 reveal that female full-time workers in Canada earn less than two-thirds of what male full-time workers earn. Table 16.2 shows median earnings for male and female full-time workers in Canada by educational level for 1979. These data show that, at every educational level, men earn more. So, in two-job couples, the wife will likely belong to a lower class than her husband.

TABLE 16.2

Median Earnings for Male and Female Full-Time[1] Workers in Canada by Education for 1979

Education	*Male*	*Female*	*Female as % of Male*
0 - 8 years	*$ 15,221*	*$ 8,895*	*58.4*
Some or complete high school	*$ 16,679*	*$ 10,530*	*63.1*
Some post-secondary	*$ 17,728*	*$ 11,446*	*64.6*
Post-secondary certificate or diploma	*$ 19,018*	*$ 12,725*	*66.9*
University degree	*$ 25,188*	*$ 17,224*	*68.4*

[1]*A full-time worker is a person who worked, mostly full-time, 50-52 weeks in 1979.*

Source: Statistics Canada. Table 6, Cat. No. 13-577, 1981.

From a legal standpoint as well, the contributions of the spouses are still not regarded as being of equal value, particularly when the husband is the sole breadwinner and the wife is in the traditional, dependent role of housewife. So, for example, the changes introduced in Ontario in laws relating to family property do little to foster the concept of equality of the spouses during marriage. These changes are aimed at a so-called equitable settlement of family assets *after* the marriage is defined legally as having broken down. In effect, then, after a marriage has broken down, the wife would be entitled to half of the family assets including the matrimonial home. What many people are unaware of, however, is that family assets, as narrowly defined in the law, do not include assets that the husband might have accumulated in other funds. In a family in which the wife has worked in the home for twenty or more years, and the husband has accumulated assets in areas not defined as family assets, including stocks, property, business profits, private pensions, investments, annuities, insurance, and the like, these funds are legally still his. Should she want to claim half of these after marital breakdown, she would have to wage an expensive legal battle in which the onus is on her to show that she was a "good girl" during marriage. Moreover, whether a wife can share these equally *in marriage* still depends on the husband's good will. So, whether the married woman works outside the home or not, equality in marriage remains more of a dream than a reality at the present time.

Many modern marriages have been caught in a cultural bind between an egalitarian ideal for which everyone is supposed to strive, and marriage as it actually exists with its social and legal inequities. What is more, the family socialisation process frequently prepares the spouses for a traditional marriage with its emphasis on male dominance and female submissiveness. One survey (Prochaska, 1977) revealed, for example, that the selection of potential dates and mates among college students is still restricted by the traditional sexist assumption of the male's supremacy. Two-thirds of the 150 young women surveyed reported feeling free to marry only a male who was more intelligent, better-paid, and better-educated than they were. Seventy per cent of the young men showed a similar bias, with the exception of an openness to marrying a better-paid woman. Further, only 3 per cent of the males felt free to date a taller woman, and only 3 per cent of the females felt free to date a shorter male. These results can be intepreted as reflecting the tradition of a woman wanting to look up to a man, psychologically and physically, and of a man wanting a woman to look down on.

As Scanzoni (1972) has pointed out, attempts to transform traditional marriages into companionship marriages inevitably result in conflict. One reason for this centres around the observation that the masculine gender role, with all of its traditional prerogatives, is being diluted. As more and more women share the role of provider, they are feeling justified in making demands on men that were not made in the past, demands which the men may not be prepared to meet. So, whereas in the past, the sole breadwinner in the family was not expected to contribute much more than goods and material things, women today are expecting more emotional involvement on the part of men as well as greater intimacy (Bernard, 1981). In this regard, the traditional male rejection of emotional expression is increasingly being challenged. Today, not only women but also some men are protesting the repudiation of expressiveness prescribed by the masculine role, according to several investigators in the field (i.e., Farrell, 1974; David and Brannon, 1976). Numerous articles have appeared in popular magazines, especially those for women, about the lack of communication between women and men, and what women can do about it. Men's inexpressiveness may be considered a product of masculine gender-role conditioning. Men may not communicate because their goal may be *winning* rather than achieving an equitable outcome. This dictates an exploitive rather than an accommodative strategy: a man withholding information while the woman discloses maintains his dominance (Jenkins and Kramer, 1978). In this regard, Baird (1976) reports a study in which men were found to be more interested in winning, and women in a fair outcome. Further, although men may not have the skills required for deep-level communication, women may be afraid to behave assertively and stand up for their own rights because such behaviours are considered deviant from those defined as appropriate for the feminine gender role, particularly by women prepared for a traditional marriage. The situation is exacerbated when women may espouse egalitarian ideals for marriage on the one hand, yet believe in male dominance on the other hand, thereby wittingly or unwittingly reinforcing traditional male dominance patterns of interaction with women. If companionship is to be achieved in marriage, the gap between women's and men's experiences is going to have to be bridged. A man may be philosophically committed to egalitarianism in marriage and may try hard to practise it, but it may not work, for the reasons noted.

The reconstruction of gender roles may affect men's health adversely. A study of engineers and accountants by Burke and Weir (1976) revealed poorer health among those with employed wives than among those with non-employed wives. Given that the man is seeking interpersonal support in marriage, when the wife is employed not only is his support system in shorter supply but also he may find that he must now take a supportive role toward his wife's ambitions and personal goals. His socialisation probably did not include training in how to be supportive (to a woman yet!), and thus he is likely not prepared to deal with his wife's needs in this area. Further, as has been noted earlier, men may regard marriage with some ambivalence to begin with. This may result in their communicating a double message to their wives: they may want intimacy on the one hand, but at the same time they may also reject the woman because of the anxiety that this intimacy arouses. In the case of the married woman who holds outside employment, if she continues to hold traditional expectations of herself as a primary support system to her husband, she will likely feel dissatisfied and frustrated. What is more, she may have difficulty in regarding her husband in a non-traditional way, namely as a support to her which she may need, given the demands of her dual role.

If companionship in marriage is to be achieved, it is not simply a matter of "opening up" communication lines, as some have suggested. A more radical approach is called for, namely, the necessity for both partners to extricate themselves from the expectations of traditional gender roles as defined in marriage. Very often, these expectations are dragged into a marriage unconsciously, like so much baggage, remnants of a socialisation process that reflects a passing but still rigid gender-role system.

Psychological researchers can make an important contribution by pointing out the contradictory expectations for marriage held by women and men. As discussed earlier, contradictory attitudes and expectations toward marriage may co-exist *within* an individual as well. Research in this area could also point to ways in which transcendence of gender roles may be achieved to maximise an individual's opportunity for greater personal satisfaction and self-fulfillment.

REFERENCES

Baird, Jr., J.E. "Sex Differences in Group Communications: A Review of Relevant Research". *Quarterly Journal of Speech,* 1976, 62, 179 - 92.

Bernard, J. "The Paradox of the Happy Marriage". In V. Gornick and B.K. Moran (eds.), *Woman on Sexist Society*. New York: Basic Books, 1971, 145 - 62.

Bernard, J. *The Future of Motherhood*. New York: Penguin, 1974.

Bernard, J. "The Good-provider Role: Its Rise and Fall". *American Psychologist*, 1981, 36, 1 - 12.

Birnbaum, J.A. "Life Patterns, Personality Style and Self-esteem in Gifted Family-oriented and Career-committed Women" (Doctoral dissertation, Univ. of Michigan, 1971). *Dissertation Abstracts International* (1972), 1834B (University Microfilms No. 71-23, 689). (Cited here as Birnbaum, 1971.)

Burke, R.J. and Weir, T. "Relationship of Wives' Employment Status to Husband, Wife and Pair Satisfaction and Performance". *Journal of Marriage and the Family*, 1976, 38, 279 - 87.

Canada, Labour Canada, Women's Bureau. *1978 - 79 Women in the Labour Force*. Table 5b, 1980.

David, D.S. and Brannon, R. (eds). *The Forty-nine Percent Majority: The Male Sex Role*. Reading, MA: Addison-Wesley, 1976.

Farrell, W. *The Liberated Man*. New York: Random House, 1974.

Feld, S. "Feelings of Adjustment". In F.I. Nye and L.W. Hoffman (eds.),

The Employed Mother in America. Chicago: Rand McNally, 1963, 331 - 52.

Feldman, H. and Feldman, M. *The Relationship between the Family and Occupational Functioning in a Sample of Rural Women.* Ithaca, New York: Department of Human Development and Family Studies, Cornell University, 1973.

Gelber, S.M. "The Underemployed, Underpaid Third of the Labour Force". In Gelber, S.M., *Women's Bureau, 1971*. Ottawa: Information Canada, 1972.

Greenglass, E.R., and Eisner, M. *Motivation for Marriage and Children — An Exploratory Study*. Unpublished manuscript, York University, 1981.

Hall, D. and Hall, F. *The Two-career Couple.* Reading, MA: Addison-Wesley, 1979.

Jenkins, L. and Kramer, C. "Small Group Process: Learning from Women". *Women's Studies International Quarterly*, 1978, 1. 67 - 84.

Johnson, F.A. and Johnson, C.L. "Role Strain in High-Commitment Career Women." *Journal of the American Academy of Psychoanalysis*, 1976, 4, 13 - 16.

Marecek, J. "Powerlessness and Women's Psychological Disorders". *Women and Psychotherapy*, 1976, 12, 50 - 4.

Meissner, M. Humphreys, E.W., Meis, S.M. and Scheu, W.J. "No Exit for Wives: Sexual Division of Labour and the Cumulation of Household Demands". *Canadian Review of Sociology and Anthropology* 1975, 12, 424 - 39.

Moulton, R. "Some Effects of the New Feminism". *The American Journal of Psychiatry*, 1977, 134, 1 - 6.

New York Narcotic Addiction Control Commission. *Differential Drug Use within the New York State Labour Force: An Assessment of Drug Use within the General Population*. Unpublished manuscript. Albany, New York: 1971.

Ohlbaum, J.S. *Self-concepts, Value Characteristics and Self-actualization of Professional and Non-professional Women.* Ph.D. Thesis. United States International Univ., 1971.

Prochaska, J. *Restriction of Range on Date and Mate Selection in College Students.* Unpublished manuscript, University of Rhode Island, 1977.

Prochaska, J., and Prochaska, J. "Twentieth Century Trends in Marriage and Marital Therapy." In T.J. Paolino, Jr., and B.S. McCrady (eds.), *Marriage and Marital Therapy*. New York: Brunner/Mazel, 1978, pp. 1 - 24.

Scanzoni, J. *Sexual Bargaining: Power Politics in the American Marriage*. New York: Prentice-Hall, 1972.

Szinovacz, M. Cited in "Health Matters". *Family Health,* 1978, 10, 18.

Walker, K.E. "Household Work Time: Its Implications for Family Decisions". *Journal of Home Economics*, 1973, 65, 7 - 11.

Williams, T.M., Zabrack, M.L. and Harrison, L.F. "Some Factors Affecting

Women's Participation in Psychology in Canada." *Canadian Psychology*, 1980, 21, 97 - 108.

Young, M. and Willmott, P. *The Symmetrical Family*. New York: Pantheon, 1973.

FURTHER READING

Burke, R., and Weir, T. "Husband-wife Helping Relationships: The "Mental Hygiene" Function in Marriage". *Psychological Reports*, 40, 911 - 925.

Greenglass, E.R. *A World of Difference: Gender Roles in Perspective*. Toronto: Wiley, 1982.

Greenglass, E.R., and Borovilos, R. "Psychological Correlates of Fertility Plans in Unmarried Women". *Canadian Journal of Behavioural Science, 17, 130-139.*

Lips, H.M. *Women, Men and the Psychology of Power*. Englewood Cliffs, NJ: Prentice Hall, 1981.

Smith, R.E. (ed.). *The Subtle Revolution: Women at Work*. Washington, D.C.: The Urban Institute, 1979.

BERT YOUNG

Looking for Lonely Men

Today's North American male has a personality like a piece of Swiss cheese — shot through with emotional holes that prevent him from forming deep friendships.[1]

The above recent statement is a sad commentary on masculinity, but one that men are beginning to confront. They are slowly moving to examine more seriously than ever before certain aspects of sexual equality, the need for change, and the importance of male friendship. Some men (including myself) have also realised that this cannot be done simply by supporting and being sensitive to feminist demands. We too must change and join with other men to challenge male dominance and promote sexual equality.

It is this dominance that pits men against women and against other men: a dominance that is fraught with distrust and endless competition among men, controlling their relationships and making of them a performance. There is little room here for the development of friendship or brotherhood and without it, men will not be encouraged to challenge themselves, let alone their patriarchal society.

My own problem in relating to men on this issue was whether other men would first admit that they were lonely for male friendship and were uncertain how to proceed. As Kavaloski notes, "the *desire for* — and at the same time, *fear of* — intimacy is usually connected with the ambivalent reserve and self-possession with which we conduct ourselves together."[2]

An example of this kind of ambivalence occurred at the Learned Societies in Guelph in 1984. Myself and three other male colleagues, along with three female colleagues, were sitting at dinner one evening discussing male friendship. The men admitted to each other how difficult it was to establish close and intimate male friends and how much we wanted these kinds of relationships. I remember joking that we were just lonely men looking for other lonely men. The colleague next to me felt very sensitive about this and noted that many of his colleagues did not take this desire very seriously. As we continued our discussion, it became obvious that this issue was important to us and one that was directly related to our questioning concerning masculinity. Our female colleagues were surprised but pleased to hear men admit they had a problem concerning intimacy with other males. I also recalled feeling envious of these feminist friends who did not seem to suffer as we did in their relationships with other females.

I believe this discussion was important to all of us because it helped us realise some of the results of our work. Over the last three years, we had all organised and participated in sessions of the Learned Societies concerning the questions of feminism, male dominance, and socialism, and these were encouraging us to reflect on our personal lives and the political importance of working towards a more egalitarian society. This to me is what "making the personal political" is all about. It also made us aware of our isolation, either because women mistrusted our commitments or motives, or because other men mistrusted us for abandoning our "manliness", or they feared our potential influence on their own lives. Those of us who are committed recognised the need to reach out to other men, as women have done together, to form friendship groups and raise our consciousness.

In order to accomplish this, it is necessary to examine the nature of male friendships, why they seem to be threatening to our manliness, and how deep sharing among men can contribute to the norm of equality between men and women.

MODELS OF FRIENDSHIP

I challenge the general assumption that the greatest bonds of friendship are those among men. Although it is true that most men in their waking hours prefer or simply find themselves in the company of other men, either at work or play, a number of studies and commentaries suggest that these relationships are anxiety-provoking and probably unhealthy.[3]

This conclusion is based on the fact that from childhood to adulthood males are encouraged to develop impersonal modes of relating to others that stress the external aspects of dealing with everyday life. Jean Paul Sartre notes that

> with men I was quite ready to stop talking once what had to be said on politics or something of that kind had been said. It seems to me that two hours of a man's company in a day, and without seeing him the next day, is quite enough. Whereas, with a woman it can go on all day long and then start again tomorrow.[4]

This impersonal style of interaction with men often seems to reinforce the demands of independence, competition, and strength; role restrictions that encourage men to fear the personal and intimate, and to hide behind the façade of the abstract and theoretical.

This stereotypic perception has been reinforced by Lionel Tiger's comparison of traits observed in male primates and male humans. Tiger argues that these traits of male dominance are maintained through "male bonding", an exclusive status-bound male-to-male relationship that excludes "non-members males and females, and which promotes a dominance-submission hierarchy; each male controls the behaviour of the one below him." The traits, or behaviours of male bonding, however, are not the prime characteristics that would create close, loving male friendships. In fact, if there is such a strong bond (biological or otherwise) between men, it may very well be predicated on reassuring males of their masculinity, rather than supporting the notion that shows that men do think their bonding is superior.[5]

Recent studies reported by Mackie showed a remarkable similarity between male and female subjects in what they looked for in same-sex friendships. However, contrary to Tiger's hypothesis of male bonding, it was the males who showed greater unfriendliness towards their own sex. In contrast, several studies argue that women's friendships tend to be more intimate and to involve more exchanges of confidence. Men typically reveal less personal information about themselves to others than do women. Women, on the other hand, receive more disclosures than men. Wives were most frequently designated as confidantes by husbands; husbands were least frequently mentioned as confidants by wives.[6]

A number of studies that looked at gender relationships in speech and non-verbal patterns of interaction would suggest that men choose speech patterns that maintain dominance and control, while women choose patterns that foster self-disclosure. It has been observed that the female style of speech is less obtrusive and uses tentative questions instead of declarative statements. Males often speak louder and with less fluency and tend to be more anxious to fill in pauses in conversations. In mixed conversations, men are more likely to interrupt women than vice versa, and women are more likely to allow the interruptions. Men also tend to complete women's sentences, and to give minimal responses to topics initiated and carried by women.[7]

The research concerning non-verbal patterns of communication is also similar in nature. Women look at one another more and hold eye contact longer with each other than men do with other men. Women also gaze more at men than vice versa and smile more than men. It has been noted that males find crowded situations more unpleasant than do women and that they expansively dominate the space around them. By contrast, women condense or compress into the space around them.[8]

While these characteristics may not be beneficial to women and may not have been freely chosen by them, it would seem that men have established interpersonal methods of communication that are functional to maintaining power and control over women and other men. Communication for men would seem to consist of making sure that others do not get too close, that personal exchanges remain restrictive and follow ritual commands.

Digressions are not allowed because of men's fear of losing control of dominance; sensitivity to issues, or the person, are to be approached with caution. As Hantover points out, while this socialisation process is "effective", it brings with it the cost of anxiety. Young boys are encouraged to alter their behavioural identification from a nurturant and dependent relationship to one of detachment and independence. Hantover also cites studies that argue that this alteration generates anxiety from the conflict of primary feminine identification with a later secondary identification with males. This conflict may be resolved by males repressing their feminine identification and exhibiting hostility toward females. In the young male's attempt to identify what is a male, he seeks out cultural clues that tend to be rigidly defined and may raise more anxiety.[9] This may explain why males are so often awkward with females and choose humour as a way of dealing with affective matters. In other words, men develop barriers to hide from others and from themselves, thereby not promoting the conditions for bonding, let alone friendship.

MEN'S GROUPS

It is precisely these barriers that encourage some men to form men's groups and relieve the traditional burden of isolation. By enabling men to expose their inner selves in the presence of other trusted and trusting men, men's groups make it possible for them to arrive at new and clearer perceptions of themselves and of women.

It is interesting to note that when men do join a men's group and experience an evening with other men, other than the bar or playing field, they are pleasantly surprised to learn that they enjoyed the encounter and often want to repeat it. It may be, as Jourard argues, that whenever men are reluctant to disclose themselves to others, it follows that men will be difficult to love,

> ...that is, it will be difficult for a woman or another man to know the immediate present state of the man's self and his needs will thereby go unmet. Some men are so skilled at dissembling, at "seeming", that even their wives will not know when they are lonely, anxious, or hungering for affection. And the men, blocked by pride, dare not disclose their despair or need.[10]

Jourard extends this analysis to self-love. If true love of self implies behaviour that will meet one's own needs, and those are blocked or resisted, then men will not know what they feel, want and need.[11] This seems to be corroborated by this divorced man's cry of anguish:

...After my divorce I realised that I had allowed all of my friendships to drop, and I had no one to talk to. It was pretty lonely. I began sleeping around a lot just to be with someone. And I started hanging around this one bar on nights. I didn't have a date. I'd always be with people but I never got what I wanted. It was like a sieve — the loneliness was a bottomless pit.[12]

or this working class man's disillusionment of his emotional core:

Although I don't see Mom and Dad you know, I do idolise them in me own way. But I can't really express the feelings. I can't really say how my feelings is...People say "bloody hard him, he's rough and ready," and all that. I don't think I am, but I've never been able to express feelings.[13]

and this cry for help from this man:

The whole goddamn business of what you're calling intimacy bugs the hell out of me. I never know what you women mean when you talk about it. Karen complains that I don't talk to her, but it's not talk she wants, it's some other damn thing, only I don't know what the hell it is. Feelings, she keeps asking for. So what am I supposed to do if I don't have any to give her or to talk about just because she decides it's time to talk about feelings? Tell me, will you; maybe we can get some peace around here.[14]

Even when men do make the effort and recognise that it is necessary to relate to others concerning their hidden selves, it is a slow and painful process. Tolson notes that at his men's group's initial meeting, "...we began to discover that we had no language of feeling. We were trapped in the public, specialised language of work...which acted as a shield against deeper emotional solidarities."[15] Donald Bell also reports that men's group relationships seem to be time-limited arrangements. The groups take on the necessary work of dealing with relevant issues and provide support. However, there comes a time when most groups seem to exhaust the possibilities or reasons to meet:

Sustaining intimate contact and dealing on a close and personal basis proved to be too difficult for us. We seemed, in effect, to reach a barrier of self-revelation which we were not equipped to transcend...we withdrew in self-defence.[16]

It may be necessary here for men to take a lesson from the consciousness-raising experiences of women and translate some of their self-revelations into political action.

Nevertheless, it has been my experience with men's groups that they provide the opportunity for us men to overcome these anxieties and work towards changing ourselves. It has been very encouraging to witness the growing numbers of men who have attended the men's workshops at the Grindstone Island Co-operative in Ontario over the last two summers, and the positive response we received at the male sexuality workshop at the Learned Societies in Montréal this year. However, there is still much work to be done to encourage men to change and relinquish their power over women and other men.

MEN'S RELIANCE ON WOMEN

One of the major reasons why men are unwilling to move forward and transcend their clogged-up emotional vents is their almost total reliance upon women to ward off their basic loneliness and fear of self-revelation. As Pleck notes, it is not a role women have wished upon themselves:

> Men's dependence on women's power to express men's emotions and to validate men's masculinity has placed heavy burdens on women...these are not powers over men that women have wanted to hold. These are powers that men have themselves handed over to women by defining the male role as being emotionally cool and inexpressive and as being ultimately validated by heterosexual success.[17]

Pleck also notes that this dependence on women's expressive powers has increased recently as a result of male friendship declining, and dating and marriage occurring at younger ages.[18] Moreover, when women are not there for men, they retreat to the bar, the television, or lash out in frustration at women or other men. Nolan states that the mid-life crisis male does not stay depressed for very long but rather, "comes fighting back. He dyes his hair; buys a sports car; starts an affair; raises hell in bars; argues with the boss; makes passes at his friends' wives; quits his job."[19] What he doesn't do is a more painful and confusing process of letting himself be known to himself and to others.

Mackie notes that "loving for men may often be channelled into a single opposite-sex relationship...placing a tremendous burden on the marriage."[20] It would also seem that men prefer younger women for this task or, at least for many men, women who do not become too familiar with their dependency and who tell men only what they want to hear. Rabkin, in an article that appeared in *Homemaker's Magazine*, reports that the women men married for the second time were basically younger and less accomplished than the man.[21] Although Rabkin relies on a small survey, she suggests that such a man knows that a younger woman will see him the way he wants to see himself. The wife he left cannot see him this way; she knows too much. Rabkin also states that only two out of the ten men interviewed who had left their wives had male friends whom they totally trusted and in whom they confided.

Rabkin's small survey is more extensively supported by Rubin's American study of two hundred men and women she interviewed: over two-thirds of the single men could not name a best friend. Of those who could, it was much more likely to be a woman than another man. In contrast, over three-fourths of the single women had no problem in identifying a best friend, and almost always that person was a woman. Among those who were married, far more men than women named a spouse as a best friend.[22] Rubin adds that when she asked the men whom they would turn to if they came home one night and their wife announced she was leaving, they stated that "there would be no friend to whom they could turn to in that moment of pain and shock." Even the thirty-year-old male who claimed he had twenty intimate friends stated that he would first call his mother: "I'd have to put myself together, you know, get over the first shock so I wouldn't just be falling apart."[23]

This constant desire to remain cool and adequate to other males is inconsistent with the goal of intimacy and self-disclosure. As Ettkin notes, men seem to "dread being known" and this creates a state of continued unhealthy tension over being found out.[24] This tension, however, may work in men's favour in maintaining power over social relations. For if men rely on women to offer emotional release, not only is it not often reciprocated, but may very well help men to maintain a subtle means of control. By ignoring or playing down their power over women, men are often surprised at women's anger directed toward them. By hiding behind a veil of rationality men often provoke and/or project their own emotional tension onto women and thereby relieve themselves of taking responsibility for their actions and their feelings. This, I believe, is a major force of male dominance, and one that ensures control and lack of intimacy among males.

This is especially true of the single male. Gilder, in his study of the American male, argues that if men do not marry and benefit from the limited intimacy they enjoy with women, society would be forced to cage them like wild animals. In the United States, although single men number 13 per cent of the population over the age of fourteen, they comprise 60 per cent of the criminals and commit about 90 per cent of major and violent crimes. Proportionately, a single man is about five times as likely as a married man to be convicted of rape. Between the ages of fifty and fifty-nine, an astonishing total of 46.1 per cent of all single men in the Manhattan survey, quoted by Gilder, suffer mental health impairment in comparison to one-fifth of all married men. This single male is often irresponsible about his debts, alcoholic, accident prone, poor, suicidal, and enjoys a shorter life span.[25]

Although these data suggest that men are highly dependent on women and marriage, nowhere does Gilder conclude that men should change. Instead, Gilder uses his damage report on single men to justify the continued subordination of women. According to Gilder, women should not be breaking away from "Kinder and Köche" but doing everything to keep men out of trouble. In other words, we are committing sexual suicide if we play around with monogamy, patriarchy and the destiny of biology; it is too dangerous for women to demand change, and even more so, for men.

The situation is further complicated by the media profile we receive on the single male. It is by no means the negative picture we get from Gilder. A very different profile, according to Nolletti, can be found in the crop of Hollywood films depicting male companionship that emerged as one of the most durable and important screen modes of the 1970s. As Nolletti points out, such popular films as *The Sting* and *Butch Cassidy and the Sundance Kid* shamelessly advocate and glamourize "cool"; the strong, silent, rugged individual who teaches us to be wary of affection and is thereby able to set aside feelings in order to be capable of decisive action. Cool becomes a value in itself — an absence of emotional expression is mistaken for strength in these films. They promote the ideal myth of manhood, encouraging men to see themselves with other men as having "a loyality that is unspoken and unasked for, and total freedom from psychological complications or involvement."[26] The same can be said for similar types of TV programmes, such as *The A-Team, Airwolf, Knight Rider*, and *Fall Guy*, plus the recent return of the Western in film.

This self-destructive mode that men seem to emulate will not be given up easily. To overcome the fear or confront the myth will involve considerable pain and uncertainty. Men will be faced with the insecurity of not knowing how to evaluate themselves and their actions. Such goals as career, power, influence, and being admired will now have to be re-evaluated, and will, to some degree, be found wanting.

FEAR OF HOMOSEXUALITY

If there is one major factor that is responsible for socially constraining male friendship, the evidence would overwhelmingly point to homophobia — the fear of homosexuality. Tognoli cites numerous studies indicating that any sense of failure regarding the masculine role is often interpreted as a sign of homosexuality. This "pseudo-homosexual anxiety" is much more powerful among males than females and encourages men to abhor feminine characteristics.[27] This anxiety, Chesler argues, acts to maintain "a system of careful surveillance of men on men to ensure that transgressions will not occur."[28]

The pervasiveness of homophobia, however, may have little to do with the real threat of homosexuality. Rather, as Lehne states, it operates to reinforce rigid beliefs in the male stereotype: "Homophobia is only incidentally directed against homosexuals — its more common use is against the 49 per cent of the population which is male."[29] Moreover, it is used directly to enforce social stereotypes of appropriate sex-role behaviour for women. Since increasing numbers of women have decided that they are no longer willing to pay the price of this sexism, it is left up to the men to decide whether they want to continue bearing the pains of this rigidity, as it inhibits love and friendship between men and between men and women.

It should not be surprising to learn that both U.S. and British gay activists were the first contemporary group of men to address the problem of male supremacy and heterosexual chauvinism, and to align with feminists on issues of sexual politics.[30] By doing so they helped to develop a theory of the contemporary structure of patriarchy and its historical importance. This seriously challenged the Marxist class analysis and chauvinism of the New Left, criticising them for skirting around the oppression of women and gays.

While the U.S. men's movement and its publicists in the 1970s ignored gay liberation arguments, gay activists were busy challenging the rigid social definitions of masculinity and demanding a reversal of the dominant sexual ideology; it was society, not gays, that needed to be cured. Their critique went beyond the defence of gay men to all straight men and to the subordination of women and children. In other words, the gay movement's analysis "had a much clearer understanding of the reality of men's power over women, and it had direct implications for any consideration of the hierarchy of power among men."[31] Contrary to the attitude prevalent in some men's groups in the United States that argue that all men are oppressed, it is particular groups of men (especially gays) who are oppressed within patriarchal sexual relations and who have a similar experience to the subordination of women to men.

This analysis offers profound insight into the problem of male friendship. Most heterosexual men are able to fall back on the traditional rationalisation of "being a man" precisely because it suits their purpose of maintaining control. Their enjoyment in maintaining a social distance from other men, while depending on women to meet their sexual and non-sexual needs of intimacy, ensures male supremacy.

CONCLUSION

I will conclude this chapter with a few personal comments and a suggestion that unless we males are willing and able to challenge male supremacy in ourselves and in other males and to admit that we have much to lose by doing so, the struggle for human liberation will remain an unreachable goal.

In my introduction, I stated that men were basically lonely and that some men, like myself, were looking for other men to share this concern. For me, my greatest fear was in facing myself; my own loneliness and the fact that I had successfully ignored being in touch with myself. I know now that this recognition may very well be the path to liberating myself from the myth of the ideal manhood; that I, the male, have to be able to perform, be in control and be strong enough to carry it all — to be cool!

Dick Vittitow, writing about this myth of manhood, notes that men are continually belittled and belittle themselves because they do not measure up; it does not matter that the demands are unrealistic. In a personal growth workshop, Vittitow experienced a great sense of pity for himself as his feelings of aloneness became stronger and stronger. At first, he denied his feeling of pity, feelings that he defined as narcissistic and selfish. He then recognised that such a prohibition was a commandment; he finally ignored it and gave in to his pity. He then recalled that his action was similar to the biologically designed system that keeps sharks alive. The shark breathes through forward, continuous movement in the water. If it stops or is stopped, it dies. It seemed to Vittitow that in his life and his aloneness, he was experiencing many of the dilemmas and restrictions of the shark. He also stated that this experience is

> similar to [the] experience that many changing men are having in their movement towards intimacy...like the shark, which suffocates if pulled backwards, the changing man cannot return to the safety of past myths. He must risk the movement forward, not always knowing where he is going, only knowing he must move onward.[32]

My own attempt to move forward came from a similar, if less profound, experience concerning male friendship. I had felt for a considerable period of time that I was not happy with the relationships of two male friends, both of whom I love dearly. I felt cheated; my love for them did not seem to be reciprocated. I felt that I was the one who wanted a more intimate relationship and they did not. I was, however, reluctant to approach them for fear that I would be rejected.

This fear was finally overcome following a conference organised by Geraldine Finn on *Reason and Violence*, held at the University of Ottawa in June of 1982. This conference made me realize if we men were going to make an effort to end our violence and control of women, we would have to begin by confronting each other as men and end the wall of silence we had built around us. Not only did we need to talk to each other concerning these issues, but we needed the support and love of friends to encourage us.

It was with these thoughts in mind that I decided to confront two of my closest male friends. When I approached the first, his response was that I was the first male friend who had ever expressed openly my feelings for him and about him. He even asked whether I wanted to strike him because I was so angry at him for being unresponsive to my needs. After a period of discussion and thought I came to the realisation that we would always be close friends, but that he would always maintain a level of reserve concerning our relationship.

Nevertheless, our discussions were fruitful, and helped both of us to focus on the topic of males and their feelings. He was also quite supportive and encouraged me to further explore these issues. The other friend I talked to had no problem relating to my feelings about him, but as the time passed, the limitations of marriage, child rearing, work and other commitments left little time or opportunity to keep a close relationship going.

It would seem, according to Stuart Miller's study of male friendship in Europe and the United States, that the great tradition of close male friendship seems dead in America as well as, to his surprise, in Europe. Many of the men Miller interviewed concluded that our bureaucratic civilisation demands that even our social life become one of strategy; "the hierarchy and conformity of modern life constantly forces you away from people, makes you choose sides."[33]

As far as my own personal situation is concerned, I too came to the realisation that there was no need to lament my own shortcomings or feel sorry for myself because of what others had or had not done for me. I also realised that there would always be some loneliness, but by expressing my concerns about the relationships I had with males, I had moved forward.

It was now only a matter of seeking out other males who felt the same and wanted to do something about it. For me, this meant joining a men's group and seeking out other men: innovative and sensitive men who have the desire to change.

REFERENCES

1 *Montreal Gazette*, April 6, 1985, p. B4.

2 Vincent Kavaloski, "Men and the Dream of Brotherhood", in Robert Lewis (ed.), *Men in Difficult Times*. New Jersey: Prentice-Hall, 1981, p. 209.

3 One of the best summaries of these findings can be found in Jerome Tognoli, "Male Friendship and Intimacy Across the Life Span", *Family Relations*, Vol. 29:3, 1980, pp. 273 - 279. See also Stuart Miller, *Men and Friendship*, Boston: Houghton Mifflin, 1983.

4 Quoted in the *New York Times Sunday Book Review*, March 17, 1985, p. 47.

5 L. Tiger, *Men in Groups*, New York: Vintage Books, 1969, and for a critique

of Tiger's theory see Tognoli, *op. cit.*, p. 275; Jack Nihols, *Men's Liberation*, New York: Penguin Books, 1975, pp. 282 - 283.

6 Marlene Mackie, *Exploring Gender Relations: A Canadian Perspective*, Toronto: Butterworths, 1983, pp. 152 - 153.

7 *Ibid.*, pp. 229 - 231.

8 *Ibid.*, pp. 237 - 239.

9 Jeffry P. Hantover, "The Social Construction of Masculine Anxiety", in Lewis, *op. cit.*, p. 91.

10 Sidney M. Jourard, *The Transparent Self*, New York: Van Nostrand Reinhold Co., 1971, p. 39.

11 *Ibid.*, p. 39.

12 James A. Doyle, *The Male Experience*, Iowa: Wm. C. Brown, 1983, p. 160.

13 Andrew Tolson, *The Limits of Masculinity*, London: Tavistock, 1977, p. 71.

14 Lillian Rubin, *Intimate Strangers*, New York: Harper Books, 1983, p. 66 and her previous study of the working-class family, *Worlds of Pain*, New York: Basic Books, 1976.

15 Tolson, *op. cit.*, pp. 135 - 136.

16 Donald Bell, *Being a Man*, Lexington: Lewis Publishing, 1982, pp. 49 - 51.

17 Joseph H. Pleck, "Men's Power with Women, Other Men and Society", in Lewis, *op. cit.*, p. 238.

18 *Ibid.*, p. 238; see also Miller, *op. cit.*, pp. 121 - 125.

19 Cited in the *Gazette*, April 6, 1985, p. B4.

20 Mackie, *op. cit.*, p. 153.

21 Brenda Rabkin, "Why Husbands Leave Perfectly Good Wives," *Homemaker's Magazine*, March, 1985, p. 46.

22 Rubin, *op. cit.*, p. 129.

23 *Ibid.*, p. 132.

24 Larry Ettkin, "Treating the Special Madness of Men", in Robert Lewis (ed.), *Men in Difficult Times*, New Jersey: Prentice-Hall, 1981, p. 36.

25 George Gilder, "In Defense of Monogamy", in Alexander Himelfarb and James Richardson, *People, Power and Process*, Toronto: McGraw-Hill Ryerson, 1980, pp. 362 - 265.

26 Arthur Nolletti Jr., "Male Companionship, Movies and the Great American Cool", *Jump Cut*, No. 12/13, December, 1976.

27 Tognoli, *op. cit.*, p. 276.

28 Cited in Tognoli, *ibid.*

29 Gregory Lehne, "Homophobia Among Men", in Deborah S. David and Robert Brannon, *The Forty-nine Percent Majority*, Don Mills: Addison-Wesley, 1976, p. 78.

30 Tim Carrigan, R.W. Connell, John Lewis Lee, "Towards a Realist Sociology of Masculinity," n.d., forthcoming in *Australia New Zealand Journal of Sociology*, pp. 10 - 11.

31 *Ibid.*, p. 15.

32 Dick Vittitow, "Changing Men and Their Movement Toward Intimacy," in Lewis, *op. cit.*, p. 295.
33 Miller, *op. cit.*, p. 123.

FURTHER READING

Ehrenreich, Barbara, *The Hearts of Men*. New York: Doubleday, 1983.
Friedman, Scarlet, and Elizabeth Sarah, eds., *On the Problem of Men*. London: the Women's Press, 1982.
Gough, Jamie, and Mike MacNair, eds., *Gay Liberation in the Eighties*. London: Pluto Press, 1985.
Jerrome, Dorothy, "Good Company: The Sociological Implications of Friendship", *Sociological Review*, Vol. 32:4, November, 1984.
Lipman-Blumen, Jean, *Gender Roles and Power*. Englewood Cliffs, NJ: Prentice-Hall, 1984.
Metcalf, Andy, and Martin Humphries, eds., *The Sexuality of Men*. London: Pluto Press, 1985.
Snodgrass, John, ed., *For Men Against Sexism*. Albion, CA: Times Change Press, 1977.

EILEEN MANION

"All Alone Feeling Blue"? Women's Experience of Solitude

I was no longer fit for the world.

Susanna Moodie, *Roughing It in the Bush*

Women alone stir my imagination.

Virginia Woolf, *The Letters of Virginia Woolf*

"Man alone": we see an image of strength, autonomy, purposefulness. "Man alone" confronts the great existential questions.

"Woman alone": we see an image of vulnerability, inadequacy, selfishness, even sinfulness. "Woman alone" confronts her own private fears.

Women are not supposed to live alone. They are supposed to be with men or with children — with family. Women, like children, need protection. Women need to be taken care of. Women ought to care for others. They want and need to look after others' needs. A woman alone seems incomplete; she behaves defensively.

Most of our ideas about women prevent us from seeing solitude or living alone as an authentic choice — for women.

***

I can't continue very long in that deadly, balanced, authoritative tone. Was living alone for me an "authentic choice"? Or did I just find myself here and try to make the best of it?

Growing up an only child, I spent too much time alone. I hated it. I was intensely lonely. I did not learn how to live alone, but I did learn how to endure loneliness and survive. May Sarton, in her *Journal of a Solitude*, remarks that "the nostalgia of the only child for what appears to most people as 'ordinary' is romantic in the extreme."[1] Just because "ordinary life" with others is so idealised, it becomes harder to achieve. Solitude, in many ways, becomes more comfortable than everyday intimacy.

When I went to university, I panicked at the promiscuous proximity of the other girls living in the dormitory. I felt constantly under observation and self-conscious. I withdrew as much as possible to the privacy of my single room, venturing out to the bathroom with its rows of sinks, showers, toilets when I thought no one else was likely to be there. I felt very lonely, but could not stand the quotidian experience of others' presence.

The other side of that discomfort was a starved need for presence, closeness, love. That unrecognised desperation pushed me into marriage as soon as I graduated. The marriage lasted less than four years. During that period, physical intimacy with another person became gradually more acceptable, but emotional closeness still triggered panic. Finally, I succumbed to the panic, and we separated.

For several years I lived alone, less reclusive than I had been in university, more "sociable". However, a perverse, self-denying puritanism prevented me from doing anything that would make the physical circumstances of my life more than minimally comfortable. I thought of solitude — when I thought of it at all — as a temporary circumstance, not a deliberate choice. I did not attempt to structure my life so that it would be graceful and pleasant for me, the only person who was there. I just waited for someone else to move in and make my life more exciting.

That did finally happen and I spent several years trying to organise the excitement into something resembling rational domesticity. Just as soon as I felt I had succeeded, the whole enterprise failed. It took more than a year to realise that the foundations had been too shaky from the beginning.

So I find myself living alone again, having "chosen" this, not so much consciously, but through a kind of irresistible internal logic. It is not entirely something that just "happened", nor entirely something I did with calculating deliberation. But I do feel as if, this time, I want to learn to live alone, and to enjoy it.

Looking at solitude from my present perspective, I see three important, interrelated aspects: (1) Living alone, with its everyday cares, concerns, difficulties. Nothing gets done unless you do it. No decision gets made unless you make it. You are to blame for all mistakes. The responsiblity for your own everyday life is total, and that can be scary, and exhausting, at times. (2) Being alone, with the dread of isolation. All kinds of fears are associated with that, from practical fears about accident or illness, to larger existential worries about "being alone in the universe". (3) Being seen to be alone, with the accompanying embarrassment, the subtle sense of failure.

The third aspect — being seen to be alone — is probably the worst for women. In our culture, we are all image-junkies, and as women we are made to worry more than men, not only about how we act, but also about how we appear. The first aspect, I suspect, is more difficult for men, who are raised to believe that somebody else is supposed to look after the everyday housekeeping details for them.

Despite all the pressures toward marriage and coupledom, thirty-eight million women in North America now are single. Many of them live alone. Who do we look to from the past to inspire us or to embody our fears?

Before the twentieth century, not very many people lived alone. In the early modern period, changing marriage patterns in Europe, and a shift to later marriage in northern Europe, meant that some women never married. Several scholars make a connection between the anomaly of larger numbers of unmarried or widowed women and the rise of the witch hunts: "If witch trials were primarily projections of general social fears onto atypical women (those who lived apart, without husbands or fathers to rule them), then the sudden growth of spinsters and an increased number of widows who did not remarry automatically provided a much larger range of witchcraft suspects than before."[2] Whatever place in the community such women could make for themselves, as healers or as midwives, for instance, did not help. In fact, their power bred terror of their anger.

It is difficult to understand why women living alone should inspire fear, but this does seem to be the case. During the industrial revolution, larger numbers of girls and women began to work outside the home, away from a family or domestic situation, and fear was expressed that they would become "too independent". The meagre wages they received made such fears largely unjustified. For most women throughout the nineteenth century, living alone was an economic impossibility. Even today it is much harder for a working woman than it is for a man to earn enough to live alone in comfort.

Nonetheless, from the past there are a few exceptions, "heroines", if we are able to accept them with their contradictions and our ambivalence. Aphra Behn, the first professional British woman writer, comes to mind. She was a very unusual woman living in the second half of the seventeenth century. After a brief marriage, her husband died. She remained a childless widow for the rest of her life and made her living writing plays, poems, and stories. Initially, she was a success, but towards the end, less favoured by the court, she died ill and in poverty. Her early success makes her atypical; her end is grimly familiar.

From the nineteenth century, there are better-known women writers associated with solitude. Emily Brontë and Emily Dickinson did not live alone, but are famous as reclusive poets, for they withdrew as much as they could from ordinary social contact. They preferred solitude and the intensity of their own contemplation to the busy distractions most people seek. Dickinson clearly understood and articulated all the pleasures and perils of her choice:

The soul unto itself
Is an imperial friend,
Or the most agonising spy
An enemy could send.

Secure against its own,
No treason it can fear;
Itself its sovereign, of itself
The soul should stand in awe.

Louisa May Alcott, who may, in *Little Women*, have done more than anyone else to idealise family life for generations of little girls, alternated as an adult between living alone and staying with her parents. She could do neither for long comfortably, nor with self-acceptance, but she courageously defended spinsterhood as an option for women in an era when unmarried women were casually referred to as "superfluous".

Mary Wilkins Freeman, a less well-known American writer, married late in life and wrote a number of stories about New England spinsters. In an unpublished story, her narrator, Jane Lennox, makes a very revealing statement: "I am a rebel and what is worse a rebel against the Over-government of all creation...I even dare to think that, infinitesimal as I am,...I, through my rebellion, have power. All negation has power. I, Jane Lennox, spinster...am a power."[3]

Two words in that passage are especially suggestive: "rebel" and "power". Against whom is the solitary woman, the single woman living alone rebelling? In one sense, against "man" who defines woman as the creature who nurtures and serves. But perhaps a deeper guilt comes from the sense that in choosing solitude, a woman at some level rejects her mother.

We may die alone, but we are born into a relationship, or we quite literally do not survive. That relationship is immediate, physical, and it is in every sense what makes us human. To live alone is not only to refuse the social role of mother, but is also to reject the internalised mother, and perhaps to feel rejected by her in turn, since any separation provokes fears of abandonment.

Paradoxically, of course, to live alone is not only to reject this internalised mother, but also to become her, to become one's own mother, both the "good Mother" who takes care, and the "bad" one who prescribes Duty. To live alone is to live with a number of people clamouring for attention and priority, but they are all within one's self. And often there are no real others outside the self to distract and bring one back to "reality".

So a woman living alone must come to terms with the heady notion that she is a "rebel" against both social prescription and against what is primary for her and for everyone else. This can provoke deep fears, but may also fill her with a sense of power that can be creative, when it is not submerged by anxiety.

Some women choose to live alone because they want to devote themselves to creative work without the distractions of family life. May Sarton has articulated the day-to-day conflicts of a woman living alone and writing poetry. For her, solitude allows time and space for reflection on the meaning of her most intense experience: "Friends, even passionate love are not my real life unless there is time alone in which to explore and to discover what is happening."[4]

Whether or not living alone has been a deliberate choice, as it was for Sarton, solitude still has its own peculiar problems. Family life imposes disciplines and rhythms. The woman who wants to integrate work or even just some independent activity of her own into her caring for others must constantly struggle for time for herself. That struggle may exhaust her so that it becomes difficult to use her time productively. She envies the solitary woman who has no such problem. All *her* time, it seems, is her own. However, in order to keep the demons of boredom, loneliness, and panicked anxiety at bay, she must structure her own time, allow for an alternation of work and pleasure, of seeing others and being alone. Otherwise having too much time can be as debilitating as not having enough. Procrastination is too tempting. Internalised others can create as much conflict as real husbands, lovers, children. But they provide none of the satisfactions of actual relationships.

The solitary woman must constantly combat the idea that she is not living "as she should", that she is not a true woman, a good woman because she is not caring for others. Such notions will prevent her from caring properly for herself or from accepting help when she needs it. We know that single people are an expanding "market" these days. The single woman must resist the inescapable refrain that some future act of consumption will make her happy, for otherwise she will be frustrated when the promise is betrayed. But she must also refuse irrational self-denial stemming from her own sense of unworthiness.

All this "good advice" comes from reflections on my own experience and on my ambivalent feelings about living alone. I would like to be more positive in celebrating the joys of living alone. There are joys to celebrate — moments of intense, ecstatic contemplation, exultation, a kind of grace. "Ordinary life does not interest me. I seek only the high moments."[5] For anyone who agrees with Anaïs Nin, solitude is a rational choice. In solitude, "ordinary life" can be reduced to a minimum; inner life can expand as far as it will go.

When I think about "woman alone" I think not only of women writers, heroines and inspirational figures, not only of my own ambivalence and unresolved conflicts, but I also think of my grandmother. Like many widows, she lived alone for the last twenty years of her life, after her husband died. She kept her own house, worked in her garden, sustained herself until the day she fell downstairs and broke her hip. She died in the nursing home she had feared all those twenty years. She had devoted herself not to the "high moments" but to "ordinary life" and she was expert at it — an excellent cook, seamstress, housekeeper. In addition, she was an active woman in her community and she had innumerable friends.

Only once, about a month before the accident, did she ever say she was depressed. I realised only after her fall how serious a statement that was. Her life had gotten completely out of control. For the previous three months, she had not cashed a cheque or paid a bill. There was little food in her house. None of her friends and no one in the family suspected that her proud indepedence had faltered. She had asked no one for help. When help came, it was already too late.

As women we constantly receive a double message: we are supposed to be the dependent sex, but we are also supposed to be the strong ones — strong enough to nurture others. "Dependence" may be some women's fatal flaw, but a rigid independence is just as dangerous, particularly for the woman living alone who fears the dependence said to be her fate and her predisposition.

Choosing solitude may be a result of temperament, of circumstance, or of a subtle interplay of both, as it was for me. The woman who chooses solitude in order to create or to devote herself to work may be nagged by the idea of what she is missing. Too much "freedom from" cares and caring can leave her with as much conflict as the woman trying to balance children and work. The work itself may never seem "good enough" to justify the lack of those real other presences.

Finally, preferring solitude *is* a matter of temperament. Since none of us chooses her own temperament, solitude can thus never be the abstract "authentic choice" I mentioned at the beginning of this chapter. The point is that living alone is less a matter of "choice" than of recognition and acceptance of who one is.

REFERENCES

1 May Sarton, *Journal of a Solitude* (New York: W.W. Norton & Company, Inc., 1983), p. 91.

2 E. William Monter, "The Pedestal and the Stake: Courtly Love and Witchcraft", in *Becoming Visible: Women in European History*, ed. Renate Bridenthal and Claudia Koonz (Boston: Houghton Mifflin Company, 1977), p. 133.

3 Quoted in Leah Blatt Glasser, " 'She Is the One You Call Sister': Discovering Mary Wilkins Freeman", in *Between Women*, ed. Carol Ascher, Louise

DeSalvo, and Sara Ruddick (Boston: Beacon Press, 1984), p. 191.

4 Sarton, *op. cit.*, p. 11.

5 *The Diary of Anaïs Nin*, Volume I, 1931 - 1934 (New York: Harcourt, Brace & World, Inc., 1966), p. 5.

FURTHER READING

Carr, Emily. *Growing Pains: The Autobiography of Emily Carr..* Toronto: Clarke, Irwin & Company Limited, 1946.

Dillard, Annie. *Pilgrim at Tinker Creek*. New York: Bantam Books, 1974.

Gérin, Winifred. *Emily Brontë*. Oxford: Clarendon Press, 1971.

Sarton, May. *Plant Dreaming Deep*. Norton & Company, Inc., 1968.

Saxton, Martha. *Louisa May: A Modern Biography of Louisa May Alcott*. New York: Avon Books, 1977.

LOUISE DULUDE

Getting Old: Men in Couples and Women Alone

The ultimate irony, for women, is that after a lifetime of having a multitude of mythical qualities and failings attributed to them because of their sex, they are suddenly told that after a certain age these differences between the sexes no longer exist. U.S. activist Tish Sommers protested against this final injustice:[1]

> Curious how we lose our sex when we reach sixty-five! Not just sexuality, or sexiness, but more basic than that. We even lose our gender. No longer are we older women and men, but we suddenly join a new category — senior citizens (or old folks, or the elderly). New bureaucracies are concerned with our welfare, new laws cover our rights (such as they are), and new councils make recommendations to an unresponsive government.
>
> Most statistics lump us together, male and female,...masking tremendous differences between the sexes, and above all obscuring how much aging is a woman's issue.

One of the most striking aspects of aging is the growing predominance of women in the older population. While older males outnumbered females in the first half of this century, this has since reversed; by the time of the 1981 census, 57 per cent of Canadians aged 65 and over were women. This imbalance in favour of women is greatest in the oldest age groups: there were 124 females per 100 males aged 65 to 79, and 187 women per 100 men in the 80-and-over group.[2]

Projections for the future indicate that the gap in life expectancy between the sexes will persist, but will get smaller as more women adopt the bad health habits of men. Most important among these is smoking, which some studies hold responsible for 75 per cent or more of the difference in longevity between women and men.[3] In spite of this, Statistics Canada predicts that by the year 2001 there will be 134 females per 100 males in the 65-to-79 age group, and women aged 80 and over will outnumber their male counterparts by more than two to one.[4]

But numbers alone do not explain why aging is a woman's issue. The most tragic fact of life for old women is that the blessing of their superior longevity too often turns out to be a curse. Instead of more twilight years of fulfillment and serenity, it brings to many of them a decade or more of loneliness, ill health and poverty. This is obvious when the day-to-day lives of elderly women and men are compared.

RELATIONSHIPS

The most obvious difference in life style between the sexes in old age is that the majority of the males live with their wives while most female seniors do not have a spouse. This seems strange at first, since it takes both a woman and a man to make a couple, but it is less surprising when we remember that a typical bride marries a man who is older than she and who has a shorter life expectancy than she does. As a result, many male pensioners are married to women under the age of 65, and most women can expect to become widowed.

As Table 19.1 demonstrates, this discrepancy in marital status is very large and accentuates with age: among Canadians aged 65 to 69, more than 80 per cent of the men are married compared to less than 60 per cent of the women; for those aged 80 and above, still over half of the males have a spouse compared to only 15 per cent of the women. As the proportions of elderly men who are married and of elderly women who are widowed have both been increasing over the years, this gap is expected to get even larger in the future.

TABLE 19.1
Marital status of people aged 65 and over in Canada, 1983[5]

Age	Married		Widowed and Divorced		Never married	
	Men	Women	Men	Women	Men	Women
65 - 69	83%	58%	10%	34%	7%	8%
70 - 74	79%	46%	13%	45%	8%	9%
75 - 79	73%	32%	18%	58%	9%	10%
80 +	57%	15%	34%	75%	9%	10%
Total 65 +	76%	40%	16%	51%	8%	9%

Before much research on these subjects was undertaken, it was widely believed that both sexes suffered a dramatic loss when they became old. Men had to give up their jobs, which had been their major source of identity and social status, and women lost their husbands who provided them with their principal life roles.[6] This was later denied by elderly people themselves, who reported that the death of a spouse was the single most critical experience of a person's life, requiring most changes and adjustment.[7] Retirement is felt to be much less disruptive, being ranked 28th out of 34 life events (with divorce ranking 17th).

The other obstacle to the neat retirement/widowhood parallel is that more and more women must go through both. In 1984, 41 per cent of all married Canadian women aged 45 to 64 had a job outside their homes.[8] The traditional view that retirement was less difficult and more "natural" for women has also been largely debunked:[9]

> First, a job may be just as important for a woman as for a man. She is just as likely to be committed to it. Retirement could therefore result in "withdrawal symptoms" for women as well as for men.
>
> Second, the assumption that women can easily refocus to "in-home" roles ignores the fact that it was because of the loss of such roles in middle age that they initially became involved in jobs. Most women at retirement have no children living at home and 30 per cent are widows...
>
> Third, because they have gotten a late career start, their retirement is likely to come before their job goals are achieved.

Another element that probably contributes to the distress of older widows is that post-retirement marriages tend to be happier than most. Little is known about the reasons for this, but it has been surmised that: (1) if a marriage lasts long enough, the spouses stand a better chance of resolving their differences; and (2) older people are marriage survivors, with less successful couples having split up along the way.[10] In any case, the fact is that older couples do more things together than younger spouses and are less restricted by traditional sex roles — for example, older husbands are more likely than younger ones to participate in homemaking tasks.

Obviously, the closer the spouses were before one of them died, the harsher the transition to widowhood. Many who went through this experience report that it left them shattered:[11]

> I was conscious of my hands dangling uselessly by my sides. I was a person with no job to do, no place to fill, no function in life.

It may be just as well that fewer men become widowed because they seem to have more difficulty in adapting to this role. For one thing, widowers are less likely to have close friends than widows.[12] For another, at least some of these men are unable to learn to cook and clean for themselves and cannot afford to pay someone else to perform these services.[13] These factors may explain why the suicide rate of elderly men who live alone is much higher than that of everyone else in the same age group.[14]

At the other emotional extreme, widowers have a much greater chance of getting remarried than widows. Given the fact that unmarried women aged 65 and over outnumber unmarried men by more than three to one,[15] the chances of a widow finding another husband are only slightly better than those of winning the lottery. Should these women — oh! horror — have relationships with noticeably younger men, they will run head on against our society's double standard of aging. Susan Sontag wrote that:[16]

> The convention that wives should be younger than their husbands powerfully enforces the "minority" status of women, since being senior in age always carries with it, in any relationship, a certain amount of power and authority. There are no laws on the matter, of course. The convention is obeyed because to do otherwise makes one feel as if one is doing something ugly or in bad taste.

Widows are also hampered from engaging in relationships with men by the myth saying that older women are no longer interested in sex. Masters and Johnson laid this to rest once and for all in 1966, when they wrote that "There is no limit drawn by the advancing years to female sexuality."[17] According to an analysis of a national American survey on sexuality:[18]

> Although the stereotype of sexless older people possibly comforts those who have no partners, and possibly reassures those who never liked sex in the first place...,the fact is that sexual response continues long into old age for many people...
>
> Members of both sexes may lose sexual desire, but this is generally a result of lower expectations, boring sexual routine, or lack of a partner — not inevitably of the lesser capacities of the body.

The author ended by quoting the following opinion offered by a female respondent to the survey:[19]

> I am 60 years old and they say you never get too old to enjoy sex. I know, because once I asked my Grandma when you stop liking it and she was 80. She said, "Child, you'll have to ask someone older than me."

None of the above comments should be interpreted to mean that the majority of widows lead isolated lives and never talk to anyone. For one thing, some widowed women enjoy the greater freedom and independence they experience following the death of their spouses.[20] For another, even though almost half of spouseless elderly women live alone, a third are living with their children or other family members.[21] Studies also show that the majority of widows have extensive social networks of relatives and acquaintances whom they see or talk to frequently.[22] Younger widows have a harder time, since they are often made unwelcome in social circles where most people still come in twos.

Contrary to rumours that children are abandoning their old parents, most elderly mothers report seeing them at least once a week. This is not necessarily a blessing, however, since the frequency of contact with their children makes little difference to old people's feelings of loneliness and life satisfaction.[23] In other words, old widows who hardly ever see or hear from their children are not necessarily less happy than those who see them every day.

On second thought, this is not so outlandish. Although parents and children are usually closer to each other than strangers, they have little in common and do not normally make good companions. The same is *not* true of relationships with other family members, friends and neighbours, who are much more likely to be equals and to share common interests and goals. Older women who were never married have an advantage in that respect, since they have long ago gotten used to making friends outside their immediate family circles.[24]

HEALTH

Numerous studies have concluded that health is the single most important factor determining whether old women and men are happy and satisfied with their lives.[25] Part of the reason for this may be that healthy elderly people who see many of their contemporaries becoming ill or disabled feel happy that they have themselves been spared. Even more likely, bad health is a strong spoiler that can drastically reduce people's activities and make them miserable.

The truth about old people's health is that it deteriorates with age. When a representative sample of Ontario senior citizens was asked whether their health prevented them from accomplishing a list of common daily tasks, it was found that only 16 per cent of those aged 65 to 74 could not do heavy housework, which was the most strenuous of the tasks listed.[26] This compared with 26 per cent of those aged 75 to 84, and 54 per cent of those who were 85 years old and above. In addition, women were more likely than men of the same age to report their health as being poor.

Although elderly women are five times less likely to commit suicide,[27] a greater proportion of them than of men suffer from depression and anxiety.[28] The classic doctors' response to such complaints is to hand out tons of tranquilisers and sleeping pills. A Saskatchewan survey found that 55 per cent of women aged 50 and over and 43 per cent of the men had doctors' prescriptions for drugs affecting the nervous system.[29] Overall, a phenomenal 77 per cent of women aged 65 and over take some type of drug, compared with 66 per cent of their male counterparts.[30]

All this would seem to indicate that women's longer lives are often bought at the price of years of unhappy discomfort. In hard numbers, it has been calculated that although women's life expectancy at birth is 7.5 years longer than that of men, their disability-free life expectancy is only 3.6 years longer. For those who survive until the age of 65, the average life expectancy of women is 4.3 years longer, but the difference in disability-free time is only 1.7 years.[31]

Very little is known of the reasons why older women enjoy less good health than older men. This is consistent with the general low priority and underfunding of all areas of medical research that concern the problems of women, and older women in particular. Dr. Robert Butler, an eminent U.S. gerontologist, has accused the medical establishment of being ageist and sexist. "All too often a woman's health problems are written off in terms of her being pre-menopausal, menopausal, post-menopausal — or, ultimately, senile."[32] Some male gerontologists have even suggested that increased efforts to improve the health status of older women might be undesirable, and that "an equally appropriate action might be to examine why women live so long, and to remove the factors that lead to this persistence."[33]

One urgent area of research relates to whether elder men's better health status is due to their being able to rely on high-quality home services and care. Most senior men have built-in housekeepers and nurses — their wives. By contrast, most old women who become sick and frail have no live-in companions and must fend for themselves. In the absence of adequate government-sponsored supports such as visiting nurses, professional homemakers and meals-on-wheels services, most widows must do without minimal comforts or must turn for help to the second most important caregivers in families, their daughters.

The plight of these daughters, who have been called "the women in the middle" and "the sandwich generation" is expected to worsen as the very old become a larger proportion of our population. Support for care-giving daughters and wives was the main theme of the first national convention of the Older Women's League in the United States in 1983.[34]

Women spoke of having to give up salaried jobs to spend as many as twenty years caring full-time for incapacitated spouses or parents. "In that time, you become a forgotten woman...You can rarely leave the house, and no one comes to visit you because it's too depressing.

The main demand issuing from the conference was for respite care legislation that would allocate state funds for temporary services. These services would "include adult day-care centres, and an arrangement where care givers would get a week, a weekend, or even a few hours' relief."[35] Even higher on the list for both care givers and care receivers are: (1) complete, well-integrated free or low-cost services allowing seniors to live on their own as long as possible; and (2) "good-quality institutions that aren't looked at with fear and trepidation."[36]

Unless these recommendations are implemented, it is feared that incidents of violence against the elderly might reach epidemic proportions. "Granny-bashing", as its name implies, is largely directed against women.[37] Its typical victims are very old, confused and physically disabled parents living with their children. The abuses reported range from insults to financial extortions to blows severe enough to cause death. Relatively few cases of this exist today, but there is every reason to believe that the situation will degenerate if the government does not step up its involvement in order to ease the burden of old people's families.

The trend now is in the opposite direction. Spurred by growing deficits, governments are deaf to the results of many surveys showing that most senior citizens of both sexes do *not* want to move in with their children or depend on them for essential services.[38] Instead, they want more formal assistance to help them live independently in their own homes as long as possible. When this is no longer feasible, more than 80 per cent prefer life in an institution within a short distance of their families rather than moving in with their children. Women are even more adamant than men on this, with 87 per cent of those questioned voicing that opinion.[39] This is confirmed by figures showing that old people who live with their children or other relatives are older, sicker and poorer than other seniors — they are the ones who are least likely to have a choice.[40]

Good institutions for incapacitated old people are presently in very short supply. A *Globe and Mail* survey of Ontario nursing homes found that most of them had waiting lists. On quality, the investigating journalists concluded that:[41]

> Of the 50 nursing homes we visited, there were six where we would have been quite happy to leave a friend or relative, and fifteen where we would not have wanted to leave anybody. The remaining homes did not strike us as either particularly good or bad.

Since more than three-quarters of nursing home residents are female, most of them in their late seventies and eighties,[42] it is women who are the most frequent losers in life's last game of chance, nursing home roulette.

MONEY

After ten years or so of intense pension reform debates in Canada, one of the few things on which all its participants agree is that too many Canadian women spend their last years in poverty. The figures are distressingly eloquent: in 1983, 31 per cent of women aged 65 and over had incomes below Statistics Canada's poverty lines. The comparable figure for men was a much lower 17 per cent.[43]

When marital status and age are taken into account, much larger differences between the sexes appear. Table 19.2 indicates that seniors who live in families, meaning most of the men, actually experience a drop in their poverty rate (from 10.3 per cent to 8.7 per cent) as they get older, possibly because the younger group includes many who are married to non-pensioner wives. By contrast, the category of people living alone or with non-relatives, where most women are found, experiences a huge increase in poverty with advancing age. At 70 years old and over, a phenomenally high 63.5 per cent of unattached women live in poverty.

TABLE 19.2

Incidence of Poverty among People Aged 65 and Over, Canada, 1982[44]

	Percentage in Poverty	
Living arrangement	Families headed by males	Families headed by females
Living with spouse or relatives		
• age 65 - 69	10.3%	23.5%
• age 70+	8.7%	23.0%
	Men	**Women**
Living alone or with non-family		
• age 65 - 69	34.7%	50.6%
• age 70+	47.3%	63.5%

The cause of this huge gap in the living standards of elderly men and women is that Canada's pension system was designed by men to benefit men. This was not done out of spite against women, but out of the traditional belief that the world is composed of only two categories of people: full-time participants in the labour market (husbands and fathers), and the people they support (women and children). If you provide adequate pensions to the first group, it was felt, the second group would automatically be taken care of.[45]

The problem is that in the real world, people do not fit in such convenient categories. About 10 per cent of women never marry, more than half of those who do marry become widowed at some point, and the rate of marriage dissolution through divorce and separation is growing by leaps and bounds. As a result, the National Council of Welfare estimated, fully three-quarters of all women end up having to support themselves and, increasingly, their children as well.[46] Since very few of these "unprotected" women had life-long full-time jobs giving them access to good pension plans and allowing them to accumulate substantial savings, it is inevitable that most of them will end up poor when they are old.

What does it mean to be old and poor? It means having to sell your home when your husband dies, because you need the money to live and cannot afford to hire people to do such jobs as cleaning the gutters, shovelling snow and fixing the roof. Because the area where you have lived for a long time has few apartments for rent, especially suitable ones for seniors (no steep stairs, low cupboards, close to the stores), you will probably have to move closer to the city centre, leaving many of your friends behind and losing most of the familiar signposts of your existence.

Being poor also means that you cannot afford a car or taxis and become dependent on public transportation. Seniors often complain about train and bus services that are less frequent when they need them most, in the evenings and on Sunday. They also have problems with physical design on most public transport facilities. As one old woman put it, one-and-a-half foot high bus steps are simply not designed for human beings, let alone for old ladies with stiff joints.[47] After a while, it becomes simpler to stay home, and even trips to the doctor become major expeditions.

Most important perhaps, having no money for extras prevents you from buying the services you desperately require when you become older and frailer. Not for you, the two-or-three-times-a-week housekeeper to help with the shopping and the house cleaning chores. Nor can you afford a private nurse to care for you, thereby delaying the time when you have to go to a hospital or a nursing home. One of the most common health hazards for old women is broken bones suffered while working in their homes.

At the very least, being poor prevents elderly women from leading a full life. Lack of money is one of the main reasons they give when they are asked why they do not see more people, entertain friends and engage in activities they would enjoy.[48] It is no wonder that the lives of so many old women come to revolve almost entirely around their television sets and their telephones.

At its worst, having too little money forces you to live like this woman whose plight is described in a National Council of Welfare report:[49]

"If you're really interested", said 67-year-old Mary S., "I'll tell you what it's like being an old woman alone who's only got the government pension to live on....It's wearing out your second-hand shoes going from one store to another trying to find the cheapest cuts of meat. It's hating having to buy toilet tissue or soap or toothpaste, because you can't eat it. It's picking the marked-down fruits and vegetables from the half-rotting stuff in the back of the stores that used to be given away to farmers to feed their animals. It's hunting the thrift shops and Salvation Army stores for half-decent clothes.

"Emergencies come up; grandchildren have birthdays; clothes wear out; cleaning products run out; bus rates go up. How do we manage? We pay our rent and utilities and we eat less.

"We live in fear. Fear of the future, of more illness, less money, less pride. Fear that the cheque won't arrive and we won't be able to work our way through the red tape in time to pay our rent. Fear that we will run out of food before the next cheque comes in.

"So, fear holds you in line. It is our punishment for getting old and sick."

WHAT SHOULD BE DONE

It has often been said that people age and die as they have lived. The facts of aging for typical men and women — the men living quite comfortably in their own homes until their death with their loving mates by their bedsides, the women condemned to a penny-pinching existence alone in small apartments before their last move to a nursing home — bear this out. Just as women are second-class citizens throughout their lives, they are also second-class senior citizens at the end of it.

The implication is that it is not a simple matter to give women equality in their old age. It requires nothing less than a complete overhaul of the dependency system on which the relationship between the sexes is based now. This does not necessarily mean that women must become more like men — indeed, men's lower life expectancy and their lesser ability to cope as widowers reveal important flaws — but that the life choices women make should maximise rather than diminish their self-reliance.

The first pre-requisite to achieving independence is a truly free choice of life style unhampered by myths about ideal feminine roles and career choices. As long as girls' ambitions are systematically dampened and they are led to believe that the most crucial activity of their existence is to find Mr. Right, they will continue to shy away from more profitable professional pursuits and to invest the bulk of their energies in their emotional lives. The idea is not to transform all women into the male ideal of the workaholic robot, but to foster the growth of their intellectual side and thereby discourage them from putting all their eggs in the increasingly fragile marriage basket.

Unfortunately, a fundamental change of this sort cannot be achieved through government policy or legislation. It requires a massive change in attitudes, especially among parents who are the main source of models for their children. The good news in that respect is that married women's entry in huge numbers in the labour market in the last decades has shattered the myth that women's only role is that of wife, mother and holy keeper of the home. Economic growth has had a great deal to do with this development, which was also stimulated by skyrocketing divorce rates that made it clear that a woman without a paid job is only a man away from the welfare roll.

The bad news is that the jobs these women took were the worst ones around. Most female earners are still segregated in low-paying, non-unionised, dead-end occupations.[50] Even worse, married women with paid jobs continue to do all the child care and homemaking tasks in their homes.[51] The message daughters now get is that a woman must have a job, as insurance if nothing else, but that it must not be so demanding as to interfere with her homemaking role. Outside of some rarefied yuppie circles, the idea that husbands could share the child care and housekeeping tasks has not yet caught on.

Faced with these obstacles, the women's movement developed alternate strategies. On the other hand, it pressed for the upgrading of traditionally female jobs through the introduction of laws requiring the payment of equal wages for work of equal value. By making it possible to compare different occupations, for example those of female secretaries and male maintenance staff, these laws raise women's wages and prevent the systematic exploitation of female employees. Most provinces have yet to implement such legislation.

Secondly, most women's organisations recommended important changes to Canada's pension system to give female employees more opportunities to save for their old age. The most important of these proposals calls for an expansion of the Canada and Québec Pension Plans, which are the only retirement programmes in which all women with earnings participate. Noting that the present retirement benefits paid by these programmes only equal 25 per cent of average lifetime earnings, which is much too low, women's groups are asking for these payments to be doubled.[52] If this were implemented, it would improve the financial situation of elderly men as well, since many of them do not enjoy adequate pension coverage now.

The other side of the coin consists of increasing the financial security of women who work only or mainly in their homes. Examples of ways in which this could be done include: the equal ownership and control by both spouses of all the assets they acquire during their life together;[53] the equal splitting of pension credits between the spouses for the time they are married;[54] the direct coverage of full and part-time homemakers under the Canada and Québec Pension Plans.[55] To this day, none of these recommendations has been fully implemented anywhere in Canada.

While each of these measures would bring some women closer to a more economically secure old age, none would strike at the crucial problems of loneliness and lack of role that so many women feel after the death of their lifetime companion. Part of these problems result from the difference in age and life expectancy between the spouses, and part from the lack of integration of old people in the mainstream of our society.

As we saw earlier, a large proportion of the life expectancy difference between the sexes is due to life style factors that are likely to diminish, but not disappear, as time goes by. Assuming that some difference will persist because it is due to the physiological superiority of women, one may ask whether it might not be appropriate to launch a campaign to discourage young women from marrying older men.

When the author tried to do this in a modest way recently by asking a predominantly female high school class why almost all of them preferred older boyfriends, she met with a unanimous answer: girls like older boys, they said, because they are more "solid" and more capable of being "leaned on". When the author challenged this and ventured to suggest that a relationship with an equal might be more desirable for both sexes, she got blank stares and no response.

A preliminary conclusion to be drawn from this episode is that sexism is even more deeply ingrained in young girls than was ever suspected. Not only are men told that younger women are preferable because they are more graceful, pliant and easier to influence, but girls internalise this prejudice themselves by seeking mates who will have a built-in advantage over them.

This age factor is even more evident in second and third marriages because men are still operating under the same youth-is-beauty-is-desirable assumption. As a result, many lonely women in their thirties, forties and older desperately cling to the remnants of their youth to attract men of their own age and more. Susan Sontag deplored this and urged an end to this disgraceful race with time:[56]

> Each time a woman lies about her age she becomes an accomplice in her own underdevelopment as a human being.
>
> Women have another option. They can aspire to be wise, not merely nice, to be competent, not merely helpful; to be strong, not merely graceful; to be ambitious for themselves, not merely for themselves in relation to men and children. They can let themselves age naturally and without embarrassment, actively protesting and disobeying the conventions that stem from this society's double standard about aging. Instead of being girls, girls as long as possible, who then age humiliatingly into middle-aged women and then obscenely into old women, they can become women much earlier — and remain active adults, enjoying the long career of which women are capable far longer.

Women should allow their faces to show the lives they have lived. Women should tell the truth.

Because of the way our society is organized, older women without mates are also very often women without roles. Survey reports show that both elderly women and men would like to play a more active role in society, would like to do more to help other people.[57] This need is not met by the New Horizons programme, which is the main federal source of funds for seniors' activities in Canada. New Horizons pays no salaries to its elderly participants, and most of the projects it funds are leisure-oriented. In 1984 - 1985, only 6 per cent of the activities it subsidised involved giving direct assistance to other people.[58]

Gerontologist Alex Comfort disagrees that leisure activities do much good to the elderly, and believes instead that working is the best way of keeping loneliness and unhappiness at bay:[59]

I am frankly disturbed by the emphasis on leisure as the prescribed state of later life. Leisure is a con. It should occupy an occasional afternoon, not 20 years...

Old citizens have as much right as the young, if not more, to sit on the porch or be hippies. But both those are in my sense occupations: they have goals, and even secession from the world is part of the world. And they rest upon choice, not rejection by society.

Leisure in our culture means not doing what you choose, but activity which is by definition goalless and irrelevant, and our emphasis on it childrenizes older people.

Examples of the types of government initiatives that could answer this need include the American Foster Grandparent Program, which pays a modest stipend to low-income people over the age of 60 who participate in projects that help children with special problems. As well as being beneficial to thousands of retarded, disabled or emotionally disturbed pre-schoolers, it was found that the programme increased the life expectancy of its "grandparents".[60] Other services that presently exist only on a sporadic and unpaid basis in Canada — often sponsored by local YWCAs — are Widow-to-Widow programmes that seek out recently widowed women, through obituaries among other means, and offer them help in coping with the range of emotional, financial and other difficulties they encounter at that time.

These and many other useful programmes could give isolated and bored elderly women and men a new purpose in life and a way of supplementing their meagre incomes. They would also contribute to making seniors better integrated and more valued members of our society. The importance of adopting such an attitude was best expressed in a presentation made to the U.S. Council on the Aging in 1975:[61]

> We can no longer ignore the economic plight of the older woman. We have three choices: (1) let her slowly starve; (2) provide her increasingly expensive, inadequate welfare services; or (3) help her to remain an independent, contributing member of society.
>
> We can give her a fish and feed her for the day...Or we can teach her to fish and she will feed herself, and perhaps some others too.

REFERENCES

1 Tish Sommers, "Aging is a Woman's Issue", *Response*, March 1976, pp. 12 - 15.

2 Statistics Canada, *Women in Canada: A Statistical Report*. Catalogue no. 89-503E, Supply and Services Canada, 1985, Table 2; Government of Canada, *Fact Book on Aging in Canada*. Supply and Services Canada, 1983, p. 20.

3 Ellen M. Gee, "Mortality and Gender", *Canadian Woman Studies*, Vol. 5, No. 3 (special issue on aging), 1984, pp. 10 - 13; G.H. Miller and Dean R. Gernstein, "The Life Expectancy of Nonsmoking Men and Women", *Public Health Reports of the U.S. Department of Health and Human Services*, Vol. 98, No. 4, pp. 349 - 355.

4 Government of Canada, *op. cit.*, p. 20.

5 Statistics Canada, unpublished preliminary post-censal estimates for 1983.

6 Judith Posner, "Old and Female: The Double Whammy", *Essence*, Vol. 2, No. 1, 1977, p. 47; reprinted in *Aging in Canada*, Victor W. Marshall (ed.), Fitzhenry and Whiteside Ltd., 1980, pp. 80 - 87.

7 Anne Martin Matthews, "Review Essay — Canadian Research on Women as Widows: A Comparative Analysis of the State of the Art", *Resources for Feminist Research*, Vol. 11, No. 2 (special issue on aging), 1982, p. 227.

8 Statistics Canada, *The Labour Force*. Catalogue no. 71-001, December 1984, Table 58.

9 Robert C. Atchley and Sherry L. Corbett, "Older Women and Jobs", in *Looking Ahead: A Woman's Guide to the Problems and Joys of Growing Older*, Lillian Troll et al. (eds.), Prentice-Hall, 1977, pp. 124 - 125; also see Maximiliane Szinovacz, "Introduction: Research on Women's Retirement" in *Women's Retirement*, M. Szinovacz (ed.), Sage Publications, 1982, pp. 13 - 21.

10 Sharon McIrvin Abu-Laban, "The Family Life of Older Canadians" in *Aging in Canada, op. cit.*, pp. 126 - 127.

11 Jocelyn Evans, *Living With a Man Who Is Dying: A Personal Memoir*, New York, Taplinger, 1971, p. 139, cited by Anne Martin Matthews, "Women and Widowhood", in *Aging in Canada, op. cit.*, p. 149.

12 Laurel A. Strain and Neena L. Chappell, "Confidants: Do They Make a Difference in Quality of Life?", *Research on Aging*, Vol. 4, No. 4, 1982, pp. 479 - 502.
13 Felix M. Berardo, Social Adaptation to Widowhood Among a Rural-Urban Aged Population, Washington Agricultural Experimental Station Bulletin 689, Dec. 1967, cited by Sharon McIrvin Abu-Laban, *op. cit.*, p. 129.
14 George K. Jarvis and Menno Boldt, "Suicide in Later Years", *Essence*, Vol. 4, No. 3, 1980, pp. 145 - 158.
15 Statistics Canada, unpublished preliminary post-censal estimates for 1983.
16 Susan Sontag, "The Double Standard of Aging", *Saturday Review*, Sept. 23, 1972, p. 38.
17 William H. Masters and Virginia E. Johnson, *Human Sexual Response*, Little, Brown, and Co., 1966, p. 247.
18 Carol Tavris, "The Sexual Lives of Women Over 60", *Ms.*, July 1977, p. 62.
19 Same as above, p. 65.
20 Helena Z. Lopata, *Widowhood in an American City*, Schenkman, 1973, p. 88.
21 Susan Fletcher and Leroy O. Stone, *The Living Arrangements of Canada's Older Women*, Statistics Canada, Cat. no. 86-503, p. 36.
22 Helena Z. Lopata, *Women as Widows: Support Systems*, Elsevier Holland Inc., 1979.
23 Greg Arling, "The Elderly Widow and Her Family, Neighbours and Friends", *Journal of Marriage and the Family*, Nov. 1976, pp. 757 - 768.
24 Joan E. Norris, "The Social Adjustment of Single and Widowed Older Women", *Essence*, Vol. 4, No. 3, 1980, pp. 135 - 144.
25 Carol Cutler Riddick, "Life Satisfaction among Aging Women: A Causal Model", in *Women's Retirement, op. cit.*, pp. 45 - 59.
26 Seniors Secretariat, Secretariat for Social Development of Ontario, and United Senior Citizens of Ontario, *Elderly Residents in Ontario: An Overview*, May 1985, p. 34.
27 George K. Jarvis and Menno Boldt, *op. cit.*, p. 147.
28 Dolores Gold, "Sex Differences in the Experience of Aging", *Canadian Woman Studies*, Vol. 5, No. 3, 1984, p. 33.
29 J. Harding, *A Socio-Demographic Profile of People Prescribed Mood-Modifiers in Saskatchewan*, Alcoholism Commission of Saskatchewan, Research Division, 1978.
30 Statistics Canada, *Women in Canada: A Statistical Report*, Cat. no. 89-503E, Table 17.
31 *Ibid.*, p. 79.
32 Elinor J. Burwell, "Discussion of Neena L. Chappel's Paper on the Future Impact of the Changing Status of Women", in *Canada's Changing Age Structure: Implications for the Future*, ed. Gloria M. Gutman, SFU Publications, 1981, p. 242.
33 E.F. Borgatta and M.B. Loeb, "Toward a Policy for Retired Persons: Reflec-

tions on Welfare and Taxation'' in N.G. McCluskey and E.F. Borgatta (eds.), *Aging and Retirement: Prospects, Planning and Policy*, Sage Publications, 1981, pp. 189 - 212.

34 Jill Johnson Keeney, ''Care-Givers: Top Issue for Older Women'', *Ms.*, Mar. 1983, p. 23.

35 *Ibid.*

36 Elinor J. Burwell, *op. cit.*, p. 248.

37 Rachel Aber Schlesinger, ''Granny-Bashing: An Introduction to the Problem'', *Canadian Woman Studies*, Vol. 5, No. 3, 1984, pp. 56 - 59.

38 S. Ciffin, J. Martin and C. Talbot, *Retirement in Canada, Vol. II — Social and Economic Concerns*, Canada, Health and Welfare Department, Policy Research and Long-Range Planning, 1977, p. 65.

39 Ingrid Connidis, ''Living Arrangement Choices of Older Residents: Assessing Quantitative Results with Qualitative Data'', *Canadian Review of Sociology*, Vol. 8, No. 4, 1983, pp. 359 - 375.

40 Statistics Canada, *Living Alone*, Cat. no. 99-934, 1984; François Béland, ''The Family and Adults 65 Years of Age and Over: Co-Residency and Availability of Help'', *Review of Canadian Sociology and Anthropology*, Vol. 21, No. 3, 1984, pp. 302 - 317.

41 James Jefferson and Mary Kate Rowan, ''You Adjust...It's Like the Army'', *Globe and Mail*, Mar. 17, 1981.

42 Statistics Canada, unpublished data from the 1975 survey of nursing homes.

43 Calculated from Table 1 of Statistics Canada, *Income Distributions by Size in Canada*, 1983, Cat. no. 13-207.

44 Unpublished data from Statistics Canada, comparing data from the 1982 Survey of Consumer Finances to Statistics Canada's low-income cut-offs as recalculated in 1978. Note that the category called ''Families Headed by Males'' cannot be compared to the one entitled ''Families Headed by Females'' since Statistics Canada uses the sexist practice of automatically including all married couples in the first group.

45 National Council of Welfare, *Women and Poverty*, 1979, pp. 25 - 27.

46 Louise Dulude, *Pension Reform With Women in Mind*, Canadian Advisory Council on the Status of Women, 1981.

47 Louise Dulude, *Women and Aging: A Report on the Rest of Our Lives*, Canadian Advisory Council on the Status of Women, 1978, p. 79.

48 Seniors Secretariat, Secretariat for Social Development of Ontario, and United Seniors Citizens of Ontario, *op. cit.*, p. 26.

49 National Council of Welfare, *op. cit.*, pp. 12 - 13.

50 Pat Armstrong and Hugh Armstrong, *The Double Ghetto: Canadian Women and Their Segregated Work*, McClelland and Stewart, 1978.

51 M. Meissner, E.W. Humphreys, S.M. Meis and W.J. Scheu, ''No Exit for Wives: Sexual Division of Labour and the Cumulation of Household Demands'', *Canadian Review of Sociology and Anthropology*, Vol. 12, No. 4,

Part 1, 1975, pp. 424 - 439; S. Clark and A.S. Harvey, "The Sexual Division of Labour: The Use of Time", *Atlantis*, Vol. 2, No. 1, 1976, pp. 46 - 66.

52 National Action Committee on the Status of Women, *Pension Reform: What Women Want*, 1983, pp. 10 - 11.

53 Louise Dulude, *Love, Marriage and Money*, Canadian Advisory Council on the Status of Women, 1984.

54 National Action Committee on the Status of Women, *op. cit.*, pp. 12 - 13.

55 *Ibid.*, pp. 13 - 17; Canada Pension Plan Advisory Committee, *More Effective Participation of Homemakers in the Canada Pension Plan*, 1983.

56 Susan Sontag, *op. cit.*, p. 38.

57 Seniors Secretariat, Secretariat for Social Development of Ontario, and United Seniors Citizens of Ontario, *op. cit.*, pp. 17 - 18.

58 Unpublished data provided by the New Horizons Programme information service, August 1985.

59 Alex Comfort, "Age Prejudice in America", *Social Policy*, Nov.-Dec. 1976, p. 6.

60 Rosalyn Saltz, "Fostergrandparenting: A Unique Child-Care Service", in *Looking Ahead...*, *op. cit.*, pp. 126 - 132.

61 U.S. Federal Council on the Aging, *Commitment to a Better Life: National Policy Concerns for Older Women*, 1976, p. 51.

FURTHER READING

Canadian Women Studies, Volume 5, Number 3, Spring 1984, Special Issue on Aging.

Dulude, Louise, *Women and Aging: A Report on the Rest of Our Lives*. Ottawa: Canadian Advisory Council on the Status of Women, 1978.

Government of Canada, *Fact Book on Aging in Canada*. Ottawa: Supply and Services Canada, 1983.

Marshall, Victor W., ed., *Aging in Canada: Social Perspectives*. Toronto: Fitzhenry and Whiteside, 1980.

Resources for Feminist Research, Volume 11, No. 2, July 1982, Special Issue on Women as Elders.

F. WORK

KAREN MESSING

Do Men and Women Have Different Jobs Because of Their Biological Differences?

Working women in North America are usually found in "employment ghettos", that is, areas in which women workers represent a large majority. In Québec, women constitute 36 per cent of the "active" population (those who are working or looking for work), but these women are distributed unequally across the job market. In the primary and secondary sectors (agriculture, forestry, fisheries, manufacturing) a quarter of the workers are women, while in the tertiary (services) sector 43 per cent of the work force is female. Moreover, the sex distribution is uneven within these sectors. For example, within the services sector, only 18 per cent of workers in transport and communications are female, but women constitute 57 per cent of those employed in finance and 56 per cent of those in personal services.[1]

As we look more closely at where women work, the work place reveals itself as a checkerboard of employment ghettos, some male and some female. In her analysis of positions in the Québec Ministry of Social Affairs, Dominique Gaucher[2] found, first, that the ministry itself is a female employment ghetto (73 per cent). This is explainable by the fact that the ministry employs most of the health care and social workers in the province. But within the ministry, the job category "stores" (care of hospital pharmacies and chemical supplies in laboratories) is a male ghetto (85 per cent). And within this male mini-ghetto, there are micro-ghettos: 80 per cent of store clerks (light work) are women but 86 per cent of storekeepers are men.

A preliminary version of this article was published in French in the Montréal-based journal *Cahiers du Socialisme* (No. 7, 1981). Part of the research was supported by the Institutional Research Fund of the University of Quebec at Montréal.

Many other examples of this kind of segregation can be found in Gaucher's study, and in our daily lives. We can see that women are secretaries, telephone operators, laundresses and sewing machine operators, while men are mechanics, truck drivers, welders, and miners. There seems to be a social consensus about what is a man's job and what is a woman's job. And there is a vague impression that these definitions come from our biology, from the different "nature" of men and women.

In fact, the prevailing ideology gives us a sort of syllogism:

1. Women and men are biologically different. Each sex has its strengths and weaknesses.

2. We can not assign the same tasks to women as to men; women can not do men's jobs, and vice versa.

3. We must protect women by giving them tasks that are adapted to their physical capacities and by excluding them from jobs that endanger their health.

4. The process of adapting job assignments to physical capacity, related as it is to biology, gives rise naturally to concentrations of women employees in those jobs which pose the least risk to their health.

Let's examine this familiar logic. As a biologist, I would like to ask the question, what are the biological differences between men and women, and do they in fact justify the existence of employment ghettos?

According to a modern textbook of occupational medicine:[3]

> In general, women's size and weight are less than men's; the hand is smaller, finer and suppler, with greater dexterity. Physical force is less developed, although it must be said that women can furnish an intense effort during a brief period of time, so that [the doctor] must not take into account any short-time measurements. The difference consists mainly in prolonged efforts for which women are more easily tired. From a genital point of view [*sic, d'un point de vue genital*] the [menstrual] periods cause physical and nervous fragility. Pregnancy and lactation get in the way of the accomplishment of industrial tasks. Women seem to be more sensitive than men to toxins. In any case their sensitivity increases when pregnant. Also, certain toxins cross the placental barrier; we must take into account the risk of the foetus....
>
> Altogether, except for dexterity, women are physiologically disadvantaged compared to men.

Unfortunately, the textbook fails to furnish scientific findings to back up these conclusions. What are the relevant data concerning the assertions made above?

Karen Messing

STRENGTH — THE "WEAKER SEX" MYTH

The first and most widespread argument used to justify the allocation of women to different tasks and jobs is that, since women are weaker, they must be given the jobs that are physically the least exacting.

What do biologists know about the respective strengths of men and women? First, they know that "strength" is not a simple concept. Strength, defined as "bodily or muscular power",[4] is a characteristic of a muscle or group of muscles. Women's muscles work the same way as men's; in both cases, the strength of a muscle is proportional to its cross-section.[5] Muscles are groups of fibres that can contract, and their strength depends on the number of fibres and the energy used to contract them. Different muscles are used when lifting, lowering, pushing, or pulling an object.

The ergonomists (specialists in the use of energy) Snook and Ciriello[6] examined the physical force used in industrial tasks and found that six components are involved: raising, lowering, pushing, pulling, carrying, and walking. Each action consists of two or more of these components. They then tested men and women by asking them to perform these tasks while varying load weights, distance transported, and speed. They recorded the largest weight each individual would accept to manipulate. For the great majority of tasks, the scales of weights men and women would accept overlapped. The average man accepted 1.5 times the weight accepted by the average woman. For pushing and pulling, the figure was 1.2 times as high; for walking, the sexes accepted equal weights. The longer the effort was sustained, and the faster the speed, the more the two sexes resembled each other.

A few points should be noted here. Even where the differences were most pronounced — in lifting — the weight acceptable to 50 per cent of women was too heavy for 20 per cent of men. In other words, it is incorrect to say that "women" can lift less weight than "men". Also, the dimensions of the weights were the same for the two sexes. This is the norm in industrial tasks; that is, tasks are not adapted to make them manageable by smaller people, but they could be if the will were there. Finally, data on *average* differences should not be used to justify allocating women to job ghettos. It would be just as logical to exclude all men from jobs requiring heavy lifting on the grounds that they are statistically more likely to have heart attacks.

Strength is not just a matter of a momentary effort. We should also consider the question of endurance, which is a function of the capacity of muscles to contract repeatedly before tiring. Since muscles get their food energy and oxygen from the blood, endurance is directly related to the efficiency of the respiratory and cardiovascular systems. On the average, men have 5 per cent more red blood cells than women, and a lung capacity 30 per cent greater.[5] However, these biological differences are not necessarily either innate or unchangeable. As weight-trainers have found, people can increase the cross-sectional area of their muscles and thereby their strength. Joggers know that it is possible to improve cardiovascular and respiratory capacities. We also know that the critical period in which the number of red cells and lung capacity are determined is between 8 and 11 years of age,[5] a time when girls are not encouraged to participate in sports, and when public facilities for their activities are lacking. Thus, it is possible that with changes in attitudes toward female performance, the difference between average male and female capacities will diminish.

In fact, if we consider Olympic performances by males and females, we observe that women are improving more rapidly than men in many sports. For example, in 1924, when women were first allowed to compete in the 400 metre swim, the best man's time was 58 seconds faster than the best woman's; in 1972, women's time had come to equal that of men in 1956 and was only 19 seconds slower than that of men in the 1972 competition. Similarly, in the 100 metre run, men improved by 0.66 seconds between 1928 and 1972, while women improved by 1.13 seconds.[7] There is no way of knowing whether these tendencies will eventually result in men and women competing on an equal basis. The physical differences that now exist between men and women may result from nature more than environment, or vice versa.

Contrary to the myth that woman's lesser strength requires that they be given less strenuous jobs, a close look at some of these jobs shows that they have not been designed to be particularly easy physically. Exertion of effort is not in itself damaging to the organism. But to furnish a sustained effort during which the muscles have no time to relax, is a stress which first tires the body and in the long term wears it out. The sewing machine operator, cramped in a fixed position, holding her fabric in one hand while she manipulates the machine with the other, contracts her shoulder muscles all day. The assembly line worker in a slaughter house, who spends her whole day cutting up chickens at the rate of 60 *per minute*, forced to stand without moving her legs, is not protected against backache and sore legs any more than is the stevedore.[8]

Moreover, many "feminine" occupations require women to lift very heavy weights. For examples, nurses' aides in homes for the aged or handicapped frequently lift their patients, some of whom weigh over 250 pounds. "On force comme des chevaux!" ("We strain like horses"), I was told by a group of these workers.[9]

We must not forget the biology of the male worker in this discussion. Women are not alone in risking their health by lifting weights too heavy for them. Seventy per cent of adults, males as well as females, suffer from backache.[10] Because of a mythology that says that a "real" man can do anything, men are encouraged to lift weights that are dangerously heavy. In a Québec firm that distributes merchandise to retailers, the young truck loaders lift 75-pound boxes at the rate of 22 tons per day. Few men can do a job like this without developing back problems.

The owner of a South Shore (Montréal) steel pylon company recently explained to me, "I could never hire a woman to work in the shop. The work is too hard. All the *men* who work here have back problems. You couldn't ask me to send a woman in there!" It seems that this employer's remarks are an excellent argument for changing the nature of the jobs in his factory, rather than a justification for employment ghettos.

DEXTERITY — THE "FAIRY FINGERS" MYTH

The average woman's hand is smaller than that of the average man — 9 per cent shorter, 12 per cent narrower, and 16 per cent thinner, to be exact.[11] This difference in size is supposed to confer a greater dexterity which, in turn, is used to justify the fact that assembly of tiny electronics components and typewriting are traditionally female jobs. Women's supposed greater manual dexterity does not explain why surgery, mechanics, and the great symphony orchestras are male employment ghettos, however.

Again, jobs calling for a woman's "fine touch" are by and large not good for her health. "Carpal tunnel syndrome" is a work-related ailment characterised by wrist pain and loss of manual sensitivity. Often it ends in loss of manual capacity. These symptoms are caused by rapid manipulation of precision tools.[12] According to scientific studies,[13] the syndrome is 2 to 10 times more frequent in women than in men.

In addition, tasks that demand great dexterity often have a large visual component. Referring to electronics industry workers, an ophthalmologist notes,[14] "It is true that in a significant number of cases an intense and prolonged visually demanding task results in visual fatigue, shown by conjunctival hyperemia [reddened eyes], tearing, a feeling of burning or pain in the eyes." Ninety per cent of telephone operators who get their information from reading microfiche suffer from headaches; 55 per cent experience pain in their eyes and 20 per cent have visual hallucinations that persist after work.[15] In this context, the fact that women are 20 per cent more likely than men to wear corrective lenses is possibly significant.[16]

Thus, we can not say that certain tasks are reserved for women because of their great dexterity. It is more accurate to say that the jobs "reserved" for women are those in which the fine manipulations are repetitive, boring, and extremely demanding visually as well as manually. In fact, these may be jobs for which male workers would not apply.

THE MENSTRUAL CYCLE — THE "RAGING HORMONES" MYTH

Dr. Edgar Berman, former surgeon advisor to the U.S. State Department, said publicly what many people think, that women cannot be trusted to hold high office since their "raging hormonal imbalances" make them unstable. As this stereotype is widespread, many studies have been done attempting to relate productivity to the stage of the menstrual cycle.

In one well-known experiment, male and female chimpanzees vied with each other for a banana. According to the researcher, R.M. Yerkes (quoted in 17, p. 8):

> When the female is not sexually receptive, the naturally more dominant member of the pair almost regularly obtains the food; whereas during the female's phase of maximal genital swelling, when she is sexually receptive, she claims or may claim the food and take it regularly even though she be the naturally subordinate member of the pair.

Ruth Herschberger found that the scientific analysis of the results of this experiment left something to be desired. She speculates on how the female chimpanzee regarded Yerkes' analysis of her behaviour:[17]

> Those words [naturally subordinate member] look like somebody decided I was subordinate way in advance. The referees are practically saying any gains I make while I'm "sexually receptive" can't be registered because the phase of maximal genital swelling is out of bounds!... *Why don't they ask what the score was?*...I was top man at the food chute for fourteen days out of the thirty-two. Jack was top man for eighteen. This means I won 44 per cent of the time, and Jack won 56 per cent. He's champion, I'll grant you that, but still it's almost fifty-fifty. If Jack hadn't been dragged in as the *biggest* male in the whole colony....

This is a good example of how scientists allow their conception of male and female roles to influence their interpretation of data relating hormonal status to behaviour. In fact, many studies of human motor function show no variation in performance with stages of the menstrual cycle. [18] One study did show that women who were wrongly led to believe they were at a "per-menstrual" stage of their cycle performed and perceived themselves in the same way as women who were really pre-menstrual and knew they were.[19] The relationship between hormones and human behaviour can be safely characterised as complex, and the stereotypes as so far unsupported by evidence.

As far as woman's jobs are concerned, data do not confirm the hypothesis that women are given tasks requiring little sustained energy or physical and emotional stability. The *Dictionary of Occupational Titles* of the U.S. Department of Labor gives the following description of the job of housewife ("foster mother"): "Rears children in own home as members of family. Oversees activities, regulating diet, recreation, rest periods, and sleeping time. Instructs children in good personal and health habits. Bathes, dresses and undresses young children. Washes and irons clothing. Accompanies children on outings and walks. Takes disciplinary action when children misbehave...." And this, all day long. It would be hard to imagine a profession that gives less respite when a woman is feeling under par — whether sick, menstruating, depressed, or otherwise — especially when there are young children. Yet the position of housewife, a 59-hour-a-week job,[20] is a female ghetto (97 per cent), as are all jobs that involve care of small children. We could also cite the positions of teacher, nurse, receptionist, or telephone operator (where women must respond cordially to over 200 calls per hour[15]) as examples of so-called female jobs that demand stability and emotional endurance of a high order.

It must be added that women are not alone in having biological cycles. The study of biological clocks is an active research area: an increasing number of biological parameters have been shown to vary in both sexes with time of day and over weeks or months. Women and men have cyclical patterns of sleep, temperature, urine production, cardiac rhythm, and production of sex and other hormones.[21 - 23] In Japan, administrators in the public transport service were able to lower accident rates by changing the work schedules of their male drivers to conform with their energy peaks.[24]

In general, the organisation of most jobs respects neither male nor female cycles. Night shifts (nurses, bookkeepers in banks, telephone operators, night cleaners, mothers of infants) gravely affect the basic biological cycles such as the sleep-wake cycle, temperature variations, digestive system cycles and eating schedules.[25] A cleaning woman at the CBC radio service told us how, as a result of 10 years on the night shift, she has lost her appetite, suffers from chronic constipation, and has to take sleeping pills to get to sleep in the morning and drink lots of coffee to stay awake at night.

And as far as the menstrual cycle is concerned, a study of poultry slaughterhouse workers has shown that 75.7 per cent of the women employees suffer from menstrual cramps, and that this is statistically correlated with, among other things, high speed of assembly lines and very cold temperatures inside the building, two factors that impede blood circulation.[8]

REPRODUCTION — "PROTECTING" PREGNANT WORKERS

There is one certain biological difference between males and females that cannot be explained away as a difference between statistical means or as a stereotype — only women get pregnant. This fact has two consequences for the pregnant woman: (a) the woman changes physically during her pregnancy and (b) the unborn child is brought into the work place and is exposed to chemicals, radiation, and germs.

First, how does pregnancy change women's bodies? During pregnancy, blood volume increases to feed the foetus, the heart has to work harder to pump the increased amount of blood, the excretory and digestive systems must work harder to clean the blood and process the extra food, and the respiratory system must supply the foetus with oxygen.[26]

Does this mean that pregnant women can not work? No one has ever proposed that pregnant women with small children take nine months off from their housework and child-care duties, so we must conclude that our society is not convinced that effort is dangerous for pregnant women. During the early months of pregnancy, women remain physically fit. In fact, 10 of the 26 Soviet women gold medalists in the 1964 Olympics were pregnant.[27] Nevertheless, during the last months of pregnancy, women have more difficulty moving around, and jobs which force women into confining positions or to make abnormally intense sustained efforts can cause problems, reflected, for example, in the greater rates of premature births among mothers whose jobs are physically exacting.[28] A paid pregnancy leave is obviously a biological necessity for these workers, as is a paid leave for the final weeks of pregnancy for all women. However, employers do not yet feel sufficiently protective toward women workers as to grant such leaves.

As far as chemical contamination is concerned, pregnant women are at a definite disadvantage in polluted work places. Their respiratory, digestive, and excretory systems co-operate to rid the body of toxins: the nasal hairs and the lungs filter the air; the liver and kidneys clean the blood. In an unhealthy work environment, these organs are overworked and suffer, just as an alcoholic's liver, unable to rid the body of all the accumulated alcohol, is poisoned by it, resulting in cirrhosis. The bodily systems that are overworked in a polluted environment are the same ones that are asked to work harder to take care of the foetus.

Lead, mercury, and cadmium are a few of the many substances which are dangerous for the pregnant woman.[10] These substances are also dangerous for the foetus. Contrary to what scientists used to believe, most toxic substances can cross the placental barrier and affect the foetus of an exposed mother. A good number of the substances which we call teratogenic (giving rise to malformations in a foetus) are used in various work places that employ women: lead by workers on automobile batteries, mercury by dental technicians, anaesthetic gases by anaesthesiology technicians, ionising radiations by radiotherapists, 2.5 diaminotoluene by hairdressers using tints, carbon tetrachloride by laundresses, etc.[29] Many of these substances find their way into the milk of nursing mothers as well.

Given that many women's jobs are not suitable for pregnant women, the traditional "solution" has been to protect them by sending them home without pay for the duration of pregnancy and lactation. But this policy has been "modernised". The period of greatest danger for the foetus has now been identified as extending between 21 and 45 days of pregnancy, a time when few women even know they are pregnant.[10] This discovery has been used to justify the exclusion of all fertile women from certain factories.[30]

But this is not a very efficient way to protect the children of exposed workers. The women are replaced by male workers who may someday be fathers. And sperm (as well as eggs) can undergo mutations that threaten the life and health of the child. In most cases, substances which are teratogenic for the foetus are mutagenic for the eggs and sperm before conception. Groups of male workers who have been identified as having undergone damage to their sperm include anaesthesiologists,[31] radiologists,[32] pesticide workers,[33] and workers exposed to vinyl chloride.[34] It must be added that most of the agents named in the preceding paragraphs have also been shown to cause cancer among male and female workers, since the mechanisms of cancer production, mutation, and teratogenesis are very similar.

We can safely say that it is not out of a yearning to protect workers and their children that certain companies have excluded fertile women; if that were the case, they would also have to exclude potential fathers. Besides, women are not excluded from *all* unhealthy work places. If there is one problem that has been well studied in regard to the possibility of damage to foetuses, it is the effects of radiation on pregnant women. Yet the profession of radiology technician (radiodiagnostics) is a female ghetto (83 per cent), as are radiotherapy (97 per cent) and nuclear medicine (76 per cent).[2] In fact, several other female employment ghettos involve recognised dangers for unborn and future children: laboratory technician, packager of contraceptive pills, print-shop worker. But employers do not attempt to exclude fertile women from these jobs, since there are no men who would replace them.

The following examples show something about the bases on which these decisions are made. In Québec, all radiology technicians are employed by the government (since medicine is socialised) and their working conditions are regulated by collective agreement. In 1979, women government workers were able to win a contract clause saying that a pregnant woman exposed to a risk for herself or her foetus has the right to a transfer, or if this is not possible, to be sent home at full pay. Among the first workers to take advantage of this clause was a radiology technician who had had two children with congenital malformations since she had started work. The employer contested her request on the grounds that there was no danger to the foetus in working as a radiology technician. The case is presently under arbitration.[35] It is interesting that, in the United States (where there is no cost to the *employer* who sends a pregnant worker home, but where the *foetus* could potentially sue for damages if harmed), it was the employer who insisted in a recent case that a pregnant radiology technician be sent home without pay for the duration of her pregnancy on the grounds that her job was dangerous for her foetus. (This case was heard by the Equal Employment Opportunities Commission,[36] which ruled that the employer had to transfer the technician to less-dangerous work.)

Could it be that the desire to protect women and children in the work place is less related to altruism than to who foots the bill? We must also wonder whether the recent policy of excluding fertile women from certain factories has more to do with affirmative action programmes and with the unemployment rate among men than with an intention to protect unborn children. A policy genuinely concerned with protecting workers and their children would provide full, paid maternity leave and clean up all dangerous work places.

CONCLUSIONS

The prevailing ideology attempts to justify employment ghettos by invoking a necessity to protect the health of women by respecting their biological specificity. But we can now reject the syllogism this ideology presents us and substitute one based on research evidence:

1. It is impossible to prove that all women are biologically weaker, less stable, or have more manual dexterity than all men.
2. It is moreover impossible to prove that the differences in mean performances of men and women are the result of biology rather than education and training.
3. Women's jobs are not particularly healthful; on the contrary, many conditions to which working women are exposed are dangerous for their health.
4. Working conditions that are used to justify the exclusion of women (exposure to pollutants, lifting of heavy weights) are also dangerous for male workers.

If the prevailing ideology has not deduced its myths from a knowledge of biology, they must come from another source. We can perhaps find their origin in the effect that the ideology has on the behaviour of women and men workers. For example, salaries in female employment ghettos are notoriously low; on the average, full-time women workers receive less than 60 per cent of the average man's salary.[37] Yet women are told that they should not try for the jobs that are more interesting and pay more, since these are not suitable for them; a "real" woman doesn't compete with men.

At the same time, men work in conditions of deafening noise, smothered with dust, exposed to the danger of fatal accidents. They are told that they are big and strong and able to "take" it; a "real" man doesn't cry.

In this way by keeping men and women in their respective ghettos, the employers can legitimise the exploitation of both women and men in interdependent ways.

REFERENCES

Acknowledgements — I would like to acknowledge the importance of conversations I have had with Donna Mergler, Monique Simard, Dominique LeBorgne, and Luc Desnoyers, and the assistance of Raymonde Pelletier.

1 Martin, C. Unpublished study drawn from data in *Statistics Canada* (Ottawa: Census of Canada, 1971).

2 Gaucher, D. "L'égalité des femmes: une lutte à finir". Master's thesis, Department of Sociology of Health, University of Montréal, 1979.

3 Desoille, H. Sherrer, J., and Truhaut, R. *Précis de médicine du travail.* Paris: Masson, 1978, p. 932.

4 Barnhart, C.L. ed. *The American College Dictionary*. New York: Random House, 1961.

5 Wyrick, W. "Biophysical Perspectives". In *The American Woman in Sport*, edited by E.W. Gerber et al. Reading, MA: Addison-Wesley, 1974.

6 Snook, S.M., and Ciriello, V.M. "Maximum Weights and Work Loads Acceptable to Female Workers". *J. Occup. Med.* 16: 527 - 534, 1974.

7 Chester, D. *The Olympic Games Handbook*. New York: Scribner, 1975.

8 Mergler, D., Vézina, N., Beauvais, A., and Everell, J. "Etude des effets des conditions de travail dans les abattoirs sur la santé des travailleurs et travailleuses". Confederation of National Trade Unions, Canada, 1980.

9 Statement given at the Annual Meeting of the Central Council of Haut-Rive of the Confederation of National Trade Unions, Baie-Comeau, Canada, October 18, 1980.

10 Hunt, V. *The Health of Women at Work*. Boca Raton, FL: CRC Press, 1978.

11 Garret, J. *Anthropometry of the Air Force Female Hand.* Aerospace Medical Research Laboratory, Aerospace Medical Division, Air Force Systems Command, Wright-Patterson Air Force Base, Ohio, 1970.

12 Tichauer, E.R. "Some Aspects of Stress on Forearm and Hand in Industry". *J. Occup. Med.* 8: 63 - 71, 1966.

13 Armstrong, T.J., and Chaffin, D.B. "Carpal Tunnel Syndrome and Selected Personal Attributes". *J. Occup. Med.* 21: 481 - 486, 1979.
14 Imbert, J.P. "Les aides optiques dans l'industrie électronique". In *International Colloquium on Vision and Work*, edited by G.E. Lambert. Rodez-Toulouse, 1978.
15 Teiger, C., Laville, A., Desors, D., and Gadbois, C. "Renseignements téléphoniques avec lecture de microfiches sous contrainte temporelle". Report No. 54. Laboratoire de Physiologie de Travail et Ergonomic, Paris, 1977.
16 Department of Health, Education and Welfare. *Characteristics of Persons with Corrective Lens*. Rockville, MD: DHEW Publ. No. (HRA) 75-1520, 1974.
17 Herschberger, R. *Adam's Rib*. New York: Harper and Row, 1948.
18 Gamberale, R., Strindberg, L., and Wahlberg, I. "Female Work Capacity During the Menstrual Cycle". *Scand. J. Work Envir. Health* 1: 120 - 127, 1975.
19 Ruble, D.N. "Premenstrual Symptoms: A Reinterpretation". *Science* 197: 291 - 292, 1977.
20 Vanck, J. "Time Spent in Housework". *Sci. Amer.* 231(5): 116 - 120, 1974.
21 Beauvais, A. "Les rythmes biologiques et le travail de nuit". Unpublished, 1975.
22 Brown, F.A. *Biological Clocks*. New York: Academic Press, 1970.
23 Briscoe, A.M. "Hormones and Gender". In *Genes and Gender*: I, edited by E. Tobach and B. Rosoff. New York: Gordian Press, 1978.
24 Ramey, E. "Men Do Have Monthly Cycles". *Ms. Magazine*, Spring 1972, pp. 8 - 14.
25 Bernier, C. *Le travail par équipes*. Bulletin No. 15, Institut de Recherche Appliquée sur le Travail, 1979.
26 Al-Aidroos, K. and Mergler, D. "La femme et la santé au travail". *Cahiers de la femme* 1: 86 - 87, 1979.
27 Scott, A.C. "Closing the Muscle Gap". *Ms. Magazine*, October 1979, p. 55.
28 Mamelle, N., Munoz, F., Collin, D., Charvet, F., and Lazar, P. *Fatigue professionnelle et prématurité. Unité de recherches épidémiologiques et statistiques sur l'environnement et la santé.* U-110, INSERM, Villeurbanne, France, 1981.
29 Shepard, T.H. *Catalog of Teratogenic Agents*, 3rd edition. Baltimore, MD: Johns Hopkins University Press, 1980.
30 Rawls, R.L., "Reproductive Hazards in the Work Place". *Chemical and Engineering News*, February 18, 1980, pp. 35 - 37.
31 Knill-Jones, R.P. et al. "Anaesthetic Practice and Pregnancy". *Lancet*, October 25, 1975, pp. 807 - 809.
32 Macht, S.H., and Lawrence, P.S. "Congenital Malformations from Exposure to Roentgen Radiation". *Am. J. Roentgen.* 73: 442 - 446, 1955.
33 Kapp, R. et al. "Y-Chromosomal Non-disjunction in Dibromochloropropane-exposed Workmen". *Mut. Res.* 64: 47 - 51, 1979.

34 Infante, P.F. et al. "Genetic Risks of Vinyl Chloride". *Lancet*, April 3, 1976, pp. 734 - 739.

35 Arbitration Hearing on the Case of Mme. Adrienne Robichaud, Before Judge Jean-Jacques Turcotte, Québec, 1980 - 1981.

36 Equal Employment Opportunity Commission. Decision 6443.

37 Conseil du Statut de la Femme du Québec. *Pour les Québécoises, Egalité et Indépendance*. Gouvernement du Québec, 1979.

FURTHER READING

Chavkin, W. (ed.) *Double Exposure*. New York: Monthly Review Press, 1984.

Chenier, N.M. *Reproductive Hazards at Work (Fécondité et milieu de travail)*. Ottawa: Canadian Advisory Council on the Status of Women, 1982.

DeKoninck, M. *La santé des travailleuses*. Ministère des affaires sociales, Québec, 1983.

Massachusetts Committee on Occupational Safety and Health and Women's Health Book Collective. *Our Jobs, Our Health*. Women's Health Book Collective, 465 Mount Auburn St., Waterdown, MA, USA, 1984.

Stellman, J. and Henifin, M.S. *Office Work Can Be Dangerous for Your Health*. New York: Pantheon, 1983.

PAT ARMSTRONG

Women's Work: Women's Wages

Women have always worked. Since Canada began, and long before, women have done what can be broadly defined as productive work.[1] They have planned and prepared meals, made, repaired and washed clothes, they have organised and cleaned the family living space, to name only some of the familiar female tasks. They have also performed what could be called the procreative work. They have borne, washed, cleaned, repaired and cared for the children. Both kinds of work have been and continue to be intimately connected, overlapping, mutually reinforcing, discouraging protest or escape. But women have seldom passively accepted the conditions of either job. Collectively and individually, they have resisted and transformed many aspects of women's work.

While men and women still do different kinds of work and while women still assume the primary responsibility for meals, clothes, housecleaning and children, revolutionary changes have resulted from developments in the economic structure, from the inter-relationship between women's productive and procreative work and from women's responses to these changes in both aspects of their job. The nature and condition of women's work, indeed the very definition of work, have been altered. The home has emerged as a separate institution as work has become socialised, as fewer people can produce within the household the goods they need for survival and as more and more must enter the market for the wages needed to purchase the necessities of daily living. Work is now defined as that which is done for pay or, infrequently, for profit. People may expend energy, get tired, complete tasks on a daily and regular basis; they may do things that are necessary for survival, things that can benefit themselves and others. But if this activity is not rewarded in monetary terms it is not considered work. This new definition reflects a new reality. It is no accident or misperception. Increasingly, money is necessary for survival and increasingly, money can be acquired only by selling the ability to work in return for a wage. The market has become the source of power, of control, of change, and thus it sets the conditions in our society. It establishes the broad outlines of what is possible, of what is real work.

Although some of women's traditional work is now carried out in a socialised way in the market, some of it continues to be done outside the market, at home, by women. Transformed by machinery, by new demands inside and outside the home and by women's own efforts to improve their lot, this unpaid domestic labour leaves many women exhausted but dependent on wage earners, doing tasks no longer defined as work. Whatever it is called, this productive and procreative work directly influences and limits women's entrance into the market, and helps ensure that most of those who do get paid jobs are restricted to women's work at women's wages. Nevertheless, as a result of the growing need for income, of the increasing market demand for female workers, of the mechanisation of some domestic chores, of women's resistance and of changing ideology, women have been flooding into the labour force.

This chapter is about the jobs and pay women get in the labour force, and about the possibilities for change. Only by placing this work within an historical context, only by looking at both women's productive work and procreative work, only by examining, however briefly, the economic, social and biological factors that keep women in their place, only by recalling women's resistance to those factors that limit their choices can we understand, and alter, the position of women. And only then can we understand the enormous effort required to bring about change.

Clearly this is an ambitious task, impossible in any comprehensive way in these short pages. Furthermore, the job is complicated not only by the scarcity of research material but also by regional and class differences amongst women, differences which themselves have a history. Canada has not, and does not, develop from sea to sea at the same pace. Viewing western Canada in the early part of this century, "a student of the growth of institutions",[2] Elizabeth Mitchell, described the great variations evident even within short distances.

> In this study something more is now possible than mere guesses, for a generation has passed since cities began to be born in the West, and they are still being born; so one can watch the whole development of the Industrial Revolution and the Nineteenth Century displayed not in a series of years, but in a circuit of communities; one can pass from the newly-settled country township, forty miles from the railway, where nearly everything has to be home-made, through the successive stages of the prairie village, the railway divisional point, and the infant city with its great ambitions, on to the city of brick and stone, established but

hardly secure, like Saskatoon, Regina, Edmonton, or Calgary; and so finally to great Winnipeg, throned triumphant between the New and the Old.[3]

While the regions have converged somewhat in more recent times, economic and social differences remain, and this historical legacy is reflected in the lives of women. And, while regional variations may have diminished, class differences may have become more exaggerated. According to Mitchell, in the early west,

the richest families have but one servant, and are lodged in brick three storey villas; the husband works at his business, the wife is busy in the house working with her hands.[4]

Social and structural distinctions existed, but women shared a common job even if paid help lightened the burden for some. But already, in the more "advanced" east,

conditions there were more like ours at home, there is competition and underpayment among women workers, and there is a class of women of leisure and cultivation.[5]

Such class and regional differences amongst women cannot be ignored. However, space and resources do not permit adequate treatment of them here. Moreover, most women still do domestic labour, whatever their class or region. And now a majority also hold labour force jobs. This chapter is about the work and lives of most women, but such generalisations necessarily leave out some important distinctions amongst even this working majority.

THE PIONEER PERIOD

Until the turn of the century, most Canadians lived in rural areas, primarily on farms. The pioneer life, fast disappearing in southern-central Canada, was still dominant in many parts of the west and north. Most goods were produced within the household by men, women and children. The work of "feeding and clothing and cheering husband and children"[6] fell to the women. In *The Canadian Settler's Guide*, published in 1855, Catherine Parr Traill drew on her experiences as a gentleman's wife in southern Ontario, to offer

the most approved recipes of cooking certain dishes, the usual mode of manufacturing maple-sugar, soap, candles, bread and other articles of household expenditure; in short, whatever subject is in any way connected with the management of a Canadian settler's house, either as regards economy or profit, I have introduced into the work for the benefit of the future settler's wife and family.[7]

Since she wrote her book for "all classes, and more particularly for the wives and daughters of the small farmers, and part of it is also addressed to the wives of the labourer and mechanic",[8] it is clear that most women were required to know how to grow everything from apples to corn to poultry and pumpkins, to make everything from beer and carpets to soap and wool, to handle everything from ague and dysentery to funerals and letters home. That this was highly skilled labour is also evident in the 1830 - 40s journals of *A Gentlewoman in Upper Canada*. A description of bread baking alone testifies to the wide-ranging talents of women at that time.

Baking is almost a daily operation but not such a troublesome one in Mary's hands as it was with our former bakers. The usual plan in this country is to mix flour with warm salt and water and set it by the fire to rise. But it must be carefully watched, the temperature must be kept even, no easy matter in cold weather. They usually put their vessel within another closed vessel of warm water, but then it requires great attention, for if the fermentation is too long delayed it becomes sour. Moreover, whenever the right degree of fermentation is attained, then and there you must mix your loaf at whatever inconvenient season it may happen to occur. If the operation is successful, you have a very good bread, but there is great uncertainty in it.[9]

Candlemaking, dress and shoe making, upholstering, soldering, shaping hams, preserving strawberries and meat, teaching children to read and write, and nursing the ill regularly appear in these journals as challenging tasks requiring constant experimentation and development.

Such skills were visible, recognised. In these same journals, Anne Langton describes a woman as "a capital help-mate for a backwoodsman, for she can do the work of a man, as well as her own domestic duties."[10] The household could not survive without womanpower, as feminist Nellie McClung's tart but telling story of life in an historically later but economically similar period in the early west makes clear.

I remember once attending the funeral of a woman who had been doing the work for a family of six children and three hired men and she had not even a baby carriage to make her work lighter. When the last baby was three days old, just in threshing time, she died. Suddenly, and without warning, the power went off, and she quit without notice. The bereaved husband was the most astonished man in the world. He had never known Jane to do a thing like that, and he could not get over it. In threshing time too!

"I don't know what could have happened to Jane — a strong young woman like her," he said over and over again.

We all gathered at the house that afternoon and paid our respects to the deceased sister, and we were all very sorry for poor Ed. We said it was a terrible way for a poor man to be left.[11]

As Elizabeth Mitchell saw it, such evident and skilled contributions to the family's survival encouraged an egalitarian relationship between husband and wife.

On the prairie the woman is the true partner as well as the wife, both in making the home and in helping with useful details about the farm — poultry, butter, etc. Sometimes she supplies useful booklearning, having "taught school" before her marriage. There is no question at all of inequality, the partners have their several departments, equally important, and the husband is the first to admit how much he owes his wife, and to own that the burden falls on her heaviest.[12]

Since a pioneering woman was "most able and competent, she applies her brains to housework, and also she has a tradition of how to do things best with simple apparatus",[13] "at the end, whatever her suffering and labours, at any rate she is not a drudge, but a strong and generous personality".[14]

The kind of pride and sense of challenge created by such skilled labour is everywhere evident in Anne Langton's journals. After a long day of household chores, she reports she "came back with the strengthened conviction of the importance of woman".[15] Two days later, "we were both bakers and butchers, and the exercise of two such important callings filled up our morning". In another letter she wrote, "I am going to exercise my skill in shaping ham tonight. That I consider my special province".[16] It is perhaps difficult in these days of corner stores and mass-produced rubber bread for us to understand her recording that "the most comfortable thing today is that I have a very nice baking, and there is nothing that affects the spirits more than the well or ill rising of your bread".[17]

But all was not rosy down on the farm, in the backwoods of Canada. While the work was highly skilled and clearly visible, it was long and hard and often lonely and frightening as well. Traill wrote her settler's guide precisely because she knew just how disastrous, especially for the new immigrant women, life in early Canada could be.

Disheartened by repeated failures, unused to the expedients which older inhabitants adopt in any case of difficulty, repining and disgust take the place of cheerful activity; troubles increase, and the power to overcome them decreases; domestic happiness disappears. The woman toils on heartsick and pining for the home she left behind her. The husband reproaches his heartbroken partner, and both blame the Colony for the failure of the individual.[18]

The usually cheerful and incredibly energetic Anne Langton writes that "woman is a bit of a slave in this country".[19] Such constant labour takes its toll and, while women's work is not obviously essential, Langton speculates that the future will reduce the workload but devalue women in the process.

I am afraid women deteriorate in this country more than the other sex. As long as the lady is necessarily the most active member of her household she keeps her ground from her utility; but when the state of semi-civilization arrives, and the delicacies of her table, and the elegances of her person become her chief concern and pride, then she must fall, and must be contented to be looked upon as belonging merely to the decorative department of the establishment and valued accordingly.[20]

She seems to have predicted Betty Friedan's problem with no name.

Even Elizabeth Mitchell, who was convinced that labouring side by side created equality between the sexes, felt that women on the farm had an extra burden to bear.

The absence of women neighbours, the impossibility of getting a hired girl to help in times of weakness, and the impossibility of affording doctor's visits are serious things for a woman and this is where the pioneer suffers, no matter how kind and helpful the husband may be.[21]

With little assistance from doctors or other women, "Many a woman dies and many a baby dies, and some lose their health and bloom".[22] Both husbands and wives worked hard to produce the things the family required for survival but it was the addition of women's other job, the bearing and rearing of children, that ensured the load was heavier, more frightening, more lonely, more dangerous and, in the end, unequal for women.

Little information on sex, birth control, pregnancy and birth, little assistance from doctors, midwives or even neighbours, made intercourse, pregnancy, birth or illness frightening and lonely experiences for women and separated them clearly and unmistakably from men. Children were essential to the household production unit. Indeed, one authority claimed that the major factor distinguishing a successful from a failed farmer was the presence of children.[23] In keeping with this economic need and the morality of the time, the law forbade abortion, the distribution of birth control devices or even the dissemination of information on contraception. And, in spite of living on a farm, many women knew little about the "facts of life". As Nellie McClung asked, "Innocence has been esteemed a young girl's greatest charm, but what good has her innocence done her?"[24] Alone on the prairie or in the backwoods of Canada, such innocence could only be frightening and dangerous. Amongst the fascinating collection of letters, diaries and interviews in *A Harvest Yet to Reap*, is one woman's description of the consequences for a western pioneer woman of inadequate information, even for those who had some knowledge of the ways of the world.

> Despite the fact that I had always regarded myself as a very modern young woman, and had known about most of the "facts of life" long before I was married, I actually knew little or nothing about the physical phenomena of human pregnancy and birth.
>
> I had no intimate friends at the time from whom to seek advice or sympathy, so that, as the time passed and my condition became physically apparent, I began to feel very bewildered, and sometimes terribly frightened, at the prospect of what was going to happen to me. I knew moments of almost breathless happiness and anticipation, but there were also long periods of intense discomfort, boredom and fear.[25]

For many the fear was rationally based, as most women knew at least one woman who had died, lost her child or been permanently injured in childbirth. Once again, Nellie McClung made the point well.

> "I can tell you" says Brother Bones, "my mother knew something about rearing children; she raised seven and buried seven, and she never lay in bed more than three days with any of them. Poor mother, she was a very smart woman — at least so I have been told — I don't remember her."[26]

Little access to birth control meant it was difficult to separate sex from procreation; high infant and maternal mortality rates meant pregnancy and birth were life-threatening processes; inadequate information and assistance meant even greater fear and danger; laws ensuring male property rights meant that married women were dependent on men. Under such conditions, whatever women's obvious and visible contributions, they cannot have been equal to men.

Of course, women's responsibility for procreation did not end with giving birth, or even with breast feeding. In his study of Canadian children, Neil Sutherland argues that "traditionally, in the home work-shop, in the small family business, and on the family farm, children grew up under the eyes of both their parents".[27] Since the household was a production unit, fathers were usually there all day every day. Thus, "as their youngster became old enough to join in the work of the household, such fathers gradually assumed an increasing share of the responsibility for rearing and educating them".[28] From an early age, children not only learned from their parents and assisted them with farm chores, they also helped take care of the younger children.

Women's child-care work was lightened too by the not infrequent presence of other relatives or a hired "girl". Nevertheless, women still bore primary responsibility for infants and for the children not well enough to work. As one western pioneer explained,

> I used a lot of home remedies. The first thing I did when I went on the homestead was to pay $10 for a doctor book. And all those little ailments children get, I took care of, because we lived 15 miles from town and travelled by horses. When you had sick children, you could kill them just by taking them on that trip.[29]

This too was women's work and separated them from the men.

Women's work was heavy. They not only contributed directly to daily survival of the family but bore and reared the next generation as well. While their productive work encouraged an egalitarian relationship with men, the conditions of their procreative work and the laws of the land prevented the realisation of this possibility. But women did not simply go passively about their daily chores, accepting the inevitability of the work and the inequality. The suffragist movement, the women's institutes, the co-operative societies and the numerous other reform organisations, the demands not only for the vote but also for changes in the conditions of birth, breast feeding and sexual relationships, for access to educational institutions and decent paid employment were visible before this century began. These collective actions of women have recently been carefully documented, and space does not allow an adequate exploration here.

Such organised resistance was more common in more settled and developed sections of the country. For many of the women isolated on family farms, there was little time or possibility for taking large-scale collective action. Nevertheless, individually, and with the assistance of some other women, they did fight to improve their lot. Nellie McClung illustrates these efforts by telling a story about

> one of the women of the old days, who arose at four o'clock in the morning, and aroused all her family at an indecently early hour for breakfast, her reason being that she wanted to get "one of those horrid old meals over". This woman had never been to a suffrage meeting — so where did she get the germ of discontent?[30]

Not only did they resist their productive work but their procreative job as well. In *A Harvest Yet to Reap*, a woman's letter to her mother explains how to make a fudge-like contraceptive. She goes on to relate a story of another woman who actively but invisibly fought both her husband and her body.

> I knew a woman in Buffalo who had a dear friend. She had a mean jealous hus-

band. They had two girls and he made his brag that he'd see that his wife never got the chance to run around. Said there would be kids in his house every year. He'd keep his brag. This was twenty-five years ago and those things weren't so popular so she said she'd fix him. So she took a good-sized piece of sponge and soaked it with soap suds and put it up next to the uterus. It worked for her and he never knew. As soon as she could do so, without arousing his suspicions she would take it out and douche.[31]

Of course, not all such resistance, either collective or individual, was successful. Although women clearly made some gains, changing economic conditions as well as male responses altered both the basis for some resistance and converted some successes into losses. Universities, for instance, did begin opening their doors to women, but women were free to take up these opportunities in part because they had lost their productive work in the household, and the selection of a few women for these honours served to emphasise the class differences amongst women. Votes for women of property had a similar effect. Declining fertility and maternal and infant mortality rates also reflected the success of women's efforts, but they were accompanied by an increase in women's child-rearing responsibilities. By the end of the century, the frontier was rapidly disappearing. So was women's most skilled productive work in the home. Their position, relative to that of men, showed little if any sign of improvement. Much changed, but much remained the same.

UNTIL WORLD WAR TWO

The family farm — men, women and children working together to provide for most of the family's needs was the dominant scene in turn of the century Canada. But not for long. Land was increasingly scarce, increasingly expensive. Machinery was replacing labour on the farm and producing cheap goods for sale in the market. There was a growing demand for workers in the urban industry and a declining demand in rural areas. Cut off from the means of producing directly what they needed for survival, more and more people had to sell their ability to work, to get a job that paid a wage. Compulsory education, itself a reflection of industrial growth, also removed the children from the home.

Of course, some people had been working for wages long before the twentieth century began. Recent immigrants and those without access to or knowledge of farming or crafts either sought employment in canal and railroad construction, in the factories and shops which were rapidly springing up particularly in Central Canada, or worked for others on the land, in the timber trade and in the households. Exactly how many women had entered the labour force is difficult to determine, but it is clear that many who were not members of household production units were forced onto the market. An 1876 article in the *Christian Guardian* pointed out that

a considerable number of unmarried females, to say nothing of poor widows, must, therefore, exist in every country, who are without fortune or friends, or any means of support but their own industry.[32]

While most of the women counted as part of the labour force at that time were single, many married women also contributed to the cash income of the family. In her report on the "Conditions of Female Labour in Ontario, 1889", Jean Scott Thomas wrote that:

In canning factories, during the summer months, numbers of married women may be found; many work in laundries; and in a mill stock factory (preparing rags for shoddy mills) visited by the writer most of the women were married. Market gardening is a means of subsistence to some. Women whose husbands are dead or are not able to support them, will not go out as long as they have children at home to care for, but prefer if they can, to engage in some work which will keep them at home. Women in poor circumstances go out washing and ironing to private homes or else take it home to do. In many cases they take in sewing or dressmaking, and do tailoring for the wholesale trade at their homes.[33]

Fewer married women than either married men or single women sought employment because they were tied to the household by their child-care responsibilities, because they could earn some cash income from their work in the home — washing, ironing, sewing, gardening and taking in boarders — and because there was still an enormous amount of women's work to do in the home. To be sure, new equipment was relieving some of the most burdensome aspects of domestic labour. Indeed, one early twentieth century writer explained the attraction of the city for the farm girl primarily in terms of the modern household conveniences available there.

The girl has seen her mother give the best years of her life in rearing a large family of children, while running at the same time a boarding house and laundry for her husband and two or three hired men. The girl has been to visit friends in the city perhaps. She has opened her eyes in astonishment at the many labour saving conveniences with which the house was supplied. The hot and cold water system, bathroom, gas range, refrigerator, furnace, and other such accessories that seem so much of a necessity in town and yet are almost wholly lacking in the majority of country homes, fill her with a longing to live in a place where such devices are obtainable.[34]

But at the turn of the century, such modern conveniences were only beginning to be available in most households. Moreover, their appearance coincided with a reduction in household staff. The men were out at work, the children at school and female domestics were increasingly rejecting household service in favour of the greater freedom offered by work in industry. Married women, particularly mothers, usually had more than enough work to do handling the household alone.

Only a minority of Canadians sought labour force jobs in the nineteenth century, but as the developments first felt in urban central Canada spread throughout the land, more and more people needed incomes to buy food, clothing, shelter and the other items now so necessary in the town. While dramatic changes were taking place in the structure of the economy, however, little change occurred in the kind of work performed by women entering the labour force. In 1899, most women who worked for pay were domestics, dressmakers or milliners, factory hands in textile, food-processing and wearing apparel industries, saleswomen, waitresses, clerical workers, teachers and nurses. By the outbreak of the First World War, "employment for women as domestics, waitresses, practical nurses, cooks, teachers, nurses, secretaries, and within the garment and textile industries accounted for over 85 per cent of the female jobs".[35] Doing women's work, they also received women's wages. Even when women were allowed to do the same work as men, they were paid less, as a contemporary article made clear.

> These women, working side by side of the male labourers, battling with the same physical struggles, full of the same higher aspirations, the value of the world's market of exchange being equal, find they receive from one-third to one-half less wages, doing the same work with as much skill as their brother workers.[36]

Various explanations were offered at the time for the ghettoisation of women and for their lower wages.

> One labour organization suggested, "We think that women should not be allowed to work in the foundaries, as it has a tendency to degrade them, to lower the wages of the men and to keep a number of young men out of work".[37]

Both employers and male workers were instrumental in restricting women to certain occupations because in this way they would not compete with men, but female wages could be kept down through the competition of women with women. "Again, women's wages are cheaper, because she labours too much in a few occupations".[38] Although some analysts were convinced that "the inferior physical strength of women of necessity almost always tells against them",[39] they also recognised that the purpose of hiring women to do unskilled labour was "of course to cheapen the cost of production''.[40] Indeed, men feared women's employment precisely because in cigar making, telegraphy and teaching ''one result of the competition of women is the lowering of salaries''.[41] When unions did insist on equal pay for women, ''the employers prefer to hire men, because they are likely to remain in the business longer''.[42] It was women's job at home, especially their child-care work, that was seen as a barrier to equal work and equal pay. So was their exclusion from training for certain trades and professions and their legal inequality. Meanwhile the demand for women workers grew. ''The very fact of there being a number of employments requiring unskilled labour has led, no doubt, to the increased employment of young girls and women''.[43] And the demand grew just as more and more women required money to survive. In the end, all these factors combined to lock them into women's work at women's wages.

By the beginning of the Second World War, most men and one in five women were officially counted as members of the labour force, and virtually all young children were in school. Home emerged as a separate institution, as a unit secondary to the market on which most members depended for survival. Money became more and more necessary to pay the mortgage, the taxes, the heating bill, in short for all the ''conveniences'' required by health, the structure of the market, and the law. Goods previously produced in the household were more cheaply and conveniently available in the market for cash. Husbands, children and servants were no longer available to perform the largely unskilled tasks that remained. Home was where most women worked, alone except for the very young. They were unwaged and unrecognised as workers.

Women's procreative work was changing as well. Birth control and abortion were still illegal but the ''combination of large-scale immigration from Southern Europe and the casualties of the First World War stimulate[d] widespread alarm over birth and mortality rates'',[44] and resulted in government and private programmes designed to change the conditions of childbirth and child rearing. More mothers and babies survived childbirth. These children were, however, no longer economic assets but liabilities as household production declined and as compulsory education took children for much of the day. Moreover, health standards and child-care practices greatly increased the work of child rearing just as the husbands, children and servants who had previously assisted in the work disappeared from the home. Child care became exclusively the mother's responsibility for the first time. The scarcity and high cost of child-care facilities, the hours and regulations of school, ensured that most women were confined to the household — excluded from full participation in the labour market — while their children were young. And these developments ensured that women remained unequal in and out of the labour force.

But once again, women were active in responding to and influencing the changes that did take place. Women organised across the country in such large bodies as the National Council of Women of Canada, The Imperial Order of the Daughters of the Empire, Women's Institutes, The Young Women's Christian Association, the Women's Christian Temperance Union, in smaller clubs to study art, music and travel, in associations related to such occupations as nursing and teaching, in trade unions and in missionary societies.[45] Broadly concerned with social and intellectual inequality, their causes seemed endless. An early report of the National Council of Women listed among its achievements the introduction of manual training and domestic science in primary schools, women factory inspectors, special provision for women in the Factory Act, the appointment of women to school boards, improved conditions for women prisoners, charities for the "distressed" and unemployed, cooking schools, the establishment of hospitals and the Victorian Order of Nurses, health talks for mothers, enquiries into the circulation of "Impure literature", the working conditions for women, the "Care and Treatment of the Aged Poor", "the Better Care and Wiser Distribution of Women Immigrants", in addition to laws to protect women and children and animal and bird life.[46] Such women's organisations also fought for access to higher education, the vote, housing and other forms of moral and sanitary protection for working women, the elimination of prostitution and venereal disease as well as better care for mothers and infants. And they were successful in many instances, although seldom simply because of their own efforts. Women did enter the universities, the vote was granted, infant and maternal mortality rates were reduced, protective legislation for women was introduced. And women did manage, in spite of restrictions on birth control, to lower the birth rate dramatically.

It was however, basically a middle- and upper-class movement. As M. MacMurchy pointed out in her 1916 article about these women's organisations,

> the need of this middle-aged, married woman for work and social co-operation, her impulse is to help others and accomplish something worth doing in the world outside, are the forces that have created the women's organizations.[47]

Because these organisations were dominated by such women, they abandoned in the end the call for equality and independence in favour of a special place for women, for a glorification of motherhood and homemaking. Wayne Roberts' study of the period leads him to conclude that

> the moralistic and maternal tangent of the new women's reform thinking became aligned with conservative notions of social order in conjunction with another social process; the conversion of the lives of upper-class matrons from the ones of ostentatious idleness to one of overseers of a social spring cleaning.[48]

With their focus on the provision of social services and on the mothering work of all women, the effects of their efforts were frequently the further cementing of unequal conditions. Protective legislation, requiring special lunchrooms, washrooms and hours for women, often either encouraged the hiring of women only or discouraged employers from hiring women at all. Women graduated in medicine, journalism, and law, but female doctors specialising in the care of women and children in separate hospitals, journalists producing women's pages crammed with fashions and recipes, and lawyers working on family law did little to alter the segregation. According to Wayne Roberts,

> women professionals were systematically shunted into specialized job ghettos which reaffirmed their subordination rather than autonomy in the world of work.[49]

Working to protect especially the maternal destiny of employed women, these organisations frequently emphasised the class differences amongst women. In a letter to a newspaper, one worker complained,

> "Our society is overflooded with such societies," she continued, "the so-called Christian workers, in many instances are like a lot of children at play. The results are invisible.[50]

The class differences were also evident in the formation and activites of trade unions. The women who worked in the factories and telephone offices did not have the time or energy to become involved in national women's organisations, but many were active participants in strikes. Although women did not develop sustained leadership in the union movement — a fact that may be primarily attributable to both their segregated jobs and their other work at home — they did gain some direct if limited benefits from their union work. Some improvements in hours and working conditions resulted from their strike action, but few were able to gain equal wages for work of equal value.

On the eve of the Second World War, Canada was a fundamentally different place than it had been at the turn of the century. Most men and single women left the household every day to work in the labour market, most married women did unpaid work in the now-separate home, most children were in school. Most goods were produced and purchased in the market, which became the locus of power, prestige and control. Women's domestic labour became increasingly secondary, isolated, unskilled and invisible. Those women who also worked in the labour force did similar kinds of work, segregated into the least-skilled, lowest-paid jobs. Women resisted both the changes and the lack of change, but their successes were often contradictory, often further locking them into women's work and emphasising the class differences amongst women. However, by the end of this period, housework was easier for most women, clothes were more comfortable, births were easier, children less frequent and healthier, women had more legal and political rights. Nevertheless, most continued to do women's work at women's wages, or no wages at all.

UNTIL NOW

The war years were an abberation. The government recruited first single, then married women without children, and finally married women with children into the labour force by appealing to their patriotic sentiments and by providing day care centres, tax concessions, part-time work and short-term contracts that permitted job change and work close to home.[51] Although women clearly demonstrated that they could perform virtually every job in the labour force, and although research at the time indicated that most women took paid employment for economic rather than patriotic reasons,[52] their widespread participation was short-lived. Since the government defined their recruitment as an emergency measure only and since returning soldiers needed jobs, the women were sent home by changing the tax laws, by closing the day care centres, by introducing family allowances to encourage the expansion of families, and by making it illegal for any married woman to keep a government job if there was a man available to do the work — first an affirmative, then a negative, action programme for women. At the beginning of the war, only a quarter of the women fourteen years of age and over were in the labour force; in the last year of the war, a third of them were there. Just one year later, the female participation rate dropped back to its pre-war level,[53] as many women disappeared again into the home.

But they did not stay there for long. The baby boom, the prosperity of the post-war years that allowed most men to get jobs and relatively decent wages, the disincentive programmes and the ideology of motherhood kept married women out of the labour force for a while. But as unemployment rates rose, as wages failed to keep pace with prices, as fewer and fewer goods made in the home could be substituted for goods purchased in the market, as more money was needed to pay things like mortgages, taxes and heating oil that could not be made at home, as technology in the home made housework lighter, as more women obtained higher education, as birth rates plummeted, married women moved into the labour market to search for paid work. Since the end of the war, women's labour force participation rates have more than doubled. More than twice as many of them have a paid job or want one. During the same period, their unemployment rate has more than tripled, passing that of men. The proportion employed part-time has increased enormously. By 1984, more than half of Canadian women were in the labour force, but more than one in ten of them failed to find any job at all, and a quarter found only part-time work.[54] Only a third of all women over fifteen years of age hold a full-time paid job. And it is clear that these figures, as dramatic as they may seem, underestimate the numbers of women who would seek such jobs under other conditions. While the majority of women want and need full-time work, only a minority find such employment, and an increasing number are unemployed or under-employed.

The typical paid worker is no longer male, and the typical female is no longer a full-time housewife. She lasted for less than half a century. However, while the changes for women have been in many ways dramatic, the jobs they do now are not all that different from those they did at the turn of the century. In and out of the labour force, women scrub floors, serve food, make beds, mind children, make coffee and clothes, answer the phone and generally wait on people.

One-third of all employed women do clerical work. A few of these women are traditional secretaries performing multiple skilled tasks but many more file, key punch, handle telephone calls, sort mail or clerk in a bank all day. In fact, many of the women who have been touted as moving into such male preserves as construction and primary industries are not pouring concrete or felling trees but typing, filing or mailing letters. Although clerical work has increasingly become women's work, the jobs in this area are decreasing as the new technology substitutes machines for workers. The occupational category that has provided a job for one out of every three employed women is becoming increasingly female, increasingly part-time, and increasingly threatened by the new machinery.

Between one-fifth and one-sixth of all employed women do service work. This broad category includes waitresses, domestics, hairdressers, hospital workers, child-care and educational workers, cooks, janitors and building superintendents. Since many of the women who take in other people's children, scrub floors in other people's homes and do hair on the side are not recorded in the official statistics, the actual number of women doing the worst jobs in this occupational group is probably significantly underestimated. Moreover, since 1975, women have become the majority of people officially counted as doing this work. In other words, more and more women are cooking, cleaning, minding children, looking after the sick and elderly than ever before.

It is true that the two highest-paid and most prestigious jobs for women — teaching and nursing — are found in this occupational category, but when the statistics are examined in greater detail, the news is not good. There are more women factory workers than teachers, and few new full-time teaching jobs are being created. Over the last several years, women have been losing ground in teaching to men but gaining some of the janitorial work in return. There are more female salesworkers than nurses, but women have been capturing most of the new hospital jobs. Unfortunately, a high proportion of these jobs were part-time, and a smaller proportion of women were doing this work in 1983 than had been the case in 1975. The jobs in teaching and nursing are also threatened, not so much by the new technology as by cutbacks in government spending and the declining birth rates.

One out of every ten women with a paid job does sales work, selling candies, underwear and groceries, not fridges, cars and stocks. When these workers are added to all the women doing clerical and service work, over 60 per cent of all employed women are accounted for. Sales work too has become increasingly female and increasingly part-time. Here there has been a decline in the number of full-time males and a substitution of part-time females.

About 8 per cent of women work in factories — packing fruits and vegetables, cleaning fish and chickens, making clothes and sorting paper — but the jobs in durable manufacturing are still primarily male. Factories remain highly sex-segregated, and women continue to do work that is very similar to the jobs they had at the turn of the century.

Not only are they still doing women's work, they are still getting women's wages. In 1981, the average earned income for male employees working 50 - 52 weeks was $22,734 while female employees working similar weeks averaged $13,382. Seventy-one per cent of employed women, but only 35 per cent of employed men, earned less than $15,000 a year in 1981. The potential average lifetime earnings of a female university graduate (even if other factors like the interruption of her employment because of domestic responsibilities are taken into account) are equal to those of a male high school graduate.[55] Those earning minimum wage are mostly women. And of course, the growth in part-time female work also means that women earn less. Perhaps even more depressing is the fact that such figures fail to take into account the exaggeration of these inequalities in pensions, unemployment insurance, vacations and sick leave that are based on hours and pay. Women still do women's work at women's wages.

And women continue to do the domestic labour. There have been fundamental changes in household production: almost all Canadian homes have hot and cold running water, refrigerators, stoves, indoor flush toilets and central heating, and even though only a minority also have other labour-saving devices like dishwashers, conveniences have lightened many of the household chores. Few goods are produced in the home today and thus the bread baking, gardening and butchering that took so much of the pioneer woman's time no longer dominate the domestic chores. The legalisation of birth control, medical advances, medicare and free compulsory education mean that fewer children are born, more survive and their education and illnesses are handled primarily by experts outside the home rather than by unpaid mothers. Household work has not, however, been eliminated. Food purchased in the market still has to be cooked and served before it can be consumed, dishes still have to be washed, clothes bought and cleaned, floors scrubbed and beds made, children taken to school and appointments made and kept at the doctor's. Indeed, infant and early childhood care remain largely within the household unit, and childhood dependency, with its accompanying workload, has lengthened along with the increase in the years of compulsory schooling. There is little need to point out who still bears the responsibility for the remaining household chores, and for the new ones as well.

Even the most egalitarian-minded couples get locked into this division of labour. She has the baby and, as recent negotiations around maternity-leave benefits make clear, she must still bear most of the responsibility for procreation and its consequences. Given the scarcity and high cost of infant and child-care facilities, one parent is usually forced to stay home to look after the child or at least be prepared to interrupt their paid labour to accommodate the all-too-frequent interruptions in child-care arrangements. Childhood illnesses, doctor's appointments or heavy snow can interfere with the most careful plans. If one partner is to drop out of the labour force for the day, week or year, it only makes sense that the lower-income earner, almost always the woman, do so. Since she is home, it also makes sense for her to do most of the household chores, especially given that she is trained for the work and probably thinks it's her job anyhow. A new cycle begins. She takes part-time work because it is the work available and because it allows her to do her other job at home, a job that receives little support from men in the form of domestic labour or from the state and employers in the form of child-care facilities, full maternity benefits and protection, decent pay and job opportunities. When her child-care responsibilities diminish, her exclusion from the better full-time jobs is justified on the basis of her interrupted work patterns, her part-time work attributed to preference. She gets women's work at women's wages.

The post-war period has not only been a time of change, it has also been a time of struggle. The women's movement was born. We have had a Royal Commission, an International Women's Year, special government committees and advisors, abortion marches and day-care marches, women's centres and a women's press. Women have flooded into the labour force, collectively and individually demanding everything from access to the top jobs and non-traditional work to equal pay and a decent wage, from freedom from coffee making and sexual harassment to paid maternity leave and child-care centres. There have been many successes. Birth control and some abortion is now legal. Maternity benefits are now part of the unemployment insurance package, and employers cannot fire people because they are pregnant. Some day care centres have been established. Women have gained some property and legal rights, especially in marriage. Divorce is easier to obtain and some men help around the house. Some women's wages have improved, and a few women have made it into non-traditional jobs and executive positions.

However, these victories too have frequently had contradictory consequences for women. The promotion of some women suggests that the segregation of most women into the bottom jobs is the result of personal failure rather than structured inequality, and thus serves not only to justify the job ghettos but also to separate women further along class lines. The movement of so many women into the labour market has forced them into competition with each other and thus helped to lock them further into women's work. The juggling of two jobs makes it more difficult to do either well, and suggests that neither can be very important at the same time as it exhausts women and thus makes them too tired to continue the struggle. The falling birth rate and separation of intercourse from procreation have camouflaged the fact that there is still no effective and safe birth control, that prevention of conception is still a female responsibility and that the "new morality" has failed to liberate women in their sexual relationships with men.

Perhaps more depressing is the fact that many of the hard-won victories that have proved beneficial for women are in jeopardy. Women's paid jobs are threatened by the new technology, by cutbacks in public spending, by the increases in part-time employment, by their position as last hired and thus first fired and by the high unemployment rates of men. Expenditures on day care centres, women's centres, maternity wards and hospital care for everyone are being cut back or threatened, thus increasing women's work at home. Job loss, low pay and cutbacks in government services can only serve to reinforce women's domestic work and place those in the labour force in greater competition with each other, willing to take any job, for any pay, under any conditions. The so-called moral majority and anti-abortion campaigners are threatening the limited control women have gained over their bodies. Even clothes have become more delicate, more "feminine", requiring more restricted activities and more care.

Fewer and fewer women can and will escape the labour force. Economic need, fuelled by rising inflation, tax rates, and unemployment, falling wages, and the increasing inability of women to substitute domestic labour for wage labour, means that more and more are forced to seek jobs that pay. Only a small minority have the luxury of choice. Most of those who enter the labour force do so because they need the income; many of those who concentrate on their household work frequently do so either because they cannot find or afford child care or because there are no suitable jobs available to them. Through their active resistance, women have gained some control over their bodies and their employment opportunities. However, as we move through the 1980s, not only these gains but also the ability to resist are being undermined. The growth in demand for female workers has dropped off. Indeed, the electronic revolution is rapidly replacing women with new machines. Thus, more women will be competing for fewer and fewer jobs. The facilities that socialised some of the domestic work, especially day care and medical services, are slowly being withdrawn, thus increasing women's work in the home. The home, family and children, with mother the one responsible and responding, are central to the new morality, and even some new legislation. All of these trends will serve to perpetuate women's work at women's wages.

CONCLUSION

Women have always worked, have always been involved in production and procreation. Their position has been and continues to be set by their work, by one in relation to the other, and by their resistance to this work. And production, procreation and resistance all take place within the context of a changing economic structure. The economic conditions in Canada are fundamentally different from those of a mere hundred years ago. These conditions and women's response to them have dramatically altered women's work. At the end of the nineteenth century, most women were involved in a household unit that produced directly much of what was needed for survival; today most sell their ability to work for a wage which is then used to purchase what is needed for survival. Then, women had little choice over the number of children they carried, and many died in childbirth. Today most women have access to some birth control, and maternal mortality rates are low. The list could go on. There have been many changes, but much has remained the same. Women are still locked into their mutually reinforcing work in production and procreation; they are still doing women's work at women's wages, in spite of many years of resistance.

Now, more than ever, it is necessary for women to work together to change the nature of conditions of women's work, but now more than ever, the struggle will be difficult. Women must realise that we have a stake in how the economy, the technology, the government and the legislation are organised. Women must recognise that the attack must encompass both productive and procreative work: we must realise that women have won only what we are prepared to continue to fight for. Through unions, women must continue to organise the unorganised, and to work for better hours, pay and benefits for all workers. Those without union protection, especially the unemployed, not only suffer as individuals but also collectively pose a threat to everyone's job. Through unions, government and research, women must develop creative ways of dealing with the new technology. The electronic revolution holds out the possibility of lightening the load for everyone, but only if the new technology is used for this purpose rather than overwork for some and no work for others. Through research and government agencies, women must work to change the legislation as it relates to unemployment insurance, unionisation, minimum wage, vacations, pensions, hours, sexual harassment, divorce and property settlements, maternity wards and other government services, education and cutbacks in general. All this legislation, not just women's legislation, has profound consequences for women and their work at home and in the labour force. We have come a long way, but we still have a long way to go. Only if women continue to resist will they maintain their hard-won gains and perhaps even improve their future.

REFERENCES

1 "Productive work" is used here in a very broad sense to refer to all things that have use value. "Procreative work" is used to refer to the process of having and rearing children, as well as sexual activity in general. Neither term is very satisfactory, and there is a great deal of debate concerning appropriate terms. I have avoided using "reproductive" because it can be applied to processes undertaken by both sexes as well as by the economic system in general. See Wally Secombe, "Domestic Labour and the Working Class Household", pp. 26 - 99 in Bonnie Fox, ed., *Hidden in the Household* (Toronto: The Women's Press, 1980).

2 Elizabeth B. Mitchell, *In Western Canada Before the War* (Saskatoon, Saskatchewan: Western Producer Prairie Books, 1981), p. ix. First published 1915.

3 *Ibid.*, p. 110.

4 *Ibid.*, p. 8.

5 *Ibid.*, p. 155.

6 *Ibid.*, p. 47.

7 Catherine Parr Traill, *The Canadian Settler's Guide* (Toronto: McClelland and Stewart, 1969), p. xviii. First published 1855.

8 *Ibid.*, p. xviii.

9 H.H. Langton, ed., *A Gentlewoman in Upper Canada* (Toronto: Clarke, Irwin & Company, 1950), p. 46.

10 *Ibid.*, p. 49.

11 Nellie McClung, *In Times Like These* (Toronto: University of Toronto Press, 1972), p. 114. First published in 1915.

12 Mitchell, *op. cit.*, pp. 47 - 48.

13 *Ibid.*, p. 49.

14 *Ibid.*, p. 50.

15 Langton, *op. cit.*, p. 92.

16 *Ibid.*, p. 83.

17 *Ibid.*, p. 76.
18 Traill, *op. cit.*, p. xvii.
19 Langton, *op. cit.,* p. 95.
20 *Ibid.*, pp. 127 - 128.
21 Mitchell, *op. cit.*, p. 48.
22 *Ibid.*, p. 49.
23 Reported in Neil Sutherland, *Children in English Canadian Society* (Toronto: University of Toronto Press, 1976), p. 9.
24 McClung, *op. cit.*, p. 84.
25 Linda Rasmussen *et al.*, eds., *A Harvest Yet to Reap* (Toronto: The Women's Press, 1976), p. 74.
26 McClung, *op. cit.*, p. 118.
27 Sutherland, *op. cit.*, p. 23.
28 *Ibid.*, p. 23.
29 Rasmussen *et al., op. cit.*, p. 68.
30 McClung, *op. cit.*, p. 44.
31 Rasmussen *et al., op. cit.*, p. 72.
32 "Employment for Women", *Christian Guardian*, 1876, pp. 169 - 172 in Ramsey Cook and Wendy Mitchinson, eds., *The Proper Sphere* (Toronto: Oxford University Press, 1976), p. 169.
33 Jean Scott Thomas, "Conditions of Female Labour in Ontario, 1889", pp. 191 - 192 in Cook and Michinson, *ibid.*
34 "Modern Conveniences for the Farm", *Grain Grower's Guide, 1910,* pp. 191 - 192 in Cook and Michinson, *ibid.*, p. 191.
35 Ceta Ramkhalawansingh, "Women in the Great War", pp. 261 - 307 in Janice Acton, Penny Goldsmith and Bonnie Shepard, eds., *Women at Work, Ontario 1850 - 1930* (Toronto: Canadian Women's Educational Press, 1974), p. 266.
36 Minnie Phelps, "Unequal Pay for Unequal Work", 1890, pp. 182 - 186 in Cook and Mitchinson, *op. cit.*, p. 192.
37 Alice Klein and Wayne Roberts, "Besieged Innocence: The "Problem" and Problems of Working Women — Toronto 1896 - 1914", pp. 211 - 259 in Acton *et al., op. cit.*, p. 220.
38 Phelps, *op. cit.*, p. 184.
39 "A Western Farm Girl Demands Equality", *Grain Grower's Guide 1910,* pp. 116 - 118 in Cook and Mitchinson, *ibid.*, p. 118.
40 Thomas, *op. cit.*, p. 178.
41 *Ibid.*, p. 180.
42 *Ibid.*, p. 178.
43 *Ibid.*, p. 172.
44 Sutherland, *op. cit.*, p. 56.
45 Lady Aberdeen, "Achievements of the National Council of Women", 1898, pp. 203 - 205 in Cook and Mitchinson, *op. cit.*, p. 203.

46 Taken from *ibid.*, pp. 203 - 205.
47 M. MacMurchy, "Women's Organizations," 1916, pp. 216 - 223 in Cook and Mitchinson, *op. cit.*, p. 216.
48 Wayne Roberts, " 'Rocking the Cradle of the World': The New Woman and Maternal Feminism, Toronto 1877 - 1914", pp. 15 - 45 in Linda Kealey, ed., *A Not Unreasonable Claim* (Toronto: The Women's Press, 1979), p. 19.
49 *Ibid.*, p. 31.
50 Quoted in Klein and Roberts, *op. cit.*, p. 213.
51 Ruth Pierson, "Women's Emancipation and the Recruitment of Women into the Labour Force in World War II," pp. 125 - 145 in Susan Mann Trofimenkoff and Alison Prentice, eds., *The Neglected Majority* (Toronto: McClelland and Stewart, 1977), passim.
52 According to Ruth Pierson, *ibid.*, p. 135, "Of the women questions, 9% indicated patriotic motives, 59% 'desire to supplement family income', and 32% 'personal needs' " as their main reason for securing paid employment.
53 Pat Armstrong and Hugh Armstrong, *The Double Ghetto* (Toronto: McClelland and Stewart, 1978), p. 19.
54 All the figures used in this section are calculated from Statistics Canada, *The Labour Force* (Ottawa: Supply and Services) Cat. No. 71-001. The historical data can be found in Pat Armstrong and Hugh Armstrong, *A Working Majority* (Ottawa: Supply and Services, 1983) and in Pat Armstrong and Hugh Armstrong, *The Double Ghetto*, revised edition (Toronto: McClelland and Stewart, 1984).
55 See R.A. Holmes, "Male-Female Earnings Differentials in Canada", *Human Resources*, Vol. xi, No. 1 (Winter 1976), p. 114. The figures on annual wages are taken from Labour Canada, *Women in the Labour Force*, Part 2 (Ottawa: Supply and Services, 1984).

Note: Since economic development happened unevenly across Canada, the references do not always fall strictly into the time period under discussion but do belong to that economic period.

FURTHER READING

Acton, Janice, Penny Goldsmith and Bonnie Shepard (eds.), *Women at Work: Ontario 1850 - 1930*. Toronto: The Women's Press, 1974.

Armstrong, Pat, *Labour Pains: Women's Work in Crisis*. Toronto: The Women's Press, 1984.

Armstrong, Pat and Hugh Armstrong, *The Double Ghetto: Canadian Women and Their Segregated Work*. Revised Edition. Toronto: McClelland and Stewart, 1984.

Kealey, Linda (ed.), *A Not Unreasonable Claim: Women and Reform in Canada*. Toronto: The Women's Press, 1979.

Trofimenkoff, Susan Mann and Alison Prentice (eds.), *The Neglected Majority*. Toronto: McClelland and Stewart, 1977.

STAN GRAY

Sharing the Shop Floor

On October 25, 1983, a group of women factory workers from Westinghouse came to the United Steelworkers hall in Hamilton, Ontario. They spoke to one of the forums on Affirmative Action sponsored by the Ontario Federation of Labour.

The women told about decades of maltreatment by Westinghouse. They were first confined to job ghettoes with inferior conditions and pay. Later, when their "Switchgear" plant shut down, they fought to be transferred to the other Westinghouse plants in the city. They had to battle the obstruction of management which wanted to exclude women. Some of their brothers in the shop resisted as well, but others helped them out. They won, but when the recession hit, they were systematically weeded out, laid off regardless of seniority and left with little or no income protection in their senior years.

THE CHALLENGE

I have worked at Westinghouse for the past 10 1/2 years and have gone through the various battles for workplace equality. As I listened to the women that night, I thought of how much their coming into our plant had changed myself, my fellow workers and brother unionists. One way unions can improve in this area is for male unionists self-critically to review these events and learn from the achievements and errors made along the way.[1]

The Westinghouse women had to come on their own behalf. The male staff officials of their union had blocked the women's committee of the Labour Council from presenting their brief. They claimed it was inaccurate, since the problems weren't really that bad and, at any rate, the brief didn't credit these male officials with leading the fight for the women's rights. But the women's committee refused to include their rewritten and sanitised version.

Originally published in *Canadian Dimension,* Volume 18, No. 2, June 1984.

And so the Westinghouse women had to come and tell their own story first-hand. When that union did give a brief of its own, it presented a theoretical and historical discussion of male-female relations and situated it in the context of the global class struggle...making no reference to Westinghouse or Hamilton or any women it represented. In fact it was a genereal research report prepared elsewhere for other purposes and handed in at the last moment.

This kind of thing has happened in other cities and with other unions. It indicates that the official union support for affirmative action is a bit deceptive. The policy briefs and unanimous convention resolutions tend to mask a male resistance within the unions and on the shop floor that doesn't surface publicly.

Too many men pay lip service to the battle against sexism and leave all the real fighting to the women. I was one of those unionists who for years sat on the fence on these matters until certain sharp events at work pushed me off the fence. I then had to take the rhetoric very seriously and try to deal fully with these issues in practice.

Male unionists have to confront chauvinism openly with their brothers in the shop and in the labour movement. This is needed in order to give meaningful help in the fight for sexual equality.

But it is important for another reason: sexism is harmful to working men. It runs counter to their interests and undermines male trade unionism. The progressive men in labour have to speak up and say so, analyse the various aspects of chauvinism in their own way and speak to the men about it from a male perspective. The process of seriously grappling with these issues has made many men better unionists.

The following chapter therefore focusses on the men rather than on the women's battle, tells about the debates and struggles among the men on the shop floor at Westinghouse. It tries concretely to bring out the men's issue and the male interest in the fight against sexism.

MY EDUCATION

My education on the problems of the Switchgear women began in November 1978 when I was recalled to work after a layoff. We had just been through a very bitter 5 month strike. We went back to work defeated, having gained little.

The union represented 1800 workers in 3 plants. Its various divisions produced turbines, motors, transformers and switchgear equipment. I had worked at the Beach Road plant where I was a union steward and safety rep. I was laid off out of seniority after the strike, a victim of an anti-union vendetta of the company taking advantage of the strike defeat and work shortage.

I was later recalled, but not to my old job. Rather, it was to an all-female department in the Switchgear plant 7 labour grades below my original one. The company was trying to keep me out of my old plant...and also, it seemed, to humiliate me.

The plant was mostly segregated. Jobs had been either male or female ones, and many departments were all-male or all-female. The women were on a separate seniority list with their own job titles and grades, and those were inferior in wages to the male ones. That system of dual wage rates and dual seniority lists was enshrined in the collective agreement — for decades signed and enforced by both company and union.

At Switchgear I heard the grievances and complaints of the women. They worked at more demanding jobs in terms of monotony, speed and work discipline. They got lower pay for that, were frequently laid off while junior males stayed on; they were denied chances for promotion and training at more skilled work. In their eyes, the majority of male workers were treated like privileged babies by the company and would not help them out.

Their complaints also applied to the union, whose leadership was thoroughly male. In frequent conflict with that leadership, they accused it of sanctioning and policing the inferior treatment of the women. The union would never fight for them, on grievances or in other areas. It was often in cahoots with management to sweep the women's complaints under the carpet. The leadership was insensitive to the problems and concerns of the female members.

From the first day it was obvious to me that the company enforced far harsher standards with the women. They worked harder and faster, got less break time and were allowed less leeway than the men. When I was later transferred to the all-male machine shop, the change was from night to day.

As for the union, the Men's Club that ran it made its views known to me very early and very clearly. The staff rep had made his spurs in that Switchgear Division. He told me the first day that he himself would never work with women. He proudly said that he and other labour leaders of his political persuasion drink at the Wellington House, the one remaining all-male bar in Hamilton.

The local President was in Switchgear and he was very upset when he heard that I was seriously listening to the complaints of the women workers. Their gripes were usually frivolous and unfounded, he stated. He told me that he always just listened to their bitching said, "yes, yes, yes...." to their faces and completely ignored it all afterwards. (This was exactly what the women told me he did.) I ought to do the same, was his patronising advice.

I had just been elected to the Executive in a rank-and-file rebellion against this Old Guard. The President seemed to assume that a common male bond would override our differences.

When I persisted in talking to the women and taking their complaints seriously, the leadership started to ridicule me. The Chief Steward began calling me "The Ambassador"...to the women. He said that he and the

President were now happy, in fact, that I was there and speaking to the women. This would save them from that distasteful task. They could from now on just speak to me and get the women's bitching relayed to them.

The new contract had for the first time integrated the male and female seniority and wage lists. This was due to the fact that it was now several years after the passing of the Ontario Human Rights Code which prohibited such discriminatory practices.

In 1979, the company announced it planned to close the Switchgear plant and decentralise production in smaller towns with cheaper wage rates. For the women, this posed a serious threat. The contract applied to 3 plants, but except for a part of the Motor Division at Beach Road, all areas were bastions of male jobs. Would the women be able to exercise their seniority and bump or transfer to those jobs, or would they find themselves out in the street after all those years?

DIVIDE AND CONQUER

Thanks to shop floor pressure by the guys, I had been recalled to my old department at the Beach Rd. by Fall 1979. There was then a lot of talk and worry in the plants over the prospect of large-scale transfers from Switchgear. When the first ones began, there were some bad incidents with male departments, refusing to show women the jobs or hassling them in other ways.

Some of us once tried to have a full discussion of these problems at a Stewards Council. We wanted the in-plant union leadership to develop common policies and strategies.

This attempt was a flop. The leadership was in no mood openly to discuss and confront sexism. Many raw nerves had already been touched. The union bully-boys went after us in their typical fashion. With a lot of shouting and breast-beating, they blamed the women for the problems and threatened us for implying the union leadership needed a fresh approach.

Having been frustrated in handling the problems through the union structures, we were left to our own resources in the shop. The Transformer Division I was in was all-male, and its management was determined to keep it that way. There were some Managers who were well known to be dedicated opponents of any women ever setting foot in their domains.

As steward, I insisted to management that the Switchgear women had every right to jobs in our department, at least to trial and training. Their seniority entitled them and we wanted them in our plant. This ought to be done in an orderly manner rather than competitively, i.e. the open jobs in Transformers to be posted in Switchgear and a gradual series of transfers rather than bumps.

Management was opposed, but they had a problem: the Switchgear women had legal and contractual rights to those jobs. Management therefore developed a strategy of Divide and Rule. Use the women in a provocative manner to push the male workers to keep them out, foster splits. Present the women as a threat to the men's jobs and livelihood and get the hourly guys to do management's job for them.

Management had a secondary objective here, which was to break our shop floor union organisation. Since the trauma of the strike and the post-strike repression, a number of stewards and safety reps had patiently rebuilt the union in the plant, block by block — fighting every grievance, hazard and injustice with a variety of tactics and constructing some shop floor unity and network. We had been doing this in the teeth of the opposition of both company and union, whose officials were overly concerned to get along peacefully with each other and have everything calmed and controlled. Fostering a war of the sexes in the plant was a weapon in management's counter-offensive against us.

For months before the anticipated transfers, foremen and their assorted rumour-mongers stirred up the pot with the spectre of the Invasion of the Women: two hundred Switchgear women would come and throw all the Beach Road Breadwinners out in the street; no one's job would be safe. Day after day, week after week, we were fed the tales: once it was that 14 women with 30 years' seniority each were coming to this department in 8 days and no male would be protected. Better start thinking now about unemployment insurance.

The first transfers in one department were some fiercely individualist women determined to keep their new jobs. When the men hassled them, they fought back. When the company told them they had to out-produce the men to keep their jobs, they did so. There was vicious fighting between the men and women. Both sides ended up ratting on the other to the boss, the "militant" steward included. The men were furious and sexist about it; they went all over the plant to warn others against allowing any "cunts" or "bitches" into their departments.

That department was next to mine. I had fought for the women to be called into the jobs opening up in our "iron stacking" area. The union's Business Agent had insisted the women couldn't physically handle those and other jobs. But I won the point with the company and we were the next on the list. The major women's influx would start here.

For weeks before their arrival, the department was hyper-alive, everyone keyed to the Invasion of the Women. I was approached by one of the guys who said that a number of them had just discussed the problem. They wanted me, as their leader and steward, to go to the company and tell them the men didn't want the women in here and are prepared to fight to keep them out.

That moment was a personal watershed for me. As I listened to him, I knew that half measures would no longer do. I would now have to take the bull by the horns.

I had been dealing with male chauvinism over the years in a limited fashion. As a health and safety rep, I had to battle constantly with some men who would knowingly do unsafe acts since it was "manly" to do so. In the inside-out mind of the male chauvinist, such dangerous work somehow affirmed his masculine superiority. The bosses certainly knew how to use guys like that to get jobs done quickly and unsafely. They would also thereby roll back the gains we had made for safer procedures in the department.

With a mixture of sarcasm, force and reason, I had been arguing over the years, "It's stupidity, not manliness, to hurt yourself; use your brains — don't be a hero and cripple yourself; you're harming all of us and helping the company by breaking the safety rules we fought so hard to establish, rules that protect all of us...."

From this I was familiar with how irrational, self-destructive and anti-collective the male ego could be. Also, I had learned a great deal from the women's movement over the years, and this included a never-ending struggle with my own sexism. On and off, I would have debates with my male co-workers over woman's liberation and related topics.

But all this only went so far. Now, with the approaching Invasion and the Great Fear that gripped the department, I had to deal with angry male sexism in high gear. I got off the fence.

I told this guy: "No. These women from Switchgear are our sisters and we had fought for them to come into our department. They are our fellow workers with seniority rights and we want them to work at Beach Rd. rather than get laid off. If we deny them their seniority rights, it hurts us because once that goes down the drain, none of us has any protection. It is our enemies, the bosses, who are trying to do them out of jobs here. There's enough work for everyone; even if there weren't, seniority has to rule for us as well as for them. The guys should train the women when they come and make them feel welcome here."

And with that reply, the battle was on. For the next few weeks, the debate raged hot and heavy, touching on the many basic questions. Workers from other departments in the plant came over and joined in.

Many men made the accusation that the women would be the bosses' Fifth Column and break our unity. They would side with the foremen, squeal on us, out-produce us and thereby force speed-ups. The women as our enemy, or at least agents of the enemy, would be used by Them against Us. And many pointed to the experience of the next department, a situation that festered and worsened every week.

The reply was that if we treated the women as sisters and friends, they'd side with us, not the boss. Some of us had worked in Switchgear and knew it was the *men* there who got favourite treatment. The women were treated like dirt by the company. Our own shop-floor unity left a lot to be desired, and so some of us sarcastically pointed out all the squealing and kow-towing to the boss that many of our male co-workers engaged in. You could be sure the women were not our equals in *this* area at least: they'd be incapable of such extremes and never be as expert as our pros at brown-nosing.

We had common class interests with our sisters against the company. This was in the protection of seniority rights and assuring that the Switchgear workers, male and female, got jobs at other Westinghouse plants rather than get thrown out on the street after twenty or thirty years of service.

It was easy to tease guys with the contradictions that male double standards led them to. They were afraid the women would come, over-produce, and result in speed-ups, yet at the same time they insisted that women wouldn't be able physically to perform our "man's work"!

Either they could or they couldn't was the answer to that one, and if they could, they deserved the jobs and it would be up to us to initiate them into the department norms. We insisted on the right to trial and training for ourselves; to deny the women a chance would hurt us. Besides, it was always brought up, no women could ever out-scab such and such a male in production.

Many of the guys said that the women would never be able to do certain of the heavy and rotten jobs. As steward and safety rep, I always jumped on that argument: We shouldn't do those jobs either. Look how long we've been fighting to make them safer and easier for ourselves. Well, they answered, the women may be able to do certain jobs, but not all of them.

Right, I would say, and how many guys in here only do certain of the jobs? Haven't we all fought to protect older and sicker or injured or pot-bellied or whatever guys from certain tasks they can't do and still keep their rates? There were enough cases of diabetes, heart problems, asthma, back injuries, etc. around the department. Stewards had even fought for exemptions for guys who found certain things personally distasteful.

If women can't do certain jobs, we treat them the same way. We don't victimise people who can't physically do everything the company wants them to do. We protect them as our brothers; and as our sisters.

Some claimed the women would never be able to work inside transformation tanks, hard work and haven of the macho crowd. Nonsense, it was proclaimed, they have smaller and more agile bodies and so can do it easier.

By having the irrationalities of the sexist double-standards picked at, the guys were being pushed to apply their class principles: universal standards of equal treatment. Treat women just as we treat brothers regarding work tasks, seniority, illness, etc.

COUNTERING SEXISM

Part of this fight to self-identity with the women as co-workers was the battle against calling them "cunts" or "bitches". It was important to set the public standard whereby the women were labelled as part of Us, not Them.

Male sexist culture strives to degrade women to nothing but pieces of flesh, physical bodies, mindless animals...something less than fully human which the males can then be superior to. Such name-calling carried the connotation, in this context, that women were in a different category than Us and so merited different and inferior treatment.

I wouldn't be silent with anyone using these sexist labels and very aggressively pushed the point. Eventually everyone referred to "the women".

After a while we established a bias in the department with most of the men. Having the women in, or giving them a chance, was the right thing to do by any standard of fairness, unionism, solidarity, of the values and principles we respected, of the basic human decency that distinguishes Us from Them.

The focus shifted to other areas. Many men came back with traditional arguments against women in the workforce. They belong at home with the kids, they're robbing male breadwinners of family income and so forth. But other men didn't agree with this. Most of the guys' wives worked or had in the past. A family needed at least two wage earners to get by these days. How can you deny for others what you need yourselves?

Some men answered that in bad times a family should have only one breadwinner and so all would have an income, share it fairly. Fine, they were told, let's be really fair and square, half and half: you go home and clean the house and leave your wife at work. Alright they countered, they could tolerate women supporting a family on their own being at work, but not single women working. Fine, I picked out 4 single men in our department and proposed they be immediately sacked.

Fairness and equality seemed to triumph here too. The guys understood that everyone who had a job at Westinghouse deserved equal protection. But then, some men developed a reaction. As one, Peter, put it, "I have no respect for any woman who would come in to work here in these rotten conditions."[2]

The come-back was sharp: What the hell are *you* putting up with this shit for? Why didn't you refuse to do that dirty job last month? Don't *you* deserve to be treated with respect?

And: is your "chivalry" going to protect the women by restricting them to minimum-wage jobs, like slinging beer where they get their asses pinched and harassed for 8 hours? Or working in textile sweat shops? Is that the Woman's Pedestal you'd like to put them on?

As the Invasion Date approached, I got worried. Reason and appeals to class solidarity had had a certain impact. Most of the guys were agreeing, grudgingly, to give the women a chance. But the campaign had been too short, fear and hostility were surfacing more and more. Looking at similar situations in other plants, it was quite possible we'd have some ugly incidents the first day or two. This would set a pattern.

A unionist's first and bottom-line priority here had to be to work to guarantee the women their right to a job. If all the men weren't fully convinced that this was the proper thing, then at least they could be forced to *behave* the right way. Much of the male hostility had been kept in check because as the official steward, I was so aggressively fighting the issue. I decided to take this one step further and use some intimidation to enforce the basics of public behaviour.

In a tactic I later realized was a double-edged sword, I puffed myself up, assumed a cocky posture and went for the jugular. I loudly challenged the masculinity of any worker who was opposed to the women. What kind of man is afraid of women? I asked. Only sissies and wimps are threatened by equality. A *real man* has nothing to be afraid of, wants strong women, welcomes women's liberation....Any man worth his salt doesn't need the crutch of superiority over his sisters...stands on his own two feet, fears no female. A real man lives like an equal, doesn't step on women, doesn't degrade his sisters, doesn't have to rule the roost at home, be a dictator, in order to affirm his manhood. Real men fight the boss, stand up with self-respect and dignity, rather than kick our sisters and wives as scapegoats.

The liberation of the women is the best thing that ever came along...it's in *our* interests.

To someone who boasted how he made his wife cook his meals and clean the floors, I'd ask if she wiped his ass too. Did he enjoy being babied? Could he survive independently?

To the porno addicts: "You like that pervert shit? What's wrong with the real thing? Can you only get it up with those fantasies and cartoon women? Afraid of a real woman? Can't handle them? Got to kick her before you enjoy it?"

There was a lot of play-acting here. I'd out-do some of the worst guys, in verbal intimidation and physical feats. Then I'd lecture them on women's equality and welcoming our sisters next week.

I zeroed in on one or two of the sick types. I physically threatened them if they pulled anything with the women. They were told to stay away.

All of this worked, as I had hoped. It established an atmosphere of intimidation on the issue. No one was going to get smart with the women. Everyone would stand back for a while. Some would co-operate, others would be neutral watchers. The "psycho-sexists" would keep out.

This tactic was effective because it spoke directly to a basic issue. But it was also effective because it takes a leaf from the book of the psycho-sexists themselves.

At Westinghouse as elsewhere, many of the men are less chauvinist and more sensible than the others. But they often keep quiet in a group context. They allow the group pattern to be set by the most sexist bullies, whose style of woman-baiting everyone at least gives in to. These "psycho-sexists" achieve this result because they challenge, directly or by implication, the masculinity of any male who doesn't act the same way. Your manhood is on the line if you don't gloat at the pornography or ridicule the women or join in the harassment. All the males, whatever their real inclinations, are intimidated into acting or talking in a manner degrading to women. The more moderate men don't speak up or challenge the sexist bullies, afraid of having their masculinity questioned.

I had done the same thing, but in reverse. I had challenged the masculinity of any worker who would oppose the women, and I scared them off.

THE DAY THE WOMEN ARRIVED

The department crackled with tension the morning The Women arrived. Two of them, to start with. The company was evidently scared by the volatile situation it had worked so hard to create. They backed off from a direct initial confrontation — they assigned *me* to work with the women, along with my younger helper George.

The women were very uptight and on their guard. Betty and Laura, in their late 30s, were expecting trouble. They were pleasantly shocked when I said matter-of-factly that we would train them on the job. They were overjoyed when I explained that the men had *wanted* them in our department and had fought the bosses to bring them here.

It was an unforgettable day. Men from all corners of the plant snuck near the iron stacking area and spied on us. I explained the work and the drawings to the women and we set about our tasks. We outproduced the standard rate by just a hair, so that the company couldn't say the women weren't able to meet the normal requirements of the work.

The strategy was to do everything to get over the hump of the first few days. I knew that once the guys got used to the women being in there, they'd begin to treat them as people, not as WOMAN, and the hysteria would go away. It was critical to avoid incidents.

I forced the guys to interact with the women. For example, I pulled over one of the male opponents. I introduced him as Bruce the slinger who knew all the jobs and was an expert in lifts and would be happy to help them if asked and could always be called on to give a hand. This put him on the spot. A big smile, and then, "Sure, just ask and I'd be pleased to show you anything, and to begin with, here's what to watch out for and...."

The morning went by. No incidents. At lunch tables, then, they all asked George: What's the verdict? What's it like to work with a woman? (No point asking me, I was prejudiced.) George looked at them all and thoughtfully pronounced: "There's no difference working with a woman, I guess it's the same as with a man. Except that you have to watch yourself that you don't swear." Silence.[3]

From then on it was easy. More guys began to talk and interact with the two women. They started to see them as Betty with 4 kids who lived on the mountain and knew wiring and was always cheerful; or Laura, who was a friend of John's uncle and was cranky early in the morning and drove 3 friends to work and could easily operate the crane but had trouble with the impact gun and liked to heat up meat pies for lunch...and so on.

After all, these men lived and worked with women all of their lives outside the plant — mothers, sisters, wives, in-laws, friends, daughters, girl friends, etc. Having one of their gender at work was no big deal once they got over the trauma of the invasion of this Male Preserve. Just like helping your sister-in-law hang some wallpaper, or changing the snow tires with your daughter, or laying some new carpet with your neighbour.

The first day, the women didn't want to eat at the same tables as the men. They were wary of them and would rather be alone. We went after the foreman to get proper tables and chairs for the women, to have their own area on the iron floor. And then, over the next days to get them all the proper facilities — lockers, hand soap, tool boxes, etc.

On the second day, their female friends from the Motor Division came over to check things out. They were proudly told that this department was okay, the guys accepted us and were showing us the jobs. We could stay here. Tell everyone. Their network spread the news to the women in the other plant — try to get into this department, these guys will help us.

More and more women came the next few months. And were integrated with minimum fuss. The same thing happened in several adjoining departments. Quickly, men and women related to each other as people and co-workers, not as enemies. Relations became friendlier, working together. People to people: rather than Man versus Woman, it was John, Mary, Sue, Peter, Alice, George and Laura, etc.

That Christmas, we had a big party at someone's home — men and women of the department, drinking and dancing. The photos and various raucous tales of that night provided the basis for department story-telling for the next three months. And this was repeated the next few Christmases.

Was this, then, the Peace Between the Sexes? The integration of men and women as co-workers in the plant? Class solidarity triumphing over sex antagonism?

Not quite. Although they were now together, it was not peace. The result was more complicated...for now the War Between the Sexes was being extended from the community to the workplace.

WORKPLACE CULTURE

As our struggle showed, sexism co-exists and often is at war with the class consciousness and trade union solidarity that develops among factory men. Our campaign was successful to the extent it was able sharply to polarise and emphasise the contradictions between the two tendencies in each individual. With most of the men, their sense of class solidarity triumphed over male chauvinism.

Many of the men had resisted the female invasion of the workplace because for them it was the last sanctum of male culture. It was somewhere they would be away from the world of women, away from responsibility and children and the civilised society's cultural restraints. In the plant they could revel in the rough and tumble of a masculine world of physical harshness; of constant swearing and rough behaviour; of half-serious fighting and competition with each other, and more serious fighting with the boss. It was 8 hours full of filth and dirt and grease and grime and sweat — manual labour, a *manly* atmosphere. They could be vulgar and obscene, talk about football and car repairs. Let their hair down. Boys could be boys.

The male workplace culture functions as a form of rebellion against the discipline of their society. Outside the workplace, the women are the guardians of the community. They raise the kids and enforce some degree of family and collective responsibility. They frequently have to force this upon individualist males. The men would rather go drinking or play baseball or do their own thing while the women mind the kids, wash the family's clothes, attend to problems with the neighbours and in-laws, and so on.

Like rebellious teenage sons escaping mother's control, male wage earners enter the factory gate; there, in their male culture, they feel free of the restraints of these repressive standards.

The manly factory culture becomes an outlet for accumulated anger and frustration. But this is a vicious circle — for the tedious work and the subordination to the bosses in the plant is in large part the very cause of the male worker's dissatisfaction. He is bitter against a world that has kept him down, exploited his labour power, bent him to meet the needs of production and profit, cheated him of a better life, makes the daily grind so harsh.

Working men are everywhere treated like dirt; at the bottom of the heap, under the thumb of the boss at work, scorned by polite society. But, the men can say, we are better than them all in certain ways — "man's work". Physically tough. The women can't do it, the bankers and politicians neither. Tough work gives a sense of masculine superiority and this compensates for being stepped on and ridiculed. There's some ways we're better than all of that Fine Society.

The Women's Invasion threatens all this.

Not all factory men, of course, share these attitudes. All one can say is that it is true for a large portion, in greater or lesser degrees. Furthermore, this male workplace culture is not one-sided — it contains a fundamentally positive sense of class value. The working men contrast themselves to other classes and take pride in having a concrete grasp on the physical world around them. The big shots can talk fancy and manipulate words, flout their elegant manners. But we control the nuts and bolts of production, have our hands on the machines and gears and valves and wires and lathes and pumps and furnaces and spindles and batteries. We're the masters of the real and the concrete, manipulate the steel and the lead and the wood and the oil and the aluminum. What we know is genuine — the real and specific world of daily life.

Working men are the wheels that make the society go round, the creators of social value and wealth. There would be no fancy society, no civilised conditions, if not for our labour. The male workers are contemptuous of the mild-mannered parasites and scornful of the soft-spoken vultures who live off our daily sweat: the managers and directors, the judges and entertainers, the lawyers, the coupon clippers, the administrators, the insurance brokers, the crooked legislators...all those who profit from the shop floor, who build careers for themselves with the wealth we create. All that social overhead depends upon our mechanical skills, our concrete knowledge, our calloused hands, our technical ingenuity, our strained muscles and backs.

The Dignity of Labour.

But society treats us like a pack of dumb animals, mere bodies with no minds or culture. We're physical labour power, the intelligence belongs in the management class. Workers are sneeringly regarded as society's bodies, the middle-class as society's mind. One is superior, the other is inferior. One is fully human, the other is less than human, close to animals...society's beasts of burden.

The male workplace culture tends to worship this self-identity of vulgar physicalness. It is as if the men enjoy wallowing in a masculine filth. Brag of being the wild men of the factory.

Sexism thus undermines and subverts the proud tradition of the dignity of labour. It turns a class consciousness upside down by accepting and then glorifying the middle-class view of manual labour and physical activity as inferior, animalistic, crude. When workers identify with the "savages", as they are identified by the boss class, they develop a contempt for themselves.

It is self-contempt to accept the scornful labels, the negative definitions, the insulting de-humanised treatment. The cartoon-like stereotypes of class chauvinism: the Supermasculine Menials; the factory goons. The industrial sweathogs.

Remember Peter: he said he couldn't respect a woman who would come here to work in this hell-hole. It's obviously a place where he felt he lost his own self-respect.

My reply to him was that he shouldn't put up with that rotten treatment, that *the men deserved better also. We* should be treated with dignity. Respect yourself — fight back like a man, not a macho fool who glorifies that which degrades him.

Everything gets turned inside out. It's seen as "manly" to be treated as less than a man, a strictly physical, instinctual creature.

Another contradiction: this is precisely how sexist society treats *women*: mindless bodies, pieces of flesh, "biology is destiny". You would think that male factory workers and the women's movement would be natural allies...would speak the same language.

They share a common experience of being used as objects, de-humanised by those on top. Men in the factory are treated not as persons, but as bodies, replaceable numbers, commodities, faceless factors of production, pieces of capital to be shuffled around at will.

The working men's and women's struggles revolve around similar things. The abortion campaigns, for example: reproductive freedom and the right to control your own body. Is this not what the fight for health and safety on the shop floor is about? To have some control over our bodies, not to let the bastards do what they want with our life and limb, to wreck us in the search for higher profits?

The demand for reproductive freedom of Choice — is this not somewhat like what the right to refuse unsafe work is about? Let *us* decide.

Male chauvinism turns many working men away from their natural allies, away from a rational and collective solution to their problems, diverting them from class unity with their sisters into oppressors and degraders of their sisters.

Robbed of their *real* manhood, they get a false sense of manhood in lording it over the women.

Many of the men at Westinghouse felt they were fighting a losing battle anyhow in trying to keep the women out of our department. Times had changed. In this day and age you couldn't stop workplace integration. It was happening everywhere, the law was on their side, most of the wives and daughters worked; the Steel Company of Canada (Stelco) across the street was now hiring women. Also, new technology was eroding the heavy manual labour. You saw the engineers and rate-men redesigning the jobs — making them simpler, easier, more standardised, taking the strength and skill out of them. We were all becoming common labour.

PLAYING THE FOREMAN AT HOME

Many men compensate for their wage labour status in the workplace by becoming the Boss at home. Treated terribly in the factory, he plays foreman after work and rules with authority over the wife and kids. He thus gains at home that independent status he loses on the shop floor. He becomes a part-time boss himself. The women are his servants and this becomes key to his identity and sense of self-esteem. Working class Patriarchs — rulers of the roost.

This sense of authority has an economic underpinning. The male worker's role as Primary Breadwinner is critical — the economic function of his paycheque is to give him power over the family and status in society. And it also makes him the beneficiary of the woman's unpaid labour in the household.

A wage labourer not only lacks independence, he also lacks property, having nothing but his labour power to sell. Sexism gives him the sense of Property, as *owner* of the family. His relation to a woman (wife or girlfriend) is critical. She is his sexual property. Workers who have nothing can find fulfillment as owners. As Elvis sang, "You are my only possession, you are my everything." This domination/ownership of a woman becomes basic to how he sees himself.

All of the above are powerful *individualist* pressures, the traits of the business class: foreman of the family, man of property, possessiveness. These elevate the wage earner above the category of downtrodden common labour, deflecting him away from the road of collective struggle with his brothers and sisters to change their conditions.

Capitalism is based on competitiveness and encourages everyone to be better than the next guy, to rise up on the backs of your neighbours. Similarly the male chauvinist typically seeks superiority over others, of both sexes. Males tend to be competitive, always putting down one another, constantly playing one-upmanship. Men even express appreciation and affection for each other through good-natured mutual insults.

Sexist culture undermines the working-class traditions of equality and solidarity. It provides a recruiting ground for labour's adversaries. Over the years at Westinghouse I had noticed that a high proportion of workers who became foremen were extreme chauvinists — sexual braggarts, degraders of women, aggressive, individualist, ambitious...ever willing to push other workers around.

Male competition is counter-productive in the context of the shop or union, where we ought to co-operate as equals and seek common solutions rather than be always bickering and out-doing the other guy. The male ego makes for bad comradeship, bad brotherhood. It also makes it difficult for chauvinistic men to look and deal objectively with situations. Their fragile egos are always on the line. They have to keep up a facade of superiority, are unable to handle criticism, no matter how constructive. Their chauvinistic crutches make them subjective, irrational...and unreliable. And often self-destructive, as with men who want to work or drive dangerously.

Male working men pay a high price for the very limited material benefits they get from sexist structures. It's the bosses who make the big bucks, have the big egos and enjoy the real power from the inferior treatment of women.

THE NEXT ROUND

For the first few months after the Invasion, the women worked mainly in the iron area. They proved quite capable and competent. Soon Betty emerged as the informal group leader and co-ordinator; even the men taking the lead from her.

The next battle was to assure that the women would get a crack at the more skilled and high-paying assembly jobs up the floor. When these became available, the company moved to exclude the women and tried to promote junior men. We had a new fight on our hands.

Now, the women were there to speak for themselves and take on their varied opponents. There were now stewards in other departments who would back up the right of women to equal opportunity, and the shop floor was less hostile, many of the men being sympathetic or neutral.

The fight was done more collectively. As their steward, I often sat at the women's lunch tables and we plotted and conspired in common. We discussed each step of the campaign, made common strategies, acted as a group, assigned everyone a special task after these sessions. The bosses were rattled by this determined collective activity they saw. We pushed and won: the women were given training up the floor. They had broken another barrier.

In the midst of all this, the "Women Back into Stelco" campaign was to have an anniversary rally on International Women's Day 1981. The women at the lunch tables objected to their leaflet: we're all for equal pay and opportunity, but we're no women's libbers; who the hell do those women think they are anyhow, and so on. I jokingly said they were all hypocrites, since they themselves had just won a big fight for female equality. That's different, they said, and so on. The lunch bell broke up our heated dispute and I left for my job up the floor. On my way back at 2 p.m., I passed the assembly area where the women were working. A Woman's Day leaflet was pinned up on every transformer a woman was working on. The males were fiercely told that the poster stands for women's rights, and that's us and we're here to stay and pity any man who tries to take these down! And the posters remained there for as long as those jobs were on the floor.

Around that time I saw a copy of *Steelabour*, the newspaper put out by the Canadian section of the United Steelworkers union. It had a big front page colour photo of a woman miner. The article inside told of a movie the union had made about the fight of women out West to break into the previously all-male mines. The paper supported the movement of women into traditionally male jobs and said the union would distribute the movie to its locals.

I was quite surprised to see this. We had had to battle the union establishment as well as the company in our campaigns. I thought of how much easier it would all have been if our union had used its considerable resources to promote workplace integration. I fantasised about how much could be accomplished by a union that backed up its shop reps, spent our union dues for things that served us.

With such support, we would be capable, as the movie title put it, of "Moving Mountains".

While all the men still maintained the women were inferior workers and could never do "men's work", they were generally co-operative with the women. There was, however, a continual bickering between the sexes. The foremen were always fostering sex divisions. They would tell the guys stories of all the mistakes the women supposedly made on the job; or spread insulting sexist remarks about them. They would play games with the work assignments — reserve the worst jobs for the men, telling them the women couldn't do those. The men would thus have their superiority boosted and also resent the women's so-called privileges. The women would be grateful for not having to do those jobs.

Some of the supervisors became quite skilled at buddying up with the guys and forging common cause against the women. They developed a masculine solidarity with some and fed their ever-enlarging male egos. They would thereby get those guys to break the safety rules, out-produce, rat on other workers and so forth. The male bond proved stronger here than the union bond, and our collective strength suffered as a result.

The women acted as part of the shop collective. When we put in a department grievance against a boss doing hourly work on off-hours, the women were the first to sign and circulate it in their areas. The same with petitions, or grievances against the company revising job descriptions and lowering the rates.

WOMAN'S WORLD

As for myself, I was learning and changing a lot as a result of these experiences. The sessions at the women's tables affected me in many ways. They were good talks, peaceful and constructive, with no fighting and argument, no competition...all of us sensibly talking about a common problem and figuring out how to handle it as a group. It was a relaxed and peaceful half hour — even when we had major problems and serious differences.

This was in marked contrast to the male lunch tables, which were usually boisterous and raucous during those months. There was a lot of yelling and shouting, mutual insults, fist pounding, throwing things at one another, making shocking noises.

When you ate at the women's tables, you sat down to rest and relax. When you ate at the men's tables, you sat down to fight.

I had read and heard a lot from my feminist friends about this so-called Woman's World of warmth, co-operation and friendship, contrasted to the men's norm of agression, violence and competition. Although I had always advocated women's liberation and respected the women's movement, I paid only lip service, if that, to this distinction, and was in fact more often scornful of this "women's world" as Sissy stuff. Over the years I had become a more aggressive male, which I saw as distinct from being a chauvinist or sexist male. In the world of constant struggle, I thought, you had to be aggressive or go under. We'll have peace and love in the new socialist society...some distant day.

As a unionist, it became very clear to me that the women almost naturally acted like a collective. And in those months of going back and forth between the men's and women's lunch tables, I took a long and serious look at this Women's World. It was an unnerving but pleasant experience to sit down among friends, no competitions and put-downs, not to have to watch out for flying objects, not be on the alert for nerve-shattering noises, in a non-threatening atmosphere. I learned from these experiences and developed some respect for this Women's World. There was obviously something genuine there and it seemed to offer a better way. It also became obvious to me that the gap between the sexes was enormous, and that men and women were far from speaking a common language.

A WOMEN'S COMMITTEE?

Even though our department seemed able to resolve these problems, from the moment the Switchgear women arrived, gender conflicts were breaking out all over the plants. Very often the men fought back and refused to train women. Here and there, all-male departments threatened to wildcat to keep them out.

These conflicts intruded into the local union divisions and politics in the strangest ways. We had developed a rank-and-file caucus at the Beach Road plant, mainly stewards and other activists.

We were in constant and bitter conflict with the conservative Old Guard of the union. Initially, we were all male. The Women's Invasion split us. Some of our stewards responded to peer-group pressure and were in fact leading the anti-woman actions!

Unionism is not male bonding, and so we had some sharp internal struggles over this. At the same time, a younger militant woman, Mary, joined us. She was a hell-raiser for women's rights in the plant. Things quickly came to a head in our group. Most of the men opted for women's rights, the strong sexists withdrew, we included a plank for women's equality in our programme, and Mary become one of our leading spokespersons.

One of our priorities was to set up a women's committee in the local. It was critical for the women to organise themselves into some sort of autonomous structure.

Such a women's committee would become an important force against the company in the shop. It would also better raise to the fore women's demands in the local, push the union to fight for equal treatment, paid maternity leave and other women's concerns. It would be a new way of combatting sexism among the male workers — in the shop and at local meetings, the men would have to deal with a group of fighting women unwilling to put up with the old crap.

The women's committee would also allow the women a forum of their own to develop a common outlook and strategy, to collectively develop their own priorities and policies. Over time a women's committee would develop independent and strong women's leaders, speaking and acting on their own behalf.

This would also remedy the lop-sided development that had occurred at the Beach Road plant. The women who had come over from Switchgear were unwilling to get involved in the union, given their bad experiences with the hostile leadership. The defence of their rights had therefore become over-dependent on a few male stewards, acting as "protectors" of the women. An autonomous women's organisation would leave all that behind: women would represent women's interests, direct their struggle themselves.

With all this in mind, we set out in the Fall of 1981 to get a local union women's committee, Mary in the lead, backed up by a group of women in the shop and our militant caucus. We knew it would be a tough fight, given the sexist and authoritarian nature of the Old Guard.

The battle extended over several months. The Old Guard was led by the union's National President and fought us tooth-and-nail. At some executive meetings and a number of tumultuous membership meetings, they railed and thundered against the very idea of a women's committee. It would split the membership, the problems were all imaginary, it was an anti-union idea, a form of separatism the union had always rejected, nothing but a foil to discredit our fine leadership, etc.

Where they had the upper hand, this was railroaded through with a lot of heavy-handed intimidation. At other times it was different. At one noteworthy membership meeting, for example, very large numbers from the shop attended and backed our position on this and other issues. The highlight was a long speech by Alice, a woman from my department. She blasted the leadership, recalled the many instances where they had refused to fight for the women, pointing to specific officials. Given that there were threats of expulsion by the Old Guard, she emphasised that all the women would back up any of our male shop leaders under the gun since they had fought for the women's rights.

The men and women of the shop floor had here forged a unity in struggle. Alice declared that none of the women would let the executive carry on like a dictatorship. When one of the bully-boys started his patented tactic of challenging his opponents to a fist fight, large numbers rose to take him on, and the platform quickly changed the subject.

We were eventually defeated on this issue and no women's committee was ever formed. Over time, however, the leadership's public rhetoric changed. By 1983 most of the local and national officials had learned how to voice a non-sexist position on women's rights...without, however, doing much to advance that cause.[4]

THE RECESSION HITS

In the Spring of 1982, the recession finally caught up with us at Westinghouse...continuous lay-offs in every division. With that, we were in deep trouble.

We had made a lot of progress in the integration of the women when the work was plenty. On this issue, as on others, the shop floor had weapons to wield against the bosses — they needed our work and co-operation. But this leverage disappeared when the work got slack. Our bargaining power shrank. With production going steadily downward, the shop floor was robbed of the means to fight the company. Our instruments of struggle were disappearing.

And once the spiral of lay-offs begins, everyone is afraid for his or her own job and this concern over-rides all others.

The company wasted no time in rolling back the clock. They vastly exaggerated the future job losses and over-posted the surplus/lay-off lists. They did this constantly, keeping workers on edge from day to day. They cut back on whatever inadequate seniority protection was in the contract. Junior workers stayed in while senior ones were often railroaded out. They manipulated job classifications, combined and re-combined jobs, put people in categories such as "loan" to avoid seniority rules, refused trial and training periods, sheltered favourites, and so forth.

Workers were pitted against workers. Everyone was in competition for the shrinking number of jobs.

The company had all the cards and it seemed futile to resist. You'd hold the fort in one area; protect 4 workers. The next week they'd arrange for massive shifts and those 4 plus 7 more would be ousted, their jobs abolished or bumped or whatever...or everyone put on short time. The company made examples of fighters and protected the suckholes.

The economy was in deep recession, there were no jobs out there, anywhere. Once out, you probably wouldn't work again. People with 30 years' seniority went out the door while others with 5 years stayed in. Better roll with the punches, please the foreman or you'd be next.

With the power relationships so altered, the company assaulted us on every front. They revived their timeless dream of a "management-controlled plant". They became arrogant and insulting to the militant stewards. They went after hard-won department traditions on wage rates and soon got people working at jobs above their labour grades. They shuffled people around at will. As the months went by, management gradually took back onto itself more and more of the power and authority it had been forced to give up to the shop floor over the years.

It was a tide you couldn't stop. Bitterness and frustration were everywhere. Seniority meant nothing, the contrast was paper protection, all our time-honoured rights were out the window. Resentment was also directed to union officialdom, who too readily went with the tide, leaving us defenceless against a vengeful management. When you really neded the union, it wasn't there. There was a lot of despair.

Management retrenched on health and safety, given the fear that gripped everyone. With the jobs disappearing, workers competed with each other to be able to weld in the hazardous gasses we had been struggling to get rid of. Those jobs became prizes, not ones to be refused. And the guy who battled for a month to be able to bump into the shipping floor was not going to refuse to spray the toxic leaded paint the moment he got the job. We were more and more forced to use other fronts for health and safety compliance — labour boards, the NDP, the government, media, etc. The shop floor was supportive, but less active.

The company went after the women. They were to be weeded out of the plant, despite seniority or skills. With few exceptions, they posted the women regardless of years of service. They claimed these women had no transferrable skills and shunted most of them to the least skilled job in the plant: "chip and grind". The job soon became almost a women's job ghetto, or more accurately, a revolving door as more senior women came in and bumped out the less senior ones. The company gave a nasty twist here. This was the worst job in the plant...heavy, dirty, rotten, unpleasant. A few women simply declined to exercise their seniority when they got their notices, being unwilling to suffer through chip and grind.

The progress the men had made seemed to vanish. From the first day of the lay-off announcements, many of them rallied to the call of Get the Women Out First. The harassers and psycho-sexists came out again into the open and campaigned full blast. They found many sympathetic responses on the shop floor: protect the breadwinners, all the women out before the men. They had no right to be here in the first place, displacing Heads of Families. Were these men to be thrown out on the street and whole families suffer while women occupy jobs that are rightfully ours? They can't do the work anyhow. No women should be allowed to bump a male since they're not physically capable of doing everything we can.

There was some baiting of the women. The atmosphere in the plant became ugly at times, a hateful place to be in, for all the workers. The company used the changed mood to try to do a job on the shop floor militants. Some of the guys loudly expressed their anger at me for having helped bring the women into the Division in the first place.

Devastating as its effect was, the recession was not all powerful. We managed to win all our health and safety battles in this period. The plant continued to re-elect militants as shop stewards. The guys in my department were noticeably more co-operative with the women when some of them were recalled later on. Many of them had by then set up a new lunch table area, distinctly more quiet and relaxed than the other.

But the most interesting and telling responses to the situation can be seen in how women acted as they were being given the gears by the company...and what this provoked amongst the men.

Some of the women gave in to the inevitable. But many fought back and fought well.

Jill was slated for lay-off and designated to bump into a heavy job in an all-male department. She had two weeks to learn. The guys were not co-operative. But Jill became more determined as the days went by and she discovered that she was capable of doing the job. She got angry that the bastards were trying to deny her her right. Her co-workers and the steward began to co-operate. Many of them pitched in, recorded her successes so they would be future grievance witnesses. Jill did well, and at the end of two weeks the manager reluctantly told her she had the job.

Big victory. Smiles all around. One week later, the company arranged to have a senior male bump her out. That department is still all-male.

This and similar incidents also show that many of the men had obviously changed a lot as a result of the women coming into our Division. There was no going back to the previous outright chauvinism. Whereas years before they fought the Invasion of the Women, they now backed up Jill and other women in trouble. Mind you, they had to be pushed and pressured at first and not all joined in, but it was nothing like the resistance of years earlier.

When the chips were down, many men took their stand with their sisters against the company...despite the recession.

Maureen is a long-service worker. While junior men stayed in our department, she was shunted to the dreaded chip and grind. But she was furious about the whole situation and decided to go out fighting. She is small and thin, but managed to do the job quite competently. The boss then called her in and said that while she is doing all right, he is worried about her. Something might happen, he was nervous and so he would have to lay her off. Maureen put up a stink. The boss then said that there were certain extra-heavy tasks a woman would not be able to do. Maureen dragged him out into the shop and in full view of all the men, demanded he try to do that task. He couldn't do it, and was ashamed and humiliated. Okay, she said, if you can't do it, then don't hold it against the women.

The men had stood aside at first, but now quickly rallied to her side. They helped Maureen out and kept the bosses at bay, the union stewards in the lead. She kept the job...and was bumped out into another plant...to another chip and grind job. But she was able to keep that job, again with the co-operation of her male co-workers.

In the midst of this battle for their jobs in October 1983, Maureen came along with Alice and the other Westinghouse women to the OFL Affirmative Action forum in Hamilton to tell their story.

BEYOND THE WORKPLACE

The women in the labour movement have made gains largely on their own, confronting their various adversaries with their organised collective power. The men have been very hesitant to give support, and have sometimes opposed them. But unions were founded to fight for equal treatment for all workers — an injury to one is an injury to all.

The men unionists ought to take on that fight for the sisters' advancement more forcefully and openly battle their foes — the employer, and also the chauvinists, harassers, sexist bullies within our own midst. Sexism is anti-labour and it shouldn't be tolerated, even passively, by the men. Take them on like we take on the squealers, brown-nosers, back-stabbers in the shop — opponents of our common struggle.

All this we do to aid the women who are the prime victims of sexist structures and behaviour. But the fight against sexism is also a fight for the men. Sexism is destructive of the labour movement and the working man's struggle. It has led men to confuse their class interests, to side with the boss time after time, to seek false and illusory solutions to their situation as exploited wage earners, to escape the injustices of class by lording it over the women, degrading their sisters.

Sexism instills the ideas and values of the enemy class in our ranks. It ingrains false ideas of manhood and strength. It cultivates individualist attitudes and competitive behaviour, when what we need is collective struggle. It deludes men and pushes them into irrational actions. It channels the men's anger and rebellion along destructive paths — destructive to themselves as well as to their sisters.

This sexist madness is part of how capitalism keeps the male workers in line, and as such men have to fight it openly. It's anti-labour, anti-working-class, it's our enemy. We should so label it and treat it. In doing so, we are fighting for our own liberation as well as that of our sisters.

That fight goes beyond the workplace. The sexist structures of family and community perpetuate those at work. And the problems are in those structures, those ways of living, not just in men's heads.

One of these is the unequal sharing of community responsibilites, particularly in the raising of children.

Another is authoritarianism. Fear of authority keeps working men down. Good unionists have rebelled against the authority of the boss and the society, but they often re-assert that authority over their fellow workers. Union office can sometimes become a power trip for male Presidents, chief stewards, staff reps. They want to run the union like the army. They become our foremen, think like patriarchs. This is harmful to the labour movement because it is anti-democratic and restricts participation, inhibits the development of a self-reliant rank-and-file, the source of real power. It is allied to the style of "business unionism", where authoritarian control and a passive workforce are part of a sweetheart relation to the boss, the staff rep substituting himself for a democratic and active membership.

Authoritarianism sets union leaders apart from the ranks. For example, rather than openly discussing mutual concerns with their brothers and sisters in the work force, such officials meet in secret and then hide their differences to confront the ranks and bulldoze or "sell" united leadership positions.

Authoritarian styles involve one form or another of manipulation, intimidation or "negotiation" with the membership. The trouble is that these are methods we develop to handle the company, our adversaries; with workers we discuss common problems as brothers and sisters. Such an approach assumes that union officials have interests separate from those of the membership. Officials ought to lead, but their function is to serve the membership, not be served by them. We draw the line of Us and Them between the workers and employers, not between union officials and workers.

I learned about the errors of authoritarianism through some of the experiences in the shop. Over the years I had always seen it important for union activists to be non-competitive with fellow workers, to talk and reason as equals, listen, learn, try to convince, make common cause, tease in a spirit of friendship. It was important not to put down, make fun of others, or threaten and intimidate. Those were the weapons you used against adversaries, not Us. We're trying to build a self-confidence and open-eyed group of workers, and you can't do that by humiliating or bullying or manipulation. Nor by pushing people around. That's how you fight your enemies.

I had taken a leaf from the book of the psycho-sexists when I challenged the masculinity of male fellow workers during the campaign to get the women into our department. But I also took a leaf from the book of the union leadership. I was *intimidating* my fellow workers. I was up against the wall and so lashed out with the weapons of the union bully-boys. I used my position as steward and my resources as a strong personality to cow and frighten the guys, to push them into a position where they behaved the right way.

It worked, in the short run. I didn't resort to those methods again. I was disturbed by what had happened and chose not to use those tactics. Because all I would be doing was to reinforce the sexism I was combatting.

Authoritarianism, intimidation, aggression are a basic part of what sexism is all about. You can't separate aggression from sexism. Aggressive ways of relating to people is part of what sexism is. To be a chauvinist is to establish a competitive and power relationship to your own people, to seek to dominate your brothers and sisters. To treat Us as Them.

You can't combat sexism by reinforcing the fear of authority, or by intimidating the men. By becoming the loudest shouter at the male lunch table. The peaceful women's lunch table is stronger because it is non-competitive and collective. During the upgrading campaigns, I saw the bosses were a lot more scared by the quiet women than they were by the mouthy men.

You can use force and authority to outlaw discriminatory practices and structures, but sexist attitudes cannot be fought with the weapons of authority. Authoritarianism is part of the problem of sexism and so it has to be challenged and undermined at the same time. The male anti-sexist fight has to be put within a democratic framework of rank-and-file interests.

The affirmative action programmes in the labour federations have often had the backing of the male hierarchy, which is fine. But it is only part of the answer. Labour has to go beyond paper resolutions and beyond placing women in top leadership positions. The struggle against sexism has to be deepened where it really counts, on the shop floor and within the locals.

The militant men in the labour movement have to organise themselves and speak out publicly: express an anti-sexist position that reflects the men's experiences, that speaks in a masculine voice and develops its own unique language. Such a position would label sexism as anti-labour and show how it is harmful to the male wage earners. This rank-and-file male current would be distinct from the women's voice but allied in the common fight.

Men need to speak to men about sexism. It is difficult for the women because they are confronting the men and are part of the problem, as the men see it. The women have been the most dynamic part of the labour movement for the past two decades — they have organised and theorised in new ways and taught all of labour. The militant working men have to learn from them and also confront on their own the big issues the women's movement has raised — equal treatment, union democracy, non-competitive formats, humanising the use of power, the relation between community and workplace problems, the family, sexuality and repression, authoritarianism. Those issues have to be debated amongst the men, in their own way, developing their own non-sexist answers.

The women's world has enriched and strengthened the world of labour in many ways. Men have to recognise and appreciate these contributions. Part of this involves recasting the conception of work and labour as something uniquely masculine, accepting and learning from the distinct methods, rhythms and styles of women miners, assemblers and machinists.

We have to declare that sexism does not come with a man's job, that pornography does not come with the work...is not part of masculine workplace culture. We have to develop and strengthen the tradition of the dignity of labour, not let it be warped and perverted by the indignity of sexism.

Working men share basic common interests with their sisters; when more of them recognise these, define and speak about them in their own way, and act on these common interests together with the women, we'll then have the ability to start moving the mountains that stand in our way.

REFERENCES

1 The OFL policy statement had called upon labour to re-examine its past inadequacies in representing women members. Many of the briefs given by local unions or their women's committees discussed their own past shortcomings. They saw such self-criticism as a necessary and helpful prelude to reform.

2 The names of the plant workers referred to here are not their real ones.

3 Betty constantly voiced her amazement at the men of this department; she said it was the only group of guys she knew who never swore.

4 The union here is the United Electrical Workers, Local 504. The "UE" is a contradictory phenomenon: its militant rhetoric rarely is matched by its concrete practices. Nevertheless, the chauvinism described here is by no means unique to the UE.

HILARY M. LIPS

Women and Power in the Workplace

During most of our recent history, the major thrust of women's struggle for power has been toward increased access to the major institutions in society. The struggle simply not to be excluded — from voting rights, jobs, organisations, full legal status as persons — has taken up much of women's collective energy for decades. A strong emphasis in the struggle has been on access to and equality in the world of paid employment, for women have intuited rightly that the income, status, knowledge and social networks that come with employment are crucial resources on which power, both individual and collective, can be based.

Power, it should be noted at the outset, is the capacity to have an impact on one's environment, to be able to make a difference through one's actions. It is the opposite of helplessness. There is no use in debating whether or not women should really want power, or whether it is appropriately feminist to strive for power. Such debates are based on a long outdated, narrow notion of power as a static quality possessed only by tyrants. In talking about women increasing their power, I am referring to an increase in effectiveness of influence, in strength.

More power for women means two things: increasing women's access to resources and to the positions from which these resources are controlled; and increasing women's impact on the formation of policy about how our institutions function. Because women have a long history of exclusion, the initial focus in the struggle to increase women's power has been to gain access for women to a variety of institutions.

The universities are a good case in point. For years, women were excluded from higher education on the grounds that we were unsuited for it and might even be damaged by it. Some "experts" even went so far as to argue that too much use of a woman's brain would damage her reproductive organs and thus endanger her vital child-bearing function (see Shields, 1975). Universities in many countries accept female students as a matter of course now. In Canada, we have come a long way from the time when the principal of a Laval University-affiliated college for women had to placate critics of her institution by interspersing piano recitals and afternoon teas with normal academic pursuits. Such activities were supposedly necessary to keep her delicate female students from breaking under the strain of uninterrupted intellectual work (Danylewycz, 1981). However, arguments about damaging the reproductive system are still being used in some quarters to exclude women from various arenas of professional and amateur sports.

We rejoice in the knowledge that women now have access to the universities as students, and that there is even a growing minority of women in faculty and administrative positions. Having increased their access to this one important institution, have women, in fact, begun to make any impact on it? And has women's access to university education increased their power to gain entry to other previously restricted arenas: employment, government, business?

The answer is yes to both questions. The universities have changed since women were admitted. The curriculum shows their influence: courses dealing with the female half of the human race are growing in number and respectability. Many Canadian universities have formal programmes in Women's Studies, and the federal government has recently moved to endow five "Chairs" in Women's Studies at universities across the country. University structure and policy reflect women's presence too. Such issues as parental leave and day care are being taken a little more seriously. Real effort is made to meet the needs of part-time students. Great transformations have not taken place, but neither has the institution absorbed women without a trace. Most interesting of all, perhaps, is the change that has been wrought in the dreams and ambitions of female students. A survey done in the U.S. in the mid-1970s revealed that no fewer than one in six female college students were planning careers in the traditionally male-dominated fields of business, engineering, law or medicine (Astin, King, and Richardson, 1975). Clearly, these women are getting the messages about the increased possibilities for access into these fields, and are exercising their newfound power to choose these professions. However, the sense of power that comes with women's perception of an increased range of career choices may be short-lived. Statistics on women's employment indicate that they may often get in the door, but no further. Females in almost every professional field, for example, are underemployed and underpaid relative to their male counterparts (Abella, 1984) and women in trade occupations still have a great deal of difficulty finding employment (Braid, 1982). Moreover, the research bleakly suggests that, as women grow more numerous in a particular profession or occupation, its status declines (Touhey, 1974).

Thus, although women's problems with access to the workplace are far from over, there is an increasing recognition that simply being allowed in — to a profession, a business organisation, a trade union — is only half the battle. How can women avoid being marginal members of the workplace community — tokens whose presence supposedly illustrates that "women can make it", but who are not at the centre of decision making and who are powerless to rise to the top of, or change the shape of, the institutions in which they work?

Much advice has been aimed at women in an effort to answer this question. Most of it boils down to a prescription that women carefully observe and follow the models provided by successful men. Successful businesswomen profiled in the media are (like their male counterparts) often heard to comment that, in the service of success, they have given up their social life, hobbies, and recreation, and find it difficult to make time for family and friendship.

Such an ideal, based on the model of a small number of high-achieving, powerful, visible men in high-status jobs, creates discomfort among many women. For some, the discomfort may stem from a fear of being labelled tough, competitive or ambitious — qualities that are incongruent with our culture's definition of femininity. For others, the idea of subordinating all other priorities to one's paid work seems unrealistic and unpleasant. The first objection is easily dealt with, at least in theory. The attention paid to the concept of androgyny in recent years has, if nothing else, shown that the qualities associated with strength are not necessarily antithetical to the traditional "feminine" virtues of nurturence, sensitivity and care for others (Colwill and Lips, 1978). It is possible to be tough without losing sight of what is fair, to be ambitious without trampling on everyone else on one's way to the top — and if women are going to make an impact in the workplace or anywhere else they are simply going to have to figure out how to blend these qualities.

The second objection, however, is one to be taken more seriously. How realistic, how desirable is it for women to adopt wholesale the myth that gaining success and power requires the subordination of all other activities, values, and interests to one's career? This model, which is held out to men as an ideal, is unworkable and destructive even for most of *them*, even though they have been socialised toward it and are provided by society with many more supports for this life style than are women (Harrison, 1978).

In order to devote all of her energy to a career, a woman needs someone taking care of the other aspects of her life: feeding her, cleaning up after her, making sure she has clean clothes, making dental appointments for her, keeping her social life organised, looking after her children, and so on. She needs, in essence, a wife. Employed women do not have wives, and it is simply impractical to try to follow the male model for career success without one. Now that fewer career men have wives who fill the traditional role, perhaps the male career model itself will begin to change. At any rate, business and professional women will have to develop their own model for career success.

The male model, presented in such glowing terms, is largely a myth. It is an ideal that is used to keep men in line, and there is no reason why women should fall in line behind them. While popular writers are exhorting women to map out career strategy years in advance the way men supposedly do, research suggests that, despite the ideal, most men do not plan their careers any more carefully than women do (Harlan and Weiss, 1980). While the advice-mongers are saying knowingly that women have not got what it takes to wheel and deal in the business world because they have never learned not to take conflict personally, many business and professional women have found to their chagrin that their male counterparts grow silent, withdraw, or become bitter and vindictive in their relationships to colleagues after being opposed on some policy or economic issue. While popular writers are fond of saying that women lack the training necessary to be good "team players" because they never passed through the proving ground of football, basketball and hockey, many a male ex-athlete will admit that his main legacy from high school football was a recurring knee injury and a sense of failure.

The writers who say these things have taken our society's definition of the male role and life pattern and elevated it unquestioningly to an ideal. If the shoe were on the other foot, if women were in the majority in business and the professions, these same writers would be telling aspiring career men that they were at a disadvantage in knowing how to be part of a co-operative business partnership because they had never gone through the "proving ground" of rearing children. Instead of advising women to bone up on football and hockey so that they would not feel left out of casual conversations with the men in the office, the experts (presuming traditional gender roles in this mythical situation) would be advising men to read romance novels, keep up with the latest recipes, talk about their children, and follow the careers of the great women runners and tennis players. Since men hold the majority of powerful business and professional positions, it is assumed that there must be something right about men's upbringing and life style — something that leads them into powerful positions — and if women would only emulate that pattern they too could make it to "the top" in large numbers. Not only does this analysis overlook the fact that our society is arranged in a way that makes it horribly impractical for the majority of women to follow the male model (i.e., not only do most women *not* have partners who fulfill the role of the traditional wife, but also they *do* have children for whom they usually have primary responsibility), but also the whole approach is rooted in our all-too-human need to rationalise the status quo.

Psychologists have been finding for years that people in general like to believe that the world is a reasonably fair and just place, that there is an order to things, and that people basically get what they deserve (e.g., Lerner, 1974). Thus, people are very good at thinking up reasons why things are the way they are — at justifying and rationalising our social arrangements rather than questioning them. It is easier, for example, to think of women as "unassertive" or poorly trained for leadership in order to explain how few women reach visible leadership positions than to think that there may be something askew with a system or an organisation in which this is the case. Since men are on top and women are the bottom, such thinking goes, what women are doing must be wrong...and men are the ones doing it right. Teach the women how to act like men, and their problems will be solved.

Perhaps the clearest way to see how this type of rationalisation works is to imagine the changes in explanation for the status quo that would be required if the positions of the two groups were reversed. Gloria Steinem provides an amusing example of this process in her article "If Men Could Menstruate" (Steinem, 1983). She fantasises that if men and not women had menstrual cycles, menstruation would be regarded as a sign of superiority. The fact that men were "in tune" with nature and the cycles of the moon would be thought to give them an advantage in making important decisions, and women's non-cyclic nature would be used as a reason for excluding them from high positions. In fact, women's menstrual cycle has been cited repeatedly (on very flimsy evidence) as a handicap that makes them unfit for certain possible positions. Here too, though, the only logic in the argument is that relating it to the status quo. Nowhere is it argued that, since women supposedly become so unreliable and irrational at certain times of the month, they should be relieved of the delicate job of caring for small, helpless children during such times. Similar logic asserts that women's allegedly superior manual dexterity makes them uniquely fit to be typists, while ignoring the possibility that it might make them uniquely fit to be surgeons or television repairpersons.

It is reasonable to be suspicious of any approach that purports to explain women's failure to advance, or their lack of impact, solely on the basis of flaws in their own behaviour. Of course there are things most women can learn to make themselves more effective, but that is also true for most men. What *may* be more true for women than for men in many organisations, however, is that support and security from the organisation is lacking. Women, while inside an organisation, often find that they are still outsiders. As Rosabeth Kanter's (1977) work shows, the issue is not whether or not women know how to play on teams, but whether a token woman can play on a team that does not want her on it.

It is becoming clear, then, that having broken down many initial access barriers, women taking up their newly-won positions in mainstream organisations often find that they are still far from the centres of power. Having dealt with many of the formal barriers to career participation, they find themselves blocked by less tangible but equally frustrating obstacles. They feel invisible. They feel (and they are often right) that no one takes them seriously. Such feelings are not limited to women in business, engineering, or other male-dominated professions, or to women in "white-collar" jobs. Women in teaching, nursing, secretarial work, carpentry and other trades, and factory work all report similar frustrations in their struggles to make an impact in their work environment. Understanding of the dilemmas faced by women trying to be effective in the workplace can be enhanced by examining their problems within the framework provided by psychological research on power.

Psychologists argue that power — the ability to make an impact or to get others to do what one wants them to do — is based on a person's access to certain resources that can be used to "back up" her influence attempts (French and Raven, 1959). In other words, in order for a person (or a group) to exert power, there have to be reasons — fear, respect, admiration, greed, loyalty — for others in the environment to co-operate or comply. The resources that provide the reasons for compliance include control over rewards (for example, the capacity to reward a person who complies with one's wishes by promoting her, giving her a raise, giving her the day off, giving her a gift) and control over punishments (such as the capacity to discipline someone, fire her, take something away from her). The resources on which power is based also include legitimacy, expertise, personal attractiveness or likableness, and the sheer amount of knowledge or information one can muster to support one's arguments. The amount of power or influence a person can wield depends at least partly on how much access she has, and is seen to have, to these kinds of resources.

A person's ability to influence others depends not only on her actual access to resources, but also on the amount of control over these resources that others see her as having. If a woman is an expert in a given field, for instance, that expertise will not provide her with a source of power with respect to others who do not recognise her as an expert. While women are often blocked from control over certain kinds of resources in their work settings, it is just as often true that the resources they do have go unrecognised. In the case of expertise, the stereotype of feminine incompetence often works against the perception of women as experts, particularly in traditionally male fields. In the case of legitimacy, not only do women rarely find themselves in positions of authority, but, even when they do, their automatic low status as women acts to contradict and undermine their authority in the eyes of others.

A consequence of these difficulties is that women sometimes find themselves relying more than they should or would like to on the resources of personal attractiveness or likableness to exert influence in the workplace. They smile a lot, try to win the friendship and good will of the people they must influence, and may sometimes use their sexuality in overt or covert ways as a basis of power. This is a strategy that often does work, but it tends to be a trap if relied on exclusively. A person using it does not enhance anyone's view of her competence and must be rather too careful about staying on everyone's good side.

It must be remembered also that attempts to exert influence do not usually involve an active influencer and a totally passive target person. The power interaction is often a complex one, involving conflict, with both parties using several bases of power at once in the effort to win the struggle. Thus, for instance, a woman who has enormous resources in terms of information, control over rewards, and personal attractiveness may find herself in a struggle with a supervisor who is not averse to using the coercive power of sexual harassment. A group of women workers that has done enough extensive research on an issue to earn the label of "experts" and has a large base of informational power may confront an employer who knows much less than they do, but who uses the power of position and status to try to delegitimise the group and their statements. Any attempt to exert influence involves making an accurate assessment of the amount and type of resistance likely to be encountered and the strategies most likely to overcome the resistance.

Not the least of the problems a person can face in trying to wield power is a negative bias in her own view of the resources she controls. If a person who is an expert lacks confidence in her own expertise, she will have difficulty exerting influence based on that expertise. Since women are continually being given the message that they are not expected to be experts, that people are pleasantly surprised when they know anything about important issues, lack of confidence is a dangerously seductive trap for them. Men too feel inadequate when they compare themselves to their colleagues. Our culture's specialised, competitive workplaces tend to foster this feeling. Men, however, have developed more strategies than women have for hiding this feeling of inadequacy. What must be kept in mind is that the exercise of power depends not only on what kinds of resources one controls, but also on the way one thinks one's own resources compare to everyone else's. In other words, how powerful a person or group feels can make a difference in how powerful they are.

A person's exercise of power is also affected by what she and others see as appropriate behaviour. Since "feminine" behaviour is, almost by definition, powerless behaviour, the woman trying to act in a powerful way is placed in a double bind. There may be times when she has the resources and knows she has the resources to wield power, but holds back out of a fear of being labelled pushy, aggressive, tough, or just plain not nice.

The three factors just described (what resources a person controls, how powerful she feels, and what she and others see as appropriate behaviour) affect not only the amount of impact she can have in a particular situation, but also the style or strategy of influence she employs. Her style of influence may be more or less direct, for example (Johnson, 1976). Someone who uses a direct style of influence asks for or demands openly what she wants, making it clear that she is the one who wants it. Someone using a very indirect style of influence, on the other hand, tries to get what she wants to happen without acknowledging that she is the source of the influence. A common example of the latter is the strategy of talking to someone behind the scenes rather than personally bringing up an issue at a meeting.

Both styles carry some risks, especially at the extremes. The person using the direct approach to influence may be viewed as abrasive, may be disliked, and may often find herself involved in conflict. The payoff is that, when she gets something positive to happen, she gets credit for it — credit that adds to her competence and expertise in the eyes of others and thus adds to the store of resources she can draw on in future situations.

The person using the indirect approach to influence, on the other hand, avoids the risk of being openly associated with an idea that turns out to be unpopular or unworkable, while keeping the opportunity for private satisfaction when she is the source of an initiative that works. However, sometimes this satisfaction can be a little too private. No matter how many good ideas she generates, a person can never build up her credibility if she is never seen as the originator of these ideas, if her influence is always indirect.

Clearly, to increase one's competence in the eyes of others, it is necessary to use influence directly and openly, at least some of the time. However, this is not to say that women should always avoid using indirect strategies. There are times when it is simply more important to get something done than to make an issue of it or get credit for it. In some organizations, for instance, people have managed to advance the cause of women considerably without ever being so obvious about it that they generated a fight.

Since it seems to be important to use influence directly and openly at least some of the time, it would seem to be a simple matter for women to get the message and start using more direct power styles in order to enhance their personal effectiveness and increase their acceptance within institutions. This, in essence, is what assertiveness training is supposed to be about: teaching people, especially women, to exert influence directly. Men rarely sign up for assertiveness training. Does this mean men have no trouble exerting influence openly? Perhaps, but it could also mean that men are more reluctant than women to accept for themselves the label of "unassertive". Also, many of the programmes are geared to women, on the unproven assumption that women need the training more. In fact, some Canadian research suggests that women are actually more appropriately assertive than men in many situations (Wine, Smye and Moses, 1980).

But while basic skills in assertiveness can only be helpful, they provide no magic cure for the power problems that women face in their working lives. How direct a woman is able to be in her attempts to exert influence depends only in a limited way on these skills. More importantly, it depends on the degree of actual control over resources that she brings to an interaction, how powerful she feels, and what kinds of behaviour she and those around her see as appropriate.

Women are often accused of relying on indirect or hidden power styles — of being manipulative and sneaky rather than open when trying to exert influence. In cases where this accusation is true, there are probably a number of factors operating that favour an indirect strategy. For example, the more resources one can command to back up one's requests or demands, the easier it is to be direct. This is particularly true of such resources as legitimacy, status and support. The more authority a person has in her position, the higher her status, and the more backing she feels from her co-workers, the easier it is for her to make strong, clear demands on people. For this reason, a teacher may have no hesitation about making certain clear demands on her students, but may be wary about adopting the same strong, direct style with school administrators. When dealing with students, she is operating from a position of recognised authority and of higher status within the institution. Moreover, she usually knows she is working within guidelines that are accepted by and will be supported by her colleagues. If she had no recognised authority over the people she was trying to influence, if she were operating from a position of lower status, if she felt isolated from her colleagues on a particular issue (all of which are more likely to be the case when she is trying to exert influence over an administrator instead of a student), it would be more difficult for her to be direct and assertive.

For women (or men, for that matter) who find themselves at the bottom of the ladder in a workplace that operates on a very hierarchical basis, it is unrealistic to expect a lot of direct, open use of power. This is doubly true if a woman has no network of support among her co-workers — a problem that plagues women who are breaking ground in a traditionally male job. Finally, it must be noted that women tend to start with a strike against them when it comes to status. The status ascribed to females in many jobs is automatically lower than that ascribed to men in the same job. Simply trying to teach or convince women to be more assertive and direct under these conditions is not the answer. Most women know how to be assertive under the right circumstances, but they avoid behaviour that is going to get them into more trouble than they want to handle.

Intervention to increase women's capacity to exert power in a direct way should not focus mainly on the behaviour of individual women. Rather, a more useful focus is on finding ways to increase women's access to resources, and to change the culture's image of femininity so that it is no longer synonymous with weakness or incompetence.

How can such changes be accomplished? They have already begun to happen. A crucial aspect of increasing women's access to resources in the workplace is the formation of support groups. Such groups not only provide much needed support (a resource in itself) for women who are isolated or ignored in male-dominated workplaces, they also enable women to share information and expertise — thus potentially increasing the competence (another resource) of all members. In some situations, these groups can also provide the political clout to help attain certain kinds of change beneficial to women (yet another resource). Also, the existence of network groups may provide a significant source of encouragement for more women to enter certain fields, an eventuality that will make it less common for women to find themselves isolated as tokens in their jobs.

It does not take a psychologist to tell most women that another extremely important aspect of increasing women's access to the resources on which power is based involves eliminating women's "double shift". Time and energy are themselves precious resources on which all attempts to have influence or make an impact on the world are based. For years, women's time and energy have been stolen from them by economic and cultural systems that have allocated to women virtually all of the responsibility for child care and the daily maintenance functions of cooking, cleaning, shopping and errand-running. Even in countries where serious attempts have been made to "socialise" child care functions, women are the ones faced with the housework when they return from work each day. And in Sweden, where new fathers and mothers are equally entitled to parental leave at 90 per cent of salary, few fathers avail themselves of the opportunity to stay home with their infants. No modern economic system has yet solved this problem of women's double day.

On an individual level, a woman is seriously handicapped in her attempts to have an impact outside of her own family by this double burden of labour. On a group level, the double shift weakens and dilutes women's impact on the values that shape the political process, the educational process, the arts, our own culture, and the future of the world. In the power terms discussed in this chapter, the cultural requirement that women perform a disproportionately large share of home-related work interferes with their access to almost every type of resource on which power can be based. Household responsibilities may make a woman less available for the extra meetings or social events where information is exchanged and contacts that lead to promotions and better jobs are made. They slow down her education, keeping her at a lower level in the job market. Thus, her access to information and expertise is curtailed, as is her access to the reward and punishment power that accompanies control over economic resources, and to the legitimacy that comes with holding a position of recognised authority. The only power base that is not guaranteed to be adversely affected by this situation is that of personal attractiveness or likability — and there is many a bleary-eyed, irritable woman with no time for exercise or sleep who will say that even that traditional source of female power is compromised by the double shift. Clearly, for women as individuals or for women as a group to have a greater impact on our cultural institutions, the relegation to women of most child care and household responsibilities would have to be changed.

The "powerless/incompetent" image of femininity would also have to be changed. While that change is beginning to happen as strong, competent women become more visible, efforts in some specific areas are called for. Ripe for revision, for instance, is the notion that women are incompetent to handle all things mathematical and technical. The pernicious stereotype of women as beings who cannot deal with numbers and who are too muddle-headed to balance a chequebook is not only wrong, it is dangerous in an age that is increasingly dominated by the computer. It will be helpful to remember that when the typewriter was first invented, it was thought to be too complicated a machine for women to handle!

It would also be useful to work against the idea that women must be physically weak. Not only is this view of women an obstacle to their employment in a variety of jobs requiring strength and stamina, but it may also be related to the general perception of women's effectiveness and their sense of power. Being weak fosters a need for protection from men — and this generates an attitude of protectiveness on men's part that generalises far beyond the physical realm into other aspects of women's lives.

A third aspect of the femininity stereotype that would-be powerful women need to challenge is that women are quiet, soft-spoken and polite. A growing body of research in psychology shows that, in the first place, people who talk more in groups tend to be accorded more status in those groups; and, in the second place, men tend to discourage women from speaking up in group situations by interrupting them and by ignoring their input. These tactics used by men tend to subdue women's efforts at participation in the discussion, allowing the men conversational control. Then, in a vicious circle, women are discounted more and more as they become increasingly silent, and they try less and less often to enter the conversation as they feel increasingly ignored. One approach to this problem is for women to try to train their male colleagues to stop interrupting them, but such training may not come easily. It is a rare and lucky woman who, after bringing the problem to the attention of the men she works with, finds she is never interrupted again! More probably, she will have to work actively to invalidate the feminine stereotype of politeness by refusing to defer to male speakers who try to interrupt her and by protesting such interruptions again and again. Since old habits die hard, and since change is more in women's interest than men's, it is unrealistic to rely too heavily on men to relinquish their conversational control tactics without continuous pressure from women.

As women gain more access to the resources on which power is based, they will find it easier to challenge the "powerless" image of femininity. And, concurrently, as the powerless image fades, women will find it easier to be recognised as strong, as competent, as experts. Thus, in a reversal of a "vicious circle", the two processes will feed into each other, ultimately making it easier for women to use such resources as expertise, information and legitimacy. These resources become springboards for acquiring access to other resources — tangible ones such as money and control over decision making — and for opening the doors to these resources to other women. This is an optimistic perspective to be sure, but one that is consistent with the way many advances for women have been achieved over the years. For women, as for any relatively powerless group, the key to starting the "non-vicious circle" rolling is to use their most available resource: their numbers, their collectivity, pooled energy and shared support. The payoff may well be not only more access to and impact in the workplace for women, but a more humane workplace for everyone.

REFERENCES

Abella, R.S. *Equality in Employment: A Royal Commission Report*. Ottawa: Canadian Government Publishing Centre, 1984.

Astin, A.W., King, M.R., and Richardson, G.T. *The American Freshman: National Norms for Fall 1975*. Los Angeles: University of California Laboratory for Research in Higher Education, 1975.

Braid, K. "Women in Trades in British Columbia". In M. Fitzgerald, C. Guberman, and M. Wolfe (eds.), *Still Ain't Satisfied! Canadian Feminism Today*. Toronto: The Woman's Press, 1982.

Colwill, N.L., and Lips, H.M. "Masculinity, Femininity and Androgyny: What Have You Done for Us Lately?" Chapter in H.M. Lips and N.L. Colwill, *The Psychology of Sex Differences*. Englewood Cliffs, N.J.: Prentice-Hall, 1978.

Danylewycz, M. "Changing Relationships: Nuns and Feminists in Montréal, 1890 - 1925". *Histoire Sociale — Social History*, 14: 28 (1981), 413 - 434.

French, J.P.R., and Raven, B. "The Bases of Social Power". In D. Cartwright (ed.), *Studies in Social Power*. Ann Arbor: Institute for Social Research, University of Michigan, 1959.

Harlan, A., and Weiss, C.L. "Moving Up: Women in Managerial Careers". Third progress report. Wellesley, Mass.: Wellesley College Centre for Research on Women, 1980.

Harrison, J. "Warning: The Male Sex Role May Be Dangerous to Your Health". *Journal of Social Issues*, 34: 1 (1978), 65 - 86.

Johnson, P. "Women and Power: Toward a Theory of Effectiveness". *Journal of Social Issues*, 32: 3 (1976), 99 - 110.

Kanter, R.M. *Men and Women of the Corporation*. New York: Basic Books, 1977.

Lerner, M.J. "Social Psychology of Justice and Interpersonal Attraction". In T.L. Huston (ed.), *Foundations of Interpersonal Attraction*. New York: Academic Press, 1974.

Shields, S.A. "Functionalism, Darwinism and the Psychology of Women: A Study in Social Myth". *American Psychologist*, 30: 7 (1975), 739 - 754.

Steinmen, G. *Outrageous Acts and Everyday Rebellions*. New York: Holt, Rinehart and Winston, 1983.

Touhey, J.C. "Effects of Additional Women Professionals on Rating of Occupational Prestige and Desirability". *Journal of Personality and Social Psychology*, 29: (1974), 86 - 89.

Wine, J.D., Smye, M.D., and Moses, B. "Assertiveness: Sex Differences in Relationships between Self-report and Behavioural Measures". In C. Stark-Adamec (ed.), *Sex Roles: Origins, Influences, and Implications for Women*. Montreal: Eden Press, 1980.

FURTHER READING

Colwill, N.L. *The New Partnership: Women and Men in Organizations*. Palo Alto, California: Mayfield, 1982.

Crosby, Faye J. *Relative Deprivation and Working Women*. New York: Oxford, 1982.

Epstein, C.F. and Coser, R.L. *Access to Power: Cross-National Studies of Women and Elites*. London: George Allen & Unwin, 1981.

Kanter, R.M. *Men and Women of the Corporation*. New York: Basic Books, 1977.

Lips, H.M. *Women, Men, and the Psychology of Power*. Englewood Cliffs, N.J.: Prentice-Hall, 1981.

III. COMMUNICATION

INTRODUCTION

Communication is one of the major ways in which our attitudes to and expectations of gender-related behaviour are developed and replicated. Language is the most readily accessible form of communication over time and space, and according to Maryann Ayim's chapter, which promises a "gender analysis of speech patterns", the way we talk and listen (and *not* listen) to others is related to gender and its relationship to power in our society.

While language might be a "basic" form of communication, the arts are the crucible through which our visual, oral and aural literacy are honed and our symbology constructed and perpetuated. To paraphrase the philosopher, Wittgenstein, "the limits of our language are the limits of our world." This becomes especially apt in discussing the influence of communication on all of our languages, such as the dialects of music, art, dance, film, photography, cinema, theatre, literature...and more.

Many people involved in the arts like to say that art transcends gender... that there is no difference between women's and men's art: there is just good art and bad art. "Art and Daily Life" and "Men, Women and Photography" both question this notion by examining the processes by which artists are trained, subjects and media are chosen, and how and where the final products are validated in our society.

There is much to say about gender and art in our culture, and this section simply touches on some of it. Further questions might be: Is there women's and men's art? Are there certain subjects, styles, and media more amenable to one gender or another? Why has there been no female Michelangelo... and does that matter? In an egalitarian society, would all members have the same possibility of achieving powerful communication? Is there a distinction between talent and power? Who really decides which art deserves to be imortalised...and why?

From the most private conversation to the most public display of communication, then, one is looking at the exercise of the power to influence and inform others. That is why, when we speak of gender, we must carefully examine what views about gender are communicated in our culture, by whom, in whose interest, and by what means.

MARYANN AYIM

Wet Sponges and Band-aids — A Gender Analysis of Speech Patterns

Mistress Anne Page? She has brown hair, and speaks small like a woman.
(*The Merry Wives of Windsor*, Act 1, Scene 1)

It is not surprising that Shakespeare has the character Slender first identify Anne Page as a brunette; by such irrelevant features as the colour of their hair or their eyes have women been labelled, evaluated, desired, or rejected by men down through the ages. More interesting for our purposes, however, is the second part of Slender's description, that she "speaks small like a woman".

This paper will first explore what it means to "speak small like a woman"; next, a distinction between the *perception* and the *actuality* of this "speaking small" will be developed; finally, the analysis of female language patterns will be integrated into a broader social structure in which the assumptions of patriarchy go unnoticed and hence unchallenged.

ON SPEAKING SMALL LIKE A WOMAN

Some Guidelines for the Uninitiated

The rules defining the language of women are for the most part acquired unconsciously, although this by no means implies that they are weak rules or that they enjoy a merely tentative or peripheral status in the language habits of the community. I shall discuss some of the features of female language typically identified in the literature; phonological, syntactical, semantical, and pragmatical examples will be included in the list, but no

Originally presented as a paper to the Canadian Society of Women in Philosophy, October 15, 1982.

attempt will be made to distinguish between them. Indeed, making a category distinction would in several instances be extremely difficult, illustrating the arbitrary nature of these very categories and their uncomfortable fit with women's speech.[1]

Whether particular features *in fact* represent genuine differences in the speech patterns of females and males will be reserved for discussion in the second part of this chapter. My purpose in this part is the simpler task of providing a clear description for each of these purported differences.

1. Inappropriate Question Intonation

The use of the rising voice or question intonation for assertive utterances is frequently attributed to female speech.[2] For example, on being interviewed by a potential employer and asked how many children she has, a woman replies, "Three?" Although she is quite cognizant of the fact that "Three" is the correct answer to this question, her use of the question intonation is taken to suggest a reluctance to make any categorical statement to that effect.

2. Tag questions

As the term suggests, a tag question is a question appended to a declarative sentence, for example, "It's very hot in this room, isn't it?" Tag questions have been associated with the speech patterns of females,[3] and taken as an indication of the need of the female speaker to solicit agreement or acquiescence from the listener.

3. The Use of "He" and "Man" as Generic Terms

Although it may seem odd to include this feature, surely characteristic of both male and female language patterns, in a list of gender *differences*, I am following here Spender's practice of collapsing sexist features of a language with sex differences in the use of the language.[4] Feminists claim that the generic status of "he" and "man" is illusory, that these words fail to refer equally to female and male human beings, and that their primary designation is "male person", allowing them to designate "female person" only by extension.[5] The male weighting of terms that purportedly refer equally to all human beings will clearly have a different impact on female than on male users of the language, suggesting that the full humanity of females is neither as central nor as obvious as the full humanity of males. Females, unlike males, must always ask whether they are included under the "aegis" of "man", and it is this feature that renders the use of "he" and "man" different for women and men.[6]

4. Vocabulary Items Indicating Fine Colour Discrimination

The lexical repertoire of females includes many more words for making fine colour discriminations[7] than does the male repertoire. Examples of such words are "heliotrope", "taupe", "mauve", "turquoise", "loden", "burgundy", and "off-white". The standard view is that making such fine distinctions is not one of the more important tasks in the course of everyday life, and hence that the characteristic use of these terms is indicative of an obsession with the purely trivial.

5. Complimentary Vocabulary Items

Adjective selection in compliment construction is also viewed as sex-coded. The adjectives "adorable", "sweet", "cute", "lovely", and "divine" are among those typically associated with female usage[8] and perceived as trivialising, sugar-coated linguistic items.

6. Extensive Use of Qualifiers

A significantly greater use of qualifiers, such as "generally", "fairly", "quite", and "really", is attributed to female as opposed to male speakers.[9] These terms are perceived as hedging, weakening terms, which allow the speaker to avoid taking full responsibility for the content of what is said.

7. Extensive Use of Modals

Extensive use of such modal verbs as "can", "could", "shall", "should", "will", "would", "may", and "might" is frequently identified as a female speech trait.[10] Furthermore, the modal construction is perceived as signalling doubtfulness or uncertainty,[11] and having a softening or more "polite-making" effect on a statement.[12]

8. Interruption Patterns

In cross-sex conversations, the interruption of female by male speakers is consistent, systematic, and largely independent of idiosyncratic features relating to the nature and disposition of the participants. This is as opposed to same-sex conversations, where the normal rules governing turn-taking apply, and interference with these rules is largely an idiosyncratic affair — that is, an instance of the "big mouth" who wants to monopolise the discussion.[13]

9. Interaction Patterns

The speech of women is more supportive than that of men, insofar as it exhibits an effort to elicit and encourage the contributions of the other speaker to the conversation. Women show a much greater readiness to develop topics introduced by male speakers, to ask questions, intersperse supportive "um's" and "ah's" in the appropriate places, and respond to explicit points made by the speaker than males show with regard to female speakers.[14] The role of women in conversational interactions is thus not unlike that of a band-aid insofar as it serves to patch up weak or strained areas and devotes itself to the general well-being of the conversation as well as the comfort of the other participant. The role of men in their conversational interactions with women, insofar as men's speech reveals a stark absence of these supportive features and very frequently manifests blatant ignoring of female conversational input and complete changes of topic, may be legitimately likened to a wet sponge.

10. "Telling It Slant"

"Telling it slant" is a phrase originally coined in a poem by Emily Dickinson, to mean telling the basic truth with no flagrant deception, but at the same time, not quite like it is, either. It is suggested that in their speech patterns women characteristically "tell it slant".[15] It is postulated that if women did not "tell it slant", men, who have no insight into female reality, could neither accept nor understand what they have to say. Furthermore, given that the language itself has been constructed and legitimised by males,[16] females must express their thoughts in a language that is not a perfect (nor even a good) match for their reality. This involves something like the application of an additional transformation rule in the generation of surface structure from the deep structure of female language,[17] another facet of the explanation for why females "tell it slant".

11. Silence Patterns

Contrary to the popular myth, women talk significantly less than men do.[18] The greater silence of women is perceived as a function of their exclusion from the making and validating of the language,[19] which is in turn symptomatic of their curtailed power in the world.

TO SPEAK SMALL OR TO BE REPORTED SMALL

The Linguistic Question

Studies dealing with sex differences in language are a relatively recent phenomenon, at least with respect to English; anthropologists of the seventeenth and eighteenth centuries exploring the language and society of "primitive" peoples reported with great astonishment language differences between males and females; in some tribes, men and women were actually reported to speak a different language.[20] The earliest that gender in language was connected with sex differences between male and female speakers of the English language was in 1900.[21] It was not until the mid-1960s that gender-based language differences among native speakers of English began to impinge seriously upon the consciousness of linguists. This new development in research was conducted almost exclusively by feminists; nevertheless, it now stands in some disrepute, challenged by other feminists on the grounds that the language differences reported involve sexist assumptions. Since most of the controversy centres around the tag question, I shall address only that feature in detail.

Robin Lakoff describes a tag question as

> midway between an outright statement and a yes-no question,...less assertive than the former, but more confident than the latter...[and] used when the speaker is stating a claim, but lacks full confidence in the truth of that claim.[22]

Thus, taking a tag question to indicate weakness or lack of confidence, she attributes its use largely to women, claiming that "this sort of tag question is much more apt to be used by women than by men".[23] It is important, however, to take note of Lakoff's admission that this belief is a function of her own impressions and that it is not based on extensive empirical research.[24]

Dale Spender criticises Lakoff's work as sexist, claiming that "Lakoff accepts that men's language is superior and she assumes that this is a feature of their linguistic performance and not of their sex."[25] Spender defends this view by pointing out that when the vehicles of empirical research did shift into gear, they showed a greater preponderance of tag questions among male than female speakers,[26] and from these real statistics no conclusions were drawn regarding male weakness or male lack of confidence in language. As a corrective to the traditional sexist bias, Spender chooses to believe that all assumptions regarding gender-based language differences that point to deficiencies in women's speech, are false. She includes differences in pitch among the beliefs to be rejected.[27] In other words, she wants to disregard all work in which the talk of women has been "reported small", as a counterbalance to the sexism embedded in the entire tradition of linguistic research.

Spender's work is extremely important insofar as it makes clear that the philosophical fact/value distinction is not nearly as straightforward as we have been led to believe — that many so-called "facts" contain implicit value judgements. She is right that sexism can be as deeply entrenched in the reporting of language "facts" as in the social interpretations based on them. Indeed, it may be more likely to occur in the former case — given a philosophic and scientific tradition that views observation as a value-neutral activity, one would naturally be less likely to suspect, search for, and identify sexist biasses in factual observations than in obvious interpretations of this data. Spender is certainly not the first to point out that "seeing is a 'theory-laden' undertaking".[28] Norwood Russell Hanson, for example, made this claim long before her. Spender's contribution lies in her application of this thesis to observations dealing with gender differences in language patterns, and her argument that the theories with which these observations are laden are those of patriarchy and male paternalism.

Nevertheless, I am more reluctant than Spender to label Lakoff's work as sexist. Given that Lakoff's observations were based on personal impressions rather than statistical analyses, they are the "observations" that one would have expected. This disadvantaged position of women relative to men in society does make it reasonable to assume that their language will be more tenuous and uncertain than that of men — that is, *a priori*, it seems a reasonable view that those in authority will speak with greater authority. Nor is such a view necessarily sexist. The belief that women's language is tentative and lacking in conviction is perfectly compatible with the further belief that such language is an index of intelligence, a crucial survival technique in a blatantly misogynist society.

In the same vein, it *need* not even be sexist to supply vastly different interpretations to the same fact where observed in female language output and male language output. For example, it would not violate any principle of fairness to provide contrasting explanations for the behaviour of two people who jumped into a river to save a drowning victim, if one would-be rescuer were a non-swimmer and the other a competent swimmer. It would not be unfair to describe the action of the first person and not the second as foolhardy. Similarly, it would not necessarily be sexist to interpret female tag questions as an expression of greater hesitancy than the situation merited and male tag questions as an expression of greater certitude than the situation merited.[29] Analogously, one could see female tag questions as a direct request for response, support, or feedback from the listener. Such a measure would be an extremely sensible one when the listener was male, given the fairly extensive research on the lack of response of male listeners to female speakers.[30] Male tag questions could be interpreted as an attempt to shape the beliefs of the listener, to pass off as more certain than it is a fairly dubious claim. This is in keeping with the observation, accepted by Spender herself, that men are typically more interested in making language an instrument of persuasion or rhetoric, and women in its use for purposes of conversational exchange.[31] Given a patriarchal context that lends greater credence to the views of males, such opposing interpretations of the same phenomenon — the tag question — do not seem to be either out of order or sexist.

This is not to say that different interpretations of the same phenomenon are never sexist, or even that they are unlikely to be. A patriarchal context points the likelihood in the other direction, and Spender is right to caution suspicion when the same datum gets interpreted differently, according to whether it is predicated of female or male behaviour. Nevertheless, it is important to be clear that such differences in interpretation are theoretically consistent with non-sexist assumptions; furthermore, attaching identical explanations to similar data does not guarantee fairness either. The appropriateness of brash, forceful language, for example, will vary with the social position of different individuals as well as with the different contextual situations of a single individual; this is true in spite of the fact that the linking of language styles with social circumstances has traditionally been done by males in accordance with sexist criteria.

This illustrates that the problem of sexism in linguistic and other types of research is even more slippery and difficult to define than Spender indicates. It cannot be separated from broader social and political issues, so to a discussion of these I now turn.

THE SOCIAL POLITICAL DIMENSIONS OF LANGUAGE

A Study in Oppression

If females are more polite and less aggressive than males in their language practices, if they are more supportive and less dominant, this is hardly shocking, for it simply reflects the reality in every other sphere of life. It meshes all too smoothly with social conceptions of male-valued and female-valued characteristics. An important difference exists between typical male-valued and female-valued features, which I shall explore now. The difference may be summarised by stating that the female-valued characteristics are universalisable, whereas for the most part, male-valued characteristics are not.[32]

Among the typical male-valued items are the following characteristics: very dominant, almost always acts as a leader, not at all easily influenced, very aggressive, not at all uncomfortable about being aggressive, very independent, not at all emotional, very worldly, very adventurous, likes math and science very much, not at all excitable in a minor crisis, very skilled in business, very direct, can make decisions easily. The following are some typical female-valued characteristics: very gentle, very aware of feelings of others, doesn't use harsh language at all, easily expresses tender feelings, enjoys art and literature.[33]

I shall now explore what I take to be a difference in logic between the bulk of the male-valued characteristics and the female-valued characteristics. The first two male-valued items in my list of examples — very dominant and almost always acts as a leader — *could not obtain without* presupposing that the opposite poles of these features were descriptive of other people. More specifically, dominant personalities require submissive people, whom they can dominate. And since dominance is valued only in males in this society, it follows logically that submissiveness will be seen as a valuable female characteristic. A similar logic holds for the leadership feature. The problem for females is that dominance and leadership are highly valued and liberally rewarded features in the realm of employment, whereas submissiveness and lack of leadership are serious handicaps. Logically, in order for males to possess these two male-valued features, females must develop the opposite characteristics which will seriously hamper their access to a wide variety of social goods. Thus maleness, as defined in this society, presupposes the oppression of females.

The next six male-valued characteristics in my list also exemplify this feature, but more weakly. While it is logically possible that the world should contain only individuals who were not at all easily influenced, very aggressive, not at all uncomfortable about being aggressive, very independent, not at all emotional, and very worldly, such a world would not be a very comfortable one in which to live. If no person were at all easily influenced, no one could hope to influence any one else without great difficulty, and much of the mutual trust and co-operative enterprise on which any social structure depends would be ruled out. Much the same point could be made concerning the other examples.

The last six male-valued features are of an entirely different type. Neither logic nor the concept of a cohesive society are jarred by the possibility that everyone be adventurous, like math and science very much, not be excitable in a minor crisis, be skilled in business, be very direct, and be capable of making decisions easily. For one set of people to like math and science very much does not presuppose that another group dislike these disciplines, unlike the dominance of one set of people, which does presuppose the submissiveness of another set. Although it may be unlikely that all individuals would develop these features, such an occurrence would not threaten social cohesiveness in the sense in which universal aggression and worldliness would. In fact, higher levels of these features would mark a healthier society, thus the more people who possessed them, the better.

It is important to note that the female-valued characteristics *all* fit under this third category. For one set of people to be very gentle, very aware of the feelings of others, not to use harsh language, to express tender feelings with ease, and to enjoy art and literature does not demand another set of people defined by the opposite poles of these features. Furthermore, the greater the number of people in any society to possess these features, the happier and healthier such a society would be.

The same description and the same implications chacacterise male and female speech patterns. Thus Spender points out,

> The crucial issue here is that if women cease to be muted, men cease to be dominant....It is necessary that there be modifications in male language behaviour as well as female.[34]

The adoption of male language patterns by females would not work, because these patterns are not universalisable. If *everyone* insisted on defining the topic of conversation her or himself, if no one were willing to develop, express interest in, listen to, or ask questions about the topic introduced by a particular speaker, conversational interactions would flounder and die. If half the pool of participants are wet sponges, the other half are required by logic to perform a band-aid function.

It is small wonder that males self-disclose to females more often than to other males.[35] The prospect of expressing your innermost feelings and concerns to someone who has developed such linguistic habits as expressing little if any interest in what others are saying, making minimal efforts even to appear to be interested, and desiring to talk strictly about his own concerns is self-defeating from the outset. In women, on the other hand, the virtues of the good listener have been inculcated from early childhood, so it is natural that men would seek out women when they wish to talk about more intimate, personal aspects of their lives.

In virtue of such self-disclosures, however, women obtain indirect access to an avenue of power — a power based on knowledge. The more limited the circulation of this knowledge, the greater the power associated with it. This explains an otherwise anomalous circumstance — the extreme disappointment experienced by someone who has been made the recipient of some highly confidential information, only to find that the "secret" has received widespread distribution.[36] The disappointment may reflect frustration at the closing off of a potential source of power.

In any case, because women talk less and listen more carefully than men do, they learn more from conversational exchanges than men. Some of this knowledge is based on what has been explicitly said and some of it is based on more subtle nuances of the situation.

That Rousseau was aware of this is evident in his description of an interchange between a wife and her husband following a dinner party. Unlike her partner, the wife

> knows what So-and-so was thinking; to what such and such a discourse or gesture related; in short, there has scarcely been a significant movement which she is not ready to explain, and nearly always to explain rightly.[37]

Rousseau's suggestion that this "delicate" power of observation is innate in women[38] is odd, however, given his view that the education of little girls ought to be based on such considerations as this:

> In order to speak, a man needs knowledge, a woman needs taste; the chief aim of man ought to be the useful, of women the agreeable. Their discourse should have nothing in common save truth. We ought not therefore to restrain the prattle of girls like that of boys with the harsh question, "Of what use is that?" but by another question, which indeed is no easier to answer, "What effect will that produce?"[39]

In spite of Rousseau's explanation of *why* women possess such "delicate observation," the fact is that they do observe more closely both overt and covert messages in conversation, and that accompanying this more careful observation is knowledge which is a source of power. In their self-disclosures to women, men render themselves vulnerable, for there is always the possibility that their listener will "tell".

This risk can be minimised, however, by minimising the likelihood that a "tattler" will be believed. So theories that define women's speech as trivial, uncertain, based not on knowledge but on taste, gossipy, bitchy, and even malicious, abound. Silent women, women who listen well but talk little, are a commodity beyond price in a patriarchal society.

Given this direction of social pressure, there were no real alternatives to Emily Dickinson's mandate to "tell all the truth but tell it slant", except the alternative of silence. The very fact that we have been able to recognise this silence and put a name to the distortion of women's truth is a measure of progress, however. Perhaps, like Plato's allegorical prisoners in the cave,[40] when men actually come to listen to what women have to say, painful as this will be, they may hear the truth in women's language, not the distorted echo of it reflected from the confining walls of the patriarchal cave.

REFERENCES

1 It is true that even in the case of men's speech, deciding whether to classify a feature as semantical or pragmatical, for example, can be difficult, but this difficulty seems to be compounded in the case of women's speech. This should

not be surprising, given that linguistic categories have been devised by male grammarians to account for the language of males. Nor should it be surprising that when women have been included in language research, they have been measured against a standard of maleness and found lacking, judged "minus male" as it were. See Dale Spender, *Man Made Language* (London: Routledge & Kegan Paul, 1980), p. 148.

2 Robin Lakoff, *Language and Woman's Place* (New York: Harper Colophon Books, Harper & Row, Publishers, 1975), p. 17.

3 *Ibid.*, pp. 15 - 17 and Mary Ritchie Key, *Male/Female Language* (Metuchen, NJ: The Scarecrow Press, Inc., 1975), p. 76. There is clear disagreement in the literature about this claim. See, for example, Spender, *op. cit.*, pp. 8 - 10. This controversy will be further explored in the next part of this chapter.

4 Spender, *op. cit.*, p. 146.

5 See Linda Harrison, "Cro-Magnon Woman — In Eclipse", *The Science Teacher* (April, 1975), pp. 8 - 11. See also Casey Miller and Kate Swift, *Words and Women: New Language in New Times* (Garden City, NY: Anchor Books, Anchor Press/Doubleday, 1977), pp. 19 - 23. The material provided in these passages from *Words and Women* provides substantial empirical support for the hypothesis.

6 Spender, *op. cit.*, p. 153.

7 Key, *op. cit.*, p. 34; Lakoff, *op. cit.*, pp. 8 - 9.

8 Key, *op. cit.*, pp. 33 - 34; Lakoff, *op. cit.*, p. 12.

9 Key, *op. cit.*, p. 75.

10 *Ibid.*, pp. 75 - 76.

11 *Ibid.*, p. 76.

12 Lakoff, *op. cit.*, pp. 18 - 19.

13 Key, *op. cit.*, p. 130. See also D.H. Zimmerman and Candace West, "Sex Roles, Interruptions and Silences in Conversation", in *Language and Sex: Difference and Dominance*, ed. Barrie Thorne and Nancy Henley (Rowley, MA: Newbury House Publishers Inc., 1975), pp. 116 - 117.

14 Pamela M. Fishman, "Interactional Shitwork", *Heresies: A Feminist Publication on Arts and Politics*, 2 (May, 1977), 99 - 101.

15 This phrase occurred originally in a poem by Emily Dickinson, in which she advised:

Tell all the Truth but tell it slant —
Success in Circuit lies
Too bright for our infirm Delight
The Truth's superb surprise
As Lightning to the Children eased
With explanation kind
The Truth must dazzle gradually
Or every man be blind —

Emily Dickinson, *The Complete Poems of Emily Dickinson*, ed. Thomas H.

Johnson (Boston: Little, Brown and Company, 1960), pp. 506 - 507, Poem 1129, C. 1868. See Spender, *op. cit.*, pp. 81 - 84, for a discussion of the significance of "telling it slant".

16 For some clear historical evidence in support of this claim, with particular reference to the "generic" status of "he" and "man", see *Ibid.*, pp. 144, 147 - 148, 150, and 158 - 159.

17 *Ibid.*, pp. 84 and 153 - 154.

18 *Ibid.*, pp. 41 - 42.

19 *Ibid.*. pp. 42 - 43.

20 See Ann Bodine, "Sex Differentiation in Language", in Thorne and Henley, eds., *op. cit.*, p. 130.

21 See J.G. Frazer, "A Suggestion as to the Origin of Gender in Language", *Fortnightly Review*, new series, Vol. 67 (1900), 79 - 90. Ann Bodine (*op. cit.*, p. 130) cites Frazer's work.

22 See Lakoff, *op. cit.*, p. 15.

23 *Ibid.*, p. 16.

24 *Ibid.*

25 See Spender, *op. cit.*, p. 8.

26 *Ibid.*, p. 9.

27 *Ibid.*, pp. 40 - 41.

28 "Observation of *x* is shaped by prior knowledge of *x*", Hanson continues. See Norwood Russell Hanson, *Patterns of Discovery: An Inquiry into the Conceptual Foundations of Science* (Cambridge: The University Press, 1965), p. 19.

29 Adams and Ware, for example, suggest that tag questions are used by men

> to make a question sound more like an assertion, so as not to appear uninformed....In addition others have found tag questions to be used as veiled threats by males, e.g., "You agree with me, don't you?"

Karen L. Adams and Norma C. Ware, "Sexism and the English Language: The Linguistic Implications of Being a Woman", in *Woman: A Feminist Perspective*, ed. Jo Freeman (2nd ed.; Palo Alto, CA: Mayfield Publishing Company, 1979), p. 496.

30 Fishman, *op. cit.*, pp. 100 - 101 and Spender, *op. cit.*, pp. 42 - 50.

31 Spender, *op. cit.*, pp. 78 - 81.

32 This same claim, as well as the following discussion which explores the different logic of the male and female-valued items, is developed in my "Women's Rights — A Pragmatic Alternative to the Inflated Price of Social Justice", a paper presented to the World Congress on Philosophy of Law and Social Philosophy, Basel, Switzerland, August/September, 1979, pp. 14 - 17.

33 Inge K. Broverman *et al.*, "Sex-Role Stereotypes: A Current Appraisal", *Journal of Social Issues*, Vol. 28, No. 2 (1972), 63.

34 Spender, *op. cit.*, p. 89.

35 Sidney M. Jourard, "Some Lethal Aspects of the Male Role", in *Men and*

Masculinity, ed. J.H. Pleck and J. Sawyer (Englewood Cliffs, N.J.: Prentice-Hall, Inc., 1974), pp. 25 - 26.

36 I suspect (but without the benefit of any empirical evidence) that this disappointment would be more characteristic of females than males. Males, after all, have access to many more forms of power than females, so it seems at least plausible to suggest that females would prize more highly than males the few inroads to power which they do have.

37 Jean Jacques Rousseau, *His Educational Theories Selected from Émile, Julie and Other Writings*, ed. R.L. Archer (Woodbury, NY: Barron's Educational Series, Inc., 1964), p. 231.

38 *Ibid.*

39 *Ibid.*, p. 227.

40 Plato, *The Republic of Plato*, tran. with an introduction by Francis MacDonald Cornford (New York: Oxford University Press, 1945), pp. 227 - 231.

FURTHER READINGS

Fishman, Pamela M. "Interactional Shitwork", *Heresies: A Feminist Publication on Arts and Politics*, 2 (May, 1977), 99 - 101.

Key, Mary Ritchie. *Male/Female Language; With a comprehensive bibliography*. Metuchen, NJ: The Scarecrow Press, Inc., 1975.

Lakoff, Robin. *Language and Woman's Place*. New York: Harper Colophon Books, Harper & Row, Publishers, 1975.

Miller, Casey and Kate Swift. *Words and Women: New Language in New Times*. Garden City, NY: Anchor Books, Anchor Press/Doubleday, 1977.

Spender, Dale. *Man Made Language*. London: Routledge & Kegan Paul, 1980.

Zimmerman, D.H. and Candace West. "Sex Roles, Interruptions and Silences in Conversation," in *Language and Sex: Difference and Dominance*, ed. Barrie Thorne and Nancy Henley. Series in Sociolinguistics; series editor Roger W. Shuy. Rowley, MA: Newbury House Publishers Inc., 1975, pp. 105 - 129.

JUDITH CRAWLEY
GRETA HOFMANN NEMIROFF
ALANNA STALKER

Art and Daily Life

In March, 1982, Judith Crawley mounted a photographic exhibit entitled *Relations* at Galerie Dazibao in Montréal. As is customary for artists exhibiting at this gallery, she was invited to give a public talk on her work:

> A collective presentation with my friends and colleagues, Greta [Hofmann Nemiroff] and Alanna [Stalker] on how our art inter-connects with and informs our daily lives was much more tantalizing to me than a one-dimensional chronological report on the development of my photography. I also wanted to defuse the cool white atmosphere of the gallery. Greta and Alanna were not only the subjects of many of my photographs, but also were artists working in different media, except with similar concerns. I wanted to reflect the feminism in my engagement with art, which I knew them to share, that extends from the subject and the social concerns of my camera's gaze to the very process that informs the making and presentations of the images.
>
> Judith Crawley

Our format combined readings from Greta's fiction with slide projections of Alanna's drawings and paintings and Judy's photographs. Encouraged by the warm reception of our presentation on that occasion, we have given other presentations, always expanding and changing our contents as our relationships and art making dynamically develop. In this article, we hope to convey the essence of our presentations in yet another medium...print. Despite the changes in content and the transformational aspects of the print medium, the essential thematic element remains: our relationships as women artists, teachers, wives and lovers, mothers and the children of our parents.

While our friendship and its shared exploration has been instrumental to our articulating the issues and arriving at some resolutions of them, the voyage of development as artists has been very individual for each of us:

Wanting to be an artist all my life, I looked forward to going to art school. Because I was single and young in art school, I was able to benefit from the facilities and unbroken blocks of time, perceiving myself as an "artist" in what I now understand to have been the conventional male manner. When I had left art school, married and had children, my time became fragmented due to the many claims imposed both by the situation and my conditioning; there was no space which could become separated from my daily life. When my conditioning regarding the roles of wife and mother came into conflict with my art school values, I felt forced to make a choice between the two. It never occurred to me to question the values underlying my art training. While I struggled to conform to the manner in which I had been trained, my "art" production (i.e. trying to do big paintings) petered out to "studies" in my journal such as drawings and writings, which I did not then perceive as art. Years later, now a single mother of two, attending graduate school at night with a full-time paid job during the day, even though I was focussing on sex-role stereotyping in Art Education, I did not apply my findings to my own work; I was still trying to produce large works of art. Because my time was even more fragmented than ever before, I was forced to realise that if I wanted to produce any art at all, I would have to question the values underlying my art school education. I had to accept this fragmentation and work within it; if I could no longer produce large works in the midst of daily life, I would work small. This led me to re-evaluate the importance of my journals as "art" itself, and also to produce paintings on small panels which recorded the events, people and places of my daily life.

Alanna Stalker

Alanna speaks of herself as an artist...one with no time, searching for ways to make art while preoccupied with family life, young children, friends and teaching. I as a beginning photographer at the same time did not conceive of myself as an "artist" or as a "photographer". My fascination for image-making...arresting moments, scenes, and fragments of life...never developed out of an interest in making "art". Nor did I have the concerns of academic art photography schools where aesthetics are divorced from meaning and personal and social implications; rather, my work came from the need to record and share the richness of our immediate lives. My camera is with me as I parent, visit, meet, travel, work and organise. My life is one of political action. I photograph events I'm participating in, and my friends alone, with their mates and children. Over the years, the lives of Greta and Alanna, among other friends, have faced my camera. Not a deliberate decision to document lives, photography provides me with a way of understanding and dealing in images with significant relationships and moments of my life. My images exploit photography's ambiguous relationship to the visible and social world. They are not built on a romantic

FIGURE 25.1
Reproduction of a journal page (Stalker).

or idealised rendering of the world, but on a day-to-day experiencing of it. Eventually my friends encouraged me to move beyond using my photographs as currency for personal exchange and to ‘‘go public’’ by exhibiting them. For me this meant acknowledging that my personal experience, life around me and my friends, had meaning to others, and therefore qualified as ‘‘art’’, as reflection on experience. A major struggle for me in exhibiting my work was how to present the images. I had great difficulty in hanging them in a row surrounded by big mats...an imitation of ‘‘high’’ art not appropriate to the intimacy of my images. My strategy became to group the photographs within one frame so that they reinforce and contradict one another, the meanings playing off and enriching each other in a circular rather than a linear manner. It is the relationships between the people, not the individuals themselves, which are the subject. The quadruple image [Figures 25.3 and 25.4] suggests some of the complexity of life and forces my photographs out of the strictly personal to the larger audience beyond my community.

Judith Crawley

FIGURE 25.2
Alanna writing in journal (Crawley).

While I have been writing and painting since early childhood, there was nothing in my formal training which really validated my own experience as viable subject matter. I studied both Art and Creative Writing at the university level and found myself forced into a double life: producing what was expected by my teachers as "art", and then producing private works for myself. I think that this pattern established itself in my life and I became an educator in order financially to support myself and my family. I relegated my art to a realm of private expression to be shared with a few friends...mainly women...who "understood". It was only through my interest in Feminism, through sharing with other women what it feels like to create and find subjects viscerally authentic for creation, that I began to suspect that my writing actually could reach beyond my own small circle. The feminist periodicals in Canada have been a very encouraging force in the publication of my fiction, although I have been published by "malestream" ones as well.[1] But it was my sharing with my friends and seeing their reactions to my work which gave me the strength to believe that my stories were more than mere personal scribblings. For example, I was once reading a story I wrote to Alanna. It is about a woman incarcerated in a car with her husband of some years. They are on a vacation trip to renew their flagging marriage and she is silently thinking about her situation:

But it must also be said that each night I dream of suffocation, choking. Some nights I am so fearful of sleeping and falling prey to my dreams that I've evolved a game or exercise that I run through as I lie beside your still, oblivious body. In my mind, I comb through the house and form an inventory...drawer by drawer, cupboard by cupboard...of all the things I can let go. I call this hoard my 'letting go' collection. As you snore softly with one arm over your eyes (to ward me off, I've always thought), I begin to extend my list to people, situations, relationships. I let go wherever I can. Eventually I drift off to sleep and awaken the next day unrested and unable to recall who and what were on the list. Somewhat hung over those mornings, I feel the way I imagine a promiscuous woman of some status feels the morning after drunken revels. She cannot remember on whom she lavished her favours, but recalls heightened scenes of pornographic essence and humiliating intent with unidentifiable people.

"We Are in a Car Going Somewhere"[2]

When I read this passage to Alanna, she began to cry; it was in this way that I found out she was planning to leave her husband. While her tears, of course, touched me with empathy, they also confirmed to me that my work could reach out to others and touch their lives. I realised that the way in which we experience alienation within marriage on a day-to-day basis is worthy of expression and must be transformed into art. From that time on, I began to write more exigently and to send my work out to journals. Eventually it began to be published regularly. It took this confidence in my viability to keep sending it out once it had been rejected somewhere, and it all finally is getting published...or most of it, anyway.

Greta Hofmann Nemiroff

By this time, the readers of this chapter must perceive that it differs from most academic writing, both stylistically and in terms of content. We do not speak from the vantage point of "one" or "they", but from the very basis of our own experience. Furthermore, our daily life is considered an appropriate resource not only for our art, but for our analyses of society. In presenting our "private" lives in a "public" arena, we are deviating from the traditional male-inspired form of academic communication, yet we too wish to teach through our own choice and style of communication.

In the history of Western culture, the prototype of the artist has always been male. In recent history, however, there has been a proliferation of women studying the arts in art schools and universities. While about 80 per cent of the students in Canadian post-secondary Fine Arts programmes are women, after graduation they tend to be under-represented in exhibitions, the juries for grants and exhibitions, in curatorships, and in full-time teaching on the post-secondary level. Indeed, over 80 per cent of all full-

FIGURE 25.3
Quartet of photos of Alanna (Crawley).

FIGURE 25.4
Quartet of photos of Greta (Crawley).

time teachers of Fine Arts at this level are male, and they pass on the historically normative values defining what Art is, how to create it and under what conditions.[3] The same holds true for Creative Writing programmes at this level where there is a similar under-representation of female teachers and a large contingent of women students. Mainstream Canadian periodical publishing of fiction and poetry continues this trend.[4] This phenomenon is further manifested in both the production of plays by Canadian women, their directors, and the number of parts for women in most Canadian plays.[5]

The values passed along about how the "artist" is to conduct *his* life contend that he must have large blocks of time committed solely to his work, separated from his personal and daily life and from the contingencies of that life. He must compose huge "major works", and above all, he must deal with the "big ideas and themes". The prevailing notion of universality in male culture is one of abstractions with the impersonal rendering of subject matter in a manner detached from the mundane facts of the artist's own daily life...unless, of course, they can become informed with the aura of "universal themes".

The phenomenon of the division of the personal from the public life followed upon the industrial revolution where men's work was removed from the home. Unless they took in work, those women who had to work for wages were also removed from their homes. On the whole, though, women were relegated to the rearing of children and maintenance of the home...forms of production that are still unrecognised as such throughout the world. This became known as the "private sphere".[6]

Women's experience, as women experienced it, was not considered worthy of comment through Art, although men were permitted either to glorify, eroticise, or romanticise women. We became the objects of men's art with little attention paid to our subjective experience.[7]

In our own lives as artists, the three of us have not been able to maintain the division of the public and private lives. As outlined above, each of us came late to this understanding from a different set of experiences and after much struggle.

Unlike male artists who are historically reputed to have had meaningful discussions in such public places as bars and cafés, our discussions have taken place in the "private" sphere...in our kitchens mainly. Our work is informed by the pervasive presence of our homes and families, a central locus of women's experience, and it is permeated with the awareness of drinking coffee on the porch off Alanna's dining room or poring together over Judy's photographs on her round oak table. Our knowledge of one another is rooted in our understanding of the minutiae of one another's lives and the shared bottom line that ultimately our children are the most important factors in our lives. From talking about whether the children need new rubber boots for the spring to talking about art with a small "a",

FIGURE 25.5
Drawing from Friendship Painting (Stalker).

our friendship enables us to bear witness to one another's lives as fully as we possibly can, and with compassion. As well we are, none of us, afraid of being fully known by the others; there is no shame involved. Hence our art is generated by the double experience of bearing witness with compassion and having witness borne without shame.

We sat there in the stillness of the child-sleeping house, looking at each other. There was a closeness between the three of us that is rare in groups of three. I suddenly realised that not one of us was really very adept at expressing sadness any more. Our tears were much more likely to be of rage or frustration. We were becoming, I suddenly realised, a bit hardened: middle-aged women with a lot behind us and well established survival patterns. I didn't mention this to my friends, though. They looked so vulnerable there in the lateness of the evening. Miraculously, and like a spirit, a smile passed through us. We clinked the dregs of our glasses in silent irony. It was time to go. The evening had gone as far as it was likely to and we all had plans for the next day.

Visitings[8]
Greta Hofmann Nemiroff

Judy's exhibition, *Giving Birth Is Just the Beginning: Women Speak Out about Mothering* (1985) builds on mothering as a shared historical experience. The project pierces more deeply into an aspect of *Relations.* The same women with their children and their men kept reappearing in her imagery over the years, as she documented the most casual of visits. She developed the idea of interviewing her subjects on their experience of mothering, and then she combined excerpts from the transcriptions of those taped interviews with images, and printed them together.

The relationship of women to their children is important in all of our work. In the novel, *Visitings*, the protagonist writes a letter to a new male friend about what really matters to her:

> Here's something that does matter to me. Today in the late afternoon I sat on the front porch waiting for Harry to come home to dinner, when my daughter, Zoë, came over to me. She was a bit runny-nosed and none too clean. She climbed onto my lap and I held her sturdy little three year old body against mine and buried my face in her dark curls. She smelled that special smell of active children and her body, usually wiry and restless, for once seemed to melt into mine. We sat there for a while heart-to-heart, her hands meeting behind my neck. For a moment I felt that the whole world...all space, time and history...had contracted to that one moment. Especially poignant was the knowledge that such moments are fewer between, that this kind of totally trusting babyhood is ephemeral...to say the least. They say that for some time after birth the child and mother share the same heart beats and body rhythmns. I felt that, even though it's three years since her birth, as I held her on the front porch this warm autumn afternoon. I felt that rare feeling of total harmony with this other being. So here's something that REALLY REALLY matters to me. My offering for the day.

Visitings[8]
Greta Hofmann Nemiroff

Alanna is very close to both her mother and her daughter, Mara. She is interested in recording the feeling of those specific mother-daughter relationships as they inform her everyday life:

> In struggling to return to producing my art, within the midst of daily life, I began to record on small panels my surroundings and the people who populate them: my parents, children and friends. The following triptych evolved through finding that three separate small paintings belonged together and could be incorporated as a window into my life. This particular work, "Mothers and Daughters", is part of a series of "windows" influenced directly by Judy's groups of four. My interest in minutiae and involvement in the many "small" things of life was further validated by the fact that Greta was absorbed with similar issues in her writing.

Alanna Stalker

We encouraged our son to express some of the so-called female qualities, his emotions, his affection, gentleness, etc. The very first day of school, he was 6 years old, he met a friend and when he hugged and kissed him, he was beaten up. He began to feel that only at home could he express his feelings, cry, be affectionate and gentle.

Mara's treatment was different. She was frozen out, ignored if her peer group didn't approve of her behaviour. I recall her going to school in a dress and doing a somersault and being totally ostracized because she was showing her underwear.

So she can't climb a tree or do a somersault, and he can't be gentle and affectionate; they are both losing valuable characteristics. *Alanna*

Nous avons encourager notre fils à exprimer ses qualités soi-disant "femelles", ses émotions, son affection, sa gentillesse. Au premier jour de l'école, il avait 6 ans, il rencontre un ami qu'il embrasse et sert dans ses bras. On l'a battu. Il a commencé à croire qu'on exprimait ses sentiments, qu'on pouvait pleurer, être affecteux, gentil seulement à la maison.

Pour Mara c'était différent. Elle était figée si ses copains n'approuvaient pas son comportement. Je me rappelle, une fois, elle est allée à l'école en robe, a fait une pirouette et a été bannie pour avoir montré ses petites culottes.

Alors elle n'a pas le droit de grimper dans les arbres, de faire des pirouettes, et lui n'a pas le droit d'être gentil et affectueux. Les deux y perdent. *Alanna*

FIGURE 25.6
Alanna with her children and text (Crawley).

I'm not always a good parent. Sometimes I'm a really lousy one, or mediocre, and you have to be able to forgive yourself for that. The post-Spock era has put so much emphasis on people being good parents that making your children happy is now the main goal, anything that happens to your child is your fault.

In the past, the infant mortality rate was so high, women's first job was to make sure their children survived. They didn't have the time, they were weaving, sewing, washing, growing and preparing food, to worry about every move they made affecting their child's psyche.

The productivity of the child, not the happiness, was the concern. The goal was to create an adult who would be able to care for you in your old age.

Greta

Je ne suis pas toujours bon parent. Parfois je suis vraiment mauvaise ou médiocre, et il faut savoir se pardonner ça. L'ére post-Spock insiste tellement sur les bons parents, où rendre les enfants heureux est le but ultime et où tout ce qui arrive à vos enfants est de votre faute.

Par le passé, la responsabilité première de la mère était de s'assurer de la survie de ses enfants parce que le taux de mortalité infantile était si élevé. Tissant, cousant, lavant, cultivant et cuisinant, elle n'avait pas le temps de s'inquiéter de l'effet de ses moindres gestes sur le psyché de l'enfant.

La productivité de l'enfant et non pas son bonheur était primordiale. Votre but était d'en faire un adulte qui s'occuperait de vous une fois devenus vieux.

Greta

FIGURE 25.7
Greta with daughter, Rebecca, and text (Crawley).

FIGURE 25.8
Drawing of her children, Mara and Kyle (Stalker).

FIGURE 25.9
"Mothers and Daughters" (Stalker).

We share common interests in our work outside of the home. We all teach in community colleges in Montréal. Greta, who is older than Judy and Alanna, was instrumental in hiring them to teach at Vanier College in Montréal because of shared attitudes to education. All of us believe in and aspire to the full engagement of both teacher and student in the holistic experience of learning:

I saw through my teaching experience that most people didn't draw, had stopped in childhood, and though they might feel a desire to express themselves, had accepted the premise that drawing was a matter of special talent. As a teacher at Vanier College, I had discovered that by using eye-hand co-ordination exercises, most people could learn to draw. As a feminist, I was struck by how much we in the women's movement dealt with theory and how little we dealt with the experiential. We as women might have studied advertising to see how we were expected to look, but there was no means for us individually to get beyond the surface to explore visually who we are.

Alanna Stalker

In teaching, I struggle against the walls of alienation built into the educational system: since losing the strike of 1983, we have longer teaching hours, bigger classes, and even more students with reduced resources and less pay.[4] I try to work closely with the students to encourage them to see their world with clarity and to articulate their vision and understanding in photographic images.

Judith Crawley

FIGURE 25.10
Alanna teaching (Crawley).

Both Judith and Alanna bring their feminism as well as their skills and general teaching philosophy together in their contributions to the Women's Studies Programme in their college. Greta, who used to teach at Vanier College with them, moved on in 1973 to become Director of an alternative programme based on Humanistic Education, The New School of Dawson College in Montréal. There she teaches English and Women' Studies:

> Like Alanna and Judith, I too believe in the holistic necessity in teaching: that cognitive and affective learning must take place at one and the same time. As a feminist, I also develop many experiential workshops designed to facilitate the empowerment of women through their own insights which they share. We all discuss our teaching; Judith and Alanna are among the few people I know outside of the school who grasp what I am talking about when I describe my work at the New School.
>
> Greta Hofmann Nemiroff

We all belong to the same public service union (the CSN) and have strong feelings about workers' rights; we also have concerns regarding the conservative direction the state is taking in education. Judith and Alanna are both active in their union local; Greta is politically very active in her college, but approaches the union with skepticism...although she invariably rallies dur-

FIGURE 25.11
Greta teaching (Crawley).

ing strikes. Judith edits the newsletter of her union local, and she and Alanna have collaborated on various projects during strikes:

During our last strike, I used my photography to provide an historical record of the Vanier College teachers during the strike of 1983. This record provided us with imagery to use in our further communications in the struggle...as posters, in the newsletter, and as an exhibit in the college when we returned to work. Eventually I gave a public presentation on this process.[10]

Judith Crawley

The photographs Judy made to document the strike in 1983 influenced me to paint a banner which we draped in front of the college when we were forced back to work. Then Judy's photo of this banner and the banner itself became further documentation of the strike...getting absorbed into the process.

Alanna Stalker

During the strike of 1983, we would talk on the phone and compare notes on our respective locals' responses to the situation. Greta wrote a story-documentation of the strike which matches well with many of Judith's photos:

FIGURE 25.12
Vanier College Strike banner (Crawley).

It is very cold during the February strike. They wear layers of clothing, jump up and down to keep warm, sometimes take refuge in a doorway with a radiator, and try to heat themselves with the soup, coffee and bagels distributed at regular intervals by the union van. Union broadsides are handed around and read like the Scriptures. The van drivers spread news from other picket lines. Rumours abound about possible scabs. One day she is so cold she can feel the imprint of her skeleton on her inner flesh; it is impossible to warm up before the next day's shift begins. Through the glass doors of her building she sees shadowy-shapes of the management; they seem to be leering at the strikers from their warm, institutional nest. One day she manages to stop two people from entering the building with her cowardly middle-aging body...or perhaps it was her words. The cold days stick together like cough drops collecting lint in a deep pocket. The picket line is paralysed with boredom...Daily their signs get increasingly tattered and illegible.

"Strike,"
Greta Hofmann Nemiroff[11]

Working for the union movement is not the only political source of our art. Beyond syndicalism is our commitment to Feminism. Feminism must always involve the striving towards political and social rights within a possible new definition of what is political...what is social. This definition is formed by re-examining what is considered to be of value in our present

FIGURE 25.13
Alanna and Mara picketing (Crawley).

political and social structures. As artists we believe in the importance of the search by women for new modes of expression in our art, modes which validate our experience as women and the views derived from that experience.

Because the bases of our daily life...friendship, mothering, teaching and political involvement as well as art...can never be static, our work always changes and evolves. Our lives and the evolution of our work endlessly provide us with subject matter which further informs each of our work. Our collaboration is not only an important expression, it is also a catalyst of change in our personal lives, our art, and our political participation. In our art, we combine one another's images and words, each work leading to others in a dynamic process.

FIGURE 25.14
Drawing of Judith (Stalker).

FIGURE 25.15
Drawing of Greta (Stalker).

Alanna in her fortieth year: her nest righting itself; children in place; sentimental detritus of her so-far life arranged the way she likes.
Easter they all went over to the Spring flower show – cool bulb scent – and home to a pretty tea.
And then there's her mother, Mrs. Stalker, who looks less than twice her daughter's age – they share a spark. Together they push aside old obstacles and explore their lives' inter-twinings in fits and starts.

10 August, 1984. Greta.

FIGURE 25.16
Photo of Alanna and her mother with written comments (Crawley/Nemiroff).

REFERENCES

1 Some Canadian feminist periodicals publishing fiction and poetry are: *Fireweed, Hysteria, La vie en rose, Herizons, Room of One's Own.*

2 ''We Are in a Car Going Somewhere'', *Matrix*, Lennoxville: Québec, No. 18, Spring, 1983.

3 For example, a recent survey at Concordia university in Montréal in 1985 indicated that about 75 per cent of the students in the undergraduate and graduate Fine Arts degree programmes are female, but only about 14.5 per cent of the faculty are female.

4 Eleanor Wachtel, *Feminist Print Media*, unpublished report submitted to the Women's Programme, Secretary of State, 20 May 1982.

5 Rina Fraticelli, "Women in Canadian Theatre", *Fuse*, Vol. 6, No. 3, September, 1982.

6 There are numerous books which discuss this subject, but perhaps one of the foremost Canadian ones is Mary O'Brien's *The Politics of Reproduction*, London: Routledge and Kegan Paul, 1981.

7 See John Berger, *Ways of Seeing*, New York: Penguin Books, 1977; Thomas B. Hess and Elizabeth C. Baker, eds., *Art and Sexual Politics*, New York: Macmillan Publishing Co., 1977; Linda Nochlin, "Introduction," *Women Artists: 1550 - 1950*, Los Angeles County Museum of Art, 1976; Joanna Russ, *How to Suppress Women's Writing*, Austin, Texas: University of Texas Press, 1983.

8 Greta Hofmann Nemiroff, *Visitings*, unpublished novel, 1983.

9 In 1983 300,000 public service workers in Québec, including the college (CEGEP) teachers, went on strike for better working conditions and pay. This "common front" lost the battle with the consequences that teachers have a larger work load and less pay than they did in 1982. We are working under a "decree" rather than a collective agreement as before.

10 Society for Photographic Education, National Conference, Riverside, California, March, 1984.

11 Greta Hofmann Nemiroff, "Strike", *Baker's Dozen*, Toronto: The Women's Press, 1984.

FURTHER READINGS

Berger, John. *Ways of Seeing*, Middlesex, England: Penguin Books, 1980.

Bradner, Su. *Committing Photography*. London: Pluto Press, 1983.

Carr, Emily. *Hundreds and Thousands — The Journals of Emily Carr*, Toronto: Clarke Irwin & Co., 1966.

Collins, Georgia, and Renée Sandell. *Women Art and Education*, NAEA Press, 1984.

"What You Staring At?" *Exposure*, 22:2 (Summer, 1984). Society for Photographic Education, P.O. Box 1651, FDR Post Office, New York, NY 10150, U.S.A.

Loeb, Judy, ed. *Feminist Collage: Educating Women in the Visual Arts*, New York: Teachers College Press, Columbia University, 1979.

Olsen, Tillie. *Silences*, New York: Delacorte Press, 1978.

Russ, Joanna. *How to Suppress Women's Writing*, Austin, Texas: University of Texas Press, 1983.

Webber, Jeannette L. and Joan Grumman, eds., *Woman as Writer*, Boston: Houghton Mifflin Comany, 1978.

CHUCK SAMUELS

Men, Women and Photography: Four Male Photographers' Approach to 'Women's Issues'

INTRODUCTION

Recently I've come across four photography projects, all produced by men, that portray women or touch on issues that have been brought to the public's attention by women, such as women's status in the labour market, women's situation in the home, and birthing. I perceive this work as part of a trend, and I'm left wondering why men are suddenly so fascinated with these issues. Are these men genuinely interested and supportive of women's struggle? Or are these issues simply *au courant* and therefore ripe for exploitation? Perhaps it's not that simple. However, by presenting photographs of "women's problems", no matter how well intentioned, these men are helping to define these issues.

I would like to examine these exhibits, whose common thread is their male authorship, their relationship to women and women's struggle, both as individual projects and as a phenomenon. Although I am scrutinising four particular bodies of work, it is my intention to build critical models which the reader may apply to other photographic or cultural events.

WOMEN AND NON-TRADITIONAL WORK

One of the projects organised by La Maison de la Culture Côte des Neiges in Montréal to celebrate International Women's Day, 1984, was an exhibit of photographs by Alain Chagnon. This exhibit, entitled *T.N.T., Travailleuses Non Traditionnelles*, was a documentary project dealing with women work-

An earlier version of this chapter was published in *Fuse* magazine, VIII: 6 (Spring 1985).

ing mainly in blue-collar jobs. Despite the fact that all of Chagnon's images depicted the same subject matter, his photographs were not, for the most part, visually monotonous. Perhaps it was the ostensibly positive nature of the show, a celebration of women who are workers in so-called "non-traditional" jobs (welders, mechanics, assembly-line workers, bus drivers, pilots, etc.) that maintained our interest; or maybe it was the women themselves, who appeared so comfortable, competent and generally happy in their occupations. It could have been the format used by Chagnon to portray these women: his handsome prints were presented in an attractive graphic style that helped keep afloat what might otherwise have been an aesthetically dull show.

Although there were approximately seventy images in this exhibit, there were only nine individually framed photographs. Most of the remaining images were framed in groups of two or three photos, each set portraying one woman in her work environment. This graphic device offered us a more complex view of each woman and her work than a single image could and strengthened the idea that this exhibit was more of a social/political statement than a collection of individual masterpieces.

In a set of twenty-four tightly knit images concentrated together in a grid of four frames, we were barraged by photograph after photograph of women posed in front of their workplaces looking into the camera, often smiling. Each photo was captioned with the woman's name, occupation and, usually, the name of her employer. There was a message being drummed into us here; we were presented with photographic evidence of a "truth" that could not be denied. The message read: Women *are* working in "non-traditional" jobs. The dogmatic repetition of this message left little room for reflection or dialogue. In the face of this numbing optimism, one would have had to be some sort of kill-joy to bring up such issues as tokenism, job discrimination in hiring, unequal pay, sexual harrassment, inadequate day care, or the high unemployment rate among women workers.

When, in his statement, Chagnon said he was making images of new situations, he overlooked the fact that women have worked in many similar "non-traditional" jobs since the turn of the century. Women have been available as a reserve work force whenever there has been a demand for extra (and cheap) labour, such as periods of rapid industrial growth or wartime. However, when the need for labour slackens (notably when the soldiers returned from overseas after World War II), women have been made to melt back into the home.[1]

Chagnon also stated that he wanted to present evidence of the capacity of women to work in fields other than those to which they are usually relegated: secretary, nurse, waitress, etc. While, of course, it is always very encouraging to see women working in blue-collar areas and presumably enjoying more benefits and higher salaries than most "pink-collar" workers, Chagnon's "postive images" imply that all is well, that women are now being accepted as equals and that no further struggle is required. For instance, there are more than a few photographs of women happily working at Pratt & Whitney Canada Incorporated, a manufacturer of aircraft engines in Longueuil, Québec. This particular company has had one charge of systematic discrimination in hiring laid against them by Action Travail des Femmes (a Montréal group that helps organise women to gain access to the "non-traditional" labour market), as well as several individual complaints by women who were refused blue-collar jobs. In fact, Carole Wallace of ATF says that she would be "hard put to name a company that pursues a more discriminatory hiring policy against women in blue-collar jobs than Pratt & Whitney". Besides a small number of token women inspectors (most of whom have since been laid off), women were usually hired there to work in one of two jobs, assembly or engraving,[2] and when this show was exhibited they were no longer being hired for blue-collar labour at all.[3]

To his credit, Chagnon did not glamourise these women. As with most humanistic documentary photography, his subjects were presented in a dignified manner, primarily as people and secondly as workers. Although their gender was addressed by the very nature of the project, their sexuality was not overly exploited. What was glamourised in the Maison de la Culture exhibit, however, was work itself, and its availability. Ignored is the fact that, owing to trends of modernisation through automation and computerisation, the number of blue collar jobs is being significantly reduced and, as always, women workers will probably suffer the greatest losses. Chagnon showed women who work on the assembly line at General Motors in St. Thérèse, a company that has been laying off blue-collar workers partially because of increased automation on the line.[4] The photographs, however, seemed to say that jobs are readily obtainable and that if a woman is unemployed or working in a low-paying pink-collar area, it is her own fault.

The women in Chagnon's exhibit appeared quite comfortable being photographed while performing their jobs, as if they were somehow used to it. If we remember that women who work in "non-traditional" jobs always have to prove themselves (at least initially, if not continually), we can understand how they might have become accustomed to this sort of observation[5] and, of course, photography has been (and is) used in industry as a mode of surveillance, advertising and reward.[6]

While women have made some progress in penetrating the blue-collar labour market, the situation is far from satisfactory (for instance, in 1982 Canadian women earned somewhere in the neighbourhood of 56 per cent of what their male counterparts earned[7]) and women's entrance into the "non-

Denise Lamarche, chaîne d'assemblage G.M., Boisbriand nov 83

FIGURE 26.1
Denise Lamarche, G.M. assembly-line worker, Boisbriand (Chagnon).

traditional'' workplace is not a *fait accompli* as Chagnon's Maison de la Culture show suggested. This exhibit, while portraying women as strong and competent, could also have been seen as good public relations material for their employers, at least one of which actively discriminates against women in hiring. It is unfortunate that the affirming qualities of the photographs have to be played down in order to look at the side of the story that Chagnon didn't tell us, but sadder still is the fact that it was *necessary* for Chagnon to omit references to unequal pay, job discrimination, etc., if he wanted to offer us a positive view of women's current position in the blue-collar labour market. However well intentioned, *T.N.T.*, as it was presented at Maison de la Culture, did not provoke discourse; it invoked closure.

Fortunately Chagnon has managed to salvage the project from what Walter Benjamin called ''the ravages of modishness''.[8] Trying to ''flesh out'' his exhibit with captions, Chagnon renewed contact with some of the women he photographed. He found that many of them were experiencing a host of problems in their workplace, while others were no longer working in blue-collar jobs. This information has found its way into the modified version of *T.N.T.* which Chagnon has since exhibited. In this show, most of the photographs were captioned by bits of information such as the low ratio of women to men workers at GM, or we find out that one woman who was

Suzanne Bairstow, conductrice d'autobus, CTCUM. mai83

"Je commence ma quatrième année comme conductrice sur une ligne, j'ai passé un an au service touristique et sept ans sur un autobus scolaire. Au début, les gars, ils voyaient pas ça d'un bon oeil, ils pensaient qu'ils seraient obligés de faire mon travail. Un matin, j'ai eu des problèmes à faire démarrer un ancien autobus, leur système de démarrage était compliqué, je suis allée les voir, ils m'ont dit: T'as voulu être chauffeur, arrange-toi avec tes troubles."

FIGURE 26.2
Suzanne Bairstow, bus driver (Chagnon).

shown smiling in her workplace has quit her job because of sexual harassment. These are facts that situate *T.N.T.* closer to the side of women worker's struggle and away from the side of management, to which it previously leaned. More importantly, many of the captions are quotations of the women describing their own experiences, and although their quotes are edited and mediated through the photographer, their voices are being heard and they speak about their struggles, their victories and their losses, dismissing the overwhelmingly positive tone of Chagnon's first show.

The revised show still skirts such important issues of women's labour as day care, racism (presumably non-white women face an additional set of problems, and there is only one Oriental worker in the show). It also avoids the social and economic forces at work pushing women into these jobs, many of which are boring and dangerous, some of which men no longer even compete for; jobs that are still pretty close to the bottom of the ladder in the production of capital.[9] Still, the addition of the captions brings the show closer to fulfilling what Chagnon originally intended it to do.

WORK IN THE HOME

Working in the home (housekeeping, child rearing, etc.) is also a women's issue indirectly referred to by Toronto photographer Michael Mitchell's project, *Staying Home*. His work came to my attention in the Fall '83 issue of *Photo Communiqué*.[10]

As the title implies, Mitchell has photographed in his home, exploring his domestic or private space. In the colour photographs published in *Photo Communiqué* he takes special interest in the traces of his kids. Their toys, strewn randomly about the home, provide Mitchell with much of his raw material. Little cowboys, tiny Indians and their miniature steeds litter a blood-red carpet in the aftermath of some imagined massacre. Hovering over the toy corpses looms the empty shell of a doll house perched precariously on a kid-size chair. In the background a child's foot dangles, amputated by the edge of the frame. In another image, a toy boat and submarine seem to have run aground on a deserted beach towel, on which also sprawls a smiling plastic survivor, his white moulded body partially obscuring an oversized handgun. The photographs are both playful and provocative, literally toying with narrative possibilities.

Along with the title, the images seem to suggest that Mitchell was able to work on this project between minding the kids and doing other household chores commonly associated with staying home. However, the title is a bit misleading, since Mitchell did not in fact stay home; most of the photographs were made when he came home from working late, while his family slept.[11] I think it is unfortunate that Mitchell seems to have passed up an

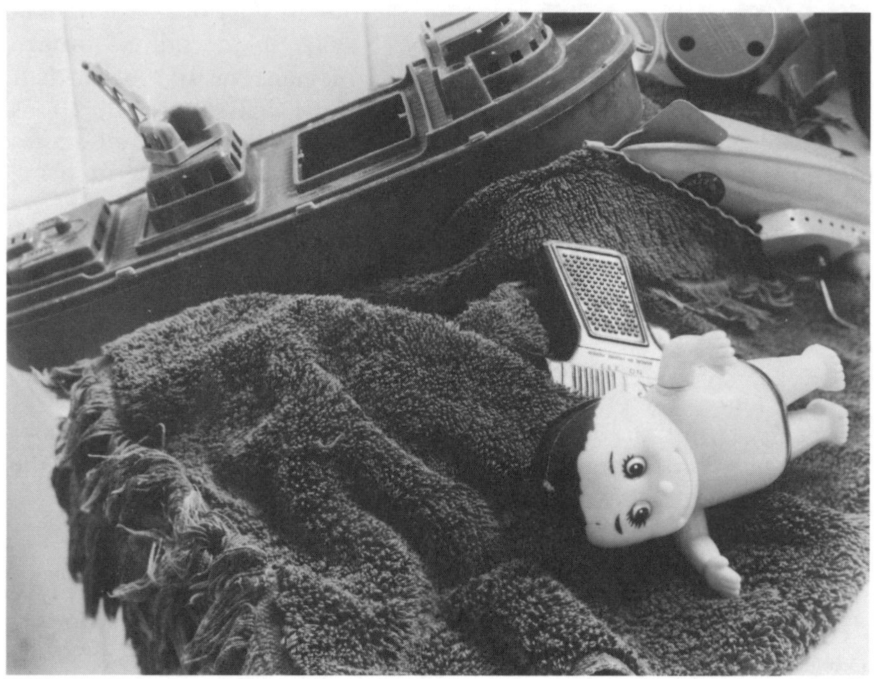

FIGURE 26.3
From *Staying Home* (Mitchell). Original in colour.

opportunity to deal with how he felt about not seeing his kids during the day or how he feels about his commitment to work outside the home versus his domestic commitments. Instead, *Staying Home* is packaged to give the impression that he is dealing with what are often considered women's issues.

His project has received a lot of attention. In the issue of *Photo Communiqué* in question, besides the fourteen-page spread on him and his photographs, there was a mention of his involvement in a photo book publishing venture; there was an advertisement for an exhibit of *Staying Home*, and two listings for his exhibits in the calendar section, as well as his photographs featured on both the front and back covers.

Exposure is a valuable commodity for an artist. Many good artists are unable to support themselves by producing art and must do other work to earn a living. To these artists, attention is a form of reward or compensation and, of course, exhibiting or publishing work often generates further opportunities for public exposure. Attention is absolutely essential to those artists who must sell works or obtain grants in order to survive. Unfortunately, many of the art funding institutions are still male-dominated. For example, from 1980 to 1984 men formed two-thirds of the photography jury members at the Canada Council, which awards approximately

$400,000 a year directly to photographers in grants to travel, exhibit and/or produce their work.[12]

A concern of many feminist photographers is how women are represented in photography, as well as other media. For years, these photographers have, among other things, experimented with producing positive images of women from all walks of life and have photographed their own domestic spaces. It seemes ironic that Mitchell, like Chagnon, has received more exposure than the women who have preceeded him.

BIRTHING IN THE INSTITUTION

The Birth Report is the title of a book by Valmai Howe Elkins, with photographic illustrations by Peter Wollheim, dealing with some of the problems and solutions of hospital childbirth.[13] It was also the title of an exhibit that was presented at Galerie Dazibao in Montréal from October 19 to November 20, 1983, featuring Wollheim's photographs with Elkin's text acting as support. The transformation of a 234-page book with 52 photographs into an exhibit of just over 80 photos and roughly 15 pages of text is necessarily one of condensation and an aestheticisation. The book deals with such complex topics as the effect of modern medical birthing technology on the people (doctors and nurses) who work with it, as well as the place of midwives, home birth, parenting, paternity leave, etc. Unfortunately the exhibit tends to oversimplify things, a common problem with condensing intricate issues into a photography show. However, the exhibit has always been presented in conjunction with talks, films and/or other presentations concerning childbirth in which, presumably, the complexity of the subject matter is restored.

As with the book, the first two captioned photographs in the exhibit compare a calm, homey birthing room — complete with its wooden rocking chair, soft light, imitation antique lamp, brass bed covered by a duvet with matching pillow shams in a print that complements the wallpaper — to a tiled antiseptic delivery room with bright operating room lights and all sorts of medical equipment. The photographs seem blandly unobtrusive. It's as if the different atmospheres of the rooms speak for themselves. Of course, in many ways they do, but, as Clara Gutsche pointed out, Wollheim's photographs possess an immediacy that lends the viewer the impression of seeing Wollheim's subject matter first-hand.[14] One could easily forget that the images are *not* neutral, that they are mediated through the photographer by way of choice of lens, distance, cropping, editing, selection, sequencing, etc. Clearly, his photographs are tendentious; they support the views advocated by Elkins in her book. The first two photographs serve as a model of what the rest of the exhibit will be; a comparison designed to prove the superiority of couple-controlled birth (preferably in a birthing room with mate and/or other family or friends, using whatever position is comfortable for the woman, management of pain through proper breathing, little or no medical intervention) over medically managed birth (in a delivery or operating room, in the "stranded beetle" position,[15] feet in stirrups, episiotomy, forceps, foetal monitoring, caesarean sections). This comparison is illustrated by Wollheim's skillfull use of the "invisible camera" style of documentary photography.

The Birth Report focusses on six separate hospital birthing experiences of six different couples. Each couple's experience is represented by a group of photographs accompanied by a written description by Elkins, quotes from the participants as well as an evaluation form filled out by the new parents. The first birth in the exhibit takes place in a birthing room, the second in a delivery room and the next is another delivery-room birth, this time after induced labour. The fourth is a second couple-controlled birth that occurs in a case room, followed by a caesarean section, and the last takes place back in the birthing room with the grandmother-to-be in attendance.

As opposed to the images of the medically managed births, Wollheim's photographs of the "natural" births show the physical closeness of the couple, featuring more close-ups of their faces. The presence of the mate is strongly felt: we see him close to his partner, supporting, encouraging, coaching her along, always in control. In one birth, the mate is shown cutting the umbilical cord. In the other, clearly less satisfactory births, a greater distance between the couple is depicted, and the baby is often pictured isolated from its mother. This distance culminates in the caesarean experience which is illustrated with photographs of the father-to-be who, along with the photographer, is "exiled to the traditional waiting room".[16] We are shown the frustration of the man who feels the anguish and disappointment of being excluded, having been banished from his privileged position within the structure of the couple-controlled birth and made to share the second-rate experience that most births are implied to be. We see, presumably from the father's perspective, the woman being rolled down the hall towards the operating room. The next photograph, again supposedly from the father's point of view, is of the baby alone in its crib in the nursery, behind glass.

I think it is important to situate Wollheim's photographs within the history of birthing in North America. Before the American Revolution, birthing in England and most of the New World was entirely women's domain. A midwife and various women from the families and communities would manage the births. Young women would learn about birth by seeing it first-hand; while the older women would comfort by virtue of their own survival and experience. By the early twentieth century, midwifery had all but vanished from America owing to the appropriation of birth by the growing patriarchal medical establishment.[17] The following observation is

First couple from *The Birth Report* in a birthing room (Wollheim).

taken from Richard and Dorothy Wertz's book, *Lying-In, A History of Childbirth in America*:

> The exclusion of women from midwifery and obstetrics had profound effects on its practice. Most obviously, it gave obstetrics a sexist bias; maleness became a necessary attribute of safety, and femaleness became a condition in need of male medical control.[18]

Wollheim's photographs, emphasising the presence of the male partner at the "natural" births, might suggest that maleness is a necessity for a superior birth. They could also argue that a woman should be granted more control over her own body in the company of her man. Seen this way, Wollheim's photographs may be described as yet another masculine voice telling women what they should do with their bodies.

The Birth Report isolates birth from a larger context of reproductive rights, which includes birth control and abortion as well as the feminist issue of the disenfranchisement of women's bodies by the partriarchy, including the medical profession. *The Birth Report* appears to have appropriated the "birthing" control issue in such a way as to empower women within the framework of the heterosexual relationship.

Although they must represent a large percentage of child-bearing women in Canada, single, poor, non-white and/or lesbian mothers are all invisible in *The Birth Report*. Non-white women and infants in North America have a much higher mortality rate than their white counterparts.[19] In fact, infant mortality among the Canadian native population is double the national rate.[20] There have also been reports that a disproportionate number of Canadian native women as young as twenty and with as few as two children have been recommended for sterilisation in northern Ontario.[21] It seems that the option of a couple-controlled birth is either unavailable or simply irrelevant to a significant number of Canadian women. In this light we could see *The Birth Report* as a celebration of white, middle-class heterosexual couples, a project that perpetrates the validation of the status quo.

HOME BIRTH

Like Wollheim, Pierre Crépô chose to photograph the birthing experience and like Wollheim's, his photographs, also accompanied by texts, are dignified, sensitive and beautifully produced images of a woman racked with the pain of labour, but most of the similarities end here. Crépôs exhibit, *Nuit Blanche Matin Rose*, presented at Espace OVO in Montréal from February 14 to March 4, 1984, took a romantic, poetic and extremely personal approach to his friend Camille's home birth.

Most of the exhibit is made up of photographs of Camille in labour and delivering her child. She is accompanied by a lover, a midwife and various friends, including Crépô. There is no mention of the child's father except a passing reference to his absence. Although supported by her group, Camille is clearly the one who is in control; she is experiencing the birth on her own terms. The exhibit, however, focusses on Crépô's impressions. The photographs, while depicting Camille's labour and birth, are also reflexive, speaking of the inner feelings of the photographer.

Although his subjects seem, for the most part, unaware of his presence, Crépô has implicated himself to the viewer through using the following techniques: the inclusion of texts that are frequently autobiographical; a self-portrait; photographs taken in his home of his roommate and of the beer they share on the eve of the birth; a photo of his car in which he will drive to the event; and portraits of most of the participants of the birth itself, in which they gaze into the camera and, of course, at the viewer. In this way the viewer is always concious of Crépô's mediation as well as his feelings concerning the birth, which remind him of another birth and two abortions in which he was involved. Crépô states in his text that his exhibit is not a clinical treatment of birth, but merely a pretext to show the irresistable force of life, a celebration of the choice of life over death. He is clearly not opposed to abortion; he simply feels the choice of birth is, in this case, a happier one.

His photographs, then, are tendentious, promoting a more humanistic

FIGURE 26.5
"The ballet of the hands frees the flow of energy like a fire ball" (Crépô).

form of childbirth, home birth with a midwife, which is still illegal in many parts of Canada today. Yet birthing is only half the subject matter of *Nuit Blanche Matin Rose*. The exhibit, with its more blatant claims to authorship and artistry than most documentary work (whose authorship is often shrouded behind a mist of objective authority), contextualised birth within a sphere of romantic prose and poetry, some excerpted from books, others written by the participants. Again, in the text, Crépô himself describes one of the photographs of Camille, leaning languidly against her semi-clad lover, perhaps between contractions, being caressed by several disembodied hands as being "the ballet of the hands [that] frees the flow of energy like a fireball".

There is a certain sexual overtone here, a mystical ecstacy or even a birth orgasm (a popular concept in birthing in the 1950s and 60s) implied by the photgraphs and text.[22] Can a woman only "achieve" this "birth climax" only in her home, or is it possible in a birth room or even delivery room in a hospital? Should women who do not or cannot participate in this mystical experience, who might suffer more banal, earthly pain, feel cheated or guilty? Ironically, it is precisely the mother's guilt of not "achieving" the "perfect" birth to obtain the "most perfect child", that has constantly been manipulated by the medical establishment to make women conform to whatever method of birthing is popular at the time.

As in Chagnon's work, although in a much lesser programmatic way, Crépô establishes a role model by producing "positive images" of the woman giving birth. Unfortunately, positive images can be problematic in that they are part of the construction of stereotypes. Replacing outdated and counter-productive clichés with new positive ones still ultimately leaves one with stereotypes. As we saw with Chagnon's work, positive images in themselves do not necessarily support or induce social change; in fact, they can easily be co-opted into a multiplicity of contexts.

ON DOCUMENTARY PHOTOGRAPHY

A convention used by humanistic documentary photographers is the *dignity* that the photographer is expected to bestow on his or her subjects. Regardless of the political, social, financial, etc., situation in which they are depicted, the subjects must seem to possess a certain indomitable human spirit, an attribute to which any audience could relate. The portrayal of universal human characteristics creates a bond, a closeness, or a sense of identification between the viewer and the subject, yet the viewer is usually not invited to effect change or communicate with the subjects. For example, a person may be deeply moved by a photograph of a (stereotypically) starving Third World child and do nothing to help change that child's (or the Third World's) predicament. In other words, the viewer is permitted the luxury of gazing at a variety of situations, including great human suffering, without risking any involvement or commitment.[23]

Although many documentary projects do little but arouse the sympathy of the viewer and advance the career of the photographer, several have actually been helpful in achieving positive social change. For example, American photographer Lewis Hine was affiliated with social work organisations concerned with child labour. Hine's photographs of young workers in the early 1900s were instrumental in the implementation of child labour laws. It has been argued that some of Hine's photographs of immigrants (a separate project) were designed to invest them with spiritual qualities that Americans could understand, in order to help alleviate their xenophobia which was activated by the huge waves of immigration in that era.[24] Nonetheless, such giants of documentary photography as Dorthea Lange, Walker Evans, Eugene Smith and Margaret Bourke-White, ardently championed this notion of dignity. The *Family of Man* exhibits and book as well as *Life* and similar photojournalist magazines, popularised and institutionalised the dignification of the "other" (the working-class person, the foreigner, the ethnic, the non-white, the woman, etc.) by the white Western media.

In the 1950s and 60s such photographers as Gary Winnogrand, Diane Arbus and Robert Frank rebelled against the *Family of Man* aesthetic and produced photographs that showed human suffering in an unheroic and undignified way.

What is the function or importance of this type of photographically and culturally induced dignity? I think it is a constructed and misleading illusion of power. Chagnon's, Crépô's and some of Wollheim's subjects seem somehow empowered by the virtue of their dignified appearance. However, it would be very costly to men (perhaps emotionally as well as financially) to share equal power and privileges with women, but it is relatively inexpensive for such documentary photographers as Chagnon, Wollheim or even Crépô to bestow dignity on the women they photograph. Some might argue that in many other areas of photography, such as advertising, fashion, pornography, etc., women are not allowed even this sort of respect. But again, it is much simpler for men to grant women this dignity than to share real power equally with them.

More importantly, the fact that photographers can give or take away someone's dignity indicates the real power that photographers have and exercise over their subjects. Therefore, although Chagnon, Wollheim and Crépô may sympathise with and support the people they portray, they are depicting them from a position of power within our social structure. In this way they are defining and thus controlling women's issues, thereby perpetuating the very structure that maintains women's oppression.

CONCLUSION

As a man (and as a photographer), I do not think it is at all inappropriate for male photographers to be exploring so-called "women's issues", since we (men) are, of course, deeply implicated in these issues. In fact, in some ways these projects are encouraging, even though there do seem to be instances of exploitation and co-optation in at least some levels of the work examined here. I feel that the intentions of the photographers were sincere, but it seems that the major problem is one of approach. It is unfortunate that all the focus of their projects is on women when there is little (if any) work produced by men that looks at us and our roles in the issues at hand. For instance, who does not validate women's work (in and out of the home) and why? Who is responsible for paying women unequal pay for equal work and how and why are we letting them? Who holds the balance of power in art granting institutions and what are they doing with that power? Who dominates the medical system that promotes medically managed birthing, and what do they gain by it?

I think that the women's movement has created various discourses that force, or at least allow women critically to examine themselves and their situation in society and history. Apart from writings by and for gay men, there has been very little in the way of parallel discourses that force all of us (men) to confront ourselves. Even though it may invoke a certain amount of anxiety, it is probably less painful for us to produce and look at photographs dealing with "women's problems" and focussing our cameras on them, than it is for us to turn and face ourselves in relation to these issues. I would suggest that our apparent need to define and therefore appropriate "women's issues", at least in the art world, is a way of avoiding more relevant and difficult problems that we must face.

Near the end of his life, Malcolm X suggested that any white person truly concerned with the plight of blacks in America should first fight to eliminate racism in white society from within before joining with the black community.[25] It is after this model that I suggest we (men) approach women's issues.

REFERENCES

Acknowledgement — I would like to thank *everyone* who discussed this project with me; without you I would never have been able to articulate and elaborate on the ideas presented here.

1 Pat Armstrong and Hugh Armstrong. *The Double Ghetto, Canadian Women and Their Segregated Work*, Toronto: McClelland and Stewart, 1978, p. 19.
2 Telephone conversation with Carole Wallace of Action Travail des Femmes, January 18, 1985.
3 Telephone conversation with a unionised male blue-collar employee of Pratt & Whitney Canada Inc. (who performs what would, for a woman, be a "non-traditional" job), March 24, 1984. He also mentioned that the union at Pratt & Whitney was not particularly concerned with "women's problems" because they were in the midst of negotiating a new contract. This disinterest comes as no surprise in view of the small percentage of women in the union.
4 Telephone conversation with Carole Wallace, January 18, 1985.
5 Pat Armstrong and Hugh Armstrong, *A Working Majority, What Women Must Do For Pay*, Canadian Government Publishing Centre, Ottawa: Supply and Services Canada, 1983, p. 198.
6 Allan Sekula, "Photography Between Labour and Capital", from *Mining Photographs and Other Pictures 1948 - 1969, Photographs by Leslie Shedden*, ed. Benjamin H.D. Buchloh and Robert Wilkie, Halifax: The Press of the Nova Scotia College of Art and Design, 1983, p. 249.
7 Rachelle Henderson, "Have Women Really Come All That Far?" *The Gazette*, July 15, 1985, p. D1.
8 Walter Benjamin, "The Author as Producer", trans. Anna Bostock, from *Thinking Photography*, ed. Victor Burgin, London: The MacMillan Press, 1982, p. 24.
9 Leah Cohen, "The Barriers to Women Seeking Non-Traditional Jobs", *Canadian Women's Studies*, Vol. 3, No. 1, 1981, p. 43.

10 Gail Fisher-Taylor, "Staying Home, An Interview with Michael Mitchell", *Photo Communiqué*, Vol. 5, No. 3, Fall 1983, p. 18 - 31.
11 *Ibid.*, p. 24.
12 The Canada Council, *23rd Annual Report 1979 - 1980 Supplement*, Ottawa, 1980, p. 63 - 70; *24th Annual Report 1980 - 1981 Supplement*, Ottawa, 1981, p. 66 - 77; *25th Annual Report 1981 - 1982 Supplement*, Ottawa, 1982, p. 70 - 82; *26th Annual Report 1982 - 1983 Supplement*, Ottawa, 1983, p. 79 - 91; *27th Annual Report 1983 - 1984 Supplement*, Ottawa, 1984, n.p.
13 Valmai Howe Elkins, *The Birth Report*, Toronto: Lester & Orpen Dennys, 1983.
14 Clara Gutsche, "Valmai Howe Elkins, Peter Wollheim, Dazibao, Montréal, Oct. 19 - Nov. 20", *Vanguard*, Vol. 13, No. 1, February 1984, p. 51.
15 Elkins, *op. cit.*, p. 3.
16 *Ibid.*, p. 103.
17 Richard W. Wertz and Dorothy C. Wertz, *Lying-In, A History of Childbirth in America*, New York: Schocken Books, 1979, p. 1 - 26.
18 *Ibid.*, p. 72.
19 *Ibid.*, p. 244.
20 Judith Nolté, "Native Canadians: A Third World Population", *Tellus*, Vol. 5, No. 2, p. 16.
21 Peter Cole, "The Sterilization Trap", *Canadian Women's Studies*, Vol. 11, 1980, p. 42.
22 Wertz and Wertz, *op. cit.*, p. 178 - 198.
23 Moira Egan and Chuck Samuels, "Claire Beaugrand-Champagne, Powerhouse, Montréal, September 10 to October 1", *Vanguard*, Vol. 12, No. 10, December 1983/January 1984, p. 45.
24 Allan Sekula, "On the Invention of Photographic Meaning", in *Thinking Photography, op. cit.,* p. 107.
25 Malcolm X with Alex Haley, *The Autobiography of Malcolm X*, New York: Ballantine Books, 1973, p. 376.

FURTHER READING

Armstrong, Pat and Armstrong, Hugh, *A Working Majority, What Women Must Do For Pay*, Canadian Government Publishing Centre, Ottawa, Supply and Services, 1983.

Burgin, Victor, ed., *Thinking Photography*, London: The MacMillan Press Ltd., 1982.

Sekula, Allan, *Photography Against the Grain,* ed. Benjamin H.D. Buchloh, Halifax: The Press of the Nova Scotia College of Art and Design, 1984.

Sontag, Susan, *On Photography*, New York: Farrar, Straus & Giroux, 1977.

Wertz, Richard W. and Wertz, Dorothy C., *Lying-In, A History of Childbirth in America*, New York: Schocken Books, 1979.

IV. POWER

INTRODUCTION

Power and powerlessness are themes that have been woven through all sections of this book. In discussing epistemology, we are also discussing how knowledge has been and can be defined, all of which implies the power of some people to define and perpetuate knowledge in a way that will validate their own interests. In looking at life's conditions, stages and choices, it becomes clear that the power of women to determine our own fertility has caused changes in our ability to achieve power in both the private and the public spheres of our lives. What is regarded as a condition or choice might very well be determined by one's sense of political, economic, social or personal power.

Power also means political power: the ability to make and carry out decisions in one's own interests which may influence the lives of other people. I had hoped to find an article by a man who consciously articulated an historical analysis of the masculinist rationale for valuing "power over" as a desirable objective for a person or a group. I was unable to attract such an article. Indeed, the only chapter in this section showing a specifically male point of view is Ned Lyttelton's article on men's liberation. This article really speaks to the advantages men might realise by *divesting* themselves of this conventional "power over" set of values.

Power traditionally is most violently and forcefully expressed through the state. To what extent is that power related to gender? Jill Vickers discusses the relationship of sex/gender to the construction of national identities. Chaviva Hosek brings us close to home in Canada by discussing how Canadian women fought for inclusion in the constitution of our country: a thoughtful account by an active participant in the struggle. Dorothy Rosenberg not only talks about the relationship of feminism to peace, but also — as an outsider to this "men's profession" — of the relationship of war to masculinist ideology. In these perilous times when we know that a nuclear holocaust could destroy us all, it is especially important to analyse the ideological assumptions that make this a possibility.

The final chapter in this book is on power and empowerment. It treats some of the themes already articulated on the power of communication as it attempts to redefine power from the notion of "power over" to that of "power to". The traditional concepts of "power over" presuppose oppression as a necessary factor of power. "Power to" envisions an egalitarian society where people can be agents of change.

Whether we perceive ourselves as free agents or as controlled by predetermined biological and social conditions, we must each admit to some area of choice where we can exercise the power to effect change, to make the society a just one, and to ensure the continuation of life on this planet. It is the earth, our home, which has the ultimate power to nurture and maintain life as we know and love it.

NED LYTTELTON

Men's Liberation, Men against Sexism and Major Dividing Lines

Gentle Men For Gender Justice — The Limits of Masculinity — The Men's Awareness Network — Readings for Men Against Sexism — The Hazards of Being Male — Holy Virility — The Men's Resource Centre — Revolutionary Effeminists — Men Against Rape — The Male Machine

These are a few of the names of books, groups and newspapers that have appeared in the last ten years, all of them presupposing or developing an analysis of masculinity, all of them in reaction to the current wave of the women's liberation movement. They range from those that are actively hostile to feminism[1] to those that pay lip-service to the reality of male supremacy, to those that attempt, however inadequately, to deal with male privilege as a reality of men's lives. The problem with all of them, including the latter, is that they have a basically white, middle-class heterosexual bias that does not recognise differing male realities, and, by extension, does not serve the interests of all women.

Unless an analysis of masculinity deals specifically with male power and privilege as its basis and starting point, it is likely to be more or less subtly anti-feminist. It will ignore or implicitly deny the basic tenet of all varieties of feminism, namely, that between women and men there is an imbalance that gives power to men and disempowers women. Using the term "anti-sexist", as opposed to "men's liberation", requires this starting point.

Furthermore, an analysis of masculinity that does not deal with the contradictions or power imbalances that exist between men themselves will be limited and biassed, and its limits and biasses will be concealed under the

Originally published in *Resources for Feminist Research* (Toronto: Ontario Institute for Studies in Education), Vol. XII, No. 4, pp. 33–34.

blanket of shared male privilege. To whom is the analysis accessible? Who is analysing whose masculinity, and for whose consumption? How, for example, is the myth of the black rapist addressed? Is the sexism of working-class men described as "worse" than that of middle-class men, and then explained by saying that the working-class man acts out the frustration of his class oppression by exercising his male power to the fullest? To what extent are the problems that anti-sexist men wrestle with really the problems of heterosexual men? How would the work of anti-sexist gays differ? And ultimately, when we think of whom anti-sexist men are, do we think of white middle-class men? When we think of whom we are oppressing, do we think of white middle-class women?

MEN'S GROUPS

These questions must be asked, not only of books and articles about masculinity, but also of the "men's groups" that proliferate all over Canada and the United States. Since I have limited space, I will focus on two kinds of "men's groups" — "Men's Liberation" groups and "anti-sexist" men's groups. For every group operates from a set of presuppositions and has an initial basis of unity, whether these are explicit or not.

MEN'S LIBERATION MOVEMENT

This "movement" sprang up in the mid-seventies in response to the new wave of feminism. It operates from several basic premises. Sexism oppresses us all, men as well as women. Men are negatively socialised — to be unemotional (except for anger), competitive, invested in the penis, etc. We have a lot to learn (or rather, steal) from women — intuitiveness, sensuality, co-operativeness — in a catchall word, nurturing. Men rely on women for emotional support and to fill our own lacks. Men must learn to give each other emotional support, learn ways of being men that are co-operative and nurturing and do not produce heart attacks. Feminists say we have all this power...look at the power that women have — the power of motherhood (they run households and influence children), the power of sexuality (the power of the "whore" to engulf and humiliate, the power of the "virgin" to tantalise and control, the behind-the-scenes, subtle power of wives). To cite one example of the way men's liberationists think, Herb Goldberg, in his book *The Hazards of Being Male: Surviving the Myth of Masculine Privilege*, has a section entitled "Prostitution as Male Humiliation", in which he writes:

> Feminists have expressed the idea that prostitution is an exercise in male chauvinism, one that results in the degradation of the female wherein she is

simultaneously being exploited by her customers, her pimps and the police.

While there is merit to this argument, there is still hardly a more humiliating, self-annihilating and less satisfying experience for a man than to visit a prostitute, an experience that thoroughly reinforces the hateful self-image of himself as a despicable animal.

Not all men's liberationists are as honest as Goldberg. Mostly their rhetoric is couched in seemingly pro-feminist terms. Who would argue with the assertion that men in general are emotionally repressed, competitive, penis-centred, etc., and that we need to change?

Men's Liberation has no analysis of sexism as political. If both men *and* women are oppressed by sexism, who is the oppressor? The System, they reply, which absolves them of responsibility. They focus on the many negative aspects of the male sex-role, but on none of the positives, and they ignore the fact that men's alienation from ourselves is in reality the price that we pay for male supremacy. In fact, being oppressors dehumanises, but does not oppress us. Men's Liberation seeks to find ways to keep the power and avoid paying the price. In other words, let's ignore the power differences and learn women's stuff, so as to get *all* the goodies, *all* the power. Then we will be able to cry and feel and be co-operative and still get the best jobs and have the freedom of the streets.

The Men's Liberation "movement" is a heterosexual, white, middle-class movement, characterised by support groups for men, the development of a so-called "men's culture" (as though western culture has not always been male), more or less suppressed sexuality with each other (referred to as overcoming the fear of intimacy and consisting of indiscriminate mandatory hugging and touching, soft-focus sexual "experimentation" with men), and a liberal tolerance of gayness (disguised homophobia), all of which is protected by the massive fortifications of heterosexual privilege. Stated most simply, the men's liberation movement is a reactionary white middle-class heterosexual backlash to feminism. It is dangerous because it is dishonest. It provides a way of having their cake and eating it for men who are afraid that women are going to take their cake away altogether. It's a kind of political tax evasion.[2]

ANTI-SEXIST MEN

I believe that it is inappropriate (or maybe appropriating) for men to call ourselves feminists. We may be pro-feminist, but that depends on how we live and act, not what words we use. Since sexism is the practice of male privilege, the acting-out of male power, anti-sexism must begin with the recognition of that power, and an intention to counteract it in whatever concrete way is possible in our lives. The intention is essential. Without it, it is easy to recognise male power, like it a lot, and fight like mad (or in the case of men's liberationists, manipulate like mad) and keep it. The intention unfortunately doesn't guarantee any action or movement, but you certainly can't move anywhere without it. At first the intention wavers, with lots of resistance, a little movement, lots of resistance, a little movement — a pattern any feminist who has pushed a man on sexism knows only too well. But ideally the practice develops the analysis, and the analysis makes sense of the practice. After repeating our mistakes over and over we learn to recognise them by ourselves and start to change our actions. Where we have always expected and taken access to women's lives and bodies, we become less obtrusive, take up less space. Where we have been used to dominating, taking over, appropriating, we listen. Where we have never had to notice that what we assume to be universal, what we take for granted, is just one reality, we become aware of more realities than our own and feel really guilty for a while. But guilt is a paralysing state that prevents action, and it quickly turns to resentment. So we start to act again, but from a new place. Instead of withholding access we give women fuller access to our groups, our thinking, our emotions, our lives. We risk making mistakes and being criticised (and we are, and will be), but we try not to be defensive or to retreat into a safe place. This is called being accountable. When we are doing this in our personal and political lives, in whatever proportion our particular process demands, we can call ourselves anti-sexist men, remembering that our conditioning and the construction of our society are such that there is no such thing as a non-sexist man.

As an aside, I should point out that for every bit of power-based behaviour that an anti-sexist man manages to surrender, he has less of a price to pay. Men's liberationists please note.

Like men's liberation groups, anti-sexist groups are joined predominantly by white middle-class heterosexual men, and the perspective that they work from and the problems that they deal with are predominantly their own. Various problems arise. There is an apparent contradiction in the notion of organising (forming groups) to surrender power, since groups tend to be empowering. The question of *how* to support the women's movement is a perennial one — should men take initiatives or act only in supportive roles? Given that anti-sexist men should be willing to take directives from feminists as to what they want us to do, which feminists should we take directives from? Socialist feminists and radical feminists will often have differing views on the role of men, and we can exploit this division to the utmost.

But the fundamental problem of anti-sexist men's groups is that the basic requirement — that they start from male privilege — is at the same time a basic limitation. Anti-sexist men's groups are organised around a contradiction in society — that of gender. This is problematic in certain ways. First, internally, if there are privilege differences within the group that are not being addressed, the unity that the group members have as males will be undermined by unresolved differences of class, race or sexual orientation. Furthermore, the norms and assumptions, as well as the style and the issues of the group, will be unexamined and will tend to be those of white middle-class heterosexuals. This will limit who will join the groups. Underlying this is the assumption that sexism is *the* major contradiction, to which others are secondary. Much political action is organised on a single front, fighting one particular oppression, and much can be achieved by the focus and intensity that this develops. But in such situations real weight must be given to the realities of other forms of oppression, and the interrelations between them all, both within the group and in coalition work with other groups. Thus gays are beginning to recognise classism and racism within our movement; women of colour are writing critiques of the white women's movement; Marxist groups are splitting apart on the issue of sexism. The anti-sexist men's group that I was most recently in collapsed when the one working-class man in the group began, after a year of not being heard, to push the middle-class men to address classism, only to be met with hostile defensiveness and refusal to move.

The counter-argument, usually put foward by the privileged group, is that dealing with the issues of class and race are divisive for a group based on gender (and experience certainly seems to bear this out, since so many groups do not survive this process). But the lines that divide are already there, dividing, and are more dangerous when unacknowledged. Group splits caused by "personality differences" often turn out, when examined, to be based in unacknowledged power differences.

Dealing with dividing lines in a constructive way is what first makes it possible to build alliances across lines of privilege-oppression.[3] If this step is not taken, if differences within are made less significant than the particular major dividing line that defines the group (in this case gender), the differences within will sooner or later split the group apart, but they will be concealed for a while by false unity which will be defined and perpetuated by those with privilege within the group, who do not have to notice.

There is too much to say. All of this needs to be thrashed out and developed. Anti-sexist white men must become anti-racist male whites. Middle-class men must start looking at class privilege. Straight men must confront their homophobia. And since most anti-sexist men are liberals, prejudices are usually harder to detect and therefore more dangerous. The paralysis that seems to plague anti-sexist men's groups is the paralysis of being stuck on one side of a contradiction that is defined as the major dividing line. But I hope that we have learned something before paralysis sets in permanently. The accountability to all women that, ideally, anti-sexist men must learn, has to work across other dividing lines as well, if it is truly to be *all* women. Even with its dangers, analogy is a good learning tool, because contradictions have some features in common, and are interrelated. Gay men can learn about our male privilege by understanding our oppression as gays. A straight man can learn about his sexism by being confronted within the group on his homophobia. Oppressions cannot be ranked, even by groups that are working on one particular front.

Unless anti-sexist men move in these directions we will stay limited by our unacknowledged assumptions, our groups will go on being predominantly white and middle-class and straight, we will not be trusted in political alliance with groups struggling on other fronts. And our usefulness to women will be as limited as our politics.

REFERENCES

1 (Their titles say it all.)
Goldberg, Herbert. *The Hazards of Being Male: Surviving the Myth of Masculine Privilege.* New York: Signet Books, 1976.
______. *The New Male: From Macho to Sensitive but Still All Male.* New York: Signet Books, 1979.
Farrell, W. *The Liberated Man.* New York: Bantum Books, 1975.

2 For scathing articles written by feminists about men's liberation see J. Snodgrass, ed., *Readings for Men Against Sexism.* Albion, CA: Timeschange Press, 1977.

3 For my developing understanding of the politics of major dividing lines I am indebted to Laura Rowe, who named them and pushed me to see them.

FURTHER READING

Davis, Angela, *Women, Race and Class.* New York: Random House, 1983.

Frye, Marilyn, "On Being White", in *The Politics of Reality: Essays in Feminist Theory.* Trumansburg, NY: Crossing Press, 1983, pp. 110 - 127.

Quest Magazine, *Building Feminist Theory*: Essays from *Quest.* New York, 1981.

Snodgrass, John, ed., *A Book of Readings for Men Against Sexism.* Albion, CA: Timeschange Press, 1977.

Toronto Rape Crisis Centre, "Rape", in Guberman and Wolfe, eds., *No Safe Place: Violence against Women and Children.* Toronto: Women's Press, 1985.

JILL McCALLA VICKERS

At His Mother's Knee: Sex/Gender and the Construction of National Identities

Women's Studies have not come to Canada's university campuses easily or without struggle. The field, its insights and its graduates are still viewed with a measure of suspicion and disdain. As Chaviva Hošek of the University of Toronto has put it:

> In the development of any discipline, you have an old guard with assumptions about how intellectual work operates. They have great fears that something called "interdisciplinary" couldn't possibly have any methodological rigour, any standards and criteria for its own verifiability, or a notion of excellence. These are reasonable worries because part of what you're developing is not just a whole new area of subject matter but new tools and techniques for thinking.[1]

Hosek's observations were about the reception of Women's Studies at the University of Toronto. Her comment, however, forces us to focus on a shared dilemma of developing new tools and techniques of thinking; of constructing new models of analysis that will ensure us an enterprise that proves the "old guard's" doubts to have been misplaced. Since the proponents and developers of Women's Studies begin with (what is to the old guard) the handicap of a political belief in the value of our venture, I will not waste space here persuading the reader that our ventures are worthwhile. Rather, I will turn to our mutual theoretical problem; that is, the development of an analytic perspective that can shape and organise our research, our insights and our findings in a disciplined but unstifling way.

Most immigrants to a field of interdisciplinary study come with a kitbag

A somewhat different version of this article appeared under a similar title in *Canadian Issues/Thèmes Canadiens*, Vol. VI, 1984.

full of theories, methods and prejudices derived from their disciplines of origin. Most, with some discomfort at first, learn to adapt to an interdisciplinary venture with judicious borrowings. By contrast, most immigrants to the realm of Women's Studies have already gone through a series of what I have elsewhere called "methodological rebellions".[2] What we have learned is that the invisibility of women in male-stream thought and research demands new tools and techniques for thinking. It cannot simply be a matter of filling in the blanks with new information which is then stuck on with crazy glue.

The outlines of our new tools and techniques for thinking, moreover, are beginning to emerge, and they offer considerable power for understanding the multi-fold Canadian experience. Obviously, other analytic structures could serve our venture; Marxism, for example, serves many Women's Studies scholars. Nonetheless, as we construct out of Canadian and comparative women's experience theories of patriarchy and of the role sex/gender plays in the dynamics of imperialism, nation building, class differentiation, racism and the construction of culture, it becomes apparent that Women's Studies requires an independent theoretical framework that builds on the indigenious insights of our own venture and movement.

In this chapter, I want to try to illustrate the value of this approach by exploring the area of nationalism and the construction of national identities through the prism of a theory that sees sex/gender as a technology for the organisation of human groups. To achieve this objective, I will first sketch briefly a theory of sex/gender and of its function in patriarchal group formation, cohesion and identity transmission. I will then explore some of the issues of cultural identity to illustrate the insights gained by this sort of theoretical de-centring or re-centring.

THE PROBLEM — NATIONALISM AND THE CONSTRUCTION OF NATIONAL IDENTITY

Nationalism and the problem of national or other cultural identities have proved remarkably resistant to coherent analysis. Any survey of the literature must leave us struck by the wide diversity of meanings placed on the phenomenon. Nationalism has been fused with so many other, contradictory ideological elements — liberationist, democratic, totalitarian, romantic, conservative or populist — that the phenomenon of nationalism itself is a most difficult beast to define.

One observer has argued that nationalism "is not a complete ideology but [is] a specific principle of human self-identification and organisation which may freely combine with others."[3] As I will attempt to demonstrate, this notion that nationalism is one among a number of possible modes of self-identification and of group organisation is one of the few consistent things that can be said about it. Nonetheless, although as distinguished a student of nationalism as Hans Kohn has argued that it is at root a psychological sentiment, little real success has been evident in understanding the psychology of national self-identification, although many attempts have been made. This difficulty in understanding nationalism as a form of self-identification and of group organisation reflects the profound difficulty that male-stream thought, in general, has had in understanding the public manifestations of the process of identity construction. Within patriarchal societies this process occurs in the private realm of the family through the child-rearing activities of male-controlled, if not always male-dominated, women. The insights offered by sex/gender theory, therefore, can illuminate both the presence and absence of strong national self-identification and both the use and misuse of sentiments that imitate the reproductive blood-tie to create identity, group cohesion and inter-generational continuity. Before I attempt to illuminate the problem of nationalism and the construction of national identity, however, I must first present the basic outlines of a feminist theory of sex/gender as a technology for patriarchal control and organisation.

SEX/GENDER AS A PRINCIPLE OF SOCIAL ORGANISATION

Virginia Sapiro recently argued that the conflict over the issues raised by making the linkages between sex/gender and politics clear and explicit "tears at the most basic structures...of society".[4] If Sapiro's insight is correct (as the intensity which now surrounds reproductive politics suggests) it is little wonder that conventional frameworks of analysis, including Marxism, have failed to illuminate the role of sex/gender in socio-political organisation and conflict. Patriarchal modes of social organisation, of maintaining group cohesion, identity and trans-generational continuity are so deeply based as to be nearly invisible. This theory of patriarchal sex/gender arrangements, therefore, begins by trying to make the invisible visible.

The principle of sex/gender obviously has two parts: the fact of sex, which means that women are the species' reproducers; and the fact of gender, which encompasses the social roles, attitudes and personalities assigned, with different content, to women and men in different societies. Patriarchy is used here to describe societies in which the balance of power and authority between men and women favours men.

Until recently, many feminist scholars have sought to discover the origins of patriarchy; to find *the* factor which is *the* key to male dominance. Comparative analysis and careful empirical research, however, suggest that neither the search for *the* origins nor key theorising is likely to be fruitful. While patriarchy is probably not universal, it is endemic. And while it takes many forms, it has important common features across time and place.

Rather more fruitful than a search for *the* origins and *the* key to patriarchy have been the explorations of the functions or purposes served by patriarchal organisations of sex/gender. (I should hasten to add that this is not a reprise of functionalism, which presumes that structures serving functions or purposes are somehow good or necessary or even "natural".) Among others, Zillah Eisenstein has argued that:

> Patriarchy...expresses the struggle to control women's options in order to keep their role as childbearers and rearers primary.[5]

Following Adrienne Rich[6] and parallelling Mary O'Brien,[7] she sees

> patriarchy as a political structure [that] seeks to control...women so that their possibilities for making choices about their sexuality, childrearing, mothering, loving and labouring are curtailed.[8]

If we ask why men would wish to limit women's autonomy and control them in this way, a range of answers are in the running. (Sheer cussedness, desire of gain, desire for sexual exclusivity, etc. come to mind.) One answer, which is ripe with insight for our purposes, lies in the fact that male groups cannot reproduce themselves without "their" women being committed to both the physical and social reproduction of the group. As Thomas Hobbes put it, in nature, the baby "follows the belly"[9]; that is, men must control reproducers if they wish to control "their" children and "their" children's values, loyalties, energies and attachments. Hence, it may be useful to see sex/gender arrangements as a technology that patriarchies employ to construct and maintain groups, group identities, group cohesion and intergenerational continuity. It is this insight I will develop and explore further in relation to nationalism and the construction of national identities.

In this paper, I am arguing that patriarchal arrangements of both physical and social reproduction are central to the maintenance of many political forms in place around the world. And yet, there are crucial historical and contextual differences in patriarchal organisations of sex/gender. And, in an analysis of these differences, lies our opportunity to understand more deeply the character of patriarchy as a technology for the organisation and replication of human groups and identities. How is sex/gender used to bond men to one another in a shared consciousness?

Earlier I rejected the view that patriarchy was a universal, homogenous form translated directly from nature. That is, the *sex* half of my analytic term sex/gender is insufficient to capture the key elements of patriarchy as an organisational technology. As Eisenstein has noted, the social construction of *gender* (the attitudes, personality traits, etc. employed to restrict women primarily to reproduction under male control) is also a crucial element.

Nonetheless, I will also argue that it is the relationships between *sex* and power which are unique and relatively unchanging because of women's physical power to reproduce male groups. The characteristics of gender are highly variable. Sex roles in relation to physical reproduction are relatively fixed. Thus male group power depends on success in the sex/gender struggle.

Obviously, the conflicts raised by caste, race and class also involve high stakes for the defenders of privilege, status, and identity. But each of these conflicts is also waged through the womb — through battles of the cradle, the nursery and the school. The white woman who chooses a black sexual and reproductive partner; the "native" woman who "collaborates" by sleeping with and bearing children for the colonial enemy; the Islamic woman who chooses a non-Islamic partner; the Jewish woman who marries outside the faith and no longer "keeps kosher": each reflects the centrality of woman as reproducers to the conflicts that prevail in patriarchal politics. Likewise, the working-class woman who rears her children to respect picket lines; the French-Canadian woman who ensures that her children keep the faith and speak French; the upper-caste woman who teaches her children abhorrence for untouchables: each reflects the centrality of women as reproducers to the forces of stable identity, group cohesion and continuity. No other "group" occupies so central a position in the dynamics of patriarchal political organisation and conflict.

Hence, what seems at first blush and what has been declared by malestream thinkers to be a private, natural phenomenon — i.e. reproduction — is revealed as the most political activity. For many, the autonomy, cohesion, continuity and identity of groups can be maintained and secured only by severely limiting the autonomy, freedom of choice and social adulthood of the group's physical and social reproducers.

To summarise my argument to this point, one technology of bonding and identity creation has been based on the appropriation of the blood-tie model of affiliation. The notions of commonality based on shared blood, ancestors, territory and a language learned "at his mother's knee" reflect the outlines of this technique of bonding men together *as if they were kin*. Now, so used are we to the conventions of male-centred kinship and residency that we might miss the fact that the younger generations of a group can be linked to it and can share its identity only through the conduit of women's bodies and women's powers of social reproduction.

Before I proceed to some illustrations to clothe my arguments with flesh, I will just briefly explore in more detail the links between sex and power —

female sex and male power. Regardless of the other purposes patriarchy has served, in most societies, men retain an ultimate power, the power to control reproduction, even when they cannot completely control reproducers. It is this power and its consequences, lodged as they are in the interface between nature and society, that must now be explored.

SEX AND POWER

Most of our attempts to understand the dynamics of patriarchy to date have been inadequate because they failed to grasp the persistence of sex/gender in our technologies of human organisation. This does not imply that I believe patriarchy to be *natural* in the sense advanced by some feminists and anti-feminists. To argue that patriarchy has a natural basis, or a basis in natural parameters, is far from arguing that it was or is inevitable, adaptive or good. Rather, I am arguing that patriarchy was derived as one solution to the human dilemma of how to construct enduring forms of social organisation, group cohesion and identity. (This is, of course, primarily a dilemma of male-centred forms of organisation. Female-centred alternatives face a different dilemma, that of integrating un-related adult males into female-centred groups.)

There are other models around which human beings could organise themselves into enduring, cohesive and relatively stable groups. In quite varied environmental circumstances, however, many human groups chose to organise themselves around the model of human reproductive ties. The natural capacity of women physically to reproduce the species and our capacity physically to nuture children (expanded into social nurturance) establishes incontrovertable links among people which can be socially elaborated to create loyalties, identities, rights and responsibilities, inclusions and exclusions. In this choice of an organisational mode, and in its perversions, we find the roots of patriarchy and of nationalism.

If, as I have argued, a core aspect of patriarchy is male control of the female biological capacity to reproduce the species, it must follow that the central organising element is the *blood-tie* or an imitation of it. To follow Hobbes: unless something intervenes with the "right of nature", the child follows the belly that gave it life. The only certain human links are those among women and their children and their children's children. Of course, it is a commonplace of male-stream thought that the blood-tie was a device of the species' infancy. We are told, for example, that it was "adaptive" that women develop deep ties to "their" men because they were dependent on them for support and protection. We are told, by Lévi-Strauss,[10] that the invention of male-centred kinship was the first truly *human* act because it created "unnatural" ties among men, unrelated to one another by blood, through the exchange of women as reproducers. We are also told that the creation of the territorial state was a great advance in human organisation because it permitted the transcendence of such blood-tie units as clans and tribes and fostered attachments to more broadly inclusive and abstract units of states and of nations. In short, it is presumed that the history of "progress" in modes of organising human groups is a history of moving away from the child-follows-the-belly mode to one that stresses abstract links among men, in which identity, loyalty and cohesion centred around male bonds to other men.

Zillah Eisenstein has suggested that the central elements of patriarchy revolve around male attempts to control women's power to reproduce the species and attempts to destroy women's consciousness of that power. Mary O'Brien suggests that the sparking mechanism involved was men's discovery of the physical role they play in reproduction. While both of these insights are important, they obscure another crucial aspect of the problem. That is, the transcendence of the blood-tie linkage in modes of human organisation was never complete. However much men may assert the "rights" ensuing from their physical paternity, "their" children continue to "follow the belly" in many crucial ways. Their language is learned "at their mother's knee"; women are still the crucial socialisers — conduits of male values, identities and loyalties.

Dorothy Dinnerstein's[11] and Nancy Choderow's[12] accounts of mothering demonstrate that the long period of infant dependence on the mother for physical nurturance forges deep links that foster identity, loyalty and emotional bonding unless something intervenes. Unless interfered with, the *natural bonds* among naturally related women and between women and their children are of great strength. Such bonding around the ties created by reproduction, however, make it more difficult for men to create bonds with "their" children (although involvement in child care can enhance such bonds). And social organisation around reproductive bonds makes it more difficult for men unrelated by blood to establish enduring bonds directly with one another. So, although it is often convincingly argued that the more "unsophisticated" forms of human organisation involve a transcendence of blood ties, this is only partially the case. The crucible of reproduction, biological and social, remains the family where the transferrence of the child's loyalty from the mother to the father occurs only with the support of law, religion, socialisation and extensive exposure to models of "appropriate" sex/gender arrangements.

The basic blood tie also remains a potent force in the establishment of identity in most of the human groupings that *move* people in a political sense. Nationalism, tribalism, ethnicity and most religions work through the reproductive mode. Our mother tongue and what we learn at our mother's knee shape to a considerable degree what identity we will adopt, what group we will be loyal to and what authority figures we will accept as legitimate. The relationships between sex and power, therefore, are unique because only women can reproduce groups and because women have been the primary conduits for the replication of identities in the years of youthful dependency. Far from being a matriarchy, however, the nursery is usually the site where female conduits transmit male-defined identities and loyalties from one generation to the next. Women limited in autonomy to guarantee their commitment to the reproductive role are rarely independent culture makers.

Many conflicts of patriarchal politics involve two central elements of the sex/gender struggle. First, each usually involves a *battle of the cradle* in which the men of each group struggle to retain the physical reproductive powers of "their" women for its cause and to "out-reproduce" competing groups. (The South African policics concerning restraints on black reproduction and the "Babies for Botha" campaign directed at white women highlight the point starkly.) The second involves a battle of the nursery to ensure that the loyalties and labour of the children reared are retained for the group. In each case, the autonomy of women is limited to some degree as is their ability to bond freely outside of the group. Women's freedom of loyalties and our freedom to establish bonds as we might choose are constrained. Moreover, this creates a gender alienation since those who claim and achieve the right to control the thoughts and actions of the others, even in a "good cause", are far less likely to acknowledge them as equals, to foster and admire the development of their inner powers or to accord them status as social adults. In some extreme cases, gender alienation leads to the view of women as sub-humans or as beings without souls. Even in milder cases, women are rarely viewed as culture makers but as conduits for the identities of others.

In this conception, limitations on women's autonomy "so that their possibilities for making choices about their sexuality, child-rearing, mothering, loving and labouring are curtailed"[13] are *central* to patriarchy and not incidental effects of purposes related to property transmission. By this definition, all patriarchies will involve male attempts to appropriate women's reproductive power, both biological and social, and to place it under male control. What is important for us to realise at this point, however, is that while all patriarchies will have some mechanisms for the control and appropriation of women's reproductive capacities, not all of them have constructed mechanisms further to control women's autonomy to achieve those other purposes that the initial patriarchal structures made possible. Hence, not all patriarchies structure sex/gender roles in such a way as to weaken female-to-female bonding or to deny women competence in the economic or sacred spheres. Nor do all patriarchies structure gender roles to permit men to appropriate or control the product of women's productive labour. Many patriarchies, in fact, did not develop forms of social organisation that attempted to transcend the blood ties. In many tribal societies, the basic reproductive bond remained central, although men claimed the right to appropriate and control the "products" of women's reproductive labour. As a result, women's value as "mothers of the nation"[14] was recognised and rewarded.

The socially constructed gender roles displayed by patriarchal cultures of different sorts to a large measure may reflect the *degree* to which a particular patriarchy attempts to constrain the autonomy of women to establish and maintain male control over reproduction. They also reflect the degree to which women are further constrained to achieve other patriarchal purposes. The *content* of these gender roles — what is deemed to be an appropriate identity and behaviour for men and women — varies so widely among patriarchal socieities that the link between the sex role and the gender role is hard to establish. Is there some central element of identity and behaviour that women must learn, for example, if we are going to live with male control and appropriation of our power to reproduce? Certainly, the evidence I have surveyed suggests little in the way of a required or standard content for *gender*.

Women can be viewed as strong but stupid beasts of burden fit only for the heavy labour of the fields; or as creatures of delicate constitution unfit for the toils of boardroom and stock exchange. They can be viewed as unceasingly sexual, distracting men from their proper labours; or as frail creatures naturally offended by the sex act. As such observers as Margaret Mead have demonstrated, gender identities and roles are highly variable from culture to culture.[15] Sex roles, on the other hand, are not. With few exceptions, women are expected to engage in reproductive labour (and hence, in heterosexual intercourse) and physically to nurture young children. The degree to which these requirements of the sex role are also linked to gender role identities that limit women's autonomy and limit our chances for social adulthood is also variable. Case study evidence suggests that, in some societies, women are expected simply to reproduce a certain number of children for the group but are also free to develop economic and social skills as they choose and to establish bonds with others (including sexual bonds) on the basis of social adulthood. In other societies, as we know, the fact of being reproducers involves severe constraints on autonomy, limits on social and economic activity and rigid exclusion from the ranks of the social adults.

Male control of women *as reproducers* may not always require marked interference with women's autonomy. If, for example, the male-defined group "need" is perceived simply as more children, it would matter little who fathered which children and thus who within the group women chose as sexual and reproductive partners, provided such partners were capable of fathering children. And, where bonding revolved around the female-child tie, few restrictions were imposed on women's sexual activities. We cannot presume, however, that women would have conceded their right, as individuals or as a sex, to control their own reproduction or to share in that control easily or without a struggle; or, perhaps, in what they too conceived of as a "good cause", such as the cohesion of the group severely threatened with disintegration because of external forces, war, invasion, etc.

SEX/GENDER AND THE CONSTRUCTION OF NATIONAL IDENTITIES

I have suggested that a patriarchal organisation of sex/gender can be seen as a technology used to construct identity, define group membership, maintain group cohesion and continuity. Clearly, however, this is not an insight of universal applicability. If it were, all groups would rely simply on the device of kinship ties and some form of ancestor worship, which is obviously not the case. Nor, however, is the employment of sex/gender in this matter entirely ideosyncratic as the reified notion of "culture" is often used to suggest. The circumstances under which groups, which identify themselves through notions of commonality, exist differ markedly. Imperial groups or nations possess far more extensive techniques for identity maintenance than do colonised groups or nations. Similarly, majority groups which are in control of state machinery are less reliant on the "private" vehicles of identity maintenance than are minority groups with inferior or no access to state machinery. Hence the importance of patriarchal sex/gender arrangements and of the related control of the group's reproducers may be expected to vary according to the availability of other techniques.

This hypothesis, stated in its most general terms, has its origins in the work of such feminist anthropologists as Peggy Sanday,[16] in the insights of such observers as Franz Fanon[17] of the psyches of colonised people and in the world-wide data concerning the fertility patterns of majority and minority groups.[18] Very briefly, Peggy Sanday has argued, in *Female Power and Male Dominance*, that "male dominance is not an inherent quality of human sex-role plans...[rather it] is a response to pressures that are most likely to have been present relatively late in human history."[19] The pressures that she identifies, both empirically and theoretically, as being associated with male-dominant sex-role plans include group migration; population pressure, especially when associated with a forced sharing of territory with stranger groups; colonisation; and individual or family emigration into a culturally strange environment. In Sanday's reading, patriarchal sex/gender arrangements are one possible device adopted by groups faced with cultural disruption. This she sees as a particularly likely response when the disruption constrains or eliminates public, trans-familial arenas for identity formation and male aggression; or when the identity-threatening, cultural disruption is of a character that it can be "blamed" on the women of the group.

Franz Fanon's psychological observations of the reactions of colonised men to "their" women and to sex/gender arrangements provide one illustration of Sanday's hypothesis. In *The Wretched of The Earth*, he explores what he sees as the "need" of men, subject to colonisation, to act out their hostility against their women who had "collaborated" by embracing either the colonisers' attitudes towards women or their men as sexual partners, or both. Algerian men, for example, viewing the family as the only vehicle for identity maintenance, interpreted all French attempts to change the status of women as a scheme to undercut the last bastion of their identity and culture. The post-independence national identity in Algeria likewise involved a rigorous and repressive re-instatement of a patriarchal sex/gender system, despite the fact that state instruments were now available.

Fertility research demonstrates that minority groups, characterised by geographic concentration, which feel themselves in a struggle to maintain their autonomy and identity, tend to pursue an intensely pro-natalist policy with stricter enforcement of patriarchal sex/gender arrangements than other groups.[20] The "mosaic" society of Lebanon provides the classic, if tragic, example. So threatened is each of the competing indigenous groups that the state has been denied any power over what are called "personal status" matters — engagement, marriage, divorce, separation, inheritance, adoption, and tutelage.[21] As Beshir Gemayel put it in an interview in *Le Monde*, Lebanon was to have a "federal structure" in which "each community should rule itself according to its own laws, and no one should impose their views on others".[22] As one Lebanese feminist noted, this represented a "gentleman's agreement" not to interfere in the manner in which each male group controlled its women and children. She also noted that currently almost no Lebanese woman, of whatever affiliation, is in a direct relationship with the state, there being as many different laws for women as there are religions and religious sects. These barriers, of course, almost totally prevent inter-marriage and serve the purpose of retaining the women of the group for the men of the group; a result fiercely demanded in a country in which no census has been possible for 50 years because of the intensity of the battle of the cradle in relation to claims on political positions.

These snippets of insight clearly require much more systematic development before we can come to understand the differential role of patriarchal sex/gender arrangements in the Canadian context. Certainly, the limitations imposed on French-Canadian women in the cause of nation, faith, language and "mission" have been well documented. Nor is the notion of the battle of the cradle alien to Canadian self-analysis. What, however, are we to make of the rapid and remarkable loosening of those fetters in the lives of French-Canadian women in recent decades? Following Sanday's hypothesis, we might speculate that the commitment to a project of independence in which the group would gain full state powers for maintaining national identity, cohesion and continuity made the traditional patriarchal technology seem less important. Or, by contrast, the intensity of commitment to the independence project may well have been heightened by the realisation that traditional sex/gender defences of language and identity could no longer be relied upon. To some degree, therefore, younger francophone women may have come to be seen as allies in the nationalist struggle to gain state instruments and as autonomous culture makers, while their mothers and grandmothers were viewed simply as conduits of group identity.

Contemporary research on Puerto Rican nationalism[23] and on the "new ethnicity" of white minority groups in the United States[24] shows clearly the links between a cult of machismo and male dominance, on the one hand, and the glorification of minority ethnic identity, on the other. An Italo-American man commenting on the over-all dynamic of the "new ethnicity" remarked, "What has driven us to our ethnicity is rejection."[25] In the American melting-pot environment, this sense of rejection by white, ethnic males is as often felt from their children as from strangers. Hence, the values supported by these ethnic men include the value of tightly-knit relationships in the family, children's respect for their father's ethnicity and male control of children's socialisation to ensure it. This dimension of new-right, moral majority politics, therefore, becomes much more explicable when we understand the link between sex/gender arrangements and the process of identity formation.

In the Canadian context, of course, this backlash against assimilationist approaches to minority groups is less pronounced. A number of ethnic groups in Canada traditionally have employed sex/gender techniques to preserve cultural identity (and to buttress male egos threatened in a strange environment) from the beginning. Obviously, however, ethnic identification has also been used in Canada as part of the process of social closure in which the majorities (anglophone and francophone) sought to restrict access to resources and opportunities to their own members, despite our political ideology of multi-culturalism and the value of the mosaic. This process involves singling out certain cultural attributes to legitimise inclusions and exclusions, the drunken Irishman or Indian versus the thrifty Scot, for instance. On the part of the minority group males, however, the counter-acting process is a more rigorous defence of ego and identity within the family. Hence it is not surprising to find traditional, patriarchal sex/gender norms more and not less rigorously enforced by some immigrant groups here in Canada than in their country of origin.

Although this brief exploration of the dynamic interaction between sex/gender and the construction of national and ethnic identities has only scratched the surface of the relevant phenomena, I hope it has been sufficient to illustrate the value of the analytic approach involved. Certainly, it is my view that women's studies research can be greatly enriched by turning its analytic sights towards an understanding of sex/gender as an organising technology. By focussing on the role sex/gender plays in the dynamics of such broad processes as imperialism, racism, class differentiation, nationalism and the construction of culture, we can begin to understand its character as the deep structure of patriarchal politics. By insisting that the insights that contribute to our theory rest on comparative research, moreover, we can avoid the theoretical *cul-de-sac* of over-generalisaton. Only thus can we develop sex/gender theory that can guide our actions as it satisfies our quest for understanding.

REFERENCES

1 Chaviva Hošek, quoted in Sarah Murdoch, "We're Not Here for Rap Sessions", *Canadian Women's Studies/Les cahiers de la femme*, Vol. 3, No. 1, 1981, p. 53.
2 See Jill McCalla Vickers, "Memoirs of an Ontological Exile: The Methodological Rebellions of Feminist Research", in A. Miles and G. Finn (eds.), *Feminism in Canada* (Montréal: Black Rose Books, 1983).
3 Konstantyn Symmons-Symonolewicz, *Modern Nationalism* (1968), cited in Symmons-Symonolewicz, "Studies in Nationalism: Old and New", *Canadian Review of Studies in Nationalism*, Vol. 2, No. 1 (Fall, 1974), p. 154.
4 Virginia Sapiro, "Research Frontier Essay: When are Interests Interesting? The Problem of Political Representation of Women", *American Political Science Review*, Vol. 75:3 (September, 1981), pp. 701 - 716.
5 Zillah Eisenstein, *The Radical Future of Liberal Feminism* (New York: Longman, 1981), p. 16.
6 Adrienne Rich, *Of Woman Born, Motherhood as Experience and Institution* (New York: Norton, 1976).
7 Mary O'Brien, *The Politics of Reproduction* (London: Routledge & Kegan Paul, 1982).
8 Eisenstein, *op. cit.*, p. 14.
9 Thomas Hobbes, "Philosophical Rudiments Concerning Government and Society" in *The English Works of Thomas Hobbes*, ed. Sir William Molesworth (London: John Bohn, 1841), Vol. 2, Chapers 8, 9 (originally published in *De Cive*). To Hobbes, in the "state of nature" ..."every woman that bears children becomes both a *mother* and a *lord*"; "Wherefore original domination over *children* belongs to the *mother* and among men no less than other creatures, the birth follows the belly"; "But in a civil government if there be a contract of marriage...,the children are the *father's*; because in all cities, to

wit, constituted of *fathers*, not mothers governing their families, the domestic command belongs to the man''.

10 Gale Rubin's treatment of the Levi-Strauss position in ''The Traffic in Women: Notes on the 'Political Economy' of Sex'' in Rayna R. Reiter (ed.), *Toward an Antrhopology of Women* (New York: Monthly Review Press, 1975),
pp. 157 - 210 presents the issues well.

11 Dorothy Dinnerstein, *The Mermaid and the Minotaur* (New York: Harper Colophon, 1976).

12 Nancy Choderow, *The Reproduction of Mothering* (Berkley: University of California Press, 1978).

13 Eisenstein, *op. cit.*, p. 14.

14 Diane Rothenberg uses this term in ''The Mothers of thc Nation: Seneca Resistance to Quaker Intervention'' in M. Etienne and E.B. Leacock (eds.), *Women and Colonization* (New York: Praeger, 1980) pp. 63 - 87,

15 Sec Margaret Mead, *Male and Female* (New York: Laurel, 1968), originally publishcd 1949.

16 P. Sanday, *Female Power and Male Dominance* (New York: Cambridge University Press, 1981).

17 Franz Fanon, *The Wretched of the Earth* (New York: Grove Press, 1963), especially pp. 254 - 259.

18 See Joseph Chamie, *Religion and Fertility* (New York: Cambridge University Press, 1981); Leon F. Bouvier and S.L.N. Rao, *Socio-religious Factors in Fertility Decline* (Cambridge, MA: Ballinger, 1975); Lincoln H. Day, ''Natality and Ethno-centrism: Some Relationships Suggested by an Analysis of Catholic - Protestant Differences'', *Population Studies* 22 (March, 1968) pp. 27 - 50; Calvin Golscheider and P.R. Uhlenberg, ''Minority Group Status and Fertility'', *American Journal of Sociology* 74 (4: 1969) pp. 361 - 72; Larry H. Long, ''Fertility Patterns among Religious Groups in Canada'', *Demography* 7 (2: 1970), pp. 135 - 49; P. Neal Ritchy, ''The Effect of Minority Group Status on Fertility: A Re-examination of Concepts'', *Population Studies* 29 (2: 1975) pp. 249 - 57.

19 Sanday, *op. cit.*, p. 4.

20 As footnote 18 suggests, there is a lively debate on the issues raised. Joseph Chamie's data on Lebanon, however, and Mikhail S. Bernstam's data in ''Demography of Soviet Ethnic Groups in World Perspective'' (xerox provided to the author by Professor T. Rakowska-Harmstone) seem compelling. None of this research takes a feminist viewpoint of the intersection of sex/gender structures, fertility and national/ethnic identities. This is more clearly exposed in Gregory Massell, *The Surrogate Proletariat: Moslem Women and Revolutionary Strategies in Soviet Central Asia: 1010 - 1929* (Princeton: Princeton University Press, 1974).

21 Chamie, *op. cit.*, p. 31.

22 Cited in Yolla Polity Sharara, "Women and Politics in Lebanon", *Khamasin: Women in the Arab World*, 6 (London: Pluto Press, 1978), pp. 11, 12.
23 See Mario D. Fenyo, Review Article, "Puerto Rican Nationalism", in *Canadian Review of Studies in Nationalism*, Vol. 1, No. 1 (Fall, 1973), pp. 120 - 125.
24 See Howard F. Stein and Robert F. Hill, "The New Ethnicity and the White Ethnic in the United States", in *Canadian Review of Studies in Nationalism*, Vol. 1, No. 1 (Fall, 1973), pp. 81 - 105.
25 *Ibid.*, pp. 92, 93.

FURTHER READING

Ardener, Shirley (ed.), *Women and Space: Ground Rules and Social Maps* (Croom Helm, 1981).
Caplan and Burja (eds.), *Women United, Women Divided: Cross Cultural Perspectives on Female Solidarity* (Travistock, 1978).
Iglitzin, Lyon B. and Ruth Ross (eds.), *Women in the World: A Comparative Study* (Oxford: Clio Books, 1976).
Massell, Gregory, *The Surrogate Proletariat: Moslem Women and Revolutionary Strategies in Soviet Central Asia: 1919 - 1929* (Princeton University Press, 1974).
Sanday, Pegg Reeves, *Female Power and Male Dominance* (Cambridge University Press, 1981).

CHAVIVA HOŠEK

How Women Fought for Equality

Women are generally perceived as having emerged among the winners in the process of patriating the constitution and entrenching a new Charter of Rights and Freedoms. A review of the history and outcome of that process, however, suggests a more qualified picture. Women had to wage a bitter battle to have their concerns recognised. At various points in the debate, gains that had seemed certain had to be fought for again. And even after the proclamation of the new constitutional provisions, there is justifiable scepticism about what has been achieved for women. The massive lobby effort in 1981 succeeded in securing a section guaranteeing all entrenched rights "equally to male and female persons". But the legal force of this section is unclear. Some see it as a symbolic and philosophical statement that will guide the interpretation of the Charter as a whole. Others reply that because the section is not part of some general statement of principles, it may well come into conflict with other sections in the Charter, and its force in such circumstances is uncertain. Clearly, any final assessment of the gains made by women in the constitutional wars will have to await the judicial and political developments of the next decades.

Nevertheless, the constitutional process itself tells us much about the position of women in the Canada of the early 1980s. This chapter examines the role of women's groups in the process of constitutional renewal from 1979 to 1982. The picture that emerges is a troubling one. It reveals the marginal role of women in politics and the forcefulness they must exert to avoid total exclusion. And this unsuccessful assimilation of women into the

Excerpt from *And No One Cheered: Federalism, Democracy and the Constitution Act*, ed. Keith Banting and Richard Simeon (Toronto: Methuen, 1983). Reprinted in *Canadian Forum*, May 1983. Reprinted by permission of Methuen Publications.

mainstream of politics raises some important questions about the quality of democracy in this country.

WOMEN AND CONSTITUTIONAL RIGHTS

A crucial moment for feminism came in 1967 when pressure by traditional women's groups on the government of the day brought about the establishment of the Royal Commission on the Status of Women. In preparing for the hearings of that royal commission, and in responding to the recommendations made in its report, the contemporary feminist movement discovered its own coherent goals. The early naïveté that assumed that the recommendations of the royal commission would be implemented quickly and that women would easily achieve equality in Canadian society is long gone. Many of those recommendations, which are crucial to women, have yet to be enacted, and further political debate and research have since discovered and articulated new goals. Nonetheless, the royal commission report remains a founding document of contemporary Canadian feminism.

The organised women's movement in Canada contains at least five identifiable types of women's groups. First, there are voluntary feminist groups devoted to improving the status of women on a large range of issues. These organisations, such as the Manitoba Action Committee on the Status of Women, La Fédération des Femmes du Québec, the Nova Scotia Action Committee on the Status of Women and many others in each province and the territories lobby primarily on the provincial level. The National Action Committee on the Status of Women (NAC) is an umbrella organisation of over 415 such voluntary groups, which lobbies the federal government on a wide range of issues. Second, there are traditional women's voluntary organisations whose primary purposes are not explicitly feminist, but who lend their support to feminist causes at significant times. These include the Canadian Federation of University Women, Imperial Order of the Daughters of the Empire, the Women's Institutes, the Young Women's Christian Association, women's church-affiliated groups, women's party-affiliated groups, and many more. Groups involved in the provision of specific services to women represent a third category. These may be largely voluntary, and include rape crisis centres, homes for battered women and their children, women's employment counselling centres, birth-control information centres, centres for immigrant women, collectives that publish books and magazines, and women's caucuses in unions. Fourth, there are advisory councils to the government in most provinces and in the federal jurisdiction. These councils are appointed by government and are meant to act as a means of liaison between government and women. Their members are always paid for their time, but their budgets vary considerably, as does their influence. The Canadian Advisory Council on the Status of Women has traditionally had a bigger budget than any other such group, and significant resources for researching policy areas of concern to women. The Conseil du Statut de la Femme in Québec has been given abundant resources. On the other hand, the Ontario Status of Women Council reported in 1982 that its research budget was $15,000. Since most other women's groups spend the little money available to them providing services to women, with little left over for lobbying governments on policy issues, the stable budgets of some advisory councils have given them substantial discretion in lobbying efforts. Finally, there are specialised national voluntary associations that lobby in areas of their own particular expertise and concern. These include the Canadian Congress for Learning Opportunities for Women, the Canadian Research Institute for the Advancement of Women, the National Association of Women and the Law and others. These organisations also join coalitions to support causes outside their own spheres of immediate concern.

These diverse organisations have lobbied on a wide range of important issues: legislated affirmative action; "equal pay for work of equal value" legislation; emergency services for women, such as rape crisis centres and transition homes for battered women; access to affordable, quality child care; access to birth-control information throughout the country; family law reform that recognises the contribution of women to the property and income of the family; pension reform to accommodate women's patterns of participation in the work force; reproductive freedom of choice; access for women to education and training; occupational health and safety controls in the workplace. It is a long list, and has involved thousands of feminists throughout the country.

Until 1980, formal legal rights did not figure largely on this list. Indeed, insofar as Canadian women have worked for legal equality, they have been sorely disappointed. In the most notable constitutional matter affecting women, the Supreme Court of Canada ruled in 1928 that women were not "persons" in the law, and only the overturning of that ruling in Britain in 1929 made women legal "persons" in this country. In the 1970s, in the Bliss, Lavell, Bedard and Lovelace cases, the Canadian Bill of Rights proved to be a deficient legal instrument for women's equality. And the struggle to reform section 12(1)(b) of the Indian Act, which discriminates against Indian women who marry men who are not status Indians, took many, many years.

Thus the drive for equal legal rights did not spring spontaneously from within the women's movement. Rather, it developed in response to the determination of the federal government to entrench a Charter of Rights and Freedoms during the patriation process. This was at once an advantage and a disadvantage. On the one hand the issue had been put on the political agenda. On the other hand, the terms of the debate and the timetable for its resolution were set by governments, and womem were able to manoeuvre only within the narrow spaces offered them by elected political leaders.

THE BATTLE BEGINS

In the spring of 1980, the federal government announced its initiative to patriate the constitution, and the women's movement mobilised to develop a policy on this major development. On May 27, 1980, the National Action Committee on the Status of Women (NAC) wrote to the Prime Minister describing a plan for regional meetings of women's groups in most provinces across the country which would develop positions on aspects of constitutional change with which women were concerned. After the provincial meetings, women's groups would meet to agree on a national policy. In effect, it was a plan for a federal-provincial consultation process within the women's movement itself.

There was no obvious consensus on what women would want in a new constitution. Women were residents of different provinces, with various political party affiliations and different views on patriation, the amending formula, the division of powers and other issues. Like all other citizens, women had different approaches to the idea of an entrenched Charter of Rights. Women in Québec, for example, largely wished to retain powers in the province, partly because the government of Québec was perceived by many women to be more forward-looking on women's issues than the federal government of the day. Women in the Western provinces, and those with more traditionalist views, tended to believe that it was not in keeping with Canada's political history and political culture to have an entrenched Charter of Rights giving the Supreme Court final say on human rights. By comparison, women in Ontario tended to be the major supporters of the idea.

The recent history of constitutional negotiations between the federal government and the provinces put active feminists on the alert. They were most concerned to find a way to include women in the new round of constitutional discussions, since the consequences of women's previous exclusion might have proven seriously detrimental to their interests. At the February 1979 constitutional meeting, the first ministers reached agreement only on the transfer of divorce jurisdiction to the provinces, a change that would have had severely inequitable consequences for women. Fortunately, massive lobbying by women's groups in Manitoba convinced the premier to oppose the change, which effectively put the issue on hold. In the spring of 1980, however, divorce jurisdiction remained a symbolic reminder of what could happen to women's interests when no informed women sat at the table where political deals between first ministers were struck.

Nevertheless, clear positions on the constitution had to be developed. To facilitate this, the Canadian Advisory Council on the Status of Women planned a conference for early September 1980. The timing was ideal because the first ministers were scheduled to meet one week later for what was billed as the last attempt to secure agreement among the governments before the federal government moved to patriate the constitution unilaterally. The women's conference was designed to pool information from women's groups across the country and to formulate a policy that could be fed into the federal-provincial process. The Canadian Advisory Council commissioned several papers on the constitution in order to focus the conference deliberations. Once again, its stable budget proved critical, since no group in the voluntary sector would have been able to fund such research or provide the travel budget required to bring women's groups together. Among the topics to be considered at the conference were the entrenchment of rights, family law, the rights of Indian women, affirmative action and overlapping jurisdiction in the provision of services to women.

Women's groups spent the summer in intense consultation about the constitution, and in great anticipation of the conference. The National Action Committee's contacts across the country that summer revealed extensive interest and a determination to ensure that legal equality between men and women would be one of the achievements of constitutional change: the publicity about the fight for the Equal Rights Amendment (ERA) in the United States helped to mobilise groups of women in Canada to fight for equal legal status, and even traditional women's groups were highly concerned. Thus, although constitutional change had not been the first item on the women's agenda, energy and commitment were available as soon as the opportunity presented itself. There was little sense that constitutional renewal alone was going to bring about all the changes necessary for women to have equal power in society. But since there was going to be significant change, women were going to make sure that their legal status would be stronger than it had been.

Regrettably, this early effort came to naught. In early September, the translators of the Canadian Union of Professional and Technical Employees (CUPTE) went out on strike for maternity-leave benefits. The CUPTE translators were supposed to be the translators for the women's conference on the constitution, and if the conference went on, women would have to cross a picket line made up almost entirely of women striking for a goal all feminist groups supported. That was impossible. The CUPTE translators were willing to translate for this conference *pro bono* in order not to force cancellation, but the Advisory Council was told by the Treasury Board that they could not have any dealings with CUPTE while it was out on strike. They could not make a separate deal with them, nor have any contact with them, until the strike was settled.

The Advisory Council cancelled the conference on Women and the Constitution, promising to hold another as soon as possible. But the disappointment, even despair, was palpable. The great concern was that the end of the strike would not coincide with a politically strategic time for another conference, and that a rare, historic opportunity might be lost.

UNILATERALISM AND THE CHARTER

The first ministers met on September 12, 1980 and were unable to agree. On October 2, the government released its proposed Resolution Respecting the Constitution of Canada and announced its decision to proceed unilaterally. The Resolution included a Charter of Rights and Freedoms which the federal government proposed to entrench in the constitution, and women's groups began to study it intensely. At this point, however, many women were caught in a dilemma. Some women strongly opposed federal unilateral action and the circumvention of provincial powers that this involved. Nonetheless, an entrenched Charter of Rights would give those rights supremacy over the laws of the provinces, and some provinces had notably bad records on women's issues. Similarly, there were women who were very reluctant to give the courts greater power in the definition of rights, because the history of judicial decisions on women's rights in Canada was very poor. Since the judiciary in Canada is appointed by order-in-council, and judges have not traditionally felt any responsibility for making social precedent, there was concern that the judiciary was less likley than the legislatures to move forward on equal rights for women. Nevertheless, such reservations were overridden by even more intense concerns about the draft charter itself. Many of its clauses were distinctly ungenerous. The proposed charter was not attractive enough or liberal enough to seduce people into supporting entrenchment without misgivings. On the contrary, the charter had so many flaws that it frightened people and mobilised women and many other interest groups into action.

The government had underestimated the intensity and extent of popular concern with the proposed charter. On October 18, the fifty-first anniversary of the declaration by the Judicial Committee of the Privy Council in Britain that women in Canada were "persons" in the law, the National Action Committee sponsored a day-long public meeting on the constitution. The meeting discussed those sections of the charter that were problematic for women, agreeing on essential changes. That evening, the group was addressed by the minister responsible for the status of women. But the minister completely misread his audience, its understanding of the issues and the intensity of its concern. He simply told the assembled group to "trust" his government to come through with a better wording of the charter. Most of the audience was outraged at being treated with such condescension. Clearly, in those early days the government was not yet aware of the strength of feeling in the country about the charter. And certainly the demand for wider public participation in the process of constitutional change was to become far stronger than Ottawa had expected.

THE JOINT COMMITTEE PROVIDES A FORUM

Under pressure from the opposition parties, the federal government agreed to refer the constitutional resolutions to a Special Joint Committee of the Senate and the House of Commons for one month. Further pressure extended that period to five months. The deliberations of the Joint Committee afforded a crucial experience for women's groups, as it did for other groups of concerned citizens. The hearings raised the political consciousness of many people, and revealed the range and vitality of the opposition to the wording of the charter and its approaches to human rights. Many people watched the televised presentations of the Joint Committee with fascination and a growing hope that the highly persuasive cases made by many civil libertarian groups would force the government to strengthen the charter. It was a source of great encouragement simply to see how fine the work done by various concerned organisations was, and with what dignity and precision they approached the problem of turning the dog's breakfast before them into a Charter of Rights of which a democratic nation could be proud.

In the five months of hearings, the Joint Committee heard from a variety of women's groups in briefs and consultations. The recommendations of the major national women's groups had many highly specific concerns in common:

1. The "limitation section", which allowed rights and freedoms to be subjected to "such reasonable limits as are generally accepted in a free and democratic society with a parliamentary system of government", was too broadly worded. It should have been deleted altogether, or at least reworded to specify the permissible limitations on rights and freedoms. Women also argued that the guarantee of equality in another section of the charter should never be subject to this limitation clause.
2. The charter should have begun with a statment of purpose, guaranteeing the equal rights of men and women.
3. The word "person" should have been used throughout the charter since its meaning is legally defined. Instead, the charter used such terms as "one", which had no clear legal meaning, and which could give rise to unnecessary legal arguments about the rights of the foetus.
4. The section that guaranteed that "everyone has the right to equality before the law and to the equal protection of the law without discrimination because of race, national or ethnic origin, colour, religion, age or sex" was too narrowly stated. The section should have indicated that equality in the

content of the laws was guaranteed and not just equality in the procedure. Moreover, the list of grounds should have been open-ended to allow for the development of new categories, and marital status, sexual orientation and political belief should have been added at the outset. Finally, the courts should have been directed to use the "strictest" legal test when assessing the validity of laws that differentiate on prohibited grounds.

5. The section providing for affirmative action programmes did not guarantee that women would qualify for such help.

6. The section that protected existing "rights or freedoms that pertain to the native peoples of Canada" was also a concern. This section would have permitted the Indian Act to continue to define band membership in a way that discriminates against Indian women who marry men who are not status Indians.

7. Another section stated that unlike any other part of the charter, the equality rights would be subject to a moratorium of three years.

8. There was concern that a new section introduced in response to multicultural groups to ensure "the enhancement and preservation of the multicultural heritage of Canadians" would conflict with the section guaranteeing equality. Cultural values have been used to justify discrimination against women before, notably in the Indian Act, and women's groups were concerned that the new section could undermine women's general guarantee of equality.

9. Women make up more than half of the Canadian population but at the time were not represented at all on Canada's highest court. The constitution should have guaranteed a representative number of women on the Supreme Court of Canada.

Even though the Joint Committee gave these concerns some visibility, it was not at all clear what the government would do with the presentations. Renewed political action would be needed to make the difficult transition from submissions to the Joint Committee to decisions of the federal cabinet. In December, the Canadian Advisory Council told women's groups that their conference would be held on February 14, 1981. This appeared to be strategic timing, as the Joint Committee would then have just finished its deliberations. The next stage of political action would then have to begin.

CRISIS IN THE CANADIAN ADVISORY COUNCIL

In January, before the Joint Committee had finished its private deliberations, the revised charter was brought to the House. The changes tabled by the Minister of Justice represented a partial response to the recommendations of women's groups but left many crucial matters in a perilous state.

The "limitation" section had been partially tightened, but the general guarantee of equality rights remained limited by the wording; there was no general purpose section with a statement about equality of the sexes; the purpose of affirmative action was partially tied to the prohibited grounds of discrimination; although the section guaranteeing equality rights had been revised in part, the word "person" was not used, but "one" was changed to "individual" as in the Canadian Bill of Rights. The rewording of the section to gurantee equality "before and under the law" also was not strong enough, since it could still mean only equality in the administration of the law and not in the laws themselves. Women's groups, along with the Canadian Advisory Council, wrote the minister of justice and the minister responsible for the status of women to insist that more changes in the Charter be made.

On January 5, however, the Canadian Advisory Council constitutional conference was cancelled and a statement was issued saying that regional conferences would be more appropriate. Rumours were rife that Lloyd Axworthy, the minister responsible for the status of women, preferred this arrangement as it would not embarrass the government at a critical juncture in the constitutional battle. Doris Anderson, then president of the Canadian Advisory Council, called a meeting of her executive, together with the minister, in an effort to reverse the decision, which had been made in her absence. But the executive insisted on cancellation. Anderson publicly accused the minister of interfering with the autonomy of the organisation, and convened the full council in the hope of getting from them the support for the conference she had not been able to get from the executive. The emergency meeting of the entire council also voted to cancel, however, and Doris Anderson resigned as president on January 19, 1981.

It is difficult to understand what advantage the government might have gained from the cancellation. The Joint Committee had already publicised the process of constitution making. The opposition parties and the provinces were so insistent on having a say in the process that a conference of women was not going to make things much worse. The process was simply not going to be as neat and expeditious as the government had hoped and wished. The political advantages of allowing the conference to go ahead, on the other hand, could have been considerable. The Liberal cabinet could have pointed to its financial support for the organisation as proof of its commitment to wider public participation in constitution making. More importantly, it might have used the conference to rally support for speedy patriation and entrenchment of the charter. Instead, the political costs of cancelling the conference turned out to be high. The women's movement suddenly had a heroine, a villain and an event, all of which symbolised its exclusion from the constitutional process. The media had a field day. The complex issues involved were reduced to a dramatic fight between a woman and a man. And as a former editor of *Chatelaine*, Doris Anderson was a particularly potent symbol around which concern about the constitutional issue could crystallise.

THE AD HOC COMMITTEE TAKES UP THE STANDARD

A few days after Doris Anderson's resignation, approximately a dozen women who were active in various women's groups met in Toronto to discuss strategy. Timing was a serious problem. Even if the voluntary women's groups decided to have conferences of their own, months of organisation would be required and the chance to influence the process of constitution making would have passed. There was a fear that after the Joint Committee adjourned, there would be no way for women's groups to have a further say.

An *ad hoc* committee emerged as the best vehicle for resolving the contradictions experienced within women's groups on the constitution. Women who were active in the Liberal Party felt that informal influence would work best. However, the cancellation of the conference made other women suspicious about this back-door route. Without public pressure from large groups of women, informal lobbying might not be very effective. Major voluntary groups, wary of leaving other issues neglected as the American ERA groups had done, worried about putting all their people to work on the constitution. Some women's groups were adamant that entrenching the charter in the constitution was a serious danger. Women's groups in Québec, seriously in conflict internally about their stance towards the federal initiative, were not prepared to submit their internal coherence to the test of a clearly stated choice on constitutional policy.

In order to avoid internal dissension, an *ad hoc* committee was formed to organise a conference on "women and the constitution" on February 14, precisely the same date as the conference that had been cancelled. Support for the *ad hoc* committee mushroomed. Women were determined to have their meeting with or without the government's resources and support, and the *ad hoc* committee poured all its energy into the conference. The women involved in the committee devoted all their efforts to it. What may be described as the training in "crisis management" that ordinary women's lives provide came into play, and a kind of feminist pride at making do with very little animated them. The group was surprised and encouraged by the astonishing response from women all over Canada.

For many, this was a time of political awakening. Women who had not been activists and had simply assumed that women in Canada were legally equal to men were profoundly insulted by the cancellation of the Canadian Advisory Council conference. There was a sense that this was a once-in-several-lifetimes opportunity in which one had to participate. The sense of historic urgency was powerful. Women were prepared to fight for their daughters' equality with men where they might not have been for their own. Some women were convinced that if enough of a political push were made, it might be possible to get a Canadian equivalent to the ERA in one fell swoop. As a result, the conference exceeded everyone's expectations, and 1,300 women attended.

Because the members of the Canadian Advisory Council were seen as having traded women's concerns for party loyalty, the *ad hoc* committee was careful to ensure that its conference would not be used for purely partisan purposes. The Progressive Conservatives were fighting entrenchment of a Charter of Rights, and there was a danger that putting the entrenchment issue first on the agenda might have the conference too neatly serve the Conservatives' needs. Discussion of entrenchment *per se* was therefore put off until discussion of the charter took place so that the meeting could generate a position on its content first. Moreover, a resolution opposing entrenchment on any grounds, which could have been recommended to the meeting after the charter had been discussed, was avoided by judicious handling in the resolutions committee. In addition, chairs and speakers at sessions were chosen to achieve balance in partisan representation. Flora MacDonald and Pat Carney, Progressive Conservative members of Parliament, and Pauline Jewett and Margaret Mitchell, New Democratic Party MPs who had worked hard and well on women's behalf in the Joint Committee, were not invited to speak on any panel.

The *ad hoc* conference passed a number of resolutions on the charter and on the process of constitutional patriation. After the conference, several key people stayed behind in Ottawa to lobby Parliament for the conference resolutions. They spoke to MPs, House leaders, leaders of the opposition parties and the minister of justice, and they issued press releases on their progress. Women across the country contacted their MPs to make their support for the resolutions known. After initial resistance, the Department of Justice began to work with the *ad hoc* committee members to draft what later became section 28: "Notwithstanding anything in this Charter, the rights and freedoms referred to in it are guaranteed equally to male and female persons."

At the annual meetings of NAC and the National Association of Women and the Law, the resolutions of the *ad hoc* conference were further endorsed. Women were making their elected representatives declare their positions on women's equality, and the three parties finally moved to support the resolutions. The NDP moved to amend the parliamentary Resolution to include section 28, and it was passed unanimously in the House of Commons on April 23, 1981.

Many women were shocked to discover how hard they had to lobby to get section 28 into the Charter. They were astonished to find such resistance to equality rights for women. In the midst of an historic opportunity to make a statement about the basic principles by which Canadian laws were to be governed, equality for women still had to be negotiated, fought for and defended at every stage.

THE SUPREME COURT AND THE INFAMOUS NOVEMBER ACCORD

The summer of 1981 was a quiet time on the constitutional front. People were tired, perhaps even shell-shocked. Everyone waited to see what the Supreme Court would say about the legal rights of the provinces in the patriation process. All along, the federal government had been wooing people interested in civil liberties and rights by claiming that it was the only level of government interested in giving Canadians rights, and that the provinces were backward, recalcitrant and otherwise unwilling to abide by liberal principles. In September, the Supreme Court decided that legality and convention could be distinguished. The federal government chose to make a final attempt to reach agreement with the provinces, and the people in the women's movement became apprehensive. The process would be opened up to bargaining once more, and again no one around that federal-provincial table would be fundamentally committed to women's interests.

The fears were justified. In the final desperate negotiations to achieve substantial agreement between the federal and provincial governments, women's interests were sacrificed, almost by neglect. The federal minister of justice and his provincial counterparts put together a new over-ride section which effectively confused the issue of whether the Charter of Rights was or was not entrenched. The supremacy of the Charter over all the laws of the country was now in question, and the over-ride section could mean that Canadian laws would *not* have to apply equally to men and women. Here, the fact that section 28 had not been made part of a first-principles section began to show its fateful disadvantage.

Confusion reigned. The Accord was reached on November 5. But when the prime minister was asked in the House of Commons whether section 28 would be subject to the over-ride, he was unable to answer. It was not until November 9 that he made clear that it was. Women's groups were appalled. It seemed impossible to believe that women had lost what had been won so recently and with such massive political effort. And it was incomprehensible that the prime minister should be so uncertain about what was, to women, a crucial matter. While Québec's rights to a veto and native people's aboriginal rights had clearly been traded away, women's rights were so invisible to the government that for several days they did not even know whether or not they, too, had been traded.

Chaviva Hošek

BACK INTO THE FRAY

With a sense of weariness and outrage, the *ad hoc* committee and other women's groups struggled to free the equality provisions of the Charter from the over-ride. This time the federal government took the view that the provinces were the culprits, and women therefore focussed their lobbying efforts on the premiers. Because the pressure was on the provinces, some of the people in the federal jurisdiction were able to help. Judy Erola, the new minister responsible for the status of women, Flora MacDonald, a leading member of the opposition, and Margaret Mitchell of the NDP gave the *ad hoc* committee access to telephones and other equipment. The *ad hoc* committee and other women's groups called across the country to inform people of the various premiers' positions and to co-ordinate the pressure. Some women who felt that they had not done enough in the previous round of lobbying came forward. There was generalised concern about Québec's loss of its veto, about the native peoples whose aboriginal rights were in jeopardy and about the whole concept of entrenchment. Canadians seemed to be getting the worst of both worlds in this particular federal-provincial agreement.

Media coverage in this period was interesting. There was elaborate reporting of the reaction in Québec and a great deal of coverage of aboriginal rights. But although the women's lobby was working actively across the country, there was no coverage of its revival at all for at least ten days. Women were ignored with a "catch-22" rationale: they were not seen as a group with political clout of their own, nor were they perceived as sufficiently weak and helpless to merit the concern of journalists. Women were neither powerful enough nor weak enough to get attention.

After the November 5 Accord, the women of the *ad hoc* committee got promises of support from the opposition parties, particularly from the leader of the Progressive Conservatives. But the main targets were the provincial premiers. Telephone calls were made around the clock; questions were asked in every provincial Legislature; ads appeared in newspapers; petitions were signed; telegrams were sent; letters to the editor were written; MPs were lobbied. The *ad hoc* committee and women's groups wished to remove the over-ride from both the general equality provisions and section 28. However, since section 28 was the only one dealing exclusively with gender, the strongest push was made there. In effect, the federal government's statement on November 9 that the over-ride did apply to section 28 narrowed the protest of women's groups. If section 28 had been declared at the outset to be outside the scope of the over-ride, women's groups would have focussed on section 15(1) and might have succeeded, together with other interest groups, in removing the over-ride from equality rights as a whole.

Nevertheless, the lobbying of the provinces served to reveal the political vulnerability of provincial governments on human rights issues, especially when they are not protected by the inter-governmental process. When first ministers negotiate as a group, no single one of them can be held responsible for the decision reached. The lobbying of women's groups shone a spotlight on each premier individually, and in that context no premier dared to refuse, as a matter of principle, to entrench equality for women in the constitution.

The mass lobbying by letter and telegram was reinforced by personal contacts around the country: someone knew Premier Peckford's campaign manager and called her; she called the head of the Newfoundland and Labrador Advisory Council on the Status of Women and a former executive member of the NAC; they all called the premier. While women's groups were demonstrating on the steps of the Newfoundland Legislature, others were talking to the premier. Newfoundland soon agreed to exempt section 28 from the over-ride provisions. In Prince Edward Island, the Status of Women Council kept in constant contact with the *ad hoc* committee. Both incoming and outgoing provincial premiers had to be lobbied as one premier had resigned from politics and was being replaced by a new party leader. In Nova Scotia, while individual women and women's groups were getting telegrams into the premier's office, Flora MacDonald, an old family friend of the premier, called him and urged him to exempt section 28 from the over-ride. In New Brunswick, Senator Muriel Ferguson, the Speaker of the Senate, and Gordon Fairweather, head of the Canadian Human Rights Commission, talked to the premier, as did Madelaine LeBlanc, head of the New Brunswick Advisory Council on the Status of Women.

Québec had refused to sign the Accord and was therefore not implicated in this action. But a network of women lawyers in Québec City and the Conseil du Statut de la Femme got the premier to support removal of the over-ride from section 28 and to state publicly that including section 28 in the over-ride provision had never been discussed by the first ministers.

Ontario received a huge number of telegrams and telephone calls, and quickly agreed to exempt section 28 from the over-ride. In Manitoba, women felt that there was no hope of persuading the premier. He was, however, in the middle of an election campaign, and women's groups made section 28 an election issue. The provincial NDP promised its support, and immediately after its victory, the new Manitoba government agreed to entrenchment of women's equality in the constitution. In Alberta, the support of the federal Conservative Party was crucial to women. All the Alberta federal Tories called the premier, as did a prominent Liberal cabinet minister who was an old friend of the Progressive Conservative party whip in the Alberta Legislature. In British Columbia women's groups' intensive lobbying and pressure from the NDP were powerful forces.

Premier Bennett, in his role as chairman of the provincial premiers, was under heavy pressure, and in the end he bowed to the inevitable.

Curiously, Saskatchewan was the last hold-out. The material on section 28, which the *ad hoc* committee had prepared for the lobby, had not reached Saskatchewan women's groups. These groups stood with the premier, and his officials trotted out old anti-ERA arguments that entrenching section 28 would mean that women would not be able to rent rooms to women only, or would endanger affirmative action for women. Indeed, at its annual meeting the Saskatchewan NDP defeated a resolution on freeing section 28. But the telegrams poured into the premier's office from across the country. When the actual text of section 28 and the over-ride clause made their appearance in the newspapers there, the tide turned. Perhaps the closeness of women's groups to the premier and the government had initially prevented them from seeing the full implications of Saskatchewan's position. But this same closeness certainly became an asset when an influential group of women, who had previously supported his position, urged him to agree to free section 28 from the over-ride. Their pressure was reinforced by the federal New Democratic Party and the federal minister of justice, and eventually the Saskatchewan premier agreed. In effect, Premier Blakeney linked women's rights with aboriginal rights by consenting to free section 28 only if aboriginal rights were restored to the charter.

The lobbying of the provincial premiers reveals interesting contradictions. The premiers were convinced by a combination of mass political pressure in the form of letters, telegrams and telephone calls from across the country, and individual contacts made by people they already knew. The provincial advisory councils on the status of women came into their own, using their bridging relationship between non-governmental women's groups and the governments in power to great effect. Here, also, the incidental but pervasive personal connections between committed women and men in positions of political power are revealed in curious light. The personal connections would never have had the desired effect without the massive lobbying. However, the massive lobbying was given a human face by the intervention of women personally connected to the premiers.

The lobbying of the premiers also reveals the difficulty of believing that contact with men in political power alone will eventually give women legal and economic rights to equality. The personal and political acquaintanceships were already in place for the women's lobby to exploit. Nonetheless, the fact that women were their wives, mothers and daughters and, more crucially, their campaign managers, party officials, and government ministers did not prevent the first ministers from signing the November 5 Accord, as it had not prevented them from maintaining the *status quo* in regard to the position of women in Canadian society.

THE UNFINISHED AGENDA

In a typically Canadian compromise, we now have an entrenched Charter of Rights, but some of our rights are more entrenched than others. The question of whether Parliament or the judiciary has final say over rights in Canada has not been settled one way or the other.

The victory which let section 28 stand unimpeded by the over-ride provision should not obscure the other changes in the charter that women's groups fought for and did not get:

1. There is no statement of purpose or governing principles in the charter within which the equality of the sexes is one of the guiding principles.
2. The power of section 28 in relation to other sections is not clear, and will surely have to be tested in the courts.
3. Fundamental, legal and equality rights in the charter can be overridden by Parliament and the provincial legislatures.
4. Equality rights generally are subject to a three-year moratorium and so cannot be tested before the courts until 1985. It is the only part of the charter subject to the moratorium. Moreover, marital status, sexual orientation, and political belief were not added as prohibited grounds of discrimination.
5. The charter does not use the word "person" throughout. It is inconsistent and will clearly be grounds for battles on the legal rights of the foetus.
6. The multi-culturalism clause remains problematic since there is no statement that gender equality over-rides cultural practice.
7. The fate of section 12(1)(b) of the Indian Act is unclear in relation to the charter's equality provisions.
8. There is no constitutional right of representation of women in the Senate, the Supreme Court, and on government boards and commissions.

In addition to these specific points about the charter, the constitutional debate had raised a wide range of other issues of concern to women: overlapping jurisdictions and their impact on the availability and funding of services for women, the spending power of governments, family law, and the reform of government institutions.

Part of the story of women and the process of constitution making in Canada is thus the progressive narrowing of the issues on which women have had a say. For the moment, the decisions on family law jurisdiction are suspended. No government institutions have been reformed, and jurisdictional matters have not yet been addressed in this round of constitutional reform. The political history of the development of the Charter of Rights and Freedoms shows women's groups addressing a steadily narrower range of issues as it became clear that fewer and fewer of their concerns would be met. It was necessary to choose the very few rock-bottom issues to address, without which the Charter would be wholly unacceptable on the issue of women's equality with men. This is also a story of the progressive exclusion of women from the process of constitutional change, and of the elaborate strategies required for them to break into the process.

Women must be centrally involved in any future constitutional change. Reforms in government institutions, decisions on the spending power and family law, changes in the division of powers between governments, cannot be made in a gender-neutral way unless women knowledgeable about the consequences take part in the process. The story of the proposed changes in divorce jurisdiction is a classic example of the problems caused by well-meaning people who simply do not, as a matter of course, consider the *differences* in impact on men and women of a given political decision. Unless the discussions surrounding such issues are open, governments will continue to make inequitable decisions and further erode the confidence of women in the responsiveness of Canadian political institutions. The many interest group representatives who testified before the Joint Committee on the Constitution expressed the legitimate concerns of the people they spoke for. Public interest groups do not usually emerge unless citizens feel that their needs are not being met by governments. The fact that women had to function as an "interest group" testified eloquently to the failure of our national institutions to represent the specific concerns of women *as women* adequately.

In November 1981, in the midst of the struggle to free the equality rights provisions of the Charter from the over-ride, the minister of justice suggested that women could deal with the dangers by being "vigilant". Women's groups are now preparing for further vigilance. Partly as a result of the political process traced here, they have become more sophisticated about rights and about the political power and strategies necessary to protect and extend them. The Canadian Advisory Council, the National Association of Women and the Law, and the *ad hoc* committee, along with other concerned women, are considering legal action funds with which to test the new provisions of the constitution on behalf of women. They have examined such models as American civil liberties funds for women, the Canadian Civil Liberties Association, the consumer's associations and the environmental law associations. Women's organisations will have to battle in new forums, and with new tools.

Already barriers are emerging. The Supreme Court is being urged on many sides to approach the Charter in a strict and narrow rather than liberal fashion. One sign of this is the stance taken by the new Centre for Human Rights at the University of Ottawa, which has received a large grant from the Department of Justice to research the implications of the charter and to advise judges on it. Already the Centre has adopted the narrow view of the force of section 28; the symbolic or philosophical approach has been given no expression in that particular forum. But women's groups knew very early in the process of constitutional change that "entrenchment of rights would only be good for women if the wording provided women's rights to equality in a way that the Supreme Court could not interpret narrowly".

Major battles lie ahead. But the women's movement engages in them more strongly than before. Women and the women's movement have become more sophisticated in their understanding of what it takes to win a political victory against serious resistance. New lobbying strategies have been developed, and the networks connecting women across the country have been extended. Moreover, women's groups now have more specialised knowledge about the constitution and the implications of future changes for them. Politically active women lawyers will have a significant and growing impact in the women's movement, partly because of the opportunities for change offered by the Charter of Rights. With its professional base, the National Association of Women and the Law will be a key organisation in women's rights politics in the next decade, and may shift increasingly into professional service for other women's groups, especially on constitutional matters.

The danger inherent in this state of affairs is the possibility of splitting the women's movement between groups interested in equality rights and the legal battles associated with them, and others interested in legislative and administrative change including changes in the design and delivery of social services to women. It would not serve the best interests of the women's movement, or its traditions, to have women lawyers professionalise concerns about the Charter to such an extent that they will be removed from the scrutiny of other interested women. Yet there is an undeniable need for professional expertise in this area. One challenge the women's movement will have to face is to combine concern for rights with the longer and more varied list of problems that have not yet been adequately solved.

Representational politics have so far not served women's interests very well. On the one hand, the changes in the constitution will make the legal system an increasingly important arena for social change that women's groups will exploit. On the other hand, the very process of constitutional change has brought into the women's movement many women who had previously believed that Canadian society was already egalitarian with respect to women. When the unwritten constitution came to be made explicit, a much less liberal set of assumptions held by Canadian governments, federal and provincial, was revealed. Because of this perception, the number of women who are willing to identify themselves as part of the women's movement has grown. In addition, partly as a result of the perceived success of the women's lobby on the constitution, political parties have become more interested in women as a voting group. Greater responsiveness to women's concerns in the area of representational politics may yet turn out to be the most important legacy of the process of constitutional change.

UPDATE — AUTUMN 1985

The three years since the time of the passage of the Constitution Bill in April 1982 have been marked by great activity within the women's movement in an attempt to realise quickly some benefits from the passage of the bill and to build structures and organisations that will be able to fight in the longer battles which will be required to transform Canadian society in the direction of women's equality.

During the three-year moratorium governing the equality rights section of the charter, governments in Canada had undertaken to audit the laws on their books to identify the ones that conflicted with the Charter of Rights and to change them. The moratorium, which women's groups had opposed because they saw it largely as a delaying tactic, proved to be just that. Women's groups all over the country urged their provincial governments and the federal government to conduct charter audits of their laws, to publish the results and to participate in public consultations on the basis of those results before the equality sections of the charter were to come into effect in April 1985. Women's groups also argued strongly that merely facial equality in the laws was not enough. Laws needed to be examined in terms of their differential impact on women and men; and laws that looked equal on the surface could in many cases *de facto* be discriminatory against women. These were the kinds of arguments women's groups had used during the time of the drafting of the charter, which had led to the inclusion of explicit phrases in Section 15(1) referring to equality "before and under the law", and "the equal protection and equal benefit of the law without discrimination". However, the audits of the law that took place during this moratorium period seem to have been marked by a very narrow definition of equality, and those jurisdictions that came up with amendments to existing legislation dealt almost entirely with issues of facial inequality.

On the federal level the report of the charter audit committee, released in January 1985, though it claimed to have worked with a definition of equality that took into account the different impact of laws on women and men, recommended legal changes of only a superficial nature and threw open the questions of *de facto* discrimination to yet further public discussion through a Parliamentary Committee on Equality Rights which was to travel around Canada for several months hearing submissions from the public. The groups of equality seekers which included, along with women, visible minority groups, organisations of the handicapped and others, viewed the parliamentary committee as a serious challenge because it required them to rehearse once again the arguments that they had made at the time of the constitution struggles of 1980 - 82 and which the revised charter was supposed to address. The equality seekers, most of them organised in voluntary associations, were being asked to explain their concerns one more time and to argue for what they thought they had already won when the charter was passed into law. The moratorium and the parliamentary committee functioned not only as a delaying tactic, but also as a demand that equality seekers — by definition those groups in society who are most disadvantaged — bear once again the burden of the struggle for equality, while the state looked on as if from a distance.

When the Equality Rights Committee toured Canada, more than sixty women's groups appeared before them. The issues raised by women's groups were: mandatory affirmative action; equal pay for work of equal value; access to job training for women; pro-rated benefits for part-time workers; an end to discrimination in hiring against homosexuals, native women and immigrant women. The immigration act was scrutinised because of the problem of "family class" sponsorships in which women sponsored by their husbands are denied access to language and other training programmes. The use of uni-sex mortality tables in pension payouts was urged, as was expansion of eligibility of part-time workers and homemakers to the Canada Pension Plan. There were a very large number of briefs calling for the inclusion of "sexual orientation" as an enumerated prohibited ground of discrimination in section 15 of the Charter. And much media attention was paid to the exclusion of women from combat by the Department of National Defence. At the time of this writing, the Equality Rights Committee has not yet reported to Parliament.

During the time of the three-year moratorium other changes in the status of women were taking place. In March of 1982 Bertha Wilson was appointed to the Supreme Court of Canada, the first woman to sit on the highest court in the land. It is clear that the political and legal changes surrounding the constitutional struggles created the environment within which the appointment of a woman judge to the Supreme Court became almost inevitable. Her appointment, nonetheless, marks an important symbolic moment in the Canadian judicial system's history — the new role of the judiciary in interpreting Canada's constitution will mean increased political pressure to appoint judges genuinely responsive to the diversity of Canadian experience, among whom must, therefore, be more women.

In June of 1985 the notorious section 12(1)b of the Indian Act was amended. The previous year the outgoing Liberal government of Pierre Trudeau had drafted a bill which it presented to Parliament in the last days of Mr. Trudeau's term as Prime Minister. That bill, seriously flawed with respect to women's equality, passed the House of Commons, but its immediate passage in the Senate was delayed because it lacked unanimous approval. Therefore, the bill failed to become law. The new Progressive Conservative government had pledged during the federal election of 1984 that it would amend the Indian Act and bring about women's equality under the Act. It brought forward a bill that restored Indian status to all the women who had lost their status as a result of marriage to someone who was not a status Indian. The bill also restored these women to band membership, which allowed them to return to the bands from which they had been sundered by the previous discriminatory law. However, the bill did not grant such band membership to the children of these women, even though the Government of Canada now recognises them as status Indians. In effect the government denied this group of women the automatic right to confer their Indian status and band membership on their children — a right that native males continue, of course, to possess. The passage of the bill was accompanied by intensive lobbying by male-dominated native organisations trying to prevent the granting of band membership to native women who had lost their status. It is highly likely that the question of the band membership of the children of these Indian women who lost their status will be decided ultimately by the Supreme Court.

Another achievement of the moratorium period was the official founding of LEAF, the Legal Education Action Fund, a voluntary women's organisation whose purpose is to help support the taking of test cases to the Supreme Court of Canada on behalf of women's equality. LEAF has embarked on a massive fund-raising campaign and is also negotiating with governments for significant grants in aid of litigation on behalf of women's equality. LEAF believes that a voluntary and representative women's organisation like their own should be one source of appropriate test cases, and that it should not be the government who has final say on which cases can be funded adequately to be brought to court, since in most cases governments will be the defendants.

At the same time that these major initiatives for dealing with the Constitution and the Charter of Rights were taking place, there was a significant change in the status of women in representational politics, as I suggested might happen earlier in this chapter. The political parties became much more interested in women as a voting group. The existence of a "gender gap" in American presidential politics and the discovery of a similar tendency in the Canadian electorate led all the parties to be more explicit in their attempts to woo women voters. In the 1984 federal election the New Democratic Party highlighted its concern with women's issues by making it one of its four major electoral planks. The leadership race of the Liberal party in 1984 involved significant attention to women delegates and to women's issues. The Progressive Conservative Party, not wishing to be cast in the negative role with respect to women that had been chosen by Ronald

Reagan in the United States, chose to highlight a commitment to women's economic equality, and not to present itself as a party opposed to changes in the status of women. All three parties during the election tried to position themselves as working to improve the situation of women. All the parties looked actively for women candidates. In the end twenty-three women ran for the Tories, forty for the Liberals and more than sixty for the NDP. It is true that most of the Tory women ran in Québec, which had, in the past, been an electoral wasteland for them, and that many women in all the parties were running in ridings that they were very unlikely to win. Yet after the election the House of Commons had twenty-seven women in it, up from fifteen women when Parliament was dissolved. The cabinet of Mr. Mulroney had six women, twice as many as ever before, several of them in key economic portfolios.

A major highlight of the electoral campaign was a televised debate, organised by the National Action Committee on the Status of Women, on issues of particular concern to women. August 15, 1984 was an historic occasion for Canadian women since on that day we led the way, and for the first time in the world called our political leaders to public account on their policies concerning women as part of a national election. The debate was a crucial moment in public education about women's concerns and acted as further legitimisation of women in the political process. It was a major step in the recognition of women in the mainstream of Canadian political life. The lobbying process that had brought about a Charter of Rights with a commitment to women's equality within Canada's constitutional structure had helped to make possible one more step in the slow process of women's development. Each step along the way has taken the combined efforts of thousands of women using limited resources and great ingenuity to try to bring about a society of greater social justice through improving the status of women.

FURTHER READING

Elizabeth Atcheson, Marg Eberts, Beth Symes with Jennifer Stoddart, eds., *Women and Legal Action: Precedents, Resources and Strategies for the Future* (Ottawa: *Canadian Advisory Council on the Status of Women*, 1984).

Audrey Doerr and Micheline Carrier, eds., *Women and the Constitution in Canada* (Ottawa: Canadian Advisory Council on the Status of Women, 1981).

Penney Kome, *Women of Influence: Canadian Women and Politics* (Toronto: Doubleday Canada Ltd., 1985).

Penney Kome, *The Taking of 28: Women Challenge the Constitution* (Toronto: Women's Press, 1983).

DOROTHY GOLDIN ROSENBERG

Feminism and Peace

This chapter will examine different ways in which patriarchal and feminist values define and address militarism and violence, peace and the possibility of non-violence. While the values I will outline are traditionally linked with the culture of one or the other gender, I am fully aware that there are female militarists and male peace makers. In my view, feminism is not anti-male; rather, it is a set of values historically and culturally ascribed to women. Such values are related to peace and non-violence. The patriarchal values we will address are found in militarism and a culture of violence.

After an analysis of violence in its most personal, local as well as global manifestations, we will examine the prevalent ideology of power and how these two values inform the practices of militarism and war...which can ultimately anihilate the planet. We will then examine various women's initiatives towards peace. These are manifested through a feminist value system and analysis of power, the experience of various Canadian and international women's peace groups, and the formulation of theories of feminist education towards peace. Finally we will look at some strategies for actions toward peace in Canada.

VIOLENCE

There are two things that men do that women don't: they make war and they commit rape. That's two good reasons for working towards a future society that derives more of its values from women.

Margaret Atwood, *Globe and Mail*,
March 2, 1983.

"Violence" in the English language is linguistically rooted in the word "viol" from the French. Consequently "rape", "violation", "violate" and "violence" are all connected in our language and society in North America. Various nuances of the word are connected through pornography and the power relationships between individuals and between various groups of people. Violence is manifested in many ways: structurally, biologically, symbolically, economically and psychologically. To deny the natural rights of dignity, self-respect and the right to live life to its fullest is the hidden premise of the logic of violence. Violence depends on hierarchical power to maintain the conditions of dominance necessary for its perpetuation.[1]

Because of our experience of oppression as women, we have been especially interested in defining violence and its relation to the power structures that oppress us:

> What is power? The world tells me that money is power, that weapons are power, that a dictator is a powerful man, that my boss has power over me, that men have more power than women. From this it seems that power is exercised through violence, that indeed, the potential for physical, economic and psychological violence is almost a definition of power.[2]

Not only must we define violence and how it acts upon us, but we must understand the logic of how violence is enacted in both the personal and public spheres of society:

> I am a member of an oppressed minority and I have no way of making you listen to me...I turn to terrorism. I am a dictator, yet I cannot force you to think as I want you to...I fling you into jail, starve your children, torture you. I am a woman in a conventional marriage situation...I feel helpless, inferior and powerless...all against my husband's constant undermining. So, I in turn undermine him, manipulate him, make him look foolish in the eyes of his children...Or I'm the president of the U.S. with all the forces at my command. I know of no way to make sure that the developing countries, especially the oil-rich nations, will dance to my tune. So I turn to witholding food as a political weapon, as well as building ever more armaments. Violence is resourcelessness.[3]

We live in a culture where violence is now accepted as normal behaviour, and has developed its own accepted forms of expression. Violence is depicted throughout the media and is integrated into entertainment and recreation, such as rock videos, pornography and widely played video games. The Canadian public's attention was drawn to how violence in a seemingly innocuous "adult video game" could draw together the elements of sexism, racism, pornography and militarism in "Custer's Revenge", a game originating in the USA in the early 1980s. In a hail of arrows and naked except for his hat and holster, The General Custer figure rides across the screen. The object of the game is for him to rape an Indian woman tied to a stake. Once mounted on her, each thrust of the Custer figure means the scoring of points. On the cover of the box, its purpose is succinctly expressed: "When you score, you score!" Women's groups, native people's groups, peace groups, community and church groups throughout Canada succeeded in pressuring the Canadian government to stop importation of this game to Canada...and in only twelve days.

Militarism enters the life of many small boys through the presence of military toys like G.I. Joe. Christmas catalogues from large stores usually devote several pages to brightly coloured and attractively displayed military toys for boys. Hasbro, the creator and producer of G.I. Joe, is becoming one of the largest corporations in world marketing of "child products". Just after the American invasion of Grenada in 1983, Hasbro re-introduced G.I. Joe to the market. It became an instant best seller. In the Christmas of 1983, Hasbro, with the help of some U.S. congressmen and the U.S. military, airlifted 23,000 toys into Grenada.[4] During the war in Viet Nam, the U.S. military stated that its goal was to win the "hearts and the minds" of the people. By proliferating military values through children's toys, the economic interests that produce armaments and promote the glory of war can be assured that such values will saturate society. These values include domination, glorification of killing and conquering, objectivication of others, racism and sexism. These values not only are evident in military toys, but are often used by the military as a way of inculcating them. Very often these values, used to help males bond, carry a strong misogynous message.

In Canada we are currently witnessing the encroaching militarism of our country. This will be discussed further on. Along with the increase in the manufacturing and proliferation of war toys, there is increasing enticement aimed at attracting young people towards military careers. Recruitment teams visit colleges and universities, armed with a very sophisticated advertising campaign. A recent brochure capitalises on the high unemployment rate of the fifteen- to twenty-four-year-old age group. Its cover shows four young people standing in a row on a roadway outside a housing project. It is in the dreary season at the end of the winter. They look bored and directionless. The caption reads: "Doing anything special?" Upon opening the brochure, one sees pictures of happy people in uniform, cheefully engrossed in several jobs in front of an armed forces helicopter. "Come with us and you'll have a choice", is the heading. The brochure concludes with the invitation to "Do something special". Only one out of the twenty-four pictures in the brochure shows active warfare and none of them shows death. The one small picture of a soldier holding a gun in front of some tanks is relegated to the last page. The whole issue of active warfare and its destruction is neatly side-stepped in the brochure in the following way:

Hundreds of young people helping our Forces maintain their "front line" effectiveness. A responsibility that may not be "front line" itself, but none-the-less a responsibility that ensures this capability, providing for the smooth operational total effectiveness of our Forces wherever they may be, what ever they may be doing.[5]

It is precisely this pretence of neutrality that makes war toys and armed forces propaganda so invidious. Where, instead, do we find recruitment and career planning for peace studies and non-violent conflict resolution? In our society there are some people who claim that much of the material in pornographic magazines and video games is merely harmless fun, recreational in nature. In the following section, we shall examine why it is important to recognise the seriousness of the motivations and implications of these cultural practices.

NAMING THE VIOLENCE

Those of us who challenge the notion of being controlled by the forces of violence in our society must analyse violence, its relation to our power structures, and each one of its manifestations. Our first step is in *naming the violence* at all its different levels. Violence is inherent in our social structures, which support privilege and maintain a hierarchy that, in order to defend its own interests, perpetuates economic violence by the few against the many. There are psychological manifestations of violence in the humiliation of various groups of people through sexism and racism; the latter are often manifested in advertising, fashion and pornography. There is also a systemic form of spiritual violence in which people are alienated from their own perceptions by a prevailing ideology that disconfirms their knowledge and replaces it with "truths", as seen by such governmental agencies as schools and social welfare institutions. Biological violence is also perpetrated by the creation of dangerous chemical wastes, acid rain and the radioactive contamination that threaten the very existence of our planet. Finally, verbal violence pervades our language, which is racist, sexist and classist.[6]

The violent use of language is an important tool in the socialisation of soldiers. This language clearly identifies the enemy through objectifying them and viewing them through the most violent forms of racism and misogyny.

"Patriarchy is a killer," says U.S. writer Donna Warnock. She connects pornography, racism, violence and military virility, showing how "snuff" films, used to entertain male viewers, are similar to the hands-on personal "snuff" offered by military work. In support of this view, she quotes veteran Richard Hale, who reported that on the way to Viet Nam, U.S. troops were told: "There's lots of loose ass over there, men, and they just love G.I. dick and best of all they are only gooks so if you get tired of them, you can cram a grenade up their cunt and waste them." Reinforced by such instruction and additional slogans ("This is my rifle, this is my gun; one is for killing, the other's for fun!"), soldiers have perpetrated many atrocities against women.

In addition to describing how violence of language helps promote acts of violence, Warnock also explains its importance in military indoctrination for creating solidarity among the soldiers by "killing the women" in them. Indeed, suggesting that the enemy is "effeminate" can often arouse extreme bellicosity:

> In reality misogyny, homophobia, and racism are the basic components of military indoctrination for creating solidarity. Such machismo exists in the highest echelons of government as well...In Henry Kissinger's 1975 appeal to congress for military and financial aid for Angola, he described the U.S. as "emasculating" itself by not sending help. After President Johnson ordered North Viet Nam PT boats, bases and oil deposits bombed, he bragged to a reporter: "I didn't just screw Ho Chi Minh, I cut his pecker off." The logical extension of this eroticized violence is articulated in a plaque which hangs on the wall of the Syracuse Research Corporation, a private U.S.think-tank with large military contracts:
>
> "I love you because:
> I love you because
> your sensors glow in the dark
> your side glows swing in the breeze
> your hair looks like clutter
> your multi-path quivers
> your reaction time is superb
> your missile has thrust
> it accurately hones in on its target
> the fuse ignites
> the warhead goes
> Sweet oblivion."
>
> If a missile launching can be sexually fantasised by leading militarists as "sweet oblivion" it follows that total annihilation would be the ultimate orgasm.[7]

PATRIARCHAL POWER

Men shouldn't vote because: 1) Men are too emotional to vote, their conduct at baseball games and at political conventions shows this, while their innate tendency to appeal to force renders them particularly unfit for the task of government. 2) Because no really manly man wants to settle any question except by fighting about it. 3) Because man's place is in the army. 4) Because men will lose their charm if they step out of their natural sphere and interest themselves in matters other than feats of arms, uniforms and drums. 5) Because if men should adopt peaceable methods, women will no longer look up to them.

Alice Dewar Miller, 1915.[8]

While there are demonstrably many political ideologies that criticise the allocation of power, feminism is the only ideology so far that has formulated a critique of patriarchal power in itself.

The word "patriarchy" in its original Latin form of "pater" means both "father" and "to own". It means in our society "the rule of the fathers". It describes a world-wide phenomenon of men's control over women, children and the economic, social and political order.

The Canadian scientist, Ursula Franklin, has refined the definition of patriarchal power as a "threat based system", and she sees opposition to both patriarchy and militarism as the task of feminist activists:

...our fundamental objection to militarism should not be related to the size of the arsenal or the destruction of its weapons. What we women are objecting to is the threat system *per se*. We have not consented to live in the "or else" world of threats, we want to build a "why not" world of respect and diversity...Threat based systems...all work under the implicit assumption that some people matter much less than others, and all people are of interest only as long as they are needed to support the system or justify it.[9]

Clearly, militarism is essential to the maintenance of patriarchal power: patriarchy is the belief and militarism the practice. It is essential for women to understand that militarism and the arms race *are* women's issues in a particular way because militarism in its practice is an extreme form of sexism and destructive to feminist aspirations and ideals. The concept of human nature underlying militarism is that humans are intrinsically aggressive and competitive. Hence,

... military strength is required to control society, to regulate nations, and to defend one's homeland. It is necessary to defend the interests of "us," the civilized good guys against "them," the aggressive bad guys ... Thus militarism and patriarchy both perceive biology as destiny. Both are based on the glorification of so-called masculine traits and contempt for so-called feminine traits. Both require sexist socialization of each generation to justify and maintain their existence. Masculine males are needed to compete, fight and rule. Feminine females are needed to support and cheer their males and to nurture the next generation of workers, soldiers and cheerleaders ... Patriarchy could not exist without the threat of force and violence to keep rebellious women and non-elite men in their places.[10]

It would be simplistic to imagine that the only place where patriarchal power shows its dependence upon and support of military violence were through the state. Other patriarchal institutions are not far behind in legitimising mass murder and destruction in the hands of the military. The relationship of the Catholic Church to the military, for instance, was well documented in an article by Sister Joan Chitister, then President of the Conference of American Benedictine Prioresses, in 1982 in the Catholic journal, *Commonweal.* Here she took the bishops of the American Catholic Church to task for failing to be ... "morally absolute in their repudiation of the manufacture or use of nuclear weapons". She was troubled, she wrote, by the contrasting ease with which they were able to take a clear stand against abortion. "What is a woman to think?" she asked. "That when life is in the hands of a woman, then to destroy is always morally wrong? But when all life is in the hands of men, then destruction can be theologized?"[11]

It is said that her questions forced the bishops to rewrite their *Pastoral Letter on Disarmament*, taking a much stronger position against nuclear weapons than they had previously taken. In a subsequent interview by the *New York Times*, she was asked about the separation of church and State, and she responded:

> When bishops bless bombs, salute the flag and pay taxes, nobody says the church shouldn't be involved in politics. But when a church begins to talk about the destruction of the planet, then they say bishops, religious and priests should stay in the pulpit, should forget the obstacles to justice. Tell that to Jeremiah and Daniel, to Deborah and Judith for me.[12]

The examples of economic and/or military sanctions imposed upon countries unwilling to bow to authority illustrate the dominant/dominated relationships of the political economy of the world. Examples of such sanctions are those recently taken against New Zealand for prohibiting U.S. nuclear weapons-carrying ships in their ports and against Nicaragua and its attempt to achieve political and economic independence.

CANADA'S ROLE IN THE ARMS RACE

Canada seems to have assumed the role of "obedient wife" to the United States, reproducing common patriarchal patterns of the dominated. Not only have two prime ministers agreed to test Cruise missiles for the U.S. without either public or parliamentary debate (not withstanding the fact that 85 per cent of the public polled opposed this), but while our government refuses officially to participate in the United States' plan for research in the Strategic Defense Initiative (Star Wars), there will still be support for universities and corporations undertaking such research. Since we are economically and militarily weaker than our powerful neighbour, we are forced to submit to a system of "security" that carries the characteristics of a patriarchal and thus militaristic definition of "security".

Obedience to authority is the cornerstone of an effective military machine and fundamental principle of the patriarchal family. Militarism and Sexism require that service and sacrifice be performed without reflection. Freedom and equality, on the contrary, require the full development of all citizens' capacities for reflection and analysis.[13]

Canada's participation in the international arms race is not only confined to agreeing to manufacture and test missiles. We are actively involved in many aspects of nuclear and conventional arms production and export. There are many ways in which Canadians are enmeshed in the U.S. war machine. Very soon after the 1984 Conservative victory, Prime Minister Mulroney and several members of Parliament went to Washington to meet with President Reagan and his Pentagon advisors. Shortly afterwards, a series of Pentagon Procurement Seminars took place in seven major Canadian cities. Under the auspices of the Canadian Departments of External Affairs, National Defence, Industry, Trade and Commerce, and Regional-Industrial Expansion, companies were encouraged to bid for military contracts under the Defence Production Sharing Arrangements (DPSA); clearly this has implications for the Strategic Defense Initiative.

The rational for war industry is always job creation. No other economic alternatives were examined or offered, nor is there any record of a Canadian study on the economic benefits of alternatives to military spending. Studies show that more jobs could be created in other sectors of the economy if equal amounts of money were invested there.[14]

There is much evidence that Canada is a major player in the nuclearisation of the world: we have become the world's largest exporter of uranium, the fuel from which nuclear weapons are made. Because we do not have enrichment facilities, we even send uranium to the USSR, our alleged enemy. There it is enriched and sent on to our customers who require it. As well, for years we have been exporting Candu nuclear reactors and nuclear technology to many countries, including Argentina, India (which exploded a bomb in 1974), Pakistan and South Korea. Despite the Non-Proliferation Treaty and other "safe-guards", Canada is encouraging Egypt and other countries to buy this technology. It is estimated that close to thirty countries now or soon will have nuclear weapons capability. Spent nuclear fuel from our reactors in Chalk river go to Savannah River, South Carolina, where it is used in the U.S. Nuclear Weapons Program, a fact vigorously denied by Canadian authorities, since our nuclear technology is not supposed to contribute to weapons.[15] In a few years, upon the opening of the Darlington, Ontario, nuclear facility, Canada will be marketing tritium, produced by

Candu reactors and necessary for the preservation of hydrogen bombs.[16]

Some Canadian firms profit extensively from the international arms trade where the United States is a major customer. In 1983 we exported ten times more military equipment to them than we did ten years earlier. Sales to redeveloping countries have grown substantially from fifty million dollars annually in the early 1970s to three times that amount in the '80s. Our military exports go to countries that are gross and systematic violators of human rights, although Canadian governmental guidelines officially oppose this practice. For example, Pratt and Whitney engines, made in Québec, are sold to Brazil, which puts them on military planes, which it in turn sells to Chile and El Salvador.[17]

The problem of our political economy and its relation to political policy is well articulated by Reverend Clark MacDonald, Chairman of Project Ploughshares and former moderator of the United Church of Canada: "As we become more dependent on military sales, especially to the U.S., our foreign policy is affected. How can we be independent when large chunks of our industries can be damaged by the cancelling of U.S. military contracts?"[18] How could we resist U.S. military proposals or demands for Cruise testing or some form of participation in SDI?

WOMEN'S INITIATIVES TOWARDS PEACE

Throughout history, women have opposed violence and wars. They have used many tactics to persuade men not to fight; one famous portrayal of such struggles is in *Lysistrata*, the ancient Greek play where women deny the men their sexual favours until they stop the war.

In the modern era, European and North American women took a peace initiative in 1915 by founding the Women's International League for Peace and Freedom. The First World War was already under way when they met in the Hague and attempted to convince the anatagonists to halt the fighting by proposing many alternative solutions for conflict resolution. They were ignored. The war continued at great cost to the men, women and children of the countries involved. In the United States in 1921, the very first speech made to the new League of Women Voters by the suffragist and League founder, Carrie Chapman Catt, was an impassioned plea to work for peace.

In Canada, one of the earliest and most consistent peace organisations has been Voice of Women, founded in 1960. At that time, many people were frightened by the threat of nuclear war as well as of radiation from the fallout from nuclear testing in the atmosphere. In the 1950s, frequent nuclear explosions were carried out in the atmosphere by the countries that possessed nuclear weapons at the time: the USA, the USSR, France and Great Britain. Women and men all over the world were very concerned about caesium and strontium 90, products of the fall-out. As a part of an international survey and under the direction of Canadian physicist Ursula Franklin, Voice of Women initiated a scientific analysis of baby teeth by asking parents to send in their children's teeth after they had fallen out. They were tested in laboratories for strontium 90, a carcinogen that behaves like calcium in the human body, settling in the teeth and bones. These studies revealed disturbing amounts of strontium 90 in the teeth, indicating its presence in our bodies, the food chain, the water and the land. Massive protests took place regarding the danger in which these tests were placing present and future generations. These protests and other political factors led to President Kennedy of the USA and Premier Khruschev of the USSR signing a Partial Test Ban Treaty in 1963.

While this treaty ended most atmospheric testing (China and France still continued for some time), it was to continue underground. The major nuclear powers went ahead and developed more dangerous and accurate nuclear weapons, such as Poseidon and Trident submarines, Pershing, MX and Cruise missiles, currently moving towards the present "Star Wars" system. The production of these weapons and their delivery systems have dangerously proliferated at an escalating rate while the arms controls talks go through the motions of mediation.

Throughout the world, women's peace movements have grown over the past quarter century. In Sweden in 1968, the women's peace movement was effective in preventing that country from becoming a nuclear weapons nation. Inga Thorrson, a key woman in this process, eventually became the Swedish Ambassador for Disarmament at the United Nations where she has written several studies on disarmament and development. These examine military economic conversion and socially useful alternatives to military spending in her own country and the world. Sweden has been represented on disarmament at the U.N. by three women ambassadors, Alva Myrdahl, Inga Thorrson and Maj Britt Theorin.

There have been many notable non-violent actions for peace throughout the world. Perhaps some of the most dramatic and innovative ones have been at Greenham Common in England, where over 30,000 women and children participated in an "embrace the base" campaign in 1982, and have continued to develop other effective action since:

> In the great traditions of pacifism, anarchy and English doggedness in adversity, they have entered the base, blockaded its gates, danced on its missile silos, made a mockery of its security systems and inspired others to set up peace camps in Britain and all over the world.[19]

The example of their non-hierarchical, feminist decision-making processes have been an inspiration to women's peace camps such as those at

Seneca, NY, Seattle, Washington, Comiso and Sicily in Italy, and at Cole Bay, Saskatchewan. Important women's initiatives for peace are taking place in El Salvador, Belau, Sri Lanka, the United States, the Soviet Union, the Federal Republic of Germany and the rest of Europe, South Africa and New Zealand.[20] In 1985 a coalition of Canadian women's groups organised an International Women's Peace conference which brought together 350 women from over 300 countries to examine the urgency for true security and women's alternatives for negotiating peace. The themes that were set for the U.N. Decade for Women (1975 - 85) were Equality, Development and Peace.

STRATEGIES AND METHODS OF PEACE ACTION

Long-term strategies for peace involve research, education and action. There is consistent technical research being done in Canada and throughout the world, not only on the effects of a nuclear holocaust, but on the effects of radioactive contaminants related to the war industry. Unfortunately, this research is not accorded the funding or respect commanded by military research and the development of armaments. Dr. Rosalie Bertell, a bio-statistician and mathematician, Director of the International Institute of Concern for Public Health in Toronto, has stated that the effects of low-level ionising radiation can already claim sixteen million direct and indirect casualties in the world as a result of Hiroshima, Nagasaki, and the current world-wide preparations for future war. According to her, World War II's nuclear bombs did not have effects only "out there", but continue to effect all of us now. We all carry some plutonium in our tissues, and we may be permanently damaging the human gene pool.[21] Women's groups, physicians and other scientists' groups, educators, and religious and community groups across the country are educating Canadians on the real dangers we face, and on alternatives to those dangers.[22] Peace research has been woefully underfunded, and the funding for women's peace research has been miniscule.

Women have also undertaken to educate people on the political economy of the arms race and its concomitant absorption of funding that should go to women and social programmes throughout the world. Through organisations, publications, press releases and the holding of workshops and conferences, women in various peace groups have attempted to involve the public in challenging the present military policies. Some women in communications have also produced material that shows the folly of military thinking and the danger in which it places all of us in the name of "security".[23]

Some feminist research conceptualises the ways in which women's world picture differs from men's, especially in our notions about power. Peggy Sanday, in her study of 156 tribal societies, found that when women exercised power *qua women*, they placed the interest of the group above individual advancement. Moreover, they tended to band together to communicate their influence rather than resort to violence.[24] Carol Gilligan, a psychologist, has formulated theories corroborating the view that male-defined morality does not really describe women's moral definitions. In her important work, *In a Different Voice*, she demonstrates that women's need for affiliation results in a morality based on feeling and caring for others. Men's, on the other hand, depends on consistency with abstract principles.[25] While this conceptual research is still at an early stage, it has already contributed greatly to women's acknowledgement of our differentiation from male values, and encouraged us to take action to change toward a more appropriate agenda for this planet.

While research is an essential element in the struggle for peace, the key to spreading it is feminist education:

> ... because we must dismantle mental as well as military weapons. The nuclear arms race is not simply madness, it is socially imposed manliness taken to its extreme....[26]

As well, feminist educators (of both sexes) have different values to impart:

> Feminist educators generally envision a world in which people's social, political and economic roles won't be determined by their sex. They try to undo traditional sex role socialization in order to develop more assertive risk-taking, competent, self-assured females and more caring, co-operative, considerate males ... militarism is really an extreme form of sexism.[27]

Peace education is beginning to take place at all levels in and oustide of school systems. An increasing amount of diverse teaching material is being produced by educators, parents and students for all levels of understanding.

SHORT-TERM GOALS AND ACTIONS

In the short term, there is an urgent need to stop all nuclear testing in the world, and there is a world-wide movement of women towards a Comprehensive Test Ban Treaty. The reasons for the emphasis on testing is that if one does not test, one cannot deploy; therefore, there will be no further building of nuclear weapons.

In Canada there has been a major move to pressure the government to urge the United States to declare that it would not be the first country to use nuclear weapons. Canadian groups have also asked for Canada to be declared a nuclear weapons-free zone; they ask for the North to be demilitarised and for a verifiable negotiated mutual freeze at the United Nations, as well as an end to the umbrella agreement that allows the testing of Cruise missiles. Operation Dismantle, Project Ploughshares, and other Canadian peace groups, have mounted a country-wide campaign to urge citizens to make their cities nuclear-free zones. To date, successful campaigns have been organised in eighty-five cities and municipalities.

Non-violent civil disobedience is another alternative. Over two hundred Canadians are participating in the Peace Tax Fund where they withhold the 12.2 per cent portion of their federal income tax that goes into defence spending. They prefer for the money to go for peace education or other humanitarian uses. Annually, the Alliance for Non-Violent Action has coordinated sit-ins at Litton Industries in Rexdale, Ontario, where the Inertial Guidance System for the Cruise missile is manufactured. Litton is heavily subsidised by Canadian tax dollars.

Scientists at many Canadian universities have signed petitions demanding that the government not participate in research in SDI, stating categorically that they personally will not participate in such work. Hundreds of Canadians are appearing before various task forces and commissions on the arms race, proposing alternatives to the current government policies.

In the last few years, there has been a growing understanding that peace, social justice and appropriate development go together. Diverse groups are working together with the understanding that the spending of a trillion dollars a year on the arms race throughout the world is destructive to development and self-determination in countries struggling towards those ends.

There are many ways to work for peace in Canada. While the participation of all Canadians is needed, the larger part of peace work is still being done by women. This fact is recognized by men as well as women: "My generation has failed to stop the arms race", stated Rear Admiral Gene la Rocque (ret.) of the U.S. Navy recently, "but it's really the men who have failed. Now it's up to the women, and I believe they can do it."[28]

An essential principle for successful peace and social justice efforts is working with other people: one can join local groups or, in their absence, form new ones. It is important to have up-to-date information on the arms race and peace issues, and to build the skills to present it dynamically. The use of film and discussion groups is a good medium of communication and quite available. Keeping in contact with other peace groups in the international community and seeing their ideas and materials is helpful and energising. Peace vigils, introduction of municipal proposals for nuclear-free zones, letters to the press, and public gatherings with invited speakers are all excellent ways of informing and mobilising fellow citizens.

Sometimes it is useful to use particular days to highlight the horrors of nuclear war and the need to engage in the struggle for peace. Hiroshima Day is on August 6; Nagasaki Day is on August 9; Disarmament Week is October 24-30; Women's Disarmament Day is October 12; October 16 is World Food Day; Remembrance Day is November 11, and March 8 is International Women's Day.

It is important to maintain a deluge of letters to legislators when important issues come up. It is vital for constituents to visit the offices of their MPs, present information and ask questions. Petitions can be useful since the people to whom they are presented do count how many people sign. Parents or teachers can insist that peace education be part of the curriculum at all levels.

Finally, it is important not only to react against war and the menace of nuclear annihilation. It is essential to hold and communicate to others a vision of a peaceful world with the benefits it would accord all people. We must keep conscious of the beauty of this planet and the people on it, celebrate them and reiterate why they are worth respecting and protecting.

Women have always been actively involved in peace work. As our technology increases, it becomes clear that our vision — our ways of doing things — may yet be factors that keep this planet alive. We must develop our moral power into a social and political force. For the first time in our history we have the opportunity to enter the political arenas of our cities, provinces, country and the world itself. The qualities of self-confidence, knowledge and competence in the public sphere, encouraged and developed in us through women's and other social movements, must now be used to redirect the policies of our governments from more death machines to meeting *life's* needs.

REFERENCES

1 "A Call to Courage for Women Everywhere" (an open letter of the Women's International for Peace and Food), 1984.

2 Jo Vellacott, "Women, Peace and Power", *Reweaving the Web of Life*, ed. Pamela McAllister, Philadelphia: New Society Books, 1982, p. 32.

3 *Ibid.*, p. 32.

4 *Calumet: The Newsletter of the Christian Movement for Peace*, Volume 9, No. 3., 1984.

5 *Doing Anything Special?* Poster/Brochure, Canadian Armed Forces, 1985.

6 "A Call to Courage", *op. cit.*

7 Donna Warnock, "Patriarchy is a Killer: What People Concerned about Peace and Justice Should Know", *Reweaving the Web of Life, op. cit.*, p. 20.

8 Quoted by Ursula Franklin, "Feminism and Militarism", *Status of Women News*, Toronto: National Action Committee on the Status of Women, February, 1983.

9 *Ibid.*

10 Lyla Hoffman, ''Feminist Education: A Key to Peace'', *Interracial Books for Children: Militarism, Racism, Sexism*, ed. Bradford Chambers, New York, Volume 13, Nos. 6 & 7, 1982.

11 Barbara Lazear Ascher, ''Hers'', *New York Times*, March 10, 1083.

12 *Ibid.*

13 Betty Reardon, ''Militarism and Sexism, Influences on Education for War'', *United Ministries for Education Connexion*, Fall, 1981.

14 Susanne Gordon and Dave Mc Fadden, eds., ''Introduction'', *Economic Conversion: Revitalizing America's Economy*, Balinger Press, 1984, p. xvii.

15 *Nuclear Free Press*, Peterborough, Ontario, Spring, 1985.

16 Energy Probe, Toronto.

17 Information compiled by Project Ploughshares, Conrad Grebel College, Waterloo, Ontario.

18 Reverend Clark MacDonald, Project Ploughshares fund-raising letter, June 1985.

19 Ann Snitow, ''Holding a Line at Greenham: Being Joyously Political in Dangerous Times'', *Mother Jones*, February/March, 1985, p. 31.

20 ''Women for Peace'', *Disarmament Campaigns: The International Newsletter on Action Against the Arms Race*, The Hague, Netherlands, no. 42, April, 1985.

21 Rosalie Bertell, *No Immediate Danger? Prognosis for a Radioactive Earth*, Toronto: The Women's Press, 1985, p. viii.

22 This work is being done by such groups as Voice of Women, Science for Peace, Physicians for Social Responsibility (winners of the 1985 Nobel Peace Prize), Educators for Peace and others.

23 The National Film Board of Canada's Studio D has produced two films: *If You Love This Planet* and *Speaking Our Peace*; CBC's *Man Alive* has treated the subject frequently on TV.

24 Peggy Sanday, *Female Power and Male Dominance: On the Origins of Sexual Equality, New York: Cambridge University Press*, 1981.

25 Carol Gilligan, *In a Different Voice: Psychological Theory and Women's Development*, Cambridge, MA: Harvard University Press, 1982.

26 Donna Warnock, ''Workshop in Non-Violence,'' *WIN Magazine*, New York, April, 1982.

27 Hoffman, *op. cit.*

28 Rear Admiral Gene la Rocque, USN (ret), *The Defense Monitor*, Vol. viii, no. 8, 1984, p. 9.

FURTHER READING

Books:

Bertell, Rosalie, *No Immediate Danger? Prognosis for a Radioactive Earth*, Toronto: The Women's Press, 1985.

Mc Allister, Pamela, ed., *Reweaving the Web of Life*, Philadelphia: New Society Books, 1982.
Regehr, Ernie, and Simon Rosenblum, eds., *Canada and the Nuclear Arms Race*, Toronto: Lorimer, 1983.
Sanger, Clyde, *Safe and Sound: Disarmament and Development in the 80's*, Ottawa: Deneau Publishing, 1982.

Journals:

Peace Magazine
Published by Candis,
P.O. Box 490, Adelaide Street Post Office,
Toronto, Ontario, M5C 2J6.

Ploughshares Monitor
Project Ploughshares,
Conrad Grebel College, University of Waterloo,
Waterloo, Ontario, N2L 3G6.

Newsletter of the Voice of Women/La Voix des Femmes
175 Carlton Street,
Toronto, Ontario M5A 2K3.

GRETA HOFMANN NEMIROFF

On Power and Empowerment

Over the past few years, there has been much discussion within the Canadian women's movement on the subject of power. Frequently, there is a preoccupation with inserting women into prominent positions within the existing power structures of organisations or within the political arena at the local, provincial or national levels. Often, women who have "made it" in the sphere of patriarchal power are invited to share their recipes for power with the less "successful" but equally ambitious; recently there has been continuing attention paid to "strategising" for power.

Less frequent, however, is dialogue on the *nature* of this power that is so earnestly sought, or by whose definition or in whose interest such power operates in our society. It is urgent for those people who strive for social change, for a society with equality between the sexes, to analyse the belief systems underlying these "strategies" for power and equality. Not only must ideology precede action and inform it with both consistency and meaning, but it is only through the discipline of a shared ideological base that the "powerless" may become empowered to assume rightful control over their own lives.

ON POWER

"Power" in our culture is customarily coupled with the words "over" and "of". Its purpose is predicated on a vertical relationship of one to another

This text is based on a speech given for the Canadian Congress for Learning Opportunities for Women (CCLOW) in Regina, Saskatchewan, in 1981 and on an article, "The Empowerment of Women", published in *Alternatives*, No. 12, Spring, 1982, Oberlin, Ohio: Oberlin College.

or others, or on a genitive relationship as in "power of attorney", which also relates to a hierarchy of ascribed values and privileges. In political terms, power has meant the concentration of strength and resources in an individual or small group. When concentrated in the hands of the majority, it is frequently presented by the media of entrenched powers as "mob rule", "chaos" or "anarchy." That hopeful slogan of the 1960s, "All Power to the People!", was consistently presented to us by the media with a visual back-up of burning cities or screaming "mobs" on the streets of Watts, Chicago or Paris. Mass-based power has had a systematically bad press in the Western patriarchy; "good" power is perceived in oligarchical terms with the built-in assumption that there must be *a* boss or leader at all times.

A central question about power is whether it creates structures that render certain behaviour and events inevitable: are individuals contorted by power or, conversely, do contorted people seek power? Indeed, when we look at the faces of those who hold positions of political power and influence in our society, we see mainly men and a small number of women who have been able to move ahead within the patriarchal hierarchy. It is often striking how quickly these people are able to take on the somewhat ritualistic rhetorical gestures and postures of power; frequently the musculature of their faces is contorted by tension. Thin, tense lines lacerate their faces where mouths used to be. I often wonder what happens to the vulnerability of small boys' lips when they grow into "powerful" adults. What in the structure of their lives so distorts the very features and movements of their bodies? Would we wish such tension and alienation for the people we love?

It is important to consider some of the ways in which the ideology of patriarchal power has imprinted itself on our expectations and perceptions. All too often people comply with the myths that surface in the obituaries of powerful men. Their raw power becomes redefined as "service"; their deaths are frequently accompanied by maudlin accounts of their "sacrifices" in the cause of their own power. These words are rarely uttered for the millions of men and women who die every day in brutal and oppressive jobs, whose very lives are sacrificed to the notions on which this or that powerful and "altruistic" benefactor, or group of benefactors, have built empires. Indeed, many resources of the powerful are directed towards the maintenance of a *status quo* to strengthen the "efficient power of conservative self-interest".[1]

Another assumption underlying the pursuit of conventional power within the existent order is that such power in the hands of "the good" is a necessary condition for fundamental political change. In reality, the assumption of traditional political and economic power by an individual or a group of individuals precludes any basic change. The moment of assumption of power has already vested the person or group with interests to conserve, with instant conservatism.

Power in Canada is vested in the patriarchal control of property, production, and reproduction. We know the terrible statistics well: that the average man earns 157 per cent of the average woman's pay in a similar job; that 71.5 per cent of all part-time workers in Canada are women, and not by their own choice. They are the last in and the first out in hard times, and because they have no real benefits, they will probably be part of that large percentage of the female population over the age of 70 who live below the poverty line. Many of these women are heads of single-parent families, 44 per cent of which live below the poverty line while only 8.2 per cent of those headed by men are in that situation.[2] World statistics are even more distressing: women do approximately 75 per cent of all the work in the world, earn less than 10 per cent of the salaries earned in the world, and own less than 1 per cent of the earth's land.[3] Throughout North America our hard-won rights over reproduction are in danger of being modified as increasingly retrogressive legislation is considered.

Women have always existed invisibly within the ideological constructs of men, been blithely included in the pronoun "he", and quietly rolled bandages and seen our loved ones perish in wars against people with whom we have had no quarrel. The fact that so often we find ourselves articulating the measure of our possible power in terms set by the patriarchy, through its own particular historical experience, indicates the extent to which we have been colonialised by an ideology based on our own oppression. In order to do justice to our own needs and objectives, we must drop all phallocentric power terms. Rather than discussing "fighting for power", we must talk of "empowerment", assuming what is rightfully ours: an appropriate share of the resources, the history, and the agenda for the world's future. Language is an essential element here: the words we use shape the nature of our thoughts and thus our acts. Empowerment must be established through the creation of appropriate terminology. I am not referring here to fashionable epithets and shallow buzz words. I mean a vocabulary that reflects the ideology of a movement that has undertaken to redress old injustices, serving the needs of all people equally.

The patriarchy has been the sole arbiter of history. Women have lived submerged by history rather than been actively involved in the creation of our own historicity. History, as it has been perpetuated by the male academy, is largely the celebration of mass death and destruction ... wars and treaties. The time has come to investigate *how* people lived, the nature and texture of their lives ... the cultural history held in such low repute by phallocentric scholarship. Not only must women retrieve the history of our culture, but we must invest it with sufficient value so that our "story" will continue to be recorded.

The patriarchal interpretation of the past allows the rulers to define as absolute social virtue those characteristics convenient to the maintenance of the power structure. A mythos then develops to give dynamic examples of these social virtues. Often a network of lies, exaggerations and omissions is developed around an historic figure in order to provide appropriate role models of such "convenient virtue".

The historical treatment of Helen Keller is an excellent example of the selective process of such "mythologisation". She is usually represented as a brave little handicapped person who rose to great heights with the help of her good friend and teacher, Annie Sullivan. Together, they met some of the most famous people of their time. We are rarely told of Helen Keller, the radical, who wrote:

> We can't have education without revolution. We have tried peace education for one thousand and nine hundred years.... Let us try revolution and see what it will do now.... The time of blind struggle is drawing to a close.... This is not a time of gentleness. It is a time for ... open speech and fearless thinking ... a time of all that is robust and vehement and bold.[4]

When "mythologisation" will not meet the goal of maintaining a sanitised version of history, invisibility is the next resort. Thus the heroines of Canada's women's suffrage movement usually remain unsung in the schools of this country, along with the issues for which they struggled. Even when the suffrage movement is mentioned, those feminists most palatable to the patriarchy are the ones mentioned. Thus in the history of the women's struggle in Québec, one is more likely to hear of Madame Casgrain, a moderate member of the upper classes, than Idola St-Jean, an activist of the left.

In our culture, history is passed along as a series of events. We are taught that there was a French or Russian revolution ... and then it was over, to be followed by a period called "after the revolution". It is salutory for those involved in the women's struggle to learn from the Cubans who, decades after the expulsion of Battista, still speak of "living *in* the revolution". Revolution is conceptualised as a process rather than an event. This distinction is especially important to women: we are living *in* a mass revolution which has been especially active for over a hundred and thirty years. When we remember this, we will not lose hope or patience. We are living in an historical process: we are creating our own historicity.

The male power complex of the state, industry and the military has found for itself a highly efficient propaganda machine in the media. The media decide when to identify an event as revolutionary, where it is and how long it should last; they can even decide who is in charge ... who are the "stars" of this revolution. Revolutionary activity can be useful in providing narrative continuity to fragmented media delivery, and often the loss of media attention can be so demoralising to a group that its fervour can dissipate.

The media create a falsified concept of time and the appropriateness of action: "That was all very well in the sixties", is a way of dismissing current "idealism". Women have an increasingly difficult time getting media coverage (or even the attention of the media) for serious political events such as was accorded the burning of one bra one night in Atlantic City. Through our manipulation by the rapid turn-over and faddism of media language, important concepts can be taken up, reduced to the absurd, and then dropped with arbitrary rapidity. As women, we must reinstate such words and concepts as "sisterhood", "women's liberation", and "consciousness raising" as viable and essential components of our political objectives. When words disappear, actions dissipate. We should learn from the world's great religions, all of which maintain their ideological roots through the use of a charged and specialised vocabulary, supported by institutions immune to successful long-term co-optation.

In the pursuit of empowerment through self-definition, then, we must create our own history, communicate and live social change without asking the permission of those who define themselves as the arbiters of the past, the present and the future. We must not look for help from those who profit the most from that lethal combination of economic avarice and the hunger for power, and who manipulate the despair of these perilous times to their own profit. We must consent neither to protest on assignment, nor to provide footage which is frequently edited for use against us. Rather, we must give ourselves and each other the mandate to struggle on each issue as it arises, but also to dare to set long-range objectives consistent with a clearly articulated ideology.

HANDMAIDENS OF POWER

Sentimental feminists will invariably argue that being female is a sufficient condition for egalitarianism and the furthering of feminist principles. However, recent efforts of women towards change within the male hierarchy in Canada have provided us with proof of the opposite. There are many styles of co-optation that appeal to the various fallacies we have accepted with too much ease. We must familiarise ourselves with them, see not only their limitations, but the disservice that co-optation has rendered women in our country and elsewhere.

The first fallacy is that of sweet reason. The notion here is that the oppressor does not realise that he oppresses. If given sufficient evidence through rigorous statistical surveys, he will see the error of his ways and reform, even if it involves the sacrifice of his own privileges. A decade after the extraordinary well-researched and federally financed *Report of the Royal Commission on the Status of Women in Canada* (1970), only one-third of its recommendations had been implemented. Information is not sufficient for change; indeed, people in power fully realise that their own power is contingent upon the oppression of others, however bland their articulated rationale of this situation may be. In a world of finite power and resources, the material gain of women must cause readjustment in male ownership. Information, then, is a necessary but not sufficient condition for change.

The appeal of "sweet reason" has now been institutionalised by the state into "consultations". With great alacrity, many groups representing the oppressed people of Canada (often coyly defined as "visible minorities") rush to "consultations" held by governments at various levels. The handicapped, native peoples, people of colour, immigrants and women are invited to carefully orchestrated meetings, often held on short notice and without prior information or agendae. Diverse groups of people are brought together, usually with no information about what other groups will be there. Hence they have no chance to caucus or strategise for a united force. Instead, they are expected to react off the cuff to ideas that have been confected at great expense with the expertise of highly paid civil servants working with the most up-to-date, sophistically acquired data. In this atmosphere of "divide and conquer", the participants are thanked for their "input" and sent on their way. While there is often an atmosphere of bland friendliness at these "consultations", little ever comes of them. The public is not informed about them, and no conclusions are reached because the "consultation is not yet over". The state's divisive strategy in bringing together those disadvantaged people in discreet and cleverly orchestrated groups, with no mechanism for accountibility, is ultimately realised when potentially controversial legislation is breezily brought to a legislature with bland assurances that there has been extensive consultation and that the interests of those most directly affected have been adequately addressed. The "visible minorities" remain in a condition of demobilisation, with only the state knowing what really happened and where to short circuit any possible insurrection from the most enfeebled people in the society.

Another article of faith is the belief in the efficacy of interventionary groups. Advisory councils are created by the state to comment on the conditions of this or that group. Appointments to such committees are often made by those groups representing the very interests responsible for the oppression in the first place ... political parties dependent on contributions from the privileged. Perhaps some Canadian feminists learned the limits of such groups during the débacle of the Canadian Advisory Council on the Status of Women in the constitutional debate of 1980 – 1981.

In the fall of 1980, the Advisory Council (which is appointed by the political party in power) scheduled a national conference to examine and recommend provisions for women in the projected constitution which Prime Minister Trudeau was attempting to repatriate to Canada. This conference was called off at the last minute, ostensibly in sympathy for the federal translators who were on strike, although they encouraged the Council to go ahead with it. It was rescheduled for February, 1981. As that date approached, the federal Minister responsible for the Status of Women, Mr. Lloyd Axworthy, attempted to have it postponed again, indicating that such a conference might be an embarrassment to the government in its negotiations for the constitution. In much-publicised moral outrage, Doris Anderson, who was then the President of the Council, resigned. She contended that the Advisory Council is a neutral body and therefore unsusceptible to governmental influence. It became obvious that the first postponement also had been due to governmental pressure. Ms. Anderson, in addition to being a well-known feminist, was also an active member of the Liberal Party. We must examine the process by which she became appointed to the crucial position of President of the Advisory Council on the Status of Women and ask ourselves how valid her injured innocence could possibly be. The only other possible construct that might be placed on her pronouncements at the time of her resignation is that she had been totally unconscious of the *modus operandi* of the Liberal Party throughout her long association with it. It is difficult to believe in such ignorance because Ms. Anderson is a very shrewd observer of the world. In either case, it is clear that there is a real danger of co-optation when working within patriarchal power structures. There are crucial issues regarding the effectuality of such "advisory" bodies hand-picked by the state, and their perhaps unintentional complicity in the perpetuation of the *status quo*.

Another way in which women have been subsumed into the power structure is through the creation of "status of women" positions. Frequently these are occupied by token women, operating in the best of faith in an environment hostile to their cause, expected singly to bear the entire load of women's struggle within large and diverse institutions. While many women have been able to effect small and hard-won changes in this situation, many have also given up. Furthermore, these jobs are frequently phased out as soon as information has been gathered and a report submitted, i.e., just short of implementation.

Most recently, various women's organisations have perceived themselves as lobbyists, making contacts with the powers within the governments. While sometimes small concessions are wrested from these contacts, usually in the form of being invited to further "consultations", there are some serious limitations in this approach to long-range and profound social change. One is that these groups are, on the whole, self-appointed and can frequently be attacked and divided on that basis. The other is that lobbying often carries with it the danger of accepting and being limited by the state's definition of the problem and its mode of redress, rather than defining the terms ourselves.

At this point, one might very well ask, "What can women do, then?" Clearly, while we must make use of whatever possibilities are available to us (all of the above), we must not lose a radical consciousness and we must plan beyond the habitual, the "tried and true". Aside from the many fascinating speculations of various feminist scholars and myth-makers, we have evidence of neither a feminist military establishment nor a feminist bloody revolution in human history. Hence, we cannot know how such a project would work. It is clear, though, that all the above models are reactive ones. As men in power survive by both reaction and combat, so must the women who are struggling for a better world. We as women do not have the material resources, armaments, or historical formation to support us in such adventurist undertakings, even if we had the inclination. Our source of power should be a generative rather than a reactive one. We are fortunate as women to have acquired through time, history and inclination many of the qualities needed for self-empowerment.

THE EMPOWERMENT OF WOMEN

There are sources other than raw "power over" available to those women who wish to change our conditions and to develop a collective ideology and set of short- and long-term objectives. The concept of empowerment defines us as drawing power in the form of energy from within ourselves as individuals and through our mutual and collective support as a group.

Throughout the world, women share many fundamental experiences, and we are all entitled to social transformation rather than the minute changes we have witnessed, for example, in the much-celebrated U.N. Decade of Women. In order to effect transformation, however, we must be prepared to live our lives with intensity and consequence, both characteristics discouraged almost everywhere in the socialisation of females. The first step towards such change is through personal and individual transformation, through the assumption of the right to define oneself, to establish our own ethical and material criteria of social organisation, and to comprehend that in so doing we are not stealing, winning booty, or destroying; we are simply assuming what is rightfully ours.

We are gifted by both biology and history with several sources for this kind of empowerment. The first is what I will call our affective base. Women are raised to feel for everyone and to cue into and transmit our own and others' feelings. This has traditionally been the role of the woman in the family, and although frequently our role as tension managers makes us repress or displace our own and others' emotions (such as turning anger into depression and passivity, for instance), we have also developed considerable skill at both eliciting and interpreting emotions. It is, after all, a characteristic of oppressed people to monitor the whims and emotional swings of their oppressors and of one another in order to survive. Rather than regard this skill as a handicap in the "real world", we must validate it within ourselves and use it to examine our values, our role models, and to help us decide what kind of people we want to be. How do various forms of behaviour make us feel in the pits of our stomachs? Do we want to replicate forms of social interaction that have caused suffering to both oppressors and the oppressed? These considerations should urge us to reject the "Queen Bee" syndrome so often imposed upon "successful" women by the patriarchy and, regrettably, often willingly assumed by "ambitious" women. Finally, our command of affective language should make us consummate communicators and political manipulators when need be.

In most parts of the world, women still preside collaboratively over the most essential events in the human continuum: birth and death. Without such collaboration, women could never have survived and raised children. Our most salient gift here is our regard for the particular, that microscopic knowledge often ridiculed by men, which tells us that each event is different and deserving of full attention. Rooted in our shared condition is the knowledge that each birth is specific and unique. Such knowledge makes us quite unlikely to sacrifice thirty thousand human lives for the acquisition of an obscure hill in a country where we do not belong.

Our oppression has made us professionals at "making do". Since our ingenuity as well as the forced ability to do many things at once has been part of our formation, we are well armed for battles of attrition. We do not need the phallic trappings of speed and warfare, nor the carapace of rigid clothing so characteristic of the male power élite. Conviction, coupled with ingenuity, is a strong form of empowerment and has been well demonstrated in several revolutions within memory.

We must not underestimate the energy trapped by women's anger; we must draw upon it. Milennia of oppression create a form of existential anger. In women this is often turned into a self-destructive sense of despair and impotence. It is important for us to touch upon this anger, vent it, dispassionately examine it, and then redirect it as energy towards transformation in our own lives and the social order in which we live.

There are concrete steps by which these attitudes can be made manifest. The first one is disciplined self-appraisal. It is disturbing to find that the words "consciousness raising" no longer are meaningful to young people. In fact, the process has been reified into becoming a better consumer ... being more "conscious" of products on the market. Since a feminist transformation is predicated on a struggle against powerful, profitable and misogynistic socialising forces of both girls and boys, we must share the consciousness-raising process with the young in much the way literacy is considered a necessary tool for young people in our culture. Consciousness raising is the feminist alphabet, and our literacy is a commitment to equality between the sexes.

It is important to foster group consciousness raising as well as individual projects. All too often, women's groups become agents of "lateral" violence between women who have been victimised by the "vertical" violence of the patriarchy. By developing modes of consciousness raising in groups, perhaps we could avoid these constricting notions of "political correctness" which so divide us and inform our judgements on everything from appearance and life style to the specialised dialect of particular sub-groups. Techniques of consciousness raising, then, must be developed, taught and practised as a continuing commitment within the women's movement in order to create the necessary trust and energy essential to carrying out long-term plans of empowerment.

From consciousness raising, we must move towards viable and appropriate actions. We must define our ideological rationale and identify a specific historical and physical location. It is important to recognise the indispensibility of groupings, alliances, and networks in carrying out the tasks we set ourselves. When we get together, we must define not only our communality but our differences. It is essential to articulate our "bottom lines", where we are prepared to compromise and other necessary conditions of our participation. All too often radical projects break up after a massive investment of energy because ideology, goals and areas of contention have not been adequately addressed at the outset. Women must check our tendency to rush into "doing", into the kind of "busy-work" that may be a thoughtless replication of male self-validation in that place men refer to as the "real world". It is also important to assess the real costs of projects in terms of time and resources before undertaking them. We cannot do everything at once, and thus our agenda setting should be based on a rational assessment of our priorities and resources.

It is also important for women to relinquish our naïvété, transcend our math and business phobias and learn how the patriarchy conceptualises the world. In order to do this, we must learn to understand and evaluate the current terms of reference upon which judgements are made. This means understanding the premises and kind of reasoning developed through systems analysis, in which categories are created and problem solving accords with those systems created to perpetuate the existing power structures in society. This view of the world, created for military analysis, must be understood by those people who seek empowerment. We cannot afford to be ignorant of how we are perceived by those in power. Only when we grasp their processes as well as their conclusions will we be in a position to assume power over our own lives and assert our stake in the future of this planet.[5]

It is essential for each one of us to identify her arena for both short- and long-term action. Serious feminists cannot always effect immediate and radical change in the workplace. We are often most vulnerable to retaliation and it is not always viable to jeopardise one's most basic needs for adventurist stances. That, however, should not stop each one of us from consecrating a tithe of her time or resources to feminist action. From the identification of a suitable arena, we can then move to specific goals, alliances and strategies. Always, though, we must foster self-monitoring and the evaluation of both our internal processes and external effectiveness. Our understanding of the conceptual framework of those in power should inspire us as well in the politics of surprise. There are so few of us that we cannot afford to expend our energy on rivalry or those unchecked assumptions about others' loyalties which can so tear at the foundations of political movements. A deeply felt and lived solidarity, expressed through objectives and modes consistent with an ideology of empowerment, is essential to social transformation.

Our processes are our most valuable asset. If we create them from our own historical and socially acquired strengths and in full awareness of how the oppressors think, we have a chance of empowering the majority of women in our society; we might also improve the quality of life for most men. If, on the other hand, we ape the structures and procedures developed for the perpetuation of the patriarchy, we will be doomed to create the conditions of our own oppression. We must not waste our energy on the insertion of the most crudely ambitious of us into those slots designated for our co-optation by the patriarchy. While we must critically analyse the system in all its tawdry efficiency, we must develop the strength to reject the few pellets of co-optation it offers to the chosen few. The very desire to excel in the terms of the patriarchy is sufficient to reduce us all to that perennial addiction to surrender which characterises the passive lives of far too many people. We must always remember that we can and must make a difference where we live and breathe, but only if we listen to ourselves, define our own standards and share our experiences and expertise with honesty, acceptance and solidarity. Our empowerment as women is contingent upon our ability to feel the depth of our pain and anger, to share it honestly, to re-direct it into well-planned actions that emerge directly from our own vision of the world, and to carry these tasks through in our traditional mode of collaboration.

REFERENCES

1 I am greatly indebted to Paulo Freire and Jonathon Kozol, who expounded at

considerable length on revolution and the idea of empowerment at a conference on "Literacy and Empowerment and Social Change", Burlington, Vermont, April, 1981.

2 Canadian Advisory Council on the Status of Women, Fact Sheets #1 (*Women and Work*), #2 (*Women and Aging*), #5 (*Working Together: Women and Unions*), #7 (*Women and Pensions*), #8 (*Women and Part-time Work*). Ottawa, 1984.

3 These statistics were presented at the United Nations Mid-decade Conference on Women in Copenhagen by Dr. Kurt Waldheim, then Secretary General of the United Nations, 1980.

4 Phillip Foner, ed., *Helen Keller: Her Socialist Years*. New York: International Publishers, 1967, p. 84.

5 I am greatly indebted to conversation and written material with and by Lyse Blanchard, Director, Women's Programme, Secretary of State, Canada, for this analysis.

FURTHER READING

Daly, Mary, *Gyn/ecology*, Boston: Beacon Press, 1978.

Kozol, Jonathon, *The Night is Dark and I Am Far From Home*, New York: Bantam Books, 1977.

Lips, Hilary M., *Women, Men, and the Psychology of Power*, Englewood Cliffs, NJ: Prentice-Hall, 1981.

Rich, Adrienne, *On Lies, Secrets, and Silence*, New York: W.W. Norton & Co., 1979.

Dale Spender, ed., *Men's Studies Modified: The Impact of Feminism on the Academic Disciplines*, Oxford: Pergamon Press, 1981.

Index